Others Before You...

The History of Wisconsin Dells Country

Dells Country Historical Society, Wisconsin Dells, Wisconsin
New Past Press, Inc., Friendship, Wisconsin

Others Before You...
The History of
Wisconsin Dells Country

Dells Country
Historical Society
Wisconsin Dells, Wisconsin

New Past Press, Inc.
Friendship, Wisconsin
Publishing Assistant:
Erika Hall
Cover Design:
Fenceline Art,
Green Lake, Wisconsin

Library of Congress Cataloging in Publication

Goc, Michael J.
Others before you...:the history of Wisconsin Dells country/ Michael J. Goc [and] Dells Country Historical Society.
Includes bibliogrpahical references and index.
ISBN 0-938627-30-9 (alk. paper)
1. Dells of the Wisconsin (Wis.)-History. I. Dells Country Historical Society. II. Title. F587.W8G63 1995
977.5-dc20 95-39319

The steamers Alexander Mitchell *and* Eolah *docked at the Larks Hotel at the head of the Narrows, c. 1880. (Courtesy, H.H. Bennett Studio Foundation).*

Previous page: *Lone Rock at the foot of the Wisconsin Dells and the bark canoe used by photographer Henry Hamilton Bennett, c. 1880. (Courtesy, H.H. Bennett Studio Foundation).*

Acknowledgements

Many thanks to those who contributed to this book:

Donna Braun
Ethel Buckminster
Carol Burgess
Edna Cone
Tom Crist, Jr.
The Crothers Family
Ross Curry
John Dixon
Jean Drollinger
Rick Durbin
Marge Ennis
Scott Fredericksen
Gail Jermier
Donna Greenwood
Bud Gussel
Gisela Hamm
Loris Harrison
Alice Hines
Julie Gussel Keller
Jan Landrum
Bob & Mary Masteller
Clarence Nelson
Jack Olson
Shirley Olson
Jean Reese
Marilyn Severson
Carol Sorg
Frank Weinhold
Cathy Wendorf
Carl Willi

Underwriters

The Bank of Wisconsin Dells
Holiday Wholesale
Tommy Bartlett, Inc.

Contents

Dell View Hotel, Lake Delton, 1929.

HOT

BEAUTY IS YOU
OTHERS BEFORE YOU LOVED THE D
Henry Hamilton Bennett, pioneer photog
pictured and named many of the scenic spo
The Witches Gulch.
George H. Crandall and his wife Nellie Bennett
acquired preserved and reforested hundre
surrounding the river. They held it in
declaring No one can own The Dells
Phyllis Crandall Connor and Lois Crand
their husbands Ralph W. Connor and H. Howard
ransferred these properties in 1954 to the Wisconsin
lumni Research Foundation that they
eautiful for posterity

Introduction

"This beauty is yours because others before you loved the Dells."

The tablet bearing these words was unveiled by Governor Walter Kohler in 1956, shortly after members of the Crandall/Connor/Musson families transferred ownership of nearly all of the most scenic parts of the Wisconsin Dells to the public trust of the Wisconsin Alumni Research Foundation. The bequest was a wonderful gesture, made to preserve a natural treasure for future generations to enjoy.

This book is the product of a similar gesture. It is the result of years of work by a generous and dedicated corps of volunteers whose goal was to preserve a historical treasure for future generations to learn from and enjoy.

The history of the Wisconsin Dells area is large. It encompasses all the broad themes of Wisconsin and American history: the alteration and development of natural resources, the coming of immigrants and the settling of the land, the growth of industry and commerce, the tragedies of crime and war, the building of schools, churches and community life. The many authors of this book have attempted to tell all these stories and more, for the history of the Dells area is unique.

No other place is like Wisconsin Dells. It is a one-of-a-kind creation of natural forces and human endeavor. Its history is, of course, equally unique. Accordingly, this book includes the most comprehensive history ever assembled of the use of the river and the tourist industry at the Dells. Several of Wisconsin's most famous Native Americans appear here, along with the high-roller who built Wisconsin's first railroad, a world-renowned photographic artist, a jurist of extraordinary repute and two recepients of the nation's highest military honor. Along with the heroes are the lesser known, but also special, people who built the communities of Kilbourn, Delton, Briggsville and surrounding areas. These are family stories and they are also told.

Years of work have gone into this volume. If it contains any errors, they are merely accidental. The people who researched and wrote this "beauty" did it because they also "loved the Dells."

Previous page: *Wisconsin Governor Walter J. Kohler unveiling the tablet acknowledging the gift of the Dells to the University of Wisconsin Alumni Foundation, 1956. (Courtesy, H.H. Bennett Studio Foundation).*

Natural Resources of the Dells

Eons of geological time are spread out in the Dells. The sandstone in this part of the Wisconsin River channel was formed during the last part of the Cambrian Period over 500 million years ago. Originally the sandy shore of an ancient sea, the weight of overlying formations compacted the sand, and percolating groundwater cemented the sand into rock. When exposed to air, the rock develops a shell. Some of this shell is quite hard and some soft enough to crumble to sand between the fingers.

Layers of deposition over the centuries are evident. The surviving layers show seemingly random concentrations of iron oxide and silica thus making some sections more impervious to weathering by wind and water over the millennia. It is this irregular erosion of differing layers of stone that give the Dells formations their unusual shapes.

Some of the sandstone layers are inclined and some horizontal. They are the result of fluctuations of the wind and water that deposited the sand along the Cambrian shore and are called cross-bedding.

The Dells are situated on the extreme eastern margin of the Driftless Area, that unique portion of the state and its three neighbors that was not covered by the last glacier of the Ice Age. The Green Bay Lobe of the glacier extended to within four miles east of the Dells about 19,000 years ago, but did not reach the Dells.

As the glacier melted, it gradually formed glacial Lake Wisconsin, which was about the size of the present Great Salt Lake. Its main basin was 150 feet deep and extended north over nearly all of Adams County to Wisconsin Rapids, west through most of Juneau County to the Wonewoc escarpment and south over the city of Wisconsin Dells. Smaller basins of meltwater formed south of the Dells with outlets in between.

Suddenly one day about 14,000 years ago, the last ice dam holding back the waters of glacial Lake Wisconsin–located in Lewiston near the Cascade Mountain Ski Area–gave way and unleashed a catastrophic flood. Water poured through the Dells from the main basin to the Lewiston basin dropping the mammoth lake as much as 100 feet, possibly within only a few days. It is likely that the gorges in the Dells area were cut in a matter of days or weeks as the swift flood waters eroded away the soft sandstone.

Probably the other river beds abandoned by the river were formed at this time. They have been called "old channels." One extends west from Coldwater Canyon, through Rocky Arbor State Park to Hulbert Creek where it joins the Lower Dells just below the dam. Another gorge encircles Black Hawk Island.

Of course, erosion still continues as the river, rainwater and tree roots enter the cracks in the rocks and change the face of the Dells.

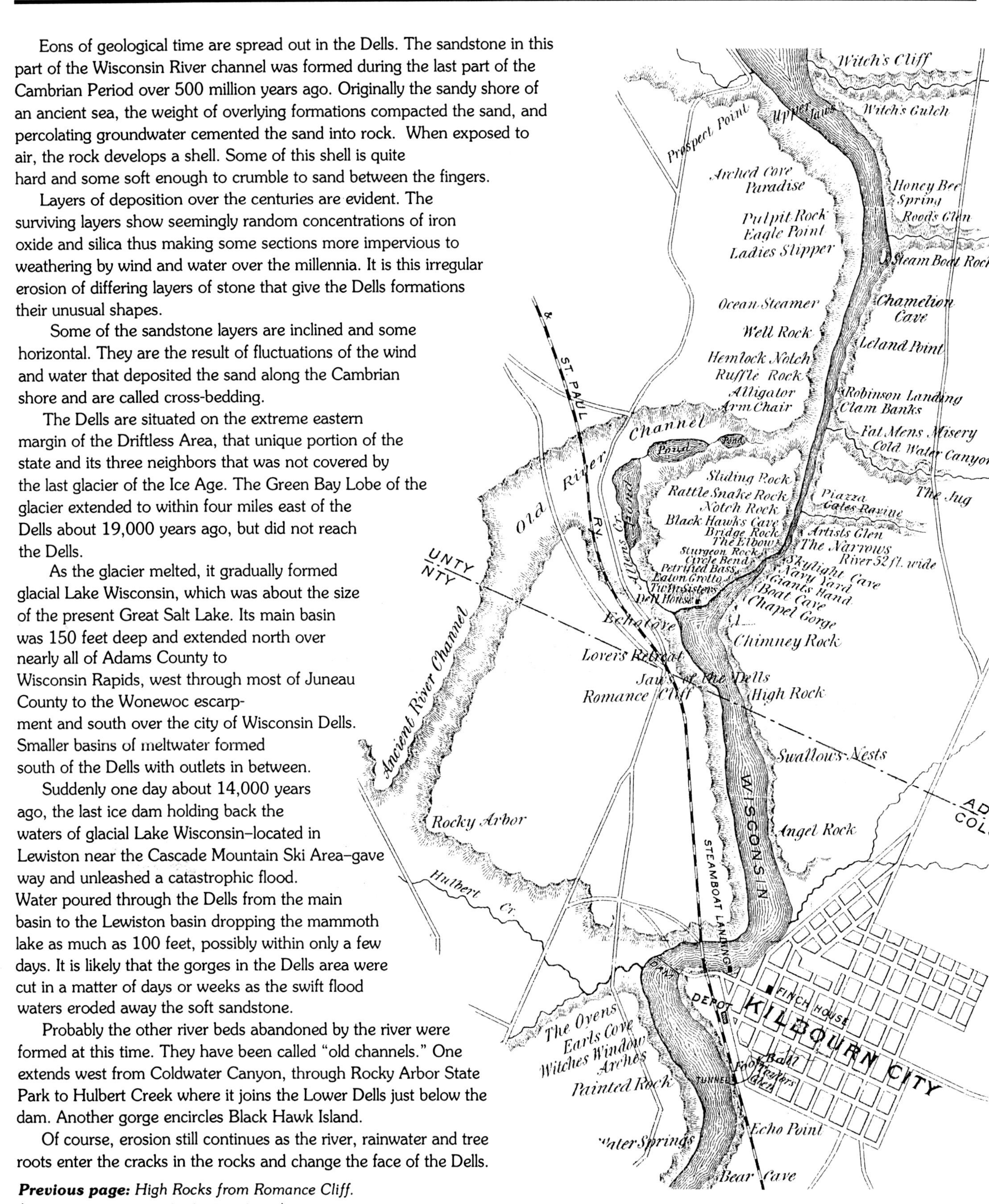

Previous page: *High Rocks from Romance Cliff. (Courtesy, H.H. Bennett Studio Foundation).*

Native People at the Dells

Ancient Earthworks

The Dells area has been inhabited by native people for at least 2,000 years, and probably much longer. Many of them left evidence of their presence in a variety of earthworks.

Hundreds of effigy and burial mounds were constructed in Dells country between approximately 300 and 1400 AD. Although numerous, they represent only a fraction of the thousands of earthen structures constructed by native people in Wisconsin in the years before Christopher Columbus initiated the European settlement of the western hemisphere. Nearly all of these mounds have been obliterated either by farming, by flooding caused by dams, or by the construction of villages and roads.

Among the most notable lost earthworks in Dells country is the "Dell Prairie Enclosure" along Cold Water Canyon Creek. It featured a double embankment with a wall 10 feet wide running from 70 to 230 feet that suggests it was used as a fort. In New Haven, many earthworks were flooded when Neenah Creek was dammed to form Mason Lake. The first settlers also recorded a large mound in the shape of an eagle and another in the shape of a bear. Mounds also once existed at Point Bluff, Crooked Lake, Wolf Lake, Jordan Lake, Parker Lake, Goose Lake and Little Lake in Adams County.

They are not mounds, but the so-called "Lemonweir glyphs" located on a bluff on the west bank of the Wisconsin just below the mouth of the Lemonweir River depicted fish, deer, buffalo and a thunderbird figure carved into the stone. They too have been lost.

Not all the ancient earthworks have been destroyed. Ancient agriculturists created the still recognizable Hulburt Creek garden beds in the Town of Delton, Sauk County. Built in about 1000 AD, the beds consist of a series of ditches, ridges and furrows designed to buffer frost and for irrigation, weed control, drainage, aeration and soil enrichment.

The Kingsley Bend Wayside on Highway 16 shelters a group of about 20 burial and effigy mounds. There are conical and linear mounds as well as effigies of two 100-feet long bears, a panther with a tail as long as a football field and an eagle with a 200-feet wingspan.

Archaeologists are uncertain what happened to the effigy builders, but surmise they were assimilated into another culture, or simply abandoned the effigy mound phase of their development.

None of the present-day Indian tribes in Wisconsin have traditions or legends which might shed light on the Effigy Mound Culture.

The Legend of Black Hawk

As a place of great natural beauty located on a major waterway, the Dells area was important to native people.

Scholars speculate that ancient people built mounds at Kingsley Bend because they appreciated its sweeping view of the river. The Ho-Chunk people, who have lived here longer than anyone else, have always held the Dells in great reverence. Spirits have resided and legends have been born in the bluffs, ravines, caves, rapids and quiet pools along the river. As Roger Little Eagle Tallmadge once said, "We are proud of this land. Indians have lived in the Dells for over 7,000 years."

Two of Wisconsin's major Indian tribes–Menominee and Ho-Chunk–have played significant roles in the history of the Dells. For more than 150 years the furs they trapped in local waters traveled east to the Great Lakes and across the ocean to Europe, making the Dells part of the international economy long before any European appeared here.

The Sauk Indians, who never had a village at the Dells, are important because of the outcome of their conflict with the United States in 1832 and in the legacy left here by their war chief, Black Hawk.

After the armed struggle with Black Hawk's band, the United States government adopted its infamous removal policy–which stated that all Indians should be moved west of the Mississippi River. The Sauk left in 1833; some of the Ho-Chunk were coerced into signing a treaty that ceded their land in Wisconsin in 1837; the Menominee signed off on the Wisconsin River Valley in 1848. Each one of these cessions opened land to white settlement–first southern Sauk and Columbia counties, then northern Sauk and southern Juneau counties, and finally Adams County.

The Sauk conflict also made the name of Black Hawk a part of the legacy of the Dells. After the massacre of his people at the mouth of the Bad Axe River on August 2, 1832, Black Hawk fled into the wild uplands of western Wisconsin. He was pursued by the U.S. Army, state militia units and their Ho-Chunk allies. Twenty-five days later, two Ho-Chunks–Chaetar and One-Eyed Decorah–delivered Black Hawk into American custody. Chaeter later reported that "near the Dalles of the Wisconsin I took Black Hawk." So the legend was born.

Where "near the Dalles" was located has led to much speculation. Is it Black Hawk's Cave in the Narrows, the stone overhang on the bluff at the

***Previous page**: Black Hawk's Rock on the Upper Dells, a refuge for the Sauk Indian chief Black Hawk when he fled from the United States Army after the massacre of his people at Bad Axe on the Mississippi River in 1832. (Courtesy, H.H. Bennett Studio Foundation).*

Spoon Decorah, c. 1888. The Decorah family was and is one of the most numerous of the Ho-Chunk people in the Dells area. (Courtesy State Historical Society of Wisconsin).

mouth of the Lemonweir, or even Seven Mile Bluff near Mauston with its lone white pine as depicted by H. H. Bennett?

General Joseph M. Street, the Indian Agent to whom the Ho-Chunks delivered Black Hawk, reported to his superiors in Washington that "The Black Hawk was taken about 40 miles above the Portage, on the Wiskinsin River near a place called the Dalle."

Shortly after his arrival at Kilbourn in 1857, George Bennett wrote that "we saw the Cave where Black Hawk the Indian Warrior hid himself when he was pursued by the soldiers and he was taken but a few miles from here."

On January 28, 1858, Henry W. Tenney, a Newport land speculator who had just lost a bundle, wrote to Horace A. Tenney, "A little while ago I was rich–now I am obliged to consider where I shall hide when I see the sheriff after me... I have thought of the cave in the Dells where Black Hawk hid after the disastrous day of Bad Ax–but that is too near Kilbourn City." If Tenney had to hide from his creditors, he didn't want to be too close to them.

General Street's report was written shortly after Black Hawk was taken, Bennett's and Tenney's about 25 years later. In between, the tradition that the Sauk leader was captured fairly close to the Dells was well established. Place names in the Dells–Black Hawk Island, Black Hawk's Head, Black Hawk's Cave and Black Hawk's Leap–all turned up on the map, along with numerous hotels, restaurants, souvenir shops and attractions featuring the Sauk leader. In typical Dells style, many places were embellished with yarns, as in the case of Black Hawk's Leap where the fleeing Indian supposedly coaxed his fearless pony to leap 52-feet across the Narrows of the Wisconsin.

The tradition that Black Hawk was captured near the Dells stood largely unchallenged until 1988, when Wisconsin's leading Indian historian, Nancy Lurie, brought to light new evidence. Lurie contended that Black Hawk was captured, not on the Wisconsin, but near Tomah, about 46 miles from the Dells. Other scholars contest Lurie's assertion and the discussion continues.

No one, except Chaeter, One-Eyed Decorah and Black Hawk himself, ever really did know for sure where the Sauk leader was captured. Perhaps no one ever shall–and that only makes a good Wisconsin Dells story even better.

Red Bird's Song

In 1994, the people who were called *Winnebago* by French furtraders more than 300 years earlier, chose to identify themselves by a shortened form of their original name–the Ho-Chunk. They were and are the largest native tribe to live in the Dells area.

Although they had fought with the American army against Black Hawk in 1832, the Ho-Chunk had not always been allies of the newcomers. Only six years earlier, violence between the Ho-Chunk and the Americans had broken out and "war" seemed imminent. Peace was preserved, at least in part, due to the responsible action taken by the Ho-Chunk leader named Red Bird.

In 1826, the United States recognized Ho-Chunk ownership of most of the southern two-thirds of Wisconsin. Nonetheless, white settlers were moving in and acting as if they intended to stay. Violence began near Prairie du Chien when a family of whites tapped sugar maple trees that belonged to the Ho-Chunk and the Indians killed them. The following year, Red Bird and three companions entered a home on the edge of Prairie du Chien, killed two men and scalped a child named Marie Regis Gagnier. The American reaction was swift and powerful. Regular army units were mobilized–some from as far away at St. Louis–and state militia called out. Led by General Henry Atkinson, the troops converged on the Fox-Wisconsin portage and threatened to attack unless the murderers surrendered.

On Sept. 6, 1827, troops commanded by Major Henry Whistler sighted a band of about thirty

Detail from the painting Surrender of Red Bird *which hangs in the Wisconsin Capitol in Madison. (Courtesy, State Historical Society of Wisconsin).*

Indians at the portage.

The Ho-Chunks approached carrying two American flags on each side of their group and in the center of the men was Red Bird holding a white flag. When they reached the river the sound of someone singing could be heard and those who were nearest said, "It is Red Bird singing his death song."

The remainder of the story is related by Thomas McKenney, later head of the Indian Service and a renowned painter and illustrator. His dramatic account has inspired the legend of the "surrender of Red Bird."

"All eyes were fixed upon Red Bird; and well they might be, for of all the Indians I ever saw he was, without exception, the most perfect in form, in face, and gesture. In height he was about six feet, straight but without restraint. His proportions were those of the most exact symmetry, and these embraced the entire man, from his head to his feet. His very fingers were models of beauty - I never beheld a face that was so full of all the ennobling and at the same time the most winning expression. It was impossible to combine with such a face the thought that he who wore it could be a murderer. It appeared to be a compound of grace and dignity, of firmness and decision, all tempered with mildness and mercy. During my attempted analysis of this face I could not but ask myself, can this man be a murderer. Is he the same who shot, scalped and cut the throat of Gagnier? His head, too, no head was ever so well formed. There was no ornamentating the hair after the Indian fashion, no clubbing it up in blocks, no loose or straggling parts, but it was cut after the fashion of the most civilized. His face was painted one side red, the other intermixed with green and white. Around his neck he wore a collar of Wampum, beautifully mixed with white. The claws of the panther or wildcat formed the rim of the collar. He was clothed in Yankton dress, new and beautiful. The material was of dressed elk skin almost a pure white. It consisted of a jacket, the sleeves being cut to fit this finely formed arm. On each shoulder he wore a preserved red bird. Blue beads were employed to vary and enrich the fringe of the leggings. On his feet he wore moccasins. Across the breast in a diagonal position was his war pipe, at least three feet long, brightly ornamented with dyed horse hair and the feathers and bills of birds. In one hand he held the white flag and in the other the calumet, or pipe of peace."

Red Bird was aware of the Indian custom of exacting personal revenge on those who committed murder. He also knew that General Atkinson had promised that the army would not harm the Ho-Chunk if the murderers were handed over for trial.

Red Bird said, "I am ready." Then advancing a step he paused, saying "I do not wish to be put in irons. Let me be free. I have given away my life. It is gone." Stooping and taking some dust between his fingers he blew it away and said, "like that."

"I would not take it back. It is gone."

He then presented himself to be executed immediately.

Instead, Red Bird and several other Indians were arrested and imprisoned. The following winter he died behind bars; some say he committed suicide, others say illness claimed him. The rest of the Ho-Chunk defendants were tried, found guilty and condemned to death, but were pardoned by President John Quincy Adams.

Marie Regis Gagnier, the scalped child, lived to old age at Prairie du Chien and occasionally showed her wounded head at public exhibitions–for a fee.

Red Bird's dramatic surrender ended the war and–along with a treaty in which the Ho-Chunk ceded all of Wisconsin south and west of the portage–insured the safety of his people for a few more years.

Yellow Thunder

Although they fought against the Sauk in the Black Hawk War, the Ho-Chunk were not spared punishment for it. In 1832, they ceded claims to land in east central Wisconsin, including Lake Winnebago and the Fox-Wisconsin portage. In 1837, a group of Ho-Chunks visiting Washington D. C., were coerced into signing a treaty that relinquished all their remaining territory in the state.

This treaty set the stage for another act in the sad drama of American Indian history and led to the emergence of the most important Ho-Chunk leader ever to appear at Wisconsin Dells.

His name was Yellow Thunder and he is perhaps best remembered as the man who would not leave. He refused to recognize the treaty signed in Washington and refused to answer federal summons to assemble for removal to the west. Four times between 1844 and 1873, the federal government hired contractors who assembled posses to round up Indians, load them on steamboats or railcars and forcibly evict them. The wisdom of this policy was inadvertently pointed out by one officer involved in the removal of 1844. "Good God," he exclaimed, "what harm could these few poor Indians do among the rocks?"

Nonetheless, they were removed. When captured and forced to go to Iowa, Minnesota or Nebraska, Yellow Thunder stayed away only long enough to turn around and walk home–sometimes returning sooner than the guards who had escorted him west. Many Indians followed Yellow Thunder, defied the removal policy and came home to central Wisconsin, where they lived as best they could among the growing white population. Other Ho-Chunks chose to stay in Nebraska and, to this day, the tribe is split into two branches.

In 1849, Yellow Thunder attempted to evade removal by buying forty acres in the Town of Delton, presuming that, as a landowner and American taxpayer, he could not be evicted. Yellow Thunder's forty became a haven for the Ho-Chunks and the site of pow-wows and dancing. Even after Yellow Thunder died, Indians continued to gather and dance at his forty. Soon tourists who wanted to see Indians dance started to appear, laying the groundwork for the Dells Indian ceremonials.

After its final attempt to remove the Ho-Chunks from Wisconsin in 1873, the federal government reversed its policy. Although they would not have a reservation guaranteed by a treaty in Wisconsin, the Ho-Chunks would no longer be hunted, rounded up and transported. In 1875, the provisions of the Homestead Act were extended to Indians and many of the roughly 500 Ho-Chunks in the Dells area filed claims to land in Adams, Sauk and Juneau counties.

Yellow Thunder died in 1874. He had lived long enough to see the government's removal policy defeated by his own refusal policy. The Ho-Chunk would remain in the Dells area that had been their home for thousands of years. All the Indian heritage on display at the Dells–from the Stand Rock Ceremonial to the "authentic" Indian souvenirs in

Why the Winnebago are the Ho-Chunk

For as long as they could remember, the people who called themselves the Ho-Chunkgra lived in the southern half of Wisconsin. They met their first European in 1634, when French voyageur Jean Nicolet traveled west from Montreal in search of the fabled Northwest Passage between the Atlantic and Pacific Oceans. He had heard of the Ho-Chunkgra as the "People of the Sea" who lived along the route and who, he hoped, would guide him all the way to China. Instead, they greeted him hospitably and, perhaps, guided him up the Fox River

The Algonquin Indians who accompanied Nicolet, had their own name for the Ho-Chunkgra. They called them the Winnebago. The French furtraders who came a few years after Nicolet called the Ho-Chunkgra, *les puans*, or "stinkards" after the strong, sulfur smell of the water at Green Bay. The English traders who followed the French preferred the Algonquin name and so the Ho-Chunkgra passed into the historical record as the Wisconsin Winnebago Indians.

They remained the Wisconsin Winnebago until November 1994, when they chose to once again be known by the name they had always called themselves–the Ho-Chunkgra–conveniently shortened to Ho-Chunk. It is not a new name. Instead, it is the oldest name of the native people of the Dells area and the first name they gave to themselves.

the tourist shops–owes its presence to the man who refused to leave.

Yellow Thunder is buried with his wife, Washington Woman, on Country Trunk A, south of Lake Delton.

Ho-Chunk men and traditional summer shelters made of reeds, early 1870s. The elderly man sitting and holding a war club is Yellow Thunder. His decision to disregard the dubious 1837 treaty with the United States kept the Ho-Chunk in their ancestral home in central Wisconsin. (Courtesy, H.H. Bennett Studio Foundation).

Getting Started

Robert V. Allen and The Dell House

In 1838, not long after they received word that the Ho-Chunk had ceded their land in Wisconsin, Robert Allen, Amasa Wilson and C.B. Smith set out from Galena, Illinois to find their fortunes in the Dells area. They built a crude cabin on the south side of Blackhawk Island and cut pine logs to be floated down river to markets on the Mississippi in the spring of 1839. After the prime timber was logged off, Wilson and Smith moved up the Lemonweir to found New Lisbon, but Allen stayed.

He became not only the first white settler on the Wisconsin River north of Portage but also the first white settler in the Town of Lyndon, first settler in what became Juneau County and the first settler in the Wisconsin Dells school district.

Not much is known about Allen's background. The federal census reports that he was born in Pennsylvania, was thirty-five years old in 1850 and had no occupation. The census differs from the inscription on his headstone, which reads that Allen was born in 1806, making him 44 years old in 1850. Be that as it may, he never married and was remembered in the Dells as a man with a thick black beard who wore heavy black boots.

Allen did have a fine eye for real estate and was familiar with the needs of the lumbermen who were just beginning to run rafts of boards from upriver mills to downriver markets. In order to fit their large rafts through the Narrows of the Dells, the river drivers sometimes stopped above Black Hawk Island at Louis Bluff to divide their rafts into smaller "rapids pieces."

After running one rapids piece through the Narrows and the rough water beyond, the lumbermen hiked or "gigged back" to the Bluff to pick up another set. Running a full shipment of rafts through the Dells could take several days and the rivermen needed a place to eat, drink, sleep and amuse themselves. Robert Allen supplied it.

He opened an inn called the Dell House that offered food, lodging, liquor, gambling and women to entertain the rivermen. By the early 1850s, the simple shack Allen and his partners built in 1838 had been enlarged into a three-story structure with a plastered fireplace in the main room on the ground floor.

The Dells was on the frontier in these years and the rivermen were typical of the time and place. Up to 100 "river pigs" slept at the Dell House, on floors and benches, indoors and out. They got roaring drunk on Allen's own concoction of the "devil's eyewater," gambled away their wages, fought with each other and had their way with the women. Allen never admitted that a killing occurred at the Dell House but he was quoted as saying, "I won't vouch for the grounds."

Allen, who hired out to pilot rafts through the Narrows, also operated a busy ferry across the river. He was one of two partners granted a charter by the state to construct the first bridge across the Wisconsin that Schuyler Gates completed across the Narrows in 1850. Busy as he was, Allen hired help to run the Dell House: the J. B. McEwen family; Mr. and Mrs. George Orcutt, who had five children there; Hannah Hurlburt; and several members of the Blaser family.

The frontier life roared on at the Dell House throughout the 1850s and '60s. The atmosphere grew more tame in the post-Civil War years as railroads replaced river drives as the means to move lumber to market and the Dells itself became a settled community visited by genteel tourists instead of "river pigs."

In 1879, Robert Allen sold the Dell House property to James W. Wintersteen. Two years later, at age 75, he was listed on the public aid roles of Juneau County and, in 1887, admitted to the county poor farm at New Lisbon. He died there in 1889. Ten years later the Dell House was destroyed by fire.

Jared Walsworth, New Haven and Briggsville

About the same time that Robert Allen was settling in at the Dell House, another frontiersman was also making a home in the Dells area. Jared Walsworth was known as a blacksmith, steamboat pilot, Indian trader, store owner, farmer and innkeeper. In 1838, he turned up in the Menominee Indian village located in what became the Adams County Town of New Haven, married a Menominee woman and made himself a home.

The Menominees had yet to relinquish sovereignty over the territory north of the Fox River and east of the Wisconsin, so white settlement was prohibited. However, the Menominee were few and scattered throughout the territory between Lake Winnebago and the Wisconsin, and could not prevent trespassers from coming across the border. Lumbermen returning upriver had already converted an old Indian trail running from Portage to Pointe Basse (near Nekoosa) into the "Pinery Road" and settlers would not be far behind.

***Previous page:** Robert Allen's Dell House, c. 1886. It was the first building constructed by a white settler in the Dells area. The women are Elizabeth Cadle Green and her daughter, Mary Lydia, the future wife of Horace J. Upham. As indicated by the scars on their trunks, the trees next to the women were used as anchor posts for lumber rafts. (Courtesy, H.H. Bennett Studio Foundation).*

A map depicts settlement in the Briggsville area in the 1850s and the location of earthworks constructed by native people.

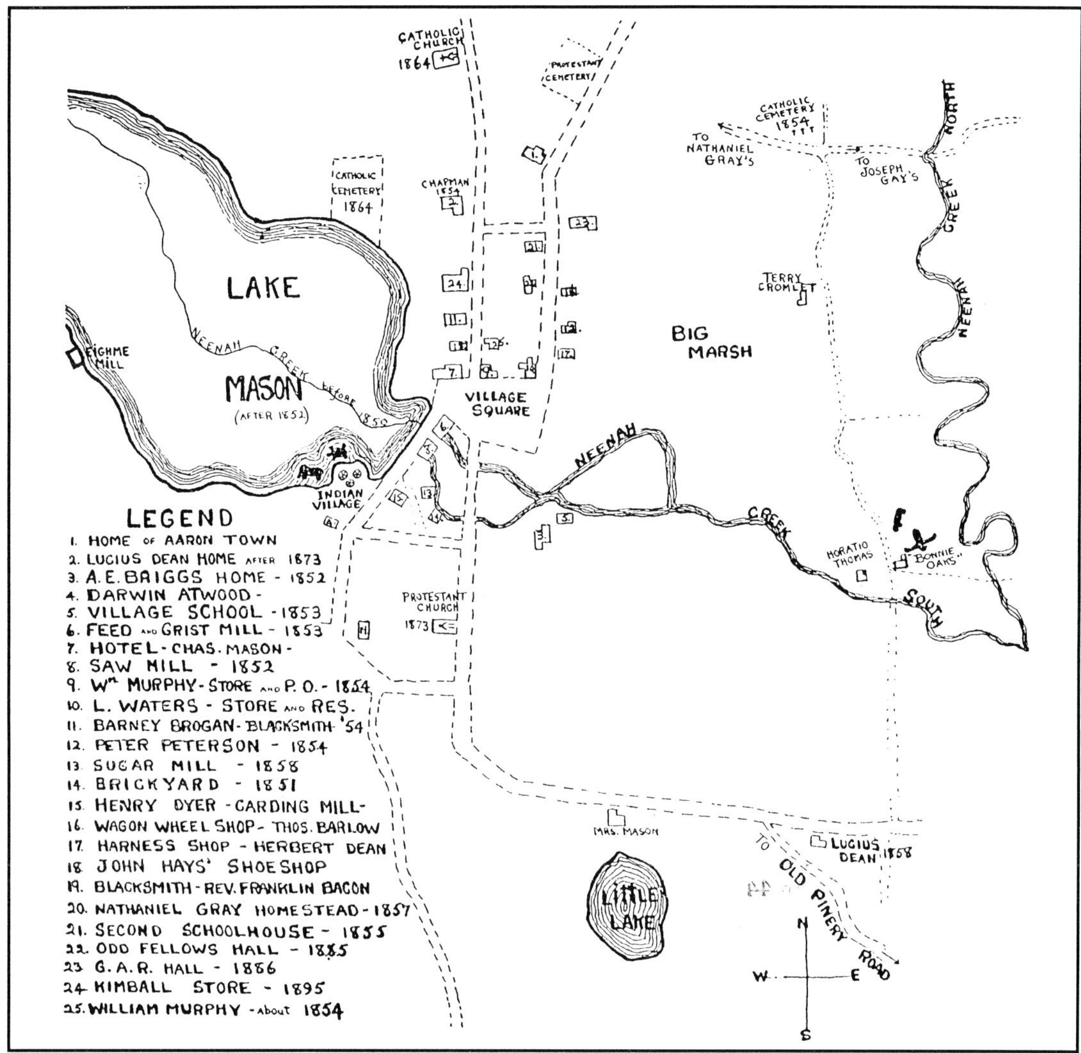

In 1848, the Menominee ceded and vacated their territory in central Wisconsin and settled, after several years of struggle, on their reservation along the Wolf River.

Jared Walsworth stayed in New Haven and his inn, which was located about one mile northeast of the junction of Highways G and 23, became a stopping point for settlers using the Pinery Road to travel north. It was a busy place, with travelers "lying so thick on the floors and in the garret that one could not walk over them." While staying at Walsworth's in 1843 a woman named Pardee gave birth to a son named Jared who is credited as the first non-Indian born in New Haven and Adams County.

Between 1844 and 1850, many settlers arrived: among them George Stowell, Amos Landt, Robert Ramsey, Ira Ward, Daniel Eighme and Uri Morse. The story is told of Morse that he "arrived with four yoke of oxen and a whip big enough to reach them all." Eighme, who left his name on the misspelled "Amey" or "Amery" Lake, opened a tavern near Briggsville and was recalled as "an ideal tavern keeper of the olden time. He had a big sign on which was painted two geese drinking from a horse trough with the words, 'Fair Play House. Peace and Plenty'."

Briggsville began when Alexander Briggs and Amphlius Chamberlain arrived. In 1850, they began constructing a dam on Neenah Creek to power a saw mill and a flouring mill. By 1854, Briggsville was a platted village with a general store, hotel and post office.

In the wake of the departing Menominee, other settlers moved into the area which was, until 1851, part of Portage County. Since the area was not surveyed and therefore could not be purchased until after 1851, these earliest of settlers could at first only "squat" on the land until it was offered for sale.

By the mid-1850s, Jeremiah Landt had built the Big Spring Mill, the Stafford and Big Spring schools were holding classes, a post office was opened and hundreds of wagonloads of settlers were traveling up the Pinery Road on their way to new homes. The population had grown large enough so, in 1854, the Adams County board organized the Town of Big Spring, later renamed New Haven.

The Bluff that bears the name of Louis Dupless, viewed from the mouth of Witches Gulch before the Wisconsin Dells dam raised water levels and flooded the islands. (Courtesy, H.H. Bennett Studio Foundation).

Louis Dupless, George Blood and Lyndon

Louis F. Dupless was born in France in 1820. Caught on the wrong side of the political struggles that shook France in 1832, the Dupless family was forced into exile. Young Louis entered the maritime service and sailed the Mediterranean Sea, the Atlantic Ocean and the Gulf of Mexico. He was in New Orleans when the United States declared war on Mexico and volunteered to serve in place of a draftee for the sum of $800.

In 1847, Dupless traveled up the Mississippi and Wisconsin Rivers to the Dells. He camped at the foot of the Bluff on the west bank of the river upstream from Black Hawk Island. He ventured up the Lemonweir to Mauston, but returned to the Bluff and staked out a squatter's claim to 183 acres of land, including the Bluff. To protect his claim, Dupless hurriedly built a shelter and stayed through the winter, visited often by Indian neighbors, and probably by Robert V. Allen, whose Dell House was only a short walk downstream.

In 1848, Dupless brought his young wife, Elizabeth Walklin, to the Bluff and together they set out to build a life there. Except for service in the Civil War, Louis Dupless would spend the rest of his life within sight of the Bluff that bore his name. In 1849, Elizabeth gave birth to a son named Charles, who was probably the first non-Indian child born in what became Juneau County. He was the first of six children born to Louis and Elizabeth prior to her death in 1869.

The Dupless family became legal owners of the Bluff in 1853, when Charles hired attorney Jonathan Bowman to turn his squatter's claim into a pre-emption certificate that prevented a speculator from buying the property out from under him. Dupless then purchased the land at the standard government rate of $1.25 per acre, or a total of $229.00 for the 183-acre parcel.

A year after Louis and Elizabeth Dupless settled at the Bluff, George and Helen Hurlburt Blood staked their claim to 40 acres in Lyndon. Had the Bloods claimed land a bit farther south and east, they would have been the first to settle within the future city limits of Wisconsin Dells.

George Tyler Blood was born in Burlington, Vermont in 1824. When he 16 years old, he and his father drove a team of little brown mares to Chicago. Later the rest of the family also came west and they settled in Evanston, Illinois, where George found employment as a stage coach driver.

In 1844 he was in Thornton, Illinois, where he met and married Helen Hurlburt. She was a half sister to Don Carlos Barry, the first white settler in Reedsburg. The Bloods moved to the Reedsburg area and then to their claim in Lyndon. Like the

George Tyler Blood and members of his family in front of the cabin he built about 1850. (l-r) Oppie Fowler, Alice Blood Fowler, Hiram Blood, Willard Blood, George, Dolly Blood and (probably) Clara Morin Blood.

Dupless family, the Bloods were squatters and had to protect their claim by living on the land and–once it was up for sale–buying it before anyone else did.

Knowing what he had to do, Blood set out for the federal land office in Mineral Point as soon as sales began. He didn't have a horse available then so he made the journey on foot. On the way he met a man on horseback who was also headed for the land office and the two decided to travel together.

When they arrived in Mineral Point, the stranger put up his horse and had lunch first, but Blood went directly to the land office and filed his claim. When the stranger got there, he was unhappily surprised to find that the land he had intended to claim was already taken by George Tyler Blood.

The Blood family remained on the farm for over 100 years and made it one of the longest continuously-occupied farms in the area. Juneau County was separated from Adams County in 1855, and the Town of Lyndon was organized by the Juneau County board in 1857.

Henry Van Wie, Dell Prairie and Plainville

The Van Wie family had already been residents of the United States for nearly 200 years before they came to the Dells area. In the 1650s, the Van Wies were among the first Dutch settlers of Albany, New York.

They arrived in the Dells area in 1847 when Henry and his son Lorenzo Van Wie staked a claim to 160 acres along what is now Hwy 13 in the Town of Dell Prairie. When the land came up for sale in 1852, Henry offered 80 acres to his brother Andrew. He accepted and, along with his wife Anna and their nine children, made a significant contribution to the growth in population of Dell Prairie.

Plainville began when James Edson migrated from New York in 1848 and built a home, hotel and saw mill along Plainville Creek on what became the Wisconsin River Road. This road ran to White Creek and Quincy where John Kingsbury's ferry crossed the Wisconsin River to Germantown in Juneau County. A later crossing just north of Plainville and south of Point Bluff was operated by the Billings family and led to Mauston.

As the names "Plainville" and "Dell Prairie" indicate, not all of the Dells area was forested. In fact, large stretches of ground were grasslands–some dry, some marshy–and the first settlers preferred them over wooded acreage. Prairie ground could be plowed and planted without the time-consuming and back-breaking labor of clearing trees and stumps. Grassland was also easier to market than forest so pioneer land speculators identified their land accordingly, which is why "Plainville" is not "Woodville" and "Dell Prairie" is not "Dell Forest."

In 1854, Dell Prairie and Springville were included in a town called Westbrook. A year later Westbrook was divided and the Towns of Dell Prairie and Springville were organized.

AMELIA ON THE MOUND

Spring, 1859

It was spring-buttercups bloomed on the slopes of Blue Mound and arbutus could be found in the shaded corners of the Elephant's Back Bluff. It was for arbutus that the Douty children were looking; it was a body they found. She was lying at the foot of a steep incline, a grotesque cariature of her former beauty. A faded blue scarf flapped desolately in the wind, pinned by an ornate brooch to the bush beside her body.

It was in the early 1850's that the story began in the rich farming country of Ohio. It was tragic tale; a tale that started with love and ended in death.

Amelia Dutcher had lived since early girlhood with her uncle and aunt and their daughter, Miranda. Amelia's parents had died when she was very young, leaving to her and her older brother, Tom, a small inheritance, a few debts, and her maternal grandmother's big gold brooch with "Amelia" written on it in flowing gold letters. Amelia received the brooch while Tom acquired the money and the debts, the first of which became smaller and the latter larger. On the fateful evening, it was a poker game that held his fascinated attention. The stakes were high-too high so to finance his evening, he "borrowed" the money his uncle kept in a brown teapot on the top shelf. And lost all of it. His uncle swore that he'd never rest until he saw Tom Dutcher in the state prison, but despite the threat, Tom came back every few months to see Amelia. They met in secrecy at the gate near the woods, but by some mischance they were discovered one day by Miranda. There was no love lost between the girls because the cousin, Miranda, was in love with Amelia's fiance. To Miranda, this was a heaven-sent opportunity. With the air of a misunderstood friend, she told the man that Amelia was being unfaithful to him. One evening when she knew Amelia was to meet Tom she summoned Amelia's fiance to give him proof of her accusations. They hid in the loft of the barn. About eight o'clock in the evening, they saw Amelia walking slowly toward the woods. They saw her meet this strange man and kiss him affectionately, saw them talk for a while, then kiss goodbye and part. Amelia hurried back toward the house - to be met in the yard by her betrothed and Miranda. He, of course, demanded the explanation Amelia could not give because of her love for her brother. She pleaded with him to believe in her, but he could not. He broke their engagement shortly afterwards and became affianced to her cousin.

When she heard the news, Amelia's despair knew no bounds. She took the little money she had and boarded the train, riding blindly on as the hours and days slipped by her unheeding. The railroad ended in Kilbourn. She came into town late in the afternoon, registering at the Tanner House. The men in the lobby saw her go out that evening. She was dressed for walking in a fine brown dress with a gold brooch at her throat and her russet hair swept down her back in a mass of flaming curls. A fine figure of a women, they all agreed! A farmer saw her walking along the highway and calling to her, offered her a ride, but at the sound of his voice, she took fright and ran across the newly harvested fields until she was only a shadow in the gloom.

And that was the last time they saw her alive. She disappeared into the night, leaving no more hint of her identity, her home, her life, then the scrawled letters on the hotel register - "Amelia Dutcher."

The wind was high that night. To the Rood farm it blew the promise of winter and from Blue Mound, a thin, high scream that could have been a coyote or a wildcat or a women. The cold winter came soon, with snow and ice. Amelia Dutcher was forgotten; her battered carpet bag lay in a far corner of the lobby, waiting for someone who never came, waiting for the owner of the high-pitched scream on Elephant's Back Bluff.

She was found in the spring, and her indentity traced with the gold heirloom brooch, first at the hotel, later to the house of her uncle in Ohio. No one knows yet how she died-whether she fell, or jumped or was pushed. Some legends whisper that another woman came to town that same day - and left the next with the fear of death in her eyes.

They buried Amelia Dutcher in the Plainville Cemetery - you can find the grave now and on it a stone "In Memory of Her Who Died on the Mound." But the story didn't end there-for some people say that if you go to the Elephant's Back on a crisp cool autumn night when the wind is high and the moon is under a cloud, you may hear a thin, high scream that might be a coyote or a wildcat - or a woman.

The Moe Settlement and the Town of Newport

The Norse immigration to Wisconsin was in its early phase when Norwegians first came to the northwest corner of Columbia County. In 1849, on the heels of the Menonimees, "Big Swen" Toralson, Osmund Jensen, Paul Anderson, Swen Thompson, Jacob Thompson, Peter Julson, Iver Ingbretson and Kettle Kettleson arrived and staked out their claims in what was not yet the Town of Newport.

These first settlers took up land in the southern part of the town. They had an eye for easy access to water, the Wisconsin River, and the wild hay ready to be cut in the marshes. Then too, here the timber was not so heavy and the land easier to clear and bring into production.

As more and more settlers arrived they had to go into the northeastern part of the town to find vacant land. Thus, two Norwegian settlements began, separated by a few Irish and Yankee farmers, among them Alonzo Stearns and Joseph Bailey. The Lower Norwegian Settlement was in the southern part of the town along the river. The Upper Norwegian Settlement was to the northeast, extending into Adams and Marquette counties.

Hospitality was a distinguishing trait of most of the early settlers. It was not unusual to find several families housed in a small log cabin. Jacob Thompson and Osmund Jensen were the first to get their cabins in livable shape. Then, as the others arrived, they found a place to stay till they could have a "duna" or house building bee, and shortly there would be another cabin seen in a small clearing, roofed with split logs, bark or sometimes clapboards and floored with split logs laid flat side up. The roof often leaked, the windows were without glass and the doors held shut by a wooden pin

The Delton Academy was one of the first structures built in the village of Delton. The original building consisted only of the Classical Revival-style rectangle beneath the gable roof with a center entrance. The center doorway was later replaced by the stained-glass Grand Army of the Republic window honoring Delton's Civil War veterans. The entrance was moved to the side beneath the belfry. The building still stands in Lake Delton and may be the oldest standing structure in the area.

inserted in an auger hole. Thus it was when Ole Armson and his wife Mary arrived they found shelter with Jacob Thompson and here their daughter Lena was born on the second Christmas Day, December 16, 1859, the first Norwegian-American child born in Newport.

The Town of Newport was organized in 1852, but the Norwegian community was already there and already known as the Moe Settlement, named after Swen Toralson's home parish in Norway.

New Buffalo and Delton

Settlement began at what became the Town of Delton in the early 1840s, when three men remembered as Mead, Bently and McNeal set up a business that sold food, drink, lodging and whatever else they could supply to the raftsmen who paused on the beach after completing their run through the Dells rapids. The preferred currency was the "whiskey shingle," which came downriver on the lumber rafts. One thousand shingles were worth one gallon of corn whiskey. The traders than exchanged the shingles to settlers whose homes needed roofs.

In the late 1840s, John T. Huntington reputedly built the first frame house along Dell Creek. Alexander Vosler is credited with having built a board shanty he called a hotel in 1849. With no sawmill nearby, it's safe to assume that Huntington and Vosler either purchased their lumber off a river raft that survived the passage through the Dells or salvaged it off the beach after the break-up of a raft that didn't make it.

Throughout the 1850s, the energies of most of Delton's settlers were directed at the development of Newport, but other things were also happening. Jared Fox and Elijah Topping built a dam and mill at what was known as the "lower" water power of Dell Creek where the Sarrington Mill later stood. Plans were made, but not executed, to utilize the "upper" water power, where Timme's Mill was built in 1860.

In 1850, Fox also established the first post office, which he named Lauretta in honor of his fellow pioneer, Lauretta Norris, wife of Edward. It was appropriate, since Fox kept the post office in a bedroom of the Norris home until he opened Delton's first store. Delton also had the first school in the area, a private institution funded by subscription, and its Baptists organized the first religious congregation, with Henry Topping as pastor.

Natives of western New York, these first settlers gave the town organized by the Sauk County board in 1851 the familiar name of *New Buffalo;* and so it remained until it became *Delton* in 1871.

Newport and Kilbourn City

There is no guillotine in this "tale of two cities," and few of its details resemble the romantic and intriguing novel of Charles Dickens. This tale does, however, speak of greed, conspiracy, wealth, poverty, the birth of one city and the death of another.

The tale begins in the newly-settled area on the east and west banks of the Wisconsin River, about two miles south of the present city of Wisconsin Dells.

Alonzo B. Stearns was the first citizen to settle in the area, arriving on the east side of the river in March of 1849. Among the other early settlers were E. A. Toles, Edmund Norris, James Kendrick, Joseph Steele, John Marshall, Joseph Bailey and the Norwegians of the Moe Settlement.

In November, 1852, apparently at the suggestion of Joseph Bailey and Jonathan Bowman, the Columbia County Board named the new town Newport. Bailey and Bowman had just completed a warehouse on the river and they hoped that a place named "Newport" would attract steamboat traffic.

Joseph Bailey had already become one of the leading characters in the tale by making a claim, in 1850, to a large section of land in Newport located along the east bank of the Wisconsin River. He had also, along with partner John Marshall, obtained a charter from the state legislature to construct a bridge across the Wisconsin at the mouth of Dell Creek.

In 1851, Jonathon Bowman, a wealthy young attorney, recently graduated from law school, and Dr. George Jenkins, a graduate of the University of New York medical college also arrived at Newport. Together with Bailey they agreed that Newport would be an ideal spot for a thriving new town and they began to work toward that end. Joseph Kendrick, John Steele and Marshall, who had located on the west side of the river, agreed that they also would work toward development of a new village.

The developers felt the river would offer power for "all the mills that could be erected on its banks." They also knew that the railroad then under construction from Milwaukee to La Crosse had to cross the Wisconsin somewhere between Portage and Point Bluff and they figured that Newport would be the best place for it.

In 1853, in addition to the charter for a bridge they already had, Bowman, Bailey and several others obtained a legislative charter to build a dam across the river.

At the same time their group was making overtures to Byron Kilbourn, newly elected president of the La Crosse and Milwaukee Railroad, to secure his promise to cross the river at Newport.

The next step for Bowman and Bailey was to plat 400 acres of land which they owned into marketable lots in the new village of Newport. The lots began selling immediately at very high prices. The village grew quickly. By the summer of 1854 many homes and businesses were constructed. By 1855, about 1500 people resided in the blossoming young village which contained 13 large stores, three hotels and other businesses.

E.C. Dixon in his "Newport, Its Rise and Fall" wrote, "Not many communities in the United States were founded with a greater promise of permanent well-being...few faded so suddenly or left behind more bitter disappointment."

According to the history of Columbia County, "As a further inducement to secure the crossing of the railroad in Newport, Bailey and Bowman agreed to make a transfer of their 400 acres and their charter for the dam to Byron Kilbourn. In return, he offered bonds worth $200,000 to insure his promise to build the dam and to cross the river at Newport."

Garret Vliet, vice-president of the La Crosse and Milwaukee, was Byron Kilbourn's representative at Newport. After the deal was made with Kilbourn, Vliet, along with Bailey and Bowman, completed platting the remainder of the 400 acres.

When the people of Newport found out about the additional land development, lots were grabbed up quickly. It was said that some parties were able to double their money in 24 hours time.

At the same time that the flourish of activity was taking place east of the river the land owners on the other side of the river were busy laying out a village they called Dell Creek. The name Dell Creek was later dropped to become part of the larger village of Newport. The entire area of Newport, east and west of the river, was originally platted for a population of 10,000.

The Steele Tavern in derelict state many years after the demise of Newport. (Courtesy, H.H. Bennett Studio Foundation).

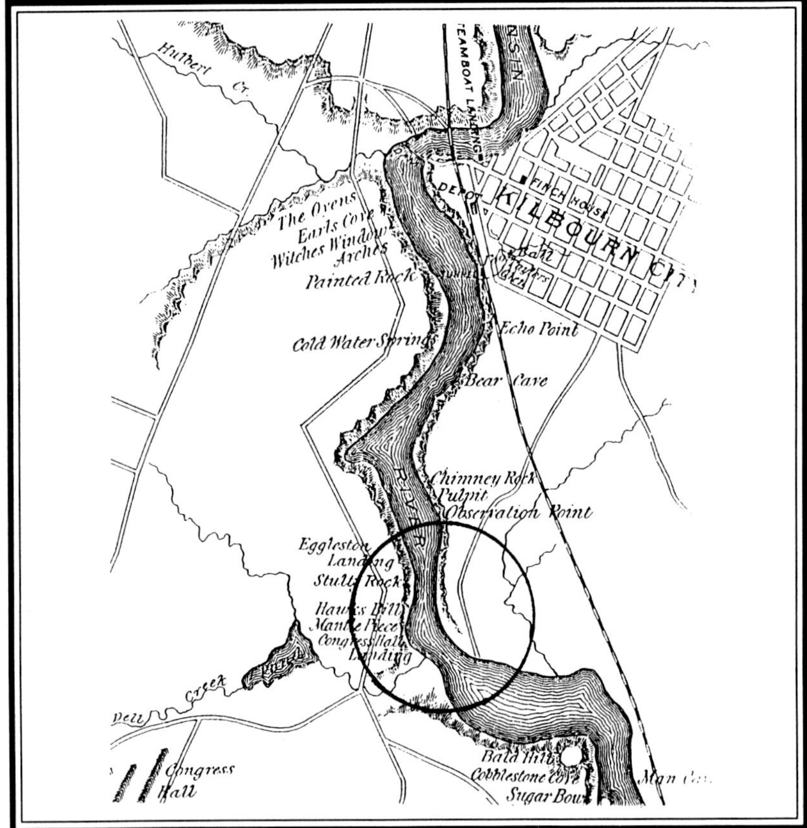

The circle indicates the bend in the river up from the mouth of Dell Creek where the grand city of Newport was to be located. The dotted line is the route of the railroad that bypassed Newport and gave birth to Kilbourn/Wisconsin Dells.

Shortly after a weak attempt to begin construction of the promised dam, Vliet, acting for Kilbourn, and on behalf of the developers, proposed the organization of a corporation, which came to be known as the Wisconsin River Hydraulic Company. The stated purpose of the corporation was to avoid individual responsibility from damage which might result from flooding upstream when the new dam was completed.

Vliet then conveyed to the new company the real estate secured from Bailey and Bowman and the charter for the building of the dam as well as the bonds given to Bailey and Bowman and their partners.

Owners of land likely to be flooded when the dam went in openly discussed the high sums they were going to demand in damages. These threats alarmed the directors of the Hydraulic Company, who feared that their profits would be eroded. Using this as a stated rationale, they asked that the $200,000 in bonds be returned to Kilbourn. Bailey, Bowman and the incorporators of the dam had faith that the Hydraulic Company would fulfill its pledge to build the dam and that the railroad would keep its pledge to cross the river at Newport.

Their faith, it seems, was misplaced. While assuring the people of their intentions to fulfill their part of the bargain, the Hydraulic Company was busy buying land two miles up river, at the site not yet known as Kilbourn.

Word spread about mysterious night time operations on the river. "Old settlers of today tell of spectral figures in phantom skiffs, sounding the river by the light of dim lanterns and pacing off the ground in the lights and shadows of the moon," wrote local newspaperman James E. Jones in the early 1900s.

Evidence of the intent of fraud has never been completely proven. Much that remains, however strongly implicating, is circumstantial.

Dixon seemed to realize this when he wrote: "Whether there was at that time an actual purpose to commit fraud or whether later events only made it appear so, only the opening of the books on Judgment Day will ever reveal."

But whatever the facts may have been, division of opinion was positive and intense, and enmities developed which lasted a lifetime. The passing years seem to indicate that the changes in location of both dam and bridge were due to reasonable causes with no intent to defraud. But it is also probably true that the investigations of an alternative route for the railroad were accelerated by reason of the exaggerated prices asked for land at the original location. John Marshall was one of the incorporators of the original dam and consequently one of the larger losers when it moved.

As Dixon recalled, "Justice Roujet Marshall, his son, told me personally that he was fully satisfied with the assurance of Colonel John B. Vliet, the surveyor, that the change in the location of the bridge and the dam was a matter of topography and that his survey west of the river proved that grading was less difficult at the Kilbourn crossing than at Newport."

"The Colonel Vliet who made these assurances is the same Col. Vliet identified as one of the "spectral figures" seen often taking measurements and making soundings on the river in the dark of the night.

"Those who believed that fraud was involved could ask some difficult questions. Was the return of the bonds requested because the Hydraulic Company actually feared suits for flowage damages or because they had already decided on the upper location? Was the change made because the upper site was actually preferable because of the width of the river, height of the banks, and the danger of flowage at Newport or was it in large part caused by a plan of land speculation relative to the new site? Was the change in the location of the bridge caused by considerations of topography as determined by Vliet's later survey or was that too brought about largely by this same idea of land speculation involving the upper site?" Dixon added.

"It is certain that secrecy was involved, but that may well have been a matter of business precaution designed to prevent panic and stampede rather

A Milwaukee Road locomotive and freight in the Kilbourn depot, 1875. (Courtesy, H.H. Bennett Studio Foundation).

than an indication of sinister purpose to complete all the plans for the change before steps could be taken to prevent it. The secrecy was related specifically to the survey for the exact location of the bridge and dam at Kilbourn City," Dixon wrote.

In the summer of 1855, while Newport was making rapid strides in its growth, the Hydraulic Company was busy buying the entire tract of land on which Kilbourn was located.

Knowledge of the purchase caused a near panic but the railroad company still gave assurance that the promise of a bridge at Newport would be fulfilled.

In the fall of 1855 a new figure entered the story, Alanson Holly. Tradition gives Holly a fairly clean "bill of health" but recently examined documents and letters seem to indicate otherwise. This information shows that Holly was made a director of the Hydraulic Company in August of 1856. Some questions about Holly will never be answered-why, when he came to the area in 1855 and everyone else believed that Newport was a booming gold mine, with a boundless capacity for growth, did he settle two miles up the river in a remote and uninhabited area? Why was he made a director of the Hydraulic Company so soon and why would the company assume the newspaper's expenses? What inside knowledge led Holly to print in the *Mirror* on Feb. 12, 1856 a statement that a definite decision had been reached to place the dam at Kilbourn rather than the Newport site–at a point, when the citizens of Newport were still sure that their site was the chosen location.

Apparently the question of Holly's involvement came up in the past because several historical writers allude to it. "His interest was at first wholly professional" wrote Dixon. "He had no involvement with either the railroad or the hydraulic company," stated one local historian.

At the time of the naming of Kilbourn, June 10, 1856, Holly stated he was in full favor of naming the town in honor of Kilbourn. It is not known whether or not Bailey or Bowman were in favor of so honoring Kilbourn. It is likely they were not.

It is not clear whether or not Bailey and Bowman were completely duped by Kilbourn or whether they went along with a scheme, if there was one, at a later point. Bailey moved his home to the new town shortly after Holly settled in. In so doing he may have seemed to align himself too closely with the decisive forces because he later received a cold shoulder from many in the community and after returning from the Civil War stayed in Kilbourn for only a short time. Bowman did not move to Kilbourn until about six years later, which probably helped to save his reputation.

Newport experienced one last hope for survival in 1858 but "resurrection" hopes did not materialize and the boom town became merely a ghost of the past, with only stone cellars and a few lilac bushes to mark its passing.

Byron Kilbourn

Byron Kilbourn. (Courtesy, State Historical Society of Wisconsin).

As President of the La Crosse and Milwaukee Railroad in the 1850s, Byron Kilbourn was responsible for the siting of the village that became Wisconsin Dells. Although originally named in his honor, Kilbourn City actually saw very little of Byron Kilbourn. It was never his home, only a potentially good investment. The following is an edited version of an article written by Russell Austin.

Byron Kilbourn's proud, obstinate nature could be read in every line of his large, strong featured face. He was "a man of strong prejudices and dictatorial disposition, at all times insistent upon having his own way, and consequently not popular," wrote Dr. Lucius I. Barber. "The man who presumed to differ with him was in the wrong, or of no account."

Byron was born at Granby, Connecticut, on Sept. 8, 1801. In 1802 his father bought 16,000 acres of land in central Ohio, around Columbus, and the next year moved there with his family.

Besides running several factories, the senior Kilbourn was a federal surveyor and boundary commissioner, a colonel of a frontier regiment and a Congressman for several terms.

The law had been young Byron's favorite subject, but his father's strong prejudice against that profession decided him against it. Byron had always liked the woods, so he coupled his interest with his mathematical training and went into surveying.

Ohio was then laying out vast internal improvements, and the young Kilbourn became an engineer on several of the projects, including the Ohio river canal, the Miami canal and the Milan ship canal. These completed, he set out for "that far off country to the west of Lake Michigan" and got a job as surveyor of public lands at Green Bay in May, 1834.

The surveying job was merely a way station for the ambitious Kilbourn. He spent most of the summer and fall of 1834 exploring the western shore of the lake, seeking "the natural commercial point."

From the moment he first looked west across the Milwaukee river from Solomon Juneau's place, he knew he had found the site for his city. The land was too swampy, and the bluffs were too steep for building sites, but these difficulties were just a challenge to the young engineer.

He moved his family to Milwaukee from Cincinnati in September, 1837, and built a log house in what is now Lapham Park. He lived in this city until his death, August 5, 1877, supporting many projects for civic improvement. Except for two terms as mayor, he avoided public office.

Kilbourn was to have his fling at railroads, but not until after he tried canal-building. The canal was to run from the Milwaukee River to the Menomonee River then cut west to the Rock River and on to the four lakes of the Madison area, the Wisconsin River and thence to the Mississippi.

Kilbourn pushed this Milwaukee and Rock River canal by every means, even founding the city's first newspaper, the *Milwaukee Advertiser*, in July, 1836, to promote it. In 1838 Kilbourn won a temporary victory when Congress granted 166,400 acres of land to be sold to finance construction and the legislature gave the company a charter. The first dirt was dug from the canal bed on the Fourth of July, 1839, and the dam and portion of the canal running parallel to the Milwaukee river was opened in 1842. That same year, however, the project's enemies persuaded the legislature to repeal the acts which would have permitted the canal's completion. Even so, there was enough canal to give water power for "75 run of millstones." Soon 24 flour mills, lumber mills and factories were humming busily on its banks. The canal cost $56,745, of which the sale of granted lands paid more than half. The fate of his canal didn't discourage Kilbourn. In 1847 a chart appeared on the wall of his office diagramming his new enthusiasm–railroads.

Kilbourn particularly wanted to beat Chicago in building a railroad to the Mississippi. He said, "If we build the first one and get to the river first, Chicago will not dare to approach our territory. Then we can defy the world to come between us and this great northwest."

As early as the boom year of 1836, Kilbourn and other railroad enthusiasts had held public meetings and circulated petitions asking the legislature to incorporate a company to build a railroad from Milwaukee to the Mississippi.

Despite repeated petitions, conservatives for more than a decade prevented any bill authorizing such a railroad from passing the legislature. Some favored canals, for water "was never known to run off the track, break down or get out of repair." They had only scorn for the "awkward engine that could not climb hills or be prevented from running headlong down them."

Kilbourn and the railroad enthusiasts countered by calling conservatives "ducks and mud hens," and by pointing out that water could not be induced to remain unfrozen in Wisconsin during the winter.

Finally, in 1847, the legislature compromised by authorizing the Milwaukee & Waukesha railroad. Kilbourn, who was elected mayor the next year, became president of the new railroad company. Alexander Mitchell, who was later to be president of the Milwaukee road, was a member of the board of directors .

The next session of the legislature amended the charter to allow the railroad to extend its lines to the Mississippi, and the company changed its name to the Milwaukee & Mississippi Railroad Company. Construction of the Milwaukee to Waukesha portion of the line began in 1849.

Kilbourn's company didn't have enough money to buy rails for this short distance, for Milwaukee investors at that time considered plank roads, with their frequent toll houses, a better investment. Many farmers along the line offered to mortgage their farms to raise capital for the railroad, but these securities sold very poorly in the east.

Money was so scarce that the railroad even accepted stock subscriptions in commodities. For the first year the grading was paid for almost entirely in orders for goods: "by carts from wagon makers, by harness from harness makers, and by cattle, horses, beef, pork, oats, corn, potatoes, and flour from the farmers," as one of the first directors, Edward D. Holton, recalled in an address in 1858.

The first trip all the way to Waukesha was made in February, 1851. Passengers even helped the train crew stack wood that first year before taking their seats.

Kilbourn's ambition was not satisfied with this first section of the railroad, and the work was pushed vigorously in the next few years. Farmers along the route loaned the railroad workers teams and implements, and often pitched in and helped without pay, some even bringing their hired men. The road pushed on to Milton in 1852, to Stoughton in 1853, to Madison in 1854, and to Prairie du Chien, on the Mississippi, on April 15, 1857.

Kilbourn was not through with railroads. He became a commissioner of the Milwaukee & Watertown railroad, then president of the La Crosse railroad, both of which were later absorbed by the Milwaukee road.

It was in the La Crosse venture that Kilbourn ran off the track of civic rectitude and got mired in a lobbying scandal of greater magnitude than any other legislative corruption ever uncovered in Wisconsin.

In 1856, while the La Crosse railroad was still under construction, Congress authorized two large grants of land in Wisconsin for railroad purposes. The state legislature was empowered to assign the grants to railroads. One grant, in eastern Wisconsin, went to the Wisconsin and Superior Co., later absorbed by the North Western railroad, and the other went to Kilbourn's La Crosse railroad.

A legislative investigating committee was created in 1858 to look into charges that bribery had been used to get the LaCrosse grant. The committee made some very shocking discoveries, which were published in a "Wisconsin Black Book" that year.

The report said that railroad officials, headed, by Kilbourn, had paid more than $1,000,000 in bonds and stocks for "expenses incident to the land grant."

Of this amount, $631,000 was paid in bribes to a majority of the legislature, the governor and a supreme court justice, the book said. The rest of the stocks and bonds went to compensate the lobbyists who had swarmed like bees around the capitol while Kilbourn's grant was pending.

The standard price paid to bribe an assemblyman was $5,000, the report stated, but state senators cost twice as much. "Key men" and those who helped line up their colleagues were even more liberally "remembered," three senators getting $20,000 each and one $25,000.

Governor Coles L. Bashford, Wisconsin's first Republican governor, received $50,000, the report showed, and Supreme Court Justice Abram D. Smith "found $10,000 in bonds in his library desk in Milwaukee" - and put them in his safe deposit box.

Some of the money went to others than state officials: Kilbourn and Moses Strong, his chief aide, each kept $25,000 of the "corruption bonds," according to the "Black Book." Alexander Mitchell, the Milwaukee banker, got $10,000 and Rufus King, editor of the *Sentinel*, $10,000, the committee reported. No one was ever prosecuted.

Some of the legislators could not be bought. Senator Amassa Cobb of Mineral Point reported this interview with a Kilbourn agent:

"I asked him what was the amount of the capital stock of the company. He replied, $10,000,000. I told him to say to Byron Kilbourn that if he would multiply the capital stock by the number of leaves in Capitol park and give me the amount of money, and then have himself, Moses Strong and Alex Mitchell blacked and give me a clear title to them as servants for life, I would take the matter under consideration."

Milwaukee was strangely lenient with Kilbourn after this scandalous expose. He had done so much in the building of the city that it seems he could do no wrong in the eyes of Milwaukeeans.

His company went into liquidation soon after the scandal, but Kilbourn was left by no means a poor man. He lived in Milwaukee like a respectable citizen until the fall of 1868, when poor health led him to travel south. He died in Jacksonville, Florida, December 16, 1870.

The Working Wisconsin River

Rafting Through the Dells

In the early days when lumbering was the state's leading industry, the river at the Dells played a leading role in the drama of rafting. Down most of its length, the Wisconsin is a placid, tranquil river but at the Narrows of the Dells, where it is confined within high rocky banks and only fifty feet wide, it can become a wild and unpredictable terror to all who try to traverse it.

Before white settlers arrived in Wisconsin much of the state was forested. White pine was the first timber considered for commercial cutting as it would float down the rivers when freshly cut. White pine in the northern two thirds of the state averaged 3 1/2 feet at the base, stood 70 feet tall and grew near the streams. As the Midwest and the treeless plains farther west were settled, lumber was needed for homes, barns and businesses. The vast northern forest seemed inexhaustible.

The first recorded logging on the Wisconsin River was by soldiers led by Lt. Jefferson Davis, later president of the Confederacy, in 1828 for the building of Fort Winnebago near Portage. In 1833, George Whitney and John Metcalf ran the first lumber raft from the mill at Pointe Basse through the Dells to Portage.

Between 1814 and 1848 lands on the Upper Wisconsin were ceded by various Indian tribes and lumbering grew rapidly. Timber was floated down many streams to mills which sawed the logs into rough lumber. In 1847, 24 mills were running 45 saws but six years later that number increased to 100. By 1872, the river's annual output was over 200 million board feet.

The Wisconsin was a great waterway to float rafts to market except for three impediments. First, there were wicked rapids at Grand Rapids, now Wisconsin Rapids. Next was the almost right-angled turn at the Devil's Elbow in the Dells and a short way downstream was the passage over or through the dam at Kilbourn. Once these dangers were past, rafts drifted peacefully on their way to their markets as far south as St. Louis.

Lumber rafts were cleverly constructed for flexibility between the cribs and stability when encountering obstacles. The art of building rafts came to Wisconsin, along with other logging practices, from eastern lumbermen who had followed the trade west.

The basic unit of a lumber raft was a crib. The framework of each crib was started by placing on the ground 3 grub planks about eight feet apart and parallel to each other. On each end and across the center of the grub planks, running the opposite way were placed the three cross planks. All of the grub and cross planks had two inch holes bored through them on each end and another exactly in the middle. The grub stakes were then inserted upward thru the matching holes on each side, each corner and in the middle of the framework. The grub was made of a small oak tree with the root end at the bottom of the planks so that the lumber would not pull through. The grub stakes were long enough so all the alternating layers of lumber were placed on top of them, each with its own hole drilled to hold them in place on the grub stakes. These stakes extended above the completed raft and served many purposes.

A crib was from 12 to 24 courses deep depending on whether the wood was dry or green and the depth of the river it was to traverse. Witch planks were laid on the final course of the lumber and a tool called a Witch was used to compress a crib by pulling up on the grub stake. The rafts rode only some two to five inches out of the water. When each crib was completed, it was slid carefully into the water or on the ice. Then the cribs were attached together with coupling slabs over the grub stakes. Seven cribs commonly were coupled together to make one *string* or *rapids piece* of a Wisconsin raft.

On the forward end of the string, a half crib was hinged to the crib behind it. The *headblock*, a heavy timber, was secured with notches to hold the springpoles. The springpoles were strong and heavy, usually made of hemlock and 32 feet long, just reaching from the bow end of the first crib to the tail end of the second one. The front end was inserted in the notch in the head block and the tail end was fitted over a grub stake at the back end of the second crib. A heavy block under the center of the pole, like a fulcrum, depressed the crib at that point so that the bow was elevated a few inches, thus slightly resembling a scow or rude boat in appearance. But the purpose of the arrangement was to give support to the raft in running dams and rapids and in safely passing heavy eddies.

Dr. E.C. Dixon of Kilbourn recounted: "I was once on a two string raft as it ran the old Kilbourn dam and the plunge of the raft over the drop was so heavy that the spring poles broke and both front cribs buckled clear under the ones behind them, thus making a raft two cribs deep. You may imagine

***Previous page:** River men reassembling a raft after passing through the treacherous Dells. Sawmills in the Upper Wisconsin Valley cut pine logs into boards and assembled them into rafts that carried them to markets downstream. The Narrows and the rapids below made one of the most dangerous spots on the river and dams built at Kilbourn only increased the danger. Rafting ended in the 1880s, when railroads in the north replaced the river as a means to market lumber. H. H. Bennett hitched a ride on one of the last rafting expeditions and created a series of images that is recognized as perhaps the first instance of photojournalism. (Courtesy, H.H. Bennett Studio Foundation).*

that there was great excitement at the time and a wild scramble of the men to escape being thrown into the river."

Each string was fitted with gigantic steering oars at either end. These oars or sweeps had a stem of carefully selected white pine 34' to 45' long, 30' inside the headblock and 15' outside of it. A blade like an enormous shingle, 15' long, 2 1/2 inches thick at the butt and 1/2 inch at the tip and 12 to 16 inches wide was fitted into a slot cut into the butt of the stem and tightly wedged into place. These oars were used only for steering the raft as their propulsion was provided solely by the flow of the current. Sometimes one man could handle an oar. The motion was lunge, step, lunge, step - not a steady push. When the water was fast all men available would be at the oars. Rafts were also furnished with grousers, tall vertical posts that could be driven into the river bottom to anchor the raft; jacks to lift it off sandbars; and Spanish windlasses to draw the strings together.

A Wisconsin raft consisted of three strings yoked together. In tight places or fast water, the strings were taken apart so each string or rapids piece could be taken through by a full crew. Such maneuvering was always necessary in going through the chute at the Kilbourn dam and often in the Narrows. After the last obstacle was past, the crew then walked or "gigged back" to the head of the Dells and then rode another string or rapids piece down to safety below the dam. This was a rough hike up hills and down ravines. A fleet could consist of as many as twenty of these three string rafts run together by one pilot. The fleets were equipped with cook stoves and their shanties called wanigans, dining tables and "dog houses" for sleeping. Shingles and lath were often cargo carried on the decks of the rafts. Thus the crew was riding the product to market.

If a fleet started above Wausau, it could usually figure on being in St. Louis in 24 days. Often it took longer–if the water was too high to go through the Narrows, or so low that it took extra time to jack off sandbars, if extra time was needed for major repairs to rafts which may have been loosened by hitting unexpected obstacles. Thus the passage through the Dells could take two or three days and a crew might make two or even three trips a season. Sometimes, acres of rafts filled the river from the head of the Dells to Lone Rock. Dr. Dixon tells of being one of the boys who ran on the rafts from the River Road bridge to High Rock.

Raftsmen were a tough and hardy band. Pilots made several trips, often earning as much as $1,000 in a season, and carried a good deal of prestige. In the Dells, we know of three "standing pilots" who took rafts through the Dells: Louis Dupless, Robert Allen and Leroy Gates, who carved his name in the Narrows. The inscription proclaims that Gates was a "Dells and River Pilot, 1849-1858" and charged $2.00 a trip or $10.00 "if he warrants the trip."

Gates was a flamboyant character who bragged that he would pilot a raft through in his full dress suit. Many were on hand to watch and chuckle when he lost his footing and was dumped in the river.

Many members of a logging crew were experienced raftsmen who worked in the logging camps in the winter and were invited to be a part of the raft crew in the spring. In 1870, the inexperienced Fred Houghton was hired as a skiffman for $100 and fare back home. This job was a boon to farm boys who very seldom saw hard cash. Dr. Dixon told that several well-known Kilbourn men had been raftsmen: Captains John and Henry Snider; Captain Bell; Dave Van Wie; Norman, Ed and Emmet Bullis; the Eggleston brothers; the Shattucks; John Lynch; Sophronius Stocking Landt; Albert Cook, who cooked on the rafts, and many others.

Hiram Sly, a raft pilot, had his young son, Martin, meet him above the Narrows, boosted him on his shoulders so he wouldn't get wet when the raft was awash and gave him an unforgettable ride downstream. The Kaleas family from Kilbourn lost two brothers who drowned off rafts a year apart. Many families were understandably reluctant to allow their young sons to associate with this rough bunch of men but adventure for the boys and money for the families were strong inducements.

On the Wisconsin, rafts ran only during daylight hours, while on the broad Mississippi, rafts of 160 cribs were 64 feet wide and 1280 feet long and ran day and night. Later they were pushed by steamboats to gain more speed.

The sharp turn in the Narrows required expert navigation but Notch Rock was an even greater hazard. It is now entirely under water. It was a near-perfect square projection of solid rock standing out ten feet into the stream on the west bank of the Narrows slightly upstream from Rattlesnake Rock. The Rock was an even greater hazard when higher water covered it and the pilot could not see it lurking just below the surface. Again Dr. Dixon tells us, "One day in the Narrows, watching the rafts pass through, I saw a three string raft hit Notch Rock, rip off the entire right hand string of six cribs, letting the other two swing and catch on the left hand rocks, breaking in two at the middle, leaving two sections of three cribs long and two wide, with both oars unhung and the worst confusion I ever saw on a Wisconsin River raft. But the swift working lumberjacks worked the three parts together and passed on down over the dam with no serious loss of any lumber."

***Previous page**: "Witching up" one of the grub pens holding together a raft at High Rock prior to running the Dells rapids. (Courtesy, H.H. Bennett Studio Foundation).*

One wonders how any man could survive a raft breaking up in the Narrows. A man had to be very nimble or very lucky to run on the wet lumber. If he was thrown in the water, he might be sucked down or if he could reach the shore, how could he climb out on the irregular cliffs slippery with wet mosses? Lives are still being lost along these banks.

A traveler in 1858 describes his journey to the river and the toll bridge at the Narrows which had been built in 1850 by Schuyler Gates.

> **"Taking a good look at the stream from the top of the bridge, I crossed, and proceeding for some distance up its side, I soon came in view of some rafts preparing to enter what to many a poor fellow has been the 'Valley of Death'. A request that I might have a passage was readily granted, and in a few minutes, by some maneuvering, the raft was started, and on we went gliding gracefully down the stream. The current appeared to me to get swifter and swifter and swifter, until the whole raft of cribs of lumber pinned together seemed to tremble and twist and be determined to go to pieces just because I was on it. We were fairly afloat on the fierce, rolling, rushing tide, speeding on or rather down toward the turn above the bridge, where projecting into the stream is the dangerous rock, on the starboard hand of the river, called Notch Rock. Having sheered too much, or given too wide a berth to the eddy, or some whirl on the opposite side of the stream, we swung too far and came too near the Notch, passing within, it seemed to me, about four feet of the savage-looking point of the rock. On we went, the men plying their sweeps or oars with a vigor that appeared to denote a danger at hand....The swift water, that here, in its narrowest limits was maddened and infuriated, writhing, twisting, whirling, seething and foaming and boiling and bubbling, like some huge watery monster that was in an agony of pain as it forced itself through the craggy passage....**
>
> **"Just as we passed the bridge, a hole or concave place appeared in sight, close ahead of the raft, looking as if some leviathan had suddenly sucked down a hollow in the water; this place of hollow water seemed at least twenty feet across, and into this eddy the two forward cribs of the raft appeared to sink and to disappear, the water rushing upon the lumber and the whole raft feeling as if it was about to turn over with a twirl and go to the bottom of the vortex. I fancied I read in the faces of two of those belonging to the raft a sign of more than common danger; and a rushing backward and forward with the sweeps as the men put out all their strength and activity, induced me to commence the process of taking off an overcoat, that under any circumstances, would have been an encumbrance in the water. This elicited a laugh from two of the 'red shirts'; however it was apparent to me that unless the craft speedily righted, it would soon be 'every man for himself and God for us all'. This was the 'Grand Eddy'. I call it the Maelstrom, on a small scale, but large enough. The author compares this experience with many storms he had sailed through on the Atlantic and Cape Horn and never felt such "perhaps it was not fear, but it was certainly a realizing sense of the fact that, had the raft broke up, and I got overboard, as I certainly should, death to me, who cannot swim a stroke, was certain. I tell the truth and say that I was thankful when we got into smooth water, and I found my feet on terra firma at the Dell House, out of all danger."**

Anyone who has seen the Narrows in high water today, has seen the vortex still sucking down a hole in which floating trees can disappear to bob up again farther downstream.

Any descriptions of raftsmen and those who did business with them is likely to sound like a tale of the old Wild West. Hamlin Garland said of raftsmen, "What skill, what endurance, what courage the smallest of them displayed....Their action was titanic, their cheer superb. A day's labor reached from dawn to dusk, and no man thought of shirking his duty, or if he did, he was shamed into action by his fellows who took a savage pride in long hours and fatigue....On Sundays or during the long evenings they joined in contests of strength or skill. You would think they would require rest, but no! They wrestled, jumped, chinned a bar, pulled sticks, tried out each other's grip, and in every conceivable way established athletic rank....It takes a man to run a raft on the Wisconsin, a man who is a mixture of wildcat and alligator."

H.E. Cole tells of their visits to old Newport. "Along the main street strode the founders of the town, discussing the news of the day, the affairs of the village, the exploits of the raftsmen in running rafts through the Dells, and listening to stories of adventurers....Here it was that rivermen frolicked away their wages at the nine or more saloons, fiddling and dancing in homes and halls, often parading up and down the streets like arrant braggarts. They were men of iron, proof against all kinds of weather, accustomed to hard fare, and no stranger to perils on land or water. The superiority of these rivermen in the town, when they congregated there in the spring at the time of running the rapids, was tacitly admitted. Not a few had acquired an abundant store of thrilling experiences on the frontier which furnished endless entertainment to village listeners."

The raftsmen's life was full of danger. In 1872, forty of them lost their lives in the Wisconsin. "The

Banks of the Little Eau Pleine" is one of their ballads which tells the story of a young girl looking for her loved one. She asks a riverman who tells her,

"If John Murphy's the name of your raftsman,
I used to know him very well.
But sad is the tale I must tell you:
Your Johnny was drowned in the Dells.
They buried him 'neath a scrub Norway,
You will never behold him again.
No stone marks the spot where your raftsman
Sleeps far from the Little Eau Pleine."

After the poor girl is aroused from her faint, she cries,

"My curses attend you, Wisconsin!
May your rapids and falls cease to roar.
May every tow-head and sand-bar
Be as dry as a log schoolhouse floor."

When the raftsmen had time or opportunity to stop and refresh themselves, these red shirts were, as Steward Edward White tells in his book, *The Riverman*, were "bubbling over with the joy of life, ready for quarrel if quarrel also spelled fun, drinking deep and heavy-handed and fearless in their cups."

The Dell House was the first inn below Pointe Basse in the 75 mile stretch from that point to Fort Winnebago. Robert Allen built the Dell House as a hotel, store and barroom, assisted by George Orcutt, who was also a partner in the venture for a time. George Orcutt and his wife lived there with their five children. One daughter was born there March 16, 1859 and had many happy memories of deer, ducks and friendly Indians. Evidently other members of their family, the Pritchards and Thatchers lived near by. The girl remembered when her mother's cousin, Daniel Thatcher, suffered a sunstroke, and she was sent for her father who attended the toll bridge certain hours of the day. Her father locked the bridge and hurried home and bled Daniel to save his life but he died before the doctor arrived. Later the family moved to Minnesota with an ox team and covered wagon. The family's prized possessions include the dinner bell and a large platter from the Dell House. It is hard to imagine this happy family home with the raucous reputation that still hangs over this hostelry.

After the dangers of Dells passage were behind them, the pleasures of the Dell House were more than welcome. H.H. Bennett says that the raftsmen would, "on landing safely at the Dell House, partake freely of the concentrated river water kept there for emergencies; if the trip had not been successful and the raft had been broke up, then something must be taken to the success of the next trip; if one of the crew had been lost in the mad waters, partaking of something in token of good wishes for his hereafter was not to be neglected by any means and sometimes like token was deemed necessary for the welfare of each of his surviving relatives, and so the old place became the scene of many a boisterous time, which may be all the foundation there is for the stories of the horrible crimes committed in and about the place in the early days."

Frank Weinhold says, "With the decline of the lumber traffic, the Dell House itself drifted into decline, although Allen had cleaned up the reputation of the Dell House somewhat and held dances and community gatherings there." The late Ross C. Curry told of seeing Robert Allen there in the 1880s. He described him as a man with a "big black beard and big black boots." He became very much a hermit and went to the county poor farm where he died in 1889.

Strange sounds and lights moving past the windows of the Dell House gave rise to stories of ghosts and the stories persisted even after the House was burned by vandals October 7, 1899, after it had stood vacant for many years.

The flamboyant Leroy Gates poses with props in Kilbourn's first photo studio. Gates helped build the first bridge across the Wisconsin at the Narrows, piloted rafts, guided tourists and inaugurated the Dells' tradition of aggressive promotion by advertising himself on the rocks of the Narrows. (Courtesy, H.H. Bennett Studio Foundation).

The classic photo of a lumber raft making its way through the Narrows. (Courtesy, H.H. Bennett Studio Foundation).

After Kilbourn was established in 1856, raftsmen also visited, sometimes to the dismay of the residents. It was said that the first thing the raftsmen did was to tie up the town marshall "so he wouldn't get hurt." Then they would head for "Bloody Run," with its many saloons and other attractions. There is still speculation as to whether Bloody Run was Eddy St. or the 700 block of Superior St. south of Broadway. The lumber companies did not pay their raftsmen until the end of the trip but–if the stories are true–the rivermen had plenty of money to spend when they hit town.

Stewart Edward White tells of some of the raftsmen's perils. "The proprietors of these places were a bold and unscrupulous lot. In their everyday business they had to deal with the most dangerous rough-and-tumble fighters this country has ever known....Men got rich very quickly at this business. And there existed this great advantage in favor of the divekeeper: nobody cared what happened to a riverman. You could pound him over the head with a lead pipe, or drug his drink, or choke him into insensibility, or rob him and throw him out into the street. The only fly in the divekeeper's ointment was that the riverman would fight back. And fight back he did....In his own words, he was 'a hard man to nick'."

Phil Sly told stories passed down from his grandfather, Hiram Sly, "king of the logging camp" who settled in Kilbourn in 1858 and piloted rafts through the Dells even when the river was "on the rampage." He once went as far as New Orleans on rafts, took a steamboat back to St. Louis where he bought a team of mules and brought them home to

Kilbourn. Hiram told of Dan McManman's store at 731 Superior Street. He sold supplies to the raftsmen and had a barrel of whiskey on his counter, offering free drinks to the crews. They might come in for a barrel of bacon, salt pork or other necessities. By the time they had partaken of several of the generous 4 oz. drinks so freely offered, they were increasing their orders considerably. Sly also told of a Madam who built a house on the cliffs on the right hand bank of the Lower Dells below the dam. She had her girls swing out over the river to tempt their potential customers below and then supplied "a ring in the rocks for the boys" to tie up their rafts.

Local people benefited from the lumber trade when they found free lumber floating in the river after a raft was broken up and not retrieved promptly. This practice was called river pirating and was legal if the rivermen made no claim to their lost product within a given time. The Lower Dells dock area became known as Pirate's Eddy. It is said that many houses throughout the area–and in other communities up and down the river–were built from this lumber.

After all the strings or rapids pieces had passed over the dam, they were pulled together three strings wide and secured for the final easy leg down the Wisconsin and the Mississippi. The pilot was often in charge of selling the lumber and some might be sold at towns along the river. When all was sold, the men had blown all their season's pay on cards, whiskey, and other diversions, they sometimes had to work their way home by planting crops as the season progressed north. Fred Houghton was given passage home on a steamboat as part of his wages but others must have had to progress on foot. The Landt family tells a story of two local men who arrived in Kilbourn, one broke and one with money in his pocket. When asked for an explanation, one man replied, "Well, on the way home, I drank river water and he drank firewater."

As railroads gradually extended through the state, they replaced the lumber raft. The necessity of drilling holes for the grub pins wasted considerable lumber, some was damaged by water and some when rafts split up. Many lives were lost also. Freight was quite cheap and soon the inexhaustible forests were stripped of their virgin pine.

H.H. Bennett had always been fascinated by this way of life and could see it passing from the American scene. In 1886, he had finally perfected his instantaneous shutter so he could stop action on his photographic plates. He obtained permission to travel on a fleet of Arpin Lumber Company rafts. His son, Ashley, went along and they photographed all aspects of the raftmen's work and play. These negatives have been printed many, many times and have been credited as the first instance of the photojournalism that was later imitated in the pages of *Life*, *Look* and other magazines.

In 1890, the last raft floated down the Wisconsin and its lumber was sold to the Drinker Mills in Happy Hollow, Kilbourn. Another chapter of the Wisconsin frontier closed.

The First Bridge Across the Wisconsin

By the mid-1840s, the Dell House on Black Hawk Island on the west side of the Wisconsin, was

The Drinker Brothers steam-powered mill was located on the river at the mouth of Crandall's Bay. It resawed for local use lumber rafted downstream. (Courtesy, H.H. Bennett Studio Foundation).

The first bridge across the Wisconsin, constructed by Schuyler and Leroy Gates in 1850. The framing on the bridge suggests that it was to have been covered with boards, but there is no record that it ever was covered. The Narrows bridge remained a vital link across the Wisconsin until it was washed out by the flood of 1866. (Courtesy, H.H. Bennett Studio Foundation).

a going concern, with 100 or more rivermen spending the night and putting coins in Robert Allen's cashbox. Allen was also running a ferry that enabled settlers traveling up the Pinery Road from Portage to cross the Wisconsin and proceed up the Lemonweir Valley. After Indian land on the east side of the river opened for settlement in the late 1840s, Allen's ferry carried newcomers from west to east.

With all the traffic crossing the river, and with a lot more likely to come, Allen and a partner named Hugh MacFarlane obtained a charter from the legislature to construct a bridge across the Narrows a short distance up from the Dell House. The partners would finance construction themselves and collect tolls set at 10¢ for vehicles drawn by one draft animal, 20¢ for vehicles requiring two animals, with another nickel charged for each additional animal. Herds of cattle or horses cost 2¢ per head, but sheep and hogs could pass for a penny. Pedestrians could cross free of charge.

Allen and MacFarlane obtained the charter, but Schuyler Gates designed and constructed the bridge. He had arrived at the Dells in 1849 and quickly acquired the land on the east bank where the bridge would touch. As a young man, Gates had worked on the Erie Canal, and had helped build and manage a canal railroad in Pennsylvania. He seems to have had the basic knowledge of construction and financing to handle the bridge project.

Although the records are not exact, Schuyler Gates, with help from his son Leroy, certainly completed the bridge in 1850. They used white pine beams–some hand-hewn, some milled–to build a simple but strong trussed bridge that spanned the 53-feet gap at the Narrows.

As the only bridge on the river, what became known as the "Gates Bridge" was a busy thoroughfare. "Being on the direct line of travel between eastern Wisconsin and the Lemonweir, La Crosse and Minnesota, there is an immense amount of

emigration now passing over it," reported Alanson Holly's *Wisconsin Mirror* in 1856.

The bridge was also a popular spot from which to watch lumber rafts make their wild ride down river. Perhaps it was the presence of this captive audience on the bridge that prompted Leroy Gates to carve into the rock nearby his self-promoting declaration that he was "Leroy Gates Dells & River Pilot from 1849 to 58." (Later immortalized in a Bennett photo and still faintly visible, Gates' carving may be the first in an long, long line of outdoor ads at the Dells.)

The Dell bridge carried settlers, river drivers, stage coaches, livestock, land speculators and merely curious visitors across the river until 1866. The spring break up came suddenly that year and the river rose to reportedly record levels that smashed dams, bridges and logging works up and down stream.

"Water the highest it's been for a great many years. It's terrible, awful, sublime, majestic and grand," wrote H. H. Bennett on April 23, 1866. Two days later, the flooding river had washed out the Dell bridge.

By then, most of the cross-river traffic had moved to the more conveniently-located and sometimes toll-free bridge the railroad had constructed at Kilbourn in 1857. There was some talk of rebuilding a bridge at the Narrows for the tourist trade in the 1880s, but no action was taken. Instead, the Dell bridge of Schuyler Gates will be simply remembered as the first bridge to cross the Wisconsin.

Railroad Bridges at the Dells

The first railroad bridge across the Wisconsin River at the Dells was built in 1857 by the La Crosse and Milwaukee Railroad at a reported cost of $100,000. It was a "home truss" wooden bridge, 450 feet long, with a tin roof to protect it from the weather and a deck of planks for horse-drawn wagons beneath the rails. Like its successors, this first railroad bridge had two decks. Trains traveled on the upper deck, horse-drawn and pedestrian traffic crossed on the lower deck in between the supporting framework.

It was one of two railroad bridges built across the river in 1857. The other one was at Spring Green and both bridges claim to be the first railroad bridge to cross the Wisconsin.

The Dells bridge carried the first train to cross the state and reach the Mississippi at La Crosse and proceed on to St. Paul. Conversely, it also carried thousands of carloads of men and material mobilized for the Civil War.

In 1866, a spark from a locomotive ignited the timbers of the bridge. Soon, the entire span was transformed into a "two hundred-foot sheet of

Kilbourn can also claim to be the site of the first railroad bridge across the Wisconsin. Built in 1857, Byron Kilbourn's bridge was destroyed by fire in 1866. The second bridge, depicted here while under construction, was also made of wood. It stood until it was replaced by an iron model in 1877. Trains ran on the upper deck, while wagons and pedestrians passed below where they could see the ad for Dixon's Store mounted on the crossbeam. (Courtesy, H.H. Bennett Studio Foundation).

flame" some of which shot downward 60 feet to the water. In minutes, the bridge crashed into the river and lodged on the remains of the old Hydraulic Company dam.

As the key river crossing point for what had become the Milwaukee Road railroad, the Dells bridge was quickly rebuilt. This second wooden structure stood until 1877, when the railroad replaced it with an iron bridge promoted as one of the largest and finest bridges in the West.

Fine and large it may have been, but the 1877 bridge was replaced by the structure still in use today. The span is a double-track, plate steel truss design, stretching 590 feet and costing $85,000 in 1896. The lower deck where horses, pedestrians, and later, autos crossed is 35' below the track and about 55' above the water.

Although built primarily to carry railroad traffic, the Dells bridge became one of the first and busiest automobile bridges in the state. It was linked to Highway 12 in Delton, the first paved rural highway in Wisconsin and, despite the sharp turn on its west bank, carried a load of auto traffic that would increase annually for more than 50 years.

Since completion of the Highway 12-16 highway bridge in 1956, the 1896 bridge has been used solely by the railroad.

Dams on the Wisconsin

"Without doubt," wrote Rick Durbin, "no dam in the state has ever had the intrigue, bitter contention, violence and financial misdeeds connected with it over such a long period as has the Kilbourn Dam on the Wisconsin River in Wisconsin Dells. Born of intrigue in 1853, it was known for a number of years as the most dangerous dam on the river. Conflicts between its developers were many, finding their way into the legislature in the late 1850's and to the courts as well during the next several decades. Between the lumbermen's efforts and the river's periodic flooding, the dam underwent a series of modifications and reconstructions that lasted until 1897. The final chapter came with the building of the present dam at the beginning of this century when hydromania was sweeping the state. Each phase of the story is replete with its own compelling elements: scoundrels, powerful antagonists, bunglers, unique problems, battles–legal, physical and otherwise–and much more. Its constructions were as much a tale of man against man as they were against nature."

The construction of the first Dells dam was intimately connected with the plans of Joseph Bailey, Jonathan Bowman and other promoters of Newport; with the dubious financial schemes of Garret Vliet and Byron Kilbourn of the La Crosse and Milwaukee Railroad; and the boosterism of Alanson Holly, newpaperman and investor in Kilbourn City. The dam was the plum in the pudding and he who possessed the state charter to build the dam decided the fate of the city to be built on the river. Ultimately, the decision was made by Vliet and Kilbourn, with the perhaps unwitting cooperation of Bailey and Bowman, who transfered the charter for the Newport dam to the railroaders.

In short, when Vliet and Kilbourn were unable to strike a favorable deal on the location of the dam with riverfront landowners in Newport, they did what was necessary to build it elsewhere–and elsewhere happened to be the village now known as Wisconsin Dells. Another site might have worked just as well. Indeed, there is evidence that Byron Kilbourn may have preferred to build his railroad bridge (and the dam) farther up river at Louis Bluff or Point Bluff.

In March 1855, Vliet, Kilbourn, Bailey, Bowman, and their partners persuaded the legislature to charter the Wisconsin River Hydraulic Company for the purpose of building a dam upriver from Newport.

Work began on this first Dells dam in October 1855 under the supervision of John Anderson and Joseph Bailey. The river was 350 feet wide at the point selected with about two-thirds of it deeper than 15 feet even at low water. Constructing a dam here would be a formidable task for men working with a steam railroad, draft animals and hand tools.

Initial progress was slow, with problems involving the dam's legislative charter, the construction of a pier for the railroad bridge and finances halting progress until 1858. In between, the Company entertained the idea of maximizing their use of the water power and the profitability of the real estate available at the Dells by diverting some of the river water into a channel dug on the west side of the river that lead into Hulbert Creek and back into the river. This loop of running water would be a powerhouse for mills and factories and the Company could sell lots and rights to the water for a good profit. The excavation involved was more than the Company could handle, so the idea never got off the drawing board.

Building and maintaining the Dells dam was enough of a challenge. In January 1858, the Hydraulic Company hired Joseph Bailey to complete the dam by the end of the year. He began by constructing a network of ten-foot-square cribs made of interlocked logs, 80 feet wide and 160 feet long, and filled with rock. Once filled, the cribs were decked over with heavy planks.

The rest of the channel was then filled with trees sunk butt-first at an angle and facing downstream, so the force of the river would drive them more solidly into the bottom. This kind of "tree-dam" was a proven and commonly-used engineering design. The trees were held in place with cross beams and stones.

Previous page: *The rapids boiled and the raft sagged in the current as the pilot attempted to line up his raft for the final descent over the partially-destroyed Kilbourn dam. Since it made the already-dangerous Dells passage even more hazardous, the Kilbourn dam was a source of conflict between lumberman and villagers for decades. (Courtesy, H.H. Bennett Studio Foundation).*

The dam also had a 25-feet wide flume down which water to power a mill was directed. By law, the dam also had to have a chute or slide, 60-feet wide, to allow lumber rafts to pass down the 8-foot drop without damage. At 160 feet, the longest on the river, the Dells slide was intended to make up for the hazard the dam created. After running the Narrows and the rapids immediately downstream, the river men would now have to steer their rafts to hit the chute perfectly or break up. As experience would show, even when they hit the chute perfectly, rafts often fell off the side or broke apart in the eddy at its bottom.

The prevailing, and correct, opinion in the upstream lumber industry was "that the dam will be ruinous to the lumbering interests on the Wisconsin river..trouble will yet grow out of this dam business."

On the day Editor Holly proclaimed of the dam that "No man who has had any knowledge of its construction has the least fear of its ever going out," a substantial portion of the crib and tree work on the east bank washed out. Repairs were made and the dam was completed in time for the rafting season of spring, 1859.

The first rafts were scheduled to pass over the dam in the afternoon of March 18. A crowd of over 100 Kilbournites lined the banks to watch. As Durbin tells the story:

"In the lead was Patrick O'Hare of Kilbourn City, who 'leaped and shouted and cheered as he was going over.' But his antics might have resulted more from fear than from joy. The rafts were 'stove to pieces' and three men lost their lives...In the following weeks the dam continued to take a fearsome toll of the lumber rafts. Included were two small German children, who in a skiff accidentally cast adrift, 'drifted over the dam, precipitating the children in to the water and drowning them'."

After meeting at Kilbourn and watching a few rafts attempt to negotiate the dam, the lumbermen promised "out it will come if men, money and powder can accomplish it." A gang of raftsmen set out to tear up the dam, but were deterred by the Columbia county sheriff. A barrel of powder was planted to blast the dam, but it got wet and failed to ignite. A lawsuit succeeded where violence failed. A Columbia County jury found the dam to be a nuisance and ordered the Company to lower its height and improve the slide. Since no one–not Columbia County, the Hydraulic Company, nor the people of Kilbourn who had once promised to do so–would pay for the work, it was not performed.

Finally, the lumberman tore three feet off the top of the dam, but so exposed the cribs and trees beneath that the dam now collected every bit of debris that flowed downstream. As one newspaper reported, "not a raft can pass without getting broken up."

Finally, in the fall of 1859, lumbermen and townspeople lowered the dam and the chute to about four feet in height. Still not satisfied, the lumbermen started to raise money to "take out said dam, with force either physical or legal." On the legal front the lumbermen petitioned the legislature to repeal the charter of the Hydraulic Company. On the physical front, lumberman Francis Biron, whose mill was at the head of the rapids at what is now Wisconsin Rapids, came down to the Dells with a crew to dismantle the dam. The Hydraulic Company, now bankrupt, could not stop either threat and in March 1860, the first Wisconsin Dells dam lost its legislative charter and was demolished.

During the course of the work, one of Biron's loggers fell in the river and drowned. As the story was told 50 years later, fueled by a barrel of whiskey, the loggers then stormed up to Kilbourn and threatened to burn down the village. They would have done so were they were not turned back by a pistol-toting Joseph Bailey.

The first Dells dam was a poorly-engineered, poorly-sited project, financed and run by a Company whose managers seemed to be pathologically corrupt. Their interest seemed to be less in building a solid dam that would act as a powerplant and magnet for industry and more in speculating in village lots sold at inflated prices.

In the words of one Milwaukee visitor at the time, "the tearing out of the great dam...has to a considerable extent damned the place."

It may have appeared that way in 1860, but in fact, the Dells dam gave birth to the village. The dam brought the railroad and the railroad made Kilbourn City a regional shipping center and farm market town. Except for Portage and Mauston on the same line of track, no other village within 25 miles had a railroad until the 1870s. By then, the railroad had begun to set Kilbourn on its course as a vacation center. No sooner were H. H. Bennett's photos of Dells scenery published, than visitors boarded the train to come and see it in person. So, despite the folly, chicanery and disaster that accompanied its short life, the first dam was successful in giving birth to Wisconsin Dells.

The Wisconsin River Hydraulic Company ceased to exist in January 1862 when only one director showed up for the board meeting. "No quorum," stated the minute book. There were also no funds in the treasury and no dam in the river.

As the Company's largest creditor, Byron Kilbourn then acquired the dam site and formed a new company whose board of directors was made up mainly of local people, most notably Jonathan Bowman. He submitted proposals to the legislature to create first the Columbia and later the Kilbourn Manufacturing Company which would build a three-foot high dam at the Dells. Much lower than the first

In 1883, with river rafting on the wane, Ellis Munger resurrected the dam and built the first mill to actually use the waterpower at Kilbourn. The Munger mill ran until 1889, when floodwaters washed out his dam. (Courtesy, H.H. Bennett Studio Foundation).

dam, the second dam would also have an extra-wide log slide with tapering sides to minimize the risk to rafts. Bowman's measure worked its way through the legislature and passed into law in 1866.

After the debris from the Kilbourn railroad bridge, which had burned and collapsed into the river in May 1866, was cleared away, work began on the second Dells dam. It was a low dam, with a fall of two-three feet. Nonetheless, the dam was still a life-threatening hazard to raftsmen and created a loss for the lumber companies of as much as 5% of the lumber shipped on the river, the equivalent of $100,000. Litigation, legislation and recriminations came downriver throughout the rest of the 1860s, yet the courts upheld the dam's right to exist.

Byron Kilbourn died in 1870. He left his Dells interests to his son Byron H., who incorporated the Kilbourn City Flouring Mills to actually utilize the waterpower which the dam was built to create.

A mill was built on the east side and opened with a grand ceremony on February 22, 1871. "Flow on mighty river," said one speaker. "No cobwebs shall bind thee." The new mill had its work cut out for it. Before it ground its first sack of flour, it already owed $75,000 in dam building costs.

Litigation continued, but at least the mill wheels were turning. In October 1872, the mill handled 53 thousand bushels of wheat. However, the burden of lawsuits and debts became too great for Byron H. Kilbourn, who washed his hands of the dam operation that had been conceived by his father.

Further weakened by the financial depression of the mid-1870s, and unable to pay court-ordered damages to the lumbermen, the owners of the mill were forced to sell out. The buyer was one of the dam's oldest and most bitter foes, lumberman John T. Kingston of Necedah. While in Kingston's hands in 1874, the mill was destroyed by a fire probably set by rivermen, who also dismantled much of the dam.

While the rivermen battled the Dells dam, railroads laid track up the Wisconsin Valley. By the end of the 1870s, railcars would all but replace river rafts as the means to move lumber to market and the prospects rose for another Dells dam. In 1883, Ellis Munger repaired the old dam once again and reconstructed the mill. The lumbermen did not harass him but the river did, sending down a flood in the fall of 1889 that washed out his dam.

Six more years passed, and William Wilmot who, like most of his predecessor's, put his hopes "on a persistent investment of cheek," built another dam. He started with a low wooden crib design which he declared to be only the first step on the way to creating a "steel dam" ten-feet high. The mill started turning again and produced Gold Brand, Roller Gem and Ruby flour. In about two years, however, with the "steel dam" as yet unbuilt and minus the uproar that had accompanied earlier dismantlings, the river washed away 80 feet of Wilmot's dam, thereby closing the mill.

As the 19th Century turned into the 20th, a new industry came to the Wisconsin River Valley. The river that had carried logs and lumber rafts, powered sawmills and grain mills, was transformed into a generator of electrical power. Starting in 1886 and ending with the completion of the Prairie du Sac dam in 1914, the river was gripped by what one historian called "hydromania." More than twenty hydroelectric power stations were built in these years, including one at the Dells. Thus between 1859 and 1905, there was a working dam in place only 11 plus years over that 47 year period.

The Dells hydroelectric dam and power plant began when Phillip Spooner, Magnus Swenson and P. M. Porter organized the Southern Wisconsin Power Company and acquired the mill property and water power rights at Kilbourn City. To generate as much power as possible, the company proposed building a dam 17 feet high that would flood the free-running rapids and keep water levels higher than ever in the Upper Dells.

Like other dam builders at the Dells, Southern Wisconsin Power faced opposition, but not from lumbermen. Some opposition came from steamboat owner Nat Wetzel who proposed that the new dam be built with a lock so boats could pass through. The old question of navigability arose here and was ultimately resolved by building the dam without a lock. A similar question arose when the Prairie du Sac dam was built a few years later and a lock was built there, but it has never been opened for commercial traffic.

Compensation for upriver landowners whose property would be flooded was also a question, and one reminiscent of the Newport conflict. Now it was settled simply, when the power company agreed to pay Wetzel and the Dells Company for flooding their property.

The most poignant opposition came from the handful of people who opposed the dam because they wanted to preserve the Dells as nature created them. In 1903, for example, Wisconsin's first state park commission drew up plans for the first state park system. Of the three parks proposed, one contained both the Dells and Devil's Lake in one large park. The other two parks were created as proposed, but the Dells portion was dropped from the Devil's Lake Park. Even though the Progressive era had begun, the environmental era had not and the legislature acceded to the hydropower interests.

The leading advocate for a Dells park and for the preservation of the Dells in their natural state was Henry H. Bennett. His role here–which has not really been recognized by historians or conservationists–should establish him as one of Wisconsin's first environmentalists.

"My energies for near a lifetime," he wrote in 1906," have been used almost entirely to win such prominence as I could in outdoor photography and in this effort I could not help falling in love with the Dells. There are few people who see them who don't become infatuated... Except with me, every rock that is to be hidden from sight is a sacrilege of

Stone and timber in place during construction of the Kilbourn hydroelectric dam in 1906.

The hydropower dam was constructed just downstream of the old Munger mill.

what the good God has done in carving them into beautiful shapes, but very few of my good Kilbourn neighbors feel this way and most of them believe now that the Dells will be quite as beautiful with fifteen feet of them under water."

As Bennett admitted, few of his neighbors–and only a few people outside of the Dells–agreed with him. The promise of jobs that would be created by the hydropower dam, the promise of industry, growth and Progress that dams at the Dells had always extended–but had yet to deliver–was too strong to resist.

Bennett's dream of preserving the Dells was overwhelmed by that of a man of equal earnestness and dedication, Magnus Swenson. A successful industrialist who made his fortune as a sugar beet processor, Swenson was one of the founders of the Southern Wisconsin Power Company and a full convert to hydromania. He hired a young Madison engineer named Daniel Mead to design a dam that would survive in the difficult conditions at the Dells.

Workers used picks, shovels and explosives to excavate a foundation in the riverbed sandstone. Some 165,000 yards of material were transported from the site by horse and wagon. The base of the dam was constructed of hewn wooden cribs matched to the contour of the river's rock bottom, floated into place and sunk under the weight of rockfill. Steam engines drove pumps to dewater cofferdams and served to power a concrete mixer, but all the concrete in the dam's base and superstructure was delivered to the forms by wheelbarrow. Among the workmen on the construction job was an energetic teenager named Newton Landt, better known as "Newt." He was destined to devote almost an entire lifetime to the operation and improvement of Kilbourn Dam and to civic duties in the community.

Although all available local men were employed on the job, more workers were needed. As many as 400 laborers–many immigrants from Bulgaria and Austria–were hired in Chicago and Milwaukee. Wages were $2.00 a day for laborers, while a man and his team could earn $4.00. Work began in December 1906 and the first power was generated in August, 1909.

The dam they built is 340 feet long, and raises the Wisconsin River 17 feet at its base. Generating capacity of the plant is 8,200 kilowatts, or 10,992 horsepower. Installed generating equipment consists of three 2,000-KW and one 2,200-KW generators. Originally, the plant generated at 25 cycles, but later was converted to 60 cycles.

During the course of construction, another problem arose. Located where the municipal dock was later built, the village waterworks would surely be flooded out by the new dam. In 1906, the power company promised to compensate the city for its loss by providing 1,000 kW a day, free, for all time.

The promise of electricity from a power plant yet unbuilt would not put water in Kilbourn's village mains. Although this offer was later modified, the citizens became irate when the power company did not commit to help the city sink new wells and replace its pumping station. In July, 1908, Horace Upham, a prominent Milwaukee lawyer and owner

The view from Stand Rock prior to construction of the hydropower dam reveals plenty of dry ground between the rock and river. After the dam was built the water rose high enough to make Stand Rock only a short walk from the river landing. (Courtesy, H.H. Bennett Studio Foundation).

of a summer home at Wawbeek near the Dells, was retained, perhaps at no charge, to fight the power company. The matter was finally settled to the village's satisfaction with a new well but not before more resentment and lawsuits by owners who objected to their land being flooded. The city even had to sue the power company for back taxes.

Unlike its predecessors, the Kilbourn hydro dam was a successful example of engineering and construction expertise. However, when it came to finances, the Southern Wisconsin Power Company had much in common with earlier Dells dam builders. In his enthusiasm to build first the Dells dam, and soon after, the dam at Prairie du Sac, Swenson apparently did not pay close enough attention to where he was going to sell the power his station generated.

It was assumed that electric railway companies in Milwaukee and its western suburbs would purchase the power at a profitable rate. Indeed, some of the first power generated at the Dells went to run trolleys in Watertown, but the railway lines–all owned by Milwaukee's electric company–agreed to pay no more for Dells electricity than the cost of producing it. This financially ruinous arrangement remained in force until the late 1920s, even after Wisconsin Power & Light purchased the station.

Another market for Dells electric power might have been the industrial development that the dam's promoters claimed would come to the village. During construction, many perspective factory owners visited the town representing companies making everything from canvas gloves to pianos. Some were even offered free land near the plant, none stayed.

No matter how ill the wind, it usually blows fairly for someone and, in the case of the finances of the Dells hydropower plants, farmers benefitted. With more power than it could sell profitably, the utility ran lines through rural Sauk and Columbia that made farmers there among the first in Wisconsin to have electricity. After it became part of the Wisconsin Power and Light Company, the Dells station helped to link Reedsburg, Baraboo, Sauk City, Spring Green and other small communities in the region into one of the state's first inter-connected utility systems.

In 1924, several southern and central Wisconsin utilities were united under the name Wisconsin Power and Light Company. It now supplies electric service in 33 Wisconsin counties, serving roughly one-third of Wisconsin, and including service to 386 communities and 39,000 rural customers.

While the construction of Kilbourn Dam had employed the best available methods, materials and design, nearly every season found the completed structure waging a bruising battle with the fury of the Wisconsin at flood stage. In 1911, fall floods washed out the apron and despite corrective measures, trouble of this nature recurred almost yearly. Scour caused the river bed below the dam to gradually lower and in low water periods the timber cribbing beneath the dam was often exposed and subjected to deterioration. By 1935, the dam was showing signs of settlement and a toe dam was built to raise the water level and deter rotting of the cribs. After the big 1938 flood, gates 11 and 12 would not open until repairs were made.

The hydropower dam–the fifth dam at Kilbourn–still stands with modifications, repairs and upgrading made over the years. Today it can produce a maximum of 10,000 KW, enough to supply 10,000 homes. The average production over a year is 6,000 KW depending on the river level.

From the river-rafting days to the hydropower era, the old saying, "it's water over the dam" has always had special significance at Wisconsin Dells.

According to the Kilbourn Advancement Association the hydropower dam would bring industry and vacationers to the Dells area. The Association even used the outside of its envelopes to promote its efforts.

KILBOURN, COLUMBIA CO., WISCONSIN

Factory Sites for Manufacturers. Grestest Water Power Poosibilities in the State. Located at Intersection of Four Counties. 20,000 Population within a Radius of Ten Miles. Large Agricultural Trade Center. Great Possibilities for Dairying, Stock Raising and Potato Culture.

100 Miles From Milwaukee Magnificant Train Service

190 Miles From Chicago Main Line C., M. & St. P. R. R.

Exceptional Inducements to Manufacturing Plants.

LOCATION OF THE FAMOUS
DELLS OF THE WISCONSIN RIVER

Good Farm Lands for Homeseekers at Reasonable Rates.

UP-TO-DATE HOTELS. FINE DRIVES. BOATING. BATHING AND FISHING. PURE AIR.

Complete System of Waterworks, Supplying

THE PUREST WATER IN THE STATE.

SUMMER HOMES FOR SUMMER PEOPLE.

FOR DETAILED INFORMATION, ADDRESS

Sec'y. KILBOURN ADVANCEMENT ASS'N. Kilbourn, Wis.

With the hydroelectric dam and power house, the 1956 highway bridge, the railroad bridge upstream, the river is at the heart of the history of Wisconsin Dells. (Courtesy, H.H. Bennett Studio Foundation).

The Brief Life of the Kilbourn Dam

1859	Dam in
1859	Dam torn out
1871	Dam in
1874	Much of dam dismantled
1883	Dam repaired
1889	Dam washed out
1895	Dam in
1897	Dam out
1905	Hydroelectric dam constructed

Though many take for granted that there has always been a dam in Kilbourn, during the 47 year period from 1859-1906, Kilbourn had a working dam for about only 11 years.

The Flood of 1938

When high water hits the Wisconsin River, as it did in June of 1993 at 18.6 feet, comparisons are made to floods of the past. On September 14, 1938, the Wisconsin River reached a record-breaking 23.8 feet. The *Wisconsin Dells Events* of September 15, 1938, reported, "East of this city in the town of Lewiston some of the lowland has been covered by the flood waters and some damage was done.

Tuesday morning the river had risen sufficiently to flood parts of highway 13 north of this city so that a detour was established.

No boats were run up river on Tuesday and the tourist business was at a standstill. The municipal dock broke from its mooring about eleven o'clock Tuesday evening and the fire company, augmented by a large number of citizens turned out to the rescue."

According to the report from the local power plant, the water in the Wisconsin River reached a height of 15.8, which is the highest that has ever been recorded since the plant was installed here. All of the gates in the dam were open and the water carrying much debris in the shape of logs, roots and trees was a never ending sight.

People came from far distant points to line the river bank and hundreds of cars lined the banks of the river at times to see the torrent as it passed.

The boiling, churning, swirling waters of the Narrows could be heard roaring as far away as River Road. Giant's Shield above Cold Water Canyon and Leroy Gates' name in the Narrows were covered. Some roads have been raised since that year but on September 14, Harold Walker pictured water over Highway 13 in Plainville and the store was threatened. The Stand Rock Road at the old river bed was closed, and water covered Highway 12 and the Lower Dells boat docks. In this area, Ed Stroede, a 12 year old boy then, walked across through 18" of water on the highway and never forgot the team of horses drowned and still in their harnesses floating down the swollen river.

In Happy Hollow, water came up in the yards of the people who lived by the slough. Colburn's cottages, where Sunset Bay now stands, stood in water and the Winnebago floated almost even with Illinois Avenue. Water came over the dam at Meadowbrook Hotel and onto their lawn.

Upstream, water came up to the windowsills of the Hacker home at the foot of Louis Bluff. Downstream, Laverne Davis took a rowboat to get to his barn. Many cattle were drowned in lower Newport.

High water washing at the foot of Leroy Gates' self-advertisement on the rocks at the Narrows in 1900, before the dam raised water levels 17 feet at its base. (Courtesy, H.H. Bennett Studio Foundation).

The Civil War

The Departure of Company E

On April 15, 1861, President Abraham Lincoln issued a call to the states to provide 75,000 militia men to suppress the rebellion in the southern states. Wisconsin's quota was relatively small, with only one regiment of 780 men requested. By the end of the year, after hostilities had actually begun, the state's levy had risen to 19 regiments of infantry, four regiments of cavalry and five artillery companies. Among these first units to muster for service was the 12th Wisconsin Infantry and the 4th Wisconsin Cavalry, both with men from the Wisconsin Dells area.

Company E of the 12 Wisconsin Infantry was formed at Delton, and its history was recorded by one of its men, Hosea Road. The following is an edited excerpt of the Company's journey from Delton to Madison on its way to active duty.

"And so it was one morning made known to us that on the 31st day of October we were to take our departure for Camp Randall, Madison, where companies like ours from various parts of the state were being organized into regiments, and where the regiments thus formed were being properly officered and drilled for active service in the field.

"Here were a hundred men and boys who had, from the conviction of duty to their beloved country, sworn to leave homes, families and friends, and give themselves to the service of their country in her time of need...

"And so, though some tears were shed, they were not the bitter tears of regret. They were tears that in an unguarded moment forced themselves to the surface from the depths of emotion that throbbed in the loving, loyal hearts of both those who were to go and those who were to stay.

"But, hark! there is Trume Hurlburt's drum? He is beating the call to 'fall in.' The boys gather promptly in front of Newman's Tavern, and at Captain Vanderpoel's order form in line for the last time in Delton.

"The brief partings over, all by common consent stand back, except two or three mothers and wives who cannot seem to find the last word. But the old Captain draws his sword, gives the order, 'Right face! Forward, counter-march by file left, March!' and the men are on the move. They march down around by Topping's store, and then file left, and there drawn up in order on the road between the store and 'The Gully,' are thirteen farm teams, and these are to take us to Madison. As the company marches alongside the wagons, eight men climb into each. In a minute all are loaded, and the procession moves forward. After crossing "The Gully" and coming up in front of the old red blacksmith shop on the left, the team in front stops, and the others draw up in close order around a wagon in the center, in which stands with uncovered head, Mr. Green, the village preacher. It has not seemed fitting to send forth our Company without public prayer to the God of battles in our behalf; and so this good man, whose life work it is to stand between the living and the dead and point the way to brighter worlds beyond this one, stands ready now to commend us to the care of Him who watches with like tenderness over country, Home and Heaven.

The prayer ended, the team in front moves forward again, the others following in order while the gathered people, not to lose sight of their departing soldier-boys, walk alongside the wagons as they move slowly toward the bridge across Dell Creek, at the lower end of the village...

'It is harder for those who stay,
Than it is for him who goes.'

"Yes, that was a jolly ride, though it was not all a ride. The rough boards laid across the wagon boxes for seats had been put by some mistake or other with their hard sides up; and before we got well across Webster's Prairie they proved rather tiresome to the anatomy. Before we came to Baraboo, Charley Briggs, Laredo Smith, Henry Marston, George Lawsha, Ed Bennett, and a dozen others, took to their heels, in order to rest themselves, and, at the same time, cultivate an acquaintance with those who dwelt by the wayside.

"It would take too much space for me to record how these jolly young soldiers, on their first expedition, would approach the door of some well-to-do stranger, respectfully knock, and, when the door was opened for them, inquire gravely after the health of the family, the crops prospects, the price of beans, or for the latest neighborhood gossip; how they kept a wide-open eye all the time for the reigning belles of the various rural communities through which we passed; how they tried to get a glimpse of the teacher, whenever we went by a schoolhouse; how they helped, with their tongues, to drive every yoke of oxen they saw at work in the fields or met on the road; how they wrought up to the highest pitch the temper of every house-dog between Delton and Madison; how they foraged upon turnip patches; how every load of the boys made it a rule to give 'three cheers' opposite every dwelling hallooed, and laughed; how they ran races,

Previous page: *Young H. H. Bennett ready to march to war and his sister Sarah Bennett McVey. (Courtesy, H.H. Bennett Studio Foundation).*

Captain Abraham Vanderpoel, builder of Dawn Manor, and Captain of Company E. (Courtesy, H.H. Bennett Studio Foundation).

and behaved generally in such a way as not only to make the journey a very jolly one, but to make the country folks remember as long as they remember anything, the time when the "Delton Company" went along that road to Madison.

"The good people of Baraboo had heard of our coming, and had got out their little Fourth of July cannon, and as we rode down through their streets, they made the welcome ring with as much of war noise as they were able.

"They hung out their flags, waved their handkerchiefs, and hurrahed till they were hoarse, and we appreciated it all in having no small opinion of both them and ourselves. Altogether, our passage through the thriving little town was a pleasant thing to remember-enough so to make the writer cherish kindly recollections of the place.

"We crossed the Wisconsin river at what was then known as "Matt's Ferry" [Merrimac]... At dark we reached the village of Lodi, twenty miles from Madison, where supper and sleeping accommodations had been engaged for us. The occasion of keeping the company overnight was an interesting one to the patriotic people of this little village that had already sent a large number of her young men to the front. Their brass band turned out and, taking the lead of the company, paraded the principal streets of the town, and so made good friends of every one of the boys.

"Early next morning the procession of wagons was again on the road to Madison. Six miles from Lodi, as the teams wound around the hill where the old Harvey post office used to stand, the colors floating from the wagon in advance, and Truman Hurlburt, Rube Green and Jim Solomon making the attention of a young man digging potatoes on the farm of Mr. Butterfield. The great question of the day, 'to enlist or not to enlist,' had been present in this young man's mind for several weeks, and demanding an answer; yet the answer he had been unable up to this time to settle upon. But the sigh of this company of men, the flag, the music, the thoughts, 'That is John Gillespie's company,' and 'I have an old school mate in that company,' brought Daniel Titus to a quick decision.

"'I'll do it!' he said.

"The procession halted, the young man made known his desire to become one of the company, wrote his name on the roll, and then with uncovered head and uplifted hand took the oath of service. Hurrying back to the house, he changed his clothing, found in one of the wagons a seat beside his old school-mate, and then went on with his newly-made comrades to camp.

"Would Daniel Titus have done all this so eagerly had he known that the day was coming–July 28, '64–when his young life would be demanded of him as a sacrifice for the bright flag floating above him that first morning in November, '61? It would have been quite like him to do so.

"About the middle of the afternoon we passed through the streets of the city of Madison and out towards Camp Randall. When near camp we left the wagons, formed into line, and with feelings alternating between soldierly pride and curiosity to see what kind of a place a military camp was, and what kind of people there were in it, we marched by the guards, through the gate, and were - in camp."

The Twelfth Wisconsin served in the western campaigns with Ulysses. S. Grant in Tennessee and at Vicksburg. Later they marched from Atlanta to the sea with William T. Sherman, and on to Washington D.C. where they took part in the Grand Review on May 23, 1865.

Isaac N. Earl and the 4th Wisconsin

The following account was written by *Illustrated Events* editor J.E. Jones in 1904.

"When the dark cloud or war gathered in the southern sky and the mutterings of the strife began to be heard among the jackpines of the old time Adams County, a company of militia was organized at Plainville. The embryo soldiers marched, and wheeled, and charged, and flanked through the streets by day, and met at Tyler's Hotel (later Armstrong's) nights to hold their campfires in the high old style of Charles O'Malley, or in jolly social dances. Out of this war nursery, this military hot house, there went now and then a few brave hearts to the front where the bullets whistled, and the cannon balls shrieked in the air, and men were dying. From this place went Newton Earl, one of the most daring and famous scouts in the union army who with others came to Kilbourn and joined Co. D, of the 4th Wisconsin Calvary. From the freedom of the forests and a courage born of danger on lumber rafts on the river these men along the 'river road' to the pineries were easily moved by a spirit of patriotism, and they never failed to make their presence known in battle."

The rest of the story is from the book *Wisconsin at War.*

Lieutenant I.N. Earl was left an orphan, without friends or means, at the age of eleven. He enlisted in April, 1861, at the age of twenty, in Company D and was soon appointed a corporal. He was captured in the charge on Port Hudson, [Louisiana] May 27th, 1863, but escaped in a few days by running past the guard, jumping into a stream, and swimming across to his friends, though fired at and wounded twice. He brought the most valuable information from the enemy's lines, was then detailed as special sharp-shooter, and at the close of the siege promoted, at the request of General Banks, to be second lieutenant for gallant conduct.

"He afterward, for some time, commanded his company with credit, and was distinguished for impetuous bravery, frequently attacking parties of the enemy larger than his own, and killing, capturing, or routing them before they could recover from their surprise. Upon one of these occasions, when he, with eighteen men, had captured twenty-eight rebels by surprising a picket post, and was conducting them triumphantly to camp, he was surrounded by a heavy force of the enemy. He released his prisoners, and ordered his men to disperse and charge the rebels by twos while he and one companion dashed down the road with drawn sabres. Breaking through the line, he plunged into a stream, and while swimming it, his horse was shot and he was captured. Only one of the party escaped.

"Earl was placed in irons, but he made a saw of a case knife, with which he severed the fetters from his limbs, and then dug out of a strong cell and escaped. He was pursued with blood hounds and captured. He escaped again, and was retaken. The next night he filed off his irons again, seized an axe at the campfire, killed one man and wounded a second, and a third time escaped.

"He now took to the swamps, waded up and down streams so that the dogs could not track him, and at length came out at the Gulf of Mexico, near Pensacola, where he found a gunboat, the officers and crew of which treated him very kindly. He was soon with his regiment again, and engaged in scouting. He was detached, by order of General Canby, as special scout, with a company of forty men. In five months they captured three hundred

The surviving members of Company E returned to Delton for a reunion in 1900. (Courtesy, H.H. Bennett Studio Foundation).

and eight-four prisoners, and seized public property and smuggled goods valued at $1,153,000.

"With sixteen men he once followed, for one hundred miles, a company of one hundred rebels, who were guarding a heavy mail on its way from Texas to Richmond, Virginia. Finally discovering the ambulance containing the mail, accompanied by four officers and four soldiers, three-fourths of a mile in advance of the remainder of the escort, he charged upon them, captured the ambulance, soldiers, and officers, and took them back to Vicksburg. General Canby said it was the most important mail ever captured in his department. It contained dispatches from Kirby Smith to the Confederate War Department, besides fourteen battle and regimental flags, captured from General Banks on the Red River. Major Smith, one of the officers captured with the mail, was one to whom Earl, when himself a prisoner and in irons, had appealed in vain for better treatment. He now expected retaliation, and begged his captor not to shoot him. Earl replied that there was no danger, that brave soldiers treat prisoners as brothers. These officers addressed letters to the War Department at Richmond, begging that if Earl were ever captured he might be insured good treatment.

"He once escaped from a party of the enemy at a house where he had stopped, by seizing a sister of one of the rebels and, holding her up before him, retreating to the edge of a swamp, where he dropped the girl and fled. November 29, 1864, he started from Natchez, with his company, to join General Davidson on his raid through Louisiana and Alabama. In passing through Fayette, Mississippi, at nine o-clock in the evening, he was shot by a mounted rebel a few rods in advance. A wound in the face, by a buck shot, was not serious, and one in the breast was pronounced by a surgeon in Fayette not dangerous. Earl sent his men back to Natchez, except John Hays, who remained to attend him. A party with a flag of truce was at once sent to bring in the wounded lieutenant, but the rebel commanding officer at Fayette would not allow them even to see him. Scouts afterward learned that he died in convulsions, twenty-two hours after he was wounded. He was dead when the flag of truce was raised in Fayette. After his death a fluid, clear and transparent as water, flowed from his wounds in large quantities, and also settled about his eyes. It is the testimony of medical men of experience that this was not the natural result of his wounds and from all the evidence obtained, it is concluded that he was poisoned by his captors.

Upon the recommendation of Major General Canby, the War Department conferred upon Lieutenant Earl the rank of brevet major, but he did not live to learn of the honor.

The illustration Harper's Weekly *used to portray the passage of Admiral Porter's fleet through General Joseph E. Bailey's dam. Bailey followed common practice for loggers in Wisconsin. He built a "driving" dam that temporarily held back water. When the dam was breached, water rushed through the opening, carrying Union gunboats over the shallows downstream just as it would have carried logs in the north woods. (Courtesy, State Historical Society of Wisconsin).*

Joseph E. Bailey and the Red River Campaign

Although the Union forces had won great victories at Vicksburg and Gettysburg in July 1863, the Civil War dragged on indeterminably. As the war entered its fourth year in the spring of 1864, vast armies on both sides were still in the field. The Union had succeeded in dismembering the South along the Mississippi River and now hoped to carry the struggle into the fertile region west of the river. It could still furnish the beef, cotton and other supplies to sustain the tottering rebellion.

Foreign intrigues were also afoot. In 1863, the French Emperor Napoleon III had sent a French army into Mexico to establish a puppet state under the Austrian Archduke Maximilian, who called himself the Emperor of Mexico. The United States favored the ousted republican government of Benito Juarez, who continued to struggle against the European invaders. Maximilian favored the Confederacy and, if he succeeded in Mexico, he posed a threat to the Union.

The federal government determined to strike in 1864 and seize the strongholds of the Southwest. Shreveport, Louisiana, on the Red River 250 miles west of the Mississippi, was singled out for capture and occupation. A joint campaign of the army and navy would subdue the Shreveport area and move into Texas. General Nathaniel P. Banks was to move an army of 25,000 men up the Red River valley, supported by a flotilla of twenty gunboats and transports under Rear Admiral David D. Porter.

From the beginning, plans did not work smoothly. There were disagreements among Union generals; preparations were inadequate and difficulties arose in establishing a functioning civil government in Louisiana. When in readiness the army moved parallel to the river in a column twenty miles long. Encountering no serious opposition on the advance, it would soon move far ahead of Porter's fleet, which crawled slowly in the shallow waters above Alexandria.

Then, on April 8, within fifty miles of Shreveport, there was a sudden attack. Led by General Richard Taylor, son of former U. S. President Zachary Taylor, the Confederates threw the advancing Union army into confusion. Banks had great difficulty withdrawing his infantry. After nearly two hours of sharp fighting the disorganized Union forces fell back fifteen miles with more than 3,000 men lost. An additional 969 were captured or killed in the two days following. Finally the army returned to Grand Ecore. The Confederate loss was never reported. The Red River campaign was doomed to end in humiliation and disaster.

New difficulties now made the military situation alarming. Just at the time when the Red River should be overflowing its banks with the spring flood, it suddenly began to fall. Fearing that his fleet would be caught on the shoals and sandbars, Admiral Porter started to descend the stream. With the Union army deprived of this support, the Confederates began a ceaseless attack. Slowly the Federal army retreated and by April 25 had fallen back to Alexandria.

Now an unforeseen crisis arose. Before Porter's fleet could reach the rocky channel above Alexandria, the river had "run out on him." Within that mile the Red River drops a total of thirteen feet in two distinct rapids. Perilous huge boulders nosed their heads above the surface. Nature had sprung a trap that obstructed Porter's return. Some of the army engineers suggested destroying the $2,000,000 marooned flotilla to prevent its capture by the Confederates. Even to Admiral Porter escape seemed impossible.

Joseph E. Bailey

On shore was at least one soldier who thought differently. His name was Lieutenant Colonel Joseph Bailey, at first a captain in the Fourth Wisconsin Cavalry with men from Plainville, New Haven, Kilbourn and Lyndon. Bailey had also served in the engineer corps and, as early as April 9th he saw the dilemma on the river and communicated his fears to General John Franklin, his superior officer.

Experience had taught Colonel Bailey lessons not found in books on engineering. Born in Ashtabula County, Ohio, in May, 1827, he had come to Wisconsin in 1849, participated in the founding of Newport and Kilbourn, and supervised the construction of the first Kilbourn dam.

General Franklin went to Admiral Porter with Colonel Bailey's idea. He proposed to build a dam that would raise the water level of the river upstream of the stranded gunboats. When the water level grew high enough, the dam would be pierced, and the resulting flood would float the fleet out of the shallows to safety. Bailey had seen dams like this one employed in the Wisconsin pineries where they were known as "driving dams" and used on nearly every stream to build a head of water to drive logs downstream. Although the Red was larger than a northwoods creek, Bailey was positive his "driving dam" would work.

"If damming it would get the fleet off, I would have been afloat long ago," a skeptical Admiral Porter is said to have observed.

The plan was generally condemned. Officers ridiculed it and engineers declared it impossible to build. But Colonel Bailey persisted.

"I am convinced that it will save the fleet," urged General Franklin, the one outstanding officer who had faith in Bailey's proposal.

"The proposition looks like madness, but Colonel Bailey is so sanguine of success that I shall direct it to be tried," Admiral Porter concluded.

So on April 26, when the squadron arrived at the shoals, Admiral Porter requested General Banks to execute the plan.

"There are 3,000 idle men and 300 wagons at your disposal," General Banks told Colonel Bailey. "Now let's see what you can do."

Requesting the pinery boys from the 23rd and 29th Wisconsin regiments and the 29th Maine volunteers, all of whom were familiar with logging operations, and the 97th and 99th Colored Infantry, Bailey set the work in motion. A dam, constructed of logs, brush, brick and stone, was run out from the left bank. From the right bank cribs of stone were built. Barges were sunk near the center.

Men worked to their armpits in water under a broiling hot sun. Night and day, they labored patiently and enthusiastically. For thirty six hours Colonel Bailey stood over the work, neither eating nor sleeping. His tall form became lank and his weight fell to 130 pounds. Eight days of incessant labor passed. Then an accident occurred to the barges and water rushed downstream. Four of the vessels escaped on this deluge of water, but the gunboats were still stranded. Undismayed, the men bent more earnestly to the task of repairs. Two wing dams were constructed up stream to lift the back water. This was a temporary application of the same engineering principles used today in flood control dam building. Up, up rose the river almost to overflowing.

On May 12 the crucial moment had arrived. An estimated 30,000 people crowded the Red River banks. One long pull and the dam center collapsed. There was a tremendous rush of current. Undamaged, the marooned gunboats swept over the rocks to make their escape into deeper waters.

Colonel Bailey's plan had triumphed. The mad thunder of the released waters through the dam bore his name to immortality.

"Words are inadequate to express the admiration I feel for the ability of Lieutenant Colonel Bailey," wrote Admiral Porter in his report to the Navy department. "This is without doubt the best engineering feat ever performed."

"Leaving out his ability as an engineer - the credit he has conferred upon the country - he has saved the Union a valuable fleet worth nearly $2,000,000; more, he has deprived the enemy of a triumph that would have emboldened them to carry on the war a year or two longer."

National approval almost overwhelmed Bailey. On June 11, 1864, Congress adopted a resolution of commendation for his "distinguished services in the recent campaign on the Red River." Bailey was one of only 15 officers–of all the thousands who served in the Civil War–so commended by Congress

"I get daily letters of thanks from all portions of the country," wrote the bewildered Bailey to a friend late in June.

The officers of Admiral Porter's fleet presented him with a beautiful gold mounted sword and a three gallon silver punch bowl valued at several thousand dollars. Before the war was over, on recommendations of Secretary of War Edwin M. Stanton, Colonel Bailey was promoted to the rank of brigadier general. At the end of the war he was transferred to Fort Scott, Kansas.

General Bailey found fame as elusive as the shadows. Within two years he was appealing to his old Wisconsin friend, United States Senator James Doolittle, to find him a position. Admiral Porter wrote to President Johnson requesting that General Bailey be appointed an Indian agent, either to the Chickasaws or Choctaws in Oklahoma.

"He is now suffering from wounds received in the war and also from disease contracted during that time, and thus is prevented leading his former life of civil engineer," urged Admiral Porter upon the president. Johnson could not help Bailey, who was one of thousands of unemployed veterans–many of them decorated heroes–petitioning him for a government position. Discouraged, Bailey removed to Nevada, Missouri and was elected sheriff of Vernon County. On March 25, 1867, while attempting to make an arrest, he was killed by two desperadoes. There he is buried.

Nearly thirty years after his death there came a pitiable sequel to Bailey's story. In want, his daughter, Ella Bailey, who remained in Missouri, appealed to the Wisconsin legislature to purchase the mementoes given to her father by Admiral Porter and his staff. An appropriation of $2,000 was rushed through the legislature and with the help of Major Guy Pierce, the golden sword and silver bowl were transferred to the State Historical Museum, Madison, where they have since been on display.

Interest in General Bailey was renewed with the news of this calamitous episode. That he might ever after be held in grateful remembrance, his portrait, with the Red River and flotilla blended into the background, was painted and hung in the governor's reception room of Wisconsin's beautiful granite Capitol.

As long as "The Hornet's Nest" at Gettysburg, the "Bloody Angle" at Spotsylvania Court House, and the "Escape of the Fleet on the Red River" are held in memory, Joseph Bailey's name and deed will be enshrined in the hearts of American citizens.

General Joseph Bailey

Joseph Bailey was born in Ashtabula County, Ohio, in 1827. As a young boy, he moved with his parents to Quincy, Illinois, where he received a grammar school education. While still in his teens, he ventured to the frontier of Western Missouri where he became a prospector. Returning to Illinois, he worked in the lead mine area of Galena where he met and married Mary Spaulding.

With his new wife and great aspirations, he moved north to the sandy shore of the Lower Dells. He staked his claim to a quarter section of land on the east bank of the river about two miles south of Wisconsin Dells. Bailey later built a fine home in Kilbourn City at 805 River Road, the site of Dr. Carlson's office.

When the Civil War broke out, Bailey enlisted a group of area farmers and raftsmen to form the Columbia County Rifles, later part of the 4th Wisconsin Cavalry. Colonel Bailey was soon recognized not only as a fine officer, but for his ability as a civil engineer. He become an overnight hero after saving the Union fleet at Red River in 1864.

Although a hero to the entire nation, he was thereafter rejected in his own hometown. The townspeople resented his fame and many connected him with the wrongs of Byron Kilbourn. In a letter to a friend in Kilbourn City shortly after his Red River success, Bailey wrote, "*I have built a dam on the Red River, my slide or shute was a perfect success, Uncle Sam's rafts rode it like a charm. But perhaps if old Byron had been there he would have defeated me in the enterprise. I have not heard from anyone in Kilbourn City. Perhaps my friends have better to do with their time than writing to a poor miserable soldier who is wearing out his life in fighting for his country.*"

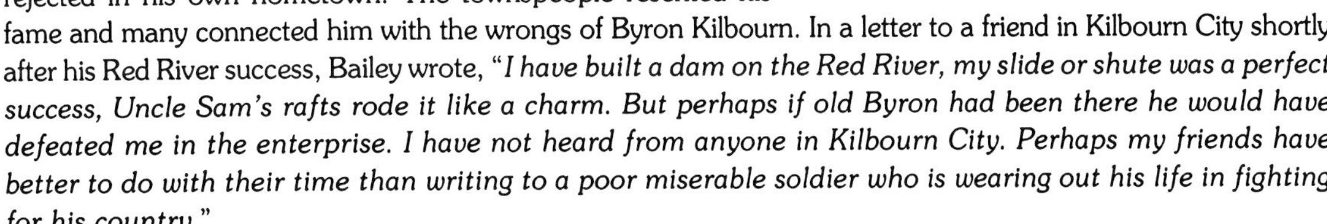

Disenchanted and unable to even get a job back at home, he decided to leave the area. Loading his family and all his belongings in two wagons, Bailey set out for Western Missouri to the same area he had prospected twenty years before. Upon arrival in Vernon County, Missouri, he purchased a farm and was determined to settle down.

There he was elected sheriff and his supporters even planned to run him for governor. In 1867, at age 40, Bailey was murdered by two desperados that he had arrested. Many southern sympathizing Bushwackers remained in Vernon County, which had been their headquarters during the Civil War, and many alleged that these political adversaries had actually plotted Bailey's murder.

General Bailey was buried in the military cemetery at Fort Scott, Kansas. Later, when Mary Bailey learned she could not be buried beside her husband, she had his body moved to Evergreen Cemetery in the same city.

The gold sword and Tiffany bowl presented to General Bailey and later preserved and presented to the State Historical Society of Wisconsin.

Major Guy Pierce

Guy Carpenter Pierce was born near Potsdam, St. Lawrence County, New York on February 13, 1840. He moved to Lenawee County, Michigan in 1844 and then to Branch County, Michigan in 1853.

When the rebels fired on Fort Sumter, Pierce was traveling in Wisconsin. On April 30, 1861, he enlisted in Captain Joseph Bailey's Company of "Columbia County Rifles" for three months of service. He was one of the first Privates who stepped to the front with a red hot patriotic speech urging all to serve their country.

He was not mustered out for that tour, but was detailed to go to Necedah and help recruit more men. For these services he was promoted to 2nd Sargeant. On June 1st he went into camp at Racine under Colonel Halbert E. Paine, and was mustered in as a member of the 4th Wisconsin Infantry on July 2nd, 1861. The company's first military work was putting down the Bank Riot in Milwaukee.

By February 1862, his company was assigned to General Benjamin F. Butler's expedition against New Orleans. 3,300 men embarked from Newport-News on the old steamer *Constitution*, the largest vessel afloat at that time.

On May 1st, the 4th Wisconsin was one of the first to land at New Orleans, and their band, playing *Red, White, and Blue*, led troops as they marched up Canal Street and took possession of the custom house. Here soldiers found endless piles of letters and papers, including the following dispatch from rebel General Lovell to General Pimberton: "The Yankees Fleet has passed the Forts, the City is doomed. My troops are on the march where to God only knows."

Not long after another battle at Baton Rouge, Pierce and one other man were left in charge of seven hundred colored refugees. On August 16th, 1862, Pierce was commissioned a 2nd Lieutenant.

Major Guy Pierce was one of General Bailey's most trusted staff officers. He was wounded four times, and chosen recipient of a Congressional Medal of Honor for brave and meritoriuos conduct at the siege of Mobile.

Pierce held numerous Civil War letters and relics and had recorded many historic incidents which future generations will value as without price. One such item was Louisiana's Ordinance of Secession, reportedly penned by an "esteemed citizen of Baton Rouge," which Union troops captured from Louisiana's Governor Moore during the war. While claiming it was only a duplicate copy, citizens of Louisiana wrote W.D. Hoard, Governor of Wisconsin, in 1889, requesting that he speak with Pierce about returning the Ordinance. Pierce declined to return the document, explaining: "This Ordinance set up her [Louisiana's] right to secede and had she been allowed to do so our republican form of government would have been a failure which moves us wants to see."

Pierce provided the State Historical Library in Madison with several General Bailey relics, including his sword and silver punch bowl.

A Harper's Weekly illustration entitled "General Sherman's Rearguard" depicts the service to Union soldiers performed by freed slaves like Tom Allen. (Courtesy, State Historical Society of Wisconsin).

Thomas Allen

Soldiers Saddened at Death of Friend

(Taken from the *Wisconsin Mirror*, January 10, 1874)

"Died: In this village on Saturday last, Thomas Allen, aged about 40 years.

Mr. Allen had been a resident of Kilbourn about ten years. He was born in Tennessee and, until the war gave him his freedom, had been a slave. When the 12th Wisconsin was in the vicinity of Humboldt, Tennessee in 1862, Tom and a dusky mate [his wife] came into camp. He served the boys of this regiment faithfully two years. When the regiment came home on veteran furlough, Tom came home here with Lt. Griffin, Henry H. Bennett and others. Since then he has earned an honest livelihood for himself and family, and was universally respected by all our citizens. He was upright and truly honest. He leaves a wife and four bright little ones to mourn his loss. His funeral was largely attended. Rev. J.C. Duncan of the M.E. Church made suitable and appropriate remarks."

Poor Tom

The wintry wind blew chill and keen,
Along the hillside's frozen sheen,
The sunlight, waning toward the west,
Fell coldly on the river's breast.
The busy village on the hill
A moment listened, and was still;
For slowly from the vale below
The hearse wheels creaking o'er the snow,
Here toward the city of the dead,
A brother man-and this was said
"Poor Tom," and as I questioned why,
I saw a brave man standing by,
A man whose valor, well I know
In many a battle faced the foe,
Yet while "Poor Tom" was passing by
To his long home, that flashing eye
Grew dim with tears, and drawing near,
These are the words I chanced to hear.
"Poor Tom was a slave, as you may know,
On a big plantation down below.
'Twas a pitch-dark night, and the boys in blue
Myself, and some more that you never knew,
Stood Picket not far from a river side,
A broken bridge swung in the rapid tide,
And at midnight down by the river bed,
The sentinel challenged a stealthy tread,
And when morning dawned, for they had to wait,
Poor Tom came in with a dusky mate,
And she and Tom, for he took her to wife,
Stuck by our boys till the end of the strife,
It may seem strange, but I can't help crying,
To think of the boys, the sick and dying,
And how faithful Old Tom, from first to last
Stood by the poor fellow till hope was past,
And when on a march, the war grew

dreary,
And many a brave lad, faint and weary,
Fell out exhausted, e're set of sun,
How Poor Old Tom would shoulder his
gun
And his knapsack
too, for Tom was strong,
And then together, they'd trudge along,
I can't tell all, nor the half he did,
But we loved poor Tom and when we bid
Good bye to the South, we brought him
here,
And now he is gone, I hold it clear,
That Poor Tom's wife and his children
four
Will beg no bread at a stranger's door,
While any are left who ever knew
What Tom did care, for the boys in blue.

Famous Names Abound in Cemetery

Death makes strange bedfellows, and four of the stranger ones are to be found in Spring Grove cemetery. Three are directly related to the Civil War, one to the American War of Independence.

The four persons you'd never expect to find in the same cemetery are Frederick Brown, the brother of the famous abolitionist, John Brown, of Harper's Ferry fame; Belle Boyd, the Confederate spy; Thomas Allen, the emancipated slave who fought with the 12th Wisconsin; and Edward Dawes, whose father rode in the opposite direction from Paul Revere.

Some of the stories were well known, and have been for years, others have been authenticated by Pat Seger, historian for the Harold B. Larkin post #187 of the American Legion.

The connection with famous people in history has been rumored long in Wisconsin Dells, particularly that of Dawes and Brown, but there was no proof.

So Seger went to rummaging around in libraries, in old newspaper files, and writing letters by the dozens.

"There's still one mystery remaining," says Seger, "and that's in connection with Edward Dawes. The tombstone is here in Wisconsin Dells. The inscription reads, 'Edward Dawes, M.D. Died April 9, 1865, aged 58'."

"The newspaper clippings from the Kilbourn papers tell how his father rode out to warn the countryside on the same night that Paul Revere made his famous ride.

"But the records in Reedsburg indicate he was buried in a cemetery there. And there's no telling if the Reedsburg records are wrong, or if the tombstone maker delivered the stone to the wrong cemetery after all the relatives were gone, or what.

"Only thing I'm sure of is that the stone wasn't put there as a practical joke. It must have cost too much money for that."

Frederick Brown's story was easier to confirm. Frederick grew up with his older brother John Brown in Hudson, Ohio. He was greatly interested in stock raising; but in 1836, when he was 29 years old, he became involved in an unsuccessful land speculation deal. He spent the rest of his life in trying to extricate himself from debt.

While Frederick was still trying to make a financial comeback, his brother John went to Kansas where he attempted to start uprisings against pro-slavery groups.

His dream was to rally the slaves to fight the South. In 1859 with 22 men, he seized the arsenal at Harpers Ferry, Virginia. His plans miscarried. The slaves failed to rally, and he was captured by U. S. Army Colonel Robert E. Lee, tried and hanged.

Frederick Brown had lived in the vicinity of Reedsburg "for some years," when he died in 1877.

Close by the grave of Brown is that of Belle Boyd, the beautiful Confederate spy.

Confederate Spy Part of Dells Area History

The only ship authorized to fly the Confederate "Stars and Bars" is docked, of all places, deep in Yankee territory, right here on the scenic Upper Dells of the Wisconsin River. The sightseeing launch "Belle Boyd" is named for the feisty rebel spy from Martinsburg, Virginia who bravely aided Confederate Generals Stuart, Beauregard, and Jackson, and risked her life for her beloved Shenandoah Valley.

She began her hazardous profession at age seventeen when federal troops occupying Martinsburg insisted upon raising the Union flag above the Boyd House. Belle's mother, firmly declaring that members of her household would die before allowing the Stars and Stripes to fly over their heads, promptly was shoved aside with a savage push and some abusive language. Unable to tolerate such action, Belle, who was still only a teenager, drew her pistol and shot the offending Union soldier, mortally wounding him.

The most famous of Belle Boyd's spying exploits was her role in Stonewall Jackson's "Valley Campaign." Using her flirtatious charms upon a romance-smitten aide to a Union general, Belle was able to learn of a secret war council to be held in the parlor of the Front Royal Hotel. Hiding in a closet overhead, she listened through a knothole in the floor to strategy intended to take Jackson's troops by surprise. Belle returned undetected to her room in the first hours of morning, encoded a note containing what she had heard, crept to the stables, saddled her horse, and set out on a dangerous moonlight ride. Making her way past two federal sentries, she delivered her message to Colonel Turner Ashly, and was home again before sunrise. This information led to the defeat of federal troops at Port Republic and a proclamation of admiration and friendship by Jackson for the daring young Belle. He later commissioned her a captain and made her an honorary staff aide.

When captured she helped confederate prisoners escape, charmed her jailers and induced the warden to shop for her wedding trousseau. Another time, carrying confederate dispatches to London, she was captured again. This time she fell in love with the young ensign who guarded her. Her escape caused his dismissal.

By the end of the war, Belle was a nationally known heroine, and spent her later years travelling the country lecturing and presenting dramatic narratives of her spying adventures. On June 9th, 1900, Belle arrived in Wisconsin Dells, scheduled to give a recital to the local G.A.R. Post. Accompanied by her third husband, Nathaniel High, she checked into room #1 of the Hile House, later the Traveler's Hotel. Two days later, at the age of 56, Isabelle Boyd High suffered a fatal heart attack. After funeral services at the local Episcopal Church, she was buried with full military honors by Wisconsin Civil War veterans.

In 1976 a memorial was completed through the efforts of Harris Botsford, a former Wisconsin Dells resident, and with contributions of funds and local labor. Previously the United Daughters of the Confederacy had brought earth from the banks of the James River in Virginia to put on the grave. At that time the care of the grave was turned over to the local American Legion.

The memorial was completed with stone from each off the Confederate states. A historical plaque with Belle's famous post-war plea, "One God, one flag, one people - forever," was unveiled at the 1976 memorial service. Since then, twice a year, on Memorial Day and on the 4th of July, the U.S. flag, the flag of the state of Virginia and the Confederate Naval Jack fly over her grave.

Members of the Wisconsin Dells American Legion Post and members of the United Daughters of the Confederacy visit the grave of Belle Boyd. (Courtesy, H.H. Bennett Studio Foundation).

MCMANMAN
1901
STORE.

Village Life, 1860s–1910s

When Wisconsin Dells Was Punkin' Town

The *Mirror Gazette* of June 7, 1888 printed the following account of the very early days at Wisconsin Dells, probably early 1856. It is the recollection of Dells resident Joe Purcell, who was "in a mood for reminiscences."

"I was working on a grade near Beaver Dam," he said, "and one night Byron Kilbourn came in where a lot of the men were having a good time. He said he wanted some men to go out on the grade at Kilbourn City. Kilbourn City, says I, and where's Kilbourn City? Oh, that's out west, he says. Well, we got up a gang and started to find Kilbourn City. When we got near Newport we found the road lined with ox teams going west and we could not get a meal at the hotel. We stopped at Hoffman's Saloon, the same man that had the brewery here, and got a lunch, some of the men taking along provisions in bottles. We came down to the ferry which was then run by George Boyd, father of Harvey Boyd. I asked him where's Kilbourn City? Kilbourn City! and he broke out in a big laugh. I don't know where's Kilbourn City, he said, but there's a place up here called Punkin Town with two or three shanties. Well, we got to 'Kilbourn City,' found the printing office and a piece of the Tanner House to be the 'city.' We crowded into a little shanty where Munger's office at the mill now stands, and sat up all night swearing at Byron Kilbourn for bringing us out here in the woods to look for 'Kilbourn City'."

Kilbourn's First Settler

The honor of being the first settler in Wisconsin Dells is generally given to Alanson Holly. Born in New York in 1810, Holly was an experienced newspaperman. Although the thriving village of Newport had a population of 1,000 souls, on November 20, 1855 he moved his family and three printers into the wilderness that became Kilbourn City. The print shop, which was located on the high bank of the river south of the River Road bridge had a dirt floor and only part of the windows were in. Holly located his printing plant and residence at this unsettled point on the Wisconsin River because he expected the railroad to go through here. There was not a dwelling within half a mile of his place, now 211 Wisconsin Avenue, and only one within a mile.

The winter of 1855-56 was an unusually severe one. It was -25 degrees outside in January and the typesetters huddled around a wood stove, standing on heated boards, setting type laboriously by hand, one ice cold piece of lead at a time. They worked until midnight, warming their fingers in warm water every 10 or 15 minutes to keep them from growing numb.

Even so, publisher Holly exulted in his position as editor of "the newspaper in the woods."

"Mrs. Holly and the girls bake potatoes and pancakes for breakfast," he wrote, "and look out the window for quails for meat; lug dry wood on our back for firewood, 24 degrees below zero and the baby crying for sleep." We wonder how Mrs. Holly liked it.

"Live in the cities if you will," Holly continued, "but give us the wild, wild woods, the rocks, the hills and majestic river, with health and friends we are content." For three or four weeks during extremely cold weather, the editor was obliged to pack all his provisions a mile and a half to supply a hungry family. Referring to this, he said: "We are getting independent now. We have pork in the barrel and potatoes (not frozen) in a box down cellar; venison hanging by the door; nice fried meat fat for our griddle cakes; a little milk once in a while for our coffee; fried pudding for breakfast; and butter-yes butter! (clean, we know, for the dirt was all on the woman that brought it) once or twice a week on warm biscuits. If this is not rich living we don't know what would be."

On January 1, 1856, the first edition was ready to be printed. People crossed the frozen river from Newport to hear speeches by Jonathan Bowman and Joseph Bailey before someone suggested that the first copy be auctioned off. Jason Weaver bought the first paper struck from the press by Holly's son Morton for $65. Abram Vliet paid $10 for the second and Joe Bailey was the buyer of the third copy for $5.

The first issue of the paper contained the following: "The forest oaks hang over our office and dwelling, the deer and rabbits shy around us and the partridges and quail seek our acquaintance by venturing nearer and nearer our doors. The noble Wisconsin River is bearing onward its immense burdens of life, majestically and silently, within sight of our windows and the snowcapped hills, covered with scattering oaks and pines, peer up in the distance. There is romance and reality in all this and

Previous page: *MacManman's, on south Superior, started as a grocery and liquor store in the 1870s and developed into Kilbourn's largest department store by the time this photo was taken in 1901. (Courtesy, H.H. Bennett Studio Foundation).*

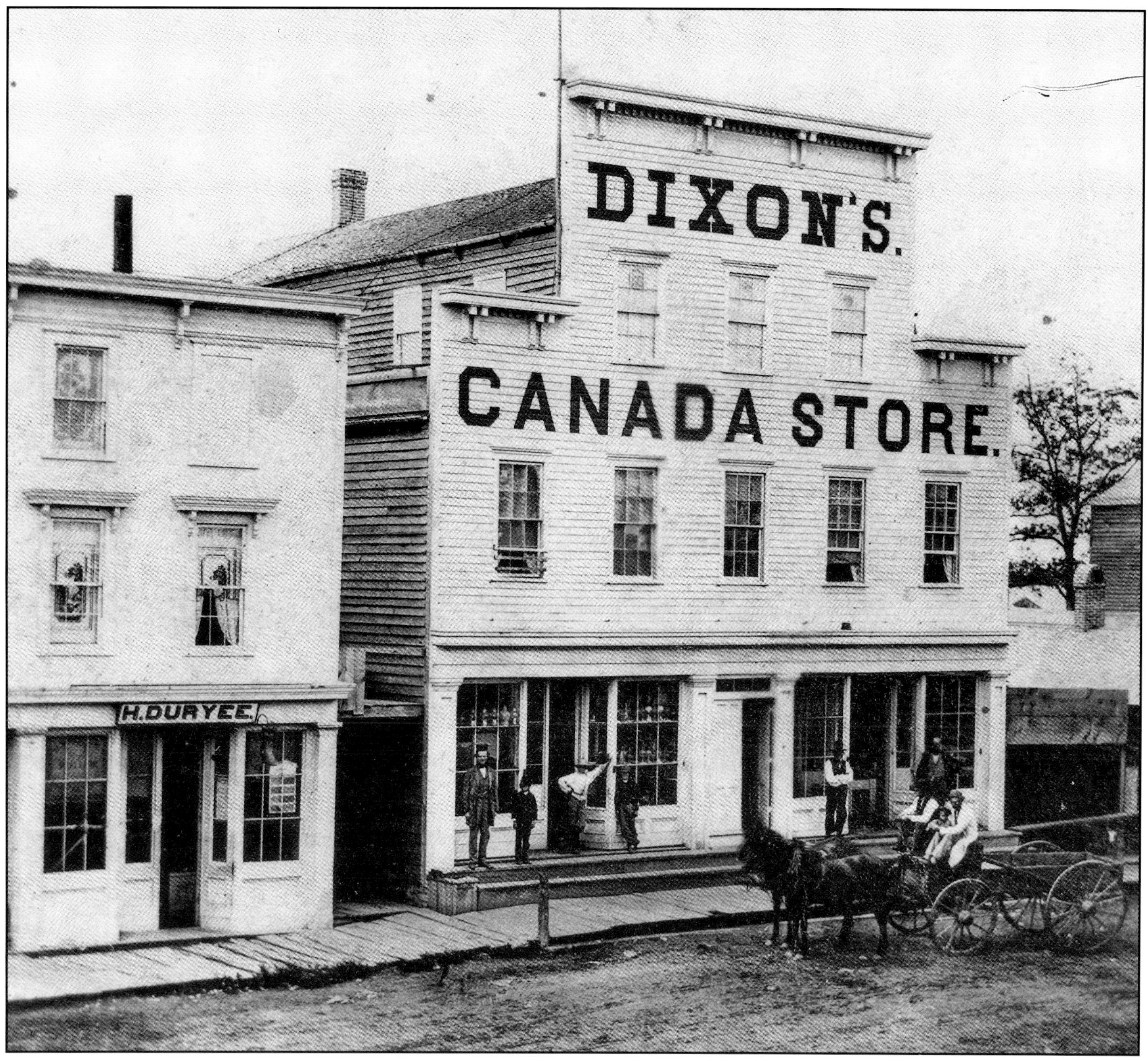

Dixon's Canada Store, Kilbourn's first general store, was on the south side of the 200 Broadway block. This building was destroyed by the fire of 1866. (Courtesy, H.H. Bennett Studio Foundation).

we feel almost willing to publish a paper in such a location just for the excitement of the thing. But most of the romance is soon to be spoiled. Already there is talk of several dwellings going up. When spring and summer shall come, we expect such a clatter of axes and spades and trowels and saws and hammers, that we shall hardly be able to write our editorials without introducing more or less of the confusion. The fact is, we expect a large village - yea, a city - to grow rapidly around us and that is why we are here - printing in the woods."

The only local person mentioned in the first newspaper was Daniel Brew who lived on the same location as his grandson and namesake lives today about a half mile upstream across the river. Brew was his nearest neighbor.

Holly continued to publish the paper, writing his news and editorials in between chopping wood, carrying water and keeping a sharp lookout for game to replenish his larder.

In June 1856, the paper announced that the location had been platted and named Kilbourn City. In March 1857, tragedy struck as son Morton Holly drowned after falling from the rocks while throwing off a cat he had killed for disturbing his sleep.

In 1860, Holly discontinued the paper and returned to New York. He was back in Kilbourn by 1866 and, in 1868, resumed publishing the *Mirror*.

During this time he was elected to the State Assembly. Like Lincoln, Holly was a self-educated man. Even though he had only 22 months of formal education, he once taught school for five years. In addition to newspapering, Holly worked for the Hydraulic Company and championed the Dells dam in the pages of the *Mirror*. He continued to publish at Kilbourn until 1872. The home he built in 1856–the first in Kilbourn–stills stands at 609 Washington Avenue.

The year of 1866 brought several tragedies to Kilbourn. High water washed out the Gates bridge at the Narrows; the railroad bridge was destroyed by fire and fell into the river; fire also destroyed the main business block of Broadway, as depicted here. (Courtesy, H.H. Bennett Studio Foundation).

Jonathan Bowman

Jonathan Bowman of Kilbourn City ranks among the most prominent of early settlers and those who gave shape to the future of this area.

Born at Charleston, Montgomery County, New York, on May 16, 1828, he first read law in the office of H & T Fish, of Fultonville, New York, and in 1850 graduated from the State and National Law School in Ballston Springs, New York.

He came to Wisconsin in May, 1851, and settled at Delton. Soon after his arrival, he opened a law office there and would enjoy a reputation as one of the area's finest lawyers.

In 1852, he started the village of Newport in company with General Joseph Bailey. In 1853 he moved to Newport, and in 1862 to Kilbourn City.

He was made President of the Bank of Kilbourn soon after its organization in 1867.

From 1875 to 1879, he served as a Director of the Chicago, Milwaukee & St. Paul Railroad Company. In addition, he served as attorney for nearly all the different corporations formed to utilitze water-power both at Newport and Kilbourn City.

Mr. Bowman was very involved in politics; in 1860 he was alternate Wisconsin delegate to the National Republican Convention in Chicago, which nominated Abraham Lincoln for President. In November, 1861, he was elected to represent Columbia County in the Wisconsin Assembly. He was elected State Senator for the 25th Senatorial District in 1862, an office he held for four years.

In 1864, he was chosen one of the Presidental Electors on the Republican ticket, and was Chairman of the Electoral College for that year. In that position he presided over the re-election of Abraham Lincoln. In 1874, he was re-elected to his previous Assembly seat by a handsome majority.

Jonathan Bowman died in 1895. He and his wife, Hannah J. Davis, of Montgomery County, New York, had five children: Ella D., Abram D., Asa, Jennie and Emma.

The south side of Broadway, c. 1880, was home to (l-r), the Beyerlein Saloon on the east side of Oak Street; west of Oak stood a store with the Odd Fellows Hall upstairs; a barbershop in the Connor building; the office/pharmacy of Dr. G.C. Jenkins in the dark-colored building; the Dixon Store, with its famous lion in front; a jeweler/watchmaker; and a billiard hall. (Courtesy, H.H. Bennett Studio Foundation).

Perry Stroud

Perry George Stroud was born in Clinton, New York, in 1834. His father, Charles Stroud, was a contractor for the State, and later moved to Canasota, New York where Perry spent his childhood. Perry was educated at the Oneida Conference Seminary at Cazenovia, New York.

In 1854, at age twenty-one, he answered the call of the era - "go west, young man, go west." He sailed through the Great Lakes to McHenry, Illinois, where he met and married Helen M. Bishop. Perry then set out with his new wife for the bustling western town of Newport, Wisconsin. In Newport Perry engaged in the mercantile business, and later operated the famous Steele Tavern.

When the railroad crossing which was promised for Newport was moved to Kilbourn, Perry, along with most others, left for Kilbourn City. Perry studied law and in 1857 became the town's first attorney. Luther B. Noyes joined him for about one year, but until the arrival of Jonathan Bowman in 1862, Perry was the only available lawyer.

In an early history, J.E. Jones reports that, "The leadership of all public matters in Kilbourn was about equally accorded to P.G. Stroud and Jonathan Bowman, and though they were frequently in bitter opposition, there never was imputed to either of them one single act of reprehensible nature. Their manhood and sense of honor was never sacrificed to an unfair advantage."

Stroud established Stroud's Bank around 1860, the first such institution in Kilbourn. Perry's son, W.S. Stroud, continued to run the bank which later became the Kilbourn State Bank.

Perry Stroud was one of the most active and influential man in the early days of this city. Besides lawyer and banker, he was active in the Methodist Church, president of the school board, and a leader in the temperance movement. When the Civil War broke out, Perry became the area's draft officer. He corresponded regularly, and became a close friend of many local soldiers, including General Joseph Bailey.

Perry died in 1887 of a heart attack. Attorney Stroud had practiced in Kilbourn City for 30 years, during which time he saved every letter, legal paper, and other bit of correspondence he received. These valuable papers were neatly filed in chronological order, packed in wooden boxes, and placed in the attic of the Stroud Bank, still standing at 314 Broadway, where they were only recently discovered in near perfect condition.

Kilbourn, 1850s-1900s

Kilbourn City grew fast. One year after Alanson Holly arrived, the village had three public houses, two dry goods stores, a cigar factory, a hardware, and one each of grocery, drug, boot and clothing stores. There was also a livery stable, barber shop, blacksmith shop, meat market, one doctor–George Jenkins, one lawyer–Perry Stroud, and one saloon.

Many homes and commercial structures came to Kilbourn from "old Newport."

To this day, Dells residents who have an old building say, "My house was moved up from Newport on the ice."

How many of these buildings are still standing today? Was it possible to move them on the frozen river? Were the winters that cold so that the river was frozen thick enough and long enough? If houses were moved this way, where could they be hauled out at Kilbourn? In Happy Hollow, at the south end of Bowman Road?

Alanson Holly, in one of the first editions of his *Wisconsin Mirror* was delighted at the thought of new neighbors coming. "The runners are all prepared on which to draw the houses and 25 or 30 yoke of cattle would pull them."

In June 1956, the Hydraulic Company offered to move Newport houses for $100.00 and sell the owners lots in Kilbourn at reduced prices. Some from the west side of the river were moved to Baraboo or Mauston, but many, especially, from the east side of the river were moved to Kilbourn. They were probably hauled up Bowman Road. Possibly the steep hill was iced and houses were winched up the steepest incline.

In 1976, a group of interested people formed the Kilbourn Landmarks Committee to try to authenticate which buildings actually did come up from Newport. Written records are scarce and abstracts do not reveal such information. J.E. Jones had written about houses which came up from Newport in his *Illustrated Events*, but most have been torn down over the years.

However, we are certain that two are still standing. The Whitney House at 809 Cedar is marked by a plaque. The front section of this house was drawn up from the east side of Newport by 12 teams of oxen. In 1862, Jonathan Bowman brought his house from the east side of Newport to 608 Broadway. In 1960, it was moved again to 618 Cedar Street.

The home with the cupola standing at 419 Wisconsin Avenue was dismantled and moved down the frozen river by ox cart from Point Bluff in March, 1867.

While most of Kilbourn City's streets were platted and named, early settlers christened some neighborhoods with names that live on today.

One of the first industries in town was the Drinker Mill, with holdings on River Road from the bridge through the Sunset Cove Condominiums in the 1100 block. On the east side of the street the mill workers built their little houses and originally all were occupied by bachelors, hence the name Happy Hollow.

Turkey Hill was two blocks east on Elm Street. It extended from the ravine to the north end of Elm then eastward. Many speculate that someone raised turkeys there but the Kliemenhagen family says the area was originally inhabited by a flock of wild turkeys.

Yankeetown was so named since it was settled by New Englanders. Its exact boundaries are lost but

Continuing down the south side of Broadway, c. 1895, (l-r), O'Neils Pharmacy, Snider's general store, a clothing store, "Kilbourn's New Surprise Store" and Fred Radandt's saloon. The saloon building was also once the office of the Kilbourn Mirror newspaper. (Courtesy, H.H. Bennett Studio Foundation).

Lith. by Doniat & Zastrow, Milwaukee.

References:

1. *Kilbourn City-Institute.*
2. *Public School.*
3. *City-Hall.*
4. *Tanner House*
5. *Sash Door & Blind Factory Walker Munger & Co.*
6. *Saw Mill. Drinker Bro's.*
7. *Brewery. C Lute & Co.*

KILB

References

1. Kilbourn City Institute
2. Public School
3. City Hall
4. Tanner House
5. Sash Door & Blind Factory Walker, Winger & Co.
6. Saw Mill. Drinker Brothers
7. Brewery. C. Leute & Co.
8. Livery Stable. D.F. Sirweri
9. Livery Stable. Frank Hill
10. Van Alstines W. & Son Blacksmith Shop
11. Weidenbacher & Co. Wagon & Blacksmith Shop

Churches

12. Baptist
13. Methodist
14. Presbyterian
15. Episcopal
16. Catholic

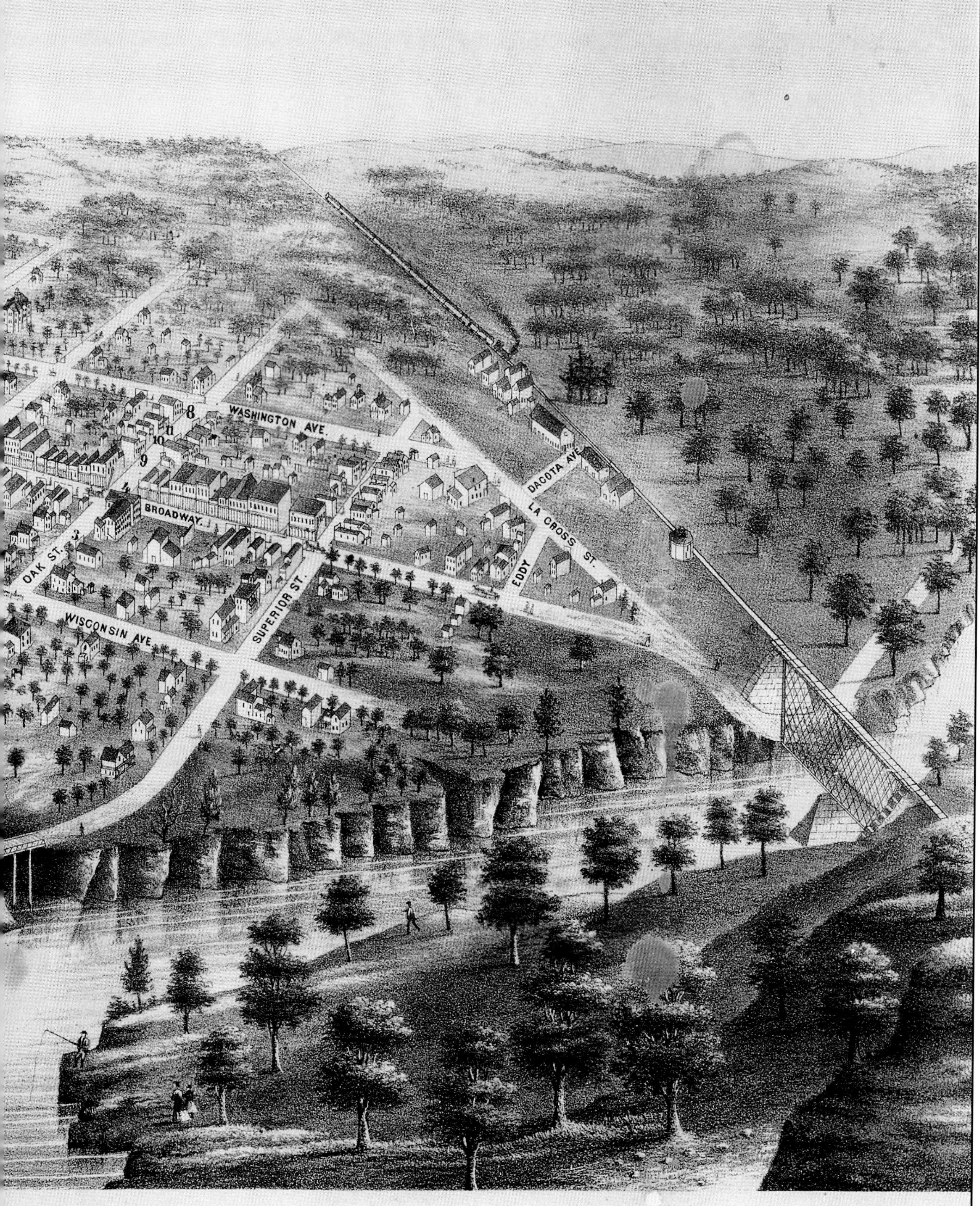

Drawn by H. H. Baile

RN CITY, WIS.

1870.

References:

8. Livery Stable D. F. SIEWERT.
9. Livery Stable Frank Hill.
10. Van Alstines W[illegible]on & Blacksmith Shop.
11. Weidenbacher & Co. Wagon & Blacksmith Shop.

Churches:

12. Baptist.
13. Methodist.
14. Presbyterian.
15. Episcopal.
16. Catholic.

The home of General Joseph E. Bailey, which stood near the northwest corner of Broadway and Superior, with the railroad bridge that Bailey hoped to see built in Newport visible out the rear windows. (Courtesy, H.H. Bennett Studio Foundation).

The E. C. Dixon House, which stood on the northeast corner of Wisconsin and Superior streets until it was destroyed by fire in 1974. (Courtesy, H.H. Bennett Studio Foundation).

The entire Martin Tofson family, c. 1900, dressed in their best and brought out their bicycles, pets and horse and buggy to pose in front of their Kilbourn home, whose porch was graced with morning-glories in bloom.

it probably centered around the 500 to 800 block of Minnesota Avenue.

Then there was the infamous Bloody Run. Some say this was Eddy Street but most agree that it was the 700 block of Superior Street. The name probably came from the early days of the rough and ready raftsmen and saloon keepers.

The Civil War slowed the pace of growth throughout the area and fires twice destroyed much of the commercial district. The first great fire occurred in the City on March 14, 1866. It began in the Dixon Store on Broadway and spread east, destroying the entire block of eleven stores. Ten families living above the stores barely escaped with their lives. The loss of goods at the Dixon Store alone was valued at $100,000. The next great fire came ten years later in October 14, 1876, when eight buildings on the south side of Broadway between the Stroud Bank and Elm Street were totally destroyed.

Kilbourn City suffered setbacks but as long as it had the railroad it had an advantage over Briggsville, Delton, Reedsburg and Baraboo, which did not. Its Wisconsin River bridges also brought traffic and trade to Kilbourn. By the end of the war the hops boom was in full swing and the prosperity it brought to Kilbourn is revealed in the number and variety of businesses here.

By 1868, there were in Kilbourn City, one Catholic, one Presbyterian one Methodist, one Baptist and one Episcopal church. There were four dry good stores, two clothing stores, two grocery stores, two hardware stores, two boot and shoe stores, two furniture stores, three paint shops, two drug stores, two bakeries, two butcher shops, two jewelry and watchmaker shops, three millinery stores, two flour and feed stores, eight saloons, one first class and two second class hotels, two harness shops, two breweries, one barber shop, two billiard saloons, six shoemaker shops, one photo gallery, four blacksmith shops, two wagonmaker shops, four tailor shops, one tinker, two cooper shops, ten carpenters, two doctors, one dentist, two livery stables, two banks, one printing office, two law offices, one insurance office, one saw mill, one sash and door factory, seven masons, one brickyard, three lumberyards, one Freemason lodge, one grain elevator, post office, express office, and railroad depot.

By the mid-1870s, Kilbourn City was an established community. The Town of Newport, including the as-yet- unincorporated Kilbourn City, had a population of 1,721 people in 1875. It was the second-largest community in Columbia County; only Portage was larger. At the same time, the Towns of Delton in Sauk County and New Haven in Adams each had about 850 people. The population of the Marquette County Town of Douglas, including Briggsville, numbered 719, while Lyndon in Juneau and Dell Prairie in Adams each had about 475 people. This area, centered on Kilbourn City, was home to over 5,000 people.

After H. H. Bennett began to publish his photos of Dells scenery in the 1870s and, with promotional help from the Milwaukee Road, tourists in large numbers began to visit the Dells. They made Kilbourn different than its neighbors. However, Kilbourn was still very much the same as any

H.H. Bennett, Pioneer Landscape Photographer

The first H.H. Bennett family, (l-r), H. H., Nellie, Harriet, Frances and Ashley. (Courtesy, H.H. Bennett Studio Foundation).

Henry Bennett, the oldest child of George and Harriet, was born January 15, 1843, near Farnham in lower Canada.

The family soon returned to Brattleboro, Vermont and by 1857, hard times had hit the area and they moved west to Kilbourn. The railroad and the town were being built, promising work for Henry and his father George, who were carpenters.

When the Civil War broke out, Henry and his brother Ed joined Co.E of the 12th Wisconsin Volunteer Infantry. A crippling injury to his right hand forced Henry to seek a new career when he returned home.

In 1865, he and his brother George purchased the photographic gallery of Leroy Gates in Kilbourn. George soon returned to Vermont and Henry built his own studio at 215 Broadway. By 1875, he had achieved national prominence as a landscape photographer.

Three dimensional stereoscopic views were at the height of their popularity as parlor entertainment and when Bennett's views began circulating, increasing crowds of visitors came to Kilbourn to see the Dells for themselves. Bennett also showed his magic lantern slides to groups in many cities.

With photography still in its infancy, Bennett had to build his own cameras and other equipment. He perfected a rubber band shutter to stop action, a revolving printing house to follow the sun and increase his time for printing and a method for printing his 18" x 66" panoramas.

The riverlands of the Dells were his first love and he returned to them year after year to get an even more artistic angle or lighting effect. He also pictured the countrysides of Devil's Lake, Mirror Lake, the rocky bluffs of Adams and Juneau Counties and the Upper Mississipp. His camera caught scenes in Chicago and St. Paul and his collection of Milwaukee views of the 1880s and '90s is the largest still in existence.

Henry Bennett married Francis Douty in 1867 and they were the parents of Harriet (Richards), Ashley, and Nellie (Crandall).

Francis helped Henry in his studio until she died of tuberculosis in 1884. In 1890 he marred Evaline Marshall and they had two children: Miriam and Ruth (Dyer).

H.H. died in 1908. At the end of his life, when the power dam threatened to cover much of the beauty he loved, he wrote, "My energies for near a lifetime have been used almost entirely to win such prominence as I could in outdoor photography, and in this effort I could not help falling in love with the Dells."

Today H.H. Bennett's fame as a pioneer photographic artist continues to grow and his beloved Dells is enjoyed by more visitors every year.

other small town in the Midwest. It was still primarily a farm service community: the place where rural people came to buy hardware, dry goods and groceries they didn't raise at home; where they could mail a letter, bank their money, hire an attorney, visit a doctor, or catch the train. Kilbourn had a high school open to rural students who boarded in town, lodge halls for fellowship, churches for worship. There was a saloon for Dad to have a beer, a millinery shop where Mom could buy a hat, a candy counter where farm kids could contemplate the jawbreakers and licorice whips.

This Kilbourn is often lost midst all the attention paid to Kilbourn/Wisconsin Dells as a vacation center, but it is just as real and important.

The Hops Boom

Between 1850 and 1860, the number of breweries in the United States tripled, with Wisconsin itself having 127 beermakers. This increase created greater demand for hops, the ingredient that gives beer and malt liquors their characteristic aroma and bitter flavor. Wisconsin farmers turned to hops growing and the Dells area was the center of the industry.

Jesse Cottington, an experienced hops grower from New York, began growing hops in the Sauk County Town of Winfield in 1852. Hops are a perennial vine with roots planted at eight-foot intervals next to a 12 - 20 foot pole for the vines to climb.

Cottington imported roots from New York and supplied them to several neighbors. The combination of hops growing experience, suitable climate and soil, and an expanding market made Sauk, Juneau, Columbia and Adams counties an important hops growing area. By the mid-1860's, market conditions would create a "hops craze" in the region.

Hops required intensive culture. Each year poles were set. In late May, women worked in the hops fields, tying young vines to the poles. At the end of the summer an army of pickers descended upon the hops yards.

The brewing process uses the fluffy, yellow-green hops flower. At harvest time, men pulled the vine-laden poles and carried them to picking stations. Each picking station consisted of four large wooden boxes. A young woman at each box laboriously picked flowers from the vines. The average picker could fill three boxes a day at 50¢ per box. At $1.50 per day, a hops picker earned a little more than an unskilled sawmill worker.

In 1867, Sauk County produced at least 2,000,000 pounds of hops and some estimates put the figure as high as 4,000,000 pounds. Hops producers recruited thousands of young women from towns along the rail line to the east to harvest the crop. From places like Beaver Dam, Watertown, Oconomowoc, and, of course, Milwaukee, 30,000 pickers came to the four-county hops region. In describing the arrival of a trainload of pickers the *Wisconsin Mirror* said that "when 2,000 pickers began to pour out of every door of those twenty cars, the scene beat all other western shows."

For a three-week period in late August and early September, the people working on the harvest overran the yellow-green hops yards. Years after hops growing faded from the scene, people remembered hops picking time. Women recalled picking hops until their fingers bled, yet spending evenings singing and stepping to the lively music of nightly barn dances. Pickers enjoyed meeting new people and learning to dance the newly invented "hops step." The dancing, singing, and mingling of men and women in the carnival-like atmosphere made the long hours of harvest bearable.

Because it was the rail shipping point, Kilbourn City was the hub of the hops region. In 1859, a farmer received 14¢ per pound for hops delivered to Kilbourn. Eight years later, increased demand coupled with the damage inflicted by hops lice on crops in the East pushed the price of hops up to 65¢ per pound. Hops fever struck many farmers in Sauk, Juneau, Columbia, and Adams counties. The rush was on to plant hops roots, build hops houses, buy hops presses, and become a hops grower.

Hops growers became rich seemingly overnight. Farmers who had known only the rough ride of the farm wagon suddenly drove fine carriages, built new houses, bought musical instruments, and wore fancy clothes. Merchants extended credit freely

Excerpt from the

WISCONSIN BUSINESS DIRECTORY
1873
KILBOURN CITY
Columbia County

Angell Wm F, Flour and Feed
Bank of Kilbourn
Barelens Charles, Baker
Barker E F, Furniture
Barker A Billy, Dry Goods
Barton Wm M, Shoes
Bennett H H, Photographs
Beyerlein John C, Saloon
Beyerlein John S, Saloon
Bowman Jonathan, Ins. Agent
Boyd George A, Grain
Brown J Jackson, Ins. Agent
Bush John, Boots and Shoes
Conner Thomas, Clothing
Corning H, Grain
Cummings Wm, Gro & Crockery
Dixon, A C, Gen Store
Drinker Bros, Saw Mill
Dunn J H, Dentist
Fuller J W, Jeweler
Hansen G J & Co, D Gds & Gro
Hansen Bros, Hdw & Tin
Hill Franklin, Livery
Hill R G Books &c
Jenkins G W, Paints &c
Langdon B, Wagons
Loomis, Gallett & Breese, Gen. St.
Lowenmeyer M, D Gds & Notions
Leute J, Brewer
McDonald Miss H A, Milliner
McManman Daniel, Gro & Liq
Markhams & Cummings, Gerocers
Martin F, Saloon
Mechler E, Tailor
Mechler Joseph, Saloon
Mylrea John, Blacksmith
Noble George F, Grain & Produce
O'Connell & Slowey, Millinery
Oswald George, Boots & Shoes
Owen A H, Saloon
Radandt Frederick, Grocer
Ribenack George, Hotel
Richardson C T & N R, Painters
Roth Jacob, Saloon
Schmitz John N, Harness
Sheahan Timothy, Hotel
Shorey Mrs R W, Milliner
Siewert D F, Livery
Slowey Ellen, Milliner
Smith George, Elevator
Snoad Wm, Shoes
Tishner Charles, Harness
Timlin John, Grocer & Saloon
Van Alstine Nathaniel, Bl'ksmith
Walker Munger & Co, Millers
Wiedenberger George, Wagons

Hops pickers separating the seed pods from the vines, c. 1870. The 1860s boom in hops brought hundreds of young men and women to Kilbourn during the harvest season. (Courtesy, H.H. Bennett Studio Foundation).

to this new wealthy class as everyone tried to cash in on the boom.

A fine line exists between investment and speculation. The price of hops in 1867 encouraged some farmers not only to invest in hops growing equipment but also to neglect other crops. Some, in the haste to plant fields of hops, mortgaged their farms to buy more land. In 1868, increased acreage and the return to productivity of eastern hops fields resulted in a glut. The price of hops crashed to 10¢ per pound and below. Growers sold their crops at a loss. Fortunes were unmade and some farms were lost. Hops acreage dropped rapidly and would fade away by the turn of the century. The "hops fever" had broken.

Area farmers returned to their traditional crops of wheat, corn and timothy hay. Gradually, like other Wisconsin farmers, they concentrated on dairying and helped make the state, "America's Dairyland."

The Great Passenger Pigeon Nesting

The hops boom and bust was followed by an equally fervent–although briefer–passion for the harvesting of passenger pigeons.

Once the most abundant bird on the North American continent, the passenger pigeon has been wiped off the face of the earth. This sad story is also an important part of Wisconsin Dells history.

The passenger pigeon was so named for its habit of passing from one part of the country to another in huge flocks. It was a beautiful bird about 17" long and pinkish gray in color. The pigeons provided meat for the table of the early colonists and the indians who would follow their migration and camp near their nesting area. They were strong fliers, often traveling a hundred miles a day looking for food.

The stories that early settlers tell about the vast number of these pigeons seem unbelievable. In 1813 James J. Audubon watched a flock of passenger pigeons pass in a stream that lasted three days. The flock was so thick that it darkened the sun. Their wings sounded like thunder. Audubon estimated the flock to be over a billion birds.

In central Wisconsin the birds nested in jack pines and fed on acorns, wild grass seeds or newly-planted wheat. In 1871, the Dells area was the focal point of one of the largest nesting of pigeons in the eastern United States. It covered 850 square miles–including virtually all of Adams County plus the Towns of Delton, Dellona, Newport and Lyndon. The number of birds in the nesting was estimated at 136 million. Almost every tree from Kilbourn City to Wisconsin Rapids contained 1 to 200 nests, the weight of which would frequently break the branches and sometimes even topple the trees.

These powerful, beautiful birds had flown from the swamps of Louisiana to our forest in Wisconsin to bear their young. Their ancestors had made similar flights for hundreds, maybe thousands of years. It was believed all the remaining pigeons in the United States nested near the Dells in 1871. Their excretion covered the ground killing the grasses for years.

By the time the pigeon harvest was finished, a total of 1.6 million birds had been shipped out of the Kilbourn City depot.

In April, 1871, the Kilbourn newspaper carried this story: "The great pigeon roost this year is in Wisconsin. For three weeks, pigeons have been flying in flocks which no man could number. On Saturday, April 22, for about two hours before nightfall they flew in one continuous flock, darkening the sky and astounding people by the noise of their wings. Hotels at Kilbourn are full of trappers and hunters. Coopers are busy making barrels, and men and children are packing the birds and filling the barrels. They are shipping to Milwaukee, Chicago, St. Louis, Cincinnati, Philadelphia, New York and Boston. From 10,000 to 30,000 are forwarded daily."

Pigeons were slaughtered in every possible way. Large nets were thrown over the birds which had been baited with grain and salt. Sometimes a live pigeon was tied to a platform as a decoy thus the term (stool pigeon). While netting produced the most birds the hunters got their share. There are accounts of some hunters bagging over 1000 pigeons in a single day. The adult birds provided excellent sport but it was the young pigeons, called squabs which were most preferred. They were fatter, more tender and easier to capture. These helpless infants were pushed out of their nests with long poles or men would burn sulphur under the trees smoking them out of the nests. The trees were even burned or cut down to harvest the squabs. Squabs were so plentiful they were sold for as low as 2¢ each. School children accompanied the hunts and were paid a penny per two dozen squabs delivered to the tents. In addition to market use thousands of pigeons were captured alive and sold to sportsman clubs to be shot when released from traps. There were other nesting areas in Wisconsin in 1871 but Kilbourn City was the most popular to the hunters. Trainloads of netters and shot gunners arrived in town in April of that year. A description of a hunt just north of Kilbourn was described as follows:

"Embarking on the 10:00 AM train we headed for the great pigeon roost stretching from Kilbourn City on the Wis. River for scores of miles beyond. Having made all needed preparations the night previous we were called to arms and headed for the roost. The idea was to get into position before daylight. The indescribable cooing produced by uncounted millions of pigeons arousing from their slumber, was heard as the hunters made up their foraging parties. Creating an almost bewildering effect on the senses, as it was echoed and re-echoed back by the mighty rocks and ledges of the Wisconsin bank. As the first streaking of daylight began to break over the eastern horizon, small scouting parties of the monstrous army of birds then darted like night spirits past our heads. Soon the skirmish line, or perhaps more correctly pigeon bummers, swept past in small and irregular bodies. Our guide now told us to get into position as quick as possible as the large flocks would follow in rapid succession. We quickly ranged ourselves along the crest of a hill overlooking a cleared valley through which the birds would fly on their outward passage.

And now arose a roar, compared with which all previous noises ever heard are but lullabies, and which caused more than one of the expectant and excited party to drop their guns, and seek shelter behind and beneath the nearest trees. The sound was condensed terror. Imagine a thousand threshing machines running under full headway, accompanied by as many steamboats groaning off steam, with an equal quota of R.R. trains passing through covered bridges - imagine these massed into a single flock, and you possibly have a faint conception of the terrific roar following the monstrous black cloud of pigeons as they passed in rapid flight in the gray light of morning, a few feet before our faces. So sudden and unexpected was the shock that nearly the entire flock passed before a shot was fired. The unearthly roar continued, and as flock after flock, in almost endless line, succeeded each other, nearly on a level with the muzzle of our guns, the contents of a score of double barrels was poured into the dense mist. Hundreds, yes thousands, dropped into the open fields below. Not infrequently a hunter would discharge his piece and load and fire the third and fourth time into the same flock. The slaughter was terrible beyond any description. Our guns became

Dells Country Century Farms

Delton Township - 1855 - Dan & Martha Mae Brew
Newport Township - 1853 - Otto & Marian Christopherson
New Haven Township - 1846 - Erwin & Ruth Crothers
New Haven Township - 1883 - Harold & Velma Gaffney
Newport Township - 1873 - Loren Lewis
Newport Township - 1853 - Clarence, Jr. & Shirley Nelson
New Haven Township - 1852 - Robert Ramsey, Kenneth Crothers
New Haven Township - 1852 - Ethel & Kenneth & Richard Huber

Threshing crew from Big Spring area, c. 1900, (front, l-r) two members of the Dye family, Fred Richter, Leonard Buckley, Tim Kane; (middle) unidentified, Robert Ramsey, Elmer Coon, Lawrence Buckley, Floyd Vanderbilt, Aris Vandervilt; (rear) Mike Kane, Tony Zeitz, Joe Donahue, Frank Gaffney, George Vroman, Evert Hageman; (at far right) John Garbarski.

so hot by rapid discharges, we were afraid to load them. Then while waiting for them others threw clubs-seldom, if ever, failing to bring down some of the passing flock.

Ere the sun was up, the flying host had ceased. It continued scarcely an hour in all. Below the scene was truly pitiable. Not less then 2,500 birds covered the ground. Many were only wounded, a wing broken or something of the kind, which disabled, without killing them. These were quickly caught and their necks broken."

Another account of a passenger pigeon nesting was written by Reverend E.C. Dixon in the 1920s. The events he recounts occurred in 1882, but are all but identical to those of 1871.

"It was my privilege to see the great flocks of passenger pigeons twice, or rather many times on two different occasions," he wrote. "The first time was in 1871, when I was but a child, and yet so great was the impression made by the masses of birds and their cries as they came into the woods at evening time, that the experience has remained in memory through all these years.

"The particular experiences which I remember most vividly began one day in the month of March, 1882. On rushing out from the schoolhouse, I saw an enormous flock high in the air and flying swiftly to the north.

"The schoolhouse faced the north so I ran around the corner to see where the birds were coming from. And there they were extending to the horizon in all directions.

"This appearance of the great flock was the beginning of a series of exciting experiences. We soon learned that the pigeons had come from Pennsylvania, for professional hunters and trappers who kept track of the movement of the flock soon appeared from the east and set in motion the whole enterprise of trapping, buying, and shipping the birds.

"The flock soon settled in a tract of pine forest about ten miles north of the city. The skies were filled every day, morning and evening, as the birds flew out for their food. In this way the pigeons covered fully one hundred miles in every direction from the roost, sweeping field and forest clean of everything in the character of small nuts, seeds and grain. They were especially severe on new seeding and later when the grain was ripe, on the grain fields. A flock would go over a field with military precision. They would light at the edge of a field and as those arriving first would be in the rear as the feeding progressed, these birds at the rear would fly just over those ahead and proceed so rapidly that the entire flock would give the appearance of a great cylinder of birds slowly rolling over the field, and when the other side was reached the farmer's grain was gone.

"It was while these flocks were out after food that the trappers got in their deadly work. The trapping was done by means of nets of about the same mesh as are used for lake fishing. The process was simplicity itself, but deadly. The netter would place his net in an open field near to the woods. Grain was thickly strewn over the place where the net was to fall. The net itself was held back by strong spring poles of hickory or ash which, in turn, were attached to a line running back to a shelter called a bower, where the netter sat waiting his victims. Further to attract the birds a light pole was placed over the space, baited with grain and to one end of the pole a small block of wood called a stool was attached. From the trapper's bower a cord ran thru a hole in the stool to a live pigeon securely fastened at the end of the cord. When a flock was seen anywhere near, the trapper loosed the cord allowing the bird attached to it to fly into the air where its loud cries would attract the flock down to the bait. This familiar fact from the pigeon-trapping days, of course, gave rise to the phrase 'stool pigeon.'

"The grain and the stool pigeon lured the flock to its destruction for the birds were no sooner down upon the ground than the net was sprung and all were taken at once. The next procedure depended upon the immediate purpose of the trapper for there was an active demand for both the live birds and the dead ones. If dead ones were desired the trapper simply pinched the heads that appeared thru the meshes of the net, loaded the bodies into farm wagons and took them to town where the buyers waited for them. As my home was located on the main highway to the nesting woods, one of my most vivid memories is that of loaded wagons of dead pigeons passing the house from day to day all thru that spring.

"If live birds were wanted it was more difficult to take them from the nets, but many thousands were taken in that way, placed in crates, taken to town and kept in specially constructed pens until desired for shipment. There was great demand for live birds at that time for the numerous shooting clubs in the east with whom the live pigeon was a prime favorite for a mark, a custom which survives in the so-called clay pigeon of today.

"The shippers sent their produce chiefly to the great cities of the east, particularly Pittsburgh, New York, Boston, Philadelphia, and Washington.

"In June, the young birds, called squabs, were ready to gather. I say 'gather' for it was in no sense hunting. The birds were taken much as apples are taken from the trees. And if the taking of the old birds was an atrocity, as I now think it was, the taking of the squabs was a still greater one. When the young were of a size to gather the woods were filled with men, boys, and teams.

"But to continue my experience. One Saturday, my older brothers, Jim and John, a schoolmate, Harry Corning, and a boy we employed, Tim O'Neil, were driven by my father, A.C. Dixon, in the farm wagon out to the nesting wood. Beside the crates in which the squabs were to be kept, father took a long light ladder which he carried from tree to tree that we might more quickly climb the trees to reach the birds. With a game bag over our shoulders we ran up the ladder, then on up among the branches of the trees. What a sight to behold from the tops of the pines! The hundreds of nests, each with its single squab, like flotsam on the ocean, and every bird facing the sun. Many question the fact as to the single egg for every nest, but there is no question of it to those who climbed the trees. We gathered eighty-one dozen saleable birds that day and felt rich indeed as we sold our filled crates to the buyer at the close of the day.

The passenger pigeon. (Courtesy, State Historical Society of Wisconsin).

"The reason for remembering that day was Saturday was that while hundreds of others were busy in the woods the next day, we chafed at home, because we must keep the Sabbath day. But more than the fact of the Sunday intermission in our squabbing was the fact as to the amazing growth of the young in the two day interval.

"Bright and early on Monday morning four of our former party were on hand to continue our work of pigeon destruction. But what a change had taken place in the squabs! On Saturday the birds sat helpless, never moving as we approached the nests, but on Monday they flew out and glided away to the ground, running off among the huckleberry bushes so that two of our party climbed the trees to dislodge the birds while the other two remained on the ground to catch as many of then as possible when they scurried away among the bushes.

"But now the beautiful birds, with their graceful flight, their brilliant, iridescent plumage, and their enormous numbers are gone forever."

With 136 million passenger pigeons alive in 1871 its hard to believe they could be exterminated in less than thirty years. Though they had few natural enemies, pigeons were vulnerable to man. They laid but a single egg a year and both parents tended the nest. If one parent was killed the egg would surely die. While the large hunts and netting during roosting killed thousands it was the unrelenting pursuit year around that destroyed the flock.

Wisconsin's last live passenger pigeon was shot near Babcock in Wood County in 1899. Two years later the last wild bird of the species was shot by an Ohio boy with a BB gun. Martha, the last living passenger pigeon died in a Cincinnati zoo in 1914.

A monument to the passenger pigeon was erected at Wyalusing State Park in 1947. Aldo Leopold gave the following commemorative address:

On A Monument To The Pigeon

We meet here to commemorate the death of a species. This monument symbolizes our sorrow. We grieve because no living man will see again the onrushing phalanx of victorious birds, sweeping a path for spring across the March skies, chasing the defeated winter from all the woods and prairies of Wisconsin.

Men still live who, in their youth, remember pigeons; trees still live that, in their youth, were shaken by a living wind. But a few decades hence only the oldest oaks will remember, and at long last only the hills will know.

There will always be pigeons in book and in museums, but these are effigies and images, dead to all hardships and to all delights. Book-pigeons cannot dive out of a cloud to make the deer run for cover, nor clap their wings in thunderous applause of mast-laden woods. They know no urge of seasons; they feel no kiss of sun, no lash of wind and weather; they live forever by not living at all.

Our grandfathers, who saw the glory of the fluttering hosts, were less well-housed, well-fed, well-clothed than we are. The strivings by which they bettered our lot are also those which deprived us of pigeons. Perhaps we now grieve because we are not sure, in our hearts, that we have gained by the exchange.

For one species to mourn the death of another is a new thing under the sun. The Cro-Magnon who slew the last mammoth thought only of his prowess. The sailor who clubbed the last auk thought of nothing at all. But we, who have lost our pigeons, mourn the loss. Had the funeral been ours, the pigeons would hardly have mourned us.

We who erect this monument are performing a dangerous act. Because our sorrow is genuine, we are tempted to believe that we had no part in the demise of the pigeon. The truth is that our grandfathers, who did the actual killing, were our agents. They were our agents in the sense that they shared the conviction, which we have only now begun to doubt.

John Muir Visits the Dells

John Muir, the founder of our national park system came to Wisconsin Dells in 1867. He had heard from botanist Increase Lapham that the rare fragrant fern could be found here. Muir and a companion located the fern in several ravines and described its aroma as most entrancing. Of the ravines Muir wrote "No human language will ever describe them." But he tried. "They are the most perfect, the most heavenly plant conservatories I ever saw." Muir and his friend stayed overnight in the Dells, then built a raft and floated the river to Portage.

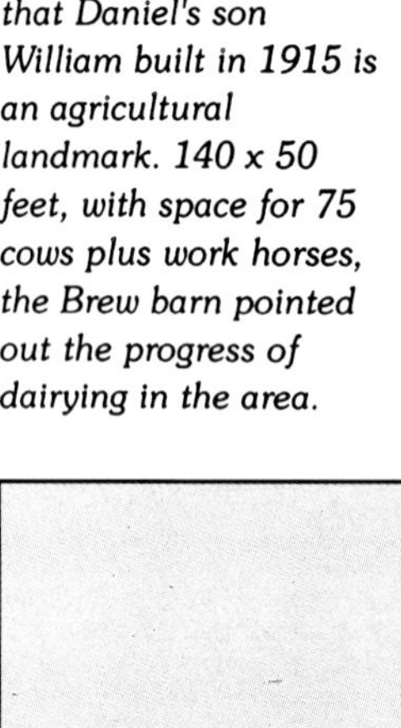

The Daniel Brew family was one of the first farm families in the Dells area. The barn that Daniel's son William built in 1915 is an agricultural landmark. 140 x 50 feet, with space for 75 cows plus work horses, the Brew barn pointed out the progress of dairying in the area.

Bloody September

(*The New York Times*, September 19, 1869)

"In Wisconsin, within a mile of Kilbourn, Gates was murdered on September 13 by a man who robbed him a year before to stop his testimony. Three days later, at Portage, 17 miles east, a lawyer shot and killed a yeoman and a mob hung him instantly. Two nights later people from far and near mobbed the Portage jail and hung the robber, Wildrick, who had robbed Gates, who was murdered five days previously. Four days later Miller Davis was robbed, murdered, and thrown senseless on the railroad tracks at a railroad Station 15 miles west of the scene of the first murder where he was mangled by the train. Three days later an Indian killed a Frenchman on a cranberry marsh. The Indian is in jail and the rest of the murderers are at large. A pleasant place–those regions of Wisconsin."

As the editor of the *Times* sarcastically pointed out, "those regions of Wisconsin" near Kilbourn could be far from pleasant. In a period of two weeks, six murders took place within a 20 mile radius of Kilbourn. Four were directly related to the village and one of its most prominent citizens, Schuyler Gates. The final two, of Davis and "the Frenchman" were coincidental, but nonetheless added to the lawless atmosphere of the times.

The tale began in 1866 when Schuyler Gates, the man who had built the first bridge across the Wisconsin at the Narrows in 1850, began to sell his property and prepare for his retirement. Gates was in his sixties, so a few eyebrows were raised a year later when he married twenty-three year old Mary Ann Cusick. In May, 1868 Gates and his wife embarked on a trip to visit Schuyler's daughter in Kansas. They loaded their belongings onto several small boats and–with $2,200 in cash and "marked" bonds tucked into a money belt–embarked down the Wisconsin.

They were camping on an island in the river near Arena when they were set upon by two masked bandits. They pistol-whipped Schuyler and left him bleeding and unconscious, then raped Mary Ann, tied her to a tree and made off with the $2,200.

Mary Ann struggled free, got Schuyler into a boat and brought him to a nearby farm where his wounds were tended. Although he lingered "on the very threshold of death," Gates recovered and was able to testify before the grand jury that he and Mary Ann had been attacked by the notorious Pat Wildrick and his partner in crime, Pat Welch.

Wildrick led of a band of cuthroats well-known in the Wisconsin River Valley and had served time in prison for assault and robbery. He was soon arrested by Columbia County Sheriff Phidelus Pool and found to be carrying $1,100 in marked bonds and cash.

In September, while Wildrick was awaiting trail, Schuyler Gates was murdered. He had walked across the railroad bridge at Kilbourn and, as the bridgetender later reported, was followed by two members of Wildrick's gang. A few hours later, a farmer traveling on the road from Reedsburg found his body.

Schuyler Gates, murdered and left to lie in the road near the Kilbourn bridge. (Courtesy, H.H. Bennett Studio Foundation).

In the communities of Kilbourn, Baraboo, Mauston, Briggsville and Portage, it was commonly believed that Wildrick had Gates killed in order to prevent his testifying at the trial. It was also commonly believed, and probably accurately too, that Wildrick could not be convicted without Gates' testimony.

Feelings were already running high when Wildrick's attorney, a short-tempered, abusive man named William Spain got into an altercation in Portage with a fellow named Barney Britt. Spain pulled out a pistol, shot and killed Britt. Hounded by a mob crying "Hang him," Spain sought protection by surrendering to the Portage city marshall, who placed him in the lock-up. The mob soon broke down the doors, dragged Spain out to the nearest tree and hanged him.

The following evening, in Lyndon Station, Mauston, Baraboo, Portage and Kilbourn, men were seen to be quietly gathering. Although the weather was warm, they all seemed to be carrying overcoats and wearing the hats low over their eyes. The train to Portage was full, as was the stage coach Jim Curry drove from Baraboo. A crowd estimated at 125-150 men gathered outside the jail in Portage. They forced open the door, tied up the sheriff and his deputy, then found the three keys necessary to open the locks on the way to Wildrick's cell. With none of the rushing and shouting that had accompanied the lynching of William Spain, the men grabbed Wildrick, placed a noose around his neck, dragged him out of the jail to a tree in a nearby ravine and hanged him.

The other murders followed in a few days, completing the roll call of death in Bloody September.

KILBOURN QUOTES

Growing up in this community, many stories have been passed down through the generations.

• *"Kilbourn City was conceived in sin and born in iniquity and no good could ever come of her." –Anonymous.*

• *One woman lived in the country and always walked even though she could afford a car. One day, Reverend Smukal stopped to offer her a ride. "No thanks" she replied, "I'm in a hurry." She was soon known as Mile a Minute.*

• *During the depression, one family had many children. When someone asked the wife why she had so many, she replied, "What is my husband going to do on Sunday afternoons?"*

• *One day Mr. McClyman gave his Indian friend a ride to town and asked him, "What kind of a winter are we going to have?" "Very cold winter", was the reply. "How do you know that?" "White man has big woodpile."*

• *Freddie Sperbeck had a speech defect and worked for Tollaksons who had accomodations for tourists. His first question to the tourists was, "Do you have your wombs yet?"*

• *Louie Miklic, a native of Austria who claimed to have been a schoolmate of Adolph Hitler, owned a general store on Oak Street. One day Louie became upset with some local Indians and said they should send those foreigners back where they came from.*

• *Henry Luettgerodt worked for Louie then left and opened his own store. Louie then said "that Henry Luettgerodt don't know nothing, all he knows he learned from me."*

The Kilbourn Library

Older residents of Kilbourn had, as far back as Old Newport days, established a reading club which took all the best magazines of our own country and of foreign countries as well.

In 1886 the germ of the present library came into existence. Miss Mylrea, Miss Bowman, and Mrs. Schofield, daughter of Editor Holly, and others, formed themselves into a literary society. This society organized and incorporated another society called the Literary and Library Association. Books were purchased, and these the Society circulated until 1895. In 1897 these books were turned over to the village and in February of the same year the village board in conformity to a new state law voted to levy a tax of one-half mill for library purposes and established the free public library of Kilbourn with an acting Library Board of five members. For five years the village council room was used for a library.

In 1902, the Tuesday Club put in a resolution to form a nucleus fund by a small annual assessment of its members, otherwise augmented by club activities, looking toward the purchase of a site for a library and the erection of a suitable building thereon. Mr. Charles W. Snider, one of Kilbourn's public-spirited citizens, hearing of this small beginning by the Tuesday Club, met them at a special meeting of the Club to make a proposition concerning the purchase of the C.A. Noyes residence on Broadway, for library purposes. The result was that Mr. Snider secured the property and offered it for purchase to the ladies of the Tuesday Club and the library board provided they would form a corporation of chosen members from both organizations and make a small payment down. Previous to this the Tuesday Club had financed and stood sponsor for the production of the opera "Mikado" by the musical talent of the town.

Over $300 was realized from this venture, which amount was accepted as a first payment by Mr. Snider who took a note at six per cent interest, for the rent. Thereafter the debt was gradually reduced to $600. Mr. Snider signed a satisfaction of mortgage for the remainder. The corporation offered it to the village as a gift, with the understanding that is was to be supported by same, which offer was accepted. The Noyes residence was shelved for library use, and there the library was conducted until application was made to Carnegie for a gift of money for a new building. Mr. Carnegie sent $6000, which sum was subsequently increased by the village to $15,000. This enabled the village to erect in 1912 a commodious building of sandstone, half timber and plaster, planned with reference to future enlargement. Frequent entertainments looking toward cultural uplift are held there and as a well patronized library it ranks very high in the state.

Thus, we see that the excellent public library at this place is largely indebted to the activities of the women of Kilbourn.

The Library Fountain

"Dedicated to Minnie Drinker Snider and Fred B. Snider. Like a cup of cold water to fevered lips is a cheerful, unselfish life in this busy world. To two such lives, which found happiness in kindness to every living creature, this memorial is a tribute." Early one evening in June of 1898 the members of the village board and many other interested citizens of Kilbourn gathered at the site of the memorial fountain on Broadway for the unveiling of this gift from Mr. Charles Snider to the memory of his wife and brother. The local paper reported, "Little Natalie Snider, a sweet little girl of five summers, a niece of the donor, pulled the cord which released the veiling, and, as the figure and outline was revealed a cheer went up." Charles Snider's son Harry then addressed the village board and presented the fountain in the name of his father and himself. For many years the lady of the fountain offered her gift of cool, refreshing waters impartially to birds, horses, dogs and people from her original location at the intersection of Broadway and Superior Streets. At that time Broadway did not continue west from Superior Street, but when the land was filled in so that Broadway ran straight west to the bridge, eventually traffic became heavy and the fountain had to be moved. After trying several different locations the memorial finally found a home on the library grounds. Although no longer a fountain its inscription still reminds us of the gracious lives of Minnie and Fred Snider.

The Snider Fountain, with newspaper editor J. E. Jones offering a cup to a neighbor. (Courtesy, H.H. Bennett Studio Foundation).

Laying a concrete sidewalk on Broadway, c. 1910. (Courtesy, H.H. Bennett Studio Foundation).

Kilbourn Landmarks

In the Bicentennial year of 1976, a group of interested citizens formed the Kilbourn Landmark Committee to investigate and mark various historic buildings and sites in the city, thus adding to the knowledge of our roots.

Many abstracts and old records were studied and by the time the group disbanded in 1979, thirty one buildings and sites had been authenticated by the committee. Owners bought plaques for their historic properties and many of these are still standing in 1995.

The committee promoted much interest in town history with two celebrations and the publication of a map showing all sites marked with these plaques and those still needing them.

These sites are as follows:

- Bailey's Eddy at the Municipal Dock
- General Bailey's homesite, 815 River Road
- H.H. Bennett Studio, 215 Broadway, National Register of Historic Places
- Tanner House Site, 229 Broadway
- Public Library, 429 Broadway, National Register of Historic Places
- Whitney House, 809 Cedar Street, moved from Newport
- Dixon Lion, 815 Cedar Street
- First Schoolhouse, 810 Elm Street, Built 1856
- G.A.R. and Masonic Hall, 817 Oak Street
- H.H. Bennett House, 825 Oak Street, National Register of Historic Places
- Alanson Holly Homesite, 211 Wisconsin Avenue
- Dr. Jenkins Homesite, Jenkins Park
- Rafting Over, Lower Dells Dock
- Belle Boyd, Spring Grove Cemetery
- Drinker's Landing, River Inn, 1015 River Road
- Alanson Holly Home, First Building in Kilbourn, Moved to 609 Washington
- Gates Gallery Site, Corner of Broadway & Elm
- Soeldner's Grocery, 306 Broadway
- Jonathon Bowman Home, 618 Cedar, moved from Newport
- Drug Store since 1866, 214 Broadway
- F. Snider Home, 532 Capital Street
- Zimmerman Home, 820 Bowman Road
- Point Bluff Boarding House, 419 Wisconsin Ave.
- Drinker Mills, 1033 River Road
- J. Harland McDonald Home, 221 Wisconsin Ave.
- Catholic Church, Wisconsin and Bowman Road
- First Catholic Rectory, 722 Wisconsin
- First Lutheran Church, 618 Washington Avenue
- Stroud Bank, 314 Broadway
- Gil Van Alstine's Blacksmith Shop, 737 Oak St.
- Corning-McManman House, 521 Broadway
- Kilbourn City, Broadway, under Railroad Bridge
- Duryee Building, 312 Broadway

William Brew and Jenny Brew York, with the mule-drawn wagon the Brews used to deliver milk, cream and butter in Kilbourn.

Bill Bauer in his meat market, which stood on the southeast corner of Broadway and Superior.

Jake Drollinger and friends in his harness shop in the 700 Block of Oak Street.

The Kilbourn Institute

The Kilbourn Institute, first a Methodist boarding school then a health spa, stood on the east end of Washington Street, c. 1880. (H.H. Bennett Studio Foundation).

In 1856, A. Bronson, a wealthy resident of Prairie du Chien, endowed the National Methodist Conference, an institute of higher education for men and women, with money for a new school. Point Bluff, a small village located on the Wisconsin River about 14 miles north of Kilbourn City, was selected as the site.

For several years everything prospered and the school was full. Fine homes were built in the area, and the future of Point Bluff and of the Institute seemed assured. But after the railroad crossing was built at Kilbourn City in 1857, the village began to decay. Many people left from Point Bluff and the school had to be closed in 1865.

Soon after, a group of Methodists in Kilbourn City secured a charter and incorporated the Kilbourn City Seminary in order to move the school from Point Bluff to Kilbourn City.

The moving contract states that the Kilbourn Methodists paid George W. Lease, A. Campbell and the Bennett Brothers $1,775 to perform the task. The contract required the men to carefully disassemble the 40' x 60' two-story building at Point Bluff, then transfer and re-erect it at Kilbourn City.

The men were required to replaster all interior walls and hang the bell in a good substantial manner. The Methodists purchased five acres of land from E.T. Hooker for $300 at the east end of Washington Avenue and reassembled the building.

The new school, which became known as the Kilbourn Institute, opened in the fall of 1866 with Rev. G.W. Case as principal. The school prospered, and in 1867 there were 140 pupils enrolled.

Apparently, however like all schools, everything was not perfect. In a letter found in the Stroud files, an irate trustee of the school complained to Mr. Stroud, "There are a number of students in the school who use intoxicating liquor, and you know that it is against the rules."

About 1:00 PM on Sunday, Jan. 30, 1868, while the dedicatory services were being held in the new Methodist Episcopal Church, the congregation was startled to hear that their institute was on fire. The fire was so far advanced that it was impossible to save the structure. A few pieces of furniture were rescued, but everything else was destroyed. The total loss was $5,000. The building was insured for $4,000, and with this money a fine new brick structure was erected. However, for some unknown reason the school was never reopened.

In 1876, Frank Straw bought the property for $800. He invested $6,000 in converting the operation into a watercure medical and surgical institute. The building then contained thirty rooms including a kitchen, dining room, bedrooms, turkish bath rooms, shampooing rooms, and hot and cold bathrooms. A five horsepower motor pumped the water from a 160' well into tanks in the attic. A steam boiler was used to heat the water. The water cure institute opened in the summer of 1878 with Dr. William Russell as head physician. Later physicians were Dr. Galloway and Dr. McElroy.

The Institute closed around the turn of the century, and was later the residence of Peter and Emma Jacobson. During the 1940's, Louis Rockoff purchased the property and operated it as an egg buyer. The building was again destroyed by fire on Christmas Day 1941. Rockoff rebuilt the structure, which now stands as Platt's Garage.

The Delton post office which, in 1910, was in the Hulbert Store, located one block west of the Methodist church visible behind the horse and buggy at lower right.

The Village and Town of Delton

In 1866, a Milwaukee newspaperman visited Delton and reported that, "This is a small but pleasant village some three miles south of Kilbourn. It has a voting population of about 300. When the St. Paul Road was being constructed through this region, it was expected to pass through this place, but failed to do so. And Kilbourn got the prize instead; consequently the village has increased but little of late years. If the inhabitants were disappointed in the railroad matter, they are in part compensated in being free from the mixed and floating population a railroad always brings with it."

It must have made a difference for, in 1880, the author of the Delton section of a history of Sauk County declared that "The people of the village and town of Delton are particularly proud of their longevity and the community boasts of a greater number of persons who have passed fourscore years than can be found in any other section of the country of equal size and population. As Squire Keyes tersely expressed it, 'The people never die; they dry up and blow away'."

The history of the Town of Delton also includes the history of Lake Delton, Mirror Lake, Newport, the village of Lake Delton, and the city of Wisconsin Dells west of the Wisconsin River.

The village of Lake Delton was not formed as a separate governmental entity from the Town of Delton until September, 1954. Prior to that it was an unincorporated village known progressively as Norris, New Buffalo, Dell Town, Delton and Mirror Lake. After the Baraboo Fire Department got confused while responding to the disastrous Morris Hotel fire in 1932 and ended up in Merrimac, the name was changed to Lake Delton.

The City of Wisconsin Dells annexed a large portion of the Town of Delton starting in 1966. Since then the city and the village of Lake Delton have annexed smaller parcels until most of the Town of Delton between the Wisconsin River and Lake Delton (the Lake) on the east and I-90/94 on the south and west, except for some farm land and wooded areas, is now part of one or the other of the two above-named municipalities. The history of the area prior to annexation remains a part of the Town of Delton history.

Of the several creeks in the Town of Delton, the most important was Dell Creek. Spring Brook (formerly Pine Creek) flowed into it and the mouth of the creek where their combined waters flowed into the Wisconsin River made a fine harbor for the small craft that then plied the river. It was also a landmark that both the Native Americans and early voyageurs watched for during their travels, as near here they could wait out storms and high water through the Upper Dells that sometimes made the river temporarily impassible.

In 1849, Alexander Vosler built a "shanty house" for his men while they built the first dam and sawmill. The following year Jared Fox and Elijah

A. M. Reynolds repaired wagon wheels and performed other iron work in Delton, c. 1910. The village had a population of about 200 and was a stopping place for the stage coach connecting Baraboo and Kilbourn.

Topping constructed a grist mill on the site of what was later known as Sarrington or Lower Mill at the junction of Spring Brook and Dell Creek. It manufactured 100 barrels of flour a week which was shipped to Milwaukee. Most of the lower part of this stream bed is now under Lake Delton.

In 1851, this rough community had 20 houses described by the wife of Dr. Jenkins as, "All consisting of boards on three sides and a blanket or canvas on the fourth side to keep out the cold and to obtain privacy."

The original settlers in the Town grew wheat as a cash crop in as great quantities as possible. This gave rise to a second mill and dam being built of logs by La Bar and Boorman in 1860 at the site of the present Mirror Lake Dam. It was later operated by the Timme family from 1893 to 1947, and considered one of the best grist mills in the state. It shipped 300 barrels of wheat flour a day to Chicago. It burned down in 1957.

The wheat trade and the hop boom which followed after chinch bugs destroyed much of the wheat crop gave rise to a machine shop and foundry which built hops stoves, fanning mills for sifting grain and other cast iron products. It was powered by a log dam with a 22 foot fall built across Spring Brook just east of the high bridge by Clement and Adams in 1858 and used iron ore mined in the Sauk County town of Ironton.

Thompson and Holmes also manufactured wagons, buggies and carts. When the heavy wheat farming died and the hops boom crashed, most of this business moved to Minnesota.

In addition to the Lower Sarrington Dam and Upper Timme Dam, and the just-mentioned foundry dam, there was also an earlier dam built in 1852 by Norris and Marshall on Dell Creek 40 rods from the river to operate a saw mill. This would place it close to the present Lake Delton dam. There was also a small dam about two miles up Hulburt Creek. Presently another dam across Spring Brook forms Blass Lake in Camp Chi and there are small dams in Trout Creek and Lower Hulburt Creek near the river that have been annexed by Wisconsin Dells.

A steam sorghum mill was built by T.J. Huntington. It had a capacity of 300 gallons of molasses a day and was probably the largest such mill in the state. A large amount of sugar cane was grown in the town at the time and in 1880 it was operating day and night and planning to make part of the crop into sugar.

After many of these industries collapsed in turn or moved away, the farm community gradually shifted from cash crops to dairying.

When farm stagnation started to set in after the turn of the century, the area got a boost to its economy with the arrival of the horseless carriage. Hundreds of motor parties came to see the Dells of the Wisconsin River, made famous by photographer H.H. Bennett. Some of these travelers also visited pow-wows held at "Yellow Thunder's Forty," the parcel owned by Chief Yellow Thunder, in Delton.

Transportation also improved. Delton native and Wisconsin Supreme Court Justice Roujet Marshall persuaded the town to contribute and himself helped pay for the paving of what became Highway 12. It was the first paved rural road in the state. He was also instrumental in getting the bridge erected over Dell Creek.

There are several cemeteries in Delton. One is next to the Copacabana and has been in constant use since it was first platted in 1854. Another cemetery, called Mount Pleasant Cemetery, was platted about a half mile away in Section 17 due north of Lake Blass in Camp Chi property. It is not known if anyone was ever buried there, or if the graves were moved, but it still appears on some maps. A third cemetery was Webster's Prairie Cemetery on Highway 12 south of Lake Delton. Yellow Thunder and his wife, called "Washington Woman," are buried in their own plot on County A.

The eastern Yankees and York Staters who first settled in the area among the Indians were later joined by a large influx of Irish and Norwegians. Today, the community has become a melting pot of many nationalities.

In 1857 the Masonic Lodge was instituted in Newport. It was known as Dalles Lodge No. 78. Upon the fall of Newport, the lodge was moved to Delton where the order built a temple in 1866, (the lower floor). It was also used at times for a drug store, post office, dance hall, ice cream parlor and restaurant. The building burned on August 7, 1931 and the new Temple as it now stands was dedicated in May 28, 1932. The Order of the Eastern Star was organized in 1921.

A crew of horse-drawn scrapers (above) worked on the roadway that became Highway 12, c. 1910. The road dips down to Spring Creek in front of what became the entrance to the Tommy Bartlett Show. Marshall Memorial Hall (below) was the gift of Delton's most famous son, Wisconsin Supreme Court Justice Roujet Marshall.

Roujet D. Marshall

Roujet D. Marshall was born December 27, 1847 in Nashua, New Hampshire. He moved with his family to Delton in 1854. Due to the ill health of his father, he spent a good deal of his childhood laboring on the family farm and evenings studying, with the encouragement of his mother. When not needed on the farm he went to the Delton Academy six months a year.

At age 14 he passed the teachers examination in Kilbourn and got a teaching certificate. He continued studying at the Academy when he could. At age 17, the care of the farm and family was largely his.

He attended Baraboo Collegiate Institute during the late fall and winter of 1865 and '66, where he met Mary Jenkins, another student. Mary was one of 80 girls who came to the farm that summer to pick hops. He entered Lawrence College in 1868, but was called home by the death of his father. For the next 2 years he worked the farm, as the price of hops had dropped and it was up to him to change the crops to something else. He married Mary Jenkins when he was 21 and spent the next 3 years studying law under N.W. Wheeler in Baraboo. He passed the bar in 1873 at age 24.

Wheeler moved his practice to Chippewa Falls and Roujet entered the law office with him, where he attracted the attention of Fredrick Weyerhauser. It was through Weyerhauser that Marshall achieved his great success as a practicing lawyer.

Marshall was a dedicated, hard working man, who spent from 12 to 15 hours per day at his practice. He took time out to make monthly trips to the farm in Delton to check on its management and see his mother, and added to the farm by buying much of the adjoining valley.

By 1888 he had been a county judge for 6 years, was a member of the Board of Regents of the University of Wisconsin and a circuit judge. He was appointed to the Wisconsin Supreme Court by Governor Upham in 1895 where he served for the next 22 years.

Many rulings that were handed down by the high court during that period still hold today. Judge Marshall is largely responsible for the establishment of workmen's compensation laws in the state. While Marshall worked in Madison, the state Capitol burned and his work cleared the way for construction of the present noble building. He also did considerable work on the law library there.

Marshall, who did considerable traveling between his home in Chippewa Falls, the farm in Delton, and Madison, helped enact the first state aid bills for highway improvements in the state. In Delton he put up one dollar of his own for every dollar appropriated for road building in the town. Delton was the first in the state to boast having a surfaced road across the township. In fact, the Judge completely paid for the entire road across his farm (Hwy 12 today) and for oiling it after that. Judge Marshall was responsible for the big fill in Lake Delton and completing the road where it is today between the Dells and Lake Delton. The fill (south of Parson's) was put in at a cost of $4500.00.

The Judge owned one of the first cars in the area and had a hired driver. He made weekly trips to the farm to visit his Mother when he was in Madison.

Judge Marshall died May 22, 1922. He was generous with friends and employees, and in his will he remembered many of them. He gave the family farm to the farm manager, William Hillman. The farm next door went to another employee, Guy House. He left money to build a Town Hall in Delton, known today as the Marshall Memorial Hall.

Maybe the Judge's success is best summed up by his motto: "I dearly love to work."

The Good Templars–a fraternal organization committed to temperance–had a Lodge of 74 members. The Templar's gavel was presented to the Woman's Club in 1958. A Woodman Lodge was formed at a later date and flourished for quite some time. Delton had such a large number of Civil War veterans that it become known as "the old soldiers' home". Not surprisingly, the Delton Camp of the Grand Army of the Republic veterans organization was large and active.

By the 1900s the bustling pioneer village of Delton had all but disappeared. The mills still served farmers, children still went to school, meet-ings were still held at the town hall, but all the business places had closed their doors. In his 1914 history of Sauk County, Baraboo editor H. E. Cole, put Delton and Newport on his list of "ghost towns."

One story is told of a man and his son who were going to Baraboo. When they reached Dell Creek bridge, the boards from the bridge floor had washed away in high water and they had to go down stream and get the boards and replace them before they could cross. The boy then asked his father where Delton was. The father replied that they had already gone through it. The boy hadn't noticed.

Delivering gasoline (above) the dependable way in Delton and a gasoline-powered launch (below) on Mirror Lake, c. 1910.

Timme's Mill and the "upside down" cantilever bridge at the foot of Mirror Lake.

Timme's Mill and Mirror Lake

August Timme took over operation of the mill on the upper stretch of Dell Creek in 1893 and it remained in the family until 1947. First built in 1857 by Horace La Bar and a partner named Boorman, the dam eventually stretched 120 feet across the stream and raised the water level nearly 20 feet–higher than the hydropower dam built at Kilbourn in 1909. The mill ground wheat into flour and the dam provided power for several industrial operations. Parts of the dam washed out in 1908 and 1917, but were rebuilt.

The clarity of its water prompted Clara Noyes, wife of Kilbourn attorney Luther Noyes, to give what was then known as "La Bar's Pond," the new name of Mirror Lake. Its beauty attracted Al and Eliza Morris Ringling, of the Baraboo circus family, and they built a luxurious summer home there. Ringling, who had traveled the world with his circus, said that he would rather be at Mirror Lake than any place on earth.

Al Ringling died in 1916 and his wife Eliza developed their Mirror Lake property. She built the Ringling Hotel in 1920 and later renamed it, in honor of her family, the Morris Hotel. In the 1920s, the Morris Hotel was considered one of the best in the state. It had a swimming pool, 18-hole golf course, dance hall and other amenities. Mrs. Ringling managed the hotel until it was destroyed by fire in 1932.

In 1956, a huge fire destroyed Timme's Mill, along with the distinctive reverse cantilever bridge constructed beside it. Most of the land around Mirror Lake has since become part of the state park.

The Grotto saloon was tucked into the rock at the end of the Mirror Lake Bridge.

Building the Mirror Lake bridge.

The Sarrington Mill

Henry Christian Sarrington purchased the Delton mill in 1882. He was the first of four generations of Sarringtons at the mill and followed by son Henry, grandson Ralph and great-grandson Robert, who took over in 1957.

Henry Christian was born at Kettering, Northhampton, England in 1835, migrated to Delton in 1867, and immediately went to work at the mill he later purchased. In its hey-day the Sarrington mill shipped countless carloads of pancake flour out of Kilbourn. The Universal Grocery chain–later part of the Kroger system– was one of its biggest contractors.

The dam went out three times through flood waters and the old wooden mill burned down in 1920. It was replaced with a stone structure in 1924. A few years later W. J. Newman bought the property and tore out the Sarrington dam in preparation for the building of Lake Delton. The dam for the lake was then built downstream of the old Sarrington site.

The Sarringtons then switched their milling operations from water to electric power and continued to grind grain and flour until about 1969.

The Sarrington mill.

Dawn Manor. (Courtesy, H.H. Bennett Studio Foundation).

Dawn Manor

Dawn Manor, built in 1855 of Potsdam sand stone, with walls three feet thick, an interior of chestnut and white mahogany and white pine, put together with brass screws and wooden pegs, is an architectural gem.

Captain Abraham Vanderpoel, rich lumber prince, signer of the constitution of Wisconsin, and friend of Lincoln, built this "Dream House." Here on its five acre front lawn Company E held maneuvers for the Civil War. Private tutors taught the numerous children in the second floor school room. Later the daughters were married from the library.

When Vanderpoel left for the West, S.H. Kerfoot, millionaire of Chicago, lawyer, member of the Board of Trade and sportsman, purchased the home, adding elaborate stables to the coach and carriage houses of the Vanderpoel era. He was extraordinary with his horses, carriages, rose gardens and fishing records.

When he died his widow left the house with the table set, her clothes hanging in the closets and her personal effects all about. She left a library full of rare first editions and autographed volumes, a legal library, fishing records and trophies plus an early D.A.R. membership, signed by Eugenie Washington, grandniece of George Washington. For thirty three years the house lay untouched. Another owner came for a short duration.

Then the owner that towered above all owners came along. W.J. Newman. He wanted a lake in front of Dawn Manor so he put one in. A 600 acre lake at a cost of $1,200,000.00. He bought all the land as far as he could see; three thousand acres for a park for Dawn Manor.

Mr. Newman never lived in the Manor; the statues never decorated it, he never swam or sailed or fished in the lake. He died broke, his finances destroyed in Great Depression.

After Newman, Dawn Manor became a hotel and the big rooms were made into little rooms and the coach and carriage houses saw a strange array of tourists check in and out each summer.

In 1942, Mrs. Helen Raab, widow of the famous artist George Raab, purchased the home. She moved in with her rare porcelains, prints, fabrics, paintings and various antiques. Carefully she restored the home as it was in 1855; removing partitions, wall paper and light fixtures, as this house was built before the development of electricity. Mrs. Raab died in 1970, and the home was passed to her son, Kirby Raab, who is also now deceased.

Briggsville, c. 1880, with the Eagle mill for feed and grain and the carding mill to process wool.

Briggsville

On a cold January day in 1950, Amphlius Chamberlain, with his wife and son, traveled from Elkhorn to begin a new life in the Wisconsin wilderness.

The family was welcomed into a large cabin along the Old Pinery Road which belonged to Silas Walsworth, who had come to Portage in 1837. In addition to building this cabin, Walsworth established a trading post and two meeting houses in Portage, and operated a ferry on the Wisconsin River.

They were also greeted by Jonathan Butterfield, who lived at Walsworth's although he had laid his own large claims in the vicinity. After enjoying a hearty meal of venison, squirrel, partridge, corn-meal cakes and scalding tea, the lively group talked of possibilities well into the night.

The next morning, Chamberlain and Butterfield set out, traveling slowly on snowshoes made by Ho-Chunk Indians, for a point about two miles northeast of Walsworth's clearing. Coming to a small break in the tamaracks, Butterfield pointed out an area within his claim which he called Little Lake.

Next they came to level ground, heavily wooded on either side but looking westward across an expanse of marsh and bog through which a dark stream meandered merrily, even in winter. At left stood ten to fifteen structures: long sapling poles, bent, with their ends firmly planted in the ground, and whole domed at top to form circular structures about eight feet in height. Butterfield explained that they were covered with deerskins or wide strips of bark in summer and inhabited by a group of friendly Ho-Chunk Indians who fished and trapped throughout the vicinity. They had joined a larger group to the north for the winter, where they held festivals and dances periodically. On a still night, he said, you could hear the tom-toms calling the young braves to dance, which they often did until dawn. Of a large, low-lying mound of irregular outline in the snow, Butterfield explained that it was an Indian mound in the shape of a turtle. Another farther on, appeared to be an elephant or possibly a bear.

The swift-moving stream which sat in the middle of all of this was Big Spring Creek, the western branch of the *Neenah*, which is Ho-Chunk for "water". It flared Chamberlain's imagination so that by nightfall he had decided to invest in Butterfield's claim, intending to harness the water power and erect a mill at the edge of the swampy clearing. He already had a portion of the money,

The Briggsville creamery and Kimball's general store, c. 1900.

and was certain that he'd find a partner to share his enthusiasm. The history of the white population of Briggsville had begun.

The claim to the south of Neenah Creek, including the land surrounding Little Lake, was Jonathan Butterfield's. To the north of the creek, much of the land had been claimed by Aaron Town, who had returned to New Hampshire shortly before to fetch his family. Chamberlain's first concern was to build a house for his family, which he did on the south side of the stream near the Indian camp. Another was built on the site of what later became the hotel, and to that cabin in 1850, came Alexander Ellis Briggs and other newcomers from Shoreham, Vermont.

A.E. Briggs became Chamberlain's partner, and together they gained from Butterfield and Town the right to build a dam across Big Spring Creek to provide water-power for a mill. Thus Alexander Briggs gave the new settlement his name, as well as a purpose.

Briggs soon returned to Vermont to bring his family to te new holdings, leaving Chamberlain to marshal building forces for the dam and the sawmill, which would supply the settlers with logs to build their homes.

The dam, which was commenced in 1850, had two flumes–(channels down which water was directed to power mills). The sawmill was finished in 1852 on the south flume. The first lumber manufactured was the heavy oak plank and joists used to build the first jail in Portage City. The lumber was taken by flatboat down Neenah Creek to the Fox River, and thence up the Fox to Fort Winnebago, which lay just outside Portage.

The dam made a lake to the west about three miles in length, which was named Mason in honor of the carpenter who built the mill and who was also the first hotel owner in Briggsville–Charles Mason. Beneath the waters of Lake Mason sleep the giant Indian mounds that Butterfield and Chamberlain had gazed upon in 1850.

All supplies for the tiny settlement were hauled 100 miles by team from Milwaukee, and the "store" was in the cabin to which, in 1851, Alexander Briggs brought his wife Robey and their four children: Lydia, Abby O., James A., and Emma R. Mrs. Briggs disliked the confusion of the log cabin beside the dam, where settlers came for provisions and newcomers frequently came for everything from information to a bed. Accordingly, the Briggs's built a new log home on the high bank of Neenah Creek, below the dam.

Building activities in the tiny village increased to a near feverish pitch. In 1851, Briggs constructed a brick kiln below the sawmill where chimney brik sold at $6 per thousand, well brick at $5, and a cheaper grade at $4. When Hiram and Lysander Chapman arrived from New York, Briggs and Chamberlain completed a flouring mill at the north flume in 1853. Ebenezer A. Corning, who arrived from New Hampshire in 1850 and made a claim in the town of Lewiston, acted as surveyor for the entire area.

In 1851, Edward B. Craig arrived and purchased Silas Walsworth's property on the Old Pinery Road. In 1853 he built his hotel, known as Menomonee House. The hotel was probably one of the first buildings built of bricks manufactured at the Briggsville yard.

West of Briggsville, Dwight E. Eighme's father had built a small mill in 1849, where Big Spring Creek ran through what later generations called Cummings Cove. The mill was later abandoned because of an insufficient supply of water.

Three or four miles northeast ofBrigsville lay a small community known as Douglas Center, where in 1849, Joseph and Betsy Cady Loomer settled. Just south of their claim, the Landgraf family settled in 1853 on a farm that has remained in their family since.

In the early days, before the government had surveyed the land into sections, all a settler had to do was to claim a piece, blaze a line around it, build a "claim shanty" and live on the claim, careful not to encroach upon another person's land. To protect their claims, Briggsville settlers organized a claim society.

A number of cases came before the society, and were settled in frontier fashion. In spring, 1852, the James Litchfield family located on a portion of Section 1, Township 13, Range 7, and erected a small dwelling. Litchfield rejected the society's "notice to vacate" on the grounds that the alleged prior claimant had selected another quarter and was therefore entitled to no more. At around midnight one Saturday in May, 1852, 10-12 masked men arrived, ordered the family out of the house, and burned it to the ground. Though five defendants were identified, arrested, and charged with arson, the case was eventually stricken from the docket.

Many other families arrived and contributed to the area's colorful history. In 1854, Joseph Gay and his family arrived at the William Post farm south of Douglas Center. Peter Peterson, a young Norwegian, opened a wagon shop and carpentry business in Lewiston. Lefavor Waters arrived in Briggsville and opened a store, as did William Murphy, who was also appointed the first postmaster the same year. The office was in Murphy's store, and the mail came by stagecoach from Portage City.

In 1855, the James Kimball family arrived from Vermont and lived on the farm that the Harvey Briggs family would occupy upon arrival in 1857. Joshua Corning built a home in Briggsville, and the Atwood family settled east across the Big Marsh from Briggsville, where a Ho-Chunk family, the Decorahs, camped nearby. Their daughter, Martha (Good Village) Decorah, would later marry Henry Dick, another full-blooded Ho-Chunk Indian who hd come from Wittenberg, Wisconsin.

Though these early days were certainly not free of animosity between the two groups, many pioneers were friendly with their Indian neighbors, who sometimes gave them indian names and adopted them into their tribes.

Pa-zee-gah and Koo-nee-kah-gah were two Ho-Chunk women well known among white settlers, and taught many a worried housewife how to use native herbs and medicines. Big Sam Decorah, John Canoe, Red Horn and Smoke Smoke were prominent men in the tribe.

Briggsville was platted on October 23, 1854 by Harvey Briggs. Amphlius Chamberlain was the first Town Superintendent, and Henry Parrott the first town clerk. The Town of Douglas was forme in 1858, named for Illinois senator Stephen A. Douglas of the Lincoln-Douglas debates. A few years earlier, however, the first election in the community was held at the Lewis farm, the first

The "old" Lake House, with the gate for the Lake Mason dam at right.

The "new" Lake House.

claim recorded in Lewiston near the present Town Hall, and included all the people from Briggsville and the surrounding territory.

The first meeting of the school district, which included Briggsville and Moundville, was held December 11, 1852 at the village store. They oted to build a log school, raise $25 to finish the building, and that it be situated on the hill behnd the A.E. Briggs home. When the school opened for 3 months in 1853, Abby O. Briggs taught 31 children ranging in age from four to twenty. Horatio S. Thomas was appointed superintendent and G.H. Chamberlain, clerk. In 1858, the English, German, and Irish settlers who did not always agree voted to separate Moundsville and Briggsville.

The village continued to develop. John Hayes conducted a shoe shop and Barney Brogan built a blacksmith shop. In 1858 a sugar mill was erected on Neenah Creek below the da, where sorghum syrup sold at 18¢ per gallon. Henry Dyer built a mill to card wool across the road from the sugar mill. Charles Mason's hotel passed through many hands, including Henry's son Hank, before burning to the ground in 1912.

Nathaniel and Julia Gray brought their seven children to the area from Corinth, New York in February, 1857. Gray was a shoemaker and also keenly interested in farming, at one point owning several hundred acres of land.

Many members of the Dean family, who arrived in Briggsville in 1858, were associated with the community's musical interests for decades. By 1873, Lucius Dean and his son Herbert were operating a harness and leather goods business.

During the early 1860s, more families came and settled east of Neenah Creek, including George and Jane Smith from Scotland, Joseph Grandy and his family, and John Hindes. In 1865 John Brenzel, whose name was later changed to Brancel, brought his family to the area, and his sons would later play prominent roles in the development of Briggsville. The Jacob Heberlein family arrived in 1868. Evan Magnus Hanson, a shoemaker and carpenter, came to Briggsville from Nee Rumarika, Norway in 1867 at age 22 and spent the rest f his life there. The Burmeister and Schwemerlein families arrived in Douglas during the 1870's. Several descenants of Alonzo W. Colburn, early Newport pioneer, later made their way into the Briggsville area as well.

In March, 1877, Joseph Champeny, born in England on October 2, 1838, arrived in Briggsville and purchased a half interest in James A. Briggs' flouring mill. I 1880 he bought the remaining interest and the mill remained in the Champeny family until its sale in 1942. few years later Joseph's son, Charles, built a sawmill a few miles south of the present mill.

On December 2, 1892, heavy frost cracked its foundations and the dam went out, after being reconstructed only the year before. Not only was the dam washed out, but also the walls beneath the mill, 80 feet on the west side of the flume, and part of the Champeny saw mill and mill shed.

During the early settlement period, services for various religions were generally held in homes. By 1856, the Catholic Cemetery was located on the original Aaron Town homestead, and a church was completed in 1864. The first Protestant Church in Briggsville was a Universalist Society organized by Joseph Franklin Bacon in 1873. That same year, the Society began constructing a church, but it was destroyed by a cyclone before it completion. The Universalist Society decided not to rebuild, and the property was sold to the Methodist Episcopal Church Society, which built a church there in 1879.

Big Spring

The Big Spring area has been described as resembling an orchard of giant oak trees on the ridges and open marshes along streams in the valleys. The Indians burned over most of the area each fall in a successful effort to discourage growth of unwanted brush. Blue stem and bluegrass on the uplands and various varieties of marsh grasses on the wetter areas, were able to thrive and provide abundant pasture for the deer herd.

The local Indian encampment was located about 1/4 mile south of the Big Spring Dam. The "squaw's hole" in the creek was near by and was regarded as theirs and theirs alone for laundry and bathing.

The Indian Cemetery and ceremonial ground was located about ½ mile southwest of the encampment site, near the center of section 27. It is a sad commentary on the treatment of Indians that this parcel of land was subjected to real estate taxation. It belonged to Jake Pretty Man, son of the old "Chief Pretty Man", and of course, the tax wasn't paid. Eventually the parcel was sold by Adams County, via the tax deed route. After all, properties belonging to the rest of us, and used as cemeteries or places of worship are not subjected to taxation.

Luke Vliet, an old resident, told of playing ball with the Indian boys, and Indian families took on land clearing projects and lived on site. At the time of the Civil War, there was concern of Indian uprisings and a group of white elders sought out Chief Pretty Man, promised him his people would not want if he would keep his braves in line. He agreed and the promise was kept.

Many of the settlers coming from Pennsylvania, Ohio or southern Wisconsin brought cattle with them and providing feed for cattle and food and shelter for the family in one summer presented a monumental challenge. The open grasslands, a scythe, fork, axe, shovel and Olympic endurance were keys to survival.

Early arrivals were Ira Ward, Daniel Eighme, D.M. Hatch, Enos Seward, Dan Clough, James Ramsey, George Marshall, James Winchell, Jeremiah Landt, Uri Morse, Jasper Stowell, Jared Walsworth, and surnames, Kingsley, Phillips, Pike, Wells, Kershaw, Pierce, Smith, Cusack, Ellis, Morey, Flook, Best, Barringer, Sargent, and Russell. The mists of time and loss of some early records obscure much of the story of the Big Spring community.

Town records indicate that the first annual town meeting was held April, 1855. It being about the first opportunity for self-expression as a township, the name was changed to New Haven. In common usage the two names have remained somewhat synonymous to the present time. At this meeting the following officers were elected: James Ramsey, Chairman; Curtis Ellis and John Best, Supervisors; David Hatch, clerk; Henry Philips, Treasurer; Seth Cole and Lycurgas Best, Justices of the Peace; Josiah Sweet, Jeremiah Landt, Peter Barringer, Constables; Samuel Ward, Sealer of Weights and Measures; Seth Mills, Town School Superintendent.

The framework of organized town government combined with vision, ability and ambition, resulted in development of a thriving community. For

The dam and the Ward mill at right, with the Hindes and Hanson general store that made up downtown Big Spring, c. 1900.

The Pierce Hotel building, Big Spring. (Courtesy, the Crothers Family).

practical purposes the town was divided into four common school districts: Badger, Big Spring, Ward and Stafford with variations over time.

In 1886, Solon Pierce wrote that in 1854 and 1855, W.S. Pierce migrated here from Canada and "bought the old saw mill from Jerry Landt. Local farmers also wanted a grist mill so the old saw mill was put in order and sawing commenced. Giles Smith put the machinery in the new mill and Big Spring had a grist mill. The mills were finished in 1856, and named Big Spring Mills."

Some time later flour milling and processing equipment was added. A Mr Irons, Ira Ward, Mr Holmes, and Emery Lapp owned and operated the enterprise at various times in later years. The building and contents burned one bright summer morning in the late 1930's.

Other enterprises developed in the immediate area or village. The Pierce Hotel was built near the east end of the dam and stands today as a residence. According to Pierce, Jasper Stowell was the first postmaster, succeeded by D.M. Hatch. The little frame buildings had the advantage of portability. If a different location was desirable, they were placed on skids and dragged wherever wanted by oxen. They just kept on adding ox teams until enough pull power was produced. In 1856, the Big Spring Post office was moved to a point about 80 rods north of the Big Spring Mills. In 1857, John Russell was commissioned postmaster. The village was platted in the same year by S.W. Pierce.

Henry Wilbur built the first building in the newly platted village. He operated a general store that was later sold and moved to various locations.

In 1865, George W. Marshall, his wife Julia, and children, Frank and Evaline, came from Vermont and purchased a site at the intersection of County G and Golden Avenue where Dexter Stone had dammed the stream and built a small factory in 1859. Marshall constructed the "Variety Works", a repair shop and small factory, and built wagons and other needed machines. He later added a foundry, a carding mill to process locally produced wool, a saw mill and a grist mill. In later years, this was known as "Tibbets", and later "Spike's Mill."

Another building just south of the corner and south of Bakeman Creek was built and later owned by Glen and Harley Lapp. They operated an extensive auto repair and farm machinery sales and service from the 1930's to 1970's and owned the local Case agency.

Winchell built another dam 1/3 of a mile north of Golden Avenue, just east of County G in section 22, impounding water at the 'Big Spring". This power was used to operate a vertical lumber saw.

Just north of the Pierce Hotel and east of the street stood the Hindes and Hanson, later the Hindes and Ward store. John Russell built a small store and Post office near the corner of Mill and Wilbur Streets, later moving it to the area west of the dam.

The Big Spring Cemetery was established in the early 1860's when it became apparent that a community was developing and that a central location was preferable to burials at numerous locations on private property. Many of the area pioneers rest here, joined by others who were later residents, including sixty-five veterans who served their country in various wars from the War of 1812 to the involvement in Lebanon.

Efforts to organize a Congregational Church focused at a properly noticed meeting held at the school house in Big Spring, on January 1, 1866. After further meetings the name Big Spring

Congregational Church was made official. Mr. Enos Seward was first of 11 people listed as desiring membership. Mr. Seward conducted the first Sunday School in the area, probably at one of the small school houses or in the homes. Discussion of building ensued with local Methodists and Baptists. Agreement was reached with the Free Will Baptist Church of Big Spring on February 22,1873, for the purpose of building a union church on land donated by John Stowell. The new building was dedicated June 4, 1875. By 1889, the Baptist records show a unanimous vote to unite with the Dell Prairie Baptists. For over 120 years this building has weathered the fury of the elements, including lightning.

The Methodists built a church east of the cemetery. It served the congregation for years and finally was torn down. Its very melodious bell now hangs in the Moundville Church, southeast of the village of Endeavor.

William Vliet erected a blacksmith shop, first west of the dam and later east of the dam. His son Luke later operated the business.

Various agricultural enterprises developed and had their time. The raising of hops, used in the manufacture of beer and yeast, became highly profitable in the mid-1860s, then went bust in 1868. Wild hops survive along fence rows to this day, and one of the buildings designed and constructed as a drying kiln still stands on section 15.

The dairy industry began to take shape in the 1880's, providing economic stimulus. At first butter was churned at home and 'traded' at stores in Portage and Kilbourn. Freeman Richardson built a cheese factory on what is now the Ebert farm in about 1890, providing a commercial market. Following this venture a Bert Janks built a cheese factory on Golden Avenue, formerly called Sneak

The Robert Ramsey farm, c. 1912 and a plat map of the Big Spring area in 1919. (Courtesy, the Crothers Family).

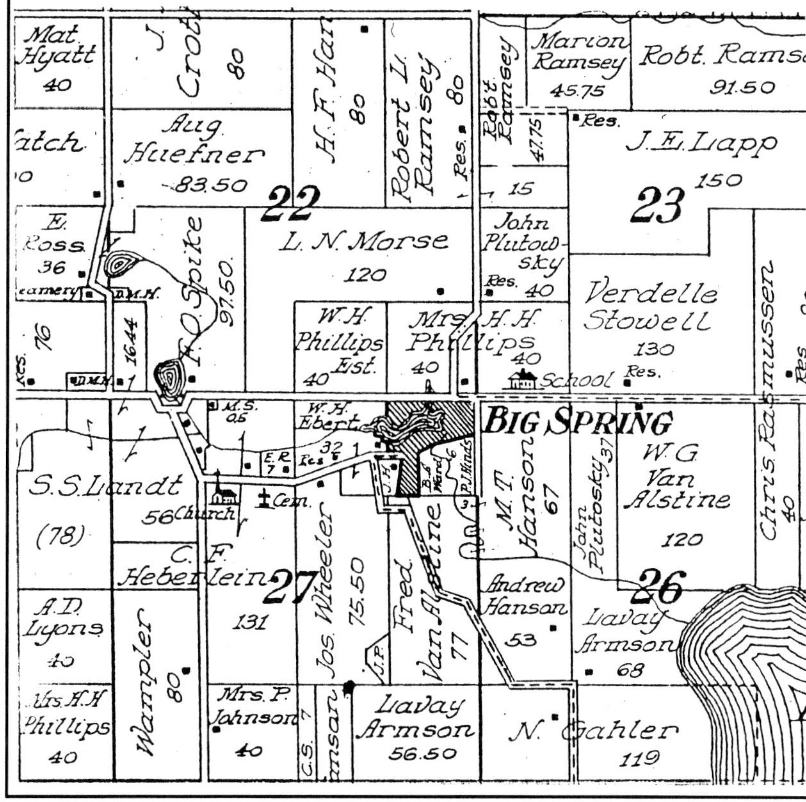

Street. This business continued operation by different owners for about 50 years.

At about the same time a Mr. Wolcott started a creamery on the north bank of the Big Spring just east of Hwy G and on section 22. These enterprises supplied a service to the area for many years and contributed immensely to the economy.

Neighbor helped neighbor in sawing wood, the only source of heat in winter, and heat for cooking in summer. Summer was threshing time. Again neighbor crews of from 15 to 25 men 'changed work'. Fall brought 'silo filling' probably the world's hardest work, then clover hulling and husking by hand or shredding corn, with the same 'changing work' system. One of the thrill days of summer for a small boy occurred on threshing day when the huge snorting, belching, hissing steam engine arrived pulling the grain separator. Sometimes the operator would invite the small boy to pull the whistle control wire. Sometimes the boy had nerve enough to do it.

September brought the confinement of bare feet in shoes and reluctant youngsters confined to schoolrooms while nice weather beckoned beyond the open window.

The stark reality of dependence on nature and ingenuity was highlighted by an account of the dry years of 1870-1872 supplied by George Crothers. Wheat straw was so short due to lack of moisture that it couldn't be harvested by "cradle". The solution was to pull it by hand to get enough grain for grinding for flour and have enough seed for the next planting.

With all of its hardships, life had its seasonings. People were involved in many social activities. Home talent shows and plays were presented from time to time. Schools and churches were focal points for exposure to various degrees of culture. Christmas and other occasions provided themes for programs at the local school.

Dances and parties were held in the homes and local halls, the latter often located above a general store. Most communities were served by local musicians who played fiddle, piano, accordion or perhaps one of the wind instruments.

Changes came with time and today small farms are consolidated into larger units or just disappear as farms, continuing the trend, while the area becomes more and more rural-residential in nature.

Davis Corners

Davis Corners was on the old stage road from Portage to Friendship. There was a neat log house very near the school house and here a widow lady kept a small store. One could buy staple groceries and kerosene, and the school children bought pink and white lozenges for a penny, as well as unpainted, rubberless lead pencils and slate pencils for the same price. Slate pencils had red, white and blue paper wrappers.

The citizens felt quite a responsibility for this good woman, and decided that she should have a post office to help out her finances as well as to add another convenience for themselves. Thinking Davis Corners too long a name, someone suggested "Glen" for the post office. Here was cause for argument, and it was to be decided by a debate at the Literary Society–affirmative for and negative against the change. This was about 1895. More than fifty years later lingers the memory of one old settler with long hair and flowing beard raising his hands above his head in his wrath and shouting, "This always has been and always shall be Davis Corners!"

The old Adams County Plat Book shows that the post office was named "Glen", but it was still Davis Corners.

Dell Prairie

The village of Dell Prairie originally consisted of three stores, a blacksmith shop, an inn, a post office and a church. The inn was located at what is now the junction of County B and Golden Court. The blacksmith shop was located south of the inn, and was owned by Jack Downy. The post office was located on the farm now owned by Mrs. William Murphy. It was run by Daniel Knox.

On the farm owned by Richard Nolan, formerly the Bert Strader farm, a church was built in early times.

Lime kilns were located on the Vanee, Carter, Bagley, and Klumpner farms.

Hops were raised in considerable quantities in early years. Hop houses were located on the Strader, Murphy, Bement and Shananhan farms.

The largest barn in the state at that time was located on the Straw farm, later owned by W. B. Markham. A carpenter by the name of Homer French built it.

One might enter this barn by the front door of an unpretentious little farmhouse standing, perhaps a bit nearer the road than does the Markham house, and facing east. A back door of this house admitted one to a hall that was like a covered bridge or sidewalk. Along this walk, on the right hand side it wore a cistern, storage places like cellars of stone and cement, and rooms and bins of wood above ground. At last, one arrived in the big barn, from the main floor of which steps, and steps and steps led up, and up and up to a cupola from which there was a view for miles in every direction.

County Trunk B was formerly the Grand Rapids Road over which many settlers traveled each year to Milwaukee for supplies.

A cemetery one-half mile west of Dell Prairie Corners is the final resting place of many of the early settlers.

Plainville

Plainville is at the junction of County Hwy K and State Highway 13. In its earliest days, it was a saw mill on the creek and the Kilbourn-Grand Rapids road. There was a set o wheel tracksthrough the sand and mud, almost impassible except in the winter, and then it was easier to go to town on the ice. At about this same time there was a furniture factory built further up the creek. Each of these were run by water power. These two enterprises, along with a Blacksmith shop and as many as three stores, were the early commercial enterprises of Plainville.

Later, a ferry and grist mill were built just north of Plainville. Much later a creamery was built and run by steam. Plainville had a school very early, but never had a churh or a baseball team in the early days. A community hall was built were plays, debates and dances were held to entertain people duing the winter. This building and the old-school house are the only two commercial buildings left. There was also a race track behind the Armour store.

Plainville was in prairie country, and the only timber was on the islands in the river. These islands, as well as the marshes along the river and creeks, were very valuable assets. Marsheswere needed for hay, and a half acre of marsh was as valuable as twenty acres of prairie.

The river was very important to the people around Plainville. It provided them with fish, waterfowl, furs, lumber for housing, ice, and in winter a road to town. Lumber that broke loose from a raft was salvaged by the residents and usd for building.

Among the memorable characters of Plainville was Hank Atcherson, the horse trader. He was mighty proud of both his horses and his big son Bert. One of his brags was, "best dam horses in Adams County, and biggest dam man. Brt hitch up the messinger mare and the beetle headed horse, and we be in town in fifteen minutes."

Clark Edmonds, Cliff Walker, and Jess Higbee were three self educated men. All served on the county board, and Higby later became a Judge in La Crosse.

Of all the old names from the 1800's, only Cook, Jerome, and Walker stayed in Plainville. Edson, Brandenburg, Billings, Dutcher, Hoffbaurer, Roirdon, Silvers, Blasic, Higbee, Atcherson, Slocum, Shattuck, Tenney, Wintermut, Sperbeck, Townsend, Wellbaum, Tyler, Armour,Edmonds, Rienhammer, White, Nickels, Whitig, Barret Geogles, Elderkin, and Crosby are all names of the past that have moved on.

The Kilbourn Meteorite

Date: Friday, June 16, 1911
Location: William Gaffney farm, about two miles from Big Spring and 7.5 miles from Kilbourn
Weight: about 1.75 pounds
Temperature: High 74, Low 60

Mr. Gaffney was in a hay field about 20 rods from his barn when he heard a rumbing noise similar to a heavy wagon passing. The day was very close and muggy with no evidence of a storm. The noise persisted not more than three or four minutes .

Mr. Gaffney walked toward the barn and upon entering, the noise ceased. All of a sudden he heard a loud report like that of a cannon. A small stone body landed about ten inches from his body, coming through the roof and second floor of the barn. It struck the manger, rebounded, and struck the stone foundation of the barn It buried itself 2.5 inches into the hard packed clay soil which formed the floor. It had penetrated three thickness of shingles, a 1 inch thick hemlock roof board and 4 feet below the roof, a 7/8 inch hemlock board forming the floor of the hay loft.

The mass when picked up was quite warm, could only be held for a second or so. The meteorite remained warm for one and a half hours. It's color when picked up was straw- like and gradually turned a shade of black. (It burned black on the outside and has a metal appearance inside, which is a gray color and sparkles at night.)

Neighbors within a radius of three miles heard both the rumbling noise and report when it struck the log barn.

The barn ran north-south and had an east-west sloping roof. The meteorite fell on the east slope.

The meteorite was on display in Kilbourn for about one year before it was purchsed by H. Conrad Meyer of the Foote Mineral Company for $350.00.

The Foote Company donated a 68 gram chunk of the meteorite to the Field Museum of Natural History in Chicago, and later another 7.5 gram piece. This museum also holds the hemlock boards.

The Academy of Natural Sciences of Philadelphia held an 85 gram piece for some time before it was discovered missing in 1964.

Another 70 gram piece is held at the Harvard University Mineralogical Museum in Cambridge. This piece was donated by a Professor Wolfe, who purchased it in 1911 for $315.00.

The National Meteorite Collection of Canada in Ottowa holds an 86 gram end portion acquired from the Foote Company in 1914, and the Center for Meteorite Studies at Arizona State University in Tempe has a 25 gram specimen, purchased as part of the Nininger Collection in 1960.

Village and Country Schools

Schools Then and Now

After the of demise of Newport and the platting of the Village Kilbourn, residents immediately made plans for their first school. In February of 1856, less than three months after the first house was built, Kilbourn built its first school. The building served the people of Kilbourn as a public school until 1867, when land was purchased from T.B. Coon for a larger school.

By then the original school had been enlarged and also other space rented for a period of time. The original building at 810 Elm St. was occupied by the Episcopal Congregation from 1871 until 1970 when it was sold to the Tofson Insurance Company, which continues to occupy it today. The original bell is on display in front of the building.

The following account, from *The History of Columbia County*, 1880, aptly describes the early history of the school district up until that date.

"The first citizens of Kilbourn City appreciated the advantages of the public school, and about the 1st of February, 1856, appointed a building committee, who at once selected a site and gave orders for the necessary material for the house, which was to be 26 x 36 feet in size, well finished and conveniently seated. In May following, the building was ready for occupancy, and Miss Julia Seville was engaged to teach a three-month term, at a salary of $10 per month. There were twenty-seven children of school age in the district, No. 6, of whom fourteen attended the school. Miss Saville was engaged the following fall, at an advanced salary of $24 per month. At the expiration of three months, Miss Lucy A. Swain took charge, at a salary of $22 per month. At the first annual meeting, a tax of $900 was voted to pay for the schoolhouse, and, during Miss Seville's first term, a bell was purchased for it, at a cost of $125. The first to fill the office of School Director of the district was Emory Wall, with John B. Vliet, Treasurer, and George F. McAlister, Clerk.

In 1857, there were eighty-five persons of school age in the district, of whom fifty attended school. The number of school age was increased to 180 in 1858. In 1861, Dell Prairie was united with this district, and it was then, and is now, known as Joint District No. 6. On account of the increase of pupils, it became necessary to enlarge the school building, which was accordingly done, at an expense of $400. But the village of Kilbourn continued to grow, and a larger and better building was demanded. At a school meeting held in September, 1867, it was voted to appropriate $1,450 to purchase, of Thomas B. Coon, Block 78 of the village, on which it was designed, in the near future, to erect a building that would be sufficiently large to accommodate all the pupils of the district. At this same meeting, a communication was received from Kilbourn Institute proposing to furnish instruction to the pupils of the high school for the sum of $800 per year, which proposition was accepted.

After the purchase of the block of ground of Mr. Coon, arrangements were at once made to build, and, in the summer of 1870, was completed the present fine structure, at a cost of $12,287. The building is of cream-colored brick, 40 x 60 feet, three stories high. There are five main schoolrooms, three recitation and one furnace room. It cost $1,400 to furnish. When first occupied, the present graded system was adopted, and the whole placed in charge of a Principal. On account of the incompetency of the Principal, the schools did not flourish for awhile, and it was not until 1877 that efficiency was attained that the expenditures warranted. In this year, Prof. A.L. Burnham was employed by the board as Principal, and his selection has been approved by the people. A fine scholar and good disciplinarian, the schools have flourished under his charge. For the session of 1879-80, there were employed: A.L. Burnham, Principal; Lizzie M. Pendleton, Assistant; Hester J. Teare, Emma Darling, Ada Douglass, Bina Loughney. The principal receives a salary of $1,000 per year, his assistant $315, and the others from $225 to $270."

For many years following the building of the first school and the first high school, only about two thirds of school age children actually attended.

In 1887 standards for high school graduation were established by the state and Kilbourn had its first six graduates, all of which were girls. This trend continued, with girls always outnumbering boys, ostensibly because the boys were required to work and assist with providing a living for the family.

By 1894, although a few boys had graduated, that year saw a class of 16 girls and only 1 boy! Not until 1921 did boys outnumber girls in the classes.

In 1901 the names of the men serving on the school board have a familiar ring: T.B. Coon, Charles W. Snider and A.C. Dixon, who would serve 39 years on the Kilbourn school board.

Previous page: *The student body in front of the Kilbourn school, which was completed at a cost of $1,400 in 1870. Although unidentified, the African-American children in the photo are probably the sons of Civil War hero Thomas Allen. (Courtesy, H. H. Bennett Studio Foundation)*

The first Kilbourn school built in 1856. After 1870 it was used as Holy Cross Episcopal church and, more recently, as the office of Tofson Insurance. (Courtesy, H. H. Bennett Studio Foundation)

In the early 1900's the cultural aspect of education began to come into prominence. Extra curricular activities included debate clubs and many plays as well as masquerades, some of which were put on as fund raisers by different classes. A small newspaper, the *Kilbournite*, was published and advertisers solicited. Ads were sold to merchants at 25¢ each. Each graduation class presented a play as part of the graduation program.

In 1906 the high school was accredited by the state and in 1909 became a free high school. In that same year a four room grade school building was built on the same site, first being occupied by students in 1910. Board members at this time were J.F. Dougherty and Messrs O'Neil and Fedderly.

In 1912 Agriculture was added to the curriculum and in 1915 Domestic Science. The Neighborhood Club and the Tuesday Club assisted in setting this program up and in teaching the girls until Miss Ruth Stanton was hired. During the 1914-15 term a new modern toilet system was installed in the school. In 1916 the Senior Class published an annual "The Arrowhead." Music courses were added.

At the grade school, an addition was added in 1916.

During the so called Roaring 20's the school system remained pretty much status quo, with politics, prohibition, and business expansion taking precedence over education or at least satisfaction being widespread with the school system.

During the depression, the school in Wisconsin Dells was hard-pressed. In 1931 it was overcrowded and lacked many facilities mandated to receive state aid of $5,000 a year. The state had given the community a deadline of September, 1932, in order to receive the aid. The necessary addition could be built at a cost of $5050 a year. At that time, two buildings stood on Block 78. On the east side of the block the building housing the high school had been built in 1870. On the west side, the grade school had been built in 1910 and added to in 1916.

The *Dells Events* devoted much space to an explanation of the problem. The new school would be built between the two existing buildings and would include a commercial room, a kindergarten, a science room, a large library, an additional classroom, a gymnasium and more storage space.

The addition would cost $70,000 over 20 years and would only add .01¢ per thousand valuation per week to the taxpayer. This building would greatly enrich the curriculum and would attract and hold many more tuition students from the rural areas. At that time, rural students could choose the high school they wanted to attend. And, of course, this construction would give employment to many during the fall and winter. Much work had been done by the school board with N.A. Landt, clerk.

The referendum passed.

In September, 1932, the new addition was ready for a greatly increased enrollment with many of these students being post graduates pursuing college work under the University of Wisconsin Extension. Plans for attracting more tuition students with a new school proved a resounding success. "Upon the close of school last June the high school had 138 students enrolled. A check today revealed that there were 183 undergraduates and in addition 21 post graduates enrolled, 204 students in all. This represents an increase of over 40 percent more pupils this year than last year when school closed."

"The faculty of the local school system for the year was: M.H. Spicer, Superintendent; Luella Retzner, Kindergarten & Music; Mary Killoran, 1st Grade; Vera Steinmetz, 2nd Grade; Evelyn Olson, 3rd Grade; Lottie Davidson, 4th Grade; Anna Vogt, 5th Grade; Dorothy Jones, 6th and 7th Grades; Mrs. Rose Tobin, 8th Grade.

And at the high school: Mary Conway, Librarian; Kenneth Counsell, Arts; William Fitzpatrick, Science; Cheridah Krause, Home Ec; Verna Mulry, English; Victor Schuman, Math, Civics, Band; Mary Swarthout, Commercial; Viola Buseth, Social Studies.

"A Fantastic Comedy", Captain Jinks of the Horse Marines, a home talent play directed by Harriet Richards was the opening play in the new gym. The audience was "Probably the largest crowd that ever assembled under one roof in the city of Wisconsin Dells...Six hundred tickets were sold with gross receipts of $164.40 and the net receipts were given to the school to furnish the stage with scenery and other equipment. Captain Robert Carollton Jinks was played by Chester Weber and the heroine, Madame Trentoni by Lucille Fitzgerald. Other members of the cast were Bernard Peterson, Harold Hansen, Lawrence Welbaum, Harry Radlund, H. Luettgerodt, Merton Tofson, Bill Hart, Ray Boynton, Roger Stroede, Dr. R.D. Boynton, Alvin Johnson, Dana Champlin, Robert Van Wie, Miriam Bennett, Hazel Tollaksen, Gertie Buckminster, Mrs. H.A. Bauer, Josephine Peterson, Olga Radlund, Ruth Dyer, Eleanor Van Ells, Marcella White, Jean Dyer, Alice Bauer, Isabel Van Ells, Margaret Shumway and the orchestra - Mrs. H.A. Bauer, Victor Schuman, I.J. Hill."

In the 1930s a new program, called "Field Days" was organized in which a program of track and field events were held and the surrounding country schools were invited to come into town and participate. In 1937 when M.E. Gribble was principal and Thomas Howley was mayor of Wisconsin Dells, the district music festival was held in the city for the first time, with 32 surrounding schools participating.

During the 1940's citizens devoted their thoughts to the war effort and little thought was given to any changes to the school. In 1948, the "Union Free" high school district was organized, and in 1955 a new Union Free High School was built on Race Street. "Union Free" meant that the townships were not required to pay tuition for their students as they had previously. Also about this time, the state required the integration of all the outlying into larger districts and efforts were begun in the Dells area to comply with those efforts. During the 1950s all of the one room country schools were closed. Only the Briggsville (now Neenah Creek) and Delton schools continue to operate as part of the Wisconsin Dells district.

During the 1960s many additions and improvements were made at the grade school, including the addition of the new Instructional Materials Center (IMC) in 1968.

Since 1968 there have been no more additions. Over the years, various referendums were held in hopes of replacing the grade school and were defeated. Efforts to build a new building, costing $5.8 million, were finally successful and the new school was completed by 1992. The old grade school was demolished in 1994.

Religious schools have also played a role in both pioneer and modern times. In Delton, the Baptist congregation had a school between 1853 and 1865 and Newport's Mary Lyon Female Seminary held classes between 1856 and 1858. The Methodist Institute began at Point Bluff in 1857, moved and became part of the Kilbourn Institute in 1867, but was destroyed by fire the following year.

Almost a century later, in 1959, Trinity Lutheran school was opened. It presently has six grades, kindergarten and pre-school. St. Cecilia's Catholic Church constructed a new parochial school in 1963, which the parish operated until 1973. In recent years that building was rented by the Wisconsin Dells school district before becoming a day care center. Emmanual Apostolic Assembly has for several years operated the Dells Christian Academy on Highway 13, near their house of worship.

One of the first graduating classes of Kilbourn High School. Female graduates outnumbered boys until the 1920s. Boys dropped out because they could find work even without a high school diploma. Girls were encouraged to stay in school if for no other reason than the fact that a high school graduate was considered qualified to teach in the rural schools, and many young women took advantage of the opportunity. (Courtesy, H. H. Bennett Studio Foundation)

The First Electric Scoreboard

Myrle H. Spicer became the Superintendent of Schools in Kilbourn in 1929. He began working on an idea in his basement. In 1935, he received his patent on the first electric scoreboard, and in 1937, refined it into an electric timekeeper as well.

He left the Dells schools in 1937, expanded his ideas and "in March, 1947 he, with several stockholders, formed All American Scoreboards, Inc. at Pardeeville which was eventually sold and is now contained within the Pardeeville Indicator Corporation. His scoreboards paved the way for one of the major industries in Pardeeville.

Kilbourn school students, (above) in geography class, c. 1910. (below) High school students, 1928, (first row, l-r) Dan Marlow, Jessie Totten, Marjorie Davies, Leroy Leissman, unidentified, Ray Cone, Helen Donnelley, Julie Kaleas, John Ryan, Clayton Stien, (second row), Clara Stien, unidentified, Dorothy Donnelley, Harry Olson, Ethel Hanson, Kathryn Huber, Roy Matthews (third row) Lillian Magee, Conrad Gaffney, Katherine Heineike, May Conway, Ruth Mulligan, Gordon Tollaksen, Mary Timlin, (fourth row) Earl Hichethier, Arlene Jantz, unidentified, Victor Ingebretsen, Adeline Kaleas, unidentified, Irese Seger, Henry Marston, unidentified, John O'Connell, Laurie Soma.

The championship football team, 1932 (first row, l-r) Chet Harrison, Eugene Landt, Dick Kaleas, Gordon Tollaksen, Cliff Cone, Howard Kimball, Robert Kimball, (second row) Bob Vasey, Francis Thom, Ken Harrison, Ray Boynton, Bud Drollinger, Ed Tangney, Ed Sperbeck, (third row) Rollie Weber, Merlin Gray, Bob Seger, Erwin Johnson, Louis Johnson, Herb Peterson, Laddie Helland, Willard Gray (fourth row) Coach Bill Fitzpatrick, George Schroeder, Wayne Strode, Mert Tofson, Forrest Heacocks, Russell Tollaksen, Bob Van Wie, Bud Lambright, Coach K. W. Counsell. (below) The high school band, 1945 (first row, l-r) Delores Playman, Donna Tofson, Jim Dixon, Joan Johnson, Phyllis Lunde, Alice Jean Hetzel, Barbara Crist (second row) Jean Knuebuhler, Marilyn Emmerich, Mary Claire Baggot, Betty Fuchick, unidentified, Gerry Murray, S. Stone, Jim Balsmeider, (third row) Lois Platt, Betty Kettleson, Jim Stephens, Theo Field, S. Peterson, Eileen Murray, Carol Holt, A. Fritz, Hans Knuebuhler, (fourth row) Jeanane Kelly, Jerry Baggot, Tom Thompson, Marion Sarrington, Mary Alice Dapp, D. Donnelly, Kathleen Platt, Dorothy Stomner, (fifth row) Joan Waltman, Joe Kaiser, D. Tucker, Beverly Counsell, C. Novak, Don Hamm, Otto Christopherson, Walter Stickford, Anthony Bacich. (H.H. Bennett Studio Foundation).

Kilbourn High School Graduates 1887–1928

CLASS OF 1887
Barker, May (Jones)
Cady, Jean H
Conway, Margaret
Davenfort, May (Reeve)
Gillespie, Cora
Nahawskil, Marie (Guier) (Pedicord)

CLASS OF 1888
Coleman, Agnes (Hamlton)
Bauer, Rose (Sharpe)
Hinman, Lola (Taft)
Johnson, Myrtice (Markham) (Fitts)
Kaufmann, Ida (Pendleton)
Schofield, Grace (Wheaton)
Snider, Harriet (Van Alstine)
Sorrenson, Lillian (Woods)
Stowell, Irene (Woods)
Timlin, Frank
Van Alstine, Manning
Walker, Charles

CLASS OF 1889
Bennett, Nellie (Crandall)
Brown, Jennie (Brown)
Gillespie, Thomas
Schofield, Marguerite (Hall)
Thorn, Mary (Randall)

CLASS OF 1890
Ahrens, Emma (Campbell) (Ball)
Bayerlein, Edward
Campbell, Harriet (Straw)
Dixon, Jennie
Gujer, Nellie (Laabs)
Hatch, Willis
Hill Ida
Loomis, Flora (Williams)
Ribenack, Bertha (Teara)
Soeldner, Anna
Timlin, Eva
Van Alstine, Lillian
Wright, Vinette

CLASS OF 1891
Baggot, Anna (Griffin)
Brown, Lydia, (Crother)
Carpenter, Mary (Owens)
Coon, Evelyn (Parsons)
Julson, Emma (Andrews) (Jenks)
Kaufmann, Benjamin F
Snider, Mamie (MacBride)
Soeldner, Carl
Stearns, Addie (Hunter)
Straw, Frank C
Weber, Claire (Kerrin)

CLASS OF 1892
Ahrens, Tillie (Rowlands)
Bayerlein, Carl
Bullis, Ira
Corning, Jen (Toates)
Deneen, Maggie
Gujer, Frank
Hanson, Emma
Johnson, Ida (Hanson) (Paulson)
Laabs, Martha
McVey, Victoria (Buskuhl)
Rork, Edan (O'Neil)
Schofield, Ha (Steere)
Schroeder, Lillian (Naber)
Smith, Ella R (Philipp)
Weidenbacker, Yetta (Lang)

CLASS OF 1893
Bishop, Cora (Latham)
Borcher, Emma (Watson)
Davies, Sidney
Flook, Edith (Wall)
Hall, Zada
Murray, Josephine H
O'Neil, Daniel T
Trumble, Julia (Huesby)
Val Alstine, Harry

CLASS OF 1894
Berry, Winnifred
Blood, George
Dixon, Anna (Fry)
Dougherty, Mary (Wright)
Gillespie, Alberta (Mertens)
Hammond, Bertha (Day)
Hoisington, Mamie (Sterns)
Leute, Mary (Waldron)
Murphy, Cecelia
Patterson, Ellen
Peterson, Laura (Rowe)
Seaman, Mary (Patterson)
Slowey, Fannie (Longstreet)
Weber, Ida (Steere)
Wooster, Josephine (Stanton)

CLASS OF 1895
Bauer, Lillian (Hollinshead)
Bayerlein, Anna (Luettgerodt)
Bulis, Effie (Arntz)
Chamberlin, Gertrude (Parkinson)
Crothers, Alma (Berry)
Van Alstine, Lucille

CLASS OF 1896
Barrows, Frank
Bennet, Mabel
Brown, Hattie (Evans)
Bullis, Ettie (Older)
Joslin, Mary (Calvert)
Murray, Tessie (Fitzgerald)
Older, Margaret
Parsons, Glenn
Pierce, Lynn
Rice, Lottie
Smith, Grace (Cretuz)
Smith, Noyce B
Snider, Harry
Stenson, Orin L
Sweet, Alma (Vogt)
Tennison, Harry
Treadwell, Glenn
Vincent, Fred
Wagner, Louise (Pore)
Woodruff,Chester

CLASS OF 1897
Bayerlein, Julia (Torley)
Gnaucks, Clara (Vogt) (Haupt)
Hollinshead, John
Joslin, Stanley
McManman, Cecelia (Smith)
McNeel, Jessie (Pierce)
Purcell, Mayme (Fancy)
Sweet, Alice (Finnegan)
Urnetle, Joseph
Vogt, Anna

CLASS OF 1898
Cavenaugh, Michael
Cooper, Jennie (Morris)
Crothers, Edna
Gillespie, Edward
Magoon, Clarence
McVey, Sarah (Cooper)
Patterson, Harry
Purcell, William
Radandt, Frank
Zimmerman Rosetta, (Dexter)

CLASS OF 1899
Armeah, Grace (Ames)
Clapper, Louise
Corning, Stuart
Cusack, May (Markham)
Dougherty, James F
Leute, Helen
Loomis, Helen (Laack)
McManman, Anna (Murphy)
Murray, John
Porte, Georgia (Campbell)
Rohner, Lillian (Kennedy)
Schofield, Robert
Smith, Russel
Snider, Glen
Vogt, Ida (Sanders)

CLASS OF 1900
Bennett, Alice (Tetzlaf)
Doepke, Anna
Doepke, Emma (Justice)
Donahue, Anna (Mortell)
Donahue, Marry (Smalt)
Dougherty, Agnes (O'Brien)
Dougherty, Katie
Hayes, Katie (Taylor)
Langworthy, May (Buckley)
Lewis, Edwin
Marston, Floyd
Murray, William
Phillips, Sadie (Knight)
Soeldner, Fred
Stowell, Warren
Sunderland, A.D.
Wilderick, Katie

CLASS OF 1901
Fedderly, Ada (Griesenauer)
Gujer, Milicent (Brady)
Hile, Mamie (Murphy)
Hoisington, Lydia (Weaver)
Loomis, Nina (Crothers)
Magoon, Norman
McNeelL, Wakelin
Metcalf, Mae
Murphy, Elizabeth
Naber,Celia
Naber, Phillip
Pepper,Alda
Smock, Florence (Van Alstine)
Thompson, Della (White)
Waterman, Carl

CLASS OF 1902
Flook, Marion (Stafford)
French, Don
Gujer, Edward
McNeel, Lydia (Tripp)
Phillips, Sybil (Fedderly)
Purcell, John
Richards, Helen (Cook)
Snider, Ray

CLASS OF 1903
Bennett, Albion
Doepke, Mignon
Hanson, Hilda (Lauderdale)
Kleimenhagen, Walter
Miller, John
Shaffer, May (Jackman)
Walker, Ray
Zimmerman, Ida (Reiels)

CLASS OF 1904
Bauer, Laura (Welch)
Belter, Ida (Howett)
Fedderly, Ray
Fox, Laura (Nelson)
French, Arba
Rothe, Alma (Garthwaite)
Harris, Ethel (Mott)
Maybee, Hettie (Wright)
Oehlers, Kate (Miller)
Oswald, Lora (Snider)
Radlund, Emma (Peterson)
Waterman, Benjamin
Whitely, Leone (Britten)
Wirtz, Fred
Zimmerman, Laura (Knebel)
Zimmerman, Lydia (Rose)

CLASS OF 1905
Adams, Rollin
Ahlhorn, Emma
Dana, Kittie (Klinger)(Welter)
Elliot, Lester
Foote, Walter
Hatch, Daisy (Cameron)
Ihde, Dena (Devereaux)
Larson, Valera
Loomis, Helen (James)
Nelson, Tena
Tollakson, Bert

CLASS OF 1906
Bauer, Nellie (Elliot)
Doepke, Martha
Fedderly, Florence (Elder)
Fehl, George
Flook, George
Hoedel, Anna
Gillespie, Hallie (Tierney)
House, Earl
Jones, Vera A
Kessler, Frank
Pribenow, Alma (Richardson)
Sullivan, John
Thompson, Charlotte (Schnell)
Vogt, Leon

CLASS OF 1907
Avery, Charles
Clough, Laura (Crothers)
Cusack, Milton
Frost, Lillian (Ducharme)
Helland, Oliver
McNeel, May (Hrobsky)
Murray, Mildred (Bullis)
Neff, Roy
Rothe, Carl
Rothe, Earl

CLASS OF 1908
Ahlhorn, Anna
Bennett, Lillie (Brower)
Corning, Corinne (Green)
Corning, Mildred (McManman)
Harris, Edna
Kleimenhagen, Arthur
Morse, Horace
Radlund, Olga
Vogt, Armein

CLASS OF 1909
Coapman, Lillian (Williams)
Conrad, Marie (Erickson)
Doepke, Edna (Sunderland)
Foster, Ollie (Oliver)
Holwick, Corain (Finneman)
Kaufmann, Irene
McNeel, Alice (Small)
Meyers, Werner
Oehlers, Albert
Smith, Keith
Stanton, Irene (Helland)
Trumble, Margaret (Marshall)
Wilderick, Celia (Calkins)

CLASS OF 1910
Armstrong, Bessie (Williams)
Bennett, Miriam
Edmonds, Jess
Field, Henry
Howley, Katie (Sullivan)
LaMar, Clifford
Landt, Rena (Palmer)
McElwain, Bertha (Peterson)
Nelson, Nettie
Rothe, Lester
Slocum, Louise, (Denzine)
Storandt, Mary (Jensen)

CLASS OF 1911
Bement, Belle (Edmonds)
Coapman, Maude (Hartman)
Gleason, Neil
Naber, Minnie (Emmerick)
Schroeder, Glen
Sullivan, William

CLASS OF 1912
Armstrong, Myrtle (Tennison)
Bradburn, Leota (Pugh)
Billings, Dana
Fogle, Sybil
French, Jessie (McDonald)
Hoedel, Ottillie (Gray)
Jacobson, Robert
Marlowe, Ruth
Shute, Dorothy
Stanton, Ruth (Kerrigan)
Van Dyke, Madge (Carpenter)
Vogt, Frank
Zwicky, Ella

CLASS OF 1913
Bennett, Ruth (Dyer)
Crandall, Lois (Musson)
Crandall, Phyllis (Connor)
Cavanaugh, Margaret (Paulson)
Halverson, Elida
Kelly, Anna
Kleimenhagen, Carl
Lynch, Anna (Laut)
Van Alstine, Clarence
Waldron, Merle

CLASS OF 1914
Baggott, Anna (Terry)
Bresnahan, Marie
Field, Floyd
Gleason, Catherine (Grieger)
Hanson, Minnie (Miller)
Jordan, Grace (Garden)
Jordan, LaVern
McClyman, Clifford
Nelson, Murtle (Walters)
Radlund, Harry
Schanke, Irma (Anderson)
Waldron, Asa
Willard, Amber (Lindburgh)
Zimmerman, Esther (Burke)

CLASS OF 1915
Ahlorn, Edith
Anderson, Oscar
Baggot, Gerald
Berning, Doris
Coapman, Veda (Miller)
Fish, Warren
Freer, Florence (Norsell)
Lloyd, Beulah
Lynch, Kathryn
Marlowe, Stella (Coyle)
Older, Thelma
O'Neil, Timmie
Purcell, Kathryn (Greenwood)
Schanke, Olga (David)
Slocum, Marion (Farnum)
Stomner, Hazel (Fotheringham)
Stowers, Mildred (Bauer)
Van Dyke, Phillip

CLASS OF 1916
Bauer, Peral (Terbilcox)
Cortright, Carl J
Donahue, Harold J
Fish, Florence (Ryczek)
Foster, Kenneth
Hawes, Bernard
Helly, Helen (Dahl)
Kleimenhagen, Joan
Landt, Geraldine (Rodwell)
McClyman, Harry
McKenzie, Vivian (Koberstein)
Rudolph, William
Schoff, Bessie (Meyers)
Thompson, LaVerne
Tolleth, Dewey
Willard, Vivan (Jones)

CLASS OF 1917
Coapman, Esther (Lansburg)
DeLong, Harriet (Leff)
Greenwood, Dan
Ihde, Beatrice (Sarrington)
Kelly, John
O'Neil, Mary
Stevenson, Marion (Larson)
Stowell, Mildred (Goebel)
Straw, Charlotte (Hillman)

CLASS OF 1918
Ahlhorn, Georgia
Baggot, Mathias
Buese, Frank
Chaffee, Perceval
Cone, Fern (Hall)
Dahl, Dewey
Donahue, Fay
Gorey, Francis
Howard, Vern
Kingsley, Marie (Landt)
Nelson, Emma (Zinke)
Nettland, Paul
Oakes, Orville
Stomner, Edna (Robbins)
Scott, Jesse
Storandt, Amelia
Stowell, Lucille
Stowers, Orville
Straw, Josephine (Young)
Tangney, Homer
Van Alstine, Gertrude (Arnston)
Waldron, Lucille (Meanny)
Waterman, Vera

CLASS OF 1919
Berry, Roland
Blzaer, Helen
Brooks, Frances (Boyer)
Crane, Catherine (Klein)
Crane, Dorothy (Kosabud)
Crothers, Rexford
Howard, Ardath (Byers
Kelly, Francis
Leissmann, Vanetta (Christopherson)
Mess, Eva
Montgomery, Thelma (Patton)
Nehls, Harold
Niblo, Blanche (Hindes)
Orton, Mildred (Cochrane)
Sutherland, Alvin
Tangney, Harry
Ukert, Lenore
Waterman, Inez (Thompson)
Wenkman, Henry

CLASS OF 1920
Berry, Carol
Coapman, Norman
Cone, Ervin
Cornwall, Bessie (Kingsley)
Donahue, Helen
Foss, Clara (Brockman)
Lynch, John
Mess, Florence
Murphy, Margaret (Wilson)
O'Brien, Vanetta (Klemme)
Orton, Leona
Seger, Henry
Spuries, Hazel (Adams)
Walrath, Kenneth
Walters, Emil

CLASS OF 1921
Cone, Harry
Gaffney, William
Hayes, Kathryn (Anderson)
Hyatt, Glen
Nelson, Anna (Gromme)
O'Neil, Ralph
Peterson, Earl
Schanke, Redlin
Stanton, Madge
Stomner, Rubye (DeNee)
Thompson, Stewart
Van Alstine, Lulu (Stanford)
Waterman, Andrew

CLASS OF 1922
Baggot, Helen
Batty, Persis
Bennet, Richard
Buckley, Luella
Coy, Veda
Donnelly, Mary
Dunham, Charles
Dunham, Olive
Flickner, Harry
Forman, Phyllis (Dunham)
Francis, Alice
Laabs, Frank
Landt, Janet
Landt, Marjorie
Lee, Crystal (Priester)
Leissmann, May (Stickford)
Lynch, Edward
McClyman, Neva (Fulson)
McClyman, Nina
Nelson, Florence (Krueger)
Olp, Majorie
Pfister, Elizabeth
Porte, Lydia
Tangney, Geraldine (O'Neil)
Thomm, Robert
Thompson, Emma
Wainwright, Robert
Woodring, Winnie (Franklin)

CLASS OF 1923
Anderson, Agnes
Anderson, Margaret (Yields)
Arntz, Adaline
Barney, Lawrence
Bauer, Helen
Berry, Robert
Botsford, Blanche (Wainright)
Botsford, Harris
Burgess, Charlotte (O'Connor)
Charlesworth, George
Crothers, Stanley
Dehmlow, Edith
Dunham, Ethel
Foster, Florence
Hacker, Martin
Heineke, Emil
Hendrickson, Sylvester
Ihde, Albert
Kuester, Bertha
Landt, Frances
Mathew, George
Morris, Wendland
Nelson, Lillian (Anderson)
O'Brien, Mary
Olson, Roland
O'Neil, CLaude
O'Neil, Lorna
O'Neil, Mildred (Jewell)(Tangney)
Radant, Esther (McTavish)
Raimer, Marie
Schilstra, George
Schoeninger, Marie
Schoff, Hazel
Smith, Eleanor
Stafford, Alma (Wohlfert)
Taft, Clifford
Tolleth, Margaret (Schumway)
Winnes, Wilma (Kaiser)

CLASS OF 1924
Avery, Marion
Baggot, Margaret
Bauer, Alice
Cook, Elsie
Cone, Herbert
Dougherty, Robert
Fedderly, Stuart
Flickner, Eva (Hall)
Foster, Ruth
Gaffney, Howard
Gottschalk, Fred
Helland, Gertrude
Kane, Arthur
Kassner, Clara
Lee, Edwin
Leege, Esther
Mathews, Florence (Meaning)
Morse, Lucille (Radue)
Murphy, Marie
Murray, Ruth (Bresnahan)
Thomm, Jesse
Tittle, Archie
Tofson, Doris, (Waterman)
Ward, Vinnie (Engrath)
Winnes, George
Winnes, Gordon
Zeitz, Leona (Stapleton)

CLASS OF 1925
Arntz, Josephine
Cummings, Myrtle (Jansen)
Dingee, Jessie
Field, Louise
Fisch, Thelma
Hanson, Hazel
Hanson, Hylda (Fedderly)
Heineke, Walter
Hendickson, Alice
Hillman, Edith
Julson, Emma (Carter)
Lee, Dwight
Lee, Henry
Markham, Lucille (Emerich)
McDonald, Clifford
McDonald, Susan
Montgomery, Marjorie
Nelson, Ray
O'Connell, Stella
Peterson, Mae
Schanke, Kenneth
Schoeninger, Madeline
Schoff, Cleo
Schultz, Avis
Swansby, Natalie
Thomas, Esther
Thompson, Flyod
Van Alstine, Ernest
Waterman, Charlotte
Wharry, Luella (Jackson)
Winnes, Anna

CLASS OF 1926
Baggot, Mary
Cone, Walter
Dingee, Mildred
Donnelly, Catherine
Duclos, Roy
Elderkin, Arlene
Gaffney, Mae
Gregerson, Edna (Stanton)
Hyatt, Amber (Plumb)
Hendrickson, Lorraine
Loomis, Damon
Lorenzon, Howard
Lorenzon, Myron
Luettgerodt, Kenneth
Morley, Irene
Morse, Lena
Mulligan, Mildred
Murphy, Helen
Newell, Percy
O'Neil, Grace
Plumb, Ellsworth
Procknow, Margaret
Rickon, Marguerite
Smith, Bruce
Smith, Robert
Storandt, Helen
Stowers, Edward
Thompson, Belva
Utter, Grace
Vasey, Gertrude
Wimmer, James
Woodring, Manis
Zeitz, Marjorie
Zentner,Wilbur

CLASS OF 1927
Barker, Dorothy (Duclos)
Blatchley, Glen
Brady, Helen
Champlin, Hazel (Pfister)
Cole, Stanley
Dunham, Gordon
Heimel, Floyd
Heineke,Edward
Knudson, Eleanor
Leissmann, Hazel
Loomis, Marion
McManman, Dan
Morse, Celia
Morse, Delbert
O'Brien, Veronica
Olson, Robert
Plump, Lois (Balsmider)
Schoeninger, Laura
Seger, Eleanor
Snider, Beverly
Snider, Charles
Stevenson, Wilma
Timme, Marguerite
Timlin, Kathryn
Timlin, Lorraine
Tofson, Donald

CLASS OF 1928
Byers, Beulah
Cole, Roger
Dingee, William
Foster, John
Foster, Keith
Gaffney, Agnes
Gnaucks, Felix
Haskins, Eylene
Heitman, John
Helland, Alice
Helley, Alden
Leege, Ruth
Neumeister, Ruffina
Peterson, Inez
Risley, Millie
Stuelke, Gordon
Thompson, George
Van Ells, Eleanor
Van Ells, Isabel
Vasey, Murray
Weidling, Corma
Wenkman, Joseph
White, Marcella

Wisconsin Dells Athletic Champions

STATE AWARD WINNING ATHLETES

James Heineke	1955	Track-discus
	1956	Track-discus, shot put
Don O'Neill	1955	Track-high jump
	1956	Track-high jump
Robert Fenske	1965	Track-low hurdles
John DeMerit	1968	Track-low hurdles, high hurdles
Stuart Miner	1970	Track-2 mile
Fran Sweeney	1975	Track-low hurdles, high hurdles
Leo Joyce	1976-77	Wrestling-Hwt. 33-0
Glenn Arendsee	1977	Track-pole vault
Andy Shumway	1977	Track-long jump, 100 yd dash
Doug Reifsteck	1979-80	Wrestling-145 lbs. 31-0
Jay Schoenbeck	1980-81	Wrestling-119 lbs. 28-2
Joe Van Dinter	1980-81	Wrestling-98 lbs. 30-0
	1981-82	Wrestling-105 lbs. 33-0
	1982-83	Wrestling-112 lbs. 34-0
Randy Zamzow	1983	Track-long jump
Greg Zander	1983	Track-pole vault
Dan Green	1983-84	Wrestling-132 lbs. 30-2
Troy Nelson	1984	Track-shot put
Pete Zapuchlak	1988-89	Wrestling-152 lbs. 27-10
Jason Maniecki	1989-90	Wrestling-Hwt. 33-0
	1990-91	Wrestling-Hwt. 34-0

STATE CHAMPIONSHIP TEAMS

1977 Track: Coach Jack Engsberg, Andy Shumway, Leo Joyce, Glen Arendsee

1983 Track: Coach Bob Johnson, Greg Zander, Randy Zamzow, Rob Conway, Bill Fandrich, Mike Jones, Karl Schultz

1984 Girls Volleyball: Coach Cyndy Collins, Catherine Breen, Kim Fisher, Vicki Grefe, Suzie Hess, Mee Lun Mak, Becky Oxnem, Debbie Polinski, Kris Schauf, Kelli Wieland, Kelly Sweeney, Sarah Koch, Paula Cleary, Rita Lentz

1986 Baseball: Coach Jim Murphy, Bill Rudersdorf, Aaron Blatchley, Travis Hilliard, Rich Weisoff, John Krueger, Pat Helland, Mike Helland, Chris Seidler, Dave Delmore, Hans Wimmer, Dale Hudack, Rob Van Wie, Jeff Van Wie, Matt Marion, Bill Tofson, Tony Beer, Dale Gray, Mark Bubon, Ed Nevar, Greg Gabris

1987 Boys Basketball: Coach Jack Capelle, Tim Bubon, T.J. Van Wie, Matt Thundercloud, Matt Marion, Brent Stowell, Brian Sweeney, Peter Flock, Tim Decorah, Rich Christensen, Jeff Van Wie, John Krueger, Ed Nevar, Jeff Diehl

CONFERENCE CHAMPIONS

Baseball

1953: *Coach Duaine Counsell,* Ken Martin, Don Counsell, Jim Holden, Jim Winn, Jim Cahoon, John Hieneke, Leo Jerome, Hans Fedderly, Jim Heineke, Bob Zamzow, Ken Gavinski, John Shumway

1954: *Coach Duaine Counsell*

1987: *Coach Jim Murphy,* Mike Helland, Aaron Blatchley, Lewis Moorehead, Robby Van Wie, Bill Tofson, Gabe DeJesus, Travis Hilliard, Hans Wimmer, Andy Nevar, Matt Marion, Jeff Van Wie, John Krueger, Aaron Tollaksen, Ed Nevar, Todd Zick, Greg Gabris, Rich Weishoff, Dale Hudack, John Leung

1988: *Coach Jim Murphy,* Brad Martens, Jason Kimball, Dan Lenahan, Shawn McMahon, Bill Engelland, Cory Cobe, Gabe DeJesus, matt Jagoe Jason Bremer, Troy Schweda, Tory Dorow, Lewis Moorehead, Fritz Elsen, Aaron Blatchley, Hans Wimmer, Andy Nevar, Chris Seidler, Dan Delmore, Travis Hilliard, Emmet Wimmer, Mike Helland, Brad Priessel, John Krueger, Todd Zick, Jeff Van Wie, Ed Nevar, Jamey Reid, Matt Marion, Russ Jenkins

Girls Basketball

1979: *Coach Dale Maher,* Colleen Cook, Torrie Procknow, Jane Marz, Christy Mawbey, Kristen Gregerson, Shelly Galitz, Chris Maher, Mary Schauf, Marian Buckminster, Carrie Cook, Carol Sturdevant, Kim Kraft

Boys Basketball

1942: *Coach William Fitzpatrick,* Joe Baggot, Duaine Counsell, Jack Doyle, Robert Field, Gordon Foster, Jack Greenwood, Jim Playman, George Schmidt, S. Stowers, Harry Weber, Jim Wenkman, Dave Fitzpatrick

1956: *Coach Duaine Counsell,* Don O'Neill, Dean O'Neill, Lee Thompson, Frit Winnes, James Heineke, James Holden, ——— Kvikman, Robert Kane

1968: *Coach Al Horn,* Dennis Dunahee, Bruce Kaiser, Larry Meyer, David Gussel, Bob Heinzelman, Ed O'Brien, Tim Tofson, John DeMerit, Steve Kahler, Dennis Sweeney, Bob Gavinski, Jim DeMerit

1969: *Coach Al Horn,* Bob Gavinski, Ken Frodin, James DeMerit, Robert Fish, Tim Tofson, Mike Sweeney, Dennis Dunahee, James Kivlin, Peter Hickethier, Gary Mattei

1985: *Coach Jack Capelle,* Scot Fedderly, Carl Thorson, Bill Rudersdorf, Tom Fedderly, Tim Decorah, Bill Fandrich, Dan Hess, Dan Anchor, Ray Mueller, Jason Tollaksen, Brian Hartley, John Waterman

1986: *Coach Jack Capelle,* Rob Van Wie, Scot Fedderly, Rich Christensen, Bill Rudersdorf, David Shumway, T.J. Van Wie, Peter Flock, John Waterman, Jason Tollaksen, Dan Hess, Jeff Diehl, Brian Hartley, Ed Nevar

1987: *Coach Jack Capelle,* Matt Thundercloud, Tim Bubon, Jeff Diehl, Tim Decorah, T.J. Van Wie, Ed Nevar, Matt Marion, Peter Flock, Brent Stowell, Jeff Van Wie, Brian Sweeney, Rich Christensen

1988: *Coach Jack Capelle*

1989: *Coach Jack Capelle,* Matt Jagoe, Aaron Waterman, Tory Eckhardt, T.J. Van Wie, Matt Thundercloud, Tim Bubon, Todd Schad, Andy Nevar, Billy Van Wie, Matt Thompson, Scott Walsh, Desomer

1990: *Coach Jack Capelle,* Jeff Hall, Jon Geyman, Billy Van Wie, Matt Thompson, Scott Walsh, Andy Nevar, Todd Schad, Mike Wood, Ben Jagoe, Cory Marston, Tory Eckhardt, Cory Waterman, Matt Jagoe

Boys Cross Country

1980: *Coach Dean Piehl,* Terry Connors, Tim Gelhaus, John Dinegan, Scott Beard, Marty Hickey, Bill Fay, Eric Gregerson, Rod Kingsley, Brian Schmitz

Football

1951: *Coach Duaine Counsell,* Ken Niebuhr, Ed Baggot, Jim Wimmer, Harvey Birkholz, John Heineke, John Shumway, Walter Smelther, Pat Gavinski, Duane Tofson, Joe Cappy, Don Counsell, Dave Fitzpatrick, Dick Kleimenhagen, Herb Bloomer, Hans Anderson, Max Cary, Joseph Farrell, Bob Zamzow, Bernie Olson, Tom Priester, Jim Anderson, Dick Wagner, Hans Fedderly, Darrell Broker, Jim Cahoon, M— Donnelly, Elmer Fisher, Victor Moon, Leonard Holt, Robert McClyman, Robert Naber, Dean Willard, Robert Gussel, Jim Winn, Ken Gavinski, Carlos Funmaker, E— Greiner, Gary DuFour, George Willard, Tom Gruman, Dave Foss, Jake Drollinger, Richard Holt, Evan Fischer, Wayne Steinhorst, Harold Rihn

1969: *Coach Fred Kuhl,* Marty Horkan, Jim Kivlin, Scott Ennis, Jim DeMerit, Tim Tofson, Mike Schultz, Larry McFaul, Randy Tallmadge, Mainert Anderson, Larry Richter, Ben Olson, Allen Timm, John Wimann, Pete Helland, Craig Richards, Jim Ashline, Jim Harper, Gary Mattei, Mike Sweeney, Al Schultz, Mark Hamburg, Dave DeMerit, Dave Heidtke, Casey Trumble, Dave Peterson, Tom Wampler, Mike Baggot, Will Nagle, Jack Ramer, Mark Hamm, Jim Joyce, Dan Fitzgerald, Ed Nagle, Dick Wampler, Ken Weber, Lyle Greendeer, Dan Warner, Robin Gray, Leo LaVigne, Paul Quinn, Richard Berg, Bill Mawbey, Jerry Carton, Tim Peterson

The 1942 Kilbourn High School boys basketball team. (front, l-r) Jim Wenkman, Jack Doyle, Harry Weber, Dave Fitzpatrick, Robert Field, Jack Greenwood, Duaine Counsell. (back, l-r) George Schmidt, Gordon Foster, Joe Baggot, Jack Doyle, E. Stowers, Jim Playman, Coach William Fitzpatrick.

1972: *Coach Fred Kuhl,* Mike Hamm, Joe Gussel, Pat Baggot, Jeff Wimann, Curt Seiler, Mike Weber, Jeff Hartman, Ted Borck, Mike Kleifgen, Mike Neubauer, Monte Mattei, Tom Luecke, Rusty Hoege, Bill Roeker, Brian Holzem, Tom Tofson, David Leege, Jim Peterson, John Huffman, Dave Corning, Paul Olson, Marv Grefe, Matt Foster, Dean Ennis, John Hamm, Doug Nate, Wayne Van Schoyck, Fran Sweeney, Keith Lytle, Don Hacker, John sobojinski, Tom Quinn, Bob Johnson, Ed Alvin, Andy Cole, Noel Mattei, Mike Larkin, Dan Gavinski, Jerry Sobojinski, Bill Harrison, Greg Fisher, Ken Christensen, Brian Ward, Bob Hudack, Jon Helland

1973: *Coach Fred Kuhl,* Steve Bloomer, Keith Lytle, Tom Tofson, Brian Holzem, Dave Corning, Don Hacker, Paul Olson, Noel Mattei, Bob Johnson, Bill Roeker, Ed Alvin, Tom Quinn, Dean Ennis, Rusy Hoege, Dan Gavinski, Chip Van Schoyck, Bob Hudack, Matt Foster, Jon Helland, Marv Grefe, Greg Fisher, John Sobojinski, Ken Wampler, Jerry Sobojinski, Dennis Snyder, Avery Tucker, Doug Nate, Fran Sweeney, John Hamm, Mike Larkin, Bob Zamzow, Jeff Buss, Pat Hilliard, Tom Hacker, Jack Shaffer, Frank Chesney, Myron Kuzyk, Bill Harrison, Jim Clendaniel, Dean Phillips, Mike Nate, Mark Zillmer, Larry Bloomer, Jim Whitson, Ken Christensen

1974: *Coach Fred Kuhl,* Jerry Sobojinski, Greg Fisher, Ken Wampler, Marv Grefe, Bob Hudack, John Sobojinski, Dan Gavinski, Dean Phillips, John Hamm, Doug Nate, Larry Bloomer, Matt Foster, Chip Van Schoyck, Noel Mattei, Pat Roth, Mike Larkin, Jack Shaffer, Bill Harrison, Mark Zillmer, Terry Marshall, Frank Chesney, Myron Kuzyk, Greg Arendsee, Dennis Snyder, Bob Zamzow, Ken Christensen, Jon Helland, Avery Tucker, Jeff Buss, Pat Hilliard, Andy Shumway, Jim Whitson, Tim Zillmer, Leo Joyce, John Dixon, Allen Getgen, Paul Anderson, Tom Hacker, Mike Heitman, Bret Anderson, Mike Hess, Mark Hartman, Mark Heitman, Jim Sturdevant

1976: *Coach Fred Kuhl,* Tim Zillmer, Jim Sturdevant, Leo Joyce, John Dixon, Mike Hess, Bob Larkin, Bret Anderson, Allen Getgen, Bill Delmore, Paul Anderson, Mark Heitman, Andy Shumway, Mike Heitman, Doug Fisher, Bob Corning, Jack Slocum, Bob Hall, Russ Howard, Dave Schwartzer, Bill Dinegan, Kevin Sarnow, Nick Tiedeken, Glenn Arendsee, Jerry Potter, Todd Olson, Jeff Larkin, Dan Runde, Dan Kuhl, Curt Marston, Jeff Olson, Dave Reifsteck, Tom Kutzke, Bob Kaufman, Bryce Knuth, Dan Strangstalein, Tom Baggot, Eugene Morse, Todd Nelson, Tim Anderson, Dave Wimann, Scott Bernander, Robin Staniszewski, Mike Strasberg, Glen Schoenbeck, Jim Johnson, Scott Sitas

1979: *Coach Fred Kuhl,* Mike Lake, Mark Honish, Bob Schultz, Tim Buss, Doug Reifsteck, Gary Thundercloud, Ralph Howard, Mike Julson, Tony Mackesey, Tim Stowers, Dave Hess, Dave Green, Toby Thompson, Rob Carlson, Ken Freel, Jim Van Dinter, Jim Connors, Ralph Corning, Dave Weiss, Tom Fisher, Dan Stroebel, Randy Gilner, Dan Marz, Larry Volkey, Bruce Nelson, Chris Larson, Matt Dixon, Paul Hess, Bob Buss, Ken Nehrkorn, Gary Harkness, Todd Geisser, Steve Schultz, Scott Beer, Jeff Johnson, Toby Stearns

1984: *Coach Fred Kuhl,* Hans Backhaus, Brian Worthing, Dave Anderson, John Vernon, Willie Wimmer, Darrin Schaefer, Jeff Morris, Rick Brunner, Tim Walch, Toby Haferman, Brendon O'Rourke, Joe Kaiser, Tom Fedderly, Jerry Schneller, Pete Johnson, Brian Hartley, Rob May, Mark Bubon, Jason Tollaksen, Dan Hess, Pat Helland, bill Rudersdorf, Brian Beard, Carl Thorsen, Tony Beer, Steve Schwartzer, Henry Little Soldier, Tim Decorah, Don Murphy, Scot Fedderly, Steve Marsich, Mike Voss, Woody Keeble, Steve Kissack, Pete Flock, Scott Hawley, David Shumway, Tim Schultz, Aaron Tollaksen, Bob Wick, John Schauf, Bill Tofson, Bob Logan

1985: *Coach Fred Kuhl,* Carl Thorsen, Mark Bubon, Tony Beer, Pat Helland, Dan Hess, Jason Tollaksen, Bill Rudersdorf, Brian Hartley, Mike Voss, Bob Logan, Steve Schwartzer, Rob May, Brian Beard, Bob Wick, Steve Marsich, Steve Kissack, Woody Keeble, Scot Fedderly, Dave Shumway, Jeff Van Wie, Tim Fish, Jeff Diehl, John Webb, Aaron Tollaksen, Trent Nelson, John Schauf, Mark Sturdevant, Aaron Blatchley, Chris Zunker, Hans Wimmer, John Krueger, Brian Sweeney, Kelly Roehl, Pete Tofson, Jeff Webb, Tim Schutte, Mike Nickel

1987: *Coach Pete Gust,* Lewis Moorehead, Russ Jenkins, Greg Montgomery, Joe Stoughtenger, Marc Henry, Manuel DeJesus, Jason Effinger, Aaron Blatchley, Jon Laundrie, Pete Zapuchlak, Rodney Winchell, Steve Turkington, Mike Ladisa, Chad Weiss, Mark Sturdevant, Bill Parfievich, James Krueger, Jeremy McIntyre, Tim Schutte, T.J. Van Wie, Mike Nickel, Dan Tubman, Chris Brandt, Brad Gussel, Mike Feldt, Chris Zunker, Tim Bubon, Scott McClyman, Brad Weidling, Jake Beard, John Koscieiniak, Mike Logan, Corey Marston, Jim Sweeney, Steve McClyman, Mike Helland, Joe Hess, Matt Thundercloud, Hans Wimmer, Aaron Kirby, Brent Stowell, Scott Walsh, Brian Sweeney, Matt Thompson, Jeff Diehl, John Krueger, Jeff Van Wie, Erik Backhaus, Tim Fish, Jeff Webb

Golf

1980: *Coach Jack Capelle,* Bob Blegen, Pat Hintze, Randy Blegen, Greg Alstrom, Mike Smith

1983: *Coach Jack Capelle,* Mike Smith, Willie Wimmer, Matt Winn, Joe Kaiser, Alan Zimmerman

1985: *Coach Jack Capelle,* Dave Anderson, Willie Wimmer, Joe Kaiser, Dan Anchor, Tom Fedderly, Alan Zimmerman

1992: *Coach John Hoenecke*

1993: *Coach John Hoenecke,* Brian Mitchell, Jeff Wojnicz, Scott Luebke, Chris Freeman, Jason Morris, Cory Rose

Softball

1992: *Coach Dale Gray*, Lara Zapuchlak, Ginny Gray, Jenny Sellmeyer, Michelle Crossley, Jen Marion, Katie Schwarze, Patty Schauf, Wendy Bereton, Emmain Bailey, Trisha Stroede, Carrie Ragan

1994: *Coach Dale Gray,* Kathy Sellmeyer, Jenny Parrott, Amy Gavinski, Debi Barker, Melanie Schoblocher, Shannon Mawbey, Connie Wampler, Carrie Ragan, Ginny Gray, Amy Warn, Nikki Wenzel, Tara Blackcoon, Stacy Hinze, Jaime Duncan

Track

1958: *Coach James Demerit*, Jack Anchor, Dean O'Neil, Ken Harrison, R— — Gruman, Tim Ryan, Edwin Heidtke, Spencer Lonetree, James Jax, David McClyman, E— Schleef, D— Goodhue, I— Blackdeer, Dick Schultz, Peter Gregerson, Alan Peters

1968: *Coach James Demerit*, Steve Ennis, David Kissack, John DeMerit, Don Kieta, Dennis Sweeney, Bruce Kaiser, David Gussel, Jim Kivlin, Luther Lonetree, Jim DeMerit, Scott Ennis, Gary Fay, Wayne Decorah, Mike Sweeney, Tim Tofson, Marty Horkan

Boys Volleyball

1969: *Coach Richard Schauf,* Ken Gray, Tim Stewart, Bill Gissal, Pete Hickethier, Bob Fish, Jurgen Pfeiffer, James Tollaksen, Bob Graack, Doug Krueger, John Kaleas, Chris Molkentine, Mark Thermes, Ken Nichols, Herb Heinzelman, Kerry Page, Don Helley, Grant Guildner

Girls Volleyball

1991: *Coach Cindy Collins,* Lara Zapuchlak, Jenny Sellmeyer, Kim Kane, Jen Marion, Lisa Haynes, Jenny Gavinski, Lisa Walsh, Rachel White, Amy Montgomery, Emmain Bailey, Kathy Zamzow, Patty Schauf, Trisha Stroede

Wrestling

1975: *Coach Glen Getgen,* Bob Hudack, Greg Arendsee, Rich Ennis, Jim McFaul, Steve Holzem, Scott Holzem, Mark Beard, Leo Joyce, Ken Wampler, Bob Zamzow, Allen Getgen, Bob Card

1977: *Coach Glen Getgen,* Duane Young, Kevin Lloyd, Rich Luke, Doug Reifsteck, Dave Reifsteck, Bob Corning, Leo Joyce, Mike Hess, Dave Rihn, Allen Getgen, Tim Zillmer, Rich Ennis

1980:*Coach Wayne Stapleford,* Dan Stroebel, Joey Van Dinter, Jim Van Dinter, Jay Schoenbeck, Doug Reifsteck, Ken Freel, Mark Obois, Pat Holzem, Larry Volkey, Tim Stowers, Brian Cahoon, Mike Julson

1982: *Coach Wayne Stapleford,* Alan Zimmerman, Joey Van Dinter, Willie Holzem, Mark Baggot, Kevin Hudack, John Getgen, Chris Baggot, Toby Stearns, Vince Volkey, Todd Geisser, Dan Park, Matt Dixon

1983: *Coach Wayne Stapleford,* Dale Gray, Mark Bubon, Joey Van Dinter, Willie Holzem, Dan Green, Rich Zamzow, Mark Baggot, Vince Volkey, Kevin Hudack, John Getgen, Alan Zimmerman, Chip Cahoon, Mark Wimann, Dan Park

1984: *Coach Wayne Stapleford,* Bob Berberich, Dale Gray, Tracy Nelson, Alan Zimmerman, Mark Bubon, Mike Platt, Dan Green, Dave Anderson, John Getgen, Tim Walch, Chip Cahoon, Dan Park

1986: *Coach Mike Kratochwill,* John Webb, Jeff Wakefield, Eugene Trimble, Alan Zimmerman

DELLS FOOTBALL PLAYERS AT THE UNIVERSITY OF WISCONSIN

1930: James Wimmer, Quarterback
1936: Ervin Johnson, Halfback
1953: John Dixon, Linebacker & Fullback, All Big Ten Scholastic First Team, All Conference Third Team, Team Record 6-2-1, Rose Bowl UW 0, USC 7
1955: Ed Baggot, Guard, 5'7", 175 lbs, Team Record 4-5
1957: John Heineke, Tackle, 6'2", 209 lbs, Team Record 6-3
1959: Jim Heineke, Tackle, 6', 218 lbs, Team Record 7-2 Rose Bowl UW 8, Washington 44
1961: Jim Jax, Tackle, 6'1", 218 lbs, Team Record 2-7-1
1965: Robert Fenske, Halfback, 5'11", 177 lbs, Team Record 6-3
1980: John Dixon Jr., Guard, 5'10", 236 lbs, Team Record 4-7
1981: Leo Joyce, 5'11", 241 lbs, Team Record 7-5 Garden State Bowl UW 21, Tennessee 28
1993: Jason Maniecke, Nose Tackle, 6'5", 290 lbs, All Big Ten Second Team, Academic All Big Ten Team Record 10-1-1, Rose Bowl: UW 21, UCLA 16

OTHER DELLS AREA ATHLETES: Dean Walker and Jim Lorenzen were both varsity members of the U.W. racing crew.

Fathers & sons who have played for Wisconsin Dells, 1958. (front, l-r) Monk Heineke, Ollie Shumway, Fat Blatchley, Jim Wimmer, Sr., Stuart Fedderly, Gordon Winnes. (rear, l-r) Jim Heineke, John Heineke, John Shumway, Pete Blatchley, Jim Wimmer, Jr., Hans Fedderly, Fritz Winnes.

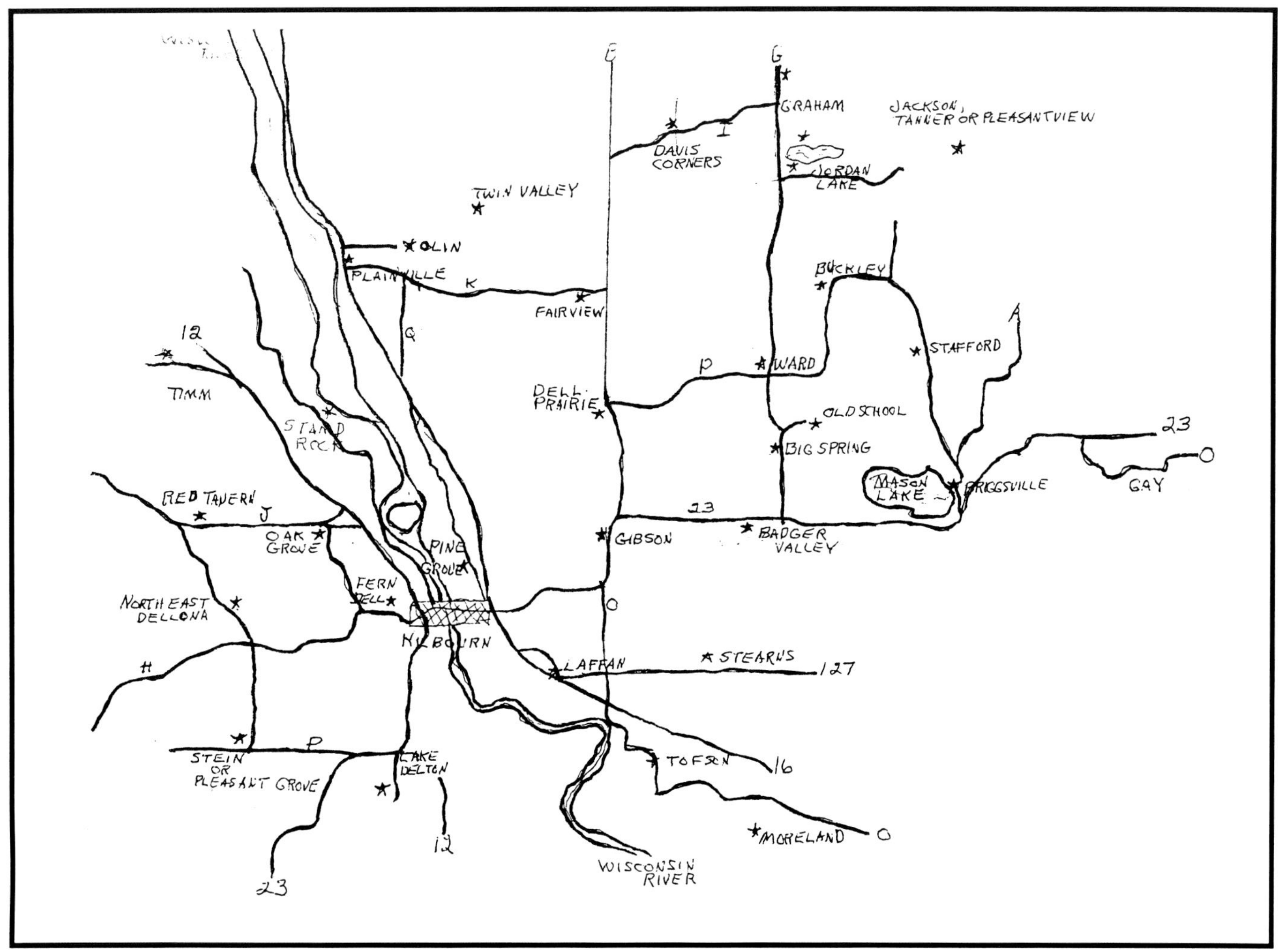

Country Schools

Settlement was already underway in the Dells area when President James K. Polk signed Wisconsin into statehood in 1848. Wherever a stream could be dammed and a mill constructed–Briggsville, Big Spring, Delton, Newport–pioneers settled with their families; and families needed schools.

The earliest history of the area mentions a school "near the Kerfoot place" or Dawn Manor, and was in the village since known as Old Newport. The school was a large two story building in the upper part of which the Congregational church held services. The *Illustrated Events*, reprinted in 1903-1905 goes on to say, "That old schoolhouse may be properly termed the point around which gathers all the sentiment of Old Newport. There with the children of the community was centered the love, hope and ambition of the whole town."

In the beginning of the settlement era, religious service and schools were often intertwined. In fact, many of the first schools were sponsored by religious organizations, as was the case of the Academy in Delton and The Institute at Point Bluff. The site of this latter is not part of the Dells school district in 1991.

As Kilbourn advanced, the area surrounding the village for miles around was also being settled and the need for schools within walking distance of the hastily constructed homes was realized. These schools, often named for the settler who had donated an acre of his newly-acquired land, were the first buildings to follow after the log cabins. Some of these schools so named were: Gibson, Tofson, Stearns, Moreland, Carter, Stein, Timm, Stafford, Tanner, Gay, Vroman and Olin. Still others such as the Oak Grove school in Lyndon township, were popularly called by the name of the earliest settler as in the case of the Blood school. Students many times selected more descriptive names for their schools, such as Pine Grove, Badger Valley, Townline, Point Bluff, Stand Rock, Pleasant View, Fairview, Twin Valley, Lower Dells and Fern Dell, (also called the Flat school, because of its location on the flat area of the old river bed west of Kilbourn). Others designated locations, such as: Davis Corners, Big Spring, Briggsville, Delton, Northeast Dellona, Plainville and Gayles Corners. The Red Tavern School took its name from an early inn of the same name located on that site. This inn, had been a landmark for early travelers on the old trail that eventually became highway 12 through Juneau County. Since 1933 this has been Juneau County J as that was the year U.S.

Country schools in the Wisconsin Dells District.

The Fair View School, c. 1890, (first row, l-r) Lydia Kaleas, Margaret O'Connell, Edward Schad, (second row) Otto Kaleas, Belle Bement, Grace Townsend, Millie O'Connell, Harry O'Connell, Lawrence Wellbaum, Leo Kinney, Anna Schad, (third row) Clarel Stowe, Albert Kaleas, Willie Kinney, Julia Kinney, (fourth row) Teacher Jennie Twist, Hazel Welbaum, Clara Procknow, Jennie Stowe, Dora Townsend, Iva Crosby.

Highway 12 was constructed through Rocky Arbor Park.

Our records are never complete on these original schools. The earliest records of the Fern Dell School go back only until 1883 when a frame building was constructed. It is assumed, however that a log building preceded it, as the abstract for the Ennis farm of which the acre was a part, states "one square acre for school purposes would be leased for ninety nine years, or for as long as used for school purposes," and is dated 1850. In 1995, the said acre is still being used for "school purposes" as it is the site of the administration offices for the Wisconsin Dells school district, one hundred and forty-five years later.

Some other early records indicate that in 1899 Ella Bullis was the teacher at Pine Grove, and in 1901 the following were serving on the school board; Neff, Berry and Fish. In that year the teacher was Grace Cook. A teacher's contract from that era states that said teacher agrees "to build her own fires."

The teachers of that day had many tales to tell. A former student of the Oak Grove school, who in 1991 operates the Dells Grill states that her teacher, Jeanette Clark, walked two miles each way, come rain or come shine. Tillie Newell says, "Yes, and she taught me and all my brothers and sisters in the same room."

In pioneer times these teachers may have been either male or female and in many instances started teaching at the age of 16, with no formal training, but they were able to pass on to their students their own country school education. Later, rural school teachers attended training sessions at "Institutes" held in the summer at the county level. The County Normal schools, which provided either a one or two year course, were in operation by 1915.

The country schools continued to be the foundation of the educational system throughout the 1920's and 30's. Confronted by the Great Depression, many closed or consolidated with another nearby. The Moreland school closed and joined the Tofson. Both these schools educated primarily the descendants of Norwegian settlers in Newport township. When the Stand Rock school closed the students were transported into town in what was probably the area's first school "bus"–a converted truck, in which the approximately 15 students, according to former student Vanita Trumble Roeker, rode. Frank Hacker was their driver, and Vanita states, there was chicken wire over the windows. This fact caused some unkind comments from their city cousins.

In the 1930s, having purchased property near the Indian Baptist Church, parents of children of the Ho-Chunk Nation sent them to the Oak Grove school. Some of these families were the Goodbears, the Decorahs, as well as the George and Melvin Miner families.

In the 1930s, merchants and educators in Kilbourn became aware of the existence of potential customers and students in the outlying areas and began offering incentives to bring them into Kilbourn. Free movie tickets to the Mission Theater were distributed to the country schools several times a year and now and then country schools were invited to participate in programs and plays at the community building.

Annual Field Days were also held. All the country school students came together in Wisconsin Dells to compete with their peers in all kinds of track and field events. Country students looked forward with anticipation to Field Days and, through this event, many became acquainted with schools in Kilbourn and became more interested in attending high school. Even in the 1930s, sending a student to high school meant quite a sacrifice for rural parents. Students had to either board in town or transportation had to be arranged personally.

In the 1940s Joe and Dorothy Nelson gradually got into the school bus driving business by first transporting Red Tavern students to Oak Grove and later the Northeast Dellona students to Fern Dell. In 1949 Joe had his first contract, which led to a career that spanned 38 years of transporting students. Joe retired in 1987 and received many awards for his work. At the time he started, only public school students could be transported but it soon became law that private and parochial school students must also be transported.

The 1950s saw great changes in public education. The state favored the integration of all of the country schools into larger districts. This led to the eventual closing of most of the outlying schools. The majority of rural residents fought hard to retain their schools and their identities. In some areas it became a time of mini "Civil Wars".

These country schools had then been in existence for over a century and they did not die easily. Those who favored keeping them were as determined and strong willed as the forefathers illustrated in the story Mary (Timm) Hall related about a major controversy concerning the location of the Timm school in settlement times. It seems some folks wanted the school located further west than it was so during the night, with the use of ox teams, they pulled the building to the location of their choice. A hearing was held to get the school moved back to its original location. The clerk complained later, "How could I write anything down with all that loud language and fists flyin." A century later it took the same type of controversy to finally integrate the country schools into larger districts with their city cousins.

By 1960 integration was complete and the Wisconsin Dells Area School District, with students from five counties, was organized and operating. The Briggsville (now called Neenah Creek, built in 1994) and Delton schools continue to operate as part of the Wisconsin Dells District.

Delton State Graded

The first school in the village that is now Lake Delton was built on the north side of Adams Street in 1850, with funds raised by subscription. Philander Fenton was the first teacher. About 6 years later, the original building was replaced by a brick building near the present location of the school.

One of the first public uses of the school building was for rallies at the beginning of the Civil War. Company "E", the Lake Delton area contingent, assembled there in October of 1861.
By 1867, public school attendance had grown and a wing was added to the brick building. Bricks used to construct the school were made in a brickyard located on the present Cheese House site. In 1880, the school had an enrollment of 91 students.

The building was replaced in 1930 by a new red brick structure near the same site. First graders in the brand "new" building included Donna Braun, Jack Scott, and Bob Sarrington. A few years later, additional rooms were added.

In 1942, there were three teachers, and in 1948, the staff consisted of 4 teachers. Enrollment increased greatly in the years of the Badger Ordnance Works. In the 1950's two more rooms were added to the south side of the building.

In 1960, the Lake Delton School District was integrated with the Wisconsin Dells School District. The staff then consisted of eight teachers and a principal. A gymnasium was added to the west side of the building during 1961. At that time the school had reached it highest enrollment; 235 students. In 1973, grades 7 & 8 were sent to the Wisconsin Dells Junior High School.

In 1991, 199 students were enrolled in grades Early Childhood through six. Some grades have two sections, including special teachers. During a 1989-90 remodeling project, the 1930's portion of the building was razed and a six classroom addition built. Where the 1930's portion had stood, a spacious cafeteria, music room, and art room were added. Twenty educators now work at the Lake Delton School.

The Red Tavern School, 1938, (students l-r) Mary Lambert, Agnes Szymanowski, Jim Lambert, Bob Laabs. The teacher is Edna Peck. (below) The Delton State Graded School. The original building, with the bell tower, was built in 1860.

The Delton School, c. 1906 (first row, l-r) Arthur Gomon, Glen House, Ernie Cole, Theodore Patterson, Roy Rodwell, Joe Gawronski, Leslie Kingsley, Emma La Foundain, Sarah Rodwell, Chester Sarrington, Ralph Sarrington, Howard ANdrews, Albert Follett, David Spaulding. (second row) Floyd Kingsley, Leon Cole, Esther Rodwell, Jennie Rodwell, Grace Kindsley, Vada Steele, Vera Sarrington, Helen Gawronski, Nettie Kingsley, Letty House, Ina Follett, Vera Evans, (third row) Frid Ayres, Frank Ayres, Guy Rice, Earl House, Louis Fox, Mign Timme, Billy Cole, Roy Coates, Ruth Reynolds, Grace Cole, Mabel Scott, Mamie cole, Letha McCabe, Genevieve Adams, Ethel Kingsley, Jessie Loomis.

Badger Valley

Badger Valley has had a school since the early 1850s.

No one says where the first school building was located, but Mr. Walter Mylrea, born in 1863, attended school there, and remembered that his first teacher was Amos Tyler. Another teacher was Johnny Stowell, an Indian half-breed. In those days the enrollment ranged from sixty to ninety. The building had two rows of seats and desks, with five or six pupils in each seat; when the one next to the wall wanted to get out everyone else in the row had to get up. This old school house was moved later to the Norman Jensen farm, where for many years it was used as a barn.

The school house site was donated by Ole Jolson, who gave a deed to one acre of ground. When all was finished, the building was too near the road. A petition was circulated, by means of which the road was set over on Gilbert Larson's land.

Melvin Kingsley is of the third generation in his family to attend the same school, as his grandmother, Mrs. Walter Kingsley (nee Laura Clark) went to school at Badger Valley.

Big Spring

It is difficult to write the history of the Big Spring School District for the school records were carelessly burned many years ago.

The original Big Springs school house was built before Big Springs was even platted, and was located outside the area on what would be part of Sneak Street before the dam was built. Just north of the town hall, marks can be seen where the Pinery Road crossed the creek, went by the site of the old school house and on through the Winchell Place. The school house was, of course, built of logs.

The Big Spring school house stood on the same ground for at least 90 years, and many believe it is the same building. Of course it has been tinkered up now and then.

When Erwin Crothers went to school, the floor had a depression about 12 feet long and 8 feet wide and 6 inches deep just inside the door. A long box-like stove stood in the center of the depression, and it would take wood about 4 feet long. The stove had raised letters on top, and at recess students burned the letters on our slate frames. There were nothing but homemade wooden desks, and a variety of things was carved on them.

The School District included the following families: Ramsey, Morse; Thrasher; Phillips; Ward; Sweet; Vleit; Powers; Wheeler; Hanson; Armson; Bowen; Stowell; Brown; Campbell; French; and Landt.

Briggsville

With the growth of the village came the organization of the district which in those days included Briggsville and Moundville. On December 11, 1852, the first meeting of the district was held in the village store. It was voted to build a log school, raise $25.00 to finish the building, and that the schoolhouse be situated on the hill back of the A.E. Briggs home. There the children when they stole a look out of the windows would often see Indians paddling down the creek. When school opened for three months in 1853, Abby O. Briggs was the teacher. There were 31 pupils ranging in age from four to twenty. Horatio S. Thomas was chosen superintendent and G.H. Chamberlain clerk pro-tem. Perry Monger was made director and G.H. Chamberlain clerk for the ensuing year.

This early community was composed of English, Irish, and German settlers who did not always agree. In 1858 the English and the Irish, from both Briggsville and Moundville, fell into disagreement about the school district, so it was brought to a vote. The English persuaded the Germans to vote with them to separate Moundville and Briggsville and so won the point!

A new school was built on the site of the present Odd Fellows Hall in 1859 and was later incorporated into that building. Later still in 1868 a third school was built on the lot back of the present post office. This building was moved to a spot north of the Catholic church; and in 1924 the present village school was erected. The Moundville school which was organized as the result of the "battle" is known as District #11, or the Gay School.

Davis Corners

There are no available records to tell just when Davis Corners school district was organized, but from old assessment rolls and land abstracts we can be reasonably sure that it was established in the early 1850s.

The first school building was constructed of logs and was for several years the only public gathering place in the community; it was used as a sort of meeting house by the settlement. Itinerant preachers held services here, having travelled long distances, sometimes with no shoes, but always with a white shirt with a stiff starched front called a boiled shirt.

Among the early homesteaders was a family of fine reputation named "Davis," who not only gave the land where the school house now stands, but also gave land for the church. The Congregational Church Society was organized in the school house and the church was built in 1880.

The first frame school house was built where the present one now stands. It was typical of the schools of that day, except that it was somewhat larger than average. It was painted white and had nice green blinds. There were trees around it and it was in a pretty spot. Wild flowers, many of them now extinct, grew everywhere. The girls gathered market baskets of mushrooms after a warm spring rain, and wild strawberries were plentiful in nearby fields.

The building had a soft pine floor, white washed plastered walls, with wainscoting about a third of the way up from the floor, and homemade desks.

There was a raised platform where the teacher sat. Wide boards painted black across the front of the room were later replaced by slate. Patent double seats were installed later. Water came from an open well with oaken buckets, on a farm near by.

At a homecoming here in 1945, Ella Briggs (Mrs. Ella Gay) of Briggsville, was asked to be present and give a talk; she was the oldest living teacher of our school at the time. Then nearing her 90's, she was as dainty and pretty as a girl and as alert as any one present. She said she had taught at Davis Corners 64 years before (1881). She told something of conditions at that time, and as best she could remember, called the roll. There was no one left to answer this teacher of that long ago. Mrs. Gay passed away in 1950 at the age of 91.

Margaret Graham Bement taught here a few years later. She passed away many years ago, having been all her life an active member of the community.

Another outstanding teacher of the old days or during the "Gay Nineties" came from Coloma Corners in 1892; her name was Lavern Richmond. She had a strong personality and a keen mind.

Miss Richmond was called just that, never "teacher" as was customary then. She was stern, yet just, and she left an impression on the community that has its effect to this day. Very public spirited and with a zeal for improvement, she worked not only in the classroom, but in the church and with the adult social life. She organized a

The Badger Valley School, with teacher Laura Kingsley Clark in the doorway and Big Spring students, c. 1925, (first row, l-r) Archie Ramsay, Lucille Smith, Lorraine Richter, Lois Lapp, Joe Smith, Eva Ramsey, Nina Ramsey, Edwin Lapp, (second row) Ivan Lapp, Earl Lapp, Gerald Brodt, Arthur Ramsey, Teacher Pearl Coon, Bernice Rasmussen.

Literary Society, a Christian Endeavor, gathered young folks for parties and always with the idea of making a better standard of manners and morals.

I often wonder who her dressmaker was. Miss Richmond was a great lady in every respect for she weighed 300 pounds. Memory still recalls her stopping along the path to church in a brown taffeta dress, carrying every ounce of herself with pride and dignity. Her clothes always fitted without a wrinkle and were very neat.

At that time it was quite customary for a mother making a trip to town, or going out to visit, to drop the very small children off at the school house–children from 2 to 4 years of age; five-year-olds attended school regularly. On one Ladies' Aid day Miss Richmond had five of these tots left to contend with. The society was meeting a short distance from school, and at four o'clock she took her charges and went to Ladies' Aid. She proceeded to wash faces, arrange hair with brush and comb, refusing to let the mothers even help, saying, "These are my guests and I shall look after them." She waited on them at the table and paid for their suppers, the price of which, by the way, was 5¢ each regardless of age. Pleasant and cheerful, she then relinquished them to their mothers.

There was much less babysitting at school during the remainder of her stay. She possessed a tact that impressed without offending. Though many years in a better world, she still lives here.

Davis Corners was on the old stage road from Portage to Friendship. There was a neat log house very near the school house and here a widow lady kept a small store. One could buy staple groceries and kerosene, and the school children bought pink and white lozenges for a penny, as well as unpainted, rubberless lead pencils and slate pencils for the same price. Slate pencils had red, white and blue paper wrappers.

Gibson-Dell Prairie school students, c. 1920.

In 1916 the school overflowed the old building and with its many scars from years of service and its memories of by gone days, it was replaced by a fine new building. In the 1940s two buildings housed a consolidated school, and Davis Corners was part of the Oxford High School District. Two big yellow buses traveled the highways bringing students to and from. The school was closed when the district consolidated with Wisconsin Dells.

Dell Prairie

The first school was built at the end of County Trunk P. It was called the Carter School. Later it was moved and called the Dell Prairie School.

The Gibson School was named for early settlers by the name of Gibson.

Fern Dell

In 1883, this "one-room schoolhouse" was constructed at a site about 1/2 mile west of the Hwy 13–12 junction.

The Town Board found it necessary to borrow $350 of the $400 necessary for its building. It was used continuously until 1956, at which time it was replaced with a larger and more permanent structure.

This school was operated without interruption for 71 years. Its teachers and their monthly wages were: Hattie Bennett, 1884-85, $18.00; Minnie Daniels, 1886, $18.00; Emil Knox, 1886-87, $20.00; Tena Luke, 1887, $20.00; Minnie Daniels, 1887-88, $20.00; Ida Kaufman, 1888, $20.00; Angie Hurlburt, 1889, $25.00; Myra Hamilton, 1890-92, $26.00; Carrie Nixon, 1893, $25.00; E. M. Timlin, 1894, $25.00; Martha Laabs, 1895-96, $25.00; Victoria McVey, 1897-98, $22.00; Martha Laabs, 1898, $22.00; Hattie Hall, 1899, $22.00; Washington Oschner, 1900, $25.00; Bertha Hamilton, 1901, 25.00; Grayce Sarrington, 1902, $25.00; Zada Hall, 1903, $26.00; Elsie Frost, 1904, $28.00; Eugene Heiner, 1905, $30.00; Mabel Scott, 1905-06, $27.00; Evelyn Smith, 1907-08, $31.00; Iva Iverson, 1908-09, $31.00; Frank Kerrigan, 1909-10, $35.00; Myrtle Kramer, 1910-12, $38.00; Margaret Trumble, 1912-13, $35.00; Will Simonds, 1913, $41.16; Myrtle Armstrong, 1913, $41.16; Helen Shoemacher, 1913, $40.00; Will Simonds, 1913-14, $41.16; Myrtle Armstrong, 1914-16, $40.59; Theresa Mulligan, 1916-17, $47.52; Leona Mack, 1917-19, $68.00; Clementine Newell, 1918, $46.53; Amelia Storandt, 1920-21, $79.50; Martina McGowan, 1921, $85.00; Vanetta O'Brien, 1922-28, $105.00; Janet Landt Holt, 1929, $90.00; Edith

Fern Dell students, c. 1930.

Hillman, 1930-37; Clara Brockman, 1937-43; Lucille Sobojinski, 1943-46; Margaret Marshall, 1946-49; Emma Rodwell, 1949-52; Lottie Fagan, 1952-53; Mary Nate, 1954-55, $225.00;

Jordan Lake

The Jordan Lake School was probably in existence from 1850 to 1890. It was located somewhere near the north lake shore, as George Crothers wrote, "It stood first, as I remember it, on a bleak hill, exposed to every wind that blew. Later, after a local civil war that nearly disrupted the community, it was moved to a sheltered nook on a sunny slope, hedged in by woods except on the south."

This later location, I believe, was near the foot of the hill, south of the lake and near to where County Highway G runs today. Its use was terminated due to eventual lack of enrollment, and finally "it burned one night."

Oak Grove School

The Oak Grove School, Joint Disctrict #7, Lyndon, Delton and Dellona, opened in the 1850s when homesteaders "pulled downed trees through the woods" with horses, to make make a trail to the "oak opening" where the school would be located. This same trail was to be the first part of Hwy 12 from Chicago to Minneapolis.

The building remembered by most sat on a triangle lot where Hwy 12 and Curry road intersect and included space for a nice playground. Other buildings on the property were boys and girls "plumbing facilities."

There were normally about 20 pupils in attendance. During the Great Depression, in addition to the usual Christmas vacation, there was also a "potato digging vacation" held in the fall.

The school board voted that during Christmas vacation, the school building was to be thoroughly cleaned by some local housewife. Other issues put to vote included who would supply the school's firewood, which would be delivered monthly for use in the large jacketed stove.

Following are some of the families served by Oak Grove School: Goman; Henricksen; Utter; Wharry; Blood; Miner; Decorah; Roderick; Good Bear; Lage; Mickelsen; Voros; Ellison; Beghin and Hagen. Other families were added when the Red Tavern School, 2 miles beyond, was closed.

Two early teachers were Margaret Doyle Dougherty and Jeanette Clark Blood. More recent

Oak Grove School students, 1938.

teachers include: Hazel Chamberlain; Helen Leberg; Hazel Peck; Anna Martin; Elane Bowman; Mary Ormson; Katherine Sweeney; Mrs. Mooney; Stella Hoile and Mary Nate.

Before automobiles were widely in use, these teachers "boarded" in neighborhood homes such as those of Dolly Blood, Zada Hall or Dave Mitchell.

Pine Grove

On the second day of April, 1877, the board of supervisors of the town of Dell Prairie, having formed a school district in the township, requested one Edwin Robinson, a taxpayer, to notify all the voters of the newly formed school district, of a school district meeting to be held at the school house. The first school meeting was held there, on April 10, 1877, at 7:00 P.M.

The newly organized school district was named "Pine Grove." The name was adaptable because the small community which was formerly located at the present entrance to Cold Water Canyon, bore the name of Pine Grove.

Mr. Irwin Berry, the father of Mr. Stuart Berry, a property owner of the community, was the gentlemen who donated the land. It was to be used for educational purposes, and the school house was to remain there as long as desired. However, if the building should be removed to a different site, the property would revert to the Berry estate.

Another school meeting was called to order at 7:00, April 16, 1877 for the purposes of raising money to pay the teacher and to cover various expenditures. The teacher's wages were to be fifty-four dollars for six months. Miss Knowlton, the first teacher, was the recipient of nine dollars a month for teaching. Then no training was required of a teacher; if she had completed the regular course of a stated number of "terms" in a rural school, she was an educated girl. Miss Knowlton was. Next, the problem of providing seats for the students arose; accordingly the sum of twenty-one dollars was raised for that purpose.

In 1879 the school house was redecorated with a coat of whitewash for which 10¢ was paid to buy the lime. Miss Freeman, the teacher that year, was provided with a new chair, for which 25¢ was paid. A box of chalk that year cost 20¢. Mr. Irwin Berry was paid the sum of 90¢ a cord for wood to heat the building.

The next year expenses had risen. It cost $100.00 to run the school.

Enrollment varied from fifteen to twenty. The ages of pupils varied more. They ranged from seven years to twenty three. In glancing through old registers and records of the school, it may be noted that one year a girl's name would be found listed in the "Upper form." The next year, the same girl's name could be found on a line at the top of the school register designated "Teacher."

The years varied as to how many months of school would be held. Some years, school "kept" for six months, other years, seven. The years were divided into a summer term and a winter term. Most years the treasurer's report at the annual school meeting showed a tidy sum in blue ink. Very seldom the end of the year showed figures in red.

In the earlier days of the school district, the citizens turned out en masse on Arbor Day. They came prepared to work, and Arbor Day really had a meaning for children and parents alike.

Glancing through the Visitor's Record, it may be noticed that parents visited school frequently. When some one from White Creek, Plainville, Friendship or Portage visited the school, it must have been quite a project to travel all those miles in a horse-drawn vehicle, or on foot.

Early residents of this community lay no claim to fame. They were too busy being neighbors and friends to think much about making a great name for themselves. The region has produced some outstanding citizens in various walks of life, however.

Among many, the name Berry is quite noted. The early Berrys were good, church-going, solid citizens.

The Morse family is one of long standing, and the boys and girls from this family who went to school at Pine Grove are widely scattered now over the United States and Canada.

This seems to be the appropriate place in this history to relate how the people in the district feel about their Country in time of war. This record appears in the clerk's report book, dated June 28, 1918:

War Stamps Sale

Meeting called to order by clerk

Roll call as follows - present are the following named families: A.P. Fish, C. Berry, U.G. Wilcox, W. Pickard, A. Priester, C. Van Wie, S. Knudson, Morse, Schoff, Van Wie, Clapp, Leute, Robinson, Loomis, Jordan, Kriegel, H. Alhorn, Leard.

Pine Grove School Jt. District No. 3 had proved itself 100%.

Plainville

Plainville's first school was built about 1855 on a plot of land just south of the Crosby farm on the west side of highway 13. There is no record of who was the first teacher. The common salary was $20.00 per month for the winter term and $15.00

to $17.00 per month for the fall or spring terms. It is interesting to note in school records that the length and number of terms varied from year to year. The annual school meeting voted on this question. The total number of months for any year was a least five and sometimes seven or eight. If there were only two terms, the winter term usually began in November and expired the last of February. The spring term began in April and expired the last of May.

Fuel was secured by the board by means of bids. Good dry solid oak two feet long was delivered and corded at the school house for .90 per cord. The school house was cleaned for $2.00 and painted for $6.50.

In 1882 the people voted to charge tuition of 50¢ per month to be paid in advance by all pupils who lived outside the boundaries of the district. The enrollment was often sixty pupils. Standard textbooks to be used for a period of five years were adopted by the board.

Community life around the school was quite active. There was a small dam east of Highway 13 on the present Ray Walker farm which furnished power for a chair factory. Cyrus Armstrong built the Wayside Inn where meals were served to people who came from farther north and stopped on their way to Portage, Kilbourn, and points south and west. There was also a small store in this same building. In the hall upstairs dances were held. As many as 100 numbers were often sold. The Good Templars, a temperance organization, held their regular meetings in this hall, too. For several years, beginning about 1863, a county fair was held on the west side of the highway near the Armstrong building. Old settlers recall seeing Sol Pierce of Friendship arrive at the fair with one of the first covered wagons they had seen.

Among the outstanding citizens who attended the Plainville School were Jesse Higbee, who became Superintendent of Adams County schools, his son Ed Higbee, who became a judge in La Crosse, and Charles Crosby, Judge of Marathon County.

Later the school was located on the east side of Highway 13 where a fine two room building was built in 1951.

Stafford

Before the Stafford School was organized, in fact, before there was an election of any kind, a sort of private school was taught for a few months each year in the home of Abraham Du Boise Smith, a log cabin built in 1848. It stood on a flat piece of ground above a spring, where the water was said to be pure. Perhaps there was more than one teacher, but old settlers speak only of Julie Van Volkenberg. Each family paid a small amount per child, and the teacher boarded from house to house as part of her salary.

The first school was built in 1858 and burned down about the spring of 1870.

Because the Buckley school burned, that district was dissolved, and the Stafford district received part of the land. In this way several families were added: Keough, Richter, Golden, Moroney, Hayes, Tangney and Gaffney. Due to the increased enrollment, the building built in 1870 was not large enough. Therefore, a new building was constructed. All that could be used of the old building was worked in. Don French, Austin Stowers, and Jerry Tangney helped with construction.

The first teacher was Fannie Crawford. It is believed that she received a salary of $18.00 a month.

The room was equipped with a bench which extended entirely around it, next to the wall. It was there that the children ate their lunch at noon. Homemade desks were provided for the pupils. A homemade table was supplied for the teacher. A long flat wood stove furnished the heat. There were blackboards, probably of painted wood.

The enrollment was, in general, quite large. The average was 42 during the winter term, and 35 during the spring term.

Spelling schools were held, and singing and music lessons were given one evening of each week by Roy MacMillan.

Because the enrollment was so small at the Pleasant View School in 1944, it was decided to close that school and transport the pupils to Stafford. Three years later, this district was attached permanently to the Stafford District.

The school was so named because, at the time the building was erected, the seven Stafford brothers lived in the school district.

Twin Valley

Twin Valley School was so named because two valleys join very close to the point where the school house was built.

The first institution of learning in Twin Valley was a log cabin. In keeping with the trend of the times, a more modern building was then constructed on land leased from Freeman G. Goff, on June 25, 1858, by the following board members: William Ward, P.W. Scott and A.S. Waterman. Adelaide Wheeler Dudley was among the first to teach this school, with a salary of $15.00 per month.

Sixteen seats and desks, each seating two pupils, were made by the carpenters who built the school house, as was also the teacher's desk, which was about six feet long. This was placed on a special platform about six inches above the floor.

There were two doors, through one of which the girls were supposed to enter, and the other one was for the boys. Behind each of these were nails upon which to hang outdoor clothing. A water pail with a tin dipper was also a part of the equipment. Someone would be asked by the teacher to "pass the water" and every pupil drank out of the same dipper. If a pupil left some water in the dipper after quenching his thirst, it was passed to the next pupil. None was wasted because the water had to be carried from a neighbor's well. There was no wash basin of any kind nor any towel. The blackboard was between the two doors, and immediately behind the teacher's desk. A long seat below the blackboard provided a place on which the smaller pupils could stand if they couldn't otherwise reach the board. A "hop stove" which burned logs four foot long furnished the heat.

The ordinary punishment for a mischief maker was confinement under the teacher's desk. As this desk was fully enclosed on the sides next to the school room, the pupils could not see the culprit who was under the desk.

Some of the early textbooks used were: *McGuffey's Readers* and *Spellers*, *Appleton Readers* and *Swinton's History*. These books were purchased by the parents.

The teachers were young people who themselves had completed the work required in a common school, and, as a preparation for teaching, had written an examination on school subjects. To receive a third grade certificate a standing of seventy per cent was required. Those who received higher grades were given first and second grade certificates.

The average enrollment, according to the early registers beginning the year 1870, was about twenty pupils. Some of the early families in attendance were: Waterman, Johnson, Willard, Donnelly, Burdick, Elderkin, Goffe, Bacon, Cook and Chamberlain.

Exhibitions were held boasting a stage and costumes for the actors. Spelling bees were also a form of entertainment. Henry Reynolds and Charlotte Waterman Bullis were noted spellers. Quilting bees were not uncommon social affairs. A Christmas program was given in 1888. There was a Christmas tree, with George Reynolds acting as Santa Claus.

Religious services were held in the school house almost every Sunday. Itinerant ministers were: Rev. North, Rev. Yokum, Mr. Reynolds and William Irish. Hugh Donnelly, Sr. also conducted funerals at times. Revival meetings were held there, too.

On September 14, 1894, a tornado destroyed the school building. This was a very narrow storm path-not more than ten rods wide. It came during the school term; Bertha Goffe Thurber was the teacher. The storm was showing in the west at the time school was out. At first the teacher thought she would keep the children until after the storm, but decided that most of them could get home before it would strike. She let them start for home, instructing them, that if the storm overtook them, to go into the first house they could get to. She, too, hurried home. Providence must have influenced her to vacate the school house; if anyone had remained he would have been killed. The tornado swept the walls across the floor of the school house, after moving the building about ten feet with a twisting motion. There was nothing left on the floor but the iron bases of the seats, broken about one inch from the floor, with three screws holding each one.

After a forced vacation of about two weeks, school duties were resumed in the Chamberlain house. The partitions were removed, and long benches and tables were constructed.

After three special meetings held at the Goffe home, it was decided to construct a new building. The district borrowed $700.00 from Adolph Rothe of Kilbourn. The contract was let to Don French for the same amount and construction started at once. Among others who helped in this work were Austin Stowers, Harry Hinman and Elmer Bacon. Some of these men boarded in the Ned Wood home. The district had a bee to help haul lumber and stone. The stone came from Fisher's Bluff.

Two dances were given in the school house: one on Christmas night, and the other on New Year's Eve, 1895. A sum of $50.00 was realized from these dances. With this money the school bell was purchased from Montgomery Ward & Co. Blackboards were also bought with a part of the money. New desks and books were purchased from L.A. Murray of Kilbourn.

On January 2, 1895, Anna Bacon with twenty five pupils, began school in the new building. It could claim as former pupils: George Reynolds, who became county superintendent of schools; Murray Hay, since governor of the State of Washington; Glen Wood, who has been a member of the county board for a number of years; and T.W. Donnelly, who served as state senator in Arizona for a number of years. In 1941 the Town Line and Point Bluff school districts were annexed to this district.

Ward

The Old Ward School was founded shortly after the country was settled during the early 1850s.

The school was named after the original owner of the land, Samuel Ward, who purchased the land from the state, this having been Section 16, and known as a school section.

The enrollment has varied somewhat from year to year, but has always been above the average for country schools. For many years this was a two-room school, and enrollment was as high as eighty pupils.

D.M. Hatch was one of the very earliest teachers. He was very efficient, an old type who believed that a good whip was one of the greatest aids to education, and who used it accordingly.

Mr. and Mrs. Harrison Churchill taught the upper and lower rooms for many years, at the time when it was a two-room school; they contributed much to the good citizenship of many who went out into the world from it.

In early days church services were held in the school building, as a church had not yet been built. Many local activities centered around the school, including P.T.A.

A "Souvenir of Your School Year" presented to her students by Ward School teacher Hazel D. Marshall, 1931 and (below) the Ward School building.

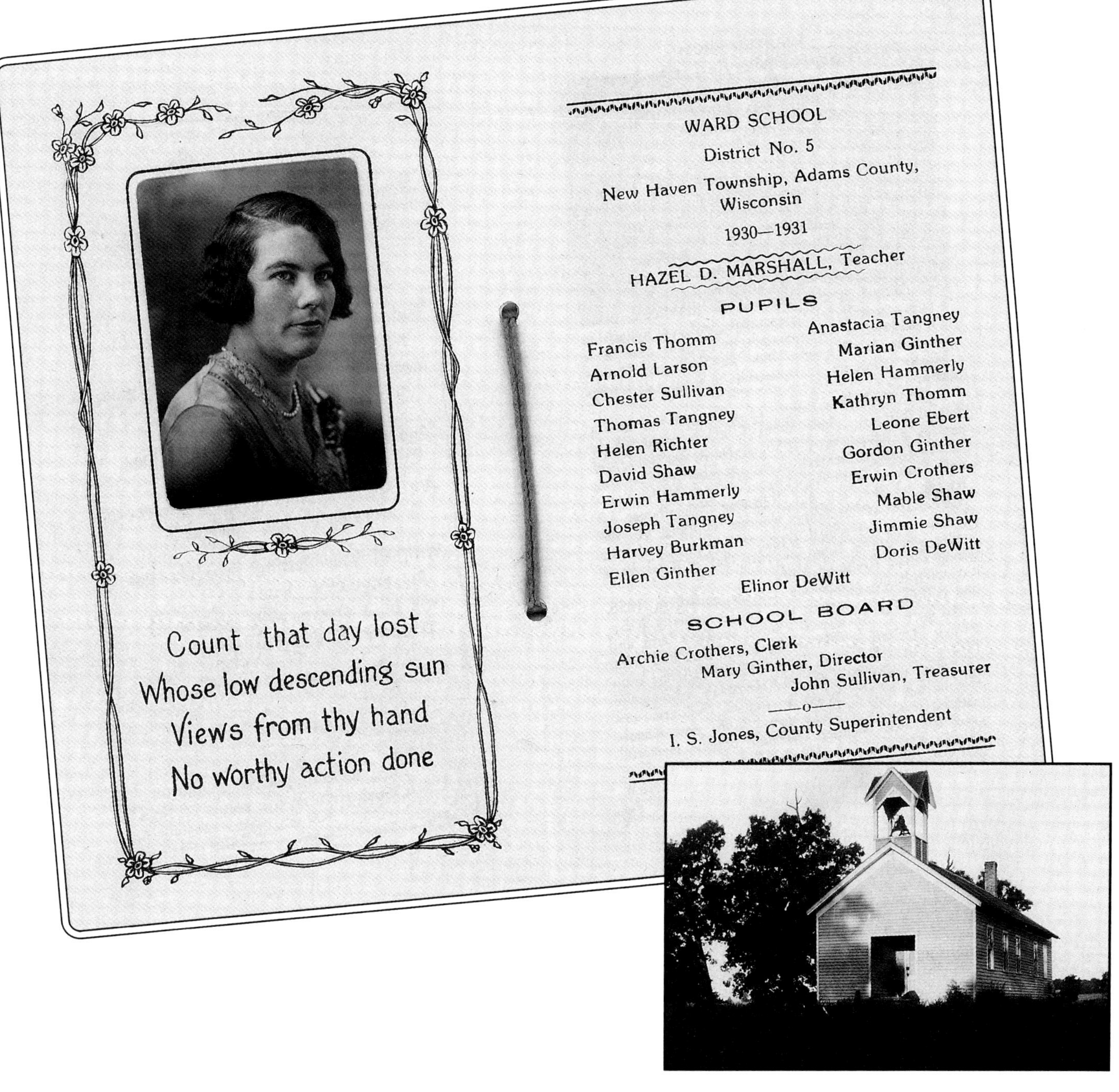

Count that day lost
Whose low descending sun
Views from thy hand
No worthy action done

WARD SCHOOL
District No. 5
New Haven Township, Adams County, Wisconsin
1930—1931
HAZEL D. MARSHALL, Teacher

PUPILS

Francis Thomm	Anastacia Tangney
Arnold Larson	Marian Ginther
Chester Sullivan	Helen Hammerly
Thomas Tangney	Kathryn Thomm
Helen Richter	Leone Ebert
David Shaw	Gordon Ginther
Erwin Hammerly	Erwin Crothers
Joseph Tangney	Mable Shaw
Harvey Burkman	Jimmie Shaw
Ellen Ginther	Doris DeWitt

Elinor DeWitt

SCHOOL BOARD
Archie Crothers, Clerk
Mary Ginther, Director
John Sullivan, Treasurer
—o—
I. S. Jones, County Superintendent

Community Churches

Newport Evangelical Lutheran Church

Originally known as Moe Settlement, the town of Newport area was settled in 1849 by several Norwegian families. Swen Toralson, who was from Moe Parish in Norway, was the first to locate in the community.

The first service in Moe Settlement, on September 11, 1851, was held at Jacob Thompson's log house, about a mile south of the present church.

Rev. Herman Amberg Preus had arrived at Spring Prairie, Columbia County, from Norway. Less than a month after his arrival in 1851, he agreed to help organize the new congregation at the settlers invitation. Rev. Preus also served several other congregations, coming to this area only four or five times a year. In the beginning, services were held in log homes or schools and people often had to stand outside. He served the Newport congregation until 1865.

People in Lewiston Township also asked Pastor Preus to serve them and St. Paul's was organized in October, 1851. Services were held in homes and later at the Oak Grove School. The church was dedicated in August, 1873 and remodeling done in 1953.

Rev. Sturk S. Reque was the second pastor to bring the word to the Newport Congregation. He also had congregations at Roche-A-Cri, Lemonweir and Lewiston. He stayed until 1871 when he was called to Spring Grove, Minnesota.

By 1890 there were approximately 70 families enrolled in the Newport Congregation. They worshipped in the little old church until 1892, when the distance to the church had become too much for many of them. Some 30 families left the congregation and organized the Upper Newport and New Haven Norwegian Evangelical Lutheran Congregation. Thus the parish was divided and two new churches built.

The new Newport church was dedicated in October of 1892, and remodeling and an addition were completed in 1968.

The Rev. E. Smukal served the congregation from May 13, 1922 until 1954. It was during his pastorate that the church celebrated its centennial anniversary.

In total, Newport Lutheran Church has been served by 17 pastors since its organization in 1851.

Saint Cecelia's Church and School

In the years following early settlement of the area that would become Kilbourn, it became more and more evident that the rapidly increasing number of Catholics needed a church.

In 1851, Father Anthony D. Godhardt came to the area from Fort Winnebago (Portage) and organized a Catholic parish. After him Father Gardner, Father Stele, Father Montague and others, came and administered to the spiritual requirements of area Catholics. Mass was often celebrated in the homes of many families and sometimes outside.

In 1851 the parish was known as St. Simon the Apostle; in 1855, as the Exaltations of the Holy Cross. In 1866, Father George Strickner became the pastor of Kilbourn City, and during his pastorate planned the erection of a Church, which his successor, Rev. Father Reindle, carried into effect.

The church, built on the corner of Bowman Road and Wisconsin Avenue, was dedicated to St. Cecilia in 1868. The parish was a mission of Lyndon Station and later of Portage, and the Pastor was Fr. Thomas Keenan. In July 1871, St. Cecilia received its first resident pastor, Father William De Kelver, and during his pastorate the rectory was built. Father De Kelver remained pastor until 1873, and then came the Rev. Fathers Gallweiler, Gonthyn, Scholter, Hackle, John Ryan, Henry Siner and William Rice.

On January 20, 1882, the Rev. Martin Smits took charge of the parish and remained until he died on February 27, 1897. His successor was Father John Holzknecht, who planned a new church and school. On July 4, 1902, the cornerstone of the new St. Cecilia's Church was laid at Oak Street and Minnesota Avenue.

The Dells Reporter, July 10, 1902 edition reported the following: "the greatest attraction of this Fourth of July Celebration was the laying of the cornerstone of the new Saint Cecilia's Church; the ceremony by Rev. Fr. O'Brien of Green Bay, delegated by the Bishop, beginning at ten o'clock, assisted by Father Kolbe, who was the pastor at this time. The hundreds who witnessed this step in God's cause bowed their heads in deep reverence, and truly all who gathered about the foundation of this beautiful structure in progress were brought more within God's teaching, and the reverence bestowed upon the faces of the innocent and all alike during these services must have been an hour

Previous page: *The Newport Evangelical Lutheran Church, built in 1871. The church cemetery nearby offers a grim reminder of the rigors of pioneer life. As reported in the Ministerial Book, 69 people were buried in the cemetery between 1849 and 1867. Of that number, no more than 4 people were older than age 60 when they died. While at the other end of the scale, 29 of the 69 graves in the Norwegian Lutheran Cemetery were dug for children who died before they reached age 5. (Courtesy, H. H. Bennett Studio Foundation)*

The first St. Cecilia church (above), built on Bowman Road and Wisconsin Avenue in 1868. (right) The pre-Vatican II main altar at St. Cecilia's.

of rejoicing to the angel in Heaven as they looked down with Heavenly love upon the Scene."

The beautiful blessing of the bell ceremony was held on August 12, 1902, and the joyful tolling of St. Cecilia's 2,200 pound bells was heard as Bishop Fox of Green Bay explained the significance and the meaning of the ceremony.

The Church was completed and the Catholic population increased, and on June 22, 1903, the church was officially dedicated. The old church was torn down that year.

The beautiful main altar and the two side altars were acknowledged as the gifts of Mrs. Thomas Sexton of Chicago, and her sons Thomas and Joseph Sexton. The stained glass windows were also gifts by or in memory of Mrs. D. M. McManman, Martha and James Baggott, Thomas and Margaret Breshnahan, John and Catherine Lynch, Mr. and Mrs. William Stanton, Julia and John Hiles, Charles Krieger, Tim O'Connell, and Patrick Baggot. The Stations of the Cross of the new church were subsequently donated by charitable persons. Much of the work of that went into building the new church was done by parishioners.

Through the persistent efforts of many people, the church and property went from a $600 investment in 1859 to about $3,000 property value in 1871, when a new parsonage was built at the cost of $1,600. The 1902 Church cost over $20,000 and today with the new school and improvement to the Church and Parsonage, St. Cecilia's has a total value of over $500,000.

In succession, the priests who have served this community were: Father DeBauck, Fr. Otto Kolby,

Fr. Bournmeyer, Fr. Nicholas Hannert, Fr. William Gensler, Fr. Thomas Riordan, Fr. Henry Novotny, Fr. Sylvester Van Berket, Fr. Timothy O'Keefe, and Fr. L. F. Strofer. The Rt. Rev. Msgr. Jerome Hastrich became the administrator of the parish until June 13, 1958, when Fr. Joseph A. Dreis was appointed the Pastor. Father Hoffelder and Father Grubba followed, and currently the parish is served by Father Cassidy.

During the pastorate of Fr. Dreis, St. Cecilia's School became a reality. The school was opened in September, 1963, staffed by the Dominican Sisters of Sinsinawa. Due to lack of finances, the school was closed in June, 1973. The building was rented by the Wisconsin Dells School District until the fall of 1991. At that time the Jack Van Wie Day Care Center was opened in the building.

Through the efforts of Fr. L. F. Stofer, the beautiful Shrine "Our Lady of the Dells" was dedicated on August 28, 1955. In June, 1973 St. Cecilia's Church was struck by lightning, and considerable repairs were made before the church could be reopened.

Father Kevin Cassidy has been pastor since 1977.

St. Mary's, Briggsville

The parish of St. Mary's Briggsville, also known as the Irish Parish, was established by the Green Bay Diocese in 1851. Priests met occasionally at homes until 1857, when Father Doyle came and the first church was erected. Doyle continued to serve the parish for five years.

The first church records are of two baptisms, one in 1875 and one in 1877, and were followed in the 1880's by a long list of Irish infants. Some members came from as far as Friendship to worship. The church and rectory were enlarged in 1883 and 1884. In 1896 the congregation had 300 members.

On May 30, 1924, the church and rectory were burned and very little could be saved. The public school was used for services that summer, and then the building which is the present post office was used. With the help of Hilliard Construction, parishioners built a new church on the basement of the old one. The land for the church was donated by Mr. Briggs who gave them two lots as well a two acre burial site at a small fee.

In 1946 the Diocese of Madison was established with Briggsville in its territory.

Through the efforts of Father I. C. Wiltzius, the Shrine of St. Philomena was established in 1948. The structure was a gift of Mrs. Thomas Flynn and friends and dedicated to the memory of Mr. and Mrs. H. Briggs and Thomas Flynn. Father Wiltzius himself donated the Italian carrera marble statue of St. Philomena.

There have been many improvements over the years. St. Mary's is greatly blessed in having four priest sons, as well as one daughter who is a nun. The priests are Father Leo A. Joyce, Father Francis J. Schmidt, Father Dale Grubba, and Father James H. Murphy, and the nun is Sister Kathleen Murphy, the only sister of Father Murphy.

The original St. Mary's, Briggsville, which was destroyed by fire in 1924.

The United Presbyterian Church

On June 29, 1855, thirteen people who had been meeting for worship in Newport and Delton petitioned the Presbytery of Winnebago to constitute a Presbyterian Church.

On Saturday, July 7, 1855 organizational meetings were held in Delton and Newport and a new organization formed–the First Presbyterian Church of Newport and Delton.

The Rev. Stewart Mitchell was the first pastor and for a few years the meetings were held in private homes. On August 23, 1857 a small church building was dedicated.

On January 21, 1863 the officers met and decided to try to build a place of worship. They applied for and received through Presbytery a loan of $200. Alanson Holly gave the lot on which to build the church and a lady from Milwaukee, Mrs. Harriet T. Smith, furnished some of the means to buy the lumber. A frame building was erected; 55x25 with 16 foot posts. The cost was $1460.54.

In 1865 a parochial school was organized. A teacher was hired to teach 15 scholars. The

The First Presbyterian church, Kilbourn, built in 1863.

Catechism was taught daily and the school was to remain open on condition of financial help from Presbytery.

On October 1, 1866 the name was changed to the First Presbyterian Church of Kilbourn City. In 1877, a small Congregational church in the city was dissolved and its 17 members united with the Presbyterian church.

By 1889, the congregation was having a hard time raising enough money to pay the minister's salary. They decided to canvass the village and $60 was raised in this way. Because of the financial difficulties they decided that it was best for the minister to resign.

In September of 1900 the Rev. Charles L. Richards was installed but, in 1905, the church was closed for lack of funds. Through the efforts of Charles W. Snider (who was not a church member), Harry Corning, Thomas Coon and Adam Dixon, the church was re-opened.

On January 17, 1906 a motion was made by C.W. Snider that a call be extended to the Rev. George H. Marsh at a salary of $800 a year. During his pastorate a fine new manse was built on the lot next to the church. With Mrs. Adolph Rothe (not a church member) as president, the Ladies Aid assumed financial responsibility for building the manse. It was a house of which they could be justly proud.

The church family has always been fortunate in having fine musical talent among its members. At

Reverend Joseph W. Davies

In 1927 Rev. J.W. Davies came to the Dells to serve as temporary minister of the Presbyterian Church. He had planned to go west, but ended up in Wisconsin Dells for the next 38 years.

Reverend Davies was born in Rhosymedre, North Wales in 1883. He was educated at the University of London and received his theological training in Manchester. In 1912 he came to America and his first parish was at Cottage Grove.

He was described by those who knew him as a 5'3" tall Welshman with a great capacity for love, and a nice word or interesting story for everyone he met. No one was turned away from his door without food, money, or a kind word. From his back porch he fed birds, squirrels and stray dogs and cats.

Rev. Davies was instrumental in organizing the first Boy Scout troop in Wisconsin Dells. He was a 38 year member and past president of the Kiwanis Club, a member of the public library board, a member of the Columbia Masonic Lodge in Wisconsin Dells and served on many civic and community committees.

He was married in 1912 to Anne Ward of Driffield, Manchester, England. They had one daughter, Marjorie, who became librarian at Kilbourn Public Library and continued until her retirement. Mrs. Davies passed away in 1944.

He retired January 1, 1963, but his retirement was short. He became ill and never fully recovered. He passed away on May 19, 1965.

A fountain in his honor stands in Bowman Park today, a memorial to a man whose memory will live in the hearts of everyone who called him friend. He was nicknamed in a poem by Captain Don Saunders "Shepherd of the Dells".

this time there was more than one choir in the church, and they put on two operettas to raise money to help pay off the mortgage on the manse. These operettas were directed by Mrs. Florence Williams.

Other members of the choir who served for many years: Lora Snider, Edna O'Neil, Nora Dixon, Florence Williams and Sylvia Bauer. These choirs sang at church services and funerals through the years, received no compensation, and even bought their own music.

The financial condition of the church was unstable and on September 28, 1919 Mr. H. A. Bauer called the session to order to consider whether to close or to call a new minister. They must have decided to remain open because in 1920 Rev. Allston was here as minister.

On November 4, 1926 a meeting of the session was called by H. D. Snider to discuss calling a new minister, one who had preached here that week. A motion was made, seconded and carried to call the Rev. J. W. Davies as pastor. The call was signed by James F. Dougherty, secretary. Rev. Davies began his pastorate in January, 1927 and was to continue in this post until January, 1962.

Many interesting events took place during the years and one which seems especially interesting had to do with the church's stained glass windows. They were memorial windows and as many years went by they needed repair. Mr. H. A. Bauer repaired them several times with cement so as to keep out the cold in winter. However in the 1930's they became so bad that the church decided to hire an expert to repair them.

As usual money was scarce, but the Ladies Aid was willing to help the church board. It seems that during the first World War the ladies had bought a Liberty Bond for $100 and put it in a window fund. Mrs. H. D. Snider, who was treasurer of the Ladies Aid, knew of this fund and when money was so badly needed she reminded them of it. The ladies offered it to the Board. Over 22 years later the original $100 had increased to over $1000. They were able to pay the window firm the $800 cash which they asked for the job.

In the late 1940's the old pump organ was replaced by a Hammond electric given by Mr. and Mrs. Fred Richter. In 1967 a larger Hammond organ was bought by Mr. D. C. Van Wie and given in memory of his wife, Clarine.

During the late 1950's the officers realized that more room was needed to carry on the church work effectively, and after much discussion, decided to build a new church. Davies Educational Hall, dedicated and named for the present pastor, came first and was dedicated on February 16, 1958. On June 12, 1960 the sanctuary was dedicated.

On December 30, 1962, the Rev. J. W. Davies retired after having served the local church for 36 years. He passed away in 1966. In 1970, the bell tower was erected in his memory.

A complete list of the pastors is as follows: Rev. Stewart Mitchell, 1855-1864; Rev. Willis B. Phelps, 1864-1870; Rev. George F. Hunting, 1870-1876; Rev. J. V. Hughes, 1878-1883; Rev. D. E. Evans, 1883-1887; Rev. Archibald Durrie, 1887-1889; Rev. A. Guliek, 1889-1891; Rev. W. J. Turner, 1895-1898; Rev. W. P. McClure, 1898-1900; Rev. Charles L. Richards,1900-1905; Rev. George H. Marsh, 1906-1912; Rev. O. E. DeWitt, 1912-1919; Rev. Allston, 1920-1923; Rev. James A. Melrose, 1924-1926; Rev. J. W. Davies, 1926-1962; Rev. Garry Kamerling, 1962-1970; Rev. Colin Webster, 1970-1974; Rev. Rex Wentzel, 1975-1982; Rev. Ray Bayley (Interim), 1982-1983; Rev. Thomas Lewis 1983-1994; Rev. Steven Keller, 1995-present.

The Dells-Delton United Methodist Church

Prior to becoming the Dells-Delton United Methodist Church we were two congregations: The Lake Delton Methodist Church and the Wisconsin Dells Methodist Church.

First records of the Lake Delton Church date back to 1855, with Delton a part of the Reedsburg-Delton Mission of the Methodist Church. In July, 1855 the mission was divided and the eastern portion became the Delton circuit.

On September 9, 1868, the Methodist Episcopal Church paid $100 for the Baptist Delton Academy property. A parsonage was purchased at

The Kilbourn Methodist Episcopal church, built in 1868.

the same time. In 1900 the Delton circuit was dissolved and Delton was on its own until joining the Kilbourn circuit in 1917. The original Lake Delton Methodist Church still stands and houses an antique mall.

The earliest record of the Methodist denomination in Wisconsin Dells states "The preaching by a Minister of this denomination in Kilbourn Village was in the old schoolhouse, in the spring of 1857, by Rev. William Muller. Another Methodist minister who preached in Kilbourn prior to the Civil War was John M. Springer. He was drafted for duty in the war and named chaplain of his regiment. In action at the Battle of Resaca, both the captain and lieutenant of his company fell, so Springer seized a musket and led the charge. He was soon mortally wounded and carried from the field. Among his last words were, "I have lived what I preached in our nothern home, and die in the favor of God."

The schoolhouse Springer used eventually became too small and various sites were used until a decision was made to build a church. While the church was being built, services were held in the old academy building known as the Kilbourn Institute at the site now occupied by Platt's Garage."

The new Kilbourn Methodist Church held its dedication service on Sunday, January 30, 1868. That same day the Kilbourn Institute burned. In 1932 the church name changed to Wisconsin Dells Methodist Church.

In 1971, a proposal to merge with the Wisconsin Dells congregation was put to vote and accepted. Dells and Delton Episcopal Churches were also merged. The two denominations decided to build one church to serve all congregations, and surplus property was auctioned off November 4, 1972.

The new church was built between the Dells and Lake Delton on the former Maiworm farm, two blocks off highway 12, on county trunk A. Construction began in April of 1971 and was completed in June of 1972. On July 16, 1972 the first Methodist service in the new church was held. Consecration services were held on September 13, 1972.

The joint building program was heralded as a very successful ecumenical venture by both Rev. Alvin Briggs of the United Methodist Church and Father David With of the Episcopal Church, the two pastors involved in the project.

St. Paul's - Holy Cross Episcopal Church

In 1856 the Reverend Hugh Miller Thompson of St. John's Episcopal Church in Portage conducted Kilbourn's first religious service at the local schoolhouse.

Father Thompson, with interested parishioners, established St. Paul's Mission in 1858. He also served Portage, Newport, and in freezing weather drove Bishop Jackson Kemper by sleigh across the icy Wisconsin River to Newport and on to Baraboo, where another mission was established.

From 1860 to 1863 services were conducted by itinerant priests, riding the Milwaukee Road Railroad, and in 1867 the Diocesan Board placed Rev. George Vernor as a railroad missionary conducting services on the first Sunday of the month at St. Paul's Mission, Kilbourn.

As the nation's leading hops market, Kilbourn now had a population of 1500. When the town had outgrown the first schoolhouse, Mary Greenly bought the building for $1,000 and gave it to the church. This building still stands at 810 Elm Street.

Byron Kilbourn gave St. Paul's an adjoining lot. In 1873, St. Paul's was accepted into the diocese and the church was consecrated in 1876. Early families included the John Jackson Browns, Charles Noyes, John Tanner, R. Herren and Thomas Coon.

The first resident priest was Rev. John Pedelupe (1875-77). The church records 27 communicants, with Adam C. Dixon as Warden and John Brown as Treasurer. Father Pedelupe had poor health, was able to serve only occasionally, and the church suffered the loss of several families but was kept alive by the efforts of a few people.

In 1896, Samuel Kerfoot, whose summer home was Dawn Manor, was instrumental in reviving St. Paul's. He contributed and collected money for the restoration of the church and, with the approval of Bishop Nicholson, the building was entirely restored and remodelled. Mr. Kerfoot gave two stained glass windows in memory of Julia Newbold Vibbert and Rev. James DeKoven, for whom DeKoven Foundation is named. The value of the church was now about $1,500.

The Rev. Arthur Gorter took charge in 1897 with 13 confirmed persons, no organist, no choir, no children or young people and an average age of 55 1/2 years.

Several families in Lake Delton established a mission there, and services were conducted beginning on June 25, 1899. Robert McCutcheon, a lay reader studying for the priesthood, was serving St. Paul's and helping the budding congregation in Lake Delton. On July 1, 1903, a lot at 127 Monroe Street was purchased for $15.00. Ground was broken for the church by R.T. McCutcheon and Milo B. Goodall, a stonemason, who later became a priest of the church.

On July 22, 1904, Holy Cross Church at Delton was consecrated at services presided over by Bishop Nicholson. On the fourth Sunday in Advent, 1907, Father McCutcheon was priested at St.

The dedication of the jointly-owned Episcopal–Methodist church in 1972.

Paul's. He also built the rectory at St. Paul's at 812 Elm Street. His Sunday schedule was such: leave on the 9:00 AM train for Mauston, return at 3:00, drive to Delton for services at 4:00 and return to Kilbourn for evening services.

By 1921, Father William Wolfe served Mauston, Tomah, Delton and Kilbourn. In 1929 the Eau Claire diocese was formed and Mauston and Tomah became part of that jurisdiction.

The parish hall was built at Delton in 1930. It was established that the rector of St. John's, Portage, would serve St. Paul's, Kilbourn, and Holy Cross, Delton. The vicar was Rev. Daniel Corrigan, who later became Suffragan Bishop of Colorado. Father Donald C. Means continued this arrangement until 1935 when the priest at Baraboo also served Holy Cross. Father George Schiffmayer served Holy Cross and Trinity, Baraboo until 1956.

Meanwhile, the rector of St. John's, Portage, became the vicar of St. Paul's. In 1956, Trinity in Baraboo requested that their priest serve Trinity only, and Holy Cross had lay readers for two years until Fr. Andrew Laabs became resident vicar, succeeded by Fr. Kenneth Martin, who lived in the newly purchased rectory in Lake Delton after 1960.

When Father Donald Radtke began his charge in 1960, he lived in the rectory in Wisconsin Dells, which had been a parish hall for a few years. No priest had lived in the Dells since 1915 and it had been rented until 1956. He was also serving St. John's, Portage, and talk of a parish hall in the Dells was revived again.

In 1966, Bishop Hallock announced that Portage should be a separate congregation and Holy Cross, Lake Delton and St. Paul's, Wisconsin Dells were to combine as one congregation. The congregations met for six months in one church building and six months in the other. It was obvious that each plant was too small for the doubled congregation. A site between the two towns was purchased, an architect was engaged, and preliminary plans for a new church were made.

By the time Fr. David With became the vicar in 1970, local Episcopalians were moving toward a unique ecumenical adventure. Pastor Al Briggs was minister for the United Methodist congregations in the Dells and Delton and they were also directed to combine. The four congregations, after numerous conferences, decided to build one building for both denominations.

Both clergymen had worked in ecumenical settings, the churches had many traditions in common and savings in building costs and space gained for both would be enormous.

The four congregations formed the non-profit Dells-Delton Building Corporation to govern the use of the building. The cost of the building and upkeep would be shared 50-50. All of the properties owned by the four congregations were sold and property was purchased at the intersection of Highway A and Unity Drive.

By November, 1970, Kenton Peters was chosen as the architect and studies were begun to accommodate the diversity in sizes and traditions of both denominations.

The church was dedicated on September 13, 1972, owned by Holy Cross Episcopal and the United Methodist Churches. The cost to each denomination was $90,000.00. Holy Cross was able to pay its share in full with proceeds from the sale of its buildings and a pre-existing building fund.

The last services in the old churches were the weddings of Holly Severson and Les Pennington at St. Paul's in 1970, and Donna Murray and Greg Georgeson at Holy Cross, Lake Delton in 1971. The first wedding in the new church was that of Linda Hattle and Doug Scott in 1972.

When David With arrived, his charge included directorship of Camp Webb, the diocesan camp in Wautoma. His successor, Bryce Hunt, also directed the camp and bought a home in the Dells.

The congregation has grown dramatically since building the new Holy Cross church, and the concept of moving toward Christian unity is admired.

After Father Hunt left, the parish was yoked once again with St. John's of Portage, and Father Robert Coval assumed both charges in 1986. Len Griffin, a member of this congregation, was ordained a deacon in 1984. A new rectory was purchased at 918 Weber Avenue in 1989.

Iness Waterman Thompson, in her unpublished family biography, c. 1918, about age 16, says, "One evangelist came to the Methodist Church and I sat through one sermon on hell, fire and brimstone. I was with Aunt Lott and Aunt Mate, two the staunchest Methodists in Christendom. I sat between them. The evangelist expounded on all the sins of the young-told of the fearful things that went on at dances, and asked if everyone in the church would stand and promise not to dance. Everyone stood but I sat staunchly in my seat. Aunt Lott and Aunt Mate glared at me but to no avail. I waited for God to strike me dead but he didn't. I knew I was going to dance everytime I had a chance. Anyway, I wanted to see all the sins committed at the dances because I had missed the excitement. That preacher must have known something I didn't. Evidently I wasn't at the dance he was at."

Trinity Lutheran Church

Trinity Evangelical Lutheran Church had its official beginning on April 20, 1918, though Lutheranism at the Dells began many years earlier.

Records show that the Bethlehem Lutheran Church was considering building a church on May 25, 1873, and that members of St. John's Lutheran Church had been worshiping for at least five years previous to 1918 under Pastor Wachholz.

Under the guidance of Rev. William Lochner, St. John's and Bethlehem joined together to form Trinity Lutheran Church.

Those present at the first meeting signed the constitution submitted by Rev. Lochner and 24 additional signatures were gathered by June. A property at 618 Washington Avenue came under the ownership of this new congregation.

Reverend Lochner served as the pastor of this new church and in October, 1919, the congregation approved a request for Pastor Lochner to serve the Norwegian Lutheran congregations at Newport, New Haven and Lewiston in connection with his duties at Trinity. Free use of the Norwegian parsonage was offered.

In January, 1921, Mr. Henry Tofson was elected chairman of the congregation and held the office for 21 years. In 1922, Pastor Lochner accepted a call to Immanuel Lutheran Church in Madison, Wisconsin.

Rev. Ewald Smukal of Muscoda, Wisconsin became the second pastor of Trinity. During his years of ministry, Reverend Smukal served five congregations. Along with Trinity of Wisconsin Dells, he served Newport, Lewiston, New Haven and also Lyndon Station which was organized in 1924.

By April 1931, church members favored the building of a new church, but not until August, 1938 were two lots on Church Street purchased for $1200 as a building site.

Ground breaking ceremonies for the new church took place on Mothers Day, May 14, 1950. On September 17, the cornerstone was laid. In December, 1951, the congregation met for the last scheduled service in the old church and dedication services were held at the new church.

After 30 years of faithful service, Pastor Smukal passed away and was buried on September 14, 1953. Pastor Fred Weber of LaValle accepted the call and was installed January 10, 1954.

In November, 1954, St. Lukes of Lyndon Station and Dells Trinity formed a dual parish. A parsonage was constructed at Bauer and Church Streets and was dedicated December 19, 1954. During 1955 many furnishings were installed in the church through memorials and gifts. The carpet was presented as a gift from the Ladies Aid, and many individual gifts made possible the altar, lectern, pulpit, pews and so forth.

The erection of an education building was approved by the voters in April, 1956 and in October, 1957, the new building was dedicated. On February 11, 1958, the voters assembly resolved to establish a Christian Day School.

Other pastors who have served the parish through the years include Reverend William Scheer from Burt, Iowa 1966-75, Reverend Leonard Thalacker, 1975, and Reverend Harold T. Steltzer from Elk Creek, Iowa, 1975-present.

The dual parish ministry of Wisconsin Dells Trinity and St. Lukes of Lyndon Station was dissolved in April, 1975.

Indian Baptist Church

The Indian Baptist Church is located 3 miles northwest of Wisconsin Dells on Hwy 12 in Lyndon Township. It was organized in 1933, the same year that Hwy 12 was built through Rocky Arbor State Park. It is believed that the church was also built that year.

Indian Baptist did, however, have an earlier beginning. It was located on Illinois Avenue near the City's pumphouse, and was known as the "wigwam" church.

The first pastor was Reverend S.R. Dunlop and some of the charter members were: Albert Yellow Thunder, Susie Redhorn, Melvin & Lucy Miner, Flora and Ray Goodbear, Tom and Grace Little Bear, Marie Kingswan Sheeka and Ed Decorah.

Although some white people, including Sarah Curry and Dolly Blood had been attending regularly, it was not until April 25, 1944 that a vote was taken which allowed white persons to formerly become members.

The most recent pastor is the Reverend Norman Miller.

The second Trinity Lutheran church, built in 1951.

Pastor S. R. Dunlop and his wife at the Indian Baptist church, c. 1950.

The Briggsville United Methodist church.

The Briggsville United Methodist Church

Reverend Joseph Franklin Bacon of Adams County organized a Universalist Society in Briggsville in the 1870s. The Society began building its first church in 1873, but it was destroyed by a tornado before it could be completed. Although the church was rebuilt, the small Society was unable to hold up under its discouraging financial situation. Lydia Briggs Atwood tirelessly fought to bring the Methodist Episcopal Church into the area. She wrote and received a volume of letters in regards to her pursuit, most of which are still held by the Briggsville United Methodist Church. By 1890 the congregation had organized and purchased the Universalist Church for the sum of $700. The land was deeded by the James A. Briggs family for $1.

A parsonage, originally valued at $1100, was erected in Briggsville in 1894 during the pastorate of Reverend H.B. Brennaman.

Twenty-eight members of the Briggsville Methodist Church formally chartered the organization in 1898. Family names included: Briggs, Blont, Brenzel, Beardsly, Clark, Douglas, Gray, Hickather, Kimball, Michaels, Mason, Richards, Stowell, Smith, Tanner, Waldo and Wood. The following Sunday schedule was given: Sunday School, 1:30 PM; Church Service, 2:30 PM; Epworth League, 7:30 PM; and Tuesday Prayer Meeting was held at 2:30 PM.

A horse barn was built in 1898 and converted into a garage in 1934. In May 1929, the church dedicated a Sunday school, built at a cost of $2500.

Continued improvements and additions were made during the pastorates of Rev. W.W. Moore, and Rev. Philip Burt. A new parsonage was purchased in 1970 which served as a home for the pastor of the Briggsville United Methodist Church, Moundville United Methodist Church and the Trinity United Church of Christ, Endeavor.

In 1940, under the pastoral leadership of Rev. L.L. Litchfield, Briggsville formally consolidated with the Endeavor and Moundview Churches to form an active parish.

In the great Methodist tradition, Briggsville Methodist women's groups have a strong history. Organized in 1896, the Briggsville women divided into two groups: the IOKA Circle and the Friendly Circle. With the merger of the Evangelical United Brethren and Methodist Denominations, the name "United Methodist Women" was adopted.

During September through May, the church school program is a strong part of the church's weekly ministry. Summer worship attracts many visiting campers who use area campgrounds. Programming throughout the year centers on adult education, family participation within the life of the church, and ministry to persons of the local community.

Big Spring Congregational Church

In June of 1866, residents in the small village of Big Spring began to hold community meetings in the log homes of settlers. Business meetings were opened and closed with prayers. On Sundays, Reverend Bridgeman conducted regular services and Sunday school was held.

Soon the congregation that developed voted to name themselves the Ecclesiastical Society. They adopted a strict constitution which outlined member requirements such as strict observation of the Sabbath Day, daily family worship, and abstention from all intoxicating drinks as beverages. When a member broke these rules, a special meeting was held and the erring member was promptly dismissed from the Society. With a formal request to reunite and a promise to abide by the rules, the member might later be readmitted.

Original members included E. Seaward, P.R. Staples, R.A. Peck, G. Wilbur, Lana Keith, Sarah Staples, T. Seward, Martha Peck, A. Keith, and J. Wilbur.

By 1867, the Society had gained many new members and had joined with Briggsville in order to hire a minister who could serve both areas. Reverend Bridgeman left the Society and was replaced by Rev. J.M. Hayes of West Salem, whose salary was $232.50 per year. Often services were held and new members received at the Ward and other area schools. In 1871 the name was changed to Big Spring Congregational Society.

In 1874 the Society voted to build a church together with the F.W. Baptist Society. John Stowell donated land for the church, and local farmers brought stones for the basement. Men traveled to Kilbourn and brought back the needed lumber using horse and oxen. Area Indians took a great interest in the building and were reportedly of great help. Kerosene lamps hung from the ceiling and the seats were all handmade. Use of the church was divided equally between the Congregationalists and the Baptists, with both agreeing to give up their time should the other have a wedding or a funeral.

In 1880, members voted to erect a parsonage across the highway from the church, on two acres of land purchased from S.S. Landt. 15 cent chicken dinners and ice cream socials helped raise money for this endeavor.

After 1891, the church was united with the Davis Corners and Jackson Churches, and all three would contribute to the salary of a minister to serve this entire circuit.

In 1905, the church hired its first and only female minister, a Mrs. Christie, who was from England. She served the parish until 1909.

Eventually, the Baptist and Congregational churches began to disagree. By 1912, the original church building and grounds were sold to S.B. Strader for $60 and the money turned over to the Baptist Society. Now the church belonged solely to Big Spring.

In 1934 the parsonage was sold to Clarence Armson with the stipulation that alcohol never be sold on its grounds. The money was used for maintenance of the church and church grounds. In 1951, the original oak heaters in the church were replaced by a coal burner.

The Big Spring Cemetery is located about a quarter mile east of the church, where more than 50 area soldiers have been laid to rest since the Civil War.

Other ministers who have served the Big Spring Congregational Church include Rev. Campbell, Rev. Hicks, Rev. Moulton, Rev. Pope, Rev. Brown, Rev. Heberlein, Rev. Hadden, Rev. Rawson, Rev. Chase, Rev. Helms, Rev. Christie, Rev. Haywood, Rev. O'Neil, Rev. Luke, Rev. Dewitte, Rev. Wilcox, Rev. Forester, Rev. Austin, Rev. Veith, Rev. Shannon, Rev. Flora, Rev. Wicks, Rev. Davies, Rev. King, Rev. Adams, and Rev. Barton.

Bethany Lutheran Church

Late in 1938 Reverend Dwight H. Shelhart, Synodical Missionary for the English Evangelical Synod of the Northwest, was called to Wisconsin Dells to work for the United Lutheran Church.

The Big Spring Congregational church, built in 1874.

The first meeting of interested people was held at the A.O. Anderson home. Other meetings followed in the Johnson and Jacobson homes. There was enough interest that the Episcopal Church on Elm Street was rented and the first services held on April 23, 1939, with 55 people in attendance. A Sunday School was organized the following June.

By October the congregation was formally organized and named Bethany English Evangelical Lutheran Church of Wisconsin Dells. The first church council was installed and 108 members were formally received, confirmed or baptized.

In December, 1941 a lot was purchased in the 600 block of Broadway as a future church site. In 1942, the church relocated to Borcher's Hall. In October, 1943, the contents of the church and Sunday school rooms were destroyed by fire. Services were then held in the City Auditorium until the following June.

On June 5, 1949, the cornerstone of the new church was officially laid and the first service held. The Dedication was held on December 4, 1949.

Ground breaking services for the erection of an educational wing were observed on September 15, 1968.

The following pastors have served the church: Dwight H. Shelhart, through 1940; John P. Shannon, 1940-1942; George R. Flora, 1942-1944; George W. Genszler, 1944-1951; Robert L. Bartsch, 1952-1954; John Schultz, 1955-1958; Robert E. Gartz, 1959-1965; Richard C. Mohl, 1965-1974; Paul E. Peterson, 1975-1989; John Krueger, 1990-present.

"Wisconsin's Most Popular Vacation Spot"

Boat Trips Through The Dells

It can be no exaggeration to claim that the Dells is one of the oldest resort areas in the state. Kilbourn was not a year old on March 25, 1856, when *Wisconsin Mirror* editor Alanson Holly wrote in an article that, "We conclude that the wild, romantic scenery of the 'Dells' will always make them a place of resort for seekers of pleasure." At that time, the city consisted of eleven dwellings and one business building housing the printing office.

In the September 23rd issue of the same year, we find the following news item, "Pleasure seekers will be interested in the advertisement of Leroy Gates who is prepared to show them all the beauties and wonders of the Dells." Gates was the "standing pilot" at the Dell Bridge whose services as a raft pilot through the Dells were apparently required in times of dangerously high water. This evidently left him time for other enterprises. Undiscouraged by the fact that it was already September, he advertises,

"*For Recreation Resort to the Dells! Where depressed spirits can be alleviated, gloom and melancholy soon be dispelled and the mind become Greatly invigorated. Leroy Gates has purchased a pleasure Boat for the purpose of penetrating the numerous occult caves of the Dells.*"

This surely was a rowboat and there is nothing to show how many passengers were shown through those "occult caves" by Mr. Gates.

Those early trips probably explored Boat Cave, Skylight Cave, Rood's Glen and other inlets. Cold Water Canyon was blocked by fallen logs, Witches Gulch was also unnamed and unexplored. Stand Rock was very seldom seen except by land and Arch Cove was probably the upstream end of the trip.

By March 10th of the following year, the railroad was advertising the Dells in the *Wisconsin Mirror*. The bridge across the river here was not yet finished. In the *Wisconsin Mirror* of August 14, 1874, Captain Kingsbury tells of the first steamboat to pass through the Dells in 1844. Kingsbury was engaged as pilot for *The Maid of Iowa* from Nauvoo on the Mississippi to Pointe Basse on the Wisconsin River. He carried passengers and freight and made stops at Galena, Illinois; Prairie du Chein; Shot Tower [Helena]; Sauk [City]; and Fort Winnebago [Portage]. The boat arrived at the Elbow of the Dalles about 2:00 PM.

"A great deal of argument ensued among the officers of the boat as to the best means of getting through the Dalles as it was feared the feat could not be accomplished safely. For steering, an oar after the manner of those used upon rafts was used without success. It was then decided that the passengers and crew should go ashore with ropes on each side to assist in pulling her through the Narrows. Everything being in readiness, with the help about equally divided on either bank, under command of Andrew Dunn, the engineer, was instructed to 'put on steam' when the boat walked along up the stream, leaving those on shore looking after her in astonishment. She went on to the head of the Dalles where she lay up for those left behind. Those parties had a laborious task in making the three miles by land. They would explore every ravine to the river, only to find they must go further upstream. After some three hours they succeeded in reaching the boat. The steamer then proceeded on her way, landing for the night at or near the mouth of White Creek. The *Maid of Iowa* was a full-rigged side wheel Mississippi river boat. She was 130 feet long, 20 foot beam and 30 feet over her guards, drawing light, about 16 inches of water. Her engines were 14 inch cylinder with a 4 foot stroke. She had 40" boilers."

The *Maid of Iowa* never made another trip through the Dells. Later, the steamboat *Enterprise* made some trips to Pointe Basse but seemed to have no regular schedule. Perhaps the changing water levels and shifting sandbars made commercial freighting by steamboat unprofitable.

In 1865, Henry H. Bennett returned home from the Civil War with a wounded right hand and no doubt felt his days as a carpenter were over. He learned the new science of photography from his uncle and brother and bought out the gallery business of Leroy Gates. Stereoscopic views were at the height of their popularity and so, leaving his wife to take care of the portrait business, Bennett spent all the time he could photographing the distinctive scenery of the Dells and Devil's Lake. Americans were endlessly curious about the country which they had never seen and now could be captured on an inexpensive photograph. As Bennett's views were circulated through his Studio and traveling agents, more visitors arrived by train to see the Dells for themselves.

Records are sketchy during the Civil War as there was no newspaper in Kilbourn. When the

Previous page: *The steamer* Alexander Mitchell *at the entrance to Witches Gulch, c. 1880. The Mitchell was named after the president of the Milwaukee Road railroad, the first major promoter of tourism at the Dells. (Courtesy, H. H. Bennett Studio Foundation)*

The first river guides used rowboats to carry visitors on Dells tours. The boats were powered by long "sweeps" or oars and designed to carry a full load of passengers, yet move easily through the water. Steamboats usually towed a string of rowboats to carry visitors where the river was too shallow for steam navigation.

paper resumed publication, tourists were evidently coming to the Dells, for Ribbenack and Lintner of the Tanner House in 1869 were said to have a two-seated buggy and a large rowboat to take hotel guests by carriage to the head of the Dells and return by boat. In August of that year, the paper printed an article about the Dells which included the following interesting comments. "Most visitors do not stay long enough to go to all the points because carriages cannot go among the ravines and none but the healthy have the courage to penetrate the depths or climb their height.....There is nothing more pleasant or health inspiring than to take a row boat on a good day and row up and down the river viewing the long rows of flowers of various colors that ornament the seams of the perpendicular rocks, noticing the shrubs and even trees that grow out of these rocks." The writer also suggested the Dells as a health resort. Later that autumn, he urged the use of a steamboat for sight seeing in the Dells. No steamboat materialized for a few years and people who wished to see the Dells took a rowboat or walked along the banks.

In July, 1870, "a party of students from Beloit College, including a gentlemen from Turkey, walked from Beloit." It was reported that they "saw the secluded falls at the head of the Dells." The story is told that H.H. Bennett, looking for more scenes to photograph, had walked up the ravine from the river and found his way blocked by the waterfalls in Witches Gulch. The following winter he skated up the river, cut steps in the ice over the falls and so was able to traverse the length of the Gulch, probably the first man to do so. He found the gorge so beautiful that in 1875, he and Captain Bell built walks through it, making it a regular stop for the steamers rather than stopping at Arch Cove on the opposite side of the river. A Mrs. Davis was said to be the first lady to visit the Devil's Jug in Cold Water Canyon. Quite a feat for anyone in those days before walkways were built. None but the agile could climb over all the fallen trees and wade the brook.

In April, 1873, the local paper advertised, "Captain Chickering will be prepared to furnish pleasure boats for all parties desiring to visit the Dells during the coming season. The Messrs Drinker have a half dozen new boats and, with those on hand, there will be at least fifteen good craft ready for use in a few days." These were rowboats, of course.

In June, 1873, the *Wisconsin Mirror* announced the arrival of the long-awaited steamboat. "Hurrah for the steamer and jolly excursions through the Dells! Captain Wood of Quincy, Wisconsin arrived at Drinker's Landing just above the dam (present site of the River Inn) on Wednesday with a Steamboat. Its advent was entirely unexpected......The boat is about 50 feet long and 20 feet wide and has a 6 to 8 horsepower engine. It is a side wheel craft built originally for a ferry boat. The Captain proposed making the experiment of running the Dells and, if successful, will probably fit it up in good shape for a pleasure boat." Captain Wood named his boat the *Modocawanda*.

Evidently, tourists were arriving in greater numbers every year as, in a few weeks, another steamer was shipped here by rail from Madison. Its original name was *Lake City* but its owner, Captain Bell, reconstructed it and named it the *Dell Queen*. Bell was also a raft pilot and was well acquainted with the currents, eddies and sand bars of the river.

From that time, there were always at least two steamboats in the Dells and occasional price wars. Someone said there was always competition in the area as soon as there were ten people in town. Rowboats were also in use for sight-seeing until the early 1900s. A rowboat and guide to row it could be hired for the round trip through the Upper Dells, or for a still pleasanter day's outing, tourists could ride up the river as far as Witches Gulch on one of the steamers, and then engage a guide and rowboat for a leisurely trip down stream. The rowboats were tied behind the side-wheel steamers or placed on the decks of the stern-wheelers at the start of the trip from docks either at Drinker's Landing or the docks downtown in Bailey's Eddy where they are today.

Early in the 1874 season, the newspaper editor asked for subscriptions for a fund to improve the walks and ravines in the Dells. In June the first notice of an excursion to the Dells appeared. This group which came from Portage probably was the first of these excursions by train which became increasingly important to the Dells traffic through 1907.

In 1874, Bell operated trips on the *Dell Queen* until the beginning of August, when he moved his operations to the Lower Dells and continued to run trips for the remainder of the season.

With two steamboats plus many rowboats now taking visitors through the Dells, the local editor made another plea for improvements in the canyons and ravines. He wrote, "Our visitors last summer stood at the entrance to these natural gates of the beautiful and were told they could not enter." In those early days, visitors could explore Artist's Glen, Glen Eyrie also called Gates Ravine, Rood's Glen and probably some even climbed over the sandbar blocking the entrance to the old river channel. Boats, either steamers or rowboats, seemed to have stopped anywhere their customers desired. In order to improve some of these walks, wooden planks and ten dollars were offered by Major Schofield of Chicago. In July of 1874, a trout pond and refreshment stand were opened in Cold Water Canyon. Here trout could be caught, cooked and served before or after enjoying the improved walk through the Canyon as far as Devil's Jug.

The *Modocawanda* passed into the hands of Captain Walton McNeel in 1875, who continued to operate her in the Dells until 1876, when she

The first Dell Queen, *a side-wheeler that became the second steam boat at the Dells in the summer of 1873. The first steamer at the Dells, the* Modocawanda, *was built upriver at Point Bluff in Adams County and arrived a few weeks ahead of the* Dell Queen. *(Courtesy, H. H. Bennett Studio Foundation)*

was sold, taken to Portage and placed on the Fox River. Meanwhile, the *Dell Queen* proved inadequate to meet the requirements of a first class passenger boat, so during the following winter, she was dismantled and an elegant and spacious boat was built to take her place.

This boat was also named the *Dell Queen.* Under Captain Bell, it plied the Upper Dells for the next three seasons. On June 4, 1878, she caught fire, but a large force of men rebuilt her in short order and on July 4, she made her first trip, after which she ran regular trips for the next two years. This *Dell Queen* was powered by two engines of twelve horsepower each and could carry three hundred passengers through the Dells.

In the meantime, Captain A. Jones brought a small steamer to join the growing Dells fleet. The 21 ton vessel, *Champion,* had been built in 1867, and originally operated at Reeds Landing, Minnesota and later at St. Paul. During the summer of 1875, with Captain D.C. Van Wie as pilot, someone wrote an account of a trip up the river on the *Champion* which steamed up as far as Arch Cove, now partially covered by water. This area was also called Paradise, probably because it offered shelter from rain and a lovely bubbling spring–an ideal place for a picnic. From Arch Cove some of the steamer's passengers walked to Stand Rock, quite a rugged hike through brush, swamps and across small streams. The steamer then took its passengers across the river to Witches Gulch where they walked from the cliff at the entrance to the Gulch, past Diamond Grotto and on to Fairy Grotto. They scrambled over logs to a "tremendous chasm" where precipitous rocks towered overhead perhaps a hundred feet. The stream was about waist deep and some logs were fastened together with planks to form a rather insecure walk. There was a ladder over the waterfall. Later in the season, an excursion from Portage enjoyed a day of sight-seeing, refreshments and dancing at Cold Water Canyon.

Early during the 1876 season, the walk was built in Witches Gulch so that ladies could safely reach this spot. In 1877, a man from Dell Prairie installed a tent and rustic house and served refreshments there.

The *Champion* ran for two seasons through the Upper Dells, and later the Lower Dells. In 1879, she was transferred to Mirror Lake.

In 1878, the steamer *Alexander Mitchell* was built in Kilbourn City by the Kilbourn Boat Company, sharing business with the *Dell Queen.* She was operated by D.C. Van Wie.

Pomeroy's *Democrat,* printed a peevish article in the summer of 1879. After praising Mr. Bell for

Wooden walkways and bridges, like this one at Artist's Glen, made it easy for visitors to enjoy the off-river sights. (Courtesy, H. H. Bennett Studio Foundation)

building his *Dell Queen*, the writer continued; "About this time a few old political hulks and men of that class who were always willing to skim the cream but never milk the cow; men who for a long time had been sneering at the men of enterprise, conceived the brilliant project of putting in an opposition boat and giving it a big name-*Alexander Mitchell*-in hopes of drawing to it the custom of those who came to see the Dells....They thought to crush the life out of and take the skin off those who were really doing something to benefit the place and to please and interest humanity,....The public, far and near, with a sense of justice that seems born of Godliness, have refused to patronize them except to a limited degree....The *Dell Queen* is kept busy making its two trips daily.... on the occasion of moonlight nights, taking moonlight trips up. The boat is generally well filled while the dog-in-the-manger fellows go tooting along, emptying the money they have earned or stolen out of their pockets in the vain endeavor to catch travel."

In the interest of accuracy, many of H.H. Bennett's photographs of the *Mitchell* show good sized groups of tourists lined up on the decks to be photographed before the morning cruise. Bennett also showed his lantern slides to visitors in his Studio on Broadway in the evenings and told many amusing stories of his adventures climbing rocks and wading streams to get the best angles for his pictures.

During the years that Bennett photographed the Dells, he named many of the rock formations in the Upper and Lower Dells as he needed titles for his views. He also photographed the crowds on the steamboats. He then took orders and sold these pictures to the passengers as an ideal souvenir of their trip in those days before amateurs could take their own pictures.

Guide books were becoming popular and one of the early ones describes a trip through the Dells in long, romantic verse beginning with-

"Summer sunlight, warm and tender, glowed with splendor on the wave
As the crowded steamer plowed it with a fare of fair and brave;
Freighted with a wealth of beauty, weighted with a world of love:
Bosoms lighter, faces brighter, ne'er were smiled on from above.
Joyously our hearts were beating as the fleeting waters fled
Swiftly past her, as yet faster toward the Jaws the Dell Queen sped
From her splashing paddles rolled the flashing waves in seething swells, As she bore us where before us lay the wild Wisconsin Dells.

"And a beautiful maiden from Baraboo
With eyes like violets bathed in dew,
Close to her Kilbourn lover drew
And gazed in silent wonder."

The Germania *beached for refitting in the late 1880s. In the background stand Munger's mill and some remnants of his dam. (Courtesy, H.H. Bennett Studio Foundation).*

The New Dell Queen, *c. 1890 with a typical crowd of excursionists. In order to promote travel to the Dells and sell train tickets, the Milwaukee Road railroad sent H. H. Bennett on tour with lantern slides of Dells scenery. As this crowd indicates, he was very successful. (Courtesy, H. H. Bennett Studio Foundation)*

An account in the *St. Louis Post Dispatch* during June, 1879 describes a most unusual boat trip–not as romantic and pastoral as the one taken by the "beautiful maiden from Baraboo." He begins, "Dells of the Wisconsin. Nowhere in America, or in the world can more wierd, wild, entrancing scenery be found condensed within so small a space. Lying as these marvelously picturesque and beautiful scenes do, within an eight hour run of Chicago....It is strange they have not long since taken rank among the world's most famed resorts for lovers of nature, but it is only four or five years since they began to come into notice. Public attention has been directed to them in great measure through the efforts of three men....H.H. Bennett is an enthusiastic artist who taught himself photography and made with his own hands many of the instruments he uses....Captain John Bell of the jaunty little steamer, *Dell Queen* is the second of the worthy trio....And the third is W.H. Finch of the Finch House, one of the daintiest little hotels in all the Northwest. This writer was pleased with the "Charming" village of Kilbourn City and continues, "After a dainty breakfast at Finch's Hotel, a council of war was held. The river was booming along under a tremendous rise at the rate of twenty miles an hour (some exaggeration here, no doubt). Immense rafts were rushing past every few minutes....Captain Bell decided it would be unsafe to attempt to run his tiny steamer up such a stream, but promptly proposed that he and artist Bennett should take a splendid four-oared rowboat to the head of the Dells, five miles above town while Mr. Finch should drive us up in a carriage. They then would take us in and, after pulling us to the chief points of interest give us the thrill of a lightening express run down the river with the current through the Narrows." All the party survived this trip with even their adjectives undiminished. The writer concludes, "Next day with Bennett, Charley Snider and Captain Jim Christy, I went over the falls (the dam, of course) on a raft, a wild plunge amid creaking timbers." It was this reporter who described the river in the Narrows as a hundred feet deep and his description of a river running on edge is still quoted today, although later soundings have shown it to be inaccurate.

A newspaper article of the 1880s quotes a price of 25¢ for a boat ride along with a description of the Kilbourn scene.

The side-wheeler steamboat *Eolah* appeared on the scene in 1883. It is possible the little pumpkin-seed steamer was later rebuilt and re-

The Apollo *running downriver at the Narrows under a full head of steam.*

named the *Escort*. She operated until at least 1891 as the *Eolah*. By 1886, F.A. Field, a local grain and farm produce dealer, age 29, bought the steamboats-*Eolah*, *Alexander Mitchell* and the *Dell Queen*. He improved the boats, built up the business and then sold his Dells Boat Company to the Dells Resort Company in 1892, after which he went into the lumber business and other enterprises.

By 1886, H.H. Bennett had perfected his instantaneous shutter, powered by a rubber band, and could take stop-action photos. He then was able to travel with a fleet of Arpin Lumber Company rafts as far as Boscobel and photograph all aspects of a raftman's life and work before that way of shipping lumber ceased.

Bennett was also able to stop the action of his son, Ashley, jumping over to Stand Rock. He entitled the scene, "*Leaping the Chasm at Stand Rock*" and it became the trademark of the Dells for many years and still evokes amazement.

F.A. Field built the *New Dell Queen*, the third steamer with this name, in 1888. She was 35 tons and measured 86'x16'x2 1/2', built in Kilbourn, and given the number 157343. She was in service until 1898 when she was listed as abandoned.

Captain D.C. Van Wie and his wife started buying property in Cold Water Canyon, which included the the open space beyond and up to the Fat Man's Misery area. Van Wie had piloted the steamers *Champion* and *Alexander Mitchell*. In July, 1895, the president of the Milwaukee Athletic Society wrote to Van Wie with final specific instructions for their excursion to the Canyon, where they were about to spend their entire day from 11:00 a.m. until 8:00 p.m."....you must have rapid and good waiters also....have everything look as clean and neat as a pin....As far as meals are concerned, don't be stingy, but have plenty of everything. I think that you will have about 85 or more guests for dinner and perhaps 120-130 for supper....I have had some pretty sad experiences in the Gulch when on my last trip to Kilbourn. If our Excursionists would have to eat such poor meals as I had there in the Gulch, they might throw me into the river and walk back to Kilbourn. Beer-I beg your pardon-Watertown Ginger Ale-you must have plenty. I bet my straw hat against a $20.00 Gold Piece of yours that you will not have enough on hand for two hours....I also wish you would serve coffee, good strong coffee all day, to people who want it, coffee and cake should be on hand at least in the afternoon...."

The summer of 1889 started gaily with the promise of more than the usual number of tourists. The Fourth of July was celebrated with dances at Cold Water Canyon and Witches Gulch. During the summer a Mr. Chanter, a member of the Agassiz Society and a professor of botany, bought a tract of fifty acres which included portions of Cold Water Canyon at the mouth. H.H. Bennett reported to an official of the railroad that Chanter planned to bring many people to the Dells who had an interest in the botanical life in the area. "He does not own any of the interesting part of the Canyon; but closing or putting a toll gate on his property would necessitate the boats landing at another point a little farther up the river to get passengers into the best part of the Canyon....A party who had a lease on the property some years ago tried the scheme of charging toll, but it didn't pay because everyone went the other way...." The Chanter project seems to have ended in failure but Bennett and the railroad were evidently worried about schemes that would detract from the beauty and accessibility of the Dells.

The Milwaukee Road worked hard to promote passenger travel along its line. It had published guide books, illustrated with Bennett's pictures. The Dells was evidently one of the main attractions between Chicago and St. Paul, since those pictures predominate, but Bennett also made photos for them in Milwaukee, Waukesha, Juneau County and along the Mississippi. His large 18" x 60" panorama pictures were displayed in railroad depots. The relationship was a close one and in October, 1890, Bennett wrote to George Heafford, the General Passenger Agent of the Milwaukee Road, "Dear Sir: I wish to present for your consideration as an official of the R.R. the desirability of your company taking an interest (the whole or in part) of the steamboat business here in the Dells. I have an offer of the present business which remains open for a time, for three thousand dollars. The receipts of the business during the season recently closed have been over three thousand dollars with expenses amounting to less than sixteen hundred dollars for the past year. With better facilities and different methods of handling it I am confident it can be made to pay nearly as large a profit on an investment of eight thousand dollars which amount I would think put it in proper shape which would include a new and better boat....and would also fix up the landings in a more attractive and comfortable shape....As it stands, it seems to me there is a possibility of undesirable boats or perhaps boats with incompetent crews and unsafe construction; but sufficient to cause a flight that would not be for the best interests of anyone, least of all the travel to the Dells, this would not be the case if it was understood the business was backed by more capital. My hands are all tied up in my own business and I cannot put any money into this, but would be glad to take the care and management for a small percentage of the profit because of the benefit an increase of travel to this point would be to my photo view business." Nothing came of this idea as the Milwaukee Road was evidently not interested.

The year 1890 marked the end of one era in the Dells and Kilbourn and the beginning of another. The last lumber raft floated down the Wisconsin to be sold to the Drinker Mills in Happy Hollow. Souvenir stores entered the scene. H.H. Bennett had placed his first order for postcards and when a souvenir salesman solicited all the stores in town, he was told to go to Bennett's as all the tourists stopped there. After much reluctance, Bennett placed a small order for sweet grass baskets and Indian dolls. The first time the Studio dared to place an order for as much as $100.00, Evaline, his wife, cried all night.

Bennett was preparing a new booklet entitled, *Wanderings by a Wanderer*, designed to be sold on the steamboats with a page to be added for passenger group pictures made that day. The publication turned out to be popular and was sold for several years. And so from that first guide book in 1891, the Bennett Studio has published guide books for the boats until the present.

Enter Dells Resort Company

John E. Godding, a real estate developer from Rocky Ford, Colorado, had been visiting his wife's relatives in Mauston. He interested his brother in the Dells and late in 1891, T.F. and J.E. Godding entered the Dells scene. H.H. Bennett was enthusiastic and wrote to them that he was releasing Mr. Field from his option to buy the steamboats. "This I hope removes any obstruction to your plans of yours as my result in putting the Dells where they should be among the resorts of the Northwest." To another correspondent he wrote, "I find that another party who seems to have lots of schekles in trying to boom the Dells....He has bought the best part of Witches Gulch, a part of Cold Water Canyon and is trying to buy other property along the Dells and I did not want my scheme to stand in the way of others on a larger scale." Bennett offered help in the way of lantern slide shows and talks around the country.

Even before the Goddings arrived to buy the property and three steamboats, Captain Bell and a crew of workmen had started to build a new pier and boat landing on the location of the present Dells Boat Company building, 11 Broadway. Godding incorporated the Wisconsin Dells Resort Company for $60,000, half of which was to be

The Dells Boat Company landing, with its "elegant reception room" at street level on Broadway, was built in 1891. The bin at lower left held coal for fuel; the Germania is in the river. (Courtesy, H. H. Bennett Studio Foundation)

spent on improvements. Most important was the new building at the landing in Kilbourn. This frame structure had "an elegant reception room" on the street level with a ticket office. A long enclosed stairway led down to the pier eighty feet below, from which passengers boarded the steamers for the river trip. A new steamer, the *Germania*, the first stern-wheeler, 86162, was brought to Kilbourn by the Goddings. She had been built in Osceola, Wisconsin in 1887 and measured 68' x 13' x 3'. She operated until 1893, then was reconstructed, given a new number and her size increased to 48 tons, 77' x 17' x 2 1/2'. The *Germania* operated until at least 1903. Then she was reconstructed again and named the *Eleanor*, 75' x 16', and operated very little.

With a new boat and boat landing, the railroad improved the approach to the Dells with plantings of grass, shrubs and trees at the depot. A gravel path led down the embankment to the landing building. The music of a five piece orchestra from Milwaukee made the trips more festive and the river guides formed an association. The railroad planned several excursions to the Dells, with tickets to Kilbourn and return at the price of a one way fare plus 50¢ for a boat ticket. A dining hall on the south side of Artist's Glen was expanded and a foot bridge built across the Glen entrance. "Wisconsin's Saratoga. Wonderful changes have produced wonderful results. The Dells Resort Co. has transformed the Dells," proclaimed the local newspaper. Evidently the *Eolah-Escort* and the *Alexander Mitchell* had outlived their usefulness as wooden boats seemed to have had a pretty short life span. At some period, the *Alexander Mitchell* was sunk in the Dells.

Guy Glazier, an "old river rat," reminesces about one of his trips working on the *New Dell Queen* or "Old Betsy" as the crew called her. "Everything went well that year. John E. Godding was owner of the boat and his younger brother, T.F. Godding, Tuff we called him, was the manager. They also owned another steamboat, a little smaller, called the *Germania*. The crew on the *Dell Queen* was Captain Henry (Hank) Snyder, Mate Robert (Bob) Howard, Engineer Otis (Ote) Earl, Fireman Ed Hiller and me Guy O. (Ring) Glazier, peanut boy, souvenir salesman, guide and roustabout. The river was not very wide at the Narrows and every few days the old boat would get stuck crossways in the rocks, the passengers would get panicky, and old Cap would send me to quiet them.

"The next season there was some little change in the crew, Captain Snyder was still with us, the new mate was Ira (Ike) Bullis, Engineer Charles W. Eggleston, Fireman Charley Murray, called Murphy. That year we got away to a good start and all was going well. Then it happened. Ike Bullis got an invitation to a wedding down at Rio or some place down below Portage and had to get some one to sub for him that day. So he chose Dee Olderr and Ike's last words before he left that morning were, "Now Dee, for God's sake, don't wreck Old Betsy.

"We made the morning 9 o'clock trip all safe. Coming back down river it was Captain Snyder's habit to steer the boat down thru the Narrows, then hand the wheel over to the mate while he would go below to collect the tickets. That is what he did on the afternoon trip. As he entered Circle Bend (near the Navy Yard) he passed the steering wheel over to Dee and he went below. I had just come up the front stairs with my hands full of those rustic pine cones which I sold as Dells Souvenirs, when all of a sudden I noticed the boat turning to the right and heading for the rocks. Captain Snyder passed me at a bound and with three strides went up the pilot house steps, grabbed the wheel and rang for reverse engines.

"When the Captain came down I went to him and said, 'Captain, shall I go for the other boat?' He said yes, so I went to the lower deck where the only skiff we had was pulled up on deck. I grabbed the bow and pushed it over the side and jumped in as it hit the water. But oh, the heart-rending wail, 'They've taken the only boat and gone with it, leaving us doomed on this shipwrecked steamer'. By now the *Dell Queen* was floating majestically down stream and was perfectly safe as her hull was not much damaged.

"There was to be a dance at the Larks that night and I knew the *Germania* would already be firing up to make the evening trip. The engineer, Dell Murray was there and had the fire going when I reached the boat near the ice house (where the DBC winter dry docks stand today) Captain Fred

The gas--burning Wisconsin was the first vessel of the Olson Boat Company. (Courtesy, H. H. Bennett Studio Foundation)

Mr. Eggleston reversed the engines and got about one turn of the paddle wheels. But the boat struck the rocks near the Lower of the Twin Sisters. The impact threw the fireman ashore and that place has always since been known as "Murphy's Landing." Charley Murray walked around past the Old Dell House, down the railroad track to Kilbourn.

"The steam pipe was broken a few inches above Eggleston's head, thereby saving his life. The crash of the impact, the noise of all that boiler full of steam escaping threw the passengers into a panic. Several of them started for the wheel house to go overboard, but I waved my canes and shouted, 'back, back, there is no danger now and no need to get wet'.

Pulver was up town. Dell blew the whistle four shorts blasts, the signal of a hurry up call and Captain Pulver soon came aboard. I told him what had happened. Dell was busy stuffing fine pine wood into the fire box and soon there was steam enough to start. We met the *Queen* at High Rock, and, although the *Queen* was still more seaworthy than the other boat, all the passengers piled over on to the *Germania* as soon as the boats were lashed togethers. And then the passengers forgave me for taking the last boat."

Guy Glazier tells where all the principal characters live in 1948 and, although Dee Olderr drove boats all his life, no one ever heard of him piloting a steamboat again.

In 1894, the first small powered tour boat

made its appearance, a precursor of things to come. The Olson Boat Company started with the *Wisconsin*, owned by Ben Olson, who had saved money earned by rowing people up river, John Soeldner and George Wenkman. This boat looked like a miniature stern wheel steamer and could hold perhaps 12 passengers.

This was about the end of the guide-powered rowboats and one marvels at the strength required for their feats. It was said that the Bennett brothers, John, Albert and Clarence, who were also carpenters, had perfected the designs of these boats with the sharp prows of canoes so that they moved easily through the water and were also very stable for the several passengers each could accommodate. The oars look long and cumbersome but were fashioned with a spoon at the ends similar to oars used in crew shells today. Many of this sturdy group had also been raftsmen and knew all the eddies and currents of the river, using them to help in powering their boats.

Annie Turner Preston describes a delightful trip to the Dells in 1894. There were two steamboats on the river but her hosts at the Finch House arranged to have H.H. Bennett, "a man of innate courtesy of manner and thoroughly acquainted with each bit of scenery for miles around" row her up the river. About 4:30 in the afternoon, the journey started in Bennett's "comfortably cushioned" boat.

As in other early stories before photographs could be reproduced satisfactorily, long descriptions of the various rock formations followed, interspersed with a few steel engravings from Bennett's photographs. Mr. and Mrs. Robinson at Witches Gulch provided a delicious supper, "It's such a quaint place. A cottage with ample piazza has been erected in a cleared space among and almost under the over-hanging rocks, and the little stream we have followed through the gorge rushes along by the very door...." They had planned the trip back down the river by moonlight but a violent thunderstorm changed those plans. "Will any of our little party ever forget that storm? It was an electric storm of unusual violence and fury. It swept through the gorge like some avenging Nemesis. One tall pine embedded in the rocks high above us, fell prostrate, the bolt of forked lightning splitting it from top to bottom....It is hardly necessary to say that we had no alternative but to accept the Robinson's proferred hospitality and spend the night with them. They made us very comfortable, even though it was a bit crowded for everyone...." The next day was fine for the trip back down the river. She says that next year (1895), the Robinsons will be in more commodious quarters in their new home, The Pines, between Cold Water Canyon and Steamboat Rock. "There are ten rooms for guests, each room commanding a river view."

Tourist accommodations were growing each year. Bennett often answered inquiries and in 1895, he writes after his investigations, "The best hotels charged $2.00 to $2.50 by the day and $10.00 to $12.00 by the week." A week in a good boarding house would cost $6.00 to $8.00, and there was nothing to be recommended for $5.00 or less.

When Louis Dupless died at his home at the foot of Louis Bluff in October, 1895, the pioneer raft pilot, farmer and veteran was singularly honored. The local paper edited now by J.E. Jones reported, "The Grand Army Post chartered the steamer *Germania*, which was the first instance known of a similar character in this part of the state. The *Germania* left the landing in Kilbourn with a large number of the Grand Army, Relief Corps and Sons of Veterans and citizens of Kilbourn, the steamer's flag at half-mast....A landing was made a few rods below the bluff and near the home of the deceased comrade....After the services at the home the casket was borne by old comrades, the Post marching with reversed arms and with muffled drums, to a grave in the family cemetery at the foot of Louis Bluff on the bank of the river...."

In October of 1895, seven thousand people visited the Dells on excursions and the boats had carried fifteen thousand paid passengers at 50¢ each. Some excursions were held over in town until after supper to the profit of the community.

The Dells Resort Company tells of its philosophy about operations in an 1896 guide book. "The changes which have been made in the Dells add to, without in any way particular detracting from the sublimity of nature. Wherever the beauty of modern adornment, the introduction of modern improvements, or the convenience of scientific invention can be applied without changing the primitive beauty or natural grandeur, these changes will be adopted. Four hundred acres of beautiful park, covering hills, dales, glens and meadows will be cleared up. There are stone walks, terraces, winding walks around precipices, wire suspension bridges over chasms, rustic seats in lovely bowers, incomparable vistas through forest groves, and broad perspectives over river, hill, woods and fields."

On July 4, 1896, the *Germania* made a trip up to the Olin ferry. It was held overnight and the passengers danced until daylight. In contrast, the newspaper had reported on February 1, that there was sleighing on the river as far as Rood's Glen.

An 1897 magazine tells of excursions to the Big Dells, upstream from Witches Gulch, that were offered two or three times a year and took almost an entire day.

The Apollo *docked at the Larks c. 1900. The Dells Resort Company christened the* Apollo *in honor of a Chicago social club that it hoped would build a large club house at the Narrows. The Company also platted Artist's Glen and Glen Eyrie, early examples of the vacation-home subdivisions that would become common in Wisconsin. Imaginative promoters, the Resort Company even "sold" property to wild west entertainer Buffalo Bill, hoping that his celebrity endorsement would help sell lots. (Courtesy, H. H. Bennett Studio Foundation)*

A party from the Apollo Commandery of Chicago visited the Dells in August of 1897, stopping at the Glen Cottage where George Crandall and the Resort Company made their stay enjoyable with boat rides, a drive to Devil's Lake and a dance at the hotel. It was hoped the Dells would become a resort of Masonic societies who were expected to establish a resort, home and sanitorium in the Dells. An Apollo club house was to be built in the Narrows, according to the sketch in the local paper of July 2, 1898. For some time the hill proposed as the site of this monstrous structure, from which there is a fine view upstream through the Narrows, was called Apollo Hill. The Resort Company had purchased much land from this hill, up the east side of the Narrows, into Artist's Glen and the north end of the Narrows where they built the Larks Hotel. Originally there was a dining room for campers on the south side of Artists Glen. The land was plotted into two subdivisions-Artist Glen and Glen Eyrie. Four cottages were built in 1898. Bill Federbusch recorded that his deed shows a sort of communal or condominium agreement for all the plot buyers. Two cottages still stand near Devil's Elbow. The July 2, 1898, ad in the *Mirror Gazette* heralds all these grand changes, "Apollo Commandery, K.T. of Chicago will spend a week at the Dells, commencing July 16. This famous Masonic organization will come in a body, bringing ladies and friends and camp near the Narrows. During the week they will have drills and athletic exercises with music. It will be the grandest outing ever given by this society, already noted for the select and high character of its social affairs. It will be the grandest week ever known in the Dells and will extend its influence over the whole season." A foot bridge was built across Gates Ravine or Glen Eyrie and now rests beneath the waters.

Add to all this the excitement of a new steamboat, the *Apollo*, named in the Commandery's honor. She was built in Kilbourn City. Her statistics were 90'x21'x4', 44 tons, number 107375. The christening and maiden voyage of the craft was set for the week in July when the Apollo was having their festive camping party in the Dells. It turned out to be a day of turbulent weather and a storm with high winds blew the *Apollo* on shore at the start of her first trip. No damage or injuries resulted and, after this rather inauspicious introduction, the *Apollo* had a long, gay and useful life; puffing and paddling through the Dells carrying crew, passengers, Tony Milano and his string orchestra, the Dells photographer and sometimes his family.

Business must have been good in Cold Water Canyon. In 1899, the D.C. Van Wie family built a fine large home in the open lowland area near the entrance. By this time, their only son, Carl, had been born and D.C.'s father also lived with D.C., his wife Jenny or Jane. This home was a two story building, also including a "commodious" lunch room for their guests, cool drinks served to picnickers under the shade trees, cigars, a fine croquet ground and a dance hall.

The Dells Company seemed to know Buffalo Bill Cody. He visited the Dells and was given property in the new subdivision, no doubt hoping to cash in on his popularity but nothing seemed to have come of this and Buffalo Bill's property was later sold.

George H. Crandall, a son-in-law of H.H. Bennett, had rented the Glen Cottage in Kilbourn from A.C. Dixon, while keeping his original job in town as night operator at the Kilbourn Depot. He also dabbled in selling sewer pipe and furniture. A family story says he didn't like the undertaking business as he felt self-conscious when greeting his neighbors and asking them how they were today. In 1898, the Dells Company asked the Crandalls to provide meals in the large dining hall they had built on the promontory just north of Artist's Glen. The next year they added 17 rooms and the Crandalls were asked to manage the whole place and give it a name. This was the famous Larks Hotel and commanded an outstanding view downstream into the Narrows.

Lois Musson tells of her parents, George and Nellie Crandall, with help from Nellie's sister, Harriet Snider, managing the Larks Hotel, which had formerly been called the Dells Inn. First consideration was the safety of their little daughters. The icehouse was converted to their "Castle" and a high wire fence "gave Nell the assurance that the girls wouldn't go tumbling into the river. One of the major problems of the new venture proved to be the feeding of the excursionists who arrived for Sunday dinners." The Inn had its own dock where the steamboats landed. "Since the *Apollo* had joined the river fleet, there were even larger crowds than in previous years. After the dining room was filled to capacity, the screen door was hooked but, more likely than not, some woman with a long hatpin would get the door open and the crowds would pour in....Freddie was their yardman and one of his duties was to look after the cow which was pastured up over the hill back of the resort. It was quite a common occurence for the cow to get loose." Then Freddie came looking for George and the two had to get her back in her own pasture. "Having a cow was quite a problem, but it wasn't practical to bring milk up from town....Of course, their guests needed to be entertained and here Hat (Harriet) was in her element. She organized a torch light parade with the guests in costume and the walk up through Cold Water Canyon and back for one evening's entertainment; a mock trial for another. She

Black Hawk's Roost, the home of the William Federbusch family in Artist's Glen. Built in 1898, the home occupies the site of the toll house of the Gates bridge. Seated in the buggy owned by Damon Loomis of Birchcliff are (l-r) Ruth Horlick with William H. and Marguerite Federbusch. Else Federbusch sits farthest right on the porch.

contructed a raft to come floating down the river past the hotel. The raft carried a dim lantern and a dummy but the dragon, which she also made, was powered by young Musson boys (the youngest was Howard) who were camping beside the Larks."

The new century brought the automobile to Kilbourn and changed the resort business and life in America forever. J.W. Fuller, the jeweler, became the owner of the first horseless carriage in town. It was a steamer and could attain a speed of thirty five miles per hour. In the same month, September, Ashley Bennett who had become the Northwest dealer for the Winton car, drove here from Mankato, Minnesota, at a speed of one hundred miles a day.

As families arrived in their automobiles, smaller boats carried smaller groups. In 1901, Mr. William Blatchley added a new boat to the sightseeing fleet, his naptha launch *Altamont*. In a few years more small launches were carrying tourists through the Dells. One of these belonged to Clarence Bennett, one of Henry Bennett's brothers G.H. Crandall planned to have two. Captain Snider, the old steamboat pilot, seeing one of these small craft moored beside the *Apollo*, exclaimed, "Polly's got a pup." In 1905, H. Goedecke and Charles Borcher reported that they had a new "vapor launch," adding to the "flood of gasoline launches which are becoming like a mosquito fleet in the Dells." Some people also knew that one could see more from a launch than from a wide steamboat, but an extra 50¢ toll was charged for using the Dells Company's landings.

That same year, Nat Wetzel came to town to manage the Dells Resort Company for the Goddings. A magazine article advertised reasonable rates at Kilbourn. "Board can be obtained in private homes or boarding houses for 6 or 7 dollars per week. Hotels are Glen Cottage, Finch House, the Markham, Schofield Cottages, Hile House, Rose House and Park Hotel." John Radlund of Chicago bought the Pine Glen Resort that year. A booklet issued by the Chicago, Milwaukee and St. Paul Railway proclaimed, "Remember the Dells, as thousands have done before you. Here in days primeval, Nature turned her water courses free and wrought out Titanic sculpture and architecture for the eternal wonderment of man."

Nat Wetzel was an interesting and flamboyant character. He was sent to Kilbourn apparently, with the purpose of increasing the business of the Resort Company so the Goddings could profitably sell their holdings here. By way of improvement, he white-washed the lower trunks of the pines at the Larks Hotel. He also put a raccoon in a cage. It escaped. He put a sea lion in a tank and it died and the alleged hippopotamus also died in the ravine north of Birchcliff Hotel. He added a tavern and sold liquor on the boats. As a result, one excursionist is supposed to have fallen from a boat near Gates Ravine and drowned. The Crandalls

The Comet *gasoline launch heading upstream with a youngster wearing an "authentic" Wisconsin Dells souvenir, c. 1910. (Courtesy, H.H. Bennett Studio Foundation).*

The Apollo at Louis Bluff. After the power dam raised the level of the river, boats had to navigate through flooded groves of trees to reach the Bluff. (Courtesy H. H. Bennett Studio Foundation)

disapproved of selling liquor in the Dells and gave up management of the Larks.

The grand plans for development in the Narrows had apparently fallen through as only four cottages were ever built in the subdivisions. But Wetzel, a man of marvelous energy and great resources, a noted and successful promoter in St. Louis and Texas, "set about the Dells to advertise with his usual energy. The Dells were elegantly set forth in literature and catchy novelties."

Perhaps it was Wetzel's vision of the Dells' future that proclaims in the local paper of August 26, 1906 that the river should be made navigable to Nekoosa. A dam should be built at Kilbourn with locks and great factories. In the Dells, cliffs will be crowned with turrets and domes in medieval architecture "occupied in splendor and ribald gayety by the newly rich."

Wetzel was one of the driving forces behind the Inter-County Fair, incorporated in 1901, which operated for several years. It was located on River Road on a level field just south of the access road to Cold Water Canyon. J.E. Jones reports this fair "would doubtless never have been established at that place but for the irrepressible energy of Nat Wetzel, president of the Dells Company, who is also president of the fair association. The secretary, G.H. Campbell, is also an indefatigable promoter of entertaining features." By November, 1905, the fair had been in operation for three years and with limited financial success. In 1904, Jones says, "The entertainment this year is said to have been more varied, numerous and interesting than at any except the two or three big fairs of the state. This included all kinds of side shows, fast races, free performances of varied kinds in front of the grand stand, balloon ascension, auto races, etc. In the agricultural building there was an unsurpassed exhibition of big vegetables, fruit, etc. The art building was about filled with the usual exhibit. L.A. Murray displayed his line of school supplies now grown to a statewide business from Kilbourn.

Bert Steele's June 26, 1906 letter to his parents in Delton gives another good look at the life of a young fellow working on the steamer. "*We leave Kilbourn at 9:30 AM get to the cannon or larks at 10:00 AM but only stop to take on passengers then go right along up to the gultch, we get to the gultch at 10:15 AM, leave there at 11:00, get to the Larks at 11:15 stay here until 1:30 p.m. (no doubt for a meal and a walk through the Canyon) get to Kilbourn at 2:00 PM, stay there until 3:30, get to the gultch at 4:15 leave there at 5:00, get to the Larks at 5:15 stay here until 6:30 get to Kilbourn at 6:45.... Yesterday I went up to the pilot room with cap and set there a few minutes and he stept down from the wheel and told me to get up and try it once, I steared it from kesslers (down stream from Swallow's Nests) through the jaws of the Dells clear up until we were going in the narrows, then after we got past the larks I steared or run it up to the gulch, and back as far as the pines, I can stear it all right only here in the narrows it is a fright now the watter is only 3 feet higher than it was when we started work, but a fellow can learn it in time. I don't work much for there is nothing to do we set still 5 hours every day when we are tied to the docks unless we have an excursion."* Steele wrote this letter on the elaborate stationery of the Dells Company which advertised the *Apollo* and *Eleanor* steamboats and "Wisconsin Dells Company, Owners of the Wisconsin Dells, capital $100,000."

As talk began about a new high dam on the river, H.H. Bennett tried every persuasion possible with his fellow townsmen and enlisted all the help he could statewide to prevent this project which would flood out so much of the Upper Dells. Opposition was in vain and Bennett died on January 1, 1908, some said of a broken heart.

In July, 1908, Nat Wetzel announced that the "Dells was closed." Wetzel claimed the refusal of the railroad to grant excursion rates was the reason. "The Dells resort will be permanently closed within the next thirty days and the property will be offered for sale. We will wind up our affairs and seek more renumerative fields." The Dells Company was said to control 600 acres along both sides of the river–including "all the beauty spots" which included parts of Cold Water Canyon, Witches Gulch and their landings. They also owned steamboats and the Larks Hotel.

And so the Dells Company used the railroad as a scapegoat. For three years they had encouraged the dam and the manufacturing it would bring, knowing that they would sell their property to the Southern Wisconsin Power Company for flowage rights. Wetzel's announcement that the "Dells was closed," brought an angry response from J.E. Jones in the *Illustrated Events.* He reported increased business at resorts and that "the launch fleet in the river with an aggregate carrying capacity of 150, have been doing good business every day. ...Things have never looked bigger and brighter for the resort than they do now." Also, there were still hopes that the Dells might be made into a state park.

The refreshment stand at Witches Gulch c. 1890. (Courtesy, H. H. Bennett Studio Foundation)

After the Dam

By October, 1908, the dam was completed and the water was rising. It would eventually raise the water level 17 feet at the dam site. There were many changes evident in the Upper Dells the following summer. Cliffs lost some of their striking height. Even today, river lovers mourn the loss of Boat Cave, Bass Cove, Diamond Grotto and Giant's Hand, drowned forever. The old river bed–formerly a creek and ponds, was now navigable all around Black Hawk Island. Occasionally motor launches run commercial trips through here when high water makes the Narrows the boiling maelstrom it always was.

Witches Gulch became more accessible when the river backed up and new walks were built. "Rood's Glen is now accessible to boats and is the prettiest nook on the entire river, being just wide enough to allow the largest launches to enter......Above the Dells for ten miles the river is like a lake and boats of any draft can easily navigate without any difficulty from sand bars or other obstructions. Stand Rock is easily accessible by boat instead of the walk of almost two miles as heretofore."

However, before the dam raised the water level, the Power Company had neglected to cut the trees on the islands at the head of the Dells. That winter, with the water raised and frozen over, farmers came out to cut the trees standing above the ice, leaving a vast forest of submerged stumps a distinct threat to boat propellers. Channels were marked, but old timers are still wary of these hidden monsters.

The dam also wrought changes in the town of Kilbourn also. Lower Broadway from Superior Street to LaCrosse Street had been a ravine, but when rock was being blasted out at the damsite the city bought this material for fill on lower Broadway with a bridge over the municipal dock area. Many businesses on the south side of Broadway had been accessible by only a foot bridge in front of their establishments and now fronted a new street, making the town more inviting. When Hoffman's moved from Newport and built a new brewery in Kilbourn at 740 Eddy

Street, they dug a vast system of tunnels to age their beer. One of these tunnels led down to the river and was now blocked off by the new street. By this time, G.M. Marshall had established his machine shop in this building so the tunnels were no longer in use.

The Southern Wisconsin Power Company had purchased flowage rights, meaning any land that would be flooded when the river level was raised. This included all of the property and boats that Wetzel's Dells Company owned. Grover Neff, of the Southern Wisconsin Power Company, had persuaded George Crandall to lease these holdings and buy the personal property of the former Dells Company. Over the years, Crandall purchased all of the property formerly owned by the Dells Company as well.

Commercialization threatened the riverbanks. Hotels and signs were going up along the river and a road was started from High Rock to the Narrows, but, fortunately, was never finished.

Tourists began coming to the Dells in their motor cars in smaller groups. Crandall had purchased a small boat, and in 1911, along with Clarence Bennett and Glenn Parsons, he formed the Dells Launch Company with the *Neptune*, the *Comet*, and the *Anona*. Two years later when Crandall bought the steamer *Apollo* and the motorboat *Seminole* and gave them to the company for $1 each, the group became the Dells Boat Company. He also gave the company free use of the boat landing which he acquired under lease and did not charge landing fees, which were part of the lease.

Trouble started when the competitive launches began to take some of the Dells business and the operators used the walks, docks and holdings belonging to the steamboat operators. "A river fight ensued." The solution to the problem was a landing fee which was placed on top of the 50¢ adult boat fare: naturally children rode free. "A half century later," Lois Musson continues, "the same arrangement prevailed despite the fact that the boat operators were making a charge for half fares. For some unknown reason, they felt that they were entitled to take the children through free and the land operator generously allowed them to do so."

While launches were increasing, in 1911 the Rowboat Livery was still doing business. The Municipal dock area was and still is city property as it is an extension of Eddy Street. Anyone could dock a boat there for a fee. In 1912, the city was requested to build a concrete stairway from Broadway down to the dock.

"Made His Last Landing," was the August 1915 headline in the Kilbourn paper. Captain Harry R. Snider, a raftsman and steamboat pilot for over 35 years, had "died in the harness" just as he had hoped to. At age 82, he had piloted the *Apollo* to the Dells Inn, formerly the Larks Hotel, where passengers were going to attend a dance. Captain Snider came down from the pilot house to sit with his fellow crew members when he died. "Like the Norse seaman, he had drifted out in his own vessel into the fathomless deeps of eternity, his hand had fallen from the wheel, the rudder was beyond his control, and was directed by a pilot greater than he, into a vast ocean from which no mariner returns."

Captain Harry R. Snider, steamboat pilot for 35 years, who "died in harness" on board the Apollo *in 1915. (Courtesy, H. H. Bennett Studio Foundation)*

World War I brought a tourist boom. Travellers came by train, bus, motorcycle and cars through deep sand on Highway 12. William Blatchley operated two steam buses and was a photographer.

By this time there were many boats and boat companies including the Olson Boat Company, the Dells Boat Company and many independent owners. Competition got fierce. Though most of the boat tickets were sold through the hotels and rooming houses, tourists were still harassed as they walked down the streets. In 1918, an ordinance was passed prohibiting any soliciting on the street for business with any hotel, boarding house, resort, steamboat, launch or other vessel or vehicle. Aggressive ticket sellers were probably already invading the bridge into town. They would

Nellie and Ben Olson, with son Grover here, were the first of several generations of Olsons to make their living on the river at the Dells.

jump on the running boards of cars approaching the bridge, urging passengers to buy boat trip tickets. Some pushed salesmanship to the limit asking, " Do you have your tickets to get into the Dells?"

Evening entertainment could be a stroll around town or up to Wawbeek. Every Wednesday evening there were band concerts by local musicians on a bandstand in the middle of Broadway near the Finch Hotel. Movies at the Electric or Crystal Theatres were popular.

For some years the Dells Boat Company also ran the *Apollo* on sunset trips as far as Louis Bluff. The 50¢ fare gave passengers a trip starting at 6:00 and returning at 9:00 PM. There was a picnic lunch, a stop at the Bluff and brief lectures on geology and "the rare and prolific history of a prehistoric race, the Wisconsin River Indians." Sometimes the music of a small orchestra accompanied the outing.In the early 1920s, Crandall went to Yellowstone Park where he met Steven Mather, founder of the National Parks Board. George told him of his dream of preserving the Dells for future generations as a national park. Mather advised him, "Buy all the property you can. You will need a tremendous block of land." He, and later his children, followed this advice.

Crandall certainly had more faith in the resort business than the city council, which voted against giving their annual appropriation for an advertisement of the Dells.

The Olson family also had faith in the Dells. In 1920, the McManman estate came up for sale and Nellie Olson was the successful bidder. Barney accepted her check for $5,000 as a down payment. This prime block of property extended from 815 River Road, 200' from the corner of Broadway and Superior Streets (Now River Road) and down 368 feet on Broadway to the Municipal dock, which is a city street. At the time all that stood on the land was the old General Bailey house, a pony barn, an apple orchard and a ravine.

Nellie, Mrs. Ben Olson, was a crackerjack business woman and had saved money she earned operating the Modern Home at 812 River Road, where she also served meals. Prior to his partnership with William Blatchley and John Soeldner, Ben had built and rowed boats and operated the first motor launch on the river. He also sold potatoes and had a tavern for two years at 217 Broadway. In 1922, the city granted permission to Grover Olson and Edward Marlow to build the municipal dock on Eddy Street "for public landing of passengers."

During the big storm of 1922, the steamer *Apollo* sunk at the landing and a new steamer was needed if large crowds were to be carried through the Dells. The *Apollo* was raised, repaired and kept at the landing as a wharf boat and occasionally made trips up the river. The Dells Boat Company consulted boat builders and closed a contract with the Illinois Steel Company and the Dubuque Boat and Boiler Company for a steel boat. The work was done in sections in the company's shops, and then shipped to Kilbourn where they were assembled. The 59–ton boat was given the number 257343, 110' x 22' x 4', and was originally a coal burner but was later converted to Bunker C oil. She cost about $30,000. Safety was provided by nine water tight compartments, convenience by electric lighting and a complete radio outfit. Its capacity seems a matter of conjecture, possibly 500 passengers but 300 seems more likely.

The first rivet was driven on May 13 and she was launched on June 13. One Saturday in early July, 1922, the *Winnebago* was formally christened. Russius Decorah invoked the approval of the Great Spirit, George's daughter, Phyllis Crandall, broke a bottle of wine on the capstan and the *Winnebago* started out on a voyage that continues to this day. After the christening, three hundred guests came aboard for the first trip up the river which turned out to be a short one. Opposite the Swallows Nests the boat nosed up on a sandbar because it drew several inches more than the *Apollo* had. Some of the passengers remembered a similar accident when the *Apollo* made its maiden voyage some 24 years before. No damage was suffered and trips on the following two days, with four or five hundred passengers, were made very successfully.

Next, the Riverview Boat Line entered the scene. Oliver and Irene Helland had purchased the Dot Bell home and river frontage in 1920. This property extended from the municipal dock to the Dells Boat Company building. The Helland family lived in the home for several years before having it moved to 320 Minnesota Avenue. The land became the property of the Riverview Boat Line which the couple, with Irene's father, William Stanton, and brother, Walter (Bud) Stanton, formed in 1921.

In addition to building docks and buying boats, Riverview built various tourist attractions along Broadway including souvenir stores, a penny arcade and a dance pavillion.

In 1923, the Tourist Boat Company owned by Harry Radlund, G.W. Gray and Fred Dixon petitioned to use part of the new municipal dock built by Olson and Marlow. They also asked for a ticket office and permission to store their boats at the Superior Street bridge. By April, 1925 the city charged the various boat companies 5¢ per passenger for use of the municipal dock. A wharfmaster was appointed by the mayor. The first to serve was J.F. Seaton with the power of a policeman.

The first meeting of the Consolidated Boat Company was held at Oak Villa on December 14, 1925. The original stockholders were John W. Ryan, Ed. C. Marlowe, Silas (Sy) Knudsen, William T. Doyle and Dee Olderr. Early minutes record that it was decided to buy glasses, if needed, for A.I. Woodring or else buy a lot more paint for the boats. By 1936, Ryan and Doyle had left the company. When Ed Marlowe died in 1936, his wife Madeline acquired his stock. Olderr and Knudsen were still stockholders.

Mort Sunderland of the Finch Boat Company requested a permit to build a ticket booth in the municipal dock area.

Many hotels along the river owned boats and ran a few trips a week for their guests. The Priesters at Rood's Glen owned the *Hawkeye* and later the *Milwaukee*. Daniels at Chula Vista had a small boat. Loomis's at Birchcliff named their boat *348*. Berry's Coldwater Canyon Hotel ran two different *Ramonas* from Berry's Eddy. Sunset trips on these boats often went above Plainville. Harry Priester remembers going as far as the present Highway 82 bridge with Marguerite Claussen sometimes singing and playing her ukelele. The Radlunds at Ravenswood had a boat in the Lower Dells.

The Dells Associated Boat Line seems to have had its beginning on July 1, 1926. This was a group of local boatmen calling for safety inspections of all boats as 150,000 people were carried through the Dells each year. Among the companies in this association were Olson Boat Co., Dells Boat Co., Harold Barrett, Walter Bresnahan, H.R. Blevans, C. Mueller, J.C. Edmonds (Pines Hotel), C.D. Berry and A.V. Waterman.

Competition between companies and their ticket agents had become even more fierce and this fact did not present a pleasant picture for tourists. The association had grown and on October 31, 1929, the company moved to eliminate solicitors on the nieghboring roads and city streets, eliminate commissions to hotels and road signs. There would be only four ticket booths and each company would honor the other's tickets with a person on the dock for an orderly dispatch of boats with each company taking turns. 5¢ from each ticket would pay for advertising.

In that year, the Olson Boat Company requested permission to build a steel elevator on their premises. In November, George Crandall bought Captain Glenn Parsons' 40% interest in the Dells Boat Company for $17,500, and bought the

By the 1920s, competition between boat companies was fierce, as indicated by this poster urging visitors to "Think" about the best deal.

Think
Don't Be Confused
You Can See
The Upper Dells Boat Trip
Including Stand Rock For 85c
INDIAN CEREMONIAL $1.15
BOAT TRIP and INDIAN CEREMONIAL
Complete Trip Including Tax $2.00
DON'T PAY $2.40 or $2.50
When You Can Ride The Best
Boats At The DELLS For Only
85c

The Winnebago, *at Witches Gulch, 1946. Built in 1922, the* Winnebago *was the first steel-hulled boat at the Dells and the last steamboat on the Wisconsin River. (Courtesy, H. H. Bennett Studio Foundation)*

present Dells Boat Company building at 11 Broadway.

In 1929, H.E. Cole's *Baraboo, Dells and Devils Lake Region* booklet reports that the construction of Lake Delton made another boat trip possible. After taking the Lower Dells trip, the boat could travel up Dell Creek to the Lake Delton dam. Here one transferred to Lake Delton boats for "another delightful trip, including a walk through Congress Hall Canyon." At the Mirror Lake dam another transfer was made "for a scenic trip up this charming body of water.

In 1931, the Lake Delton Development Company also applied to use the municipal dock for a launch landing.

That same year, the steamer *Apollo* was burned and sunk near the mouth of Witches Gulch. The *Events* recalled its long life since 1898 when Captain Pulver was in charge for a year, through the year that Captain Snider manned the wheel until his death. Charlie Ruch had been its captain for the last 10 years.

This left the *Winnebago* the last steamboat on the Wisconsin.

In 1932, the country was in the depths of the depression. Visitors who could afford a vacation had to pinch their pennies. A non-stop trip met this need. Bob Olson, Ed Ryan and Howard Heitman competed with Norman Coapman for about a year until Glenn "Fat" Blatchley bought these men out and started the Silver Dollar Boat Line. The docks were in the slough or Crandall

Bay in the 1100 block between Illinois and Indiana Avenues. The charge was $1 for the trip while the three stop trips, at Cold Water Canyon, Witches Gulch and Stand Rock, were $1.50. Tourists saved time also. Ed Tangney vividly recalls those days.

In 1933, after he graduated from Kilbourn High School, Ed Tangney was hired to drive a boat for Glenn "Fat" Blatchley. The Siver Dollar Boat Line was only a year old and had one boat, the *Silver Arrow* purchased from Bob Olson, the originator of the no-stop trip.

As a guide, Tangney bought his guide books from the Bennetts for 12 1/2¢ and sold them for a quarter. At one time, he found some Dells scenic cards at Sam Weber's second hand store and restaurant. His gift for salesmanship soon developed when he bought these cards for 1¢ and sold them for 10¢ or 3 for a quarter. He was very sorry when this source of supply ran out.

The Silver Dollar's ticket salesmen, Bud Colburn and Tommy Ryan, sold tickets from the sidewalk outside Bauer's Meat Market. It wasn't legal to solicit on the sidewalks or streets at that time but they got away with it. They also sold tickets at their dock. Tommy Ryan's, "Dells Boats," was a familiar cry in Happy Hollow.

There were times when these men didn't get to work in the morning because their nights turned into days. Ed declares, "Tommy was a crackerjack salesman when he was sober but he wasn't sober a lot." Another neighbor declared that Tommy watched out for all the neighborhood children so he must have sobered up more later.

So by mid-July, Ed had become a full time ticket salesman. And he made money. He received a 25¢ commission on each $1 ticket. If he sold ten in a day, he made $2.50. Many men were working for $1 a day then. His expenses were minimal. He slept in a tent where the public boat launch now stands. He got his meals at Wenkman's restaurant at 741 Superior Street because he recommended Wenkman's to his passengers. After Fat married Jo Arntz, he sent customers to Arntz's restaurant at 207 Broadway and ate there free. It was a common practice for guides and ticket salesmen to recommend the restaurants owned by the boat owners or their relatives in return for free meals.

Ed credits his success as a ticket salesman to copying the style of Cliff Zahler, "the greatest salesman of them all." Cliff worked for the Riverview Boat Line in a booth on the far side of the bridge. He dressed as much like a policeman as he dared, with some kind of badge on his boat cap. "He had a way of stepping out and throwing out his cane. Cars would stop. It worked. Cliff always had something complimentary to say about people's cars to break the ice."

Of his pitch to potential customers, Ed said, "Well, of course, if they didn't know about the $1.50 trip, I didn't bring it up. But if they did and if they were older people, I said, 'Of course, there's some pretty heavy climbing to do out there. We have smaller boats and they get in closer and you can see better. We did go into Rood's Glen....and I told them we take you into one that they can't. You can see Stand Rock better than you can by walking up there. It wasn't hard to switch them. Our biggest problem was the old boat we had." Sometimes it was hard to start and many misfortunes could befall it once it did start.

Phil Sly worked a ticket booth for the Dells Boat Company at Lake Delton on the west side of what is now Fischer's Restaurant. The boat company closed this booth on Labor Day but in the fall of 1934, people were returning from the World's Fair in Chicago and Blatchley rented this "Great White Arch" which was facing south and a prominent landmark. A large sign over the arch said, "Gateway to the Dells." Ed did a terrific business way into October. There was nothing but a dead-end bullpen behind the arch. "I couldn't stop them at the entrance but, of course, they couldn't get out. I just let them go but I caught them when they came back out. One of the funniest things that happened out there, three elderly ladies drove up in one of these old Cadillacs and, of course, I sold them on going over and taking a boat trip. Well, in about an hour they were back. Zahler had stopped them on the top of the hill and convinced them that they shouldn't take this river ride. They should take the complete boat trip. So I had to do my work all over again and I convinced them they should keep their tickets and go back and give Mr. Zahler his but he turned them around and sent them back again. By this time it is quittin' time. It's five o'clock and I didn't have a car out there. I convinced them again that they shouldn't take this trip where they would have to crawl around these cliffs and in the woods. So I got in the car with them and you know I had a helluva time getting them past him with me in the car. That's how great he was. He had them slowed up again."

Tangney went to work in Milwaukee but in 1936, Fat convinced him to come back and work for him again. He was given the booth at Wrezinski's corner. At that time, Hwy 16 came into town along Vine Street and made a 90 degree turn at Broadway to go through town. This was an excellent corner for a salesman as the traffic had to slow down at that corner. One night he says, "I got one car stopped and all of a sudden, I had six cars stopped. Well, now, I can't talk to all of them so I jumped up on the bumper of the front one and, of course, with my roaring voice, I had them all leaning out the windows–thought maybe it was an accident or something. Then I went along peeling off the tickets." Fat witnessed this incident and later told people, "He sounded just like a foghorn." Today there are still some people who call Ed, "Foghorn."

There was another sales angle on Wrezinski's corner. Many people did not want to buy a boat ticket until they got their rooms for the night. Most rooms were $1 but those on the back streets rented for 50¢. So Foghorn filled all the rooms around the area also. First he filled Wrezinski's house by the corner. Many rooming houses sold Ed's tickets for him.

Ben Olson, Sr. was mayor in 1936 and he hired Daisy Thomas as police chief. The Silver Dollar Boat Line was competition for the Olson Boat Company so he probably told Daisy to keep a good eye on Foghorn and catch him if he stepped out of his booth to solicit boat tickets. "Doggone it," says Tangney, "I got pinched three times that summer." He was fined $15.00 and went back to work.

"They had no police car and old Daisy didn't drive very much. His son used to drive him. If he came up in that black car, I couldn't see him coming." So Fat hired Ken Murray, who was ten years old. "He gave him a dollar a day to shadow Daisy. If Daisy started up Broadway where I was, Ken called the gas station. The gas station would call over and wave at me. I'd get back in the booth. I never got pinched again."

"The last time Daisy caught me was a Sunday morning. I was having a ball, traffic was good. I was stopping everything that came through and I was peeling off the tickets. There was corn planted on the north side of Broadway and Daisy was hiding in the corn." Ed had a hard time stopping some ladies in a Cadillac. "I'd almost get them stopped and then they'd go again. I finally got them stopped at Landry's Funeral Home (halfway down the block). And here comes Daisy out of the cornfield."

"Doggone you, Tangney," says Daisy, "get back in the booth."

And so Ed Tangney learned salesmanship and as he says, "We were definitely needed in this town in the 1930s. If we didn't stop these people they'd have drove right on through. We were definitely needed."

On June 29, 1933, the *Events* listed tour boats who received licenses from the city. They were *Silver Arrow*, G.C. Blatchley; Launch *Jerry B.*, Walt Bresnahan: *President, Lady O'Lyons, Beverly, Mary Jane, Queen*, Olson Boat Company; *Juanita*, E.V. Avery; Steam Boat *Winnebago*, Motor Boat *Commander*, Motor Boat *Captain*, Dells Boat Company; *Flying Cloud*, Finch Boat Line; Launch *Lassie*, John Heitman; *Sea Gull*, John Ryan; *Arbitus, Beaver, Helen, Helen II*, Consolidated Boat Company; Launch *Red Wing*, John Wanderer; *Black Hawk, North Star, Viking, Kiwanis, White Eagle, Virginia*, O.P. Helland of Riverview; *Pastime*, J.H. Soeldner.

Boat owners were often at odds with each other over rights to keep the municipal dock open to all but many differences were worked out in their Dells Associated Boat Lines organization and action by the city.

In 1934, all the property of Jennie Bowman's estate was sold. George Crandall purchased a half interest. Walter Stanton, with Irene and Oliver Helland, owned the other half. This included properties at the four corners at the Lower Dells landing. Riverview operated a free campground where Riverview Park is now located, as well as a gas station formerly leased from Jennie Bowman.

The Lower Dells boat trips were the special concern of Walter "Bud" Stanton. This was a shorter no-stop trip which had been popular since the beginning of tourist travel. The steamer *Modocowanda's* trip in 1874 with Captain Wood started from the Railroad Ravine and the *Mirror* decribes the Double Echo, Bear's Cave, Pulpit Rock, Observation Point, a stop at the site of the village of Newport, Signal Point, Sugar Bowl, Grotto Rock full of caves, Ink Stand and Lone Rock. Probably there were times when the dams were gone that a boat could travel the Upper and Lower Dells all in one trip.

Some of the boats in the Lower Dells were *Na-Hu-Nah, Josephine, Ramona, Red Bird* and *White Eagle*.

Sunset trips were especially popular often with an Indian singer guide such as Johnny White Eagle. Herb Campbell, Herb Droste and Don Saunders on the *Dawn* were outstanding guides for many years.

In 1936, a few new boat owners applied for licenses. They were G.D. Parsons, Charles Ruch with the *Iris, Alvin, Wanderer*, and Finch Boat Line owned by Mort Sunderland, for a total of 30 launches. Most of these wooden launches were built by the Nehls Boat Works of Portage.

Any man or boy and later girls who has ever worked on the river in the summer can name a confusing list of boats, owners, drivers and guides. Olson Boat Company renamed the *President, Ben Jr.* and added the *Chief, Wisconsin* and *Kumbimini*. Dells Boat Co. added the *Commodore*. Boats were bought and sold, such as John Ryan's *Sea Gull*, sold to Allen Dearborn and then to Mark Trumble. Some went to the Lower Dells.

Many men spent their lives working on tour boats. They trained many of the young guides and drivers and in the off-season many worked at carpentry, wood-cutting and odd jobs before the

The Clipper Winnebago *at the Dells Boat Company Landing. (Courtesy, H. H. Bennett Studio Foundation)*

days of unemployment insurance. They loved the river and the people and were fondly called "old river rats." Some owned a boat and some were loyal to their favorite employers over many years. Some of these men were Arnol Priester, John Jones, Hooky Radandt, Tom and Harold Barrett, Hoot Schanke, Cliff Zahler, Bill Doyle, Charlie Ruch, Phil Sly, Cotton Stephans, Jack Morse, A.I. Woodring, Dee and Lyle Olderr to name but a few.

George Crandall died in the winter of 1938 and his daughters and sons-in-law, Phyllis and Ralph "Doc" Connor and Lois and Howard Musson, carried on his dream and his businesses.

In 1941, Ingebert Soma bought Fat Blatchley's Silver Dollar Boat Line and named it Soma Boat Line and became "Cap" Soma from then on with an expanding fleet.

Jack Morse had been piloting the *Winnebago* until World War II, following Tom Gorman and Percy Newell at the wheel. Arnol Priester replaced Jack and stayed on the boat until almost the end of his career. After the war, Arnol trained Oliver Reese, cub pilot, fulfilling Ollie's boyhood dream of piloting on the river at age 22.

In the 1930s and '40s, warm summer evenings were wonderful downtown. Tourists and natives alike might start out the evening lining the sidewalk on the railroad bridge to watch the steamboat load up for its evening trip to the Stand Rock Indian Ceremonial. Ralph Connor would wave from a window high up in the Dells Boat Company building, the final warning whistle would blow, lines were thrown off and the boat was on its way. The crowd gradually moved up town where they might play bingo near the theater and perhaps win a radio or an "Indian" blanket. Movies and dancing at the Wharf were popular and an ice cream cone at Bauer and O'Neil's was 5¢. There were band concerts one night a week and occasional water fights when the Kilbourn Fire Department challenged nearby towns. The rules were changed somewhat when Hugo Van Ells lost the sight in one eye to one of those streams of water. One of the favorite sports was watching the funny tourists and no doubt they equally enjoyed watching the funny natives.

During the war years from 1942 to 1945, gas was in short supply and was rationed. It was a problem to get enough to run the launches. The steamer *Winnebago* was used more because the oil was easier to come by. As many men joined the services and others went to work at Badger Ordnance, younger and younger boys were allowed to guide on the river.

The crowds waited in long lines for Greyhound buses, service in restaurants outside the movie theater and on the ramp leading down to the docks for a boat trip. On weekends the crowds were usually swelled with soldiers on weekend passes from nearby camps. On V-J Day, there was dancing down Broadway with a snake dance and some even said that Miriam Bennett, who never drank, got drunk and blew the steamboat whistle. If she did, it was stone-cold sober exuberance.

The Sunday of Labor Day weekend, 1945, Wisconsin Dells was so crowded with tourists that guide boat captain Roger Stroede and his river guide, Bud Gussel, ran five complete Upper Dells trips, with the first starting at 7:00 AM.

Ownership in the Consolidated Boat Company was changing. Ralph Hines bought into the corporation in November, 1943 and Mark Trumble bought Dee Olderr's stock in May 1947. Fat Blatchley bought the stock of Silas Knudsen in January, 1948. Mike Uphoff bought Madeline Marlow's stock the following year. They were known as the "Big Four."

Postwar prosperity brought more visitors and new ideas. Attractions were built and the Chamber of Commerce increased its efforts for a wider base of contributors and more advertising.

In the early years, guides had jumped the gap at Stand Rock on the Upper Dells trip but by late 1947, that practice was forbidden and dogs leapt over for every boat load of passengers.

Steam was becoming a thing of the past and not many were still skilled in its maintenance except the aging John Jones, the *Winnebago's* engineer. It also takes a large crew to run a steamboat. In the winter of 1948, the Dells Boat Company converted the *Winnebago* to diesel and it became the *Clipper Winnebago,* still in service. Following the tradition of bad luck on first trips, the boat was steering all wrong until Arnol Priester figured out that the steering cables had been reversed.

When Jack Olson came home from the Navy in 1946, he urged his father, Grover, to buy steel boats to replace the wooden launches. Olson's *Chief* was the first double-decked steel boat in the Upper Dells. In 1952, Oliver Helland of Riverview had the next steel boat and by the end of the 1950s, all were steel boats and all still in service.

Olson Boat Company owned the *Chief, Yellow Thunder* and *Red Cloud.* Riverview operated *Marquette, Joliet* and *Belle Boyd.* Dells Boat Company had the *Captain, Commodore,* the *George I. Haight* which was re-named *Commander* and the *Clipper Winnebago.* The Consolidated Boat Company owned by Fat Blatchley, Ralph Hines, Mark Trumble and Mike Uphoff, operated the *Dell Queen, Duchess* and *Empress.* Mark Trumble built the *Mark Twain.* The Silver

Built to carry troops to storm the beaches of the Pacific during World War II, the amphibious DUKW was transformed into the DUCK at Wisconsin Dells. Mel Flath brought the first Ducks to the Dells in 1946 and they quickly became one of the area's most popular attractions. (Courtesy, H. H. Bennett Studio Foundation)

The Lower Dells Boat Dock, c. 1950, prior to the construction of the Broadway Bridge. (Courtesy, H. H. Bennett Studio Foundation)

Dollar Boat Line owned the *Badger* and the *Wisconsin*.

Charlie Ruch and Manny Wanderer built the *North Star*, later sold to the Dells Associated Boat Line. In the Lower Dells, steel boats owned by the Riverview and Dells Boat Companies were *General Bailey, Voyageur, Viking* and the *Chicagoan*.

George Crandall's heirs, the Connors and Mussons had long been concerned with the future of their holdings in the Dells since they had no children. They were also worried about the preservation of this great natural resource and hoped it could be made a national park but there were too many unconnected small parcels. The state didn't know how to manage the commercial operations.

Finally the best solution at that time was found. On January 16, 1954, the Crandall holdings of 1200 acres of land, the assets of the Dells Boat Company, the Hotel Crandall and an undivided half interest in Lower Dells properties were given to the Wisconsin Alumni Research Foundation.

The Fred Harvey Company managed the properties for five years until WARF took over management in 1958, appointing Tim Johnson as manager. WARF had also pledged that they would try to acquire more properties along the river.

Illness forced Oliver Helland to resign as manager of Riverview Boat Line and his son, Peter, took over. Oliver died in 1957.

On May 14, 1958 Helen Raab and her husband, Herman Brietenbach, entered into an "arrangement similar to the Connor-Musson gift for a one-half interest in their Dells Corporation" which held a 200 acre parcel of land on the west bank of the Lower Dells to Dell Creek. The other half interest in this parcel was purchased from Dr. R.O. Ebert.

In 1954 Grover Olson sold his company to his sons, Jack and Ben.

Ducks, the army surplus land and water vehicles, were first brought into Lake Delton by Mel Flath in 1946. He operated a tourist trip from land near the present Mexicali Rose until 1952. Dr. Ebert bought out Flath and operated through 1954. Also in 1954, the Olsons and Hellands bought three ducks and ran them in Mirror Lake. Don Pagel owned a few ducks on Mirror Lake and Lake Delton. Ed Baggot and Clark Winn operated Aquaducks on Mirror Lake for six years before selling out to the Wisconsin Ducks in 1976.

In 1954, Dr. Ebert built a duck dock on Hwy 12, 1890 Wisconsin Dells Parkway. After the Raab-Brietenbach-Ebert purchase-gift to WARF in the Lower Dells, the Original Wisconsin Ducks, owned by the Dells Associated Boat Line, leased that property for their trips. These World War II vehicles gave their passengers a fun ride through the woods up hill and down dale, splashed into the Lower Dells below Echo Point, into Lake Delton, past Dawn Manor and old Newport and wind through the woods and canyons. The trip grew in popularity every year. Dan Gavinski succeeded John Dixon as General Manager.

Flath's Dells Ducks was sold to Wisconsin Ducks in 1965 and 1966 with a lease on Flath's property until 1977.

As the area kept expanding, even the conservative bank of Wisconsin Dells decided that loaning money to summer businesses would be a good investment.

In 1957, Ed Baggot, his father Leo, and Clark Winn bought the Soma Boat Line, operating from the slough. In 1958 they also started a Lower Dells boat trip entering the river across from the Sugar Bowl. When they bought the company, there were the small boats and gradually they replaced these with seven steel ones. Some of their names were *Wanderer, Leroy Gates, Kilbourn* and *Red Eagle*. The shorter no-stop trip was still popular, they had several ticket offices and rivalry continued with the companies making the three stops. One of their problems was the Illinois Avenue bridge which allowed these boats only a two foot clearance at a normal stage of water. When the water was high, they were locked in. In October, 1970, Ed Baggot and Glenn Blatchley requested that the city raise this bridge. The city refused to take action and finally the Soma Boat Line appealed to the courts. The Circuit Court ruled that the bridge was not an obstruction citing the Northwest Ordinance and the Supreme Court backed this decision. In 1974 the Soma Boat Line offered to pay $10,000 toward abatement of the Illinois Avenue bridge and the possibility of a road around Crandall Bay near Meadowbrook Motel was discussed. By 1983, fill was dumped to start this road but the DNR stopped this project over a navigable stream.

Ardell Abrahamson and Jerry Matthews, art teacher, tried to revive steamboating by building the *Apollo II*, 541106, at Wisconsin Dells. She was an exact replica of the first *Apollo*. "this was accomplished by the salvaging of artifacts from the sunken boat, working from old photographs and diving to the hulk in order to obtain acurate measurements. Both engines were brought up to be copied by the Nekoosa Foundry for use on the new boat. The construction began in 1968 and was completed three years later. Her measurements were slightly larger than the original boat, being 108' x 24' x 4'. She was built with a wooden hull, consisting of plywood planking over fir framing and was complete with intricate jigsaw trim around the decks, pilot house and railing. The *Apollo II* was built at Catfish Bay near Plainville. Her first trip down to her dock under River Road bridge foretold more troubles yet to come. Captain Kelly, a St. Laurence River pilot, would take no advice from Jack Morse, an experienced Dells pilot, when it was evident that Kelly knew nothing about the Narrows. So Morse stepped back and watched Kelly order his helmsman, Bernie Bennett, who also had no steamboating experience, "A little more tight, a little more right." Finally Bennett said, "It won't turn any farther." First the boat hit trees in the Navy yard, then hit Circle Bend on the other side of the river. When the landing was attempted in town, the dock was at the wrong angle and the *Apollo* was drifting stern first downstream toward the Olson and municipal docks. In desperation, Kelly ordered the anchor to be thrown out. It held and the boat swung around and was finally landed.

The first formal trip with 150 passengers made an unscheduled landing at the beach across from the Canyon.

Design faults and clumsy handling limited its trips to the Old Dell House and back. In the following years rudder depths were changed and extra keel was added to the prow. Meanwhile the owners were insolvent and the Reedsburg Bank attempted to run her.

The boat was required to carry a licensed steam engineer and when others quit, Norman Sandley filled this role. Old steamer captains Jack Morse and Charlie Day came out of retirement to advise or train a new pilot. Young Joe Edmonds was the most successful pilot in its final years.

The *Apollo II* sat and rotted on dry land near Holiday Shores Campground. Finally it burned on June 9, 1991. As Ardell Abrahamson left town in defeat, he told his friend, "It was a noble thing to have done."

One could write a whole book of river stories. Competition was sometimes dirty for the tourist dollars. One boat would try to cut another off at the Narrows or spray the rival boats with water, but they helped each other also. Owners fought tooth and nail and then joined in a round of golf as their employees lifted their glasses together after hours or joined in the annual boat party.

Fat Blatchley was a well-loved river man. His son, Peter, says, "A sure sign of spring and the beginning of another boat season was Dad falling in the river. It got to be quite the event. People would ask, 'Has Fat Blatchley fallen in the creek yet?' And if not they would say, "Well the boating season can't be too far away, he's bound to go in.' I think it got to be such a talked about event, Dad would fall in on purpose and, even though drenched, he would head right up town to one of the watering holes to show everyone a new season was here."

Employers hired as many local people as they could. Many still take pride in the students who worked their way through college in their employ. And the students learned responsibility, ease with the public and salesmanship.

Ownership in the Consolidated Boat Company changed again when Fat Blatchley died in

The Upper Dells fleet, c. 1960. (Courtesy, H. H. Bennett Studio Foundation)

1975 and his shares passed to his five children. Peter Blatchley became the manager. Ralph Hines died in 1977 and his shares went to his wife, Alice. Mark Trumble died in August 1979 and his shares were inherited by his wife, Delores and then their children. After Mike Uphoff's death in 1991, his stock went into trust with his son, Jack, as trustee.

In 1994, Consolidated Boat Company was sold to the Dells, Riverview and Olson Boat Companies. Peter remains close to the river, owning Carps Marine with Gary "Carp" Fish, selling and servicing boats.

In 1984, Ben and Jack Olson sold their boat company to Ben's son Paul.

In 1985, Ed Baggot and Clark Winn sold their boat company to Wisconsin Ducks, a subsidiary of Dells Associated Boat Lines, who later sold the property for the Sunset Coves Condominiums, retaining the boats.

When Tim Johnson retired in 1991, he had managed the WARF interests in the Dells for 23 years. Jack Anchor served from 1969 to 1978. John Dixon, long a member of the operations under WARF's control, including Fort Dells and Wisconsin Ducks, was named General Manager.

WARF had continued to buy riverbank property until they increased the Crandall gift from 1200 to 1800 acres. Through 1976, they had spent about $950,000 buying among others, the Pines Resort, Echo Point in the Lower Dells, the north side of Witches Gulch, Snider and Potter property near the Narrows, Avery's, Bowden's and Sunset Lodge near Swallow's Nest, Ravenswood and Pine Glen resorts in the Lower Dells. Buildings on the riverbank were removed.

WARF never pursued property owners but many came to them as they wished to retire and were interested in preservation. Many sellers were allowed to live out their lives in their old homes.

In 1986, WARF managed to outbid a group of Texas people for the Cambrian Lodge on Stand Rock Road. This group was planning to build a high rise condominium and a 500 foot boat marina on the 17 acres with 12,300 feet of river frontage.

During the later years, burning and demolition of buildings was limited by many environmental restrictions. Taxes on the properties were going up and were a great burdem.

By 1991, the only private properties not owned by WARF or Upham Woods were Chula Vista with restrictions on the riverbank, the Bird Cottage, Federbusch's at Devil's Elbow and the Grail descendants.

In the Lower Dells all property on the west bank down to Dell Creek is preserved and on the east bank only the Sisters of Charity acreage is privately owned. This leaves some private properties down stream from the old Pine Glen property.

Private boats have increased over the years and are launched at the end of Indiana Avenue into the slough. The city has built docks for private owners in this area also.

Tourists who come to the Dells now are often in too much of a hurry to take a two-hour boat trip or are more interested in the newer attractions that have grown up around an area of natural beauty. Many bewail this trend, but the river, its majesty and beauty have been enhanced over the years.

Two sportsmen relaxing at the Pines resort.

The Wisconsin Dells Hotel Industry

The Early Days: Raftsmen and Settlers

There were hotels in this area long before Kilbourn or any other town existed. The first were taverns and stopping places for lumbermen as they rafted down the Wisconsin and hiked the long road back to the northern pineries. The earliest and most famous of these was the Dell House, standing at the foot of the Devil's Elbow. Robert Allen, the first settler in the area, built it when he arrived in 1838; it was one of the first frame houses on the river north of Portage. Jared Walsworth put up his log tavern near Big Spring a year or so later. Soon there were a number of stopping places scattered along the pinery road: Roswell Bullock's place, also near Big Spring; Thomas Rich's house on Dell Prairie, Whit Sayer's place at Point Bluff; and William Ward's hotel at White Creek. Down by the mouth of Dell Creek, Joe Kendrick ferried men, machinery and supplies across the Wisconsin River on their way to the north woods, and kept a log hotel as a sideline.

These were crude places, built to house rough men. The lumbermen slept on the floor, packed so close it was impossible to step over them. While awake the men took part in "many jolly revels", as editor and historian J.E. Jones later discreetly put it. Other sources mention drinking, gambling, fighting and prostitution.

The local Ho-Chunk resisted this encroachment on their territory. Walsworth and Bullock, who had married two Native American sisters, were grudgingly tolerated by their in-laws. But within months of Allen's arrival, the tribe protested to the American government about his presence. There was no reply from Washington. By the late 1840's, the Ho-Chunk were being driven off their land by a combination of dubious government dealings and straightforward force, and the lumbermen were followed by a flood of more respectable settlers, eager to carve permanent farms and towns out of the newly available land.

The hotels that sprang up to accommodate them aimed for a more respectable reputation, too. When Daniel Eighmy built his traveler's home about 1849, east of the Briggsville road, he put up a sign showing two geese drinking amicably together from a horse trough, with the words "Fair Play House. Peace and Plenty." Each newborn village spawned its own hotel. James Edson, one of the first settlers in Plainville, built a hotel there in 1848. In 1849, Alexander Vosler put up a board shanty to house the men building Delton's first mill; a year later he built the more substantial Delton House. Charles Mason established the first hotel in Briggsville in the early 1850's; the lake created there behind the dam was named after him.

Newport especially was booming. Joe Kendrick's log hotel was soon superseded by larger frame hotels on both sides of the river. On the east bank stood the Bradbury Hotel; the west side boasted two more. The Clark House was a two-story business block with hotel, stores and saloon. The Steele Tavern, built by William and James Steele in 1852, was the political, business, and social headquarters of Newport. An early settler, Mary Markham Jenkins, remembered her days as a young girl with pleasure. The town was filled with bright young men attracted by "rose-colored visions of what Newport was to be..Parties were generally held in the old hotel..Everyone danced that knew how."

There were a number of smaller boarding houses and plans for still more hotels. But then the railroad was routed through Kilbourn, and Newport's rosy future dissolved.

Kilbourn's First Hotels

"In the formation of new villages, the usual order is first a blacksmith shop, then a sawmill, and after that other enterprise demanded from the situation," noted an early Columbia county history. "In Kilbourn City, the first thing was a newspaper, second a carpenter shop, and third a hotel." The hotel arrived in the winter of 1855-56, hauled by oxen from Newport to what would be the corner of Oak and Broadway. The owner, Captain John Tanner, had decided to go into the hostelry business when visitors told Mrs. Tanner her cooking was "so excellent that she should open a hotel." Legend has it that the first paid meal in Kilbourn was served while the building was still on the mover's rollers.

Known successively as the St. Nicholas House, the Tanner House, and the Finch Hotel, this was the premier hotel in the Dells for much of its long life. Through the years it underwent many additions and remodellings; by the time it was torn down in the 1950's, nobody was sure which part was the original building.

Other hotels were soon established. The Forest City Hotel flourished briefly before disappearing with the forest. The Railroad House (later known as the Commercial, the City, and Stanton's) was built by Carl Moeller in 1857, across the street from the depot. The American House went up next door in 1860; it eventually became the Hile House.

These were commercial hotels; the early tourist traffic was too sparse to support a seasonal establishment. Before the mid-70's, when steamboats finally appeared on the river, it took a great deal of effort to tour the spectacular Dells scenery. The Tanner House provided a two seated buggy to drive its guests upriver, and a rowboat for their return down through the Dells, but capacity was obviously limited. Most people, one guidebook noted, "had to content themselves with standing on the bridge and admiring the beautiful but comparatively tame scenery observable from that point."

However, young Kilbourn City was a thriving market town and crossroads. Lumbermen who had safely negotiated the Narrows celebrated with an overnight stay at one of the hotels on LaCrosse Street, "merging next morning looking slightly dazed and quite 'Broke'," according to an early townswoman. Travelling salesmen arrived by train armed with samples to show local merchants and customers. Many commercial hotels provided a special sample room where drummers could invite potential clients to inspect their goods over a friendly drink. Before the Chicago and NorthWestern line siphoned off Sauk County business in 1872, merchants drew trade from as far away as Baraboo and Reedsburg. When farmers made their monthly trip to town to buy supplies and ship produce, they also needed a place to spend the night. These hotels were located in the heart of the business district, convenient to the railroad, and open year-around. Iness Waterman Thompson had fond memories of growing up after the turn of the century in the Hotel Waterman, which had begun as the "Farmers Home" in 1877. "It was a typical farmer's hotel," she recalled. There was a big barn and an hostler to tend the horses; first-class barn accomodations "for farmers and transients" cost from $1.00 to $1.50 per day. Her mother served hearty meals of meat, potatoes, and a plain vegetable – "no fancy salad" – plus pie for dessert, all for 35¢.

When the Civil War broke out, the hotels became recruiting centers. A company of militia was organized at Plainville, when "the embryo soldiers marched, and wheeled, and charged, and flanked through the streets by day, and met at Tyler's hotel...nights to hold their campfires...or jolly social dances." In Kilbourn City, S.S. Landt

The Tanner House, the first hotel in Kilbourn, was moved from Newport by oxen in the winter of 1855-56 to the corner of Broadway and Oak. A hotel would remain on this site for nearly 100 years. (Courtesy, H. H. Bennett Studio Foundation)

recruited volunteers at the Tanner House; he later recalled that staunchly patriotic Captain Tanner provided him with "the best accomodations at a reasonable price." In Delton, Vosler's hotel was now owned by Justus Freer, who changed its name to the Union House and housed the rambunctious boys of Company E in the big ballroom upstairs. The recruits who would become some of Sherman's toughest soldiers tested his patriotism severely. They staged nightly pillow fights and midnight initiations, jumped on the beds, and generally wrecked the place. "There was not one bedstead left standing when the boys left for Madison," recounted Freer years later. "Everyone was sleeping on the floor for the last week at least."

Even in less stirring times hotels served as gathering places for men of the town. Some local businessmen lived there - the shoemaker next door, the blacksmith, the telegraph operator. Others might stop in for a meal or a drink, to check out the drummers' wares, or just to sort over the news of the day. "They had a pole up in the center of the office," remembered Iness Thompson, "and they sat..with their feet on the pole and...talked about all the things that should be done in the town."

Tourist Hotels

By the 1870'S, the steamboats and publicity from H.H. Bennett's stereo views had increased the tourist traffic significantly. The hotels took advantage of it. The Tanner House, newly purchased by Reedsburg innkeeper W.H. Finch and rechristened the Finch House, advertised widely that it had been "remodelled and refurnished throughout" to appeal to the more fastidious tourist trade. The Kilbourn City Cornet Band was engaged to serenade guests from the balcony. Finch's improvements paid off; by 1880, he was entertaining 3500 visitors a year.

Glen Cottage was the first truly seasonal tourist hotel. It began as the seven-room home of John Vliet, president of the Wisconsin River Hydraulic Company. Like the Tanner House, it had been hauled from Newport in 1856, to the corner of Superior and Wisconsin. And like the Tanner House, it gained many piecemeal additions over the next hundred years. By 1875, J. H. Dunn was advertising its beautiful view of the river and convenient location near the steamers' landing. It operated intermittently for some years, but once the G. H. Crandall family took charge of operations, it soon challenged the Finch as the best hotel in town.

When the Crandalls first leased the property from James Dixon in 1895, success was by no means certain. Previous tenants had failed and left their furniture behind to cover the rent. At the Ladies Aid Society, another member told Mrs. Dixon, "I suppose, Cora, that you and Jim will have some more nice furniture when the Crandalls go out of Glen Cottage." Inevitably, the remark reached Nellie Crandall's ears, and stiffened her

The Finch House, which followed the Tanner House, was the premier hotel in Kilbourn. Like other fine hotels, the Finch House operated its own horse-drawn "hack" whose top-hatted driver met the travelers at the depot and drove them to their lodgings. (Courtesy, H. H. Bennett Studio Foundation)

resolve. "There was no work too hard and no hours too long for Nell or George," wrote their daughter, Lois Crandall Musson, years later. "They won't get our furniture," said Nell to herself and they didn't." In fact, they were so successful that a 20 room addition was built in their second year. In 1901, after experimenting with other ventures including the Larks Hotel up the river, they bought the property from the Dixons and renamed it the Hotel Crandall. It eventually surpassed the Finch as the top hotel in the Dells, and outlasted it, operating until the 1970s.

Then as now, the newspaper regularly announced new establishments with a flourish of great optimism - establishments which were never heard of again. But a handful of other hotels followed Glen Cottage with some success. As its name implies, the Farmer's Home (later the Rose House/Hotel Waterman/Kilbourn Inn) began as a year-round farmers' hotel when Dick Rose remodelled a group of buildings and barn on Superior Street in 1877. But it welcomed summer visitors too. Later, from the 1920's until its demise in 1952, it was known as the Kilbourn Inn and given over to the tourist trade.

The old American remained open year-round, but was transformed from a farmer's hotel into the stylish Hile House after Adam Hile bought it. The Hile House (later called the Traveler's Motel) is gone, torn down in the 1980's.

Across town from the Hile House, Schofield Cottages had been founded by another Civil War hero. Colonel Robert Schofield had risen through the ranks from private, eventually being wounded and taken prisoner at Gettysburg. After the war he married Alanson Holly's daughter Josephine; and when his sight finally failed as a result of his harrowing war experiences, they returned to Kilbourn City. On a big tract of land at the outskirts of town, just north of Broadway, the Schofields opened their quiet vacation resort. Today, it is the only early Kilbourn hotel still in existence; after passing through many hands, it is now called Indian Trail Motel.

The Markham also stood on the far east side of town, atop the hill at the end of Washington Avenue. It had a long and misfortune-plagued history, only a small portion of which was spent as a hotel. Originally built at Point Bluff in 1856 as a Methodist seminary which went bankrupt, the building was moved to Kilbourn in 1866 by a group of local Methodists. They reopened it as the Kilbourn Institute. Two years later it burned to the ground; it was rebuilt, but never reopened. Instead, the property was sold and remodelled into a water-cure medical institute, which opened in 1878 and was overseen by a succession of doctors, including the husband and wife team of Drs. George and Amanda McElroy. The Hygienic Institute was a health spa, not a hospital. "As many scholars and professional visitors make it their rendezvous, the cultured and gifted gravitate there also, where the best eating and drinking can be had with choice conversation and lively

The Crandall Inn, began as the home (left) Hydraulic Company President John Vliet hauled from Newport to the corner of Superior and Wisconsin in 1856. In the 1870s, it was a hotel called Glen Cottage. In 1895, the Crandall family enlarged and renamed it (center), eventually adding the pillared entranceway (bottom) for which it was known until it was destroyed by fire in 1974. (Courtesy, H. H. Bennett Studio Foundation)

discussions on the literature, politics and philosophy of the day," read a contemporary account. "Every facility for calisthenics and out-door sports is found on the lawns, and impromptu musicales, readings or charades form pleasant pastimes during these cool evenings." By 1890, the institute was closed and J. B Markham and his son Henry were running it strictly as a summer hotel. That closed, too, around the turn of the century. Thereafter, the property was used as a private residence. In 1941 it was again destroyed by fire. It was rebuilt and Louis Rockoff operated a junk business and sold eggs until 1958 when it was sold to Platt's Garage.

The old City hotel also burned down in 1892. The Park Hotel was built where its barn had stood, across from the depot on LaCrosse Street. In 1902 the Park in turn was wrecked by fire, but enough remained to rebuild it. Later, it became the Hotel Helland.

Fire was clearly a constant peril in the hotel business. Before electricity, light was provided by kerosene lamps, which were a source of both work and worry. "The office had large baseburner lamps and individual rooms each had an ordinary kerosene lamp with glass chimney," wrote Lois Crandall Musson, who grew up in Glen Cottage/ The Crandall. "These chimneys had to be cleaned each day, wicks had to be trimmed and bases filled with kerosene." The kitchen was another danger spot. On one occasion, a fire started under the big wood stove while lunch was being served. According to Lois Musson, "There wasn't a delay in the service. The cook kept right on working, even adding a few sticks of wood to keep the heat up, while men with axes chopped a hole in the floor beside the stove and extinguished the fire underneath." Only one guest noticed anything wrong. Ironically, the Crandall survived these hazardous years only to be destroyed by a suspected arson fire in 1974.

These seven hotels handled the tourists and business travelers of 19th century Kilbourn. The largest could house a hundred guests, the smallest about twenty. There were also a number of boarding houses. But as late as 1905, the newspaper warned that an anticipated party of four hundred Masons from Milwaukee "would tax hotels in the Dells and overflow into Kilbourn hostelries."

You could pay from $1.50 to $2.50 per night, depending on where you stayed; there were discounted weekly rates of $7.00 to $10.00, and most tourists did stay at least two weeks, and often all summer. Boarding houses were a little cheaper. "One important consideration of a summer at the Dells is economy," according to one guidebook. "A season here costs no more than it does in ordinary homes or boarding houses."

The Dells was never a classic Victorian resort. At fashionable summer resorts such as Lake Geneva, Waukesha, or Oconomowoc, elegant ladies rocked on the hotel veranda in refined idleness, keeping one eye on the children and the other on the ever-present fashion parade. They whiled the lazy days away sewing, chatting, changing their clothes three times a day, and waiting for their husbands to join them on the weekends.

In contrast, Kilbourn was middle-class and unpretentious. It emphasized comfort over elegance. The Finch proudly advertised it had been called "one of the rightest, freshest, home-likest houses we ever saw." Glen Cottage was "an attractive and pleasant home." You needn't worry about being in the latest style. "The very best people appear in check or drab travelling dresses," a travel writer assured anxious visitors. "The journey up the river...is made in a steamer and can not be satisfactory if encumbered by the restraints of dress." "Here is seen no display of equipage, no extravagances of dress or other evidences of fashionable life" wrote a contemporary Kilbourn native. Men often came along with women and children. Days were spent exploring the natural beauties of the river, hiking, picnicking, fishing or even braving the rutted roads and taking a bicycle or carriage ride through the countryside.

In the 1890's, this style of pastoral vacation began to gain popularity across the nation. People now sought to be revitalized by the beauties of nature and refreshed by wholesome food and clean country air. "The summer is not for the summer hotel, it is for the closest possible association with Nature," admonished the *Ladies' Home Journal*. This was where the Dells' strength lay, and soon a new type of summer place, the farm resort, began appearing up and down the river, promising "pure, sweet, holy rest and recreation - atordinary prices."

The Resorts

All along the road that would become Highway 13 and then River Road, farmers began taking in summer boarders. As they gradually abandoned the struggle to wrest a living from the sandy soil, their farms evolved into full-fledged resorts. A few resorts grew up elsewhere - Walmar Lodge across the river (later known as Pa-lea-rida/ Raftsmen's/Rustic Pines/Cambrian Lodge); Pine Glen and Ravenswood in the Lower Dells; the Blue Mound Resort; and later Multnomah on the east end of town - but "Lucky 13" was the heart of resort country. Meadowbrook, Birchcliff, Orchard Farm, Leute's Dells Farm/Artist's Glen, The Larks/ Dells Inn, Berry's Cold Water Canyon, Butternut Lodge, The Pines, Rood's Glen, Chula Vista, Kriegel's, Tenney's Riverdale Farm, Atcherson's - from the edge of town up to Plainville, the highway was lined with resorts. Leute's was the

The Crandall Family enjoying the river at the Narrows. As the photo indicates, from its earliest days the Dells has always been a place where people of all ages can enjoy nature and relax together. (Courtesy, H. H. Bennett Studio Foundation)

oldest, and may have been taking in boarders as early as the 1870's. The former farms were set close to the road. Only places like The Pines, which had been planned as resorts from the first, were built close to the river.

The story of Birchcliff was typical. In 1916, Harry and Clara Loomis bought thirty acres of farmland on Highway 13, put up a house and barn, and began taking in guests two years later. In those early days, the Loomises and their three children turned their own bedrooms over to the paying guests. Clara was both cook and waitress. "When we were starting out," remembered Damon Loomis, "my mother would be in the kitchen cooking, and guests would come into our living room; (we'd) pack 'em in there plus the front porch." It wasn't long before the Loomises were adding on a main lodge, dining room, and cottages "like Topsy grew up..all around the place", and hiring help. But Birchcliff remained a working farm, which meant the summer help had quite a variety of duties. Bernice Loomis came to work as a waitress in 1936 and later married Damon. "I remember having to drive the truck while they were trying to put hay in the barn," she said. It was also a chore preparing chicken dinners twice a week. First the chickens had to be caught, butchered, and dressed; then the waitresses had to pick out all the feathers before the birds could finally be cooked. "I was never so glad in all my life as when they got rid of the chickens and we could buy them all prepared," she recalled. "Well, it got to the point where you couldn't find a girl who would pick a chicken."

That good fresh farm food ws a major drawing card of the resorts, which provided three hearty meals a day on the "American Plan". In the days before reliable refrigeration, top quality food was not something to take for granted. Adolph Priester's family operated Rood's Glen Resort, and they bought only as much meat as they could use each day. Stores in town were two and a half miles away and they opened early, he recalled. "I remember my grandfather going down to get fresh meat from the butcher shop about 5:30 in the morning." But most food came straight from the farm itself. Every resort had a big garden; Kriegel's farther from town, butchered and smoked their own meat; and Ravenswood promised "Plenty of milk and cream from our own herd." We maintain our own supply of fresh farm, garden and dairy products, which are tastily and generously served," advertised Birchcliff. When a guest wanted eggs for breakfast, "My sister Marion would go out and chase the hen off the nest and grab the egg," recalled Damon Loomis. "And that's what you'd call a fresh egg!"

The farm wives were used to cooking for crowds, and they were all known as wonderful cooks. "Well, they had to be," pointed out Adolph Priester. "Otherwise people didn't stay there." As the resorts grew, they began hiring professional chefs. "We had one who changed our menu considerably," remembered Audrey Berry Fisher, whose family owned Berry's Coldwater Canyon Resort. "We had never had Italian food of any kind, but he was Italian, which would have been all right of itself..however, they did object to a couple things...He kept wanting the waitresses to stand against the door while he threw knives at them. He fancied himself quite a knife thrower." Both the resort and the waitresses survived the summer.

Guests had plenty of other activities to choose from as well. Among them were tennis, archery, horseback riding, badminton, croquet, horseshoes, shuffleboard, ping-pong, bowling, and dancing. Berry's put in one of Wisconsin's first golf courses in 1923. One could go fishing, or go swimming in the river near Birchcliff and some other resorts. Starting with Multnomah in the twenties, a few resorts put in swimming pools.

The river was the main attraction, of course. Berry's, Rood's Glen and other resorts operated their own launches and boat trips. Hiking was another big activity. "Beautiful walks to Cold Water Canyon, Artist's Glen, Rood's Glen, and Witches Gulch" advertised Butternut Lodge; as many people walked into Witches Gulch and Cold Water Canyon as landed from the river. Paths along the river were well-worn and easy to follow. "You could actually walk all the way down to the Dells (from Berry's) if you were ambitious," recalled Audrey Fisher. And in the evenings, guests could walk over to Parsons Indian Ceremonial, or sometimes rest their feet and enjoy the music from their cottage. "On a clear warm evening we could hear that beautiful All American Quartet singing over there in the hollow," remembered Damon Loomis.

Vacationers stayed at least a week or two–some stayed all season–and they usually came back to the same resort year after year. "In the middle of the summer, when there were so many 'old-timers' as we called them, we'd put on a skit," recalled Damon Loomis. "People would go all the way to Baraboo, Portage, and Reedsburg to find costumes and everything, and they had more darn fun than a picnic, I tell you." At Birchcliff, a different group activity was scheduled each day of the week - a first night get together, the boat trip, the Indian Ceremonial, a picnic at Rocky Arbor, marshmallow roasts, square dancing. "When the Ducks first started, they would come right up here to the lodge and pick up our guests...as many as one and a half Ducks would fill up right on our property and then take them on down," remembered Bernice Loomis. At the end of the day everyone would gather at the snack bar porch. "They'd come in the evening, you know, to talk about the things they'd done during the day and have a sundae or a snack...and that's the way they got to know each other."

As the years went by, people changed, and the resorts changed with them or disappeared. Stays decreased from weeks to days to overnight. A week of hiking, swimming and shuffleboard was no longer lively enough. There were new attractions to take in, and a smorgasbord of restaurants to sample. The American Plan gave way to a European Plan–meals not included–so you could eat where you pleased. By the mid-sixties, vacationers no longer spent enough time at the resort to get acquainted with their hosts or fellow guests. "People would just check in and you'd never see them again," recalled Bernice Loomis with regret. Some resorts adjusted to modern tastes and changed their emphasis; others sold their riverfront property to WARF and shut down.

The resort on Blue or Elephant Mound, northeast of Kilbourn.

The automobile changed the type of lodging visitors sought and made popular cottages like those at the Pines Hotel (above) and the White House on Vine Street (below).

Motorcars, Motels and Rooming Houses

The heyday of farm resorts located miles from town had been possible because the automobile brought them within easy reach. But that same automobile gave birth to the competition that eventually outstripped them - the motel.

The early years of this century were a time of change and doubt for the Kilbourn tourist business. The dam was changing the very look of the river. The railroad was phasing out the big low-rate excursions which had brought thousands of people to the Dells each summer. "Dells Will Be Closed" announced an alarming newspaper headline in the summer of 1908.

That was overstating the case, but the loss of the excursions was a blow. At the turn of the century, if you travelled any distance, you travelled by train. Rural roads were a nameless patchwork of muddy rutted lanes, maintained by farmers who had no training for road construction, and even less enthusiasm. In 1915, when Louise Stettin was a little girl, her family took a trip by horse and buggy from Chicago to Lyndon Station. Their odyssey took nine days. "We didn't know the roads," remembered Lou, and the roads in those days were often unmarked. So at every little town, her father would buy a few provisions at the grocery store, ask how far it was to the next town and get directions. "And the roads were all sand and stones, and lots of times we had to get out of the buggy and walk up a hill, or the horse couldn't pull it." The roads were so narrow they had to pull over whenever they met another team of horses. Near Bristol, "we had thundershowers and the bridges were out," said Lou, which delayed them several days; they also had to buy a new horse when theirs took sick. None of it fazed an eight-year-old girl. "It was a great adventure," said Lou.

There were no hotels in the country. "Every night we stopped at different farm houses," said Lou. Late each afternoon, her mother and father would look for a clean well-kept place and knock on the door. The farm families welcomed travelers all the way from Chicago with interesting stories to tell. The children, who fancied themselves actresses, would put on impromptu shows for their hosts, and Lou would play piano. "They thought that was wonderful," she recalled. "Lots of places didn't want to take money–my mother had to throw it down on the table. And then they would give us breakfast and supper and maybe a basket of fried chicken for the next day."

Early motorists were daring dventurers who had to carry everything they might need–food, tents, gasoline, and of course repair tools. Like Lou's family, they had to camp out or find private lodging along the way. But they revelled in their freedom from railroad routes and timetables, and they heralded change. As automobiles became more affordable, motoring grew rapidly from a sport to an accepted middle-class mode of travel. In 1905, when Wisconsin began registering motor vehicles, there were fewer than 1500 in the state; by 1918, there were over 200,000.

In 1918 Wisconsin established a state trunk highway system. It took one week in May to mark 5,000 miles of state highways, using the number system which was later adopted nationwide. Most of the system consisted of sand and dirt roads, and hundreds of miles were in poor condition. But at last signs and maps pointed the way from town to town, and the state had assumed some responsibility for road maintenance.

Thanks to the Wisconsin River bridge, Kilbourn was once again an important crossroads on the main route between Chicago and the Twin Cities. "This season Kilbourn has been full of automobiles from all over the middle west, and from eastern and southern states," reported the *Kilbourn Weekly Events* in 1920, estimating that 3,000 cars visited the Dells that Fourth of July. "Hotels have had to equip themselves with bathrooms for the convenience of the dusty travellers," wrote a Kilbourn native.

In general, however, motor tourists didn't like the established railroad hotels. Arriving dirty and dishevelled from a day on the road, they were uncomfortable in the formal lobby of a good hotel. The meals and checkout times were geared to railroad timetables, not motorists' needs. The car had to be parked in a garage blocks away.

An alternative was developed to meet the needs of early travelers, who were already accustomed to camping by the side of the road. Towns began offering free campgrounds with fireplaces, picnic tables, and rudimentary sanitary facilities, hoping to attract tourist traffic and dollars. Within a few years most municipal autocamps began charging a fee, partly to finance improvements expected by increasingly demanding tourists, and partly to weed out riff-raff with no money to spend. This provided an opening for private entrepreneurs, who soon took over the business. In Kilbourn, the Crandall family bought the property across the river from the Upper Dells Boat Docks, and opened the Dells Park autocamp. Riverview offered free campsites conveniently adjacent to their boat landing, and there were other campgrounds along Highways 12 and 16.

Competition was unrelenting. Autocampers compared notes about facilities and rates, and standards rose rapidly as each owner tried to top the camp down the road. Privies were the norm one year, flush toilets the next. Cold showers gave way to hot. One idea that spread quickly was providing cabins, which protected both traveler and owner from the vagaries of bad weather. In places like Kilbourn, where tourists were likely to stay a week or more, cabins were especially popular. Soon amenities such as private bathrooms, mattresses and even sheets and towels were expected. At the Dells Park, the Crandalls offered another imaginative and unique option–the chance to sample Native American crafts and culture.

The cabin camp rearranged itself into a row or a horseshoe, and became the "motor court"; and as separate cabins were linked by carports and finally merged into one long low building, the "mo-tel" was born.

Soon non-camping tourists discovered the advantages of the motor court over the traditional hotel - informality, economy, convenience and privacy. This last was a source of considerable ambivalence, however. While the average traveler enjoyed coming and going from his room or cabin without trooping through a central lobby under the scrutiny of a watchful hotel clerk each time–he wondered what the fellow next door was up to when no one was watching. J. Edgar Hoover didn't mince words; he called these places "camps of crime" and "dens of vice and iniquity." His concern was not entirely unjustified. In 1935, when sociologists recorded arrivals, departures, and license plates at motels and motor courts in one big city, they discovered at lest 75% of the business consisted of local couples staying for suspiciously short times.

The Rest-Wood Grill and Cabins, on Highway 12 in the Town of Lyndon.

The Olin Cottages on Highway 13 in Dell Prairie.

Anderson's Rooms on Broadway.

This aspect of the business was less of a problem in vacation areas like the Dells. But all motels had to battle the image of the seedy "No-tell Motel" at the edge of town. Owners reassured prospective guests that they maintained high standards by advertising familiar brand names such as Simmons Beautyrest mattresses and Congoleum flooring, and they provided visible evidence of cleanliness by placing a "sanitizing" strip across the toilet and wrapping glasses, and everything else possible, in paper or cellophane.

Virtually all motels and courts at this time were Mom-and-Pop operations; a few companies tried to start nationwide chains, but couldn't keep up with evolving tastes. Innovation and experimentation continued. Did motel guests prefer baths or showers, a garage or an adjoining parking spot, a kitchenette or a nearby diner? Slowly, a standard plan took shape during the decades between the world wars.

Many of these developments first appeared in southern states, where motels could make money year-round, and only later spread to seasonal motels in the north. As a result, names evoking Florida and the southwest carried a special prestige. The Finch Hotel proclaimed its up-to-date "CALIFORNIA BUNGALOW COURT" was "The Only Bungalow Court of its Kind in the Dells". This legacy survives in the number of motels plunked down in the pine woods of Wisconsin with incongruous names like "Del Rancho", "Aztec", and "Flamingo." Even in the mid 1990's Chula Vista is advertising itself as "A Southern California Style Vacation Resort."

The automobile reshaped the Dells in many other ways. Tourist traffic increased dramatically. "From the beginning of June to the middle of September all previous records of summer visitors have been broken," reported the *Kilbourn Weekly Events* in 1920. "Some of the big days the town has overflowed, not only hotels and private boarding houses were full, but about every private house in town that could do so have taken roomers...one of the leading hotels in Portage said his biggest trade came from the overflow at Kilbourn."

The people of Kilbourn cheerfully set about providing lodging for all these new visitors and their dollars. In 1906, before the impact of the car, the paper noted that Kilbourn now boasted a record number of hostelries - which added up to about a dozen hotels, resorts, and places to stay "of more or less pretension" and half a dozen more private boarding houses. By the 1920's, a tourist brochure listed 46 hotels, resorts, cottages and camps, and no less than 99 private homes which rented rooms to tourists. All in all, there were over 1200 rooms available, plus campsites and cottages. Prices ranged from $8.00 a night (American Plan) at the prestigious Crandall to autocamps where you could stay for free.

And that didn't include the Morris Hotel on Mirror Lake (built by Eliza Morris Ringling, widow

The filling station at the Old Newport Resort on County A in Delton.

of one of the Ringling Brothers, and also known as the Ringling Hotel), or the Dell View, which soon followed in Delton. In 1920, Delton had been called a ghost town, but the automobile brought it back from the dead.

Thanks to Wisconsin Supreme Court Justice Roujet Marshall, the Town of Delton had one of the best road systems in the state. He had been a forceful proponent of good roads at the state level, but he was especially active in his boyhood home of Delton, cajoling farmers and town fathers for support and paying for improvements out of his own pocket. He was often on the spot as the county roads were laid out and built, a familiar figure in his Prince Albert coat, derby hat and custom high-top boots. He masterminded the Delton Cutoff, which brought the road through the village and clipped a mile off the distance to Kilbourn by filling in a deep ravine. "Almost entirely through the interposition of Judge Marshal, the Delton-Kilbourn Road in the Town of Delton was changed from a desert waste of sand and sandstone to a modern macadam road," wrote the state highway engineer.

As a result, the Delton-Mirror Lake-Lower Dells area was within easy reach of Kilbourn tourists. Chicago millionaire William J. Newman spotted the possibilities and laid the foundation for further growth by buying up land creating Lake Delton in the twenties. The Dell View was built as part of his vision of a first-class luxury resort. Cap Parsons moved his Indian ceremonial and trading post from the heart of the River Road resort country to the up-and-coming Lake Delton area in 1938.

But by then the Depression had intervened. When Newman went bankrupt in 1929, his associate Ralph Hines managed to keep the project alive, but further growth was put on hold. A few small resorts clung to the shores of the new lake, but it would be decades before other tourist businesses joined the Dell View and Parsons' on Highway 12 and "the strip".

Weber's Cottages and Cabins on Broadway.

Many other Dells Country resorts were hit hard. Fred Dixon had built Multnomah Lodge during the booming twenties, with the help of family and friends, but he wasn't quite in the clear when the Depression struck. "Financially, it was a very difficult situation, not only for Multnomah but for every business in the area," recounted his nephew John Dixon. "The beauty was that the bank didn't have any need for resorts or businesses. They were better off letting people operate them rather than taking them over, because they wouldn't get any money out of them then...But it was nip-and-tuck." Some, like Tenney's Riverdale Farm, didn't make it. "Things just went from bad to worse," recalled Georgia Tenney Foster. "A real good friend of my dad's offered to lend him $10,000 - which would be like a million, you know, back then - and my dad was just too proud to take

The Dell View Hotel, Lake Delton.

Uphoff's Rotunda Restaurant and Motel, on Hwy 12, Lake Delton, c. 1955. (Courtesy, H.H. Bennett Studio Foundation).

it...He said, I'll lose the place before I'll take charity,' which was the way he thought of it."

Tourists who could no longer afford a week at a nice resort might be able to manage a weekend in a rooming house, though. This had always been an option. "For such as prefer the quiet of a home, private boarding houses offer all that can be desired," advised an 1875 guidebook. When the tourist traffic mushroomed in the twenties, so did the number of rooming houses. "You know, there were no cabins or motels or anything then," explained Celia Drollinger, who helped her mother-in-law with summer boarders. Building cabins took money, but it only took a spare bedroom and a sign to turn a home into a rooming house. That's what Louise Stettin's parents, Ann and William Hinz, did. "They had a light bulb out front and a sign over it saying 'Tourist Home," remembered Lou. Some visitors wrote ahead for reservations, but others might come knocking on the door after midnight. "Usually they'd come and stay a couple days," recalled Patricia Field Bannen, whose mother took in roomers at The Maples and later in the house where Pat still lives. "Quite often they came on the train. Everything was right in town, so you didn't need a car."

Most places went beyond renting the spare room; often the family gave up their own bed-rooms to paying guests. At the Maples, Pat and her brother and sisters lived in a cottage in back for the summer. "When the tourist season was over, and we were allowed back in the parlor and so on, my mother said I'd go in and sit on every chair–sort of saying hello to them again," said Pat. "In this house, we were all up in what my mother called the third floor–it was really the attic. We liked that. It was so hot up there, my mother felt sorry for us–so we got to stay up late and sit on the porch." In some houses, the family slept in the living room, getting up and out of the way early each morning before the guests woke. Lou Stettin remembered one night when twenty-eight people crowded into her parents' four bedroom, one-bathroom house, while her parents spent the night dozing in rocking chairs on the porch.

"My folks weren't poor, but they were looking for a few extra dollars," explained Lou. So were many others; roughly one out of three houses in town rented rooms for the summer. Many tourists, in turn, were pleased to find a place to stay for only 50¢ to $1.00 per person. Others haggled and complained even at those prices. It covered room only, not board, although some places (including both The Maples and the Hinzes) offered breakfast for a little extra. Lou's mother served eggs, toast, coffee, and maybe home-canned peaches for 25¢, getting up at 5:00 AM to fire up the old cookstove.

The Hinzes would also serve dinners on request, which was quite unusual. "There weren't very many (who did)," says Celia Drollinger. She remembered helping her mother-in-law Nora move her furniture out in the summer to make room for dining tables. "She probably was the only rooming house of that type that did serve regular meals."

Nora Drollinger later worked as manager and hostess of the Bowman Home, which also operated as a full-fledged boarding house. "They used to have wonderful meals," recalled Celia. "Just imagine, those women could come and stay for two weeks and not raise a finger and not pay a cent." The Bowman Home was unique. Under the terms of Jennie Bowman's will, working women over 45 were offered a free vacation stay in the gracious house that had been her home, asking only that they tidy their own rooms. For several years, it operated year-round, boarding teachers in the winter, but high heating bills eventually put an end to that.

The Bowman Home may have been a charity, but other places were not, and they used a variety of strategies to bring in business. Some tried a hard sell approach. Freddie Sperbeck worked at Bert Tollaksen's cottages near the corner of Broadway and Vine. It was his job to deliver a sales pitch to incoming visitors who had not yet found rooms. Unfortunately, Freddie had difficulty pronouncing the letter "r". Women tourists who pulled up to the cottages were startled when a strange man approached them and asked "Do you have your wombs yet?"

Smaller places might cut their rates as low as 10¢ a person, especially when business was slow, according to Lou Stettin. And Patricia Field Bannen described a feud between her grandmother, Nell Field, and Nell Olson, who were competing for roomers. "They'd each tell tourists...that the other had bedbugs," said Pat, laughing. "Which neither did...That's the Dells; always ready to give someone a hand down."

While competition with each other could be lively, many hotels and rooming houses joined forces with the boat companies and other summer businesses, in order to snare as many tourists as possible. Ed "Foghorn" Tangney earned his nickname selling boat tickets for Fat Blatchley. "Now, there was another angle to these ticket sales," he explained. "We also filled the rooms all around the area." The overlapping arrangements could get complicated. To begin with, he worked at the corner of Broadway and Vine on property owned by the Wrezinskis, so "of course my first obligation was to fill Wrezinskis' house and then I could do whatever I wanted with the rest of them."

Since many visitors wanted to find a place to stay before buying boat tickets, Foghorn worked out a deal with other rooming houses. He sent them roomers; they sold those roomers his boat tickets; then he got the commission on the sales. "And of course, I did lose some because (the rooming house operators) also had dollar-and-a-half tickets (from other boat companies) and I think they got the commission on those," remembered Foghorn. "But those that I really took care of, they all paid me whatever they sold."

As the Depression came to an end, so did the rooming house era. People had been happy to find an inexpensive place to stay during hard times, but as the number of cabins, motor courts and motels increased, the demand for private rooming houses diminished. Most had stopped taking in summer visitors by the forties.

World War II presented a new set of obstacles to the hospitality industry. Just when people had money again for a summer vacation, gas and tire rationing severely restricted automobile traffic. Food was also rationed, and many locals were off to war or making good wages at the powder plant. "During the war years it was difficult to get help, and that's when we started discontinuing the noon meal (at Birchcliff)," remembered Bernice Loomis. At Rood's Glen "it kind of tapered down to not running during the war, when they could not get food and so on," recalled Adolph Priester, "plus (my grandparents) were getting older at that time." The resort never resumed operation. At Multnomah, Fred Dixon found a way to solve the problem of meat rationing. "Well, I remember during the war that my uncle would raise beef on a farm outside the Dells - illegally, because beef was rationed," said John Dixon. After buying a calf, feeding it, and having it butchered, "we'd bring it back to the hotel in the trunk of his car and put it in the freezer..because (otherwise) he couldn't get enough meat for the guests."

The Blackhawk Hotel on River Road, c. 1955. (Courtesy, H.H. Bennett Studio Foundation).

After The War: Growth and Expansion

The end of the war meant prosperity and growth, but it didn't last long for little motels all across the country. Big motel chains like Holiday Inn and Ramada were being organized and taking their business. The chains incorporated the successful features that had been hammered out by pioneer motel owners, plus they could offer standard reliable accomodations from Maine to California, operate less expensively due to their size, and afford prime locations near the new interstate highways. Nationwide, many Mom-and-Pop motels found themselves elbowed out of business just when good times had finally arrived.

But not in the Dells. Some of the big chains did reach the Dells eventually, but they competed amid a thriving throng of independent motel, campgrounds and resorts. The enormous potential which had been held in check during the Depression and war years had finally been released. New tourist attractions–Tommy Bartlett's ski show, the Deer Park, the Ducks, Storybook Gardens–sprang up along Highway 12. By 1962, the new interstate highway ran without a break from the Illinois border to the Dells; tourists spilled out four exits from Lake Delton to Rocky Arbor. The story of the hospitality industry from then until the present is essentially a story of remarkable growth and ever inflating expectations and prices. Motels, campgrounds and resorts spread out along the highways, filling in "the strip", and encircling Lake Delton. By the mid-1990's there were almost 130 places to stay listed in the area vacation guide. Amenities which had once been unheard of became more common, making the gradual transition from luxury to standard fare: swimming pool, heated pool, indoor pool, air-conditioning, queen-size beds, king-size beds, TV, cable, HBO, Jacuzzi, sauna, microwave, wet bar...

Many of the new places were operated by hard-working families originally from the Chicago area, familiar with the Dells from their own vacations. Robert Kelley had been coming to Wisconsin and Minnesota to fish long before he started the Musical Acres Resort north of the Dells. In 1961 he bought some property on a trout stream with a partner, who later sold out to him. "She and I bought the place together to have a place for our families to stay," he explained. A few years later they decided to turn it into a resort. Other incoming entrepreneurs may have simply seen an inviting business opportunity, or a way to finance vacation property. Bob, who is African American, had another reason. "Some friends had not been able to find a place to stay," he said. "For minorities...there were very limited places in the Dells where they could stay."

Other newcomers came from tight-knit Ukrainian and Polish communities, helping relatives and compatriots get started once they themselves were established. Family support was critical. Bob, his wife Chris, and close friends worked together clearing woods, building a pond, and putting up a recreation hall in the early years; the women pitched in with the heavy work as well as the men. "Every weekend there for a while, we were up cutting out forest and burning brush," he recalled. Like many others, the Kelleys continued to live and work in Chicago. Bob had the advantage of working as a teacher for the Chicago Board of Education, so he was free for the busiest part of the summer season. "When school was out, I'd come up," he said. They were able to get the resort ready in the spring and closed down in the fall by coming up weekends. For those with year-round jobs, juggling schedules was more difficult, the pace even more grueling until the summer business became self-supporting. Logistics aside, the new generation of entrepreneurs faced the same challenges that Dells hotelkeepers had always faced, and they needed the same qualities to succeed. Bob Kelley summed up what it took: "Patience, and a lot of work, and a love of people, and a love of what you're doing."

The hotel industry in the Dells has grown beyond all recognition since Robert Allen built the Dell House in 1838. And yet, although the Dell House and the earliest generation of hotels are gone, today's visitors can still find a surprising number of remnants and connections with the past. The old commercial hotels have been torn down. But there are still year-round hotels where modern-day drummers can show their wares at conventions and home shows, and where the Kiwanis and Jaycees meet to talk about all the things that should be done in the town just as they did at the old Hotel Waterman. The rooming houses are gone, but there are bed-and-breakfasts for those who want a homey atmosphere. Visitors can still find resorts on the river and along River Road. They can choose between Leute's where four generations of the Leute family have been taking in guests for over a century, or a family-run motel in the heart of the strip. Every stage in the evolution of the motel is still represented, from campgrounds, cabins, and the Dells' first "California bungalow courts," to the Holiday Inn and the latest in luxury suites. And over 150 years after Robert Allen first charged unruly lumbermen for a shot of whisky and a sleeping space on the floor, the flood of visitors still overflows the Dells every Fourth of July, and the hotel industry continues to grow.

Wisconsin Dells Resorts 1906

Finch House
proprieter Mrs. A.F. Sunderland
accommodates 75
$2.00-$2.50 a day
special per week
(*NW Corner Broadway & Oak*)

Pine Glen Farm Resort
proprieter John Radlund
accommodates 35
$8-$10
(*End of Bowman Road in Lower Dells*)

Blue Mound Resort
proprieter W.E. Dillon
accommodates 25
$8-$10
(*E. End of Blue Mound or Elephants Back, top of Mound*)

Scofield Cottages
proprieter Mrs. Fred Richards
accommodates 25
$8-$10
(*1013 E. Broadway - Indian Trails Motel*)

Dells View Home
proprieter Mrs. C. Luettgerodt
accommodates 25
$8-$10

Cold Water Canyon Boarding House
proprieter Mrs. D.C. Van Wie
accommodates 25
$8-$10
(*in Cold Water Canyon*)

Hotel Crandall
proprieter G.H. Crandall
accommodates 100
$2.00 a day
$10-$12 a week
(*SW Corner River Road and Wisconsin Ave.*)

The Pines
proprieter Wallace Robinson
accommodates 75
$2.00 a day
$8-$10 a week

The Larks
proprieter Nat Wetzel
accommodates 60
$2.00 a day
$12.00 a week

Coldwater Canyon Farm
proprieter Mrs. I. Berry
accommodates 30
$1.25 a day
$7-$8 a week

Oak Villa
proprieter Mrs. J. Timlin
accommodates 30
$1.50-$2.00 a day
$8-$12 a week
(*Corner Oak and Wisconsin*)

Park Hotel
proprieter J.F. Bresnan
accommodates 75
$1.50-$2.00 a day
$7-$12 a week
(*Corner of LaCrosse and Eddy Streets*)

Hile House
proprieter Adam Hile
accommodates 75
$1.50 a day
$7.00 a week
(*Washington Ave. and LaCrosse Streets*)

"Summer Tourist Round Trip Rate from Chicago $8.85 weekend. Excursion Tickets sold Fridays, Saturdays, and Sundays, good returning until the following Monday. $6.70 via the Chicago, Milwaukee and St. Paul R'y."

An Auto Trip To Kilbourn

The following first person account gives a graphic story of the slow growth of auto travel as a popular means of coming to the Dells. On August 3, 1906, five Winton cars containing "happy autoists," including women and three children, started from Minneapolis to "the Delles of the Wisconsin, the party being in charge of that indefatigable worker and all around hustler, Mr. A.C. (Ashley) Bennett, ably assisted by "Dr." Dave Thomas in charge of the repair car."

The party left at 8:15 a.m. and arrived at Winona at 11:30 p.m. There were many hills, and a broken spring in one car had to be repaired by a local blacksmith. Townspeople and farmers turned out all along the way, even at 11 p.m., to see five cars.

On the second day in the rain, some of the cars lost their way beyond Sparta and "plunged back into the wilderness and found innumerable trails thru sand and scrub oak, but little or no road....." The cars then dragged their weary way thru the sand for two or three miles, when they discovered the hottest proposition seen in many a day. The Larabee car was half way up a sand hill, buried to the axles in sand, and impossible either to back down the hill or pull up the hill. In a few minutes seven husky men were stripped of coats and collars and with a united push and shove the car was finally raised out of the sand and pushed to the top of the hill, only to find that the sand was getting deeper and wetter every minute. The distance from Sparta to Tomah was only 22 miles, but it took four hours....the day's run of 92½ miles was the hardest day's work of the entire trip."

It was still raining on the third day. "We had been warned of a very steep and slippery clay hill about five miles outside of town, but the first two cars negotiated it successfully. The Larabee car, however, came to grief by breaking her driving chain about half way up the hill, much to the delight of the various countrymen who passed up or down the hill on foot or in buggies. Bennett and Dave, however, in forty minutes had the chain repaired and followed by Little 'C' carrying all her freight and five extra passengers, got safely to the top. The hill on the other side of the ridge was even worse than the going side and it was quite a problem whether we could stay on the road or would slip down the gullies, but we finally reached the valley without any mishap and then had sand and mud, sand and mud through Clifton, Hustler, New Lisbon to Mauston, where we arrived at five o'clock, 31 miles out....we landed in Kilbourn at 7:20 p.m. tired, wet, hot and hungry."

The fourth day was spent enjoying Upper and Lower Dells boat trips in Mr. Olson's launch and buying souvenirs. On the return trip, the fifth day, there was another breakdown but they enjoyed dinner at the Sherman House in Tomah.

After spending a day in La Crosse, the travelers ventured forth for the seventh day of their journey. There were a few more breakdowns and more rain. Two of the cars had to be shipped by freight to Minneapolis and their occupants also took the train home. Others had left the caravan earlier and the last two cars were separated for the final leg of the journey.

By the ninth day, the one remaining car left Owatonna to Minneapolis and the writer reports, "completed a tour of 601 miles in which we experienced every kind of weather, good, bad and indifferent and over roads that were good, bad and impassable but with a party of people who never once were 'grouchy', never complained but enjoyed the trip to its fullest limit without one cross word or unpleasant look."

Minneapolis-Kilbourn Trip Log

Total Mileage	601 miles
Actual running time	51 hours
Average MPH	11.8
Average MPH	7.5
Rain	4 Days
Good Roads	210 miles
Heavy Sand	90 miles
Trails	40 miles
Mud-Chuck Holes	240 miles
Clay Hills	20 miles

Women dancing the Swan Dance, Stand Rock, c. 1960.

The Stand Rock Indian Ceremonial

At the turn of this century, the Dells was already renowned for its natural beauty.

About the same time, there was a revival of interest in Indian people and culture, and as early as 1919, Indian dances were held at Stand Rock for the tourists. The August 5, 1920, *Kilbourn Weekly Events* simply states, "Several from here have been to see the Indian dances at Stand Rock."

The dances were generally held in July and ran for 10 nights. The Dells Boat Company sent steamers to the ceremonial nightly: the 1922 fare, including admission to the dance and all expenses, was $1.25. By 1924, the Indian dances had become a major attraction, and that year the event was expected to attract thousands over its 10 day run.

Captain Glenn Parsons, with George Crandall and the local Ho-Chunk group, helped to organized the first ceremonial dances for tourists at Stand Rock. Parsons was general manager of the Dells Boat Company. Area Ho-Chunk appreciated his efforts to re-establish the ancient custom. Their ancestors had danced at Stand Rock for centuries, but before this revival, it had been ninety years since the tribe had practiced the annual ceremonial there. They were also honored when the boat company named one if its steamers *Winnebago*. Thus, in 1924, the Ho-Chunk gave Parsons the name Zazamanega, meaning Thunder Bird, and adopted him into the tribe as a chief in a very traditional and dignified ceremony conducted by Chief Little Bird, who was 101 years old. According to some Ho-Chunk, Parsons was only the second white man in Wisconsin to receive this highest honor.

In 1929, the Parsons/Crandall partnership was dissolved and Parsons developed a new Indian pageant site near his Indian Trading Post at Indian Hill on Hwy 13, now River Road. Crandall remained and the Stand Rock Indian Ceremonial was officially named and designed by his daughter, Phyllis Crandall Connor, who directed the show for the next 25 years.

That year the dances were held from June 27 to September 3, and included Indian entertainers from across the nation. According to the July 11, 1929, *Kilbourn Weekly Events*, some of these were "Chief Silver Tongue, a tenor of supreme quality...Evergreen Tree, an impersonator of birds and animals that has no equal...Little Moose, a dramatic reader of a type hardly ever seen, and not to be slighted is Blue Bear, a baritone singer with a voice as clear as crystal." Chief Lone Tree presided over the ceremonial and Chief Daybreak, better known as Jim Smoke, took the role of announcer. Several of these performers appeared at Stand Rock for over 30 years.

The natural amphitheater at Stand Rock has been the site of the ceremonial dances every year except 1933, when the majority of the program was taken to the Chicago World's Fair. For five months the Ho-Chunk people lived in a village built at the fairgrounds. Here the world was invited to witness the daily life of the Ho-Chunk and view the traditional dances of these proud people. As many as ten thousand visitors went through the village every day. It was here at the Century of Progress that Phyllis first met and worked with a group of Zuni Indians, the Edaakie's, from Zuni, New Mexico. The Zuni joined the ceremonial in 1935 and introduced the Zuni Sunrise Call which was considered the most spectacular event of the show.

Chief Evergreen Tree

The Dells was not without an Indian pageant during the Fair, however. A pageant was held across the river from downtown Wisconsin Dells at Dells Park. Chief Yellow Thunder, Little Moose and other old timers, as well as many new ones, were featured performers.

The Stand Rock Indian Ceremonial has always prided itself on presenting the finest and truest in Indian performers. Since its inception, all of the performers at Stand Rock have been of Native American descent. In 1940 the ceremonial had the distinction of being the only all-Indian show in the country. The Ho-Chunk have presented the main part of the program and groups from other tribes have participated by special invitation. Other tribes performing at the ceremonials have included the Apache, the Pueblos of the Southwest, the Ojibwe and many others.

Chief Silver Tongue

Perhaps the best remembered entertainer was bird and animal impersonator, Chief Evergreen Tree of the Cochiti Pueblo of New Mexico. Chief Silver Tongue was a Hoopa from Northern California. Little Moose was an Ojibwe and Laughing Boy was a Zuni.

Over the years, there have been few changes in the management of the ceremonial. In 1941, the Crandall's invited the American Legion Post to sponsor the ceremonial, which they did until 1955, and then successfully assumed its operation through 1978. During those years members of the Legion and its Auxiliary volunteered their services free of charge: parking cars, selling tickets and ushering. Before and after the show season, volunteer parties were organized to clean up the grounds. A number of improvements were also made including a paved parking lot, increased seating capacity, and lighted concrete walkways. Much rebuilding, modernizing, and overhauling was completed.

Following the 1978 season, the Wisconsin Alumni Research Foundation did not renew its contract with the American Legion Post 187, and operation of the show was turned over to the Neesh-la Indian Development Corporation, headed by local Ho-Chunk woman Alberta Day. This was the first year that the operation was under the control of a Ho-Chunk-based company. Along with her cousin, Robert Funmaker, she had began developing Neesh-la in the late 1970s. After Funmaker's death, Day and two other women, Jerry Decorah and Lilian Thundercloud, continued working on the project.

Over the duration of its tenure, Neesh-la was able to realize an important goal. It replaced all non-

Chief Daybreak

Chief Albert Yellow Thunder

Roger Little Eagle Tallmadge

Photos Courtesy H.H. Bennett Studio Foundation.

Indians in management with Native Americans. By 1987, the ceremonial was completely run by Ho-Chunk people, from its board of directors to the majority of the performers. Neesh-la failed to realize its economic goals, however, and following the 1987 season, passed the ceremonial to another Ho-Chunk controlled company.

A partial list of performers who danced, sang or recited at the ceremonials includes: Chief Albert Yellow Thunder, Russell Decorah, Andrew Black Hawk, Little Moose (an Ojibwe), Chief Silver Tongue, Evergreen Tree and dog, Daybreak (Jim Smoke), Eddy Lucero, Tony Lucero, Leonard Shika (Zunis), Blowsnake (Sam Carley), Jasper Carley, Blue Bear (Francis Lamero), Blue Bird (Joe Johnson), Ed Lone Tree, Sam Lone Tree, Jacob Lone Tree, Spencer Lone Tree, Albert Yellow Thunder, Sr., Albert Yellow Thunder, Jr., Chadwick Yellow Thunder, Miles Yellow Thunder, Marie Yellow Thunder, Mary or Nahni Yellow Thunder, Grace Decorah, Edward Decorah, George Johnson, John Bearskin, John Smoke, Charlie Smoke, Hester Decorah, Suzie White Eagle, Lucy Lone Tree, Lucy Winneshiek, Gertrude McKey, Suzie Redhorn, Belle Hopinka, Mary Smoke, Mary Brown, Florence Little John Lamere, Stella Johnson, Andrew Black Hawk (Little Thunder), Sarah Lone Tree Kenjockety, Henry White Bear, Phil Decorah, Frederick Lone Tree, George Lone Tree, Calvin Coolidge Decorah, Jerry Redhorn, Frank Lincoln, Nellie Decorah (Mrs. Rufus), Mary Brown (Mrs. Tom), Louis or Lewis Decorah, Jay Ironcloud, Jesse Wells, Melvin Miner, Lucy Miner, Ruby Miner, Bernadine Miner Tallmadge, Alberta Miner Day, Marion Miner, Tom Walker and family, Bosa Decorah, Mrs. Fred Miner, Smoke Smoke, Chief Alex Lone Tree, Tony White Cloud (Pueblo), Francis Shika (Peachy), Marie Decorah Shika, Suzie Redborn, Bill Lewis (Zuni), Maude Brown Eagle, Sanborn White Eagle, John White Eagle, Josephine White Eagle, Wendland White Eagle, Winslow White Eagle, John Swallow, Cecilia Black Deer, Ken Funmaker, Yvonne Wells, Henry White Bear, Roger Tallmadge (Little Eagle), Redstone, Pete Lamere, Carolyn Young, Annette Miner, Richard Day, Randy Tallmadge, Hotonga, Douglas Ladd (Zuni), Russell Decorah, Ebenezer Russel, Wilson White Eagle, Fred Mallory, Alvin Cloud, Joyce Funmaker, Owen Cloud, Percy Greendeer, Matthew Cleveland and Bobby Bird.

Brochure for the Stand Rock Ceremonial, 1929.

Steamers Winnebago and Apollo
Leave The Dells Landing At 7:45 P.M.
FOR
THE INDIAN CEREMONIAL DANCES
AT
STAND ROCK AMPITHEATRE
THE DELLS, KILBOURN, WIS.

CHIEF SILVERTONGUE
Hoopa Indian Tenor

THE INDIAN CEREMONIAL DANCES
AT
Stand Rock Ampitheatre
THE DELLS OF THE WISCONSIN

JULY AND AUGUST 1929

The Crandall Family

In March of 1892, a young man stepped off the train to begin his new job as night operator at the Kilbourn Depot earning $45.00 a month; good wages for a youth. George Crandall never dreamed that his life would be devoted to the Wisconsin River.

George married Nellie Bennett on November 28, 1893, and was soon looking for ways to add to the family income. In 1894, he advertised as an agent selling sewer and drain pipe. In April, 1895, the Crandalls made their first venture into the summer resort business. They rented Glen Cottage, a seven room house on the southwest corner of River Road and Wisconsin Avenue, and converted it into a small hotel. In 1898, George tried the furniture and undertaking business.

In 1898, the new Dells Resort Company asked the Crandalls to manage their Larks Hotel, later the Dells Inn, at the head of the Narrows between Artist's Glen and Cold Water Canyon. George also managed hotels and properties in Texas.

In 1908, the Dells Resort Company sold their Dells holdings to the Southern Wisconsin Power Company, which was buying riverbank property rather than pay flowage fees for land that would be covered by the water backed up by the power dam. The power company persuaded Crandall to manage these properties, along with other riverfront land threatened by logging. Where trees had been cut, he reforested. His land purchases halted plans for roads, hotels, cottages and signboards along the riverbanks.

By the time George purchased Stand Rock and the Hotel Crandall in 1914, he was also a partner in the Dells Boat Co., owner of the steamer *Apollo* and several small launches.

Crandall family, 1906, (l-r) Harriet Bennett Snider, Phyllis Crandall Connor, Lois Crandall Musson, Nellie Bennett Crandall, George H. Crandall, George O. Crandall. (Courtesy, H. H. Bennett Studio Foundation).

Crandall saw that the Dells area was in danger of being defaced by commercial practices. Though he worked to have his and other riverbank property preserved in a national park, it was not to be.

George Crandall died March 4, 1938, on a golf course in Phoenix, Arizona, where the family had spent many winters. Nellie was active until ill health forced her retirement. She died November 22, 1952 after a long illness.

George Crandall's life exemplified his words, "No man can own the Dells. He can only be its custodian for a time."

The Crandall daughters and their families, before and after George's death, were involved in management of the riverfront properties and also the Stand Rock Indian Ceremonial.

Lois, born June 30, 1896, married Howard Musson on June 9, 1917. He became associated with the Crandall companies in 1921 and gradually took over management of the Hotel Crandall. Lois entered the family business in 1934, designing the financial structure of the Stand Rock Indian Ceremonial and later serving as treasurer of the Dells Boat Company and G. H. Crandall, Inc.

On April 1, 1923, Phyllis, born November 19, 1894, married Ralph "Doc" Connor, a dentist from Wilmette, Illinois. Phyllis designed and directed the Stand Rock Indian Ceremonial from its inception in 1929 until the year of her death. She and her assistants sought out talent and staged the lighting effects which still dramatize the production.

In 1933, Phyllis, assisted by Lois, was asked to direct a group of 200 American Indians from various tribes at the Century of Progress Exposition in Chicago. They were joined by 75 Dells Indians. The welfare of native Ho-Chunks was an abiding concern to the family.

"Doc" Connor managed the Dells Boat Company and its operations. He was also known as an excellent golfer.

Since neither couple had children, they grew concerned over the future of their properties. In the early 1950s they took up George's efforts to have the Dells riverbanks become a national park, but were again refused. The state noted the many small unconnected parcels owned by others and expressed concern for existing commercial involvements. State officials did, however, lead them to the Wisconsin Alumni Research Foundation.

On January 16, 1954, after much thought, the Connors and the Mussons gave most of their Dells properties to WARF. These holdings included 1200 acres of land along the river, mostly in the Upper Dells, the Dells Boat Company with three launches, the *Clipper Winnebago* and supporting equipment, the Crandall Motor Inn, the Stand Rock amphitheater and interests in the Lower Dells. Provisions were made that these operations would continue to pay federal, state and local taxes in the four counties and five municipalities. The only building allowed on the river bank would support tour boats and their passengers. All of the donors received a small income during their lifetimes, but their greatest reward was in the knowledge that their legacy was secure.

A bronze plaque erected in Witches Gulch sums up the profound contribution of the Crandall-Connor-Muson family to our community: "This beauty is yours because others before you loved the Dells."

Souvenirs

Souvenirs at the Bennett Studio, c. 1920. Indian baskets and beadwork were among the first souvenir items sold at Wisconsin Dells. (Courtesy, H.H. Bennett Studio Foundation).

Resort areas are promoted and known for the souvenirs that visitors bring home from their vacations.

In the Dells, there were first stereoscopic and other views of the area photographed and sold by Leroy Gates and H.H. Bennett.

Post cards were a novelty in 1900, and the Bennetts soon sold sweet grass baskets and Indian dolls as well, as there was a great deal of interest in Indian culture. By 1903, Bennett reported selling various crafts made by local Ho-Chunk such as miniature birch bark canoes, beadwork, bow and arrows, moccasins and some relics. Blankets from the Navajoes, pottery from Santa Domingo and crafts from many tribes were also popular.

As time went on, other families opened souvenir stores along Broadway and in shops along the boat trip, and many of them continue in that business today. These include the Van Wie, Borcher, Tollakson, Stanton-Helland, Bennett, Buckminister and Counsell families.

Winnebago baskets were sold in almost every store and in stands along the highways. Children ground area sandstone of various colors and created designs in sand bottles which sold for 10¢.

By the 1920s and '30s, plates with Dells scenes, ashtrays, salt and pepper shakers, headdresses, bows and arrows and tom-toms were made in Germany, Japan and later Hong Kong. All of these items had to say, "Kilbourn" or "Wisconsin Dells." "Silk" pillowtops with verses sold for $1.00 and were ideal for "Mother" or "Sweetheart."

Heitman's Nifty Novelty Company on Oak Street manufactured many small unfinished wooden items such as wishing wells, outhouses and plaques with Dells post card pictures. Today silver and turquoise jewelry continues to be popular–some handmade by southwestern tribes and and some mass produced. Moccasins still sell but now are made in factories.

After World War II, fudge shops gained popularity and later came cheese shops. Old Time Picture Studios have expanded since 1976 and local artists make "hand-blown" glass miniatures. Today there is a great increase in t-shirt shops that sell other items of summer wear also.

Local merchants continually search for something new with which to tempt the public.

Taylor's Glen

Children in Kilbourn could always earn money in the summertime; the boys shined shoes and children guided tours for visitors. They often played at and guided tours through Taylor's Glen, otherwise known as the Schoolhouse Ravine (because it ran behind the school).

One area native, Iness Waterman, recalls the area she played in around 1914. "The rock formations were as pretty as any in the Dells, and we named many of them. There was a Fat Man's Misery and a spot where the children jumped from cliff to cliff like the men at Stand Rock. We carried lanterns or flashlights through the dark tunnel beneath the railroad fill. Tramps lived down there but never bothered the children."

Today, Taylor's Glen has been partially filled and the Post Office stands on portions of it. This beautiful but sometimes dangerous playground still winds around behind area homes to the dark tunnel beneath the bridge.

The Chamber of Commerce

Following is an edited version of articles by Jack Olson:

In 1947, the Dells was poised on the edge of the post-war boom in vacation travel. A vast backlog of travel-for-pleasure had built up during World War II. If the Dells were to take advantage of the possibilities of this market, we had to define our market, and expand it, and position ourselves through advertising to benefit from it.

This was the situation when I got involved with the Chamber in 1947. Chamber officers that year were Tom Howley, mayor of Wisconsin Dells; Dr. Connor, representing Crandall-Dells properties; Bert Tollaksen; and Claude O'Neil.

Chamber offices were in the old Soeldner Bank Building, the former Stroud Bank, at 314 Broadway. Advertising by the Chamber on behalf of Dells attractions was handled by Reineke, Meyer, & Finn of Chicago, and Bellman Jones was our account executive.

A committee was formed to explore the possibilities of changing the contribution level per member, which at that time was $15 to $35 per year, with an annual budget of $4,000. Members of the committee were Val Baggot and Ralph Hines for Lake Delton; Paul Fedderly, Bud Stanton, and Jack Olson for Wisconsin Dells.

We created a Dells Chamber Holding Company, the purpose of which was to attempt to raise the contribution level to $40,000.00 for 1948, a very ambitious goal for a town of two thousand people. We needed to assure the business community that we would work very hard to attain our goal; that contributions would be fair for each category of members; that we would spend the money wisely; and that they would be kept fully informed and involved.

The next step to assure the businessmen that we meant business, was to rent a lock box at the bank. We put all the checks and written commitments at the new pledging levels into that box, as they arrived.

Then we went to work. As an example of our approach, Bauer & O'Neil Drug Store, later Bork &

Helping visitors at the Chamber of Commerce, Mrs.Lucille Albertson and Les Albertson. (Courtesy, H. H. Bennett Studio Foundation)

Kane, were giving $35.00 a year as Chamber membership. We asked them for $300.00. Bork & Kane wanted to know what Stuelke's Drug Store was going to give. We told them–and everyone else we approached–that we would bring them a list of pledges after we had worked for six months. They would then have a chance to reevaluate whether they had pledged too much, or less than other people in the same business.

Each person who was a Chamber member in this period was an important contributor, both personally and financially, to the success of the Dells/Delton area.

Space constraints, unfortunately, will not allow listing of each member, but only those who agreed to spearhead specific areas of need but all share equally in the satisfaction of a difficult job well done.

Bud Stanton was a key member of the new Chamber Contributions Committee, and he was extremely effective and hard working. Everyday Bud would come and pick me up at 6:00AM, and we would go the entire day, calling on people who might be willing to be involved in the effort to increase the income from the tourist industry through higher contributions to the Chamber for the advertising program we felt was crucial to the continued success of the Dells area.

At that time, Lake Delton was not incorporated. The Chairman of the Town of Delton was Ernie Volz, who together with Ralph Hines and Val Baggot headed a parallel program within the Lake Delton Chamber of Commerce, separate from the Dells. That Chamber had its office on Ralph Hines' property close to what is now Fischer's Supper Club.

Those of us in the two Chambers decided to try to unify the efforts of the Lake Delton/Dells area, so we could speak with one voice in advertising ourselves to our mutual market. Members exploring that possibility were Val Baggot, Ralph Hines and Mike Uphoff from Lake Delton; and Russ Tollaksen and Jack Olson from the Dells.

If we were to be successful, then the matter of creating a Dell Creek watershed to begin rebuilding water quality for Mirror Lake and Lake Delton was of vital importance. Baggot, Hines, Volz, Tollaksen, and myself went to work . We enlisted the support of a powerful State Senator who represented the area. This was Jess Miller (R) of Richland Center. He agreed with our concern, and went with us to the Conservation Department (now Department of Natural Resources). We convinced them to make a commitment of $10,000 a year for twelve years, a total of $120,000, to rebuild the Dell Creek watershed, and to create two islands in Mirror Lake to dump fertilizer run-off that was going into the Creek. This run-off came about during the Depression of the 1930's, when the trees along the shoreline of Dell Creek were clear-cut by farmers who couldn't afford to heat their homes otherwise.

As later years were to show, this was one of the most important actions to be taken in this area. Most people today are not aware that Lake Delton would not be a viable body of water for recreation, had there not been the commitment to clean up the watershed. With Senator Miller's help, the Conservation Department was convinced of the necessity to begin the clean-up at once.

Meanwhile, the Chamber collection program was a success. After six months, $40,000 in checks was in the lock box at the Bank, ready to be turned over to the Chamber Board for the planning of the 1948 promotional programs.

Not everyone agreed with our program. Bud Stanton and I asked ten souvenir operations to come to a luncheon to discuss individual pledges and our program. Of the ten operators attending, we were able to secure pledges averaging $200 each from nine of those present. The tenth person had not yet come into the Chamber.

Other beginning contributions were $2.50 per chair for the restaurant division. The cottage and cabin division contribution was to be at $5.00 per bed.

The Lake Delton Chamber of Commerce joined us in the new Dells/ Delton Area Regional Chamber of Commerce, and Les Albertson, the Vice President of the Kilbourn State Bank, was hired as the new Executive Director of the expanded Chamber at $3,000 per year.

Among the key players in uniting the two Chambers, two stand out. Mike Uphoff of Uphoff's Rotunda (now the site of the Copa Cabana Resort Suites), and Joe Kaminksi of Chula Vista worked extremely hard in the mutual best interest of our two communities.

Bill Kelly, Dell View Hotel properties, and Peter Helland, Riverview Boat Line, were very active in the expanded advertising and publicity committee which now spearheaded the Chamber's efforts. George Cappy became the President as the Dells Businessmen's Association was absorbed into the Chamber for resort promotion purposes.

Many individuals made great personal contributions as time went on. One of the strongest and most effective was Russ Tollaksen, who became Chamber President about 1960. Russ worked almost daily on bringing in new members and contributions in both Lake Delton and the Dells.

Meanwhile, in 1954 the non-profit Wisconsin Alumni Research Foundation became the operator of the Dells Crandall Properties via a most generous gift by the Connor/Musson families. WARF sent Tim Johnson to the Dells to manage WARF interests here. Tim was an invaluable addition to the growing Chamber of Commerce team.

Bud Lackore, a chamber executive from Mason City, Iowa, was hired as Executive Director of the Dells/ Delton Regional Chamber of Commerce with Bernie Olson as his assistant.

Ben Olson became chairman of the committee which worked on pamphlets, 4x9 inches in size, which covered such areas as housing, restaurants, attractions, and things to do in the area for which there was no charge.

Between 1952 and 1960, a great expansion of the area took place, with the inception of such outstanding new attractions as Storybook Gardens, developed by Tom Egan; the Wisconsin Deer Park, developed by the Tollaksen family; Tommy Bartlett's Water Ski, Sky and Stage Show, Fort Dells..... all were early and highly successful additions to the area.

All of these developments chose the Dells as their operations headquarters because of the growing number of vacationers coming to the Dells for the boat trips on the Wisconsin River, and the Stand Rock Indian Ceremonial.

In the early 1960's it became obvious that the Chamber Visitors Bureau needed additional advertising funds to be competitive with other vacation areas of the Upper Midwest.

It was decided to place most of the divisions of the Chamber on a gross percentage membership basis. In order to preserve the confidentiality of individual income figures, we arranged an account in a Stevens Point Bank. This account was the repository for payments from individual members, with a monthly check being sent to the Dells Chamber. John Okey, a Madison Certified Public Accountant, was in charge of the details of this program. Under John's competent management it worked smoothly and well. The resulting cash flow allowed substantially larger annual budgets for Chamber promotions.

It was also at this time that I became an officer and director of the Wisconsin Good Road Association. The Interstate Highway System was being developed nationwide over this ten year period. We saw that this new system was of paramount importance to the future of the Dells/ Delton area. I was fortunate in obtaining the commitment for three I-90/94 interchanges for our Dells area (the same number as allotted to the City of Madison), with a guarantee of a fourth interchange at Rocky Arbor to be added in five years.

We were lucky in the years after the war, but luck means nothing unless it is accompanied by hard, consistent effort. We all worked very hard to expand on our natural "big ticket" to build a better Dells area. And we succeeded.

The Chamber of Commerce office on Broadway, c. 1960. (Courtesy, H. H. Bennett Studio Foundation)

Chamber of Commerce officers, 1960, (l-r) Jack Olson, Russ Tollaksen, Jack Gray, Tim Johnson.

During the years leading up to the 1980s, visitors came to Wisconsin Dells as a result of neighborly recommendations or family tradition. But, the onset of increased competition for vacationers' discretionary income played a major role in shaping the future of Wisconsin Dells and influencing the direction of business operations.

Today, the Wisconsin Dells Visitor & Convention Bureau (WDV&CB) is truly distinctive, mainly due to its unique membership fees structure, requiring members to pledge their fees based on their gross revenues, and the initiation of cooperative marketing programs which serve to maximize advertising investments in a highly competitive marketplace. The Bureau has been extremely successful in congealing the area's business owners, increasing levels of funding for joint programs and making a positive impact for its members.

Cooperative advertising, for instance, was first initiated by the Bureau in 1976 under the leadership of its Advertising Committee. And in 1977, the first cooperative television advertising program was executed by James Jeffords & Associates with a $70,000 budget. In comparison, in 1994 the Bureau's marketing budget of $2.6 million was leveraged into nearly $8.2 million, through the use of a cooperative marketing strategy.

Cooperative advertising was employed as a means of pooling both public and private resources to effectively disseminate the Wisconsin Dells message. It also provided an opportunity for private businesses to participate in advertising programs that would have been an impossibility to afford on one's own–particularly in reaching the Chicago market.

An additional example of cooperative marketing occurred in 1976 when Tom Gussel first presented the idea for a combined Dells/Delton Directory to replace four or five separate in-area advertising pieces. The Directory, which later became known as the "Travel & Attraction Guide," became an important vehicle for fulfilling inquiries. There were more than one million Travel & Attraction Guides distributed in 1994 versus 600,000 in 1981–a reflection of advertising and public relations success.

Another innovation in funding, the introduction of a room tax, initially was met with tremendous local opposition, particularly from hoteliers. Chamber Board members were instrumental at the local level, while Jack and Ben Olson worked at the state level, to install a program wherein the village of Lake Delton and city of Wisconsin Dells would apply a room tax of 2% – 1.5% of which would go directly to fund Bureau tourism promotion and development programs. This tax went into effect in 1969, and was then increased to 5% for both municipalities in 1991.

The Bureau of the '90s has made a conscious commitment to technological advancements and contemporary facilities in order to remain competitive and maintain its position as a leader in the industry. The installation of an 800 number and the Bureau's telemarketing facilities require staff of up to 60 to serve as "ambassadors" for the area, answering questions and ensuring literature is mailed overnight. The WDV&CB expects to accommodate 475,000 inquiries in 1995, in contrast to 156,000 literature requests handled a decade earlier in 1985.

In 1976, the Bureau moved from its location above Hans Helland's law firm on Oak Street to the Dells Boat Company building overlooking the river on Wisconsin Avenue. It remained at that location until finally purchasing its own facility on Superior Street in 1988. In 1995, the Bureau completed an expansion to increase its office space to 10,800 square feet to accommodate the unprecedented demands of phone and visitor inquiries.

The changes in physical space that have occurred over the years are indicative of the Bureau's direction in being a consumer and inquiry-driven agency. In keeping with that mentality, the Bureau officially changed its name from "Wisconsin Dells Regional Chamber of Commerce" in 1980 to "Wisconsin Dells Visitor & Convention Bureau, Inc.," reflecting the change in attitude and commitment on behalf of the membership.

The recognition that members of the Bureau have received on the state and even a national level are a reflection of its success and an indication of where it is headed in the future. Within the state, Wisconsin Dells has received a new found respect mainly because of the leadership the area has displayed in meeting the needs of the consumers and its willingness to share that knowledge with tourism leaders across the state.

Tom Diehl, in addition to serving as president of the WDV&CB since 1982 and president of Tommy Bartlett, Inc., has been chair of the Governor's Council on Tourism, which administers all of the state's major tourism promotion, since 1987. He has been credited by many, including State Senator Joseph Leean, for "bringing the state's tourism into the modern era."

The Bureau has spent the last decade maintaining and advancing its credibility – a major initiative of Kelli Trumble Gavinski, who joined as Executive Director in 1985. Having an advertising and public relations education and background herself, she worked diligently to direct both the public relations and advertising agencies, to create a formula that worked to the advantage of the membership.

Boelter & Lincoln, later changing its name to Advertising, Boelter & Lincoln, became the advertising agency of record in 1982 and continues to represent the WDV&CB in a contemporary and highly effective fashion.

The Bureau's public relations efforts during the '70s and '80s were handled by a variety of different agencies, headed mainly by Joan Collins or Herb Kraus. Upon entering the '90s, the Bureau made a conscious decision to seek a public relations firm that could make a greater media impact within its most important market – Chicago. In 1991, the Bureau hired Chicago-based Minkus & Dunne Communications, headed by Raymond Minkus, whose firm provided a more targeted, comprehensive media relations program than ever before.

In 1990, the Bureau added another component with the incorporation of "Wisconsin Dells Festivals, Inc." This individual entity provides the structure and the attention needed to accomplish a variety of marketing and financial goals for the membership. The three main festivals directed, managed and developed by the Bureau today – Flake Out Festival, Automotion and the Great Wisconsin Dells Balloon Rally – are used as a means for expanding on the fall, winter and spring seasons by garnering the media attention that ordinarily couldn't be reached during those months.

A somewhat recent phenomenon for the community, due in part to the Bureau's efforts, is the increase in business from September through May. In the last five years alone, area businesses have reinvested approximately $80 million into the community, much of which has gone toward larger, more modern facilities oriented toward year-round business.

The hard work of the Bureau, driven by advertising, public relations and the positive word-of-mouth of millions of satisfied visitors from previous years, result in more than 3 million visitors a year. It represents the attitude and sophistication that the WDV&CB has acquired during the past two decades. Focused management, award-winning marketing and communications programs, modern technology and management commitment not only has repositioned Wisconsin Dells, but has elevated it to leadership status within the travel and tourism industry.

There is no doubt the Bureau has grown and advanced in many significant ways during the past two decades. As a tribute to its success, there are more than 700 member businesses, responsible for a total $3.3 million budget in 1995. These funds compare to less than $580,000 in membership funds nearly a decade ago. The Wisconsin Dells Visitor & Convention Bureau, along with its member businesses, have demonstrated what it takes to lead the travel and tourism industry into the 21st century, as evidenced by the 78% of visitors who return to the area.

Chamber/WDV&CB Presidents

Claude O'Neil	1945-1947
Tom Howley	1948-1949
Henry Field	1950-1952
George Cappy	1953
Grover Belton	1954-1955
George Brooks	1955
George Cappy	1956-1958
Arnold Borcher	1959
Russ Tollaksen	1960-1969
Charles Thompson	1970-1972
Richard Schauf	1973-1975
M.D. Newson	1976-1978
Bob Koch	1979-1981
Thomas Diehl	1982-present

Advertising Chairmen

Jack Gray	1966-1973
Dudley Newsom	1974-1975
John Dixon	1976-1983
Turk Waterman	1983-1994
Ben Borcher	1995-present

General Managers/Executive Directors

Jack Gray	1963-1966
Bud Lackore	1966-1975
Bernie Olson	1975-1984
Kelli Trumble Gavinski	1985-1995
Romy A. Snyder	1995-present

DRUGS
HARDWARE

World Wars and Great Depression

World War I in Kilbourn

The United States entered the war against Germany and Austria in April 1917 and Kilbourn, like other communities across the country, mobilized for the war effort.

Men who belonged to the National Guard joined their units, others volunteered for service, while still others registered for the nation's first draft of soldiers since the Civil War.

A total of 50 men registered for the draft in Kilbourn in the first three hours of the sign up. "There was not the first word of protest," reported the *Weekly Events*, and few claims to exemption." After a man registered one of the women of the Tuesday Club would pin an "honor band" on his arm. The bands became "a frequent mark in the passing crowds in Kilbourn."

The final draft registration took place in September 1918 and included previously ineligible men between ages 18 - 21 and 31 - 45. A total of 106 men, "the flower of Kilbourn youth and manhood," signed up then mustered for a parade down Broadway. Led by the surviving veterans of the Civil War and the high school band, the registrants assembled in front of the fountain, heard a brief speech, and sang the national anthem.

Mobilization of the local home front was also underway and so successful that in less than a year after American entry the newspaper was reporting that, "So complete and universal is the organization for war work that the man, woman or child who is not a member of some kind of committee is not considered to be in their full duty."

A local unit of the Red Cross was organized, with newspaper editor J.E. Jones as chairman. In June, he reported that Kilbourn had raised $1079.25 for the Red Cross and more than met its quota of $1000 in the national campaign to raise $100 million. Women who wished to knit garments for men in service could pick up a "kit" containing enough yarn for a sleeveless sweater, a scarf, and a pair each of wristlets and socks. Phyllis Crandall and Ruth Bennett were in charge of the knitters and kits could be picked up at the Bennett Studio "any afternoon."

Later on in the war, the local Red Cross also sponsored a "Melting Pot" and asked people to donate gold, silver, copper, brass and tin to be sold or melted down for the war effort. Members of the Melting Pot committee were Phyllis Crandall, Ruth Bennett, Vera Jones, Anna Baggot and Herman Knippel.

Kilbourn also had a chapter of the Loyalty Legion, headed by Reverend Walter French Scott. Loyalty Legion members were pledged to observe and report "anti-American" activities to federal prosecutors. Scott was also the community's "Four-Minute-Man," who promised to give an oration on the war and patriotism - lasting no more than four-minutes - at any assembly or meeting he attended.

Kilbourn did not see any extreme examples of the anti-German feeling exhibited in many other parts of the state. However, Reverend Diekvoss told editor Jones that the correct name of the "German Methodist Church" was "Zion Evangelical" and that, as of March 1918, all services would be conducted in English.

Service flags - with stars designating the number of men in service - were hung for the village, the high school and the members of the Methodist Church. The first offical village service banner was an "all-wool bunting flag, 6 x 9 feet." It was emblazoned with 48 stars and mounted in the window of the post office. The newspaper printed letters from men in service for the entire community to read. It also printed the death notices of the seven men who died while in the military.

Kilbourn was also the scene of an odd accident that claimed the life of a young soldier named King Henry. In the early days of the war, National Guard troops were activated to guard important bridges and highways. On one night in June 1917, a car packed with seven soldiers rumbled over the Kilbourn bridge, violating the speed limit of 5 MPH and failing to follow the sentry's order to halt. As the car sped past him, the sentry fired and - with one bullet - wounded Privates Steve Kamowski and Joe Kaiser and killed Private King Henry. An investigation later revealed that the men in the car had been drinking heavily before they got in the car, that the auto itself had no tail lights and but one headlight. The sentry also testified that "someone in the car called out an unprintable remark in reply to his command to stop." The result was a fatal accident.

On the day the Armistice was announced, Kilbourn paused. The war had taken its sons and daughters to faraway places, revealed ethnic tensions at home, and claimed the lives of at least seven young men. Peace brought much to be thankful for.

Previous page: *A parade during World War I led by the local unit of the Red Cross, chaired by J. E. Jones, who may be leading the march here. Next in line are the Red Cross women, followed by the village band and the fire department. The service flag, with 70 stars for men in service, plus two more for men who died, hangs over the street. (Courtesy, H. H. Bennett Studio Foundation)*

Looking down Superior from Broadway at the damage wreaked by the Washington's Birthday ice storm in 1922. (Courtesy, H. H. Bennett Studio Foundation)

The Glory of Kilbourn In Ruins

On February 22, 1922, an unprecedented ice storm wrecked the famous tree-lined avenues of Kilbourn. A heavy fall of rain turned to ice that so heavily weighted the limbs that they broke under the strain. All the next day and during the night Kilbournites heard the crash of falling limbs and trees. Thursday morning revealed a sight that appalled the younger generation and was heart-breaking to the older settlers who had grown up with the trees, planted by hands long since folded in the silence of the graves.

Kilbourn's pride of beauty, its incomparable foilage and shade trees lay before them a heap of icebound rubbish. Broadway Avenue, nearly a mile long, was said by visitors to have one of the most beautiful stretches of oak trees in the state. Now it was a wreck of tree tops and branches, bare trunks and splintered tops. The storm, the most severe of its character within the "memory of the oldest inhabitant" was general throughout the state. It caused hundreds of thousands of dollars in damage to traffic and business interests of all kinds, the telephone, telegraph and electric companies being the heaviest losers, aside from the inconvenience experienced by patrons and public.

Many basements in Kilbourn were flooded by the continuous rains that fell while the icy conditions of the surface prevented the volume of water from going into the ground or passing off in its natural channels. The ice melted in a few days, but Broadway would never be lined by great oaks again and decades would pass before the other streets of Kilbourn saw trees like those lost in the Washington's Birthday storm of 1922.

Prohibition, 1919-1933

After World War I, the Volstead Act and a constitutional amendment made the experiment called Prohibition a reality. The sale or consumption of any alchoholic beverages had become illegal. Many, however, refused to obey this law and enforcement was nearly impossible.

In this area, those places which sold illegal liquor were called "blind pigs" and were often a farm house kitchen with a few chairs around the table, although often the customer bought his bottle as a "carryout". Sometimes the apricot brandy, bathtub gin or other drinks were made in the barn and sometimes "imported". In Dell Prairie, near Roc O'Connell's farm, manufacturers would try their product on the two Gaines brothers. If they lived, the product was safe to sell.

There were probably thirty blind pigs within a ten mile radius of Kilbourn. Some of the most popular were Ma Gannon's, Bonfoys on Cty J, (then Hwy 12), Ott Raymond's, and Eddy White's in the Lower Dells near the Beach Hotel, later Echo Point. Bootlegging was common and even semi-respectable. Of course, many people needed a little drink once in a while for "medical purposes."

The Millers lived across the street from the Catholic Church on Oak Street and engaged in several businesses. They broke broncoes, shod

Jake Drollinger at the small tavern near the Larks, which featured Cream City Beer c. 1910. In the 1920s, sale of beer and other alcoholic beverages was illegal.

horses, and did some bootlegging on the side. The day the *revenooers* came, young George Miller ran out the back door, across the railroad, down the hill and swam the river to escape.

Eugene Blood is probably the last witness to a raid on Wisconsin's largest still. Eugene was six years old on the November day in 1928 when he and his father, Willard, saw a group of men running through a nearby farm field. Some of them were wearing uniforms. Shots were fired and the uniformed men came back with handcuffed prisoners. The farm was on the Sauk and Juneau County line and now belongs to Dean Dorow, W960 Lage Road.

The equipment was smashed, including eleven vats for working the mash. Each held about 5,000 gallons. "Then there were two good sized boilers and two copper columns for the distillation of alcohol....The officers stated that the plant had a capacity of about one thousand gallons a day, and, as the product was alcohol, this would mean about two thousand gallons of ordinary 90 proof whiskey a day." The officers estimated it would have cost about $75,000.00 to install and probably had been in operation from two weeks to two months. The product was sold for five or six dollars a gallon so it would not take long "to pile up quite a neat sum of money from the venture."

Kilbourn newspaper editor William Drumb was tired of the whole sham. Evidently some still favored prohibition but Editor Drumb opposed the "moonshiner who makes the stuff in a dirty old barn where swarms of flies and bugs drown themselves in the mash tubs and barrels...The people have had thirteen years of prohibition in its most virulent form. It had been possible all that time to get intoxicating liquors in some form or another..." Drumb favored giving up the hypocrisy, letting the government tax a safer product and ridding the country of the type of crime that prohibition spawned.

Prohibition ended in 1933, not long after the inauguration of Franklin D. Roosevelt.

Lake Delton, Its Creator and the Man Who Made the Dream Reality

William J Newman, a Chicago contractor/ millionaire, visited the "Dells area" in the fall of 1925, and stayed at the Sarrington House (Dell View Hotel). Newman loved to walk through the hills, valleys, and gorges at sunrise to feel the sheer exhilaration of the charm and splendor of this area. He was so pleased and thrilled with the natural beauty and healthful atmosphere around the present Lake Delton site that he decided to buy the Sarrington House. He had visions of making it an ultra-modern resort.

One year later, partially because his children wanted a good place to swim, Newman decided to expand his dream and create a lake where the cows once grazed, or, as his slogan said, "up where the pines begin." He expanded his dream to include an

GOLF COURSE
MIRROR LAKE PARK
MORRIS HOTEL
MIRROR LAKE
FORMERLY
DELTON
BOAT LANDING
GOLF COURSE
DAWN MANOR HOTEL
BOAT LANDING
CONGRESS HALL
SPECTACULAR SCENIC CANYON
TO BARABOO
SAND BATHING BEACH
TO BARABOO

KE DELTON
$1,000,000 Spring-Fed
Artificial Lake
HWAY-12-13-23
LAKE AREA
400 ACRES
SHORE LINE
5 MILES
5 MINUTES
DRIVE TO
UPPER DELLS
TO KILBOURN
PROPERTY
OFFICE
G BEACH
SAND BATHING BEACH
COUNTY HIGHWAY-A
DAWN MANOR
HOUSE
BOAT
LANDING
HAWK'S BILL
PAVILION
LOWER DELLS WISCONSIN RIVER
KILBOURN

Excavation work for Lake Delton (above) near the Highway A bridge and (below) the Dawn *on the lake bearing a sign advertising "Lake & River Front Lots."*

exclusive, luxurious community targeted at Chicagoans, a place where the elite would come, play, and live year round.

Newman contacted county Judge Jim Hill, drew a pencil line on a map and told the judge, "buy up all that land within my pencil line." Confident that he could get Public Service Commission approval for a dam, Newman went ahead with plans to create a resort-lake area. He chose Ralph M. Hines, who was then in Chicago, to supervise all construction phases. Hines became Newman's right hand man.

Crews of men under R.M. Hines, engineer and general manager, began work on the creation of the lake. Much surveying and calculating was involved in deciding the exact spot to locate the dam and its dikes on this spring fed Dell Creek. Hines sent for Newman's revolutionary steam shovel and other heavy earth moving equipment from Chicago. This equipment arrived late in January, 1926. Excavation started that February.

The biggest job was the dam itself. Thousands of yards of dirt were filled in on both sides of the dam to form a strong embankment to hold the water. Enough cement was needed to allow for the expansion of the dam area to serve the power plant that was scheduled. Water directly behind the dam was 26' deep and the spillway of the dam was about 50' long. The dam and the dike extending in both directions together totaled more than 1,000 feet. One day Newman's community would be exclusive and self-sufficient.

The building of the lake was no small task either. Most of the land was perfect for a lake as it was used for grazing. However, many pines lined the south and west perimeters of the lake to be and had to be removed. Dell Creek, that ran from the Sarrington House and Mill toward the Wisconsin River, needed to be dredged and widened. Working diligently in early spring the lake began to take shape.

With the construction of the lake well under way Newman set out to complete his vision of making Lake Delton one of the most - if not the most beautiful place in Wisconsin. Mr Newman's property covered 2,000 acres and offered the perfect setting for clean outdoor recreation. The Sarrington homestead was enlarged, improved, and expanded until there was a spacious lobby-living room, additional porches, and comfortable furnishings throughout its rooms. Renaming it the Dell View, Mr Newman wanted this to be the ultimate in accommodations. Newman graced the entrances to the Dell View Hotel, on Hwy A and on Hwy 12, with the great griffins and gargoyles that once stood on the Board of Trade Building in Chicago. Marble balls that once decorated the Chicago building were placed at the hotel entrance. Newman had investmenst in other hotels and cottages in the lake area that offered accommodations to those who did not wish to make this area their permanent home.

Things were moving fast. On June 27, 1927, Lake Delton was formally opened. Many from surrounding towns crowded the grounds at the Dell View to listen to the praises and speeches for Newman, and his dream come true. Bands from Baraboo and Portage made the afternoon delightful. Chicago City Attorney Sawtelle spoke many words of appreciation for Mr. Newman, who was responsible for the production of the new lake and beautifying the surrounding country. Governor Zimmerman was on hand to speak to those attending. He was quoted to say, "When I heard that some man created an artificial lake in Wisconsin where there are already eight thousand lakes, I thought it was my duty to come and take a look for myself." It was reported that he was not disappointed in what he saw. Mayors from Baraboo, Wisconsin Dells, along with W.C. Simons of Mirror Lake, and Adolph Kannenberg, a member of the State Railway Commission also expressed praise and gratitude to Mr. Newman for his accomplishments. E.S. Hall, State Conservation Commission, gave his talk on the subject of artificial lakes. Mr. Hall had much to say about the distribution of fish fry and fingerlings throughout the state. He spoke of the advantages of a lake like this that planned for two fish hatcheries. This would make Lake Delton just perfect for breeding fish, and would keep anglers happy for some time. Captain Parsons gave a short talk, and Chief Silver Tongue sang a number of songs.

Later that evening a banquet given by Newman, was held at the Dell View. Again speakers praising Newman's accomplishments were Atty J.F. Doughtery from Kilbourn, Al Smith, Atty. Sawtelle, Ex-senator Staudenmayer, W.C. Simons, chairman of the county board, Arthur Cheek. From Wisconsin Dells Mayor Luettgerodt, Charles Borcher, Peter Emmerich, J.M. Drollinger, Dr. Duclos, A Schoeninger, J. C. Fitzgerald, H. Tofson, W.A. Drumb, Ben Olson, K.K. Johnson, J.H. Dixon. J.F. Dougherty, and H.D. Snider. All had expressed appreciation for what Mr. Newman has done for the area. The fact that he had left a considerable amount of land for public use emphasized that fact that he has not had the making of money his sole objective. Mr. Newman stated that if he was to live up to all that had been said about him during the evening, he would be more than satisfied with his venture. He also stated that he had invested more than $600,000.00 in the project to date and that before it was completed that total may well be more that a million dollars.

Mr. Newman saw to it that the two fish hatcheries located just east of Lake Delton near Hwy A kept Lake Delton well stocked. It was reported that a million and one half baby pike were in the hatchery. This hatchery of Newman's was a fascinating place , and was planned according to the most up-to-date methods of the time. The baby fish were 'grown' in the upper fish pond, located nearer Hwy A. The upper pond was drained by gravity into a lower pond when the fish were large enough, allowing the upper pond to be restocked. When the fish were of size they would be added to the lake. Water for the ponds was secured from Lake Delton via a tile inlet. Newman had visions of building another lake devoted exclusively to trout.

With Ralph Hines, working as manager since the project began, Newman had expanded his dream to include the farm that was adjacent to the Dell View (formerly owned by the Von der Heides - originally owned by the C.A. Sumner family) The farm located near Congress Hall Canyon (Lost Canyon) was managed by Fred and Frances (Fanny) Hines (Ralph's parents) who sold their farm in Ohio in 1929 to move here to Wisconsin. The poultry farm was no small affair. This farm provided the freshest of cream, and eggs, and young broilers for the Dell View Hotel. Bert Washburn operated that portion of the Newman properties and boasted that 2,000 chickens were to hatch out in the spring and that he had at least that many in the yard. At the farm two Shetland ponies, 11 riding horses, a duck pond with 150 ducks including some wild ones, and 12 pheasants offered more entertainment for visitors.

Dell View now had its own nine-hole golf course. It was an interesting course in perfect condition, with greens among the best in the world. Henry Titus, the club's professional laid out much of the course. Nine more holes were planned in 1929.

Camping was also available between Lake Delton and the Wisconsin River. Entrance to the camp grounds was just across the Newport bridge. There was no charge for the use of the grounds where dozens of tents were pitched. A ball diamond was adjacent to the camp grounds, and a deer park adjacent to that. Across the street from the Camp grounds was the beginnings of the Lake Delton Zoo.

The east shore of Lake Delton, with (l-r) Newman's Stadium, a diving platform, boat landing, beach and what was the first water slide at the Dells.

The next project was the airfield, the Lake Delton Air Port. South of Hwy 12, it was built to handle the tri-motor Ford transports of the day. Daily scenic flights were made and a complete service station was maintained for airplanes. The airport opened May 15, 1930. A crowd of better than 5,000 was present at the Lake Delton Airport on Sunday June 30, 1930 for the dedication. Judge Hill of Baraboo gave the dedicatory speech followed by a short speech by Mayor Prothers of Baraboo. Twenty planes were in attendance making quite a showing when a flock of them went up at once, the likes of which many local people had never seen. Spectators who had never flown before went up and experienced the thrill of their first flight. Various stunts were done by visiting pilots with trophies given to those participating. Newman's airport was the subject of much praise by the visiting pilots, who pronounced it one of the best to be found anywhere. The new hanger was large and the surrounding grounds seemed sufficient to accommodate large groups of people as well as many visiting planes. Plans were to develop the airport as a terminal for aerial tourists to the Dells region of Wisconsin, and it was expected that regular air lines would make use of this field. Pilot Paul F. Koehn, of Sheboygan, was named chief pilot at the Lake Delton Airport, in 1930. Keohn would serve as instructor as well as pilot for chartered airplane trips. (The airport was later owned by John McBoyle.)

By 1931, Newman had invested more than $1,500,000.00 into the project and had 300 men working. Already in operation were the Purple Grackle - a dance pavilion enjoyed by many who came to listen to the internationally, nationally, and locally famous big bands of the era. Kerfoot House and Cottages (presently Dawn Manor and Pine Beach Resort) was being run by Ralph's sister Hazel Mae Hines Marshall and her husband Clayton Levi Marshall. In 1936, after the passing of Fred, Frances (Fanny) joined Hazel and Clayton in this operation. This accommodation ran for 12 years. Just to the south and east of Dawn Manor was that enormous public sandy beach. Its high diving tower, covered pavilion, boat launches, and docks made Lake Delton the perfect retreat on the scorching summer days.

Two 55' launches equipped with glass enclosures, life preservers, electric lights, automobile controls and 80 horsepower engines operated on Lake Delton. These launches each had a capacity of 60 passengers. Newman planned to add 11 more to the fleet, along with row boats for the summer tourists. Speed boat rides were also given. Tennis courts, a riding academy, and canoeing offered still more diversions for the tourist coming to Newman's healthy resort area 'up where the pines begin'.

In an effort to add even more entertainment and pleasure to his complete community, the Newman Stadium was built near the west bank of the Wisconsin River--just north of the Purple Grackle. It was to be the site of many exciting spectator events. It boasted 5,000 free seats 1,000 of which were covered.

One of the first spectacular events slated to take place there was Wisconsin's very own Spanish Bull Fight, on August 23, 1931. Publicity hitting all newspapers in Chicago and throughout the state of Wisconsin showed action pictures of the 'death defying struggle between man's skill and brute strength'. Also to appear was Carr's Horse Circus Rodeo featuring 10 big acts, plus a polo game on horses - Shorewood Hills vs Carr's Circus team. Promising two hours of thrills and spills, spectators would witness a exhibition of Spain's national sport at the W.J. Newman stadium on Lake Delton at the Dells at 2:30 and 8:30 PM.

Lake Delton and the featured bull fight made the headlines across the nation. Because of its controversy, the bull fight came very close to 'getting into the talkies'. All the commotion was not because the sight was to be so spectacular, amazing, and breath-taking. On the contrary, most people were upset that such a horrible, inhumane, and gory form of entertainment could possibly be shown anywhere in the Unites States. State District Attorney C.M. LaMar received telegrams, letters, and orders from Lieutenant Gov. Henry Huber, acting governor, and State and National Humane Societies demanding that such a spectacle not be permitted stating, "Wisconsin will not tolerate such brutality. Bull fights were in violation of the statues of Wisconsin and will not be sanctioned." As District Attorney, LaMar was to see to it that no such event took place. In 1931, the crime of baiting an animal without killing it was a misdemeanor carrying a fine of $10 to $100.00. However, if the animal died, someone could spend from 10 to 30 days in jail. State Humane agent George Comings, stated in an interview, "no toreadors flaunting red cloaks will jump nimbly around the Newman Stadium Sunday if I have anything to do with it." Letters written to humane officers in Reedsburg and Baraboo by Comings demanded that the laws of Wisconsin be upheld. Statutes prohibiting animal baiting entertainments were cited from all over, including Kentucky and Tennessee.

When all was said and done the following appeared in the local *Dells Events* August 27, 1931: "Because of the much heralded "Spanish style bull fight" the stands were fairly well filled when the program got under way. The chief attraction was Pete Carr, owner of the show, who did excellent work on the jumping horses and demonstrated the abilities of his trained high school horses. J.E. Smith directed the event as ringmaster, while Bushbaum Brothers furnished some excellent comedy as the clowns.

The only dark cloud on the entertainment's program was the inability of the management to present the widely advertised bull fight because of pressure brought to bear upon them by acting Governor Huber, who directed that the prosecutor of Sauk County stop the exhibition at that point. The bull that was to have been used, however, was paraded around the arena.

The scheduled night performance was canceled because attendant difficulties entailed. Both Paramount and Metro-Goldwyn-Meyer had cameraman on the grounds with sound equipment, but when the feature of the show was called off, they packed up and left." However this performance, or lack of one, was viewed, good or bad, it brought much attention to Newman's Lake Delton-at-the Dells.

Things appeared to be going great for Newman and his dream. But suddenly, Newman faced tax difficulties blamed on a bumbling accounting firm. Newman needed to pay the government several hundred thousand dollars and thus had to liquidate some of his assets. Being hit hard by the depression, Newman neared bankruptcy. Judge Hill, Helmer Amundson, a county surveyor, and Hines gathered nearly $50,000.00 to aid Newman.

The three men formed a corporation, Lake Delton Development Company, and with the approval of Newman and the Federal Court, acquired Newman's Lake Delton holdings by assuming Newman's debt in 1932. Newman was given a three year buy-back option, but never was able to buy the holdings back.

Lake Delton Development Company, with Ralph as operative agent, sold lots and cottages, built roads, enlarged and leased out the hotel's golf course. Hines took on other construction jobs with WPA, and in other communities, to keep his equipment operating and bring in needed money. By borrowing and pooling their earnings, the partners raised another $250,000 for development.

But they weren't earning enough to keep ahead, and by 1940 were $10,000.00 behind in taxes. They sold the Dell View to stay above water. Promotion of the area through air shows, rodeos and sports events at the new arena (located nearer to Hwy 12 off Hwy A); and big name bands performing at the Purple Grackle helped publicize the area. By the end of World War II, lake property was booming, as was the tourist industry, and the Lake Delton project progressed rapidly. Playing his hand close to the vest, Hines was able to keep the project alive. What began as Newman's dream, became reality through the courage and perseverance of Ralph Hines and the Lake Delton Development Company.

A poster advertising the notorious bull fight that did not take place in 1931.

Tales are woven and legends are told that Mr. Newman died a broken man, neither seeing the finished product of his labor and investment, nor living in Dawn Manor, or swimming in the beautiful lake. The reality of the situation is that Newman still visited Lake Delton-at-the-Dells for many years. Although, he had never intended to live in Dawn Manor, he did enjoy the beauty and tranquility of his lake 'up where the pines begin'. William J Newman died in Chicago, at the age of 78, on June 2, 1943.

Over the years businesses have come and gone, land has been purchased and sold, developed or returned to its natural state, all in an attempt to make the Dells a place where the tourists will want to visit and return. This area's early popularity started with H.H. Bennett's advertising the 'natural beauty' of the Dells. However, the Dells area flourished in the 1920s, '30s, & '40s due largely to the foresight, diligence, and hard work of the developers and builders of this man-made beauty, Lake Delton. Little acknowledgment or honor has been given to William J. Newman or Ralph M. Hines for their contribution to this community's development and growth, but their efforts are left for posterity to appreciate.

The Purple Grackle

It is believed that the Purple Grackle, as part of W.J. Newman's dream to develop Delton into an exclusive country colony, was built around 1927. What is certain is that it remained Wisconsin Dells' most popular dancing pavilion for more than 20 years.

The pavilion was built on large cement pillars which are still visible on the west bank of the Wisconsin River in the Lower Dells, and was the site of many evenings of ballroom dancing at its best.

The Grackle had a massive bowed roof supported by wide eaves that kept the rain out and provided anchorage when the large, unscreened windows were tilted up and hooked to let in the cool river breezes. The main entrance to the long, rectangular building was also bowed and finished with a Stucco type material that appeared to be purple and glittery.

The building, stretching nearly from the river to County Hwy A, had entrances at both ends. A large wooden archway and pillars near the highway marked one entrance, and at the river there was a boat dock and heavy wooden steps leading up to the hall.

Inside, the dancing area was expansive with a hard wooden floor, two orchestra pits–one at either end, and a sparkling crystal ball which hung in the center of the ceiling. With an addition to the building in 1929, the dance floor could hold an enormous crowd without overcrowding the building. A new cooling system added in 1931 made the Purple Grackle an even more delightful place to dance.

The Purple Grackle was operated seasonally with Joe Maes and his Studio Ball Room Orchestra performing nightly for the first season. For the next four years others appearing at the Purple Grackle included Victoria Spivey, noted blues singer and star of the motion picture "Hallelujah." She and her 13 piece Brunswick recording orchestra opened the 1931 season on Memorial Day.

Manager Ray McKavis brought back by popular demand Louis Panico and his celebrated radio recording orchestra and world famous trumpet players during August of 1931. All were informed that 'Park Plan of dancing will be in effect during most performances'.

McKavis, keeping his promise to provide the best music obtainable for dancers in the Dells region, scoured the country for such other leaders in the dance world as Maurie Sherman and his nationally famous College Inn 14 piece orchestra and Marty Stone and his thirteen-piece orchestra from the Schroeder Hotel in Milwaukee. Their snappy dance music made them daily radio favorites on WTMJ.

Also apppearing were Jack Ashe and his internationally-famous orchestra of the noted Parisian revue, the Follies Bergere. They toured Europe, and featured a chorus of light opera stars. Lanky Neal and his noted Milwaukee Athletic club orchestra which was featured on the R.K.O. vaudeville circuit and numerous radio stations, also played here. Neal's dance on Saturday, June 10, 1931 inaugurated the 10¢ a dance season at the Purple Grackle. Other innovations to the Grackle that season included Tuesday nights devoted to nationally famous orchestras. Plans were formatted to broadcast from the Purple Grackle, but never materialized.

On Sunday, September 27, 1931 at 5:00 AM, the Purple Grackle was destroyed in a spectacular blaze. The owners believed that the building was set afire but no proof was ever discovered. Others claimed that the recently installed new furnace was to blame. The caretaker, however, maintained that the last fire in the furnace was built at 5:00 PM Saturday, and had been out long before the last dance was over. Some who danced that night said that they had smelled wood smoke, but that there had been no cause for alarm as no source of fire was found.

The Original Blue Aces was one of many dance bands that played at the Purple Grackle over the years.

On the Way - - They'll be Here

WHEN?

PLAYING HERE FROM

Date May 28th to June 10th

WHO?

They'll Sing for You

They'll Entertain You

Chas. Herbert

AND HIS

ORIGINAL BLUE ACES

THE ACE OF DANCE BANDS

Direct from Chicago — Don't Fail to Hear These Masters of Rythmn

At Purple Grackle at Lake Delton

Ladies — Gentlemen

An aerial view of the east side of Lake Delton shows the original Purple Grackle standing on piers on the shore of the Wisconsin River. This building was destroyed by fire in 1931 and another Purple Grackle built away from the water. This structure, then known as the Crossbow, was destroyed by fire in 1966.

The caretaker and his wife, who lived in one of the cottages just a few feet from the dance hall, discovered the blaze and immediately reported the fire to the manager. He returned and tried to enter the building to obtain the fire extinguishers that were inside, but the smoke was so thick that it was impossible to enter. At 6:30 AM the Wisconsin Dells fire department was called, but by this time the building was so far gone no attempt was made to save it. The Baraboo Fire Department reached the blaze at 7:30 AM, but there was little for them to do. Ralph Hines, manager for the Newman properties, said the loss of the pavilion and the equipment neared $25,000.00, which was only partially covered by insurance.

The three cottages which had sat overlooking the river next to the pavilion were moved across the road to Kerfoot House and Cottages not long after the blaze.

The second Purple Grackle was built and ready in time for the 1932 season. It was closer to County A, with a more modern exterior which featured a gable roof and few windows. It still boasted a massive dance floor and nationally famous bands continued to entertain there. Among those were Cab Calloway, Wayne King, and the Dorsey Brothers.

After the war began, dancing gave way to more practical things, like the production of materials to support the boys over seas. During the war the Purple Grackle was leased to Ray-O-Vac who used it for a warehouse for their batteries. After the war the building was used for an Italian restaurant for a short time. The Purple Grackle dance pavilion lived only in the memories of those who frequented there.

The building housed several manufacturing concerns after that. The last known company to occupy the building was the "Bug Light Company", which manufactured light bulbs with dents in the top during the 1950s. Tablets were place in the dents, and as the tablets heated they melted, chasing bugs away.

Don Zinke purchased the property and vacant building in 1965 from the Lake Delton Development Company on a land contract. To restore the building to its original dance pavilion atmosphere, extensive rebuilding was required both inside and out.

Times change and the Big Band era gave way to Disco and Rock. Now called the Cross Bow, the Purple Grackle was once again deemed one of southern Wisconsin's most popular teenage dancing spots. The Cross Bow was very successful that first year and Zinke was able to pay off the land contract. He planned for the business to be open year round. Though Zinke meant the hall to provide a 'good clean place for teenagers to go', with uniformed policemen on the premises to card all who entered, the Cross Bow met with great disapproval by area residents.

On June 2, 1966, while County Hwy A was unaccessible due to reconstruction, a fire was discovered about 8:00 PM. By the time the Dells and Lake Delton Fire departments reached the building, not much was salvagable. Estimated insured loss in this fire was $50,000.00, and arson was suspected.

After an intense investigation by the Dells Police Department, an arsonist was determined but charges were never filed for reasons of mental instability. Don Zinke sold the property to the Uphoff family in 1967.

Today the site of the famous Purple Grackle lies vacant. Returned to its natural state, it is used by the Original Wisconsin Duck Company as part of their "Duck" trail ride.

Looking down Broadway west towards the bridge, c. 1925.

The Great Depression

Black Tuesday, October 29, 1929, the day the stock market crashed, signaled the end of 1920s prosperity. Probably the biggest loser in this area was W.J. Newman, but others suffered as well.

Jennie Bowman was the last survivor of the wealthy Jonathan Bowman family. She was always known as a shrewd businesswoman who knew how to pinch pennies. Stories abound about haggling over the price of a half dozen eggs, the division of a banana with her household help and the precious penny she gave to little Bobbie Wainwright. On a rainy night, Oct. 10, 1931, her drab, bedraggled figure knocked on Roy Weber's door, asking him to buy a farm she owned near town. Her price was $1,500. Mrs. Weber was opposed to the purchase, being fearful of the Depression. Finally Jennie said she would sell the property for $1,000. The lonely recluse had survived the crash with lots of worthless stock and property that no one could buy. She needed cash. Today this farm is known as the Oak Lawn subdivision on the east end of Broadway.

The Depression gradually deepened across the country. The Bennett Studio was a good indicator of the situation. Business declined until the low point was reached in 1933, when their total sales were 75.2% below their 1929 receipts.

All families have their own stories of the Great Depression. Tom Howley and Leo Baggot had been in the gasoline and fuel oil business but when sales declined dramatically in the early 1930s, Leo moved his family to a farm in Adams County. He established a dairy and delivered milk to town at 5¢ a quart. Many people were never able to pay him, but his deliveries never stopped.

When Celia Morse and Jake Drollinger were married in 1930, they couldn't afford $15 a month for rent so they moved in with her parents on their farm. Sometimes they had pancakes three times a day but they always had side pork and potatoes. Years later Celia told Dr. Thompson that when he and a friend came to their house one day, the Morses were so embarassed to be eating pancakes that they didn't invite the men to eat with them. Dr. Thompson replied, "You don't know how much we wished you had." Even dentists were hungry.

Celia's brothers and Jake pooled their money to buy a pack of cigarettes. The Morses were a musical family and they often earned 25¢ for each member of the band when they played for dances. Celia says, "We had an awful good time."

The events of 1932 often carried articles telling of the plight of hobos and others out of work. By May 1st, the city had provided more than 1,000 meals, about 7 a day since January 1. Wisconsin Dells did not have a soup kitchen, but meals were served at the city jail. This was at a time when many communities–large and small–were running "tramps" out of town, not feeding them.

Columbia County's poor relief was forced to borrow $10,000 from the Reconstruction Finance Corporation by August, 1932, to meet April and May bills. Half of the county's bills were paid by the state. That winter Portage established a soup kitchen and shelter. The paper of October 13 says, "During the summer months the hobos take care of this matter themselves gather in jungles and other places where community meals can be cooked at a minimum of cost and a maximum of satisfaction. But when winter comes stalking down from the north covering the old camping ground with snow, then it is a different thing and there is nothing to do but give the wayfarer the shelter and sustenance of some sort of a city charity. The soup kitchen supplies the needed sustenance at a minimum of cost and the result is that a much larger number can be fed at a much lower cost."

Conditions gradually improved. In the *Events* of February 7, 1934, Editor Drumb explains the shelter given to the destitute wandering the roads near the Dells in those days. "TRAMPS ARE FEW AT CITY HOTEL." Chief of Police Jack Willard reports that he has very few callers at his place of repose these nights in comparison with what there was a year or so ago. An average of not more than one a night has been the number listed since the first of the year, and the indications are that there are but few of these wanderers on the road to what there has been since the depression first started.

"In the days before employment was given to the wanderers there was often times when the local calaboose would have seventeen or eighteen customers of a night, and when you come to put eighteen men into a place where the normal capacity is about half a dozen, the last two or three have to be put in with the aid of a shoe horn or a hay baler. The quarters were probably not overly comfortable, but once in a while there would be some hyper-sensitive hobo who would voice a protest about the prevalence of bedbugs in the jail, but outside of this things were generally all right.

"Jack says they used gallons of insecticide in their effort to keep down the insect population in the cells, but the visitors brought them in faster than modern science could kill them off, so there you were."

"While the efforts of the government to take all the tramps off the road has probably not been entirely successful, it is considerably different from what it was a few years ago."

Meanwhile, local merchants offered sales. When school opened in 1932, Borcher's store ran a special sale, "2 tablets for 5¢, one pencil free." In October the H.H. Bennett Studio, "Announces it will accept wood or other farm produce in payment for portrait work. For the Holiday Season up to December 17."

Jim Dixon traded clothes from his store for groceries from neighboring merchants.

On the day after his inauguration, Franklin Roosevelt proclaimed a bank holiday–March 5, 1933. The *Events* proclaimed, "Closed Banks and No Cash Meant Nothing". In the March 16 edition, the headlines announced that both banks "Open For Business Tuesday. Money is Coming In." The article goes on "The Farmers & Merchants Bank, 232 Broadway, has passed thru the stabilization plan before the moratorium was called, so there was nothing to keep it closed any longer, and the Kilbourn State Bank (201 Broadway) was in such condition that there had been no call for closing it at any time, but it was closed in accordance with President Roosevelt's call.

A dispatch from Madison stated that the Kilbourn State Bank was the only bank outside of Milwaukee, aside from those under stabilization, that was released to open without restriction on Tuesday, which is a pretty good work for our local bank and one that it is be hoped that the people of this city and vicinity appreciate." When the two banks reopened, depositors at the Kilbourn State, a private bank, could receive 100% of their money. Many people still talk of losing all their money in the Farmers and Merchants State Bank. Perhaps a percentage was paid to some.

The Riverview Boat Dock, c. 1925.

On the morning the banks closed, Charley Murray asked his neighbors, Dorothy and Bill Phelps if they had any cash in the house. He had only 50¢. The Phelps family had written $200 in checks and it took a long time to pay off those bills.

The Depression did not hit the area as hard as many parts of the country. People around here were used to "hard scrabble". Everyone had a garden and canned fruits and vegetables. The men hunted and trapped. If you had a quarter, you could feed your family for a day. Hamburger was 3 pounds for a quarter and bread was a nickel a loaf. Many families charged their groceries all winter at Oehler's Grocery and gradually paid off the debt when money started coming in with the tourists.

Some men had secure year-round jobs. Others worked summers on the boats or at the resorts. In the off-season they picked up odd jobs and carpenter or cabinet work. Women cooked, made beds, cleaned rooms and waited on tables in the many hotels and resorts during the summer. The Crandall and Finch Hotels seemed to have employed almost every woman in the area at some time. Of course, this included meals and often lodging, especially at the resorts north and south of the town. The starting wage was 15¢ an hour. Many women took in washing or sewing and roomers in their homes in the summer. The going rate for years was $1.00 or 50¢ per person, depending on their location. Most women sewed the family clothes or remodelled those they had bought at a rummage sale.

"Use it up. Wear it out. Make it do or do without". Hand-me-downs were especially trying for the children. One little navy coat was passed down through at least five children in three families.

Girls from neighboring farms often worked as "hired girls" in town. Their wages might be $5.00 a week and they also got room and board while they cooked, cleaned and cared for the children.

Children, especially boys, often supplemented the family income. When Carl "Shoudy" Slocum was a boy his family lived at 620 LaCrosse Street, an ideal location for fun and profit. Born in 1922, he probably explored every avenue open to him until he entered the army in World War II.

The south end of Superior Street was a ravine used as the city dump. He says it was a "Happy Hunting Ground" for kids. Whiskey bottles brought a nickel and beer bottles a penny when sold to bootleggers. The boys stripped junked Model T's and sold parts. The Equity or Farmer's Exchange was nearby and boys could gather the shelled corn cobs and sell them for fuel. The going rate was a nickel a bag. Shoudy's Aunt Lu Purcell thought her nephews should give her a special rate–6 bags for 26¢ or 13¢ for each brother. When the boys refused, she was furious but years later, she allowed Shoudy to mow her lawn for a quarter.

A neighbor hired him to buy and deliver her groceries from Miklics for 2¢. Sometimes he tried to run his 2¢ into a nickel on the local slot machines. Then he could have an ice cream cone.

Dingee's Pickle Factory was nearby. A huge, open salt water vat held the cucumbers dumped in by the farmers. Anyone could help themselves if they didn't mind the drowned rats, mice and bats also floating in the brine. George Miller's blacksmith shop and blind pig on the east side of the block generated a lot of traffic and excitement.

Taylor's Glen and the tunnel under the railroad sheltered many hoboes. The Slocum house was probably marked by the hoboes to show that they would get a handout at the back door. No matter how tough things were, almost every home would give handouts, sometimes in return for household chores. These hoboes built their fires in Taylor's Glen and made stews from scraps of meat and vegetables found along the way.

Shoudy's career extended to delivering telegrams for 12 1/2¢ an hour, 50¢ a day. He peddled theatre programs for Frank Fisher and was paid with free admission to the movies. Programs changed three times a week then. The ride to Briggsville in Fisher's convertible and the free candy bar added to the charm of the job. Like most boys he had a shoeshine stand one summer near Olson's pavillion. The hardest part of this job was Grover Olson's two-toned shoes at 15¢ a pair.

This led to work at the refreshment stand in the pavillion. Other jobs followed-Gordon Winnes' delivery boy, pin setter at Wenkman's bowling alley but at Thompson's Restaurant he finally got high pay at $20 a week, plus hamburgers and cigarettes.

Some boys hauled ice for Gray's or Kaiser's. This job built athletic muscles for the football season. Older boys looked forward to caddying on the golf courses and later guiding on the river-the cream of the jobs then. Teenage girls clerked at stores or waitressed.

Everyone was in the Depression together and there was little difference between rich and poor, although some of the more affluent had to forego their winter trips to Florida or California.

There was card-playing, dancing and lodges for the adults. Admission to the Mission, later the Dells Theatre at 123 Broadway was 25¢ for adults, 10¢ for kids. Some boys worked here as ushers.

On summer evenings a family might play Bingo at the big stand at 119 Broadway. Crowds stood on the railroad bridge to watch the steamer go off to the Ceremonial mid whistles and steam. Later there might be an ice cream cone and tourist watching.

Boys played baseball and marbles, girls jumped rope, played hopscotch and jacks. One could roller skate on all the sidewalks in town. The hills were great to roll down unless one lost a wheel en route. Some kids had scabs on their knees all spring. There were Radio Flyer wagons in summer and Flexible Flyer sleds in winter. Other favorite street toys were classic balloon-tired cream and brown Ranger bicycles, scooters and Irish Mails. There was ice skating at the Slough or on the school grounds, tobagganing and skiing when skiis only had a strap over the instep. It was fun to slide down the ice on the sidewalk in front of the Van Hotel on the way to school but by noon, someone had spoiled the fun by putting ashes on the walk.

If one was lucky, the parents might be able to afford a season ticket to the Multnomah swimming pool where Fred Dixon taught kids to swim, dive and swing on the rings. The big top in the middle of the pool was great for groups of kids to twirl or tip until all fell off. A good wool Jantzen suit from Dixon's store cost $5.00 and would last a girl all summer.

After Franklin Roosevelt's inauguration, many federal programs were put in place to provide jobs for the unemployed. Relief rolls had mounted to nearly 1,000 in August, 1933. The Civil Works Plan (CWA) gave jobs to many by November 23. The paper announced that $13,000 would be spent in the Dells before February 15 with 75% of the allotment to be used for labor. In December of that year the work force grew. "The city now has four projects, namely, the reconditioning of Wisconsin Avenue, Fremont Park, sewer work at Washington Avenue and Cedar Street, and filling in the ravine and general improvements back of the school." Many other needed civic projects were funded in this way. Free afternoon and night school courses were offered to give unemployed teachers work and extend adult education. Nursery school was provided during class times with a full time nurse. Classes offered in December, 1933, included typewriting, business English, home economics, American social problems and recreational classes.

Lake Delton also benefitted from CWA funds when an airport project was approved with the expenditure of about $12,000. This airport was known as McBoyle's in later years and stood with its hanger across from the entrance to Dell View Hotel on Highway 12.

Another federally funded project was the Ranger Station. In 1936, the city purchased land and gave it to the Wisconsin Conservation Department to erect a substation as headquarters for the fire district. The department had formerly operated out of a cabin at the Pines Hotel.

Construction of the station at 1242 River Road started in 1937 with labor costs paid by the Works Progress Administration (WPA). Local men found work cutting the pink sandstone for the building at a quarry owned by Morses at the intersection of Waubeek Road and 9th Ave (the old Field Road). The state supplied the materials building a handsome and functional building with an apartment for the chief rangers on the second story. The first ranger was Leigh Hilliker, followed by Dayton Woodward, Roy Kelly, Frank Palenik and Robert Oxnem.

Fire control from this station today extends over 10 townships in four counties. These townships include Lemonwier, Kildare and Lyndon in Juneau County, Springville, Jackson, New Haven and Dell Prairie in Adams County; Newport and the west end of Lewiston in Columbia County; Delton and Dellona in Sauk. The southern part of the state uses planes for spotting fires. The fire tower on Elephant's Back or Blue Mound is the southernmost in the state. The first steel tower was built on Leute's property on the mound. In 1938 it was replaced by a wooden tower on Chula Vista property. In 1958, the present steel tower was erected. The Home Owner's Loan Corporation (HOLC) saved many homes with a mortgage through long term low interest loans.

Cockeye Hoisington

When stories of the "old days" are told, someone always says, "Do you know about Cockeye Hoisington?"

He was one of those old time ticket sellers for the boat companies who stood on the Sauk County end of the bridge. When a traveller's car approached, he followed the custom of the day trying to stop the cars, then jumping on their running boards inquiring, "Do you have your tickets to go into the Dells?" If that didn't work, he would lie down in the road to stop the cars.

The Wisconsin Dells Events of February 11, 1932, tells the story of Cockeye's last adventure. "Hoyt Hoisington and John Bauer Drowned". Mr. Drumb never told all the facts if the story might hurt the family's feelings and Cockeye's father was a very respected old member of the GAR. John Bauer was Mrs. Jake Wirtz' son.

The men drowned in Dell Creek on what is now Country A. "The accident is supposed to have occured about eleven o'clock last night, when it is supposed the two men were on their way to Baraboo and missed the turn at the bridge and went into the creek. It was more or less foggy last night and somewhat rainy, and an accident of this kind might easily have happened, as there is a sharp turn onto the bridge going south that might easily prove disastrous to a motorist driving at any speed along the road.

Dell Creek at the bridge is quite deep, having been dredged out to allow pleasure boats to go up to Lake Delton, and at normal times there are five or six feet of water there, and when the river is high it is much deeper, as the creek is on a level with the river at that point."

What the paper did not report was that the men had a "skinful of booze" and had just robbed Mrs. Hall's roadhouse. Their pockets were full of coins from the slot machines and they sank like rocks. Old tales say the third man with them pulled himself out of the river and was drinking at the scene when the sheriff came to arrest him.

Duststorm in Dell Prairie, 1925. The light soil of the Dells area was always vulnerable to wind erosion, especially in the drought years of the early 1930s.

The Great Depression On The Farm

After threatening for some time, the 1930s Great Depression was finally brought on by the stock market crash of 1929.

In the rural areas here things didn't change much immediately but as the reality of what was happening hit home, there was a feeling of "sorrow, consternation and despair," as recorded by Msgr E. C. O'Reilly, of Baraboo, in his memoirs "Look Back 50 Years". He goes on to say "We are going through a national panic, factories are closing and banks are shutting their doors, jeopardizing the savings of millions of hard-working people."

Most people in the countryside were not "in the market" on Wall Street, but some had modest savings which were lost in the closing of the Farmers & Merchants Bank in Kilbourn.

The main concern in the farm communities was the drought of those years and the concern that farms, one by one were "going under" when mortgages couldn't be paid, not even the interest.

This was finally stemmed to some extent after Franklin Delano Roosevelt became president, as he was instrumental in establishing as one of his programs, the National Land Banks, thus allowing farmers to refinance and hang on.

Country children of the depression seemed to be on equal standing with their neighbors. Everybody went barefoot during the summer months, and everybody got new shoes from the Sears catalog as fall and a new school term began. One of the memories of children of the depression was a program in the country schools to enable children in grades 1 through 8 to be vaccinated. Small pox vaccinations were given and a new shot, then called "Toxin-Anti Toxin" was given for the first time, as a preventive for the dreaded disease diptheria. Children were transported to a central location (in Lyndon township, it was the Red Tavern School) where all were unhappily vaccinated. All children's diseases in that era were dreaded, as penicillin was far in the future. scarlet fever and polio were two of the worst and measles and mumps were just endured by all.

Even though at the beginning of the depression, most farm people did not have radios and many did not have telephones, neighbors who were a little better off were willing to share their newspapers. The daily gave graphic accounts of the Lindbergh kidnapping in 1932, the election that same fall, Edward VII and his affair with socialite Wallis Warfield Simpson in 1935 and the disappearance of flyer Amelia Earhardt in 1937.

Meanwhile in the rural areas of Wisconsin Dells, now that prohibition was over, a common crime was chicken stealing. This may appear humorous today, but at that time farmers depended on their flock, not only for meat but for their daily egg supply. The thieves, of course were stealing the chickens to sell for cash.

"Tramps" were a fact of life during the depression years. These desperate, out-of-work beings literally tramped the countryside hoping for work or food or a hand-out. Some of them, also called "hobos" would linger awhile or hop a freight for the west, in time for the grain harvest. Most farm wives fed the itinerants, but had them enjoy their meal on the back porch.

Football At $4 A Game

"Professional" football came to Wisconsin Dells long before televised NFL games became a Sunday afternoon ritual. In the early 1930s, a team quarterbacked by Glenn "Fat" Blatchley brought out the fans to the high school field and was actually paid for it.

"We used to pay Ollie [Shumway] four bucks a game," Blatchley later reminisced. "That was because he had a job in Wisconsin Rapids and we had to chip in for expenses."

Local players were paid less than Shumway, who was a bonecrusher of a fullback. However, it was the Depession era and all the players were glad to have every nickel they could earn.

"We didn't have any money. But, believe me, we had a football team." The roster read as follows:

LE, Monk Heineke; LT, Toby Tofson; LG, Jake Drollinger; C, Paul Fedderly; RG, Joe Berthing; RT, Frank Schultz; RE, Claire Graham; QB, Glenn Blatchley; RH, Jim Wimmer; LH, Ed Heineke; FB, Ollie Shumway.

Alternates included Thor Peterson, Don Hamm, Sr., Buff Mathews, Art Tobin, Jim "Butterball" Johnson, Greg Charlesworth who coached the team and substituted for Blatchley as alternate quarterback, Vern Sharpe, Charles Van Wie, Dick Swansby, Ted Leute, "Cuffy" Lyons, Francis Botsford, Harry Flickner, and Joe Wenkman.

"There were times when Portage's Rebholz brothers played with us, sometimes against us," Blatchley said.

"The older Rebholdz–Harold–was probably the finest fullback, pound for pound, this area has ever seen. Given three inches more height and 20 pounds more weight, he'd have rated with the greatest power runners of all times and as a linebacker, even Nagurski couldn't match his defensive play."

Blatchley said the only game the Dells aggregation lost in its initial season–1931–was to Portage.

The Dells team, Blatchley continued, managed to wangle a $300 loan from city funds for uniforms before the start of the 1932 season.

"We had a big year and ended up with $240 after expenses. The city, in a gracious gesture, charged our loan off to advertising."

"We played both ways, offense and defense, in those days," Blatchley said.

"Our offense, in reflection, was fairly simple. We ran from a single wing, alternating Shumway who did our punting and ran low with great power and the highkneed Wimmer, our break-away back, hitting at the same holes until something gave in the defense. Eddie Heineke was our speedster–our 'Roadrunner.' Wimmer did most of the passing."

The "Iron man" of the team, according to Blatchley, was Dells hardware merchant Paul Fedderly, a quick-tempered, explosive center from St. John's Military Academy.

"Our right tackle, Frank Schultz, who later became city street commissioner, was scouted for us by Jerry Baggot, who saw the young Frank pick up a punctured cattle truck tire–wheel and all–and flip it in a single motion over the rack rather than roll it around to the loading gate."

In the fall of 1933, backed by a syndicate of local business men, the Dells team drew the services of several "bonus" players including All-American half back Mickey McGuire.

"I think they drew something like $25 a game," Blatchley said. In those days, $25 would have bought shoes for the entire team. The "high-priced" new talent, however, failed to meld with the local players. The team disbanded at the end of the 1933 season and brief era of pro football at Wisconsin Dells ended.

The Wisconsin Dells "professional" football team, c. 1932, (front l-r) Charles Van Wie, Charlie Glassel, unidentified, Bud Peterson, Francis Botsford, Monk Heineke, Nick Weber (rear) Ollie Shumway, Rosie Gottschauk, Joe Wenkman, Fat Blatchley, Dean Ostrander.

Camp Wawbeek

Camp Wawbeek is located east of Wisconsin Dells on property originally purchased by a Milwaukee attorney H.J. Upham as a summer retreat. In order to receive a tax deduction Upham established The Wawbeek Company, Inc. which produced and sold bottled water. Mr. Upham died in 1935 leaving the property to his daughters Elizabeth and Caroline. In 1938 the daughters donated the land and buildings to the Wisconsin Easter Seal Society as a camping facility for the physically handicapped. The first season benefited 91 campers. The camp includes boys and girls dormitory, kitchen, dining hall, swimming pool, nature trails, rifle range, and horseback riding. In 1970 attendance was 646 campers and in 1991. In 1944 President Franklin Roosevelts wife Eleanor wrote the following article:

My Day: Easter Seal Sale in Wisconsin

Every Easter we are asked to buy Easter seals, and the proceeds of these sales in the State of Wisconsin are used by the Wisconsin Assocation for the Disabled. A boy who is a cripple wrote to tell me the story of the reclamation runs near Wisconsin Dells, and sent me copies of a little paper called Smiling Through. This camp is known as Camp Wawbeek for Crippled Children.

The estate, including several buildings, was the gift of Mrs. Charles Upham Davis and Carolina Upham Hughes to the association which has invested more money in proper equipment. Children come from all over the state, suffering from many crippling diseases, but whether they are in wheelchairs or are only partially afflicted, the program is adapted to give them both pleasure and education.

Previous page: *The Wawbeek Cottage (above) and (below) disabled children and staff, 1943. (Courtesy, H.H. Bennett Studio Foundation).*

Blowsnake and Daybreak (above) welcoming a young person to Wawbeek, c. 1950 and (below) Marvin Hanson and 4-H members at Upham Woods, 1957. (Courtesy, H. H. Bennett Studio Foundation)

Upham Woods

Camp Wawbeek was a wonderful gift and Upham Woods another, given through the generosity of Elizabeth Upham Davis and her sister Caroline Upham Keen. Upham Woods encompasses Blackhawk Island, 320 acres of unspoiled forest on the Upper Dells.

The gift specifies the land is to be used as an outdoor laboratory and camp for youth, such as 4-H clubs and other people cooperating with the University of Wisconsin in the advancement of conservation, of agriculture, or of rural culture.

Camp policy is the responsibility of the Upham Woods committee of the University of Wisconsin faculty. Buildings and facilities of Upham Woods are financed through the Wisconsin 4-H Foundation, Inc. Matters relating to operations, finance, and programs are the responsibility of 4-H Youth Development Programs, University Extension.

Upham Woods is the State 4-H center, owned and operated by the University of Wisconsin. The Center serves as a model and demonstration area for youth and leadership development, using the natural environment as the place and materials of learning.

It is not a camp, forest, conference center, natural preserve, bird sanctuary or game refuge. Rather, it is a combination of all of these–an area where all living things are of importance, even weeds, insects and snakes, because they are a part of the Upham Woods ecology. Participants may gain further insight in human relations, knowledge, and appreciation of the out-of-doors and an understanding of the outdoor education movement, and leadership responsibilities. Such insight is provided through small group living, sharing of responsibilities, practical experience in outdoor skills, and conservation practices.

During the summer months, this facility is used by county 4-H youth groups for camping on a 3–to–5 day basis. Approximately 32 different groups use the facility during the summer season.

The Home Front in World War II

News that the United States would be thrust into war shattered the peace of a Sunday afternoon when word of the Japanese attack on Pearl Harbor and the Phillippines reached Wisconsin Dells on December 7, 1941.

The first newspaper story printed in the *Wisconsin Dells Events* following the attack stated, "President Roosevelt asked that the newspapers not give out news which they do not know to be true, and if this matter were observed religiously, nothing could be given out at the present time, because nothing is known as to what the exact truth of the matter is."

Although news of the war may have been slow in arriving, mobilization of the home front was not. Soldiers who had formerly been drafted by lottery were now all called to service. Deferments for reasons of health, hardship and occupation became increasingly fewer. Many enlisted without waiting to be drafted, hoping to get a better choice in the service. A seventeen year old boy could enlist with parental consent.

The impact of the war locally was seen in many different ways. Charles Van Wie had to close his bakery when he was inducted into the army. High school students were fingerprinted so their bodies could be identified in case they became war casualties. General Douglas MacArthur was inducted into the Ho-Chunk tribe by Chief Albert Yellow Thunder, Sr. A large Roll of Honor billboard with a background of the Jaws of the Upper Dells and the names of all local servicemen on it, was displayed on Broadway next to the Finch Hotel.

Some of the farmers with large operations were deferred. "We are feeding the free world," was the popular expression. Even so, those who were drafted resented and ridiculed those who had deferments of any sort. If a farm had more than one able bodied man on it, the youngest was liable to be drafted. The local ag class that started out in 1943 with 15 boys only graduated 5 of them, as boys dropped out of school to help out on the farm when older brothers were drafted.

Many farm girls dropped out also, to marry their boyfriends who were going overseas. A few joined the WACS, the WAVES and the SPARS.

The demand for farm goods increased and farm families worked seemingly non-stop to produce what was needed. Even so there were shortages--cars, farm equipment, baling wire, barbed wire, even baling twine.

Consumer goods were rationed, especially sugar and rubber which were imported from east Asia. Local schools registered sugar users, so much sugar according to the number in the family. Some newspapers said this shortage was bound to make the nation healthier, but even Val Baggot's Coca-Cola plant was affected. When Japan took over Singapore, Columbia County's allotment for tires and innertubes each month was 24 each.

Each family received sugar stamps, shoe stamps and a letter: A,B,or C, in the window to tell how much gas was allowed. A good case had to be made to the ration board to get a C stamp. Coffee, tea, fuel oil and meat were also scarce and sweet sorghum was planted to boost sugar supplies.

To help combat these shortages, all automobile drivers were asked to turn in their old license plates when receiving new ones. There were scrap drives for metal, rubber, tin foil, rags, paper and virtually anything that could be recycled.

Victory gardens were started to increase the food supply. Dresses became much shorter to save cloth. Landlords were required to register all rental units to fight the housing shortage. Wood was used in place of fuel oil when possible. Hunting was used to replenish the meat supply, although ammunition was strictly rationed out, one box per customer each year. Drivers were urged to travel no more than 35 miles per hour to save tires, tubes and rubber. When synthetic tires and tubes came on the market, they were of such poor quality that they sometimes blew before they were fully inflated.

There was no let up on the home front in Wisconsin Dells. Red Cross units were organized and, with the Women's Relief Corps, made bandages, knitting and sewing for our servicemen. The following month a Defense Council was appointed for the city. There were Bundles for Britain, a Bomber drive to buy a bomber, a Victory Book Drive to get books for servicemen, air raid block wardens appointed in Wisconsin Dells, Navy Relief Drives, five percent Victory tax, early Christmas mailing to servicemen and a Labor Control Office.

Men and women flocked from all over to work at Badger Ordnance Works. Some of them lived here and many of them recreated in Wisconsin Dells. Highway 12, which had already made history as the first paved rural road in Wisconsin, now became the first four-lane rural highway in the state.

The *Wisconsin Dells Events* carried letters from servicemen on the front page for the duration of the war. In September, 1942, 64 servicemen received the *Wisconsin Dells Events* free every week.

Defense stamps were sold in the school every week for 10¢ each. When the book was full it could be exchanged for a war bond. War bonds sold for $18.25 and matured in ten years to $25, paying about 2% interest. Larger denominations became available, but the $25 bond was the staple of the bond sales.

Newspaper sales flourished and the *Events* printed four pages of boilerplate each week, which was pre-printed paper on one side that mostly

Waiting for the bus on Broadway during World War II. (Courtesy, H.H. Bennett Studio Foundation).

contained news of the war's progress, or lack of it. Editor Drumb made constant referrals to it in his popular column, "Tales By The Wayside."

Popular slogans were, *Uncle Sam Needs You! Keep 'em Flying! Remember Pearl Harbor! Your dollar may be the one to win the war!* and for Badger Ordnance workers, *Loose Lips Sink Ships!*.

People were urged to turn in knives and field glasses to help soldiers and an Army Day parade was held in town. The junior prom colors were red, white and blue. There were blackouts at night and a national election in the middle of the war, in which traditionally Republican Wisconsin Dells voted against Franklin Roosevelt and Harry Truman. By 1945, school was held on Saturday in some of the Dells school districts as boys were needed on the farm and teachers got summer war plant jobs.

Nearly every issue of the *Dells Events* contained a notice of promotions, medals, commissions, and citations. Also reported were local men who were wounded, missing-in-action, prisoners-of-war or dead.

Finally, as the war started to draw to a close, news of freed prisoners of war was often found in the columns of the newspaper. There were also many memorial services for those who did not come back.

On April 12, 1945, the Dells area, as well as the rest of the world, was shocked by the death of President Roosevelt. The death of war correspondent Ernie Pyle in the Far East brought an article about his comments on his visit to the Dells.

After V-E Day (Victory in Europe), the outdoor lighting ban was revoked. Reports of deaths and injuries to troops became less frequent compared to news from those in Europe who had relatives in America. Letters from servicemen in the *Events* told of prison camps and war-torn cities that they had overrun.

On V-J Day (Victory in Japan) the city of Wisconsin Dells wildly celebrated the peace. The bands played, car horns honked and there was dancing in the streets.

But perhaps more ominous were the comments of the *Events* editor following the dropping of the atomic bombs on Japan:

"Death lurks in the ruins of the destroyed cities for 70 years through the effects of irradiation."

"Man now has in his possession the means of world destruction. It is a terrifying thought."

The Wisconsin Dells area Roll of Honor with the names of men and women in service superimposed on a river scene. (Courtesy, H. H. Bennett Studio Foundation)

Men Who Gave Their Lives

World War I

Harold B. Larkin
Keith W. Morris
Lawrence S. Christianson
Hubert Coon
Otto Christopherson
Ray T. O'Connell
Merton Dunham

The Korean War

Durlin Morse

The Vietnam War

Dennis Beard

World War II

Edward B. Armson
Carmon M. Cole
Maurice H. Finnegan
Ralph Haralson
Oliver P. Helland, Jr.
Bernard E. Leake
Leo S. Lavigne
Thomas W. Mulligan
Orriel O. McDonald
John G. Nelson
Donald G. Oeftger
Eugene J. Prouty
Archie Ramsey
C. Arnold Stowers
Leslie L. Spence
Peter Szymanoski
Lloyd C. Utter
Willard L. Van Schoyck

WORLD WAR II
ROLL OF HONOR

Raymond G. Albert, Eugene P. Amann, Charles M. Anchor, Arthur Anderson, Clifford G. Anderson, Maynard H. Anderson, William N. Anderson, Blake Armson, Duane L. Armson

Harold E. Bacon, Roy J. Bacon, Joseph P. Baggot, M. Helen Baggot, Harry D. Bahr, Leroy R. Bahr, Newton O. Bahr, Roland D. Bahr, Ruben Bahr, Harold J. Barrett, Frank R. Barrier, Winston B. Bartells, Bernard H. Bass, Floyd R. Bass, Leon O. Beard, Ruben N. Bearskin, Kenneth L. Beghin, Kenneth E. Berry, Alvin L. Birkholtz, Edward C. Birkholz, Henry L. Birkholz, Burnell C. Bixby, Daniel O. Bixby, George D. Bixby, Gerald M. Blank, Raymond E. Blaser, Eugene M. Blood, Edward H. Bloomer, Isaac C. Bloomer, Ralph J. Bonini, Arnold B. Borcher, Charles A. Borcher, Jr., Harris F. Botsford, Russell R. Bowser, Robert K. Boynton, Adrian M. Brandt, Melford L. Bressler, John E. Brickwell, Joseph Brickwell, Corwin R. Brown, Edward J. Brown, Ralph H. Brownell, Robert W. Buckelew, Chester A. Buckley

Claude L. Cahoon, Harold H. Campbell, Herbert A. Campbell, Eugene A. Carter, Carl R. Christensen, Norman Colburn, Jr., Roland H. Colburn, Royal O. Colburn, Robert A. Colby, Albert H. Cole, Freeman F. Cole, Milford L. Cole, Orville E. Cole, Archie R. Cone, Walter F. Cone, Dennis W. Connor, Harold W. Cook, Robert L. Cook, George W. Coolidge, Charles Coon, Lawrence Coon, Walter Coon, Daniel B. Corr, Duane K. Counsell, Lowell M. Cozart, Thomas D. Crist

Ralph G. Dahl, Charles G. Day, Allen B. Dearborn, Jr., Glenn Dehler, Harold Donahue, Buford V. Donovan, Robert Dougherty, John T. Doyle, Boyce R. Draper, Floyd A. Drinkwater, William Dusel, Henry B. Dyer

Harley C. Edmonds, Paul M. Ellison, Allen G. Erdman, Edwin Erdman, Lawrence J. Evans

George A. Farley, Floyd A. Field, Robert F. Field, Morris H. Finnegan, Earnest S. Fisher, Chester T. Fisher, Norbert L. Flemal, Jack Flickner, Leonard W. Foote, , Edwin C. Foster, Gordon J. Foster, Lee J. Foster, Edward L. Fox, Lloyd T. Frank, Robert J. Fuchiek

Conrad J. Gaffney, Robert D. Gahan, David L. Gasser, Conrad M. Gavinski, Stanley R. Gavinski, Henry E. Goebel, Merlin O. Gray, Olaf T. Gregerson, Oleus Gregerson, Kermit T. Grey, Arthur Grezlak, James T. Grieger, Robert I. Griffin, Herman H. Groothoff, Kenneth L. Gross

Frank P. Hacker, Keith J. Hall, Kenneth J. Hall, Stewart E. Halverson, Arvin J. Hammerly, Verdine R. Hammerly, Harold E. Hanson, Chester Harrison, Anton Harwick, Henry R. Haves, Arthur F. Hawalleck, Arthur H. Hays, Buster A. Heath, John J. Heimel, Emil Heineke, Gustave A. Heineke, James W. Heineke, Hans O. Helland, Oliver P. Helland, Stanton P. Helland, Dale N. Helley, Carl S. Hendrickson, Edmund A. Hendrickson, Albert Henriksen, Clarence D. Henriksen, William Henricksen, Kenneth C. Hetzel, Constance N. Hinterberger, William G. Hinterberger, Donald F. Hoeller, Francis R. Hoeller, Clifford C. Holden, Carroll A. Holliday, Edward J. Holton, Albert O. House, Orlow Hove, Lester E. Howland, John E. Howley, David A. Hudzinski

Albert J. Ihde, Victor E. Ingebretson

Carl M. Jacobson, Jesse W. Jacobson, John Jacobson, Edward K. Jahn, Loris M. Jermier, LeRoy N. Jesse, Kenneth A. Jimson, Robert E. Jimson, Kenneth K. Johnson, Louis G. Johnson, Arnold M. Jones, George H. Jones, Kerwood G. Jones, Robert R. Jones, Albert Jonikas, Claude W. Jordan, John R. Joyce

Wayne W. Kaleas, Richard A. Kaleas, Frank W. Kaminski, George R. Kaminski, Henry S. Kaminski, William F. Kassner, Frank M. Kelly, Arthur V. Kimball, Merle E. Kimball, George King, Jr., Milton J. Kingsley , Archie Kinney, Ernest Klicko, Phillip E. Knippel, Howard G. Koelle, John R. Kremer, Carl L. Kuntz, Raymond J. Kuntz, Carl Kwasigroch

Edward G. Laabs, Adolphe Lage, Henry E. Lage, Jacob P. Lahni, John R. Lahni, Eugene F. Landt, Earl J. Lapp, Ivan c. Lapp, Arnold L. Larson, Arthur T. LaVigne, George T. LaVigne, Leo S. LaVigne, Bernard E. Leake, Ernest J. Leake, Irvin A. Leege, Eugene J. Leute, Thaddeus J. Leute, Durward L. Lindquist, John Lobotski, Alfred Lombard, Richard T. Lucke, Kenneth W. Lueck, Thomas A. Luke, Arnold W. Lumby, John J. Lynch

Leo D. Mac Kessay, Arthur P. Marlow, Daniel C. Marlow, George P. Marlow, James J. Marlow, Henry F. Marston, Charles W. Martin, John P. Martiny, Roy E. Mathews, Orriel O. McDonald, Vernon McKee, Delbert D. McQueen, Donald A. McQueen, Hans R. Mickelson, Gordon A. Mitchell, William J. Mitchell, Carl A. Moldenhauer, Henry J. Mommen, Dick Morris, Robert G. Morris, Thomas W. Mulligan, Clarence A. Murray, Edsel H. Murray, Kenneth M. Murray, Robert Murray

Marcel L. Naber, David B. Nelson, Henry P. Nelson, John G. Nelson, Lawrence O. Nelson, Orville Nelson, Roy C. Nelson, Robert C. Nemitz, Robert D. Neubauer, Anton P. Neumeister, Henry W. Neumeister

Donald G. Oefger, Edward R. Oefger, Grover C. Olson, John B. Olson, Richard P. Osborne

Leon C. Peck, Arliss P. Perkins, Bernard L. Peterson, Herbert M. Peterson, Thorl A. Peterson, Walter K. Peterson, Paul S. Pfister, Hilbert W. Pickel, Clarence A. Platt, James R. Playman, Harold F. Poppie, John G. Poppie, Robert E. Poppie, William H. Poppie, Donald J. Powell, Adolphe Priester, Harry L. Priester, William J. Procknow

Carl J. Radant, Cyril J. Radl, Don L. Radlund, Robert M. Ragan, Robert M. Rockoff, James M. Roderick, Norman A. Roeker, Leslie A. Roesler, John Rohrbeck, Merle E. Ross, Ralph S. Rothwell, John Russ, Raymond J. Russ, Thomas W. Ryan, Harry R. Ryczek

Donald O. Sarrington, Robert R. Sarrington, Laverne G. Schaitel, Arnold V. Schank, Agnes E. Schmidt, George W. Schmidt, Warren G. Schneider, Milton L. Schulte, Nelson B. Schultz, Norman W. Schultz, Robert E. Schultz, Vern A. Schulz, Donald J. Scott, John C. Scott, Robert F. Scott, Bernard Seger, Carl R. Seger, John J. Seger, Raymond J. Seger, Laurence M. Severson, James E. Shepard, Vern V. Sherd, Edward G. Sickenberger, Carl G. Sigafus, Lester G. Simons, Robert L. Simons, Carl M. Slocum, James W. Slocum, Arnold G. Smart, John F. Smart, Bruce H. Smith, Clifford Smith, Leon D. Smith, Raymond L. Smith, Robert F. Smith, Theodore A. Smith, James A. Smoke, Gerhard G. Smukal, Luther W. Smukal, Robert G. Smukal, Laurie P. Soma, Nenford N. Soma, Sherman S. Soma, Edward A. Sperbeck, Leland L. Standiford, Walter A. Stecky, Clayton N. Stein, Elbert G. Stein, Howard E. Stein, Nicholas W. Stein, John W. Steinmetz, James L. Stephan, James W. Stephan, Claire M. Stomner, Homer A. Storandt, Clarence A. Stowers, Herbert E. Stowers, Dennis J. Stroede, Edwin C. Stroede, Robert E. Stroede, Roger A. Stroede, Chester J. Sullivan, Richard A. Swansby, Peter Szymanoski

Homer F. Tangney, Thomas R. Tangney, Edward Templin, Shirley M. Tennison, Frederick K. Thomas, Merlin E. Thomas, Stuart E. Thomas, Jesse C. Thomm, Floyd M. Thompson, Stewart A. Thompson, Wayne D. Thompson, Chadwick T. Thunder, Miles A. Thunder, Arthur R. Tobin, Ingval O. Tofson, Merton W. Tofson, Herbert A. Tollaksen, Woodrow C. Tollaksen, Charles A. Tucker, James G. Tucker, Lloyd E. Tucker, Keith W. Turner

Clarence R. Utter, Earl A. Utter, Franklin E. Utter, Howard J. Utter, Lloyd C. Utter, Wilfred S. Utter

Gerrit K. Van Beck, William E. Van Ells, David C. Van Wie , Robert H. Van Wie

Robert L. Wainwright, Lawrence R. Walther, Frank Wampler, Mary G. Waterman, Harold J. Weber, James H. Weber, John M. Weber, Ted D. Welch, Gilbert A. Wenker, James F. Wenkman, John H. Wenkman, William G. Wenkman, Bert R. Wharry, John H. White Eagle, Wendland S. White Eagle, Tony Wiach, Joseph F. Will, Harold Williams, Vernon J. Williams, Vincent E. Williams, Chester R. Wilms, Waldon E. Wilms, Wilbur J. Wilson, Ben T. Wolfram, Daniel M. Woodard, George W. Wrezinski, Norman H. Wyzcsinski

Albert Yellow Thunder, Robert C. Zahler, Leonard Zelner, Gordon F. Zinke, Raymond R. Zinke

YOUR
COMPLETE DELLS TRIP
'THE IDEAL WAY'
Riverview Boat Line
ARCADE
DO-NUTS
DO-NUT BAR
ARCADE
WHARF
DANCING
BAR
OLSON
BOAT CO.

The Modern Era

The Wisconsin Centennial

Wisconsin was 100 years old in 1948 and the Dells, along with every town in the state, planned a gala celebration. The local Civic Club spearheaded interest and Ruth Dyer was named general chairman to explore interest and cooperation among local clubs. By March an organization had been set up and Ruth Dyer accepted chairmanship of the group. The first objective was fun for all with the widest possible participation and interest was stirred by articles in the *Dells Events* about plans and history of the area.

Besides Mrs. Dyer, the following chairman were appointed for various events. Dancing, Mrs. Bob White; Music, Mrs. Elmer Armson; Ways and Mean, Don Deakin; Cooperation with business houses, Mrs. Raymond Moravek; Advertising, Jack Olson; Local newspaper publicity, Miss Fidelia Van Antwerp; Historical displays, Mrs. K K. Johnson; Socials, Mrs. Carl Meyer; Parade, Percy Newell. The dates of the celebration were set for June 23-27. Men grew beards, women searched attics for period costumes, floats were made for the parade and everyone remembers the clothes they and their families wore and events they participated in.

Many people wore their costumes to work or to the special events. Four people portraying historical figures were constantly on the street. They were Dr. Ed Dixon as Abraham Lincoln, Roland Dyer as Buffalo Bill, Ruth Foster as Belle Boyd and Bob White as General Joseph Bailey. A group in costume arrived on the train from Portage.

The program began on Wednesday, June 23 with an Alice in Dairyland luncheon and an evening program at the high school with an address of welcome by Mayor Howley, a Minstrel Show and dance contests. On Thursday, a Centennial luncheon at the Hotel Crandall, a steamboat ride free to all in costume with one stop. In the evening the firemen staged a Water Ball Contest, and the Minstrel Show was followed by dancing. On Friday the steamboat ride was again repeated and the evening featured a Musical and Variety Program free including a Style Show west of the Finch Hotel with dancing in the street. An exhibition of birling drew spectators to Illinois Avenue in Happy Hollow. The parade included many old time vehicles and people in costume and many prizes were awarded. The evening program included a band concert, a Musical and Variety program followed again by a street dance on Broadway. On Sunday there were Centennial observances at the churches, another exhibition of birling, Indian Day in the Dells Park with an address by Chief Yellow Thunder and much dancing. The Twilight Hymn sing at the school capped off this great celebration.

Horse and Buggy Days, 1949

Everyone had such a good time at the Centennial celebration that the townspeople decided to have a similar event from June 24-26 in 1949.

Ruth Dyer was again named General Chairman with many committees. Chairmen of these groups were Ways and Means, Don Deakin; Displays, Mrs. Clifford McClyman; Advertising, Clifford Cone; Arrangements, N.A. Landt; History, Marion Fremlin; Parade, Gerald Baggot; Dancing, Mrs. Elmer Armson; Swimming Meet, Oliver Reese; Group Reunions, Mrs. Stuart Fedderly; Ice Cream Social, Iness Thompson; Style Show, Irene Greenwood; Music, Dorothy Ziegenhagen.

Again, interest was created through weekly articles in the *Events* urging everyone to be in costume or participate in special events.

The official program had its Grand Opening at the Depot where Mrs. and Miss Kilbourn, descendants of Byron Kilbourn, were met by a large costumed crowd and welcomed by Mayor Henry Field. At 2:00 PM was the dedication of the Veteran's Memorial Park Swimming Pool followed by a swim meet. At 8:00 PM, Adolph Kieger's Aqua Capers performed at the new pool. Dances at the high school grounds with dance contests were enjoyed by all. On Saturday, June 25, boat rides with one stop were again offered free to anyone in costume. A reunion luncheon for older high school classes was held at the Hotel Crandall followed by the huge parade of old fashioned vehicles, floats and walkers and prizes were awarded. In the evening a music and variety program and dance with dance contests took place at the school grounds. On Sunday, all the churches held special services followed by reunion lunches. The festivities moved to Bowman Park in the afternoon with an ice cream social, band concert, style show and spelling bee. The Twilight Hymn Sing in Bowman Park again climaxed the old fashioned celebration.

There had been talk that this might turn into an annual affair but those who had worked so hard at these celebrations the past two years did not feel they could devote the time every year and no others volunteered to take over and so the plans were dropped but a good time was had by all.

Previous page: *A traffic jam on Broadway, 1949.*

Telephone Service in the Dells

First it was Farmers Intercounty Mutual Telephone Company, on Broadway, and Bill Doyle served as manager. Next, it was Commonwealth Company, located in 1942 over the Bauer & O'Neil Drug Store at 214 Broadway.

Customers went up the stairs, down a long hall, opened a door and walked a little furthur to a payment counter behind which the cashier had a desk. Behind her desk was another for the manager, Phil Eberlein. In the next room was the switchboard and enough room for two operators, or three during the busiest hours.

Phones had to be cranked manually in order to place a call. The operator would put a plug in the number calling, say, "number please," and put a corresponding plug into the number called. The switchboard was marked with dots which told the operator who had a private line and who had a party line, as well as how many rings to make so that those on the same line knew who the call was for. One long ring and a short ring or two longs, for example. This system entertained many country folk on the party line who didn't really need a newspaper when they could quietly put a hand over the mouthpiece, take the receiver off the hook and hear all of the local news.

Chief Operator Gert Tolleth and Margaret Donovan made sure that all of the calls coming in from servicemen went through, no matter what it took. If a mother was at home, then the operator would connect. If she was out however, Gert told the long distance operator that she was ringing. Margaret kept the other operator chatting until the two could think of where the mother could be, church, club, store, etc. Gert kept calling until she found the mother, whom she instructed to tell the long distance operator that she was at home when the operator asked. It was an exciting time. Jean Reese recalls a time when Ollie called home while he was in service. Earlier that day in the grocery store, the operator had overheard her mother, Mrs. Dyer, say that she and Jean were going to the movie theater that eveing. The Dells operator called the theater in Baraboo, they paged Jean, and she got Ollie's call.

As their part of the war effort, telephone operators had to learn to dismantle some portion of the telephone. How this knowledge was to help make the world safe for democracy, the operators never knew. Maybe it was because Morris Anderson was the only repair man and they might be able to step in if his load ever got to great? No one ever did find out.

Night operators like Anna Ziegenhagen received 10 cents more per hour than day operators. Anna would turn the buzzer on and set up a roll-away for herself. If a call came while she was sleeping the alarm went off and she would answer. Others like Marilyn Severson, who filled in on Anna's day off, were too scared to sleep in the dark phone room. She remembers only dozing lighly at the switchboard. Listening in on tourist calls that came through at all hours of the night helped to keep these operators alert and awake.

The phone company never hired married women and if a woman got married while she was employed she was expected to quit. The war changed these expectations as more married women entered the workforce. For benefits, operators received double pay on Sundays and holidays, and nice gifts at Christmas. Many felt very lucky to have a year round job.

In those days, the town had one policeman. He was night, day, regular, part-time, and Chief of Police all rolled into one. He walked the streets–never rode in a car. All police calls, fire calls, noon whistle, and 5:00 PM whistle were activated through the switchboard. When a fire call came through, operators had to call the firemen. Operators turned on two red lights located on top of high poles when they needed to get the attention of the policeman, who would then call in for the message. One light was located over the police station and the other was probably over the post office. Doctors called in to let the operators know where they were as they were still making house calls in those days. The telegrapher, Howard Winter, often called for help in locating tourists he had received telegrams for. The ice man was also provided with an answering service."Not much got past us," says one 1940s operator.

When people used pay phones, operators would ask for the money after the call was completed. They had to be quick to catch the callers before they left without paying. When coins were dropped in, operators listened carefully for the distinct sound each type of coin made in order to count the amount inserted. Margaret Donovan once caught a sneaky caller who inserted slugs when asked to deposit coins. She called Officer Daisy Thomas who captured the telephone bandit: it was pay up or go to jail. The story made the front page of the local newspaper.

Operators never gave out their names when asked, only their operator numbers. One disgruntled customer demanded Margaret's name, but got only her number. The next day, the customer called to report operator #2 and Margaret took the call, and hence was reported to herself.

Eventually, General Telephone bought the company and installed dial phones, marking the end of an era.

1. Hiawatha Bar
2. Riverview Gift Shop
3. Stantons Sweet Shop
4. Badger Restaurant
5. Barretts Bar
6. Postcard Shop
7. Barretts Gift Shop
8. Kneubuhler Garage
9. Wigwamn Gift Shop
10. Totompole Curio Shop
11. Dells Boat Company
12. Riverview Boat Line
13. Riverview Arcade
14. Municipal Dock
15. Wharf Dance Hall
16. Olson Boat Company
17. Barnhill Gift Shop
18. Dells Arcade
19. Sylvias Resrarant
20. Dells Theater
21. Pure Oli Station
22. Stuelke Drug
23. Kleimenhagen & Magoon
24. O'Connors Bar
25. K & G Restaurant
26. Schultz Brothers Variety
27. Bork & O'Neil Drug
28. Fedderly Hardware
29. McClyman Hardware
30. Nigs Normande Bar
31. Quality Market
32. Broadway Market
33. Borcher Gift Shop
34. Roekers Bakery
35. Browns Restaurant
36. Dells Cafeteria
37. Farmers and Merchants Bank
38. Petes Barber Shop
39. Arntz Restaurant
40. Uptown Trading Post
41. Post Office
42. Bennett Studio
43. Ryans Restaurant
44. Finch Hotel
45. Kicks Bar
46. Dalles Apparel
47. Oehlers Grocery
48. Stomner Grocery
49. Oehlers Jewelry
50. Dr. Bohlinger Office
51. Balsmeider Beer Depot
52. Wisconsin Ducks Terminal
52. Dells Grill
54. Texaco Station
55. Deep Rock Station
56. Greenwood Chevrolet
57. Snider Insuarance
58. Dells Events
59. Wenkmans Restaurant
60. Bowling Alley
61. Ford Garage
62. Anchors Restaurant
63. Baker Pontiac
64. Shell Station
65. Sinclair Station
67. Standard Oil Station
68. Sand Bar
69. Wagner Hotel
70. Helland Hotel
71. Brooks Hotel
72. Hile House
73. Timlins Restaurant
74. Landry Furniture
75. Dells Cleaners
76. K & F Dept. Store
77. Gussel Distributing
78. Fishers Tavern
79. Kilbourn Creamery
80. Austins Grocery
81. What Not Shop
82. General Telephone Office
83. Browns Studio
84. Martiny Dairy
85. Olson Motel
86. Dells Clinic
87. Dell House
88. Kellogg Lumber Co.
89. Dells Body Shop
90. Fedderly Funeral Home
91. Harrison Electric
92. Helland Law Office
93. Monks Bar
94. Schultz Plumbing
95. Coast To Coast
96. Gaffney Electric
97. Roser Plumbing
98. Zinkes Grocery
99. Carters Tavern
100. Bobs Barber Shop
101. Dells Ice Cream Co.
102 Anderson Shoes
103. Platt Garage
104. McClyman Garage
105. Little Norway Bar
106. City Auditorium
107. City Hall
108. Fire Station

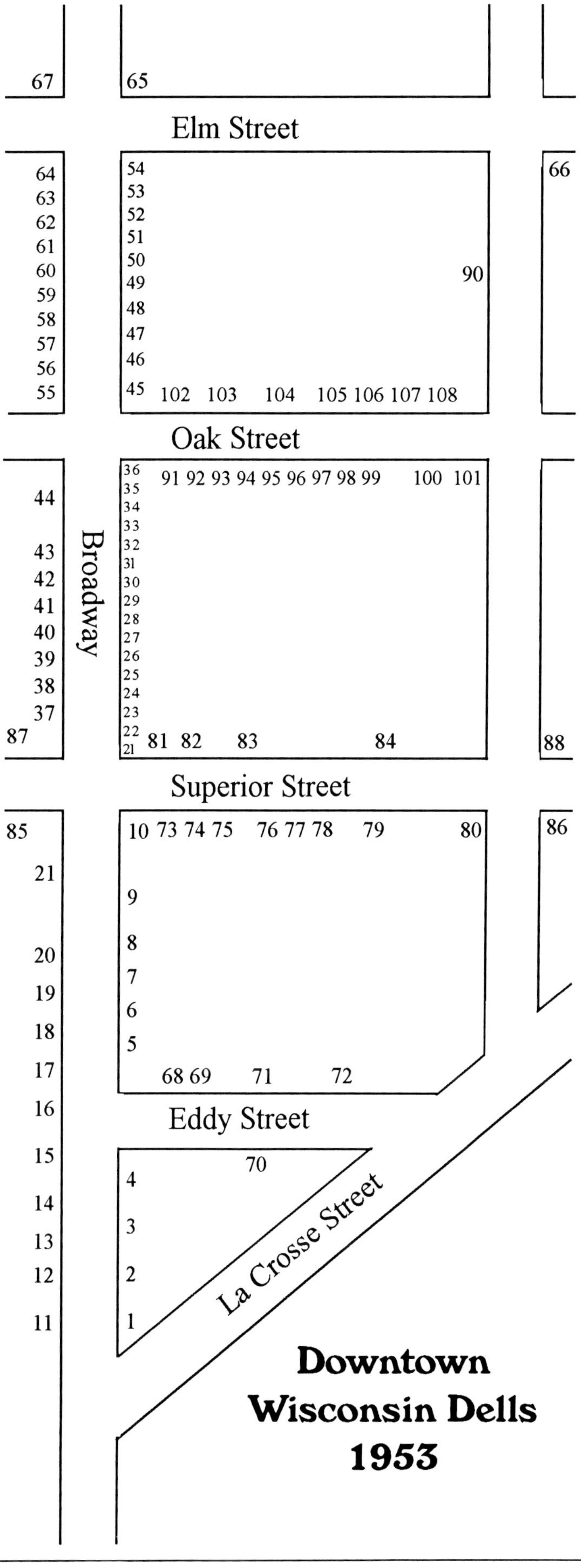

Elm Street
Oak Street
Superior Street
Eddy Street
Broadway
La Crosse Street

Downtown Wisconsin Dells 1953

Waiting for the last span of the new Broadway bridge, 1955.

The Highway 12-13 junction, with Fort Dells under construction on the southwest corner.

"The Million Dollar Bridge"

One hundred years after the founding of Kilbourn, a new Highway 16 and 13 bridge was completed. It was dedicated on June 16, 1956, when a million dollars was still "real" money.

The need for a new bridge had been evident for many, many years. The old bridge, built by the railroad in 1903, carried the railroad tracks above and a roadway and pedestrian walk on the lower level. The roadway was narrow and had right angle turns at either end. In order to avoid hitting the corner trusses supporting the upper deck, semi-trucks had to ride in the middle of the roadway. If

other traffic forced them to the side, trucks got stuck on the trusses and the drivers had to let air out of the tires before they could move on.

Even when trucks were moving, the bridge was a narrow bottle neck. Traffic often backed up for blocks, especially in the height of the summer season and gave the Dells bridge a reputation as the "worst" in Wisconsin.

By 1950, engineers were planning a new bridge and considering three different sites for it. One was an extension of Wisconsin Avenue into Dells Park on the west side of the river. A second would cross downstream at Echo Point with traffic passing south of the city. Frank Lloyd Wright offered to design a bridge for this site free of charge.

However, Dells residents and business people preferred extending Broadway west across the river and keeping traffic and business in the center of town. The completion of the 1956 bridge expedited traffic through town and helped keep the old Kilbourn business district as the heart of the Dells commercial district. It was also one of the leading factors in the growth of tourism that took place in the late 1950s and '60s.

So much growth occurred that even the 1956 bridge eventually became a bottleneck. To ease the strain an entirely new two-lane bridge named the Kilbourn Bridge was built alongside the older span in 1993.

Dedication of Interstate 90-94

On October 6, 1961, a 52.6 mile stretch of the Interstate highway was officially opened. Fourteen separate ribbon-cutting ceremonies were held, five in this immediate area.

The program started at the "H" intersection with a concert by the Dells High School band; an invocation by Rev. Davies; an introduction by Jack Olson, Secretary of the Wisconsin Good Roads Association; and Harvey Grasse, State Highway Commissioner. Governor Gaylord Nelson cut the ribbon aboard a Fort Dells stagecoach. Many other Dells and Lake Delton officials were present.

A circus theme marked the Highway 12, Baraboo and Lake Delton interchange. Tommy Bartlett's water skiers and the Reedsburg High School band were featured at the ceremony held at the Mirror Lake bridge. Another ceremony at the Highway 23 interchange featured the cutting of a giant piece of cloth from the Reedsburg Woolen Mills. The fifth dedication in the area was the 12-16 intersection at Rocky Arbor with Juneau County officials.

Construction of the highway north was delayed for several years, so Rocky Arbor became the "end of the Interstate" for drivers traveling north from Madison, Milwaukee and Chicago.

Storybook Gardens, c. 1955, which was, along with Fort Dells, one of the first theme attractions targeted at the post World War II baby boom generation. (Courtesy, H. H. Bennett Studio Foundation)

BARABOO NEWS

Baraboo is the Hub of the Devils Lake-Dells Resort

READ THIS PAPER FOR ALL THE LATEST NEWS EVERY DAY

UNITED PRESS INTERNATIONAL LEASED WIRE

BARABOO, WISCONSIN

MONDAY, AUG. 21, 1961

Member of the United Press International

ESTABLISHED 1855

Jantz Killed, Kohl Wounded

MADISON, WEDNESDAY, AUGUST 23, 1961

MORNING FINAL 5c

1 Captured—Manhunt On For Two Others

Lake Delton Is Scene Of Early Morning Shooting

Every available officer in Sauk and Juneau counties was today engaged in a manhunt—to seek two escaped robbery suspects who early today shot and killed Traffic Officer James G. Jantz, 26, of Baraboo and seriously wounded Police Chief Eugene Kohl, 45, of Lake Delton. A third suspect was ... Lyndon Station when ... to flee

At another roadblock at Lyndon Station, a shotgun from an officer broke the window of the car and it went out of control to crash. The ... man, reported to have both ... broken, was first taken to Mauston hospital but arrangements were being made this morning to convey him by ambulance to Madison.

Kohl had first become suspicious of the men when he noticed their car carried two different license plates. During last ...

3rd Man Still Sought

SUSPECT IN SLAYING CAPTURED NEAR DELLS

Charges Into Posse When He's Cornered

By JUNE DIECKMANN

WISCONSIN DELLS — A hunted police-killer suspect ... members of a converging posse like a trapped animal Tuesday ... captured in dense underbrush just north of this resort city. He identified himself as Larry G. Fletcher, 27, Chicago ... early today learned he is Lawrence J. Nutley ... Sauk County Dist. Atty. James ... said Fletcher ... charged for being one of three gunmen who early Sunday killed Sauk County ... James C. Jantz ...

More Photos of Manhunt, Pages 2, 3

Unfrightened, Woman Spots Suspect as He Asks for Pop

Murder In The Dells

Most residents of Lake Delton and Wisconsin Dells will never forget the events of the early morning hours of August 21, 1961 and the week that followed.

Residents of Lake Delton on that night remember the wounding of their police chief, 46 year old Bob Kohl, in a gun battle that took the life of Sauk County traffic officer, James Jantz, 25.

A witness entering the nearby C-Der-Del Motel on Highway 12 in Lake Delton saw officer Kohl's squad car pull the black Oldsmobile over, then witnessed the gun fire and saw Kohl fall. Officer James Jantz came to Kohl's asistance and three men with guns blazing leapt from the car and Jantz fell dead. (According to the witness 30 shots were fired)

Residents west of Wisconsin Dells remember the night of August 21, 1961 as a night of wailing sirens as the escapees led a chase up highway 12 toward Mauston. The chase ended when the assailants vehicle crashed while trying to negotiate a u-turn. In that crash one of the men, Richard Nickel, sustained two fractured legs when he fell from the car. He was taken to the Mauston hospital where he was kept under guard. In the confusion that followed the other two men fled into the darkness. They were later found to be Lawrence Nutley and William Welter.

While the families mourned, the search continued for Welter and Nutley. Police departments from throughout the area were joined by hundreds of civilian volunteers, while residents in outlying areas lived in fear that the assailants would walk out of the woods or hide in their barns. On Tuesday Nutley did in fact walk out of the woods near Stand Rock.

The proprietor of Stand Rock Resort cooly served pop to the bedraggled Nutley and was able to alert law enforcment as to his whereabouts.

Throughout the week search for Welter continued as searchers combed the wooded and marshy regions northwest of Lyndon Station. On the following Sunday, searchers with the aid of blood hounds tracked the suspect, who was wounded and somewhat delirious, to a dump near a creek in that vicinity.

A joint sigh of relief was breathed by residents and a sense of normalcy returned to the area, although the loss of services and the loss of life will never be forgotten.

500 SEARCH FOR SLAYERS OF POLICEMAN AT DELTON

(Wisconsin State Journal)

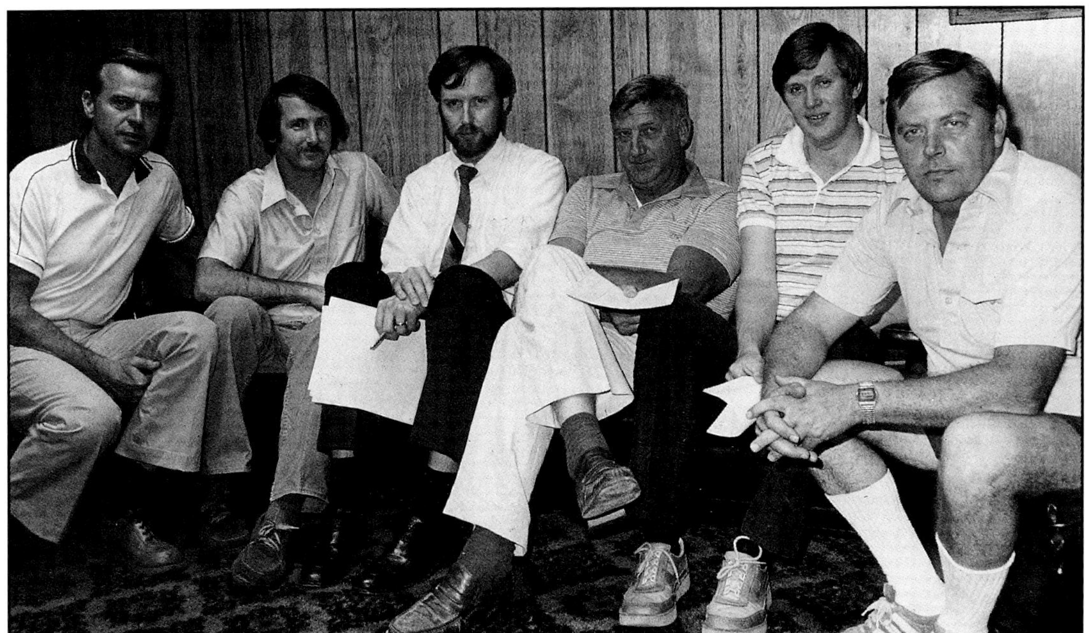

The Wo Zha Wa Committee, 1982 (l-r) Bud Gussel, Dave Foster, Steve Toepel, Gus Never, Ben Borcher, Bob Gussel.

Wo Zha Wa

In 1966, a group of civic minded citizens founded the fall festival organization. The name Wo Zha Wa was offered by a local Ho-Chunk man who said it meant "time of fun." The first festival which included Maxwell Street Days, a carnival, art show, food stands, 16 mile run and parade was an immediate success. The event has grown to become the busiest weekend of the year. Charles Van Wie was the first chairman and Bud Gussel has chaired for the last 28 years.

The Dells Rotary Club (below), c. 1960, (sitting, l-r) Oliver Tofson, George Willard, Harold McKuen, Jack Gray, Jack Olson, John Kremer, Floyd Field, Dick Richardson (standing, l-r) Bob Field, Jim Walsh, Howard Gaffney, Merlin Gray, Mert Tofson, P. A. Carey, Norm Fedderly, Dr. F. W. Gissal, Jim Tollaksen, Will Shute, Jerry Kivlin.

The Wisconsin Dells city council, 1970 (front, l-r) Roger Gruman, Bernie Olson, Roy Kelly, Leon Beard, Howard Heitman (rear) Wilbur Walucks, Duke Weber, Carl Slocum, Don Hamm, Jr., Bob Hillman.

The Fate of Dell Lake

In 1968 N. E. Isaacson and Associates of Reedsburg announced plans to build a lake on Hulbert Creek two miles west of the Dells. The lake would be developed by construction of a 50-feet-high, 700-feet-long earthen dam across the creek.

Isaacson optioned and purchased most of the land for the project area which was 1300 acres with 13 miles of shoreline. The lake itself was to cover 310 acres with 1500 residential lots on or near it. The developer purchased most of the land and removed the timber before the Department of Natural Resources issued a permit to construct the dam.

The day before the hearing for the dam permit was held, the City of Wisconsin Dells, in order to provide sewer service, annexed the land around the lake. The hearing started March 10, 1970, lasted ten days, with about 150 people in attendance. Many conservation groups opposed the lake. They expressed concern over pollution, the loss of wildlife habitat and the destruction of a natural stream that produced brook trout. After a long wait, on December 2, 1970 the DNR denied the permit for a dam. Isaacson appealed the decision to the circuit court but did not get a permit.

Without the permit to build the dam, the land along Hulbert Creek was of little value to N. E. Isaacson, and the company let it revert to the bank holding the mortgages on it. In 1978, the remaining landowners were able to secede from the city and and returned to the townships. At that time the DNR purchased 550 acres of the wetland from the bank to be used as a natural area for hunting and fishing.

The developer had removed the buildings on six of the farms he had purchased and planted trees. The remaining land has been sold to individuals, but the farms are gone, along with the big pines and other timber cut out of the lake bed area.

The Depot

On a scorching hot July 4, 1982, the railroad tracks had buckled and a coal train from Montana to the power plants in Portage derailed hitting the southeast corner of the depot built here in 1856 and 1857. The railroad crossing the river here, due to Byron Kilbourn, who was president of the railroad at the time, was the reason for the founding of the town. At the time of the accident, the Milwaukee Road was in bankruptcy and had no interest in repairing the damage. The City of Wisconsin Dells offered to repair the station. Since there were no vital services such as water or heat involved, the cost would have been minimal-$18,000. However, the Milwaukee Road seemed glad to get rid of one more depot, although Amtrak continued to stop here twice a day.

In 1983 the remains of the depot were torn down. The Milwaukee Road, Amtrak and the city were not able to reconstruct the depot.

The townspeople got the idea to build a new station through volunteer effort. Russ Porter had painted a picture for Ollie Reese of a train coming in to the old station. The Bank of Wisconsin Dells had been successful in selling lithographs of Eagles in the Dells by Owen Gromme so the idea of selling lithos of Ollie's picture came to realization with a great deal of help from Russ Porter.

Initially, the Dells Boat Company, the Bank of Wisconsin Dells, Bud Gussel, Arnold Borcher, Oliver Reese and David Jahnke contributed $5,500 to start the community effort to rebuild the depot. In October, 1984, the Wisconsin Dells Community Transportation Association, Inc. was formed as a non-profit corporation with Oliver Reese as president. The directors were Bud Gussel, Vice President; Orrin Anderson, Treasurer; and Alice Toepel, Secretary. Other directors were Karen Baggot, Arnold Borcher, Donna Greenwood, Gisela Hamm, David Jahnke, Tim Johnson, Paul Olson, Norman Sandley and John Van Wie. Later additions were Eugene Landt and Donna Labrenz.

The first efforts of the committee were to build shelters on each side of the tracks, a telephone and restoration of the signal light to alert passengers to cross the tracks to board the eastbound Empire Builder. The committee coordinated offers of labor in construction. Residents were invited to vote on the style of depot they preferred-a wooden board and batten building, a brick veneered structure much like the demolished building or a contemporary depot. The brick veneer of 1878 style was the choice.

On November 3, 1984, the 1200 prints all numbered and signed by the painter, Russ Porter went on sale. #1 was given to the Bank of Wisconsin Dells. Three of the Jaycee women camped in front of the bank overnight so they would be first in line to buy print #2 which they later raffled off and contributed the proceeds of $502 to the depot fund. A print was given with each contribution of $50. Over $25,000 was raised in the first three days and many volunteered their labor.

By January 30, 1985, two 1880s-style shelters had been constructed by volunteer labor from plans by Norman Sandley, local railroad historian. The cost was $2,089.02.

Bob Nagel of Southwest Engineering, later Architectural Design Consultants, was drawing plans for a brick faced depot.

Lists of volunteers and print buyers regularly appeared in the *Dells Events*. Ollie Reese checked on #8 train arrivals and when it was late coming from the West Coast, met passengers every day to advise them on time of arrival and send them to the neighboring Sand Bar on Eddy Street, later called the Winter Depot, to warm up and possibly order refreshments rather than stand out in the cold for hours.

The restored Wisconsin Dells railroad depot. (Courtesy, H.H. Bennett Studio Foundation).

Then the delays began. In April, 1985, the federal budget crunch threatened to cut off all Amtrak funds even though Amtrak had asked for less money every year.

In the summer of 1986 the Committee was negotiating for a site for the depot. The Soo Line and later the Canadian Pacific Railroad bought out the Milwaukee Road. Amtrak seriously considered abandoning the use of the Soo Line through Wisconsin as the bad tracks caused delays. A test using the Burlington Northern tracks through Illinois to the Mississippi River proved they could not make better time on this route. But all of Wisconsin was alarmed at this prospect of losing the service going through the state. U.S. Representative Robert Kastenmeier and U.S. Senator Robert Kasten helped to keep the trains running on the present route in 1988. Senator Kasten got an appropriation of $6 million in federal funds matched by an equal amount from the Soo Line to upgrade the tracks between Milwaukee and Minneapolis.

In the meantime, the city agreed to take over ownership of the future depot in July, 1986. With assurances of a railroad, ground breaking for the depot was begun on October 13, 1988. The building was 24' x 40' housing a waiting room, office, utility room and two restrooms. John Van Wie was the head of the building committee. His Dells Lumber furnished the building materials at cost. D.L. Gasser Construction donated the excavating and backfilling. R.F. Young Construction volunteered the labor for masonry, footings and concrete slab. Bob Anderson was foreman of the construction crew. Beard Plumbing and Heating and Norman Schultz, retired, worked on plumbing. Many other volunteers now contributed their expertise, time and materials. A complete list is posted in the depot today. Norman Sandley provided the historically authentic details of an 1880s depot.

It was cold when many of these men worked to close in the structure but it was in use for the Christmas season. The official opening was January 1, 1989.

In the spring of 1989, Larry Volkey and his crew were laying up the used brick veneer. Probably Larry and his son, Vincent, put in the most time on construction as they worked at this for 23 weekends.

The official dedication was held on June 10, 1989 with a large crowd present. Tommy Bartlett emceed the proceedings with many dignitaries present headed by Representative Bob Kastenmeier and Mayor Richard Schauf. The program also featured spike driving, Barbershop singing, a band, refreshments and special thanks to Ollie Reese and John Van Wie. The kids still put their pennies on the tracks and the Empire Builder arrived on time.

Fred Becker, former Dells agent, served as caretaker for a time, then Peggy Pitts. Ed and Billie Long have filled the role since January 3, 1990 keeping the station clean and opening it for arriving trains. They add their own personal touches with hot coffee and cookies for passengers, long hours when trains are late and many other services to their patrons not required in their job descriptions.

The total cost of the project was $42,236.07 and not one dollar of tax money. The money was received from 730 individuals in 19 states.

The example of the Dells Station has inspired many other communities along the line to spruce up their own stations but passengers from around the country declare this depot the best they have ever seen.

Fire Guts Dells Business Places

A fire which started in a projector room in the Haunted Mansion in Wisconsin Dells gutted the popular attraction and resulted in smoke, water and fire damage to several other Dells business places during the summer of 1985.

The fire started at about 1:00 PM Saturday, and was noticed by some patrons of the Haunted Mansion, who notified owner Buster Reinboldt. Reinboldt called in the Kilbourn Volunteer Fire Department, and before the blaze was brought under control, firemen from the Dells, Lake Delton, Reedsburg and Lodi were on the scene.

Chief Dennis Dorow said that the fire probably started when the projector, which casts images of witches on the walls, overheated, but he added that he wasn't sure whether the fault lay with the tapes or the projector itself.

Dorow said that the blaze spread quickly because of a ceiling fan, spreading to adjacent buildings which housed the Wisconsin Dells Fudge store, the Candy Factory, Professor Porter's, the Skreemer, and the Sand Bar tavern.

Dorow said that since there is no suspicion of arson, the state fire marshall's office will not be brought into the investigation. Losses as the result of the fire were significantly less than originally thought because of quick action by the firemen and by area businessmen, according to Toby Tofson of Tofson Insurance Agency and a member of the KFD.

Tofson said that a number on the amount of damage was difficult to arrive at because adjusters were still working on their reports. "But the fact that the businessmen went to work and got ready to reopen so quickly is a big factor in keeping the cost down, he said.

The building which housed the Haunted Mansion, a 40 by 80 foot structure, was built in

The 200 Broadway block, c. 1965.

1948 by the Kilbourn Machine Co. It is a concrete block building, and was built to the codes that were in existence at that time. The building which housed the Skreemer adjoins the Mansion building at the rear, and forms a T-shape. It was probably built around 1860, according to Ollie Reese of Bennett Studio, which owns the Mansion building.

The worst damage was inflicted on the Mansion, which was almost totally gutted, and did not reopen that season. Reinboldt built most of the figures in the Mansion himself, by hand, and said he plans to reopen again next summer, "better than ever."

Most of the other businesses involved in the fire suffered mostly smoke and water damage, and reopened over the next few days. The ceiling at the rear of the Sand Bar over the rest room area collapsed because of water, and delayed the reopening of the tavern. Apartments above the Sand Bar and the fudge store were badly damaged in the fire.

Dorow said that firemen from the Dells and Lake Delton had the fire contained within about an hour after it started, but that firemen had trouble getting to the point of the fire to extinguish it. Reedsburg was then called to bring in their snorkle truck, which was able to get at the blaze from above. The snorkel made the 17 mile trip to the Dells in about 24 minutes from the time of the call.

In addition to the Reedsburg and Delton units, four firemen from Lodi heard about the blaze, and drove up in their car to assist. Several honorary Dells firemen, including five retired chiefs, joined in the battle, along with many area employers and some tourist bystanders.

Dorow said that there were no injuries to any patrons of the businesses involved in the fire, but that two firemen were treated for minor injuries. "There were a few cases of smoke inhalation, too," he said.

Dorow said that at one point shortly before the blaze was brought under control, firemen lost water pressure, and water was transported to the scene by trucks from the Dells Concrete Plant. Firemen also used the KFD's big tank trailer for additional water.

"Part of the water problem was due to the time of the season; there have been lots of toilets flushing," Dorow said. "We didn't run out of water, though, the pressure was just low."

While firemen were battling the fire–on Broadway, Eddy Street and in the alley behind the Haunted Mansion–traffic coming into the Dells on the Broadway bridge was rerouted, and the entire two block area from the River Road corner west to the bridge was blocked off to vehicles.

Tourists who were unable to leave this area because of the street closings lined the north side of Broadway and the west side of Eddy Street.

Isabelle Drumb, who could write, edit and typeset a newspaper article all at once on the linotype at the Wisconsin Dells Events.

The Newspaper Business

The *Wisconsin Dells Events,* with its predecessor, the *Wisconsin Mirror*, holds the distinction of being the oldest business in Wisconsin Dells.

The founder of the *Mirror*, Alanson Holly, was the first settler and first businessman in Wisconsin Dells. Holly moved his family and three printers into the wilderness on November 20, 1855, and set up a dwelling and connected print shop.

On January 1, 1856, the first copy of the *Wisconsin Mirror* was ready to be printed. People crossed the frozen river from Newport to hear speeches by Jonathan Bowman and Joseph Bailey before someone suggested that the first copy of the press be sold at auction. Jason Weaver bought the first paper struck from the press by Holly's son Morton for $65. Abram Vliet paid $10 for the second and Joe Bailey bought the third copy for $5.

Holly discontinued the paper in 1860 and returned to New York. He returned to Kilbourn in 1866 and resumed publishing the *Mirror* with his sons in 1868.

Frank C. Wisner was the next publisher of note, the paper having passed rapidly through the hands of several people after Holly sold it in 1872. Wisner was probably the first to make a successful venture of it. In 1876 Wisner sold it to W.M. Cole, but it burned down after three months.

In this vacuum several newspapers sprang up under various owners. The *Kilbourn Guard* started in 1876 and lasted three years. The *Kilbourn Gazette* was formed in 1883 and the *Wisconsin Mirror* was revived for the third time by former owner Frank Wisner and James Elliott Jones, better known as J. E. They bought out the Gazette in 1885, forming the *Mirror-Gazette*. The *Dells Reporter* was started in 1901.

In 1903, after J.E. Jones sold the *Wisconsin Mirror-Gazette,* he founded the *Illustrated Events*, which was more of a monthly history and literary journal. In 1907 he made it a weekly paper and changed the name to *Kilbourn Weekly Events*, a name that was to last until shortly before the city changed its name in 1931. For awhile the city had three newspapers.

This all changed when Jones bought the *Dells Reporter* in 1906 and, in conjunction with B.E. Tollaksen, purchased the *Mirror-Gazette,* in 1911 thus giving the present newspaper continuity back to the original *Wisconsin Mirror*.

J. E. Jones remained publisher until 1923, one of the longest tenures of any publisher. Jones had led a full and exciting life even before he came to the Dells. Jones sold the newspaper to C.F. Fredricks, who only operated it a couple of years before selling out to William A. Drumb, publisher of the *Grand Rapids (Wisconsin Rapids) Tribune* in 1925.

Drumb was an avid outdoorsman, but because of a bad heart condition was comparatively inactive in his later life. He once operated a photography studio and played in bands and orchestras in Sturgeon Bay and Grand Rapids. He was also active in Kiwanis. At the *Events* he was read far and wide in his column *"Tales by the Wayside."*

In 1931, several months before the city made the formal name change itself, he changed the name of the paper to *Wisconsin Dells Events*

Around 1936, the *Events* moved from the east side of River Road near Broadway, where it remained for 45 years before moving to its present location on Elm Street.

Also in 1936, W.A. Drumb's wife became ill and his daughter Isabelle, who had been secretary for a law firm in Wisconsin Rapids, came to the Dells to help with the paper and care for her mother. When William died in 1942, Isabelle became editor and publisher of the *Events*.

She set all the type for the paper herself on a linotype, without writing or typing the stories before hand. She was a reporter, editor and typesetter combined. She also did the bookkeeping, acted as receptionist and did her share of the job printing, which at this point was the larger part of the printing business.

Isabelle loved newspapering at the Dells, but was chagrined that the city forced her to tear down the old-fashioned canopy in front of *The Events*, only a few years before canopies came into style again and every business had one.

Among her accomplishments is the fact that, for a time, she was the only woman member of the Kiwanis Club in the United States, When she retired in 1956, the speaker at her retirement party was United States Senator Alexander Wiley.

Isabelle sold the *Events* to Jim and Pete Walch. They were no strangers to the newspaper business. Their family had published the *Manawa Advocate* for 60 years, and Jim had published another paper in Weyauwega. He was a former president of the Wisconsin Press Association and was publicity director of the Wisconsin State Fair during five of its most successful years. He was also secretary to former Congressman Reid Murray and handled publicity during one of Jack Olson's campaigns for governor.

In 1960, Jim Walch bought out his brother and went on to be one of the most popular publishers in the history of the newspaper. He spent his entire life in the newspaper business except for service in World War II where he received special commendation for meritorious service in Leyte in the Phillipines. He was active in many community activities including the American Legion and the Masonic Lodge.

Walch had a great many friends and was the type of person who could sell ice to an Eskimo. He expanded the paper to a large size, 16-page publication with summer and holiday editions often running from 24 to 32 pages. He started the *Dells Area Guide* and had four press operators doing job printing with seven part-time bindery workers in the summer. In 1970, the *Wisconsin Dells Events* took first place for general excellence in the state in its size category. Jim's wife Betty was also active, assisting her husband with many duties connected with the publishing business.

When Walch retired in 1976, his place was taken by his son Jay who, like his father and uncle, was also an officer in the Wisconsin Newspaper Association. Jay was the first publisher who was locally raised and educated, and as a result was one of the best known publishers.

Except for time off for school and service in Vietnam, he had worked continuously at the newspaper since has family had moved here in 1956. He also won several awards for the paper and was active in many activities.

In 1986 the newspaper was sold to Bill and Dolores Griffith of Printed Communications Group. "We have been in love with the Dells for many years," said Bill Griffith at the time, "We know

Newspaper editor, historian and writer, J. E. Jones.

many wonderful people here and will enjoy working with them."

Bill and Dolores Griffith now own 14 publications, seven weeklies, six shoppers, and a Minnesota monthly. Among these papers is the *Wisconsin Dells Events* and the *Dells Area Guide*.

Locally, the job of editor was separated from publisher and was handled by Lonni Lown. The paper is printed in Mauston where the company owns its own web printing press. Currently, Kay Jones serves as editor.

Lake Delton had a newspaper in 1882. Little is known about it except that it was a weekly and that Levi Cook was editor.

The *Dells-Delton Dispatch* was published in 1985 until it merged with the *Wisconsin Dells Events* the following February. Patrick F. Sweeney was the publisher.

The *Dells-Delton Daily* was started in 1992.

Jim Walch

Jean Dyer Reese, Oliver Reese and the plaque recording that the Bennett Studio is on the National Register of Historic Places. (Courtesy, H. H. Bennett Studio Foundation)

H.H. Bennett Studio Foundation, Inc.

The studio that H.H. Bennett founded in 1865 has been continuously owned and operated by successive generations of his family. It is the oldest family business in the area and is the oldest family-owned photographic studio in the United States.

When H.H. died in 1908, his widow, Evaline, was 44 years old with two school age daughters. She had worked with H.H. and learned photographic processes, and continued this work as well as the publication of guide books and postcards.

The Bennetts had been persuaded to sell the first Dells souvenirs about 1900–Winnebago baskets and beadwork, pottery from the Southwest and other trinkets. This trade grew in the studio at 215 Broadway and was expanded into the building next door at 213 Broadway and the Post Card Shop at 112 Broadway.

When daughter Miriam returned from college she joined her mother in these businesses. Daughter Ruth married Roland Dyer on December 30, 1922, and soon that family was spending summers in the Dells. Roland expanded the Post Card Shop until he took over operation of the Dells Park Trading Post for the Crandalls. Ruth joined the firm in 1930.

Ruth and Roland (Pipe) had two children, Jean and Henry.

The Bennett women were active in community affairs. Evaline was the first local chairman of the Wisconsin Anti-Tuberculosis Assocation in 1925 when the disease was a dreaded killer, especially among the Indians. She was a charter member of the Tuesday Club, and also in the Civic Club, DAR and the Library Board, and her daughters followed these interests as well. Miriam wrote many historical articles and filmed many early amateur movies of the locality and its activities. Ruth chaired the local Wisconsin Centennial celebration and Horse and Buggy Days in 1948 and 1949. The two sisters were named *Women of the Year* in 1970.

Evaline died on March 25, 1949. Meanwhile another generation was joining the firm. Jean Dyer married Oliver Reese on October 27, 1945 and he began his apprenticeship in 1946. They became the parents of three daughters, Deborah (Kinder), Betsy (Grant) and Lisa (Henrickson).

Roland left the Dells Park Indian Village in 1955 and owned and operated the Winnebago Indian Village on Stand Rock Road, currently the KOA Campground, from 1956-1961. The Bennett Studio branched out to include the Dells Minirama at 112 Broadway from 1960-1969, and the Red Wing Pottery Shop and Table Talk Cheese Shop at 213 Broadway from 1969-1983.

Jean returned to the business to manage Bennett's Gift Shop from 1963-1984. The Studio produced its last portrait in 1971 when Ruth photographed wedding pictures for her oldest granddaughter, Deborah, who married James Kinder.

Miriam died June 3, 1971, Roland Dyer died Nov. 29, 1973 and Ruth on May 11, 1982.

In 1950, the Bennetts had built and gradually expanded a museum of H.H. Bennett's vintage prints, negatives and equipment. Today this museum also sells contemporary prints made from his original glass plates and his vintage stereoscopic views. When Bennett's work was featured in a major show at the Museum of Modern Art in New York in 1963, interest in the work of this pioneer photographer was revived and continues to grow.

Jean and Oliver Reese have retired from the retail businesses but continue to produce guide books for river trips. They manage the Bennett Museum in the Studio that H.H. Bennett built in 1875 and continue to catalogue his negatives and print from his original glass plates.

In 1990, the Studio received Foundation status in order to preserve the complete Bennett collection which also includes his handmade cameras.

H.H. Bennett's statement that "I could not help falling in love with the Dells" has echoed down through the generations.

Medical Profession at the Dells

The first doctor to serve in Newport and Kilbourn was Dr. G.W. Jenkins. He died November 3, 1913 after he'd been retired for about 14 years.

Dr. Jenkins' brother-in-law, Dr. H. Markham was associated with Dr. Jenkins in the drug business during 1862 and 1863.

They were followed by Dr. Stillman and Dr. Wintermute. For a time, Dr. Wintermute opened a hospital in the "old institute" building at the east end of Washington Avenue.

These doctors were followed by Dr. John McGovern, who served the community during the 1920s and 1930s. He was born in 1872 and died in Wisconsin Dells in 1941 and is buried in Calvary Cemetery.

Dr. Albert Duclos, a native of Quebec, Canada, was born there in 1862. He was educated at McGill University of Montreal. After a bout with illness he continued his education at Bennett Medical College in Chicago. Upon graduation in 1895 he came to Kilbourn where he opened an office and practiced for many years.

Dr. Clarence Treadwell, a native of Reedsburg, located in Kilbourn in 1898 where he conducted his practice in the years following.

Dr. Taylor lived and practiced in Kilbourn starting in 1903. He was married with no children and lived at 719 Cedar Street. Mrs. Marjorie Lapp of Big Spring stated, "There were seven of us children, and no matter what, we always felt better after his visits. He even cut off and sewed up the leg of our pet dog after it was injured by a mower in the hay field."

During the 1920s and 1930s Dr. R.D. Boynton made a name for himself in Kilbourn and Wisconsin Dells, especially in the field of obstetrics. Dr. Boynton was a native of Menasha, where he graduated from high school in 1906. He then attended Lawrence College and graduated from Marquette University in 1913.

Before coming to Kilbourn he had practiced at Waupaca and Grand Marsh. Dr. Boynton was also active in local civic affairs including Kiwanis and Boy Scouts. He was fatally injured in a traffic accident in Forest County on August 28, 1951.

Dr. Homer W. Krehl came to Kilbourn in 1930, but stayed for only 4 years.

The next doctor to practice in Wisconsin Dells was Dr. Radl who, along with Dr. John Houghton, had offices located upstairs on the main block of Broadway, above Kleimenhagen & Magoon's Store.

In 1947 the Dells Clinic took over the entire upper floor of the new Kilbourn Co-op Exchange building at Washington and LaCrosse Streets.

Dr. Houghton was in Wisconsin Dells from 1932 (four doctors were here at that time) until 1936, when he left to attend the University of Pennsylvania medical school. During that time Dr. Houghton married, and also served a year's residency in surgery at St. Joseph's Hospital in Milwaukee. He returned to Wisconsin Dells where he became associated with Drs. C. F. Broderick, F. W. Gissal, H. L. Conley, and D. W. Van Gore in the Dells Clinic. Dr. Sandeno was also a doctor there for a short period.

Dr. F. W. Gissal came to Wisconsin Dells in 1946, after his return from the armed services. He practiced here for 37 years before retiring in 1985. Dr. Gissal was born in 1917 in Wisconsin and received his education at Marquette University in Milwaukee. He was very active in civic affairs and was for many years the team physician for the Wisconsin Dells football team. He was one of the founders of Continental Manor Nursing Home in Wisconsin Dells. Dr. Gissal passed away in 1993.

In 1957, a new Dells Clinic building was built and occupied on Vine Street. Dr. H. L. Conley joined the staff in 1960 and Dr. Renato Faylona in 1972. Dr. Broderick had been on the staff since 1946.

In 1935 Dr. C.F. Broderick was the youngest student to ever graduate from the Marquette University medical school. He interned in Milwaukee and practiced there from 1937 to 1945. During World War II he served as a navy lieutenant and came to the Dells in 1946. Dr. Broderick underwent heart surgery in 1970 and retired from the clinic in 1971. He passed away in Atlanta, Georgia.

Dr. H. L. Conley was born in Illinois in 1929. He was educated at the University of Illinois and first practiced in Wisconsin Dells in 1960. In 1974, he was board-certified in family practice. He, with wife Virginia and son Patrick, lives in Wisconsin

Dr. F.W. Gissal

Dr. J.H. Houghton

Dr. C. F. Broderick

Oldest Businesses In The Dells

At the time of the state centennial in 1948, the *Events* reported the oldest businesses in town still in operation. The following were established as follows:

H.H. Bennett Studio, 1865
Hansen-Snider Lumber Co., 1884
Oehlers Grocery, 1883
O'Neil's Drug Store, 1898
Stuelke's Drug Store, 1908
Arntz Restaurant, 1914

The Finch Hotel is the oldest hotel, brought over from Newport as the Tanner House. The Kilbourn Inn is the second oldest.

The Kilbourn State Bank on the northeast corner of Superior and Broadway. (Courtesy, H. H. Bennett Studio Foundation)

Dells and he continues to practice at the Dells Clinic.

Dr. Renato Faylona first came to practice at the Dells Clinic in 1972. He was born in Luzon, the Phillipines, in 1937. He was educated at St. Thomas, Manila, and at St. Joseph's in Milwaukee. He is practicing today at the Dells Clinic and resides in Baraboo with his wife Marta (Schultz) and two daughters Kristi and Julie.

Dr. Maureen Murphy-Greenwood has been a member of the Dells Clinic staff since 1984 and also had an office in Lyndon Station. Dr. Murphy-Greenwood was born in St. Louis, Missouri in 1954. She received her education at St. Louis University and at the University of Arizona. She married Jim Greenwood in 1988 and in 1990 had a daughter, Kelsey Margaret.

Another doctor on the Dells Clinic staff in 1993 is Richard K. Westphal who resides in the Dells with his wife and four children.

Dr. Jerry Miller, born in Colorado in 1961, has been at the Dells since 1992. He served his residency at St. Luke's in Milwaukee.

In 1988 the Dells Clinic occupied a new building on East Broadway and in 1993 had the following doctors on staff: Conley, Faylona, Westphal, Murphy-Greenwood and Miller.

There was also a Dr. Carey who retired to Wisconsin Dells and carried on a limited practice here in the 1950s. Also Dr. Carson was with the Dells Clinic in 1990 but now practices in Madison.

Banking at Wisconsin Dells

Perry Stroud, a young attorney from New York opened the first bank in Kilbourn City at 314 Broadway in 1865.

In 1867, John McGregor opened a bank on the northwest corner of Broadway and Elm which he sold to Jonathan Bowman the next year.

The Stroud Bank was incorporated in 1884 as the Kilbourn State Bank with W.S. Stroud, President and L. N. Coapman, cashier. The bank later moved to a new building on the northeast corner of Broadway and Superior.

The Bank of Kilbourn, also called the Bowman Bank, was chartered as the Farmers and Merchants Bank in 1910. In 1911, it moved to Superior Street and in 1923, moved again to the corner of Broadway and Oak. In 1944 the Farmers and Merchants Bank purchased the assets of the Kilbourn State Bank and relocated in their facility on Broadway and Superior. In 1961 the bank moved to the present location at Superior Street. The Lake Delton branch opened in 1968. The bank directors in 1944 were E.C. Amann, Valentine Baggot, Robert Dougherty, John Kelly, John J. Kremer, C.R. McFarland and H.M. Tofson. Directors in later years were Lawrence Buckley, Edmund Hart, Dan Greenwood, Joseph Dunne, Merton Tofson, George Hoffman, Jack Olson and Arnold Borcher. Directors in 1995 are President Orrin Anderson, Peter Helland, John R. Kremer, Bud Gussel, Otto Christopherson, Tom Diehl and Gary Gilliland.

The Baraboo Natonal Bank opened a branch at 41 W. Monroe St. in Lake Delton in 1994.

Bork and Kane Drug Store

On the night of March 14, 1866, the big fire destroyed Seth Knowles new store. One tenant was C.D. Woodruff, druggist. F. Radandt and C. Borcher rebuilt this "block" in 1867. In 1886, Dr. Stillman, also a druggist, bought the building which later became Bork and Kane's, dispensing advice and cures around the hot stove.

In 1898, Daniel O'Neil, with help from his foster mother, Judith Landt, bought the building and in partnership with Herbert Bauer, established the Bauer and O'Neil Drug Store. That summer their ad read, "Come and see us if you want what you ask for, we never substitute. Our soda fountain turns a cold shoulder to this warm weather."

Prior to 1923, when Tom Crist established the Kilbourn Ice Cream Company, the drug store bought cream from the Landt farm and made ice cream. The soda fountain is one of the few still serving in a drug store.

Claude O'Neil, Dan's son, became a pharmicist and took over the business. In the early 1930's Claude became the first Greyhound bus agent, an association continuing until today. Claude bought the building in 1947 and for some years it was O'Neil's Drug Store. Rueford Bork began working with Claude in 1946 and, in 1955, when Rueford purchased a half interest in the business and the building, the name was changed to Bork and O'Neil.

In 1962, Bob Kane joined the firm and bought Claude's half interest in the business in 1970. The business is still known as Bork and Kane. Bob purchased the business and building in 1987 and Rueford is now semi-retired.

Malted milks, prescriptions and advice dispensed until the business closed in 1995.

Rueford Bork and Claude O'Neil on the first day of their partnership in 1955. (Courtesy, H.H. Bennett Studio Foundation).

Roeker's Bakery

Roeker's Bakery was founded in 1919 at 228 Broadway in Wisconsin Dells, where it still stands today. All products are hand made, scratch-baked, without preservatives, and original recipes continue to be used.

The formulas and production techniques used by founder, Arthur Roeker, were passed down to his son, Norman, who passed them down to his son, Bill Roeker. Satisfied customers have come as many as 100 miles out of their way to buy from the bakery.

The Roeker baking tradition started with Arthur, who worked in a bakery in Portage and baked in the service during World War I. When he opened the bakery in 1919, he lived in the upstairs quarters. He and his wife had three children, Norm, Betty and John, who is currently a baker at Triggs in Madison.

Norman also baked for Uncle Sam, during World War II. He and his wife, Vanita, had six children: Gay, Jack, Kathy, Andy, Bette, and Bill, all of whom put time in the bakery. Gay's son Tim, worked at the bakery for 10 years and still comes in to help out during a rush. From 1941-1982, Norman and Vanita operated the business, and then Bill and Joyce took over.

"The love of baking seems to be in the blood of this family," Joyce Roeker observed. "My husband, when he was little, was just like our four year old son. When Bill was only five, Norman had to sneak out of the house when he left for work early in the morning because Bill wanted to get up and go along. Our son, Joel, is the same way, he just loves to get his hands in some dough."

The Kilbourn Cooperative Creamery at 715 Superior Street, 1950. (Courtesy, H.H. Bennett Studio Foundation).

The Kilbourn Cooperative Creamery Company

On February 19, 1921, the Kilbourn Cooperative Creamery Company was incorporated at a meeting held in the Grand Army Hall in Kilbourn City and $15,000 in capital stock was sold. Farmers from Adams, Columbia, Marquette, Juneau and Sauk counties were instrumental in the Creamery's organization.

The business was purchased from William Blumingstein at 302 LaCrosse Street in Kilbourn where he had been manufacturing butter, and a new office was later added to that location.

When the Creamery opened there were three plant employees, a bookkeeper and three cream haulers. They gathered cream in 30 gallon jacketed cans, and hauled them with horses hitched to wagons which had cabs. The cabs protected drivers from the weather, and in the winter were heated with small kerosene heaters. The first price paid for the butterfat in cream was 47¢ per pound.

On September 9, 1922, the directors voted to join the Baraboo Valley Creamery Association. On August 22, 1925, stockholders voted to erect a new building, and they soon moved to 717 Superior Street.

In 1937 the Creamery went into the bottling and resale of fluid milk. The milk was collected in ten gallon metal cans. In 1940 they purchased the Leo Baggot bottle milk firm, and milk became the main source of income. A new intake was added to handle the increase in milk. In 1955 the creamery decided to handle Grade A milk and in 1958 the pickup of bulk milk was added.

Because more equipment was needed to process the increased fluid milk operation, it was necessary to discontinue churning butter and begin selling whole milk. The whole milk was sold to the Wisconsin Cooperative Creamery Association until 1959, and later to Hillpoint Cooperative Dairies of Reedsburg.

By that time there were 20 employees including bottle milk route men and 12 milk haulers. Milk was trucked to the plant from Arkdale, Brooks, east of Highway 51, and west of Reedsburg. The changes paid off and in 1958 the Creamery enjoyed a business year which exceeded $1,300,000, compared to $199,000 in 1921.

In later years, however, the bottled milk business became very sensitive to price wars.

Unable to diversify on their own, the creamery sought to make changes in order to remain competitive. In March, 1965 a special meeting of the members of the Kilbourn Cooperative Creamery Company overwhelmingly voted to merge their operation with The Wisconsin Dairies Cooperative of Union Center, Wisconsin. The merger proposal was approved by 92% of those voting, and on April 1, 1965 about 240 creamery producers became members of Wisconsin Dairies.

Two years after the Kilbourn Cooperative Creamery Company merged, the Hillpoint Cooperative Creamery of Reedsburg also merged with Wisconsin Dairies. Unable to compete with the bottled milk business, the Kilbourn Cooperative Creamery Company closed its doors in 1967.

Edna Cone was employed as bookkeeper for the creamery for 44 years.

The groundbreaking for the Colonial Manor, 1970, (l-r) Tim Johnson, Hans O. Helland, Robert Sarrington, Thomas Crist, Sr., K. K. Johnson, Roy Kelly, Bud Gussel, Arnold Borcher, Dr. F. W. Gissal, Jack Olson, Warren Schultz.

The Kilbourn Ice Cream Company

The Kilbourn Ice Cream Company was opened in 1923 by Tom Crist, Sr., a Walton, New York native who came to Wisconsin when his father became manager of the Pet Milk Company in Middleton, Wisconsin.

The original Oak Street building had no refrigeration, and ice cream was made using Wisconsin River ice and salt. The original capacity was 60 gallons per day and by 1950, 80 gallons per hour. In 1923, the only flavor was vanilla, and in the 1980's it was common to have 32 flavors to sell.

Tom Crist's business started with a sale to Bauer-O'Neil Drug Store, who had been making their own ice cream. Then G.H. Crandall promised all his business to Kilbourn Ice Cream, which in 1932 became the Dells Ice Cream Company.

Local restaurants frequently needed freezer space, and the frozen food locker business began in 1929 with 50 lockers, eventually expanding to 750 lockers including meat cutting facilities.

Many people were employed over the years. Maurice Tofson worked for 20 years through the Depression; Tom Crist, Jr. spent 19 years following World War II in business with his father; by 1989 Joe Kleifgen had worked and managed the business for 38 years.

In 1989, the ice cream business was sold to Cedar Crest of Cedarburg, Wisconsin, the locker plant was closed, and the real estate was to be sold separately.

Tom Crist, Sr. was very active within the community. In 1969 he formed the Dells Housing Authority and with the aid of a low cost 50 year U.S. government loan, constructed a non-profit, 41 unit apartment building for the elderly called the Dells Colonial Apartments. A board of directors, with Crist as building manager, operated the complex, located close to "downtown" Dells, without pay.

In 1972, Crist was instrumental in the construction of the Continental Manor nursing home in the Dells. He was unsuccessful in attempting to make Continental Manor a non-profit venture as well, but as a member of the Columbia County Housing Authority, he was able to help construct another non-profit senior citizen apartment building in Wyocena.

Tom also spent 51 years as President of the Spring Grove Cemetery Association and was a member of the Wisconsin Dells Water and Light Commission for 25 years. He is quoted as saying "I get all the non-paying jobs."

Center State Industries

Center State Industries, a furniture manufacturing company, was originally called Beno Boy Manufacturing Company. The company was founded by Beno Gussel and Wayne Boyington in 1945. A dry kiln was built in 1948 and the company sold in 1950.

Holiday Wholesale/Vacationland Vendors

Company President Bud Gussel started Gussel Distributing in 1951. His warehouse was an unheated, one car garage at 513 Capital Street. A 1938 Desoto with the back seat removed was the delivery "truck."

He purchased candy and tobacco products from other wholesalers and sold them to retailers in the area. The business prospered and in 1956 moved to a larger facility at 727 Superior Street. Six years later the company moved again to 316 Broadway.

In 1970 Bud purchased the John I Hahn Co. of Baraboo, built a new warehouse and changed the name of his company to Holiday Wholesale.

The present facility on Pioneer Road serves much of the state and employs over 200 year

Bud Gussel in his 1956 Chevy, in front of the first downtown location of Holiday Wholesale and Vacationland Vendors.

round employees. Company success is credited to the support of Bud's wife, Joyce, his mother, Julie, and early key employees, Helen Koepcke, Aaron Anchor, George Thompson, Bob Neubauer, Maurice Tofson, Herb Cone, Art Gibson, Pat Jagoe and Hugh Gaston. Present directors include Joe Gussel, Pat Jagoe and Ed Wojnicz.

Vacationland Vendors, a branch of Holiday Wholesale, began in 1953 when Bud purchased 18 used cigarette machines. Cigarettes sold for 23 cents a pack in 1953. The customer would put a quarter in the machine and receive a pack of cigs with two pennies in the celliphane. The tedious job of inserting the pennies in the packs was handled by Joyce Gussel.

In addition to candy and cigarettes, the company now provides thousands of other items including confections, paper goods, chemicals and food products. Vacationland Vendors now operates a full variety of vending machines as well as music and games. Food products are prepared daily in the company's modern kitchen.

David Gussel, Betty Wegert and Matt Bubon are now principals in the company. Special recognition is given to Alden Helley for his many dedicated years with Vacationland Vendors. Most importantly, the company could never have succeeded without the early support of businesses in Wisconsin Dells and Lake Delton.

The Dells Park Trading Post

In 1922 the Crandall family bought property across the river from the Upper Dells Boat Docks from the Milwaukee Road. The few buildings that were on the river bank were removed and visitors to the Dells Park campground pitched tents and creature comforts were minimal.

The Stand Rock Indian Ceremonial was growing in popularity and many Indians returned to the area each summer to dance at the show. They set up summer camps at Stand Rock and on the flats below the dam where Hulburt Creek flowed.

Summer visitors were interested in the Indian's life and culture so the Crandall's invited Indian families to set up their camps in the Dells Park.

In 1932, the Crandall family built a Trading Post and hired Roland Dyer as manager. He really did some trading, but the log structure with its huge fireplace had a distinctive character; many Indian crafts were sold--Ho-Chunk baskets and beadwork, Navajo rugs, and turquoise jewelry. There were also small trinkets and souvenirs, a small grocery, ice cream and pop. A Zuni silversmith was at work and sometimes a basket maker.

At 2:00 PM drums started to pound, luring tourists and townspeople across the river, and the moccasin game began. Two teams of four men each faced each other and a marble was hidden under one of the four pieces of fur - the moccasins. The opposing team guessed where the marble was hidden. The songs sung to the beat of the drum were supposed to distract the other team. Many side bets and much giggling and teasing added to the fun. Of course, this was all done in Ho-Chunk so visitors could only surmise what they said.

When these parties were held, the pounding of the drums carried so well across the river that it often kept people from their sleep.

An archery range and a fortune teller's tent drew people. It was fascinating to walk through the park and buy baskets or beadwork from the women who made them in front of their wigwaums. A Baptist wigwam church was built in the valley.

Thus the Dells Park was one of the earliest attractions aside from the boat trips. In the depths of the Depression, Roland Dyer, the manager, could not afford his favorite cigars so he smoked a pipe. Eventually, his friends at the Park called him Da-Nee-Hoo or Pipe.

His work continued there until 1955. In 1956, the new highway bridge was completed and the roadway under the railroad bridge was vacated. The Dells Park was cut off from the main stream of traffic and was closed after the 1956 season.

The Tommy Bartlett Show

The Tommy Bartlett Show first came to Wisconsin Dells in 1952 as a touring company sponsored by the Wisconsin Dells Chamber of Commerce and free of charge.

A prominent radio & TV personality, Bartlett turned his talent to the production of water ski shows after seeing a ski performance at the Chicago Railroad Fair in 1949.

The local show was presented on the Wisconsin River north of the River Inn as 1,500 spectators watched two mahogany Correct Craft tow boats, four Mercury outboard jumping boards, a pick-up boat, and 12 men and women who performed.

The following year, Tommy Bartlett, his partner Dick Rowe, Chamber of Commerce President Jack Olson, and Peter Helland found a permanent location for the show on Highway 12. The front entrance and parking lots were provided by Priscilla and Duaine Counsell of Parson's Trading Post for $1.00 per year plus the gift shop rights. The show itself was performed on Howard's Motel property for $1.00 per year and the food concession rights.

The first year, four shows a day were performed. Admission was 75¢ for adults and 25¢ for children. There were no lights for a night show and no running water, so outhouses served as toilets.

The Dells Park Trading Post on Stand Rock Road, c. 1955. (Courtesy, H. H. Bennett Studio Foundation)

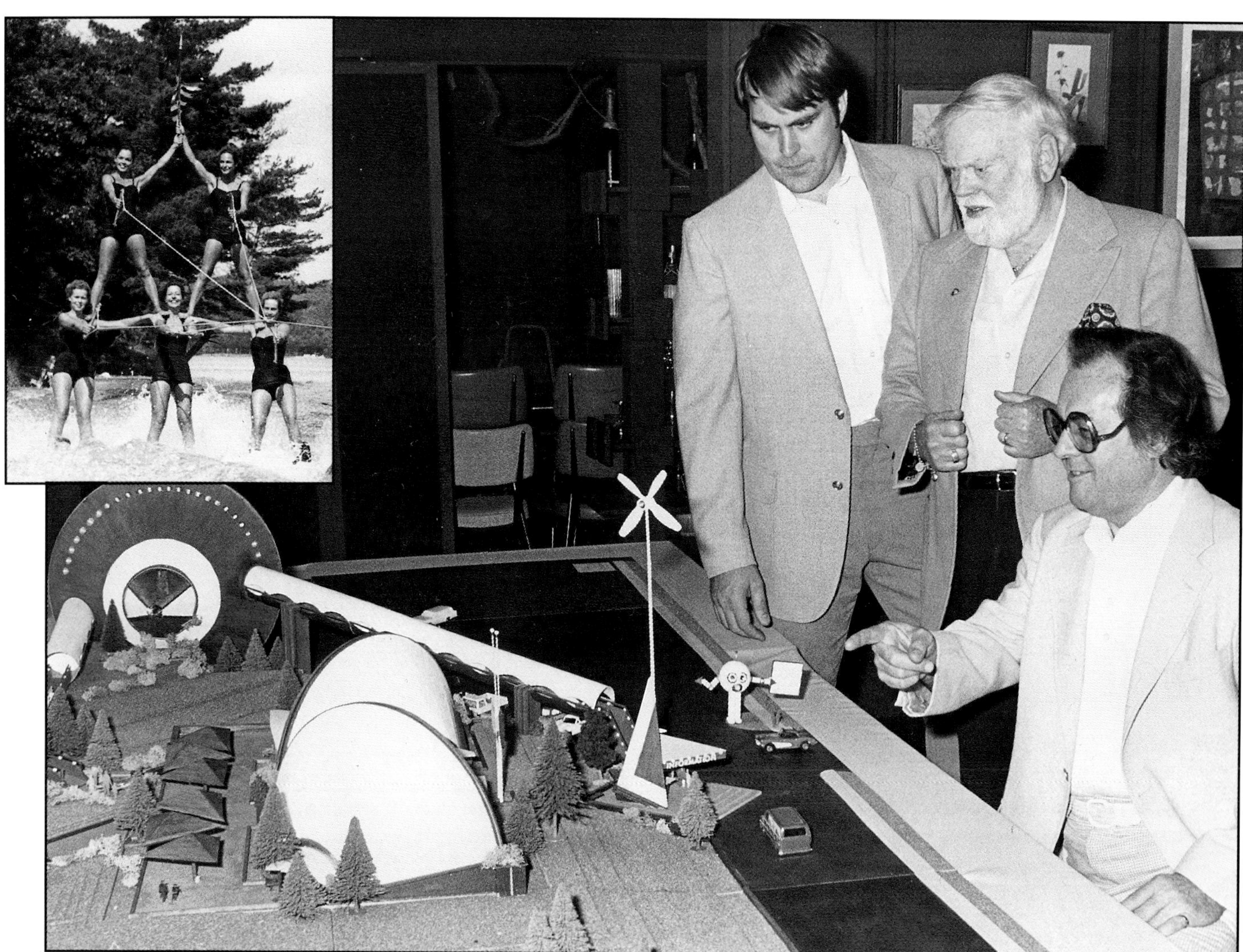

Tom Diehl, Tommy Bartlett and Jim Dresser examine a model of the Robot World attraction, 1982 and (inset) skiers at one of the first Tommy Bartlett shows. (Courtesy, H. H. Bennett Studio Foundation)

There were five rows of planks and plenty of hillside space for blankets and picnic lunches. Bartlett estimates that by 1979 the show was taking in as much in one day as it took in its entire first year of 1955. The second year business doubled.

The third year night lighting allowed for an evening performance in addition to the two daytime shows. The fourth year Dancing Waters was added and Bob Chase joined the group as Master of Ceremonies. Cliff Conley was the general manager.

While in Hawaii on a USO Water Ski tour to Southeast Asia in 1959, Bartlett saw Polynesian entertainment and the Tahitian dancers became a popular part of his show.

Bob May and his son Matthew were part of the show in the early years. Matthew, at age four, was one of the youngest skiers ever to perform. Other acts were added over the years. In 1957, the cast of the Lawrence Welk Show performed on a rotating basis. Bartlett recalls that when the Lennon Sisters performed, there were so many people watching that many were seated on the sand beach on peach crates.

Skip Gilkerson was the first waterfront director as well as a performer in the show. Tom Diehl joined the organization in 1957, aggressively promoting and marketing the show. Diehl was named president of Tommy Bartlett, Inc. in 1981. His wife Margaret and their children, Jill and Jeff, were involved in the daily operation of the show.

In 1959 an ice rink was built where the present stage is and three ice shows were performed daily, some in 110 degree heat.

The first of two covered grandstands, enabling performances rain or shine, was built in 1966. The amphitheater can seat over 5,500 people with more than 3,000 seats under cover.

Later additions to the show were a skydiving performance, the Helicopter Trapeze "Sky Flyers"; Wes Harrison, Mr. Sound Effects; the Nerveless Nocks; the Argentine gauchos; Harlan & Huntzicker, "The Wizards of the Trampoline"; and Dieter Tasso, juggling while balancing on a suspended slack wire. In 1987 the Laser-Rama light show was added to the evening performance.

In 1982, Tommy Bartlett added a Robot World and Exploratory to his show. This trip to the future, with over 90 "hands on" experiences, is located next to the site of the Ski-Sky and Stage Show.

The front entrance to the show grounds, the "Water Walls" were originally designed by James Dresser, a Frank Lloyd Wright protégé. He was also the architect for the administration building with trees growing through the roof and the working house of the future where visitors can explore future styles of living. A restaurant was added in 1984 and in 1991 a walkway was redesigned and crafted to resemble a deep space experimental command station.

The philosophy of the Tommy Bartlett organization is to "continue to renew and revise the house of the future concept" and to present family entertainment to the estimated 500,000 visitors who annually enjoy a two-hour, live extravaganza.

The Dells Lumber & Construction Company, Inc.

Dells Lumber & Construction Company, Inc. was founded by R. Jack and Dorothy F. Van Wie on November 24, 1947. The original name of the company was Central Insulation Roofing & Siding.

After attending Ripon College, Jack was called to serve his country in 1943. Due to hearing problems, he was unable to serve in the war but went to work at Badger Ordnance.

Following the war, Jack went to work for Downing Insulation Company in Baraboo and was soon one of the company's top salesmen. After a year with the company, Jack and his wife Dorothy started their own Central Insulation Roofing & Siding Company.

In 1952 Jack hired Hans Georgeson to start his building material supply and construction business, and the name soon changed to Dells Lumber & Construction Company, Inc.

Following Jack's death in 1978, his son John purchased the company from the family estate. John, who had grown up in the business, continued to operate the company with the same premise his father had founded it with: price, quality and service.

In 1985 John's wife Joanne joined him in the operation of the company. In 1991 John turned his contractor yard into a contractors and consumers store by adding the Ace Hardware franchise.

Today Dells Lumber & Construction Company, Inc./Ace Home Center continues to operate at 931 Michigan Avenue, employing more than 40 full time employees and 100-plus subcontractors. The company provids a full line of building materials, general contracting services, Del-Co Metal Building Co, kitchen design and home decorating, floor covering and the Ace Home Center.

The Dells Lumber Company crew in 1954 (l-r) Andy Anderson, Dutch Weishoff, Al Wittig, Frank Kanus, Julius Polak, Ralph Stroede, Hans Georgeson, Bob Procknow, Howard Page, Jack Van Wie, Mike Pietrzak, John Wagner, John Stroede, Elmer Hoesly.

Pine Beach Resort

Pine Beach Resort, on County Hwy A adjacent to Dawn Manor, celebrated its 30th year of existence in December 1993. The Pine Beach property was originally plotted in the town of Newport. In 1855 Abraham Vanderpoel built the historic Dawn Manor for his large family. He turned the adjacent land into a back yard where he entertained many famous people.

Samuel H. Kerfoot, a millionaire from Chicago, purchased Dawn Manor in 1886. Kerfoot saw something in the area that he liked, even though the new town was across the river. Dawn Manor and the surrounding properties were to be a summer retreat for his family. He started purchasing most of the land on the west side of the river, heading north and south including land with Dell Creek to the west.

By 1893 Kerfoot owned 260 acres of the land around Dawn Manor, including one and one half miles of river frontage. Kerfoot believed that vacationers would enjoy a healthful retreat in the area, and built coach and carriage houses as well as servants' quarters near by.

Before Samuel, Sr., died in 1896, he sold some of the property to his son, Samuel Kerfoot Jr. In 1897-8 Samuel's widow sold Samuel Jr. the remaining property. History has it that the main house sat idle until Annie's death in 1908. It is guessed that the 10 cottages, still part of Pine Beach Resort, were added to the property around 1901. The Kerfoot children, John Barrett, Samuel Humes, Jr., and Alice Gray Kerfoot formed the Wisconsin Dells Holding Company in 1891 and operated Kerfoot House and Cottages until 1914.

The Kerfoot's sold the property on July 3, 1914 to Harley Bement and his wife Eliza. Harley died 10 years later, leaving the property to Eliza and their daughter Belle Bement Edmonds. After a quit claim sale from Belle during June of 1924, Eliza was sole owner.

In late summer of 1926, H.S. and E. Louise Moeller of the Dells Area Development Company entered into an agreement with William J. Newman to purchase from Eliza 86 acres of land to construct and maintain a dam across Dell Creek. Newman also entered into a contract with Eliza Bement to purchase for $32,000.00 the total acreage containing the cottages and Dawn Manor. The purchase was to be handled in 15 acre increments, passed to Newman on the 10th of every month for $4000.00 each.

In March of 1927 Newman owned all the land and the lake was filled that June. By 1931 Newman was in great financial difficulty, but 'Kerfoot House and Cottages' was still maintained throughout the '30's by various managers. The Lake Delton Hotel Company was incorporated in March of 1930 for this purpose, with Fred and Fanny Hines as its officers. Two years later the corporation's name was changed to the Lake Delton Development Company, and it purchased lands from the government in the Newman proceedings. Hines took up where Newman left off, trying to develop Lake Delton's surrounding area.

The three cottages that sat next to the Purple Grackle were moved to the resort complex early in the 1930's following a fire at the Grackle. The cottage property now contained 13 cottage buildings. The cottage property including Dawn Manor stayed complete until 1943 when Mrs. Helen Raab purchased Dawn Manor and surrounding acres from the Lake Delton Development Company.

The company then sold the 'cottage property' to Leland and Gertrude Shaw under a land contract for $16,000.00 in May, 1944. This property was to contain 16 acres west of Dawn Manor to Hiawatha Drive. The Shaws constructed and operated a store/residence near County A on the resort property.

In 1949 the Shaws sold the property under a land contract to Charles and Mary Pech for the sum of $38,000.00 The Shaw's kept a 4 acre parcel of the land west of Dawn Manor as their personal residence, acquiring a 25 foot right of way between the cottage property and Dawn Manor from Mrs. Raab.

In 1958, Charles and Mary Pech granted to their daughter, Lorraine and her husband, Robert Walden, the property containing the cottages. It was now known as Bobby's Resort. Over the next 13 years the Pechs and Waldens made several mortgages in order to modernize and expand the resort, adding eight motel units.

In 1963 the Pechs and Waldens sold 7.5 acres of the property to the family partnership of Joseph and Georgianna Curcio and children; Georgianna's parents Otto and Rose Musil; and their son Robert Musil and his wife Sylvia, for a total of $55,000.00. The Waldens kept the remaining acreage and the motel units, turning the new division into the Tiki Motel, now Aloha Beach Resort.

The resort-cottage property, consisting of only the 13 original cottages, was renamed Pine Beach Resort. Under the partnership's management the resort continued to expand and prosper. Rose Musil passed away in 1977, followed by her son, Robert in 1979. Shortly after Robert's death, Sylvia sold her shares to the remaining partners. Otto passed on in 1982 leaving sole ownership to Joseph and Georgianna.

Joseph and Georgianna Curcio, with their daughter, Janet Curcio Landrum and her family, operated the resort for three more years. Facing retirement and crippling arthritis, Joseph and

Georgianna sold the property, now containing 13 cottages, 5 cabins, and 6 motel units, to Janet and her husband Larry on December 31, 1985. The Curcio's sectioned off the south west corner of the property for their personal residence, where Georgianna still resides. Joseph died on April 29, 1987.

During the next nine years the Landrums modernized the resort, removed the motel units, the cabins, and 3 of the orginal cottages, and expanded Pine Beach Resort to include 20 cottages, (10 of the original ones refurbished and modernized, 10 new cottages - 5 added in 1986 and 5 added in 1987) a swimming pool, and 8 family suites added in 1993. The Landrums, with sons Jason and Justin, believe as the resort's originator did, in 1901, that this property still is a relaxing retreat for vacationers to enjoy.

Big Joe Manufacturing

On April 28, 1955 the Big Joe Manufacturing Company, Inc. purchased the building located on Stand Rock Road owned by the Dells Area Building Company. The building, built in 1947, was originally rented by the Anderson Milking Machine Company and then by the Disston Saw Company. Big Joe manufactures hydraulic lift trucks.

Lift trucks from Big Joe Manufacturing. (Courtesy, H. H. Bennett Studio Foundation)

Dells Pioneer Village

Gerald Baggot opened the Pioneer Village in 1948, the culmination of a life-long collecting hobby. He started with 5 acres of land and two big tents.

Later he added 16 buildings, including the revolving print house which H.H. Bennett built in 1875 and the Fern Dell country school.

Visitors could take in the Pioneer Auto Show, Art Gallery, Old Post Office Vehicles, Tread Mills, Jail, Bull Moose Saloon, Blacksmith Shop, Livery Stable and more. Over 150 unusually fine wild life specimens were also on display.

Gerald Baggot sold the Pioneer Village in 1966.

Kilbourn Fire Department

The Kilbourn Volunteer Fire Department was founded on September 5, 1891. It was formed after the city of Kilbourn laid the first water line from the pumping station along main street to the O.E. Loomis residence, in 1889.

F. R. Snider was elected the first "Foreman" of the Kilbourn Fire Department during the inaugural meeting in 1891, and his title changed to Chief in 1895. Other officers of the original department were F. H. Marshall, J. F. Dixon, H.D. Snider, L. H. Fogel, and T. J. Larson. There were six additional members.

Throughout its history, the Kilbourn Fire Department's ranks have been represented by men from all walks of life within the community. Among them have been bankers and plumbers, electricians and tavern owners, lawyers and cooks, bakers and pharmacists, funeral directors, insurance men and carpenters.

In April, 1893, the Kilbourn Fire Department purchased an Oak Street property for $375, and in July the department deeded the property to the city. The fire station building stayed there until 1927, when it was moved off and a city hall and the first stall of the fire station were constructed. An addition to the fire station was completed in 1958, and another, fronting on Washington Avenue, in 1974. A fourth addition to the fire station is presently being planned by the department.

The original land purchase and equipment were financed through proceeds raised at annual plays and dances, along with the member fine system which still exists today. Members were fined 50¢ for missing a fire or drill, 15¢ for missing a meeting, and $5.00 for missing the Memorial Day parade, which is also the annual inspection.

The department held its first play in March of 1892, netting $79.51 and raised $38.82 at a dance held in July of the same year.

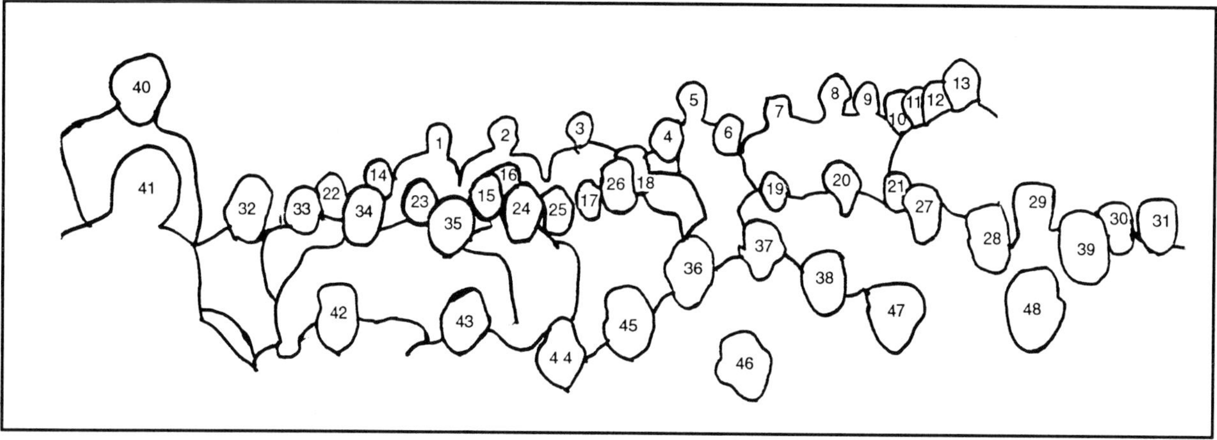

The Wisconsin Dells Fire Department, 1957. 1. Norm Roeker 2. Almer Soma 3. Walter Wimann 4. Monk Heineke 5. Floyd Thompson 6. Val Baggot 7. Leon Beard 8. Ken Lueck 9. Jack Fish 10. Bert Tollaksen 11. Merrill Meltz 12. Stacy Anchor 13. George Gray 14. Dr. Houghton 15. Dick Kaleas 16. Louie Wrizinski 17. Ed Brown 18. Jack Greenwood 19. Paul Jacobson 20. John Wenkman 21. Bob Gavinski 22. Pete Helland 23. Orville Stomner 24. Roy Kelly 25. Art Kane 26. Jim Tollaksen 27. Gordon Zinke 28. Butch Stomner 29. Sog Wimann 30. George Bixby 31. Bud Gussel 32. Stuart Fedderly 33. Herman Knipple 34. Jake Drollinger 35. John Kelly 36. Hans Kneubuhler 37. Arnie Borcher 38. Percy Newell 39. Kicker Thompson 40. Stewart Thompson 41. Mert Tofson 42. Hans Helland 43. George Thompson 44. Bert Wharry 45. Bo Hattle 46. Red Foster 47. Chuck Anchor 48. Norm Schultz. (Courtesy, H.H. Bennett Studio Foundation).

The first fire fighting equipment consisted of hose and ladder carts, which were pulled to the scene of a blaze by members of the department. Horses were later used for the pulling until the first motorized fire truck was purchased.

The Kilbourn Fire Department continues to raise funds through its annual dance, as well as through its Wo-Zha-Wa beer stand and nickel pitch projects. The department also receives funding through the city of Wisconsin Dells and from area service organizations, most notably the Harold B. Larkin American Legion Post, which has purchased several rescue vehicles and other equipment.

The Kilbourn Fire Department's first annual banquet was held on February 1, 1912 on a regular meeting night, and originally included election and installation of officers.

The Hansen's Department Store fire, 1962.

The first annual fireman's picnic was held on June 16, 1918, and annual ladies' and guest nights also continue to be held.

In addition to fire fighting, the Kilbourn Fire Department has become heavily involved in rescue operations. While modern equipment and vehicles have made both rescue and firefighting operations easier than in the early days, the amount of training and knowledge necessary to be a member has increased with each year.

Members of the Kilbourn Fire Department must be at least 21 years of age, with mandatory retirement at age 50. Firemen must serve a minimum of 15 years to be eligible for a vote to the honorary list.

Present members of the Kilbourn Fire Department are: Mark Hamm; Steve Lueck; Bret Anderson; Jim Pugh; Dave Parkhurst; Paul Gregerson; Durlin Morse; Dave Hall; Tom Anen; Eric Gregerson; Bob Anderson; Rob Holmes; Rick Warren; Mark Procknow; Tom Heller; Bill Kurz; Marc Playman; Pat Helland; Roger Henry; Perry Mayer; Tim Gavinski; Steve McClyman; Todd Swansby; Mark Sturdevant; James McClyman; Scott Holzem; Shawn Newell; Scott McClyman; Steve Licht; Dave Hess; Terry Richards; John Schauf.

Honorary members include: Aaron Anchor; James Beard; Peter Blatchley; Doug Bloomer; Arnold Borcher; Ben Borcher; Bill Brown; Edward Brown;Robert Cunningham; Lawrence Dickman Jr.; Dennis Dorow; Hans Fedderly; Tom Fisher; Ron Galitz; Dick Galitz; Robert Gavinski; Les Grant; Jack Greenwood; Bud Gussel; Keith Hattle; Hans Helland; Peter Helland; Jim Holden; Robert Holmes; Robert Kane; Bob LaVigne; Robert Lueck; Robert McClyman; Ron Newell; Marvin Platt; Norm Schultz; Elmer Soma*; Harold Sturdevant; Mike Swansby; Lee Thompson; Stewart Thompson; Tim Tofson; Toby Tofson; Robert Wick; George Willard; David Wimann; Walter Wimann; Jerry Wolfram; Don Wrezenski; Dick Zamzow; Gordon Zinke.

Deceased firemen include: F.H. Marshall; J.F. Dixon; L.H. Fogel; T.J. Larson; A. Miklic; M. O'Neil; Charles Anchor; Stacy Anchor; Morris Anderson; Fred Auerbach; Val Baggot; James Baggot ; J.J. Barrett; H.A. Bauer; Walter Bauer ; William Bauer; Leon Beard; Aug. Belter Sr.; George Bixby; C.A. Borcher; A.O. Brown; F.A. Burnham; Rev. J.W. Davies ; James Dixon; J.F. Dougherty; W.J. Doyle; J.M. Drollinger; Ronald Drollinger ; A.A. Duclos ; George Fedderly ; Stuart Fedderly; Jack Fish; J.C. Fitzgerald ; Ed Foster; A.C. French; George Gray; Monk Heineke; Oliver Helland ; Adam Hile; Paul Jacobson; Carl Jansen; A.P. Julson; Richard Kaleas; Art Kane; John Kelly; Roy Kelly; Merle Kimball; Hans Kneubuhler; Herman Knippel ; Art Koberstein ; Donald Krey; A.W. Luettgerodt ; F.P. McManman ; John Murphy; L.J. Naber; Percy Newell ; Ralph O'Neil; J.W. Ryan; W.J. Schultz; Leonard Sly; Fred Snider; H.D. Snider; E.J. Stillman; Charles Stomner; Orville Stomner; Ernst Storandt ; Richard Storandt ; A.C. Stowers; M.H. Stuelke; A.D. Sunderland ; Alvin Thomas ; F.T. Thomas ; Floyd Thompson; George Thompson; Jack Thompson; Stewart Thompson; Henry Tofson; Merton Tofson; B.E. Tollaksen; W.C. Tollaksen ; D.C. Van Wie; Harry Van Alstine ; H.A. VanElls; Paul Volkey; Joe Wenkman; John Wenkman; Bert Wharry; Jacob Wirtz; Fred Witt; Fred Wolter; Louis Wrezinski; Galitz, Robert; Lueck, Kenneth; Meltz, Merrill; Ryan, Robert; Roeker, Norman; Wimann, Fred;

*Oldest Living Fireman

The Delton Fire Department, 1982, (front, l-r) Maurice Delmore, Jr., Les Bremer, Dan Witecha, Ember Adams, Mort Rodwell, Al Asp, Gus Felt, Tom Peters, Larry Kimball, Guy Krueger, Larry Fish, Mike Brandt (rear) Jeff Woodruff, Tim Brandt, Don Riggs, Lee Doucette, Dick Blada, Paul Bremer, Ron Blegen, Robert Kaufman, Jerry Trumm, Darrell Klicko, Robert Fawcett.

Delton Fire Department

In 1932 America was still in the grip of the Great Depression. Franklin D. Roosevelt was elected President of the United States in the November elections; the city of Kilbourn had just, a year before, changed its name to Wisconsin Dells and the community in and around the Township of Delton was growing and quite proud that had it been selected to be the site of the new Dell View Hotel, one of the grandest vacation resorts of the time.

On February 2, 1932, the Delton Fire Department, consisting of six men and one third of a fire truck, was organized. According to Ember Adams, the only living original member, the Delton Department owned the truck with the Kilbourn and Newport Fire Departments.

"If we had a fire, the men from the Dells would bring it over here, but then we would have to go back to the Dells to hang the wet hoses and somehow find a way back to Delton," Adams said.

Other members of the six man organization included Chief Bill Cole, Ed Goman, Charles Retzlaff and Clarence and Glen Simons.

One third of a truck remained the department's only asset until 1944 when the town board approved some ropes, a ladder, and a trailer to haul the ladder and some pike poles. This approval came after the department was unable to save a drowning victim due to lack of equipment.

Also in 1944, the Sarrington Construction Company (presently Scott Construction) donated the use of a water truck for several months. This action allowed the department to receive its own charter in the fall of 1944.

The following spring, the department bought the water truck from Sarrington, and initially stored it in Bill Cole's garage at McBoyle's airport. Around 1949 the department bought its first rescue vehicle, an old Packard funeral hearse previously owned by Fedderly Funeral Home of Wisconsin Dells.

"We started using the town garage to store the truck, then when the township built a new garage in 1951 they gave us two stalls in the old part to store our water truck and a new Persh Pumper, which we had purchased from the Dells Fire Department in 1950," Adams said.

When the town built its own garage outside of the village of Lake Delton, Delton gave the fire department its old building. The fire department then shared the building with the Lake Delton Police Department until 1974 when the Village Hall was completed. After Lake Delton became a village, the department continued to serve both the village and the town of Delton and maintained the name Delton Fire Department.

As the years went by the department gradually added to its firefighting and rescue equipment. In 1961 they purchased a Ford van to carry firemen to fires, then later turned it into a rescue vehicle. This vehicle and the next one purchased, a 1969 Suburban, purchased jointly by the town and the village, both became obsolete when the state enacted new regulations for rescue vehicles.

The department's first state approved rescue vehicle was purchased from West Baraboo in 1976. In 1982 when the town and village purchased a more modern ambulance, the vehicle was used as a back up. In 1972 the Lake Delton Lions presented the department with a snowmobile and rescue sled and, in 1979, with "The Jaws of Life."

In 1961 the department purchased a 750 gallon pumper, in 1969 a used tanker. In 1974 the Legion bought the department a tanker and in 1980 the department purchased a 750 gallon pumper. At the present time the department owns nine vehicles: two 750 gallon pumpers, two 1800 gallon tankers, one rescue unit, one brush/grass fire unit, one utility vehicle/chief's car and two ambulances.

In June 1932 one of the worst fires ever fought by the Delton Fire Department occurred at the Morris Hotel. Although the firemen were assisted by the Dells Fire Department, the large two story hotel on Xanadu Road could not be saved.

Another terrible fire occurred in February of 1956 at Timme's Mill next to the Mirror Lake Dam. According to Ember Adams the fire was so hot that no one could get near the fire.

"In addition," he said, "it had been a very dry winter and there was no snow on the ground, so sparks kept setting the surrounding woods on fire, making our job even more difficult." The fire destroyed the mill and a grain elevator and damaged the bridge over the dam.

Other large fires fought by the department include the Reedsburg Big Store fire in 1958, which Delton firemen helped to fight for more than ten hours; the Reedsburg Woolen Mill fire in March of 1968, several fires fought at the Purple Grackle, later the Cross Bow, in 1967 and in 1974, and assisted the Dells during the January 1974 Crandall Hotel blaze.

There are still no fire hydrants in the village of Lake Delton but the firemen say they can get along without them. There are two old cisterns filled with water under the present fire station which remain from when the fire trucks were first stored there. "If we ever run out of water from our two tankers we can always use water from the area's many pools or the lake," Fire Chief Larry Fish said. "The cisterns would be used if the lake was frozen in the winter," he added.

At the present time the Delton Fire Department consists of 30 members. The firemen meet every first and third Monday night at the Firemen's Drill Hall and serve the community in whatever way they can.

The fire at Timme's Mill which destroyed both the mill and the bridge. (Courtesy, H. H. Bennett Studio Foundation)

Briggsville Fire Department

Until 1961, the Briggsville area relied upon surrounding communities for fire protection. Not long after a building burned on the shores of Lake Mason on January 30, 1961, residents voted for their own fire department. Harold Dunahee, was elected fire chief and 41 members of the community volunteered to become the first fire fighters.

Wisconsin Dells gave Briggsville its first fire truck, known as the "Purish Engine", in 1961. The townships of New Haven and Lewiston were assessed $100.00 for fire protection. Today each of these communities is assessed over $1,500 per year.

In 1962, 450 persons purchased Fireman's Ball tickets, and the proceeds purchased the first fire station. From 1962 to 1987 additional rooms were added to the station. In 1989, a new fire station was built, which now holds 6 trucks, a large water well to fill water tanker trucks, and meeting and training rooms.

The David Garrick Company

The local chapter of the David Garrick Company was formed in 1913. These amateur performers produced such plays as *In India, Holy Innocents, Our Wives, Princess Kiku, Florinda,* and *Twelfth Night.*

The proceeds from these plays paid for many civic projects. The gates at Spring Grove Cemetery and probably other improvements there were built with the company's help.

Actors for many of these plays included Dr. Boynton, Art Kane, Art Kliemenhagen, Harold Barrett, Charlie Ruch, Lawrence Welbaum, Bill Wimmer, Sr., Norm Magoon, Anna Baggot, Hazel Tollaksen, Gertie Buckminster, Olga and Harry Radlund, Miriam and Ruth Bennett, Mrs. Wintermute, G. Schroeder, Earl Rothe, Laurence Fogle, Dr. Wintermute, C. Van Alstine, Mrs. Rothe, Mrs. Bement, Valera Larson, J.E. Jones, O. Anderson, J. French, Mrs. Murphy, and H. Wiedenbacker. Harriet Richards directed and played parts in most of these plays.

Some of these plays had very large casts and one wonders how they could all fit on the stage of the old G.A.R Hall, now the Masonic Building.

The group's last major production was *Captain Jinks of the Horse Marines,* performed on December 6, 1932, to open the new High School Gym before a crowd of 600 people.

Kilbourn Chapter #120

Kilbourn Chapter #120, Wisconsin Dells Order of the Eastern Star, saw its beginning in the year 1901, when eight persons were initiated into our "mother chapter" at Baraboo in order to institute Kilbourn Chapter. The charter was received from Grand Chapter on March 21, 1901.

The first corps of officers included: Martha Wintermute, W.M.; G. E. Wintermute, W.P.; Nellie Crandall, A.M.; Cora Dixon, Conductress; Harriet VanAlstine, Associate Conductress; May Goedecke, Treas.; Evelyn Parsons, Adah; Vinnie Patterson, Ruth; Mae Kessler, Esther; Lillian Ramsey, Martha; Mary Teare, Electa; Mertice Johnson, Warder; and Frank Snider, Sentinel.

Chapter meetings were first held in a hall on the second floor of the Borcher building. In 1926 the present temple building was dedicated to the use of the Blue Lodge. Before the Masons purchased the building, it was known as the G.A.R Hall.

In 1920, several members demitted from our chapter in order to organize a new chapter at Delton. In October, 1921 Mirror Lake Chapter #238 received its charter from the Grand Chapter. Thus our "daughter chapter" was founded.

In 1944 our chapter sponsored the institution of the Order of Rainbow for Girls which included girls from Baraboo, Lake Delton and Wisconsin Dells. Rainbow remained active in the Dells until the 1980s.

On October 15, 1970 the consolidation of Mirror Lake Chapter #238 and Kilbourn Chapter #120 took place. Fifty-nine members of Mirror Lake Chapter were united with our chapter to make a membership of 178.

Through the years many of our members have had the honor of being active at Grand Chapter.

At one time the woman officers of Eastern Star were required to wear "white only" for Installation, Inspection and Initiation. Since the late '50s "color" has become accepted but long dresses are still required for all special events and skirts for all meetings.

In the '30s one highlight of a Matron's year was the annual May Ball. During the second world war, fuel shortages saw a few meetings held in the basement dining room to save fuel. Members assisted at the community USO Snack Bar during these years.

During the Golden Anniversary Celebration program in 1950, cast members wore the very first set of jewels owned by Kilbourn Chapter, which were handmade in 1900 by chapter member Nellie Crandall.

Badges worn by the present officers of Kilbourn Chapter are the badges first used in Mirror Lake Chapter so that parts of both Chapters remain to remind us of our past.

Extension Homemakers

The Homemakers Creed

We, the Homemakers of Wisconsin, believe in the sanctity of the HOME, the cradle of character, blessed by motherly devotion and guarded by fatherly protection.

WE PLEDGE ourselves:

To work for the preservation and improvement of home and community life.

To strive for healthier minds and bodies and better living.

To promote the welfare of our boys & girls, the nation's greatest asset.

To be true to God and country and of lasting service to our homes and communities.

– Mrs. John Meise, Sauk County

All over Wisconsin, the *Homemakers Creed* is used to open meetings as well as the closing prayer.

In the Dells area, homemakers clubs have come and gone, but many have endured, growing with the times and updating their concerns while the years passed.

Adams County's Gingham Girls Homemakers Club was organized on October 9, 1935 when the Home Demonstration Club met at the home of Mrs. Sybil Douglas. The "Plain Point Home Demonstration Club" was so named because some members were from Plainville and some from Point Bluff. Their dues were 10¢ and all the expenses they would have would be for Leaders expenses. They elected their officers. Leaders were also voted for their next lesson.

Their lessons were on a 1½ minute patch, sofa pillows made from monks cloth, toys and many pretty collars. Pamphlets were handed out for hooked rugs and a child's apron, how to put a patch on worn elbows and how to use a pattern for enlarging the waist on a skirt and how to fix a worn armhole.

On September 22, 1936, twenty ladies met at the home of Mrs. Irwin, in Easton, for a half day meeting. New ladies were asked to join. On October 9, 1936 the club met with 30 members present. Lessons were on personal care, facial packs and pure cleansing cream. Models included Elsie Schoff and Mary Barnes for shampoos – massaging neck and scalp, and Maude Bacon was set the ladies hair after the shampoo.

With membership growing, the ladies decided to get a hall for their meetings. Woodman Hall, in White Creek was their meeting place on October 27, 1936 with the name of Plain Point Club. By December 1, 1936, forty five members had joined. They held a dinner for flood relief and the sum of $27.25 was sent to County Red Cross for the flood sufferers.

They discussed dividing the Club into 2 or 3 smaller clubs, and the Plainville members formed their own club, with twelve members, on October 5, 1937.

In 1940 they changed the name of the club to "Gingham Girls". Around 1990 the Gingham Girls disbanded as a club connected with the Adams County Extension, but many continue to meet as an independent group each month and some have remained members at large.

In Juneau County the first home agent employed by the state was Mildred Olson, and the Stand Rock Homemakers was among the first clubs to form, in 1945. The charter members were: Phyllis Dunham, Ruth Hagen, Clara Beghin, Mabel Holden, Doris Naber and Anna Mitchell.

In Sauk County the first home agent was Myrtle Smith who arrived in 1942. However by that time eight clubs had already been formed and it took some urging of the county board by the clubs before the need for an agent was demonstrated.

The Dells based Ferndellettes Club has been in existence since 1956, when the Northeast Dellona Club and the Fern Dell Community Club, both of which had been in existence prior to that date, were merged. Early members included: Gert Horkan, Pat Wendorf, Gerry Potter, Edith Tesser, Isabelle Thompson, Lee Ludeking, Sally Lackore, LuAnn Duplayee, Bette Jones, Alberta Day, Marge Ennis, Ruth Raedel and Robin Raedel.

Present Ferndellette officers include Monica Waltman, President; Arlene Marslender, Treasurer and Marge Ennis, Secretary.

Since as far back as 1930, there was a Homemakers Group in Columbia County. Then called "Woman's Home Economics Work," Gladys Meloche, Nellie Kedzie Jones or Gladys Stillman would come from the U-W Madison and conduct all day meetings. They taught subjects like "Home Canning" where charts told how many bushels were needed to make 20 quarts and "Butchering and Curing of Meats."

On September 17, 1938 at the Courthouse in Portage, the beginning of the first "Home Demonstration" organization was made. Mr. Hovde, County Agricultural Agent was present and offered his guidance and assistance. Mrs. Herman Bahr was elected first county chairman.

Columbia County hired its first Home Agent, Stasia Lonergan, in 1942. She stayed for 14 1/2 years and said in a recent letter to the county, "During the 40's much of the emphasis was toward the war effort. Homemakers were told to make do, make over and to extend the use of everything. Victory gardens were planted and preserved and emphasis was on good nutrition and the food values of those homes produced fruits and vegetables."

In 1957 Mrs. Melvin Pulver of Columbia County was elected Wisconsin Extension Homemakers President.

During the Korean War, women were urged to set up Civil Defense shelters in or near their own homes, equipping them with food, water, battery radios, etc. The favorite lesson that year was, "Foundation Garments." An undergarment salesperson gave the lesson and taught women to "lean forward into your bra when you put it on, and to try a little baby powder when your girdle just won't slide."

Often the vice president of a club was assigned the job of "Health Chairman." After 1959, she was called "Civil Defense and Health" chairman, and given articles to share with club members throughout the county.

Margaret Patchett of Columbus was hired as the new Home Agent and the Civil-Defense-Health Chairman became the "Safety Chairman." Guidance for children was introduced and the study of a country, Hawaii, began an International Study tradition that continues today.

Columbia County hosted Farm Progress Days at the Christopherson farm near Wisconsin Dells in 1976. Everyone studied history and heritage and many made long skirts and bonnets for the many celebrations around the country.

Local Homemakers Earn 50 Year Awards

Two local women received awards for 50 years of membership in the Juneau County Extension Homemakers on Tuesday, May 3,1994 at the annual awards banquet.

The two women are Ruth Hagen and Clara Beghin of the Stand Rock Homemakers Club. The club was started in 1944 by women living on Stand Rock Road. Their first meeting was at the Dunham home and meetings rotated from home to home.

Leader training sessions were held in Mauston and were attended by volunteers from the club who brought the information back to teach the other members.

Beghin and Hagen were active in these leader trainings, taking their youngsters and a dish to pass to the nearly day long sessions.

Although is wasn't called recycling at the time, much of the training dealt with making things over, reusing things, sewing, gardening, and canning. Other training sessions included crafts, nature, ecology, and finances.

For Beghin, sewing was a favorite and at age 89 she is still busy making quilts and gifts for her family using skills she learned through Extension Homemakers.

Both women have held every office in the club at least once, some many times, over the past 50 years. Hagen now has three daughters, a daughter in law, and a grandduaghter active in the club. Beghin's daughter in law is a member, too, and is also Hagen's daughter.

Homemaker Activities

1930s: cabbage cookery, dress shoes tied with a stocky heel and a brochure on "How to Make a Burlap Shopping Bag".

1940s: Crocheted collars, $1.49 Sears leather handbags, sailor dresses, lockets to carry sweetheart pictures, turbans and parkas. Five cent stain removing charts, fuses, repairing cords, and how to buy a freezer. Hair in pompdours, saddle shoes and fur collars. Pasteurizing milk, short skirts and jitterbugging. Shoes without a ration coupon, baby dolls, and sling pumps. Page boy hair and pearls. Good posture, good work habits and work surfaces. "Good Grooming": making deodorants, hand lotion, and face cream. The first mental health topic, "As We Grow Older," was studied. Rhinestone jewelry, velvet trim.

1950s: Window Treatments, Floor Coverings, Closets, and the first lesson on Town and County Government, Family Fun, Soaps and Detergents, Accessories in the Home, and Buying Small Appliances. Wisconsin Driving Laws and Social Security. A Columbia County Chorus was organized and twenty six ladies raised their voices in song. Breadmaking and Textile Painting, "Buying the Correct Pattern Size" and just to round it out, "Housecleaning". "Managing the Food Dollars" combined with "Outdoor Cookery", and clothing lessons were on "Decorative Stitches", "Advanced Basic Sewing" and "Repair of Clothing."

1960s: Bouffant hair-dos, narrow leg pants. Decorating with houseplants, matting and rehanging pictures, and weight control. Lady Van Huesen shirts with hiphuggers and hawain print shirts. The Beatles and a Kitchen Band that played at community events. Mental Health as it Affects the Family, Manners Away From Home, Shopping, Menopause, Drugs and Narcotics, Advertising and the Consumer, lessons on food and the country of Puerto Rico.

1970s: Long hair and ponytails, boots with short skirts, turtleneck sweaters and pants with cuffs. Platform shoes with striped hose, bodysuits and ankle length winter coats. Pointed shoes and courderoy; handbags and earings went small. Haircuts with bangs and fuzzy sweaters.

1980s: "Color Me Beautiful"; everyone wants to know their season. Driving Defensively, Communication Techniques, Energy Saving Window Treatments, Helping Children Handle Peer Pressure, Natural Grain Baking, and Recycling. High heels with jeans, shoulder pads and huge pierced earrings. Co-Composting, Handling Conflict, Osteoporosis, Laws for Women, Haiti and a lesson on Child Abuse. Wok Cookery and Garnishes, HMO's, and Ireland.

Kay Miller became the new "Home Economist" (new title) in 1977 and the Executive Board of Columbia County Homemakers wrote a Mini-History of Columbia County.

In 1978 special interest meetings were offered to both men and women, who need not be Homemakers, including "Baby Food at Home, and "Financial Planning." In 1979 Diane Bender joined the County Extension staff and the program flourished.

The 1980s brought renewed interest in College Week for Women at the University of Wisconsin-Madison and council members eagerly attended annual conferences. Members got acquainted with their libraries, helped parents through the aging process, and helped them understand health insurance.

Cheryl Rew became the Extension Home Economist in 1982. The Cultural Arts Contest was becoming more popular and five first place winners went to the state conference contest in 1984.

The 50 years gala on October 27, 1988, included plays, skits, a parade of banners by club presidents, a style show and other entertainment to encourage reminiscing. Recent lessons on "Diet and Cancer", the special interest meeting on "Should Mom and Dad Live at Home After Age 75?" and cultural arts meetings on quilting were well received.

Dells Jaycee Organizations

The Junior Chamber of Commerce

On January 21, 1920, in St. Louis, 29 clubs from around the nation met and officially gave birth to the United States Junior Chamber of Commerce. The Wisconsin chapter of this group was organized in 1930.

In September, 1956, Adolph Priester, a J.C.C. from Columbus, extended the organization to Wisconsin Dells. The founding officers: President, Dan Colby; Vice-President, Bud Gussel and Ollie Reese; Secretary, Frank Haas; Treasurer, Howard Rockoff; and directors, Tim Draper and Harley Edmonds.

The purpose of the organization, as stated in the charter, is one of "civic service through the organized efforts of the young men of Wisconsin Dells and vicinity: to promote the welfare of the community and its citizens through active, constructive projects, to provide the young men constituting its membership, training in leadership and civic consciousness to better their usefulness as citizens."

Members had to be over 18 years old, and retire from service at age 36. The J.C.C. creed summarizes the J.C.C. concept as: "We Believe: That faith in God gives meaning and purpose to human life; That brotherhood of man transcends

The Jaycees raft race, with Brodhead in the lead.

the sovereignty of nations; That economic justice can best be won by free men through free enterprise; That government should be of laws rather than of men; That earth's great treasure lies in human personality; and that service to humanity is the best work of life."

The group held many fund raisers, some of which are still in successful practice today. The first project devised (1956-57) was called Benches on Broadway, today known as the Bench Program. which continues to allow local merchants to rent benches for the comfort of their summer visitors.

In 1958 the J.C.C.'s sponsored the Spring Sports Banquet. Every service club in the area was to choose a season to honor the athletes of our community. The J.C.C.'s chose the spring banquet. This project had many names, in 1959 being called the All Sports Banquet, and was run until 1986 under the title of Spring Sports Banquet. It honored the participants of basketball, baseball, golf, track, and wrestling. Today the project is under the direction of the Wisconsin Dells Sports Boosters.

Also in 1958 the J.C.C.'s participated in their first Halloween Party for grade school children and a Halloween Dance for the junior high students. Currently students of these age groups enjoy a safe Halloween Party and Dance.

The group organized the Wisconsin Dells Raft Race, which attempted to revive the pioneer art of river navigation, in 1960. The rafts were to be fashioned after the old rafts that came down the river some 75 years earlier. These modern day rafts, however, could be made out of any material that would float, but were restricted to a 8' by 9' size. Twenty nine rafts from all sections of the state partook in the experiment. The first rafts for the Dells J.C.C.'s was a replica of those log rafts - including the pike poles - that earlier floated the river. The very first raft was manned by Aaron Anchor, Hans Fedderly, Bud Gussel, Jake Drollinger, and Ed "Dad" Loofboro. The emblem for this project - Reggie Rafter - was known throughout the state. In consideration of rafter safety on the uncooperative river, the project was taken over by the Wisconsin State Jaycees for insurance purposes in 1985.

In 1963 the group cooked brats at a community involvement project called Maxwell Street Days, now called Wo Zha Wa weekend. Today, the Jaycee Brat and Corn Stand still nets the group the majority of their annual operating funds.

The group operated fairly smoothly through the years, boasting an average annual membership of 25 and holding many fund raisers: The Fisheree 1956-1972; Free Saturday Night Movies for Kids 1959-1963; Bowling Sweepstakes and Tournaments; Bloodmobiles and Polio Clinics; Barbershop Sing into Spring Afterglo; several Parades of Homes; Punt, Pass and Kick Program 1964-1989, (still sponsored by the State Jaycees).

Annual social functions for members included a Christmas Party since 1956; a family picnic since 1963; and a Boat Party since 1963. In 1973 the first Smoker was held to meet and recruit new members, and is now called an M-Night.

In 1965, the National Organization officially changed its name to the United States Jaycees. Hence, the Dells group became the Wisconsin Dells Jaycees. The group participated in the national project of Outstanding Young Farmer, choosing an outstanding local entry to represent the Dells area in the program. In 1963 the Dells Jaycees extended the organization to Reedsburg. With the group growing, and 12 more projects added, the donations the club made were also extended.

Jaycees donated the first High School Score Board in the early 1960's, and money for a warming house to the Wisconsin Dells Hockey Program in 1963. They donated funds to have the playground blacktopped at the Grade School, to buy a bus for the Park District in 1975, and the United Fund, Camp Wawbeek, the Boy Scouts, and the Junior Ski Program.

Since 1979 they have provided an annual scholarship to a high school student, and since 1974 have donated funds to help with the Lunch with Santa Program. The Wisconsin Dells Jaycees have participated in the M.D.A. Telethon since 1978. In 1980 they participated in the movement to save the Bowman House which later became the Dells Country Historical Society.

The Wisconsin Dells Jaycee Women

In 1963 the Wisconsin Dells Junior Chamber of Commerce Auxiliary was organized that year for the sole purpose of providing support to the Wisconsin Dells Jaycees. A prerequisite to membership was that your husband had to be a Jaycee. There were 19 original members.

This women's group assisted with Jaycee projects such as the bloodmobile, Barbershop Sing into Spring after Glo, Raft Race, and the Polio Clinic. They also organized their own community service projects: A Christmas Sale, Cowboy Eddie Show, White Elephant, and Candy Sale, Fisheree and a Style Show. They participated in the Special Ed Room with time and money, provided Chest X-Ray and Polio Clinic assistance and made a female scholarship donation as early as 1966.

Through the years the membership dwindled, averaging about 12, but the service projects increased. In 1969 they added to existing programs the following: Measle Clinic, Butternut coupons, magazines and cards to central Colony, PKU pamphlets for the clinic and drug store, and Red Cross Training Classes. They continued to provide scholarship donations and added a Girl Scout and Camp Wawbeek Donation. Their lunch with Santa program is still held today. They assisted the Jaycee Assocation with the Fireman's Jubilee, the Halloween Party, the Jaycee Brat Stand, and more.

When the men's organization changed its name in 1965, the Auxiliary followed suit and became the Wisconsin Dells Jaycee Auxiliary. Under this name the group organized the Fire Prevention Week Red Ball Stickers, and a Baby Sitting Clinic.

In 1973, by national decree, the organization's membership was able to accept women, ages 18 to 36, whose husbands were not Jaycees. The group now became the Wisconsin Dells Jaycettes. The old auxiliary ceased to exist and the new group organized. This should have been a boom to the membership, but it was not until 1980 that the membership grew. While continuing to operate existing projects, the Jaycettes added the Continental Manor Valentine Party, and made donations to the United Fund. A new name followed the ruling about membership.

This was an exciting time for women aged 18 to 36. Another National decree soon followed, stating that the "ette" on the Jaycette name denoted that the women belonging to the group were still considered "less than a Jaycee". Hence, the Wisconsin Dells Jaycettes dissolved once again and became the Wisconsin Dells Jaycee Women. Membership grew to 22.

This new group added a Children's Finger Printing for safety project, as well as spring and fall bake sales in conjunction with their craft fairs. The Holiday Craft Fair is still very popular today, bringing in over 50 crafters to the area for a two day craft show in November. The Jaycee Women also participated in the 1980 movement to save the Bowman House.

The Wisconsin Dells Jaycees

In 1985, the United States Supreme Court ruled to uphold a Minnesota public accomodations law that said "no place of public accomodation" may deny access to anyone "because of race, color, creed, religion, disability, national origin, or sex. Therefore, both groups, because their membership was divided, had to be revised. The Wisconsin Dells Jaycees and the Wisconsin Dells Jaycee Women had to dissolve and form a new co-ed group with new by-laws and constitution. The National Organization also changed the age qualifications ruling, to ages 21 through 39, allowing older members more time to help the new ones keep the organization strong.

As a final act, before disbanding forever, the Wisconsin Dells Jaycee Women made a donation to recondition the Davies Memorial Fountain in Bowman Park. Holiday Wholesale made a matching $1550.00 donation to the rededication ceremony in May, 1985. Making a final statement to the community that the group did exist and have purpose, the plaque simply reads "Restored by the Wisconsin Dells Jaycee Women 1985."

Officers from both groups worked diligently to combine the two important community organizations into a single new group. After weeks of deliberation a new constitution and by-laws were completed, projects and fund raisers were combined, and elections were held.

Today the club is as strong as ever, with a membership averaging 34. The new Jaycees kept the major fund raisers: Halloween Party & Dance, Bench Program, Holiday Craft Fair, Wo Zha Wa Brat & Corn Stand, Afternoon with Santa, Boy & Girl Scout Sponsor, and Sandbox Fill. They continue their socials - Christmas Party and Family Picnic, and together they continue a relationship on a regional, state and national level with other combined Jaycee groups, and they still feel "That service to humanity is the BEST WORK OF LIFE!"

The Kiwanis Club

The Kilbourn Kiwanis Club received its charter from the president of its sponsor, the Portage Club, on October 30, 1922. When the community changed its name in 1931, the club did also. Thirty five charter members elected Carl Orthman the first president and C.F. Francis the first club secretary. Club meetings were held at Larson's Restaurant on the corner of Broadway and Eddy Street.

Later meeting places included the Helms Restaurant, the Hile Hotel, Pat Stowers Restaurant, the Kilbourn Inn, the K & G Restaurant, the Beaver Building, Camp Upham Woods, Field's Steak & Stein, Bethany Lutheran Church, Otto's Supper Club and the Holiday Inn.

The longest tenure was in the Beaver Building which was owned by the city. The club rented the basement meeting and dining facilities, hired cooks, bought groceries wholesale and enjoyed home-cooked meals complete with home-made pie for $1.25 a meal.

Club membership remained in the 60s until the 1970s when four additional service clubs were chartered in the Dells-Delton area. Membership has since fluctuated over the years, but has never fallen below 35 members.

Though Miss Isabelle Drumb, the Editor/Owner of the *Dells Events*, was an honorary member of the club for 30 years, official membership remained all male until September 19, 1988, when the first female was inducted into membership.

Records indicate that in the past 73 years, the club has undertaken over 200 different individual and community projects. Fund raisers have included auctions, barbeques, pancakes, fruit cakes, tree sales, peanut sales, gum ball machines, concessions at civic events, Kiwanis revues, and more.

The annual Kiwanis Cystic Fibrosis Walk has raised almost $100,000 over the past 14 years and has provided camping experiences for CF victims at Camp Wawbeek. The Wishing Well at Cold Water Canyon, a fund raiser unique by Kiwanis standards, has netted tens of thousands of dollars over the past 35 years.

For many years the club owned and operated over 40 postage stamp machines which produced excellent revenue in a tourist community. Their annual "service" budget remains in the $25,000 range.

In 1955, the Kiwanis began sponsoring the Key Club at the high school, which continues to provide students with leadership training and an introduction to the "service" philosophy. In 1984 they chartered a Builders Club at the junior high but that program proved far less successful.

The club has presented scholarships to deserving students, made annual contributions to local, state and national fund drives, made donations to individuals facing critical surgery, to victims of fire, the handicapped, the elderly, the local fire department, the City of Wisconsin Dells, and has provided many hours of volunteer service and labor.

Ward and Harold Larkin, 1911.

The Wisconsin Dells Kiwanis Club has provided leadership for the Wisconsin-Upper Michigan District by providing two District Governors, one District Secretary, 17 Lieutenent Governors and nine District Chairmen. The club scored a first in 1966 when three Dells residents served as Wisconsin-Upper Michigan District Governors for that year; no similar situation had ever occurred in Kiwanis International.

One member has served Kiwanis International for several years including one year as the International Chairman for Key Clubs.

The personal commitment, leadership and unselfish service rendered by several hundred past and present members should serve as an inspiration to present as well as future Kiwanis members.

American Legion Post #187

Corporal Harold Weedin Larkin, son of Mr. & Mrs. J. R. Larkin, was born in Rockford, North Dakota, March 29, 1891. His family came to Davis Corners in 1904, and then moved to Kilbourn in 1909.

Harold enlisted in the U.S. Army the first time on June 23, 1916 and was sent to Waco, Texas for training. He served in Company F, 3rd Wisconsin Infantry, National Guard until he was discharged December 14, 1916. He re-entered the U.S. Army on March 26, 1917, was assigned to Company F. 128th Infantry Regiment, Cavalry Unit of Wisconsin National Guard, 32nd Division, and guarded bridges. He trained at Camp Douglas, Wisconsin and later at Waco, Texas. He was promoted to the rank of Corporal, July 17, 1917.

From Texas he wrote his mother that he was in a base hospital because he had a fine spring bed and could sleep as long as he wanted, and enclosed money for her to buy herself a Christmas present.

Harold landed in France in the early spring of 1918, and after training there his company went into the front lines. After three months of conflict he died in action on August 30, 1918, in Soissons, France. Corporal Larkin was cited for bravery during the Battle of Chateau-Theirry.

His remains arrived in Kilbourn by train on Friday, December 31, 1920. Funeral services were held in the G.A.R. hall on the morning of January 1, 1921 and conducted by Rev. E.L. Grau.

The American Legion was formed following World War I, and Wisconsin Dells Post 187, chartered January 5, 1920, was named after Harold Larkin. The *B* middle initial is an error stemming from some confusion over the years. Family members knew it to be *W.* but did not think it was necessary to cause a stir, and, to complicate matters, his army records refer to him as Harold William.

Corporal Larkin's uniform, his service revolver, some items of his cavalry harness equipment, the flag that draped his casket and other items are on display at the Post's meeting hall. He was one of 4,734,991 Americans who served in World War I.

In recent years, Post 187 has been happy to welcome the veterans of the Vietnam War, who are now wearing the Legion's blue caps, and are beginning to take an active part in Legion activities. Women who served in the Armed Forces are also eligible for membership. Legion Post 187 recognized its women veterans by electing a woman as Commander in 1979. In 1995, Korean War veterans became eligible as well..

While the Legion is primarily concerned with the veteran and his family's welfare, the Post also engages in community affairs and seeks to promote patriotism and good citizenship. It is involved in sponsoring oratorical contests, Badger Boys' State, Columbia County Government Day, Memorial and Veteran's Day celebrations, Legion baseball and dedication ceremonies.

Post 187 Legionnaires also provide a firing squad and honor guard at veteran's funerals. The Post presents a flag to the next of kin and provides a permanent marker for the grave. On Memorial Day all veterans graves are decorated with an American flag. Money given to the city of Wisconsin Dells has, among other things, provided playground equipment at Bowman Park and helped purchase fire and rescue vehicles for Lake Delton and Wisconsin Dells.

Post #187's money has been primarily accumulated through the efforts of the veterans and their auxiliary who, for over 30 years, sponsored the Stand Rock Indian Ceremonial. Hundreds of volunteer hours helped make this project an outstanding success and has enabled the Post to contribute generously to the community.

Working closely with Post #187, and also developing many areas of community service on its own, is the American Legion Auxiliary. It was organized in 1929 with Mrs. Nora Dixon as its first President; John C. Van Wie, Commander; and Carl R. Seger, Adjutant.

VFW Post #9387

Wisconsin Dells Memorial Post #9387 was chartered on May 15, 1966, with 35 members. Membership has reached 60, 17 of which are charter members.

The charter officers were Commander, Mainert Anderson; Quartermaster Patrick Walsh; Sr. Vice Commander Richard Mlsna, Jr.; Vice Commander John Kremer; Judge Advocate Hans Mickelson; Chaplain James Flickner; Surgeon Monk Heineke; and post trustees, Arnold Jones, Jack Olson and Robert Funmaker.

Deceased charter members are Patrick Walsh, Richard Ennis, John Rathka and Robert Funmaker.

Present officers of Post #9387 are: Commander John Stroede; Vice Commander Eugene Blood Sr.; Vice Commander Dan Jones Jr.; Adjutant Mainert Anderson; Quartermaster Robert Jones; Chaplain Arnold Jones; Advocate Barney Richter; Officer of the Day Frank Gray; Service Officer William Rubin; and Trustees John McCauley, Augie Stroede and Ray Smith.

The Auxiliary to Post 9387 was chartered on February 26, 1967. The original members were: Leona Anderson, Rachel Carley, Helen Coon, Alberta Day, Marge Ennis, Lena Flickner, Ruby Frost, Stella Funmaker, Bette Jones, Elnora Jones, Julia Kaleas, Norma Lytle, Marion Miner, Katherine Mlsna, Clarice Stroede, Lorraine Stroede and Georgia Wood.

The Auxiliary had 48 members in 1991, and in 1992 it celebrated its 25 year anniversary.

1991 Auxiliary officers are: President Joan Kaiser, Sr. Vice Billy Long, Jr. Vice Diane Keyes, Treasurer Bette Jones, Conductress Norma Lytle, Assistant Conductress Grace Jordan, Guard Sally Gray, Historian Helen McCauley, Chaplain Sue Proeber, Patriotic Instructor, Mid Cloyd and Trustees Angie Warneke, Leona Anderson and Marge Ennis.

Kilbourn Scouts

The first Girl Scout troop was organized in 1926 with Mrs. Drumb as leader. Jo Arntz, later Mrs. Glen Blatchley, was also an early leader and remained with the organization in many roles for 35 years. It is simply impossible to find records of or remember the hundreds of women and young girls who have made the Girl Scouting program a success since then. Mrs. Edna Crist and Mrs. Eleanor Anchor led the troop for many years.

In 1995, there are 100 girls in nine troops throughout our area.

Sponsored by the Presbyterian Church, Kilbourn Boy Scout Troop #66 was organized on January 10, 1929. The first troop committee was chaired by Rev. Joseph Davies and included B.E. Tollaksen, Newton Landt and Dr. R. W. Boynton.

K.K. Johnson served Troop #66 as Scoutmaster from 1929 to 1937 and was assisted by Thomas Crist Sr.

The original troop registration included: Ray Boynton, Willard Gray, Chester Harrison, Kenneth Harrison, Robert Kimball, Allison Landt, Leroy Liessman, Henry Marston, Robert Seger, Gordon Tollaksen, Roland Weber and Ervin Johnson.

The boys established both summer and winter camps and in 1932 constructed a log cabin at the end of Elm Street for a meeting site.

A National record was set in October, 1931 for the advancement to the highest rank in scouting by the most members of one troop. Eagle Scouting Awards were presented to eight scouts: Oliver Helland, Robert Van Wie, Ray Boynton, Kenneth Harrison, Chester Harrison, Roland Weber, Robert Seger and Allison Landt. Leader K.K. Johnson was presented with a Golden Palm to add to his Eagle Award. These scouts and leaders were rewarded with a trip to Washington D.C. in March, 1932.

In 1995, there are 52 Cub Scouts in six dens and 19 Boy Scouts.

The Explorer program includes boys and girls ages 14-21. The Police Explorer troop has 19 members, 10 of which are High Adventure Explorers.

Dells Country Historical Society And The Bowman House

The founding of the Dells Country Historical Society was the result of the effort to save the historic Bowman House. Located in Bowman Park on the corner of Capital and Broadway in downtown Wisconsin Dells, the Bowman House was built in 1904 by Abram Bowman, son of Kilbourn pioneers Jonathan and Hannah Bowman.

One of the founders of Newport and a practicing attorney, Jonathan Bowman moved his family and house to Kilbourn in 1862. This original Bowman house was located on Broadway only a few blocks west of the present home. It is still standing at 619 Cedar Street in Wisconsin Dells.

The young Bowmans prospered in this new and growing community. During the next few years their family grew to include five children: Ella, born in 1859; Abram, 1861; Asa, 1863; Jennie, 1865; and Emma, 1867. As Kilbourn's leading attorney and one of its most successful businessmen, Bowman was one of the wealthiest men in the community when he died in 1895.

In 1902, at the age of 40, Abram Bowman married Alberta Griswold. Two years later, Abram purchased the one block square piece of land that became Bowman Park from his mother. The new Bowman House was ready for occupancy by the fall of 1906. Abram and Alberta shared the home for less than one year when Abram died.

Hannah Bowman and her two remaining children, Jennie and Emma, purchased the home from Alberta in 1908, and lived there with their servants until Hannah passed away in 1916. The two daughters lived alone in the home, without servants for 5 years, until Emma passed on in 1921, leaving Jennie the only surviving Bowman.

Since all her siblings had passed on without leaving heirs, Jennie gave great thought to the disposition of her property after her death. She was a thrifty woman, known as the financier of her family. She had also traveled extensively, and it was on one of her trips to California that she got the idea of turning her brother's home into a guest house for working women not younger that 45. Guests who qualified could stay in the house for two weeks free of charge. She painstakingly rewrote her entire will stipulating that the house–as a memorial to her father–be set up for working women.

Jennie passed on in 1934, at the age of 69, but not before she gathered enough wealth to set her plan into motion. By the close of the tourist season on October 1, 1945–21 years after it opened–between 800-850 women had enjoyed the privilege of being a guest in the house. The Memorial Guest Home was in operation for a total of 44 years until the funds ran out. In the fall of 1978, all the interior belongings were auctioned off. Money collected went to distant relatives of the Bowmans.

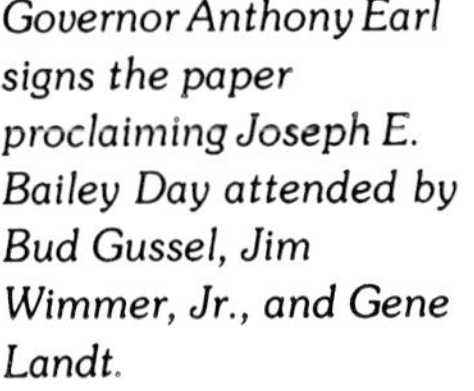

Governor Anthony Earl signs the paper proclaiming Joseph E. Bailey Day attended by Bud Gussel, Jim Wimmer, Jr., and Gene Landt.

The Jonathan Bowman Home, c. 1950.

The home sat empty for a year. The city then gave permission to the Neeshla Indian Association to use the home for one season. By April, 1981, the city decided to dispose of the home, due to the costly upkeep, by allowing the Wisconsin Dells Fire Department to use it for a "practice burn".

In May 1981, one last plea was made to area service clubs and individuals to see if Wisconsin Dells couldn't find something more constructive to do with this beautiful and historic building. Hence, on that day in May, the Historical Society was formed on a "We'll see" basis: to see if perhaps, one day, the home could be enjoyed again by many–not just as a memorial as Jennie wished–but as a learning place for the future generations to step through a doorway to yesterday.

During its first year, the organization took the name of Dells Country Historical Society. "Dells Country" was chosen to include the surrounding areas of the community. With major donations of electrical work, some eve and gutter repair, display cases, flowers, and money the Society held its first open house on June 14, 1981. This was meant to be an appetizer to the community to "come and see" what was started and what could be accomplished.

During that same month officers were chosen: President Bud Gussel, Vice-President Charlie Van Wie, Secretary Betty Heller, Treasurer Jerry Karaus, and committees were formed: Restoration Jack Heller, Personnel Ed O'Brien, Security Charlie Van Wie, Curators, Clara Hauser, and Gene Landt, Publicity Jan Landrum, Fund Raising Joy Bartol. 40 members joined that year. During one of its first meetings, the Society discovered the Bowman silverware hidden in a secret place known only to those who worked in the Bowman household.

The Society also became affiliated with the State Historical Society, set a budget, and regular meeting dates were chosen. Due to generous donations the home was partially furnished for the Society's second open house during the Wo Zha Wa fall festival in September, 1981. A total of 864 people shared the experience of stepping into the past that first year.

During its still growing second year, the membership grew to over 70. In an attempt to raise funds for the much needed security system, the Society published its first newspaper containing a collection of articles on the early histories of the people, places and times of our area. A quilt show in the spring and a bake sale, also helped to raise funds. During this second year the Society also arranged to hold a community wide 'Heritage Day' in June, 1982, to help promote its cause and to evoke the community's historical interest.

Today, the Museum is quite filled with many artifacts and historical mementoes leading all on a journey to the past. The current officers are: President Bud Gussel, Secretary Jan Landrum, Treasurer Shirley Olson, Curators Gene Landt, and Donna Greenwood. Major restorations to the exterior and interior with funds raised and donated have also been accomplished. Fund raisers are still held, and Heritage Day is an annual part of the community's celebration in Spring. The Society has, thus far, succeeded in preserving that doorway - a learning place for the future generations to step through to yesterday.

Wisconsin Dells Attractions
1950s – 1990s

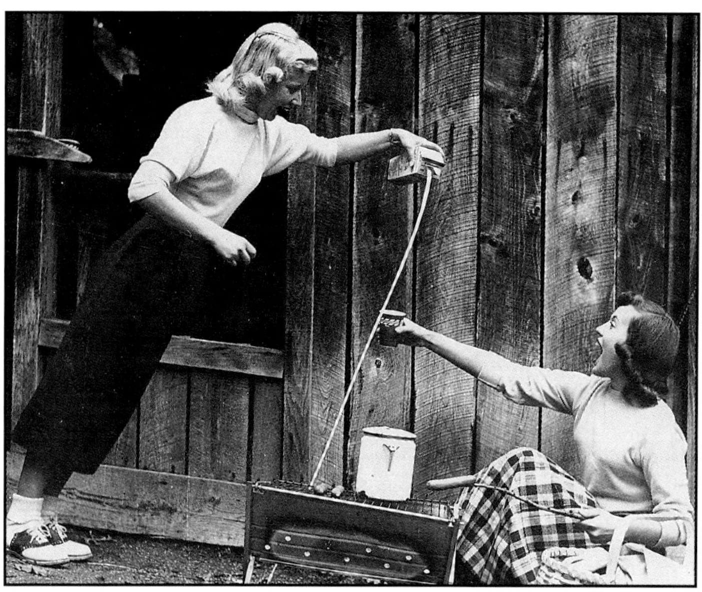

The Wonder Spot, 1957. (Courtesy, H.H. Bennett Studio Foundation).

Beaver Springs Fishing Park 1955–
-Owned by Brent Tollaksen
-Located on Trout Road
-Everyone catches a fish! Seven spring fed ponds with trout, bass, pike and panfish. Services include bait, tackle and packaging

Biblical Gardens 1961–
-Owned by Arthur Donaldson
-Located on Wisconsin Dells Parkway
-The life and times of Jesus in 16 sculptural scenes

Big Chief Go Cart World 1976–
-Owned by Demetrias Laskaris
-Located on Hwy A & Hwy 12
-Nations largest go cart complex, featuring 13 uniquely designed tracks

Dells Auto Museum 1976–
-Owned & operated by Dick & Donna Tarnritzer
-Located on Wisconsin Dells Parkway
-An array of antique, classical and special interest automobiles. Also featuring antique dolls and toys

Dells Park Trading Post 1932–1956
-Operated by Roland (Pipe) Dyer
-Located across the river from Upper Dells Boat Dock
-Featured authentic Indian Village including silversmiths, headwork and basket making

Dungeon of Horrors 1981–
-Owned by Bill Nehring
-Located on 325 Broadway
-Haunted House

Enchanted Forest 1956–1990
-Owned by Charles & Robert Van Wie
-Located northside of Wisconsin River at the Bridge
-Fairytale attractions, dinosaurs and children playground

Familyland 1974–
-Owned by Noel Mattei
-Located on Wisconsin Dells Parkway
-A 60 acre water and amusement park with wave pool, lazy river, water slides, mini gold and u-drive-em rides

Fort Dells 1959–1989
-Owned by Dells Associated Boat Lines
-Located on corner of Hwys 12 & 23
-Featured indian dances, mini railroad, big bonanza mine, Dells Fargo Stage, haunted house, childrens farm and the Totem Tower

Charlie Van Wie's souvenir shop, c. 1955.

The Riverside and Great Northern Railroad of Elmer and Norman Sandley, 1954. (Courtesy, H.H. Bennett Studio Foundation).

Ho-Chunk Casino
-On Hwy 12 between Lake Delton and Baraboo
-Blackjack, keno, video poker and bingo

Lost Canyon Tours 1955–
-Owned by R. Kissack
-Located on Canyon Road-Lake Delton
-Horse drawn wagon tour through a beautiful canyon

Lower Dells Boat Tour
-One hour tour on portion of the river below the dam

Minirama 1960-1969
-Owned by Oliver Reese
-Located Downtown Dells
-Model of the Dells built to scale of ¼" to one foot. Depicted Upper and Lower Dells and main points of city. Scale model trains and boats ran through the display

Molly's Dinner Show 1978–
-Owned and operated by Bruce & Joanne Christoph
-Located on Wisconsin Dells Parkway
-Dining, cocktail lounge and music America stage show

Noah's Ark
-Founded by Jack & Turk Waterman
-Located on Wisconsin Dells Parkway
-65 acres of family activities 2 wave pools, 2 lazy rivers, 31 water slides, 4 kiddie water play areas and 15 restaurants

Olde Kilbourn 1975–
-Owned by John Tollaksen
-Located on Wisconsin Dells Parkway
-Mini golf, bumper cars, amusement rides and haunted house

Original Wisconsin Ducks 1956–
-Managed by Dan Gavinski
-Located on Wisconsin Dells Parkway
-Featuring a one hour, 8½ mile tour aboard amphibious vehicle from World War II. The trip takes sightseers through Red Bird Gorge along Lake Delton and past the beautiful Lower Dells of the Wisconsin River

Reptile Gardens 1954–1960
-Owned by Sam Peroni
-Located on Wisconsin Dells Parkway
-Snakes and reptiles on display

Peter Tollaksen's Wisconsin Deer Park, c. 1965.

The Lake Delton Balloon Rally, 1995. (Courtesy, W.D.V. & C.B.)

Ripleys Believe It or Not 1990–

-Operated by Concept Attractions Inc.
-Located Downtown Wisconsin Dells
-Museum features the strange and unusual. Numerous video presentations and two sit down theaters. Puzzeting illusions and special effects

Riverside & Great Northern Railway 1954–

-Owned and operated by Elmer & Norman Sandley (1954-1981), now operated by the Riverside Great Northern Preservation Society
-Located one mile north of Wisconsin Dells on Cty A
-Miniature railroad carries passengers two miles on the former right of way of the LaCrosse and Milwaukee Railroad

Riverview Park

-Owned by Riverview Corp.
-Located on Wisconsin Dells Parkway
-30 different water activities, u-drive-em ride, amusement rides, roller coaster and grand prix racing

Santa Claus Town 1958

-Owned by Lloyd Atkinson
-Located on Wisconsin Dells Parkway
-Featuring Santa and his helpers

Sea Lion Village 1956–1962

-Owned by Norman Olson
-Located on Wisconsin Dells Parkway
-Live seals and sea lions for viewing

Storybook Gardens 1956–

-Operated by Noel Mattei
-Located on Wisconsin Dells Parkway
-Characters, landscaped gardens, kiddie rides, animated displays and live performances

Timber Falls Park 1990–

-Owned by Arnold & Ben Borcher and Greg Van Wie
-Located on west end of Wisconsin River Bridge
-Mini golf, log flume ride, restaurant and shops

Tommy Bartlett Show 1955–

-Founded by Tommy Barlett now operated by Tom Diehl
-Located on Lake Delton
-Featuring waterskiing, skyflyers, acrobats, Mr. Sound effects, Tahition dancers and Dancing Waters

Totem Tower 1965–1990

-Located at Fort Dells
-330' tower with revolving gondola to carry 60 people

Upper Dells Boat Tour 1873–

-Located Downtown Dells
-2½ hour tour with three scenic stops

Wax World of Stars 1969–
-Operated by Raycax Investments
-Located Downtown Wisconsin Dells
-Everchanging exhibit offers over 100 life like wax figures created in England, Spain and United State

Wisconsin Deer Park 1952–
-Owned by Peter Tollaksen
-Located on Wisconsin Dells Parkway
-See them alive-deer, elk, buffalo and game birds. Feed, pet and photograph in a natural 28 acre park

Wisconsin Dells Greyhound Racing 1990–
-Owned by Thomas & Margaret Diehl
-Located on Hwy 12 and I-90/94

Wisconsin Dells Trolley Tours 1987–
-Owned by Brent Tollaksen
-Located on Trout Road
-One hour narrated tour of Dells area

Wisconsin Opry
-Owned by Virgil Dickenson
-Located on Hwy 12, south of Lake Delton
-2 hour country music show

Wonder Spot 1948–
-Owned by William & Debra Carney
-Located on Wisconsin Dells Parkway
-A guided tour through a topsy turvy world that will leave you questioning the laws of nature

World Wide Animal Kingdom 1972-1975
-Owned by Earl Jordan and Leo Rothe
-Located on Wisconsin Dells Parkway
-Displayed mounted animals from Africa'

The Kowabunga Water Slide at Noah's Ark, 1995.

Xanadu 1988–1993
-Owned by Tom Gussel and Ken Forsythe
-Located at west end of Wisconsin River bridge
-Foam house of tomorrow

The Wisconsin Dells Automotion Auto Show, 1995.
(Courtesy, W.D.V. & C.B.)

1954 PHONE BOOK
WISCONSIN DELLS, WISCONSIN

A

Abrams Albert
Accola William J
Acott Jane
Acree Bruce
Adams Mackey
Adams W E
Adams Ember
Adams Brothers Builders
Adams Alfred E
Adams John L
Agema John T Rev
Ahlhorn William
Ahlhorn Adolph
Ahlhorn Georgia J
Albertson L H
Algeo Herbert E
Amann E C
American Motor Court
American Legion Hall
Anchor Bay Resort
Anchor Charles
Anchor Stacy
Anchor's Restaurant
Andersen Patricia
Andersen A O
Anderson Henry
Anderson A W
Anderson Oscar
Anderson Alfred
Anderson Norris
Anderson Leone D Mrs
Anderson Lloyd
Anderson Lester
Anderson M M
Anderson Harry
Anderson Alvin
Anderson Walter
Anderson Fred
Anderson Cliff
Anderson Russell
Anderson Clarence
Anderson Robert
Anderson Carl
Anderson Gordon
Anderson Wallace
Anderson M H
Armson Elmer
Armson Duane
Arntz Restaurant
Arrowhead Shop The
Auck Leon G
Auerbach Fred
Auerbach's Shady Lawn Resort
Austin's Grocery
Avery Gordon H
Avery's Edgewater Lodge

B

Backeberg Omar
Badger Restaurant
Baggot James
Baggot Leo
Baggot Gerald
Baggot Valentine
Bagley Archie
Baker C P
Baker Peter Mrs
Baker Lester
Baker John
Baker Pontiac
Ballweber J C
Balsmeider Charles Sr
Balsmeider Lois
Balsmeider Charles Jr
Bannen Francis R
Barney R D Mrs
Barnhill Helen
Barnhill J K
Barrett J J Mrs
Barrett's Souvenir Shop
Barrett's Bar
Barrier John
Bartness Todd R
Barton William
Bartsch Robert Rev
Bass Ben
Batty Arthur B
Bauer W F
Bauer H A Mrs
Beahm Ralph H
Beard Louis
Beard Leon
Beasley John Co
Beckerleg Laverne
Beghin Jacob C
Beghin Julius
Beghin Louis
Behn Ernest A
Belcher Bennett
Bell W H
Bell Arthur
Bell Gerald
Belton G E
Benes Wensel
Bennett H H Studio
Bennett Miriam
Berkley E E
Berry Roland
Berry's Dells Golf Course
Bethany Lutheran Church
Biermeier Louis J
Bill's Shell Service
Birchcliff Hotel
Birkholz Louie
Bixby Fred
Bixby George D
Bixby Lillian Mrs
Black Forest Inn
Black Oaks Motel
Blackhawk Hotel
Blackhawk Cottage Court
Blank Gerald
Blaser Helene
Blatchley Glen C
Blighton Nellie
Blood Eugene
Bob's Sinclair Service
Bogh Ed
Bogh Laurence
Bohlinger W H Dr
Bohn Kenneth
Booth Standard Service
Booth R L
Borcher Charles Mrs
Borcher Arnold B
Bork Lottie Mrs
Bork Rueford
Borud John
Botsford Hazel Mrs
Bowden B R
Boyington W L
Brandt L C
Braun Raymond B
Breezy Hill Motor Court
Bremer Helmuth
Brenson George
Brereton W R
Bresnahan Walter
Bressler Melford
Brew Dan
Briggs Duaine
Brill Marguerite H
Brink E W Mrs
Broadway Market
Brockman Clara Mrs
Broderick C F Dr
Broker R H
Brooks Hotel
Brown John
Brown Rolland E
Brown Jane
Brown Edward
Brown's Restaurant
Brown's Studio
Bruhns Robert
Buckley A L Mrs
Buckley Charles
Buckminister E Herbert
Burgess Fletcher
Burke Michael
Burke Harold A
Burns Fred G
Burris Mark
Byers Etta

C

C M St P & P Ry Co
Cady Alton E Sr
Caflisch Alymer
Cahoon Paul
Cahoon Claude L
Camp Chi
Camp Wawbeek
Campbell Herbert
Cappy George V
Cappy's Department Store
Carbide Carbon Chemical
Carey Earl Stafford Dr
Carley Jasper
Carnrick John
Carter's Court
Cary Williams
Casperson Robert
Cauley Leroy
Cavanaugh Mary
Center State Industries
Central Insulation Roofing
Chamber of Commere Lake Delton
Chamber of Commere Wis. Dells
Chap's Cabin Motel
Chaplin Mary E
Chapple's Pine Drive Cottages
Charlesworth G T
Charm Beauty Shop
Chase Gene Beer Distributor
Chevrolet Sales & Services
Chicanich Anthony
Chief Evergreen Tree
Christensen Jens R
Christensen Hans A
Christenson Walter J
Christopherson Nels
Chula Vista Resort
City Market & Grocery
City Yellow Cab
Clark Lester
Clark James E
Clark's Willard Log Cabins&Tavern
Clauslus Elmer
Clendaniel Mae Mrs
Clufo Theodore
Coapman Norman L
Coast to Coast Store
Coca-Cola Bottling Co
Colburn Clarence E
Colburn Norman
Colburn Arthur W
Colby Dan Mrs
Cold Water Canyon Gift Shop
Cole Emery
Cole W.H. Garage
Cole Ernest
Colonial Motel
Commonwealth Telephone Co
Cone Frank
Cone Ervin
Cone Archie R
Cone Walter
Cone Fred
Connor Ralph W
Conway Mary Miss
Conway Mike
Cook Raymond
Cook Carl
Coolidge George
Coon Francis
Coon Howard
Cornwell Roy
Cornwell Leo
Coughlin Edward
Counsell Duaine K
Counsell K W Mrs
Cox Lorenzo W
Crandall Hotel
Crist Thomas
Crist Thomas D Jr
Crothers Stanley
Crothers Edna L
Crothers Archie
Curry Ross Mrs

D

Da Walt Verne
Dahl Norman
Dahl Marvin
Dalles Womens Apparel
Daniels Karen
Dankert Emil
Daoust J J Mrs
Davies J W Rev
Davis Ruth W
Day Frank
Day Charles
De Merit James A
Deakin D S
Deans J N
Decker David
Deckert John C
Decorah Joe
Deep Rock Service Station
Deer Park
Dehler Norman
Dehler Glen
Del-Aire Beauty Salon
Del-Bar
Dell House
Dell View Hotel
Dells Trading Post
Dells Transfer
Dells Sign Service
Dells Theatre
Dells Clinic
Dells Concrete
Dells Cooperative Boat Line
Dells Cafeteria
Dells Air Tours
Dells Beer Deport
Dells Area Television Center
Dells Body Shop
Dells Grill
Dells Boat Co.
Dells Motors
Dells Manor Bar
Dells Park
Dells Superior Cleaners
Dells Lumber Co
Dells-Mound Lake Resort
Dellwood Rooms
Delmore Maurice
Delton Town Hall
Delton Fire Department
Delton Outdoor Theatre
Dick's Restaurant
Dinckler Fred
Dittrich Kenneth
Dixon Fred
Dixon James Hall Mrs
Donnelly Don
Donnelly James
Donnelly Hugh
Dopp George
Dorow Edward H
Dorow Henry
Dorow Sidney
Doud Roy
Dougherty Robert Atty
Dougherty J F Mrs
Dougherty Thomas H
Douglas Marion
Douglas Rufus
Dowd Henry
Down Town Motel
Doyle Phillip
Doyle William T
Draper B R Jr
Draper B R Sr
Drew R A Mrs
Drockner William
Drollinger Ronald M
Drollinger Nora Mrs
Droste Herb
Droste Frank
Drumb Isabelle
Duck Line Boats
DuFour Earl
Dunham Kittie
Dunham Gordon R
Dunham Henry A
Dunham Wm Harold
Dunn W R
Dunn's Drive In

Dunne Jos
Dusell Wm Lt
Dutch Mill Motor Court
Dyer Roland M
Dzekunskas John

E
Ebert Gus
Ebert R O
Echo Point Hotel & Resort
Eckert Carter
Edmonds Jess
Edmonds Harley
Edmund's Rock Cliff Resort
Edmunds Electric Shop
Edwards Joseph E
Eichelman J M
Elderkin Dana
Elderkin Clark
Elledge Leroy B
Ellenz G B Dr
Ellis Willard
Ellison Elmer
Emmerichs Peter
Englebretson Clarence
Engnath Frank H
Ennis Joe
Ennis Richard
Enz E C
Erickson Kenneth
Erickson Eric
Erickson Irvin
Evans Max
Evans Harvey
Events Office
Evergreen Motel
Everson Adelbert
Everts Frank G

F
Fairview Cabins
Family Park Resort
Farmers & Merchants State Bank
Farrell Walter
Fedderbusch William
Fedderly Funeral Home
Fedderly Hardware
Fedderly Stuart
Fedderly Norman S Insurance
Fedderly Paul H
Fenske Robert
Ferge John
Ferge Richard
Fern Dell School
Field Henry A
Field R F
Field Henry
Field George
Field F F Dr
Field & Field Drs Dentist
Field Motor Lodge
Field F A Dr
Field's Texaco Service
Finch Motel
Finnegan Dan
Fischer Francis
Fischer's Cocktail Bar & Rest.
Fish Louis
Fish John
Fisher Stanley
Fisher Ira
Fisher Ed Mrs
Fitzgerald E P
Fitzgerald J C Mrs
Fitzpatrick William
Flickner H M
Flock Leonard
Florida Water Ski Show
Flying Bar-B-Q
Ford Frank A
Foss Carl S
Foss Ernie
Foss Levi
Foster Edwin
Foster Gordon
Foster Ray
Foster Keith
Foster Kenneth
Fowler Jennie
Fox E L
Frankfurth Wencel
French D W
French A C Mrs
Fritz Charles
Fritz Wilbur
Frodin Eugene D
Frodin Elmer E
Fuchiek F J
Fuller W J
Fullmer Warren Mrs
Fullmer Daniel A
Fulton Mary Lee

G
Gables The
Gaffney J H
Gaffney William
Gaffney Electric Store
Gaffney Stanley
Gaglione Anna
Galitz Robert W
Gant W R
Ganther George L
Ganzi Michael
Gardens Motor Lodge
Gasser Gordon B
Gasser David L
Gavinski Stanley
Gavinski Peter
Gavinski Stanley Robert
Gavinski Walter
Geibel Ferd
General Realty Inc
General Telephone Company
Gibbs Theodore
Giebel Robert
Gift Mart
Gissal F W Dr
Gleason Frank
Glencoe Cottages
Globe Rendering Co
Gloede Ray
Gluth Walter
Goerlitz Carl C
Golding Joseph
Goman Edward
Gonzagowski Walter
Gorman's Chalet Motel
Gotthardt Katherine
Gould Alma Soergel
Grabowski Albert
Grade School
Graff Anna L
Graham Betty J Mrs
Gray Merlin O
Gray John A
Gray George
Greenwood Jack
Greenwood D A
Greenwood Motor Sales
Gregerson Ole
Gregerson Jens Mrs
Greiner Henry
Grey Kermit T
Greyhound Bus Station
Grieger John T
Grieger Fred Mrs
Grieger William
Grieves Donald
Gross Common Carrier
Gruman Raymond
Gudenschwager Await
Guildner Sam Jr
Gussel Bernard
Gussel Bud Wholesale Dist.
Gustafson Fred N Mrs
Gutzler Stacey F

H
Hacker Frank
Haferman Leonard
Hagen Lee
Hagen's Tavern
Hale William
Hall Jack
Halverson George O
Hamm Donald
Hammerly Erwin
Hammerly Marvin
Hammerly Jost
Hammerschmidt Emil
Hansen Vivian
Hansen-Snider Lumber
Hanson Tom
Hanson Kenneth W
Harding Kenneth
Harding's Standard Service
Harger Jennings
Harms Armand F
Harrison Kenneth C
Harrison Marshall
Harrison Marden E
Harrison John
Harrison's Gas & Electric
Harritt Lyle E
Harvey Fred
Haynes Russell F
Hays Art
Hays Lloyd K
Heckendorn Fred L
Heckendorn Arthur
Hecock Ralph
Heidel Roy J
Heidenrich C A
Heidtke Edwin E
Heimel Mary
Heineke G A
Heitman Howard
Heitman Fred
Heitman Adolph
Helene Beauty Shop
Helland O P
Helland Hotel
Helland H O Mrs
Helland Hans O
Helley Dale
Helley Alden
Helm Walter
Hemming Arthur P
Henriksen Harry Mrs
Henry Clifford
Hensel Lewis
Herman's Off The Highway Cabins
Hetzel O L
Hewitt Harry E
Hiawatha Bar
Hickathier Earl
High School
Hill George B
Hillebrandt J A
Hilliard H S
Hillman Fred
Hillman William H Jr
Hilltop Motel
Hindes Lauren
Hines Ralph M
Hinterberger William
Hinterberger Esther Mrs
Hodge Foster J
Hoesly Elmer
Hogarth's Fountain Motel
Hogenbirk Albert
Holden William
Holden Clifford
Holiday Motel
Hollinshead John S
Holt Carl
Hopper Clifford
Houghton J H Dr
House Agnes Mrs
Howard Joe
Howard's Lake Resort
Howley Dan
Howley James
Howley Elizabeth
Hudzinski Frank
Hudzinski Roman
Huefner Carl A
Hueston William
Huntley Arthur O
Hurley Eugene

I
Indian Baptist Church
Ishnala Beach Supper Club
Iversen Arthur

J
Jacobson Carl
Jacobson Peter
Jacobson Harriette
Jahn Edward
Jahn Commodore
Janata Irvin
Jansen Carl
Jansen Matt
Jantz Ernest
Jantz Leroy
Jensen Harvey
Jensen Robert
Jermier Lois
Jewell Leonard
Jimson Albert
Johnson Robert
Johnson Althea E
Johnson K K
Johnson Theodore
Johnson Louis
Johnson Truck Bodies
Jones Engle
Jones Robert
Jones Lew
Jones Arnold
Joyce M E

K
K & G Restaurant
Kaiser Joe Jr
Kaiser J J & Son
Kaleas Richard
Kaleas Kenneth
Kamin John H
Kaminski Frank
Kaminski Joe
Kaminski Frank S
Kane A M
Kasdorf John
Katz Sam
Kay J Roland
Kazanecki Louis Jr
Kellogg Bros Lumber
Kelly Perry
Kelly Denis G
Kelly John J
Kemp John
Kepple Floyd
Kerwin George W
Kesler Arthur
Kettleson Carl
Keubke Edward
Keubke William J
Keubke Delmar
Kick's Bar
Kilbourn Cooperative Creamery
Kilbourn Public Library
Kilbourn Machine & Repair
Kilbourn Ccoperative Exchange
Kimball Howard
Kimball R J
Kimball Merle E
King Jay
King George
Kingsland Frank
Kingsley Alwyn
Kingsley John
Kinney Nig
Kinney James
Kivlin Jermoe
Kleimenhagen Arthur A
Kleimenhagen & Magoon
Kleta Joseph S
Klicko Bernard
Klicko Charles Jr
Kneubuhler Hans
Kneubuhler AAA Garage
Knippel Marjorie
Knippel Donald
Koberstein Arthur
Koehler Jerry
Koepcke D G
Kozlowski Raymond
Kozlowski Clarence
Kozy's Resort
Kramer James
Kraus John
Krejsa Caroline
Kremer John
Krenz Edwin W
Krey Donald R
Kriegel Max
Krueger Les
Krug John
Kruger L P Mrs
Kuikman Melvin

L
La Mar Cliff Mrs
La Mar Percy
Laabs E S
Laabs Arthur
Lage Henry
Lake Delton Trout Farm
Lake Delton IGA Super

Market
Lake Delton Grade School
Lake Delton Beach Cottage
Lake Delton Corner Restaurant
Lake Delton Cities Service
Lake Delton Beauty Salon
Lake Shore Cottages
Lake Delton Development
Lakeside Cottages
Lambert Katherine
Lambert J H Mrs
Landeck's Auto Court
Landry H J Furniture
Landt Newton
Landt Bryce
Lane Ethel Mrs
Lange Ronald
Langer Lester
Langer Leo
Lapp Harold W
Larkin Ward
Larson's Motel
Last Round Up Tavern
Laundry H J
LaVigne Robert
Lazy M Dude Ranch
Leary Catherine
Lebica John
Lee Chris C
Leege Chris
Leege Ernest
Leege Arthur
Leege Harold
Legion Hall
Leute's Artist Glen Hotel
Lewis L M
Lewis Joseph B
Lewis Addys
Lewis Earl A
Lindloff Albert Pure Oil Station
Lindloff August
Lindloff O A
Lindloff August Cabins/Oil Station
Log Cabin Tavern
Lone Tree Sam
Loofboro Edwin
Loomis Damon
Loomis H W
Lorenzen Howard L
Lorenzen C M Mrs
Louck Lloyd
Lowe Robert D
Lower Dells School
Lower Dells Drive In
Lower Dells Boat Landing
Lucke Richard
Lueck William
Lueck Kenneth
Luettgerodt Henry C
Luke Austin C
Luke Kenneth
Lumby Ralph
Lumby Arnold
Lunde Mary Mrs
Lunde Carlyle
Lundgren Linnea V
Lusby Gerald
Lynch's White Pines Cottage
Lytle Arnold

M

MacGowan Francis Mrs
Mackesey Leo
Mackesey John
Mackey James W
Manges Ray N
Manis J W
Mann Ralph
Maples Motel
Markham W B
Marlow Henry Mrs
Marshall Ruth
Marshall-Wells Store
Marsich Victor
Marslender James
Marston Hazel Mrs
Marston Henry
Marten's Rooms Hotel
Martin Louis
Martin William H
Martiny Pierce Mrs
Martiny Dairy Company
Maschek Ella Mrs
Mason Allen C
Masonic Temple
Mass H H Construction
Massey Dick
Mattei Noel
Mattei's Pure Station
Mau Charles F
Maukstad Palmer B
Mawbey Mary
Max's Garage
Maxfield Marshall
May Milton B
McBoyle John
McBryde Robert
McCarron Joe
McClyman C A
McClyman Garage
McClyman Harold A
McClyman Hardware Co
McCullough William M
McDonald Ida Mrs
McFarland C R
McFarland Hardware
McFarlin Brothers Trucking
McFaul Ira D
McGuinness Mae Mrs
McMahon James E
McManman F P
McNutt Verl F
Meadow Brook Lodge
Meenagh C M
Meltz Merrill E
Merten Elmer E
Mess Louis
Meyer Carl
Michael R D
Mickelsen Hans
Millard Edward H
Miller Joe
Miller William F
Monk's Bar
Monohan Robert
Montanye Mae
Moore Wanda I
Moore Elmer A
Morovek Raymond
Morris Wendland B
Morris Bess Mrs
Morse John J
Morse Clinton
Morse D E
Mortimer W S
Morton Wallace
Mossholder Equipment & Supply
Mueller Ernest C
Mueller Edmund
Mulligan Thomas
Multnomah Manor
Multnomah Lodge
Murray Walter
Murray Robert
Murray K M
Murray Thomas J
Murray Joseph P
Murray Lester
Murray William S
Murray's Texaco Service
Musson H Howard

N

Naber Lawrence
Naber M L
Nadel Leo
Nate Neil
Nauruhn Robert E
Nehring William
Nelson Donald C
Nelson David W
Nelson Ada
Nelson Oscar
Nelson Clarence
Nelson Joe H
Nelson S Robert
Nelson Palmer
Nelson Wm O
Nemitz Robert
Neumeister A E
Nevar Gus
Newell Percey
Newman Edgar
Newport George
Nickel Alfred
Niebuhler Lester K
Niles Grace
Norling Livera Mrs
Normandie Bar
Noyes J M

O

O'Brien L E
O'Connell Roc
O'Connell Mary Mrs
O'Connell John
O'Connor Henry
O'Connor Dennis
O'Neil Mary Miss
O'Neil D T
O'Neil Claude T
O'Neil's Drug Store
Oak Villa Cottages
Oeftger Gerald
Oeftger Gus
Oehlers Herman
Oehlers A H
Oetzman Bertha
Old Newport Resort
Older L W
Olp Frank
Olson Anna E Mrs
Olson Ray E
Olson N P
Olson Ben
Olson Boat Co.
Olson Harry
Olson Gaylord L
Olson Earl
Olson Jack
Olson Grover
Olson's Motor Lodge

P

Padley Donovan
Page Bunnell M
Page Howard
Pagel Donald
Pagel Arthur J
Palmer Otis
Palzer John
Paraszuk Adam
Parkside Cabins
Parkway Motel
Parson's Indian Trading Post
Parsons G D
Patterson C A
Patterson Donald R
Patterson Richard
Pearson Fred
Pech Charles
Peck Ovel
Pennington Paul
Peplin Anthony V
Peters Walter
Peterson Harry
Peterson J H
Peterson Robert
Peterson Walter
Peterson Harry A
Peterson Arthur
Peterson Blanche Mrs
Peterson Bernard A
Peterson Clarence
Peterson Earl
Peterson Earl W
Peterson Effie
Pfister Paul
Phelps Willis
Phillips Keith
Phillips Willard
Pickel George
Pickeral Slough Resort
Pietrzak Mike J
Pike George M
Pine Glen Hotel
Pine Grove Cottages
Pine Dell Trav-O-Tel
Pines Hotel
Pioneer Village
Platt Martin
Platt Marvin
Platt Garage
Platt Clarence
Platt Lewis C
Platt Service Station
Playman William
Playman William
Plumb Ellsworth
Plumb F V
Popp's Beach Resort
Portage-Wyocena Ready Mix
Post Card Shop
Post Office
Powell Otto
Priester Adolph

Q

Quality Food Market
Quick Service Laundry

R

Raab H H Mrs
Rachey Earl
Radlund Harry
Radlund Emil
Rady Frances Mrs
Ragan Maurice
Railway Express Agency
Rainbow Cabins
Ralph's Lazy B Lodge
Ramer Joe
Rand Frank
Rasmussen Chris P
Rau Edward
Ravenswood Hotel
Red Star Oil Service
Red Owl Agency
Reese Oliver W
Rehbein Albert
Reich Edward
Reidelbach James W
Reimers George
Reineke Willis
Reineking Frederick C
Reinhardt Amelia M
Replinger Richard
Rest Haven Resort
Restwood Cabins
Retzlaff Harold C
Retzlaff Gilbert W
Reynolds Emmett C
Reynolds Floyd
Rhinehart Phillip R
Richards A S
Rickon Roger E
Rickon Frank
Riese A T
Rihn Otto Mrs
Riley Spencer W
Riley Walter A
Risley Harold
Riverview Curio Shop
Riverview Work Shop
Riverview Boat Line
Rockoff Louis S
Rockoff Produce & Salvage
Rocky Arbor 21 Auto Courts
Rocky Arbor Shell Service
Rocky Arbor Tavern&Restaurant
Rodwell Mort
Rodwell Everett
Roeker Norman
Roeker Arthur
Roeker's Bakery
Rogers Katherine
Rogge Richard
Rohde August F
Rohrbeck WM F
Roney Harley
Rooney Morris
Rosenthal Jules
Roser H W Plumbing & Heating
Rothwell Ralph S
Rotunda Bar
Roudebush Fay
Rubado Richard
Ruch Charles
Ryan Edmund
Ryan John
Ryan John Mrs
Ryan's Restaurant
Ryczek Edward

S

Sand Bar
Sandy Beach Cottages
Sarrington H L Mrs
Sarrington Grace Mrs
Sarrington Milling Co

Sarrington Ralph
Sauger F A
Saunders Don W
Schabow D A
Schaitel L G
Schank Vincent
Schanke Kenneth
Schaumburg Herman
Schleef Walter
Schmehl Frank
Schmidt Florence
Schmidt John
Schmidt Leo
Schoenfeid Walter F P
Schoeninger Frank Mrs
Schoeninger William J
Schofield Hotel
Schroeder Charles
Schultz & Weiss Contractors
Schultz Norman
Schultz Kenneth P
Schultz W J Mrs
Schultz Harold A
Schultz Warren R
Schultz Frank H
Schultz Brothers
Schultz W J & Son
Schultz Arthur
Schutz Gustav E
Schwark Edward J
Schweda Edward
Schwedisky Stephan
Scotch Pine Roller Rink
Scott Virgil
Scott John C
Scott Harry L
Scott Don
Seger Joseph P Mrs
Seger Alois
Seger Raymond
Seger's Grocery
Selander R C Rev
Selchow Alfred
Selchow Max
Selchow Marvin
Semrow Edward
Shady Grove Cabins
Shea Edward J
Sheaffer J B Rev
Shepard Henry L
Sherer Clifford
Sherod C O
Shoemaker Corrine
Shumway Oliver A
Sickenberger Carl
Simons C C
Simons Glen
Slocum Louis J
Slocum Carl
Slocum James W
Slocum Carl M Jr
Slumber Hill Cabins
Sly Philip
Smale William B
Small Lester
Smatlak Frank J
Smith Lou
Smith Edward W
Smith Gerald A
Smith Arthur
Smith N M Mrs
Smith Reynold
Smith Ray
Sneen M A
Snider Charles W
Snider Charles Insurance
Snider H D
Sobojinski Ervin
Sobojinski John
Socony Vacuum Oil
Soeidner J P
Soma Elmer
Soma's Capt Resort & Boat Dock
Sommers Paul
Sorensen E T Dr
Sorenson Edwin J
Southern Wis Breeders Coop
Spatz Peter
Spaude Henry Jr
Sperbeck Mayme
Spiegel Howard L
Sprague Fred
Spring Hill Motor Court
Spychalla Edward
Squires Betty Mrs
Squires Evergreen Retreat
Squires Harold Mrs
Stand Rock Resort
Stand Rock
Stand Rock Souvenir Shop
Standard Service Station
Stanton Madge L
Stanton Walter W
Stanton Edward Motel
Stanton Thomas
Stanton's Sweet Shop
Stanton's Service Station
Starr Howard E
Stearns School
Stebbins Paul E
Stecky Dominic
Stecky Walter
Steele Deane Block Works
Steele A P
Steele Elmer
Steffeter Alphonse
Stein Adolph
Stein Howard E
Steiner Louis
Steinhorst Fred
Steinweg Walter
Stephan James
Stevens Alfred C
Stickfort William
Stomner George
Stomner O H
Stomner Charles
Stomner's IGA Supermarket
Storandt E F
Storandt Richard
Storandt Harold
Storandt Wm A
Stowers Herbert E
Stowers Fred
Stowers Roland
Stowers Clara M Mrs
Stozek Stanley
Stroede Jean
Strofer L P Rev
Strong Thomas
Stuelke Gordon A
Stuelke's Drug Store
Sturdevant Clyde
Sugar Bowl Retreat
Sullivan J R
Sullivan Edward
Sullivan James
Sullivan Dan
Sunderland Mort
Sunset Lodge
Sutherland Motel Court
Sutter Ethyin Mrs
Svejcar Frank U
Swallow's Nest
Swansby Michael
Swedish Coffee Shop & Motel
Swets WA Painting & Decorating
Sylvia's Coffee Shop

T

Tallmadge Roger J
Tallsman Process
Tangney John
Taylor Everett E
Teeple S U
Texas Co
Theisen's Millwork
Thiede Walter Mrs
Thomas Albert C
Thomas Edmund
Thomas Stuart
Thomas Charles F
Thomas Faye Mrs
Thompson Frank
Thompson B J Dr
Thompson Lillian Mrs
Thompson Harry
Thompson Lafe Mrs
Thompson Herman
Thompson Stewart
Thompson's Flowers
Thompson's Ranch House
Thurber Harry
Tice H Jay Mrs
Tilton Betty
Timlin Margaret Mrs
Timlin Sisters Cafe
Timm Ernest Jr
Timm R F
Timme Herman Mrs
Timme Otto
Timme Bros Inc.
Timme's Ranch
Titus Lillian Mrs
Tobin Rose
Tobler John L
Tofson Maurice
Tofson Oliver
Tofson Otto Tavern
Tofson Otto
Tofson Henry
Tofson Merton W
Tofson H M & Son Insurance
Tollaksen Russell B
Tollaksen B E
Tollaksen W C Jim
Tolleth Gertrude
Tolleth Fred
Tolleth Hale R
Totem Pole Curio Shop
Townley Rena M
Traxler Perry L
Triangle Bar Tavern
Triangle Fixture Co
Trinity Lutheran Church
Trumble John A
Trumble Mark
Trumbull A G
Tucker James
Tucker Lloyd
Tufts Oliver B
Tufts Woodland Motel

U

Ufnowski Edward
United Farm Agency
Updike Robert
Uphoff M K
Uphoff's Rotunda Rest. & Motel
Uren Delos
Utter Emma H Mrs
Utter Clarence R

V

Van Ells Clara Mrs
Van Schoyck Wayne
Van Winter Grace Mrs
Van Schoyck Edna
Van Houghton Wm
Van Zile G E
Van Alstine Fred
Van Dyke S P Insurance Agency
Van Wie Charles
Van Wie Carl Mrs
Van Deuren H L
Van Alstine Harry
Van Wie Jack
Van Volkenburg Ray
Van Alstine Louis
Van Matre Joseph E
Villa Motel & Restaurant
Village Inn Tavern
Vodvarka Frank J
Voelcker Carl K
Vogt B P
Vogt Harold
Voights Louis
Volkey Vincent
Volkey Paul
Volkey Charles E

W

Wagner Pat
Wagner O C Mrs
Wagner Hotel
Walker Orval
Walker E L
Walker Emma J Mrs
Walker Ray
Walmar Lodge
Walters Theodore
Waltman Paul A
Wampler A B Mrs
Wampler Frank A
Wampler Harlan
Ward Charles
Wareham Ellen
Washburn Walter
Waterman Vinnie
Waterman Andrew
Waterman Ray
Weaver E A Rev
Webb Eugene
Weber John
Weber Fred H Rev
Weber Roland
Weber Dorothy
Weber James
Wegert William H
Wegner Ewald
Weidling Stanley
Weidner John A
Weiss R M
Welch Ted
Wenkman Henry
Wenkman Henry J
Wenkman James
Wenkman William G
Wenkman Joseph J
Western Union Telegraph
Weyh Floyd
Weyh Orville
Whaley Robert K
Wharf Bar
Wharry Bert Taxi
What Not Shop
Wheeler F M
Wheeler's Red Tavern
Whipp Garland
White Bert
White Eagle John H
White House Hotel
White Howard Rev
White Construction Co
White S R
White Eagle Sanborn
Whiting Ralph W
Wick Margaret
Wickus George
Wies John
Wiese Eula
Wigwam Gift Shop
Willard George E
Williams James R Mrs
Wilms Henry
Wilson Arthur
Wimann Walter
Wimann Fred G
Wimmer J W
Winn Janet Mrs
Winnebago Drive In Theatre
Winnes Gordon
Wisconsin Power & Light
Wisconsin Deer Park
Wisconsin Dells Realty
Wisconsin Conservation Dept.
Wisconsin Dells Ice Cream
Wisconsin Dells Amphiblan Lines
Wisconsin Dells Chamber of Commerce
Witt Charles
Wittig Blanche
Woerz Frank
Wolcott M J
Wolfram A E Cabins
Wolfram Ben
Woodard Grace V
Woodruff Anna
Wormet Dennis
Worofka Charles
Wright Vinette
Wrzesinski Norman
Wrzesinski Frank & Sons
Wrzesinski Ted

Z

Zahler Clifford
Zeitz Clarence
Zelner Leonard
Zeman J C
Zentner John
Ziegenhagen Anna
Ziegenhagen Arthur
Ziegler Harold L
Ziegler Loren
Zimmer Frank W
Zimmerlee William
Zink's Pure Oil Truck Stop
Zinke Fred
Zinke Robert
Zinke Gordon
Zinke George
Zouski Joseph

Dells Country Chronology

300-1000 AD
• Native people of the Woodland Culture erect hundreds of earthern effigies and mounds in the Dells area, including the eagle, bear and panther at the Kingsley Bend site.

1634
• Jean Nicolet reaches Wisconsin from Montreal.

1673
• Joliet & Marquette cross the Fox-Wisconsin Portage.

1827
• Chief Red Bird of the Ho-Chunk surrenders into custody of U.S. Army and averts further bloodshed in the "Winnebago War."

1828
• First commercial lumber is cut on the Wisconsin River.

1829
• Lieutenant Jefferson Davis cuts white pine timber on the Wisconsin and floats it through the Dells to build Fort Winnebago at Portage.

1832
• The Black Hawk War begins and ends; most records indicate that after the final battle, Chief Black Hawk is captured by Ho-Chunk Indians One-Eyed Decorah and Chaeter near the Big Dalles in Juneau County.
• Daniel Whitney builds the first sawmill on the Upper Wisconsin at Pointe Basse.

John Kingston's Adventure

One of the first accounts of the Dells area was penned by young John T. Kingston who had "heard of a very extensive forest of pine timber" on the Lemonweir River. In December 1837, Kingston and Sam Pilkington set out to find the timber and make their fortune.

"We packed our Indian pony and started out from Racine," Kingston wrote. "Our outfit consisted of a Mackinaw blanket and butcher knife, an ax, a box of matches, and provisions for a week [and] a small fly tent."

They reached Fort Winnebago where they stopped at a tavern kept by an Italian immigrant named "Ubeldine, who had an Irish woman for a wife." After spending the night they set off up the Pinery Road past the Indian camp where Jared Walsworth would soon live, "then struck west across the head of Dell Prairie and reached the Wisconsin River at the foot of Big Dell." There the explorers found "the ice running in the river and the crossing impracticable."

They returned to Ubeldine's and waited a week "until the river closed." Before they left, "Mother Ubeldine handed us a bottle of Medicine with the remark: 'if you get frost-bited, try this; it came from Auld Ireland'."

Thus fortified, Kingston and Pilkington set out but "at the edge of [Dell] prairie, and facing a cold west wind, we soon felt unmistakable evidence of the frosty atmosphere, so much so that we concluded to halt and try the remedy in the bottle; but here found a difficulty– how to apply it. After mature consultation and reflection, we concluded to try an inward application and I must say the result was equal to our highest expectations." The "Irish" carried the men over the prairie and across the ice-bound river at "McEwen's Rock" [Louis Bluff]. On their fourth day of travel they reached the mouth of the Lemonweir and with much difficulty "followed up the river, on the ice, broke through two or three times, went ashore, built fires and dried out clothes,then continued on."

They traveled as far as present-day New Lisbon then turned back after "learning that our extensive pine forest was a myth."

A few years later, Kingston returned to the area and found his pine forest on the banks of the Yellow River. He logged much of it and helped turn Necedah into a busy sawmill town. As a leading owner of lumber rafts, Kingston was a bitter opponent of the first Kilbourn dam and, in the 1860s, became a part owner of it in order to tear it out.

1833
• Daniel Whitney and John Metcalf float the first raft of rough-milled pine lumber through the Dells.

1835
• The *Frontier* becomes the first steamboat to come up the Wisconsin to the Dells.

1837
• The United States signs a treaty with Ho-Chunk (Winnebago) Indians that cedes the last of their land in Wisconsin. Yellow Thunder leads the "non-abiding" faction of the tribe that refuses to accept the treaty. Nonetheless, land on the west side of the Wisconsin is soon open for settlement.
• John T. Kingston and Sam Pilkington pass through the Dells on their way up to the Lemonweir River.

1838
• Robert Allen builds a cabin on Black Hawk Island to become the first white settler in the Dells area.
• Jared Walsworth marries a Menominee woman and settles near Big Spring.

1840
• The Wisconsin legislature creates Sauk County.
• Federal government attempts to remove the Ho-Chunk to reservations across the Mississippi.

1841
• Wisconsin legislature charters the first state road to the Dells; it runs north through Sauk County from Honey Creek.
• Robert Allen completes construction of the Dell House and operates a river ferry.

1843
• Jared Pardee, Big Spring, becomes the first white child born in Adams County.
• H.H. Bennett is born.

1844
• The *Maid of Iowa* becomes the first steamboat to navigate through the Dells.

An artist's rendition of the "dogtrot" style double log cabin Jared Walsworth built in the Menominee village near Big Spring, in 1837. (Courtesy, NTG)

1845

• Joe Kendrick builds a log cabin at the mouth of Dell Creek.

1846

• Wisconsin legislature organizes Columbia County.

1847

• Federal surveyor J. G. Norwood canoes through the Dells on his way south from Lake Superior.

• Louis Dupless arrives at the bluff that will bear his name and stakes out a "squatters" claim to the land.

• First claims are made in New Buffalo, later to become the Town of Delton.

• Ephram Hecocks settles at Davis Corners.

1848

• Menominee Indians cede their land in central Wisconsin, opening the east bank of the Wisconsin for white settlement.

• State of Wisconsin admitted to the Union.

• Wisconsin legislature creates Adams County.

• Elizabeth Walklin Dupless joins her husband Louis and begins to make a home at Louis Bluff.

• The Stafford school meets in a private home.

• John Meade, a local Daniel Boone, lives in the Dells area.

• James Edson is the first settler in Plainville.

1849

• Amey Lake is built near Briggsville by D.W. Eighme.

• A Claim Protection Society is formed in Briggsville.

• Uri Morse locates in New Haven.

• Hannah Hurlburt, mother-in-law of George Tyler Blood, "squats" on the future Blood homestead.

1850

• Schuyler Gates builds the first bridge across the Wisconsin at the Narrows.

• The steamer *Enterprise* passes through the Dells and travels up to Pointe Basse.

• The Wisconsin legislature grants Joseph Bailey and John Marshall a charter to build a bridge across the Wisconsin at the mouth of Dell Creek.

• Country schools open throughout area.

• Amphlius Chamberlain and Alexander Briggs, along with the Slowey and McDonald families, settle in Briggsville.

• Neenah Creek is dammed to form Mason Lake.

• Joseph Bailey and Jonathan Bowman plat their village, Newport, on the east bank of the Wisconsin River.

• The first post office is established in Delton, Jared Fox is postmaster.

• The first school is established in Delton, on the north side of Adams Street.

• Alexander Vosler builds the Delton House, the first hotel in Delton.

1851

• Norwegian immigrants organize the Newport Evangelical Lutheran Church.

• Fox & Topping build the first dam and mill on Dell Creek.

• Alexander Briggs brings his family to Briggsville.

1852

• Increase A. Lapham, "Wisconsin's first scientest," visits the Dells area and climbs to the top of Louis Bluff.

• Joseph Kendrick and John Steele each file plats for villages named Dell Creek on the west side of the river.

• Joseph Bailey builds a warehouse on the Wisconsin for Jonathan Bowman and, hoping to attract steamboats, Bowman christens it Newport.

• Iron works and foundries go up in Delton.

• Jonathan Butterfield dies in Briggsville.

1853

• Wisconsin legislature grants Kendrick and Steele a charter to build a dam across the Wisconsin at the mouth of Dell Creek.

• Louis and Elizabeth Dupless purchase 183 acres of land, including Louis Bluff, at $1.25 per acre.

• The Delton Academy opens.

• Delton & Newport grow in anticipation of the railroad.

• A flouring mill opens in Briggsville.

• George Tyler Blood acquires Town of Lyndon property.

1854

• John Marshall and Edward Norris plat a third village adjacent to the two Dell Creeks on the west side of the river, and call it Newport.

• Bowman and Bailey plat a village on the eastside of the river and also call it Newport.

• Alexander Briggs plats Briggsville.

• The William Murphy store operates in Briggsville. Murphy also serves as postmaster.

1855

• The Wisconsin River Hydraulic Company is organized and begins work on the first dam to cross the river at the Dells.

• Plainville builds its first school.

• Peter Peterson operates a wagon shop in Briggsville.

• Abraham Vanderpoel builds Dawn Manor in Newport.

• Alanson Holly, who will publish the first area newspaper, arrives in what will soon become Kilbourn City.

• The Brew family farm is established on the Stand Rock Road.

1856

• Leroy Gates advertizes to row sightseers through the Dells.

• Salesmen for the LaCrosse and Milwaukee Railroad sell mortgage bonds on farm land in the Dells area in order to finance construction.

• Kilbourn is platted and named. Miss Julia Seville is hired to teach school there for $10.00 a month. 14 students attend.

• The first school in Kilbourn opens.

• Catholics purchase land in order to build a church in Briggsville.

• Nettie Munger is the first white child born in Kilbourn and dies 8 months later.

• The Mary Lyon Female Seminary is founded in Newport at a cost of approximately $3500.

• The first dam is built in Kilbourn City.

• The Leute family buys a farm at Artist's Glen.

A toast by the secretary of the Hydraulic Company, December 15, 1857:

"The Pioneers of Kilbourn. May their shadows never be less nor their dish bottom side up when good luck reigns."

1857

• The railroad is completed to La Crosse, and the first railroad bridge is completed at Kilbourn City.

• Bypassed by the railroad and the dam builders, Newport begins to die.

• Then known as Dells Lodge #78, the Masonic Lodge is instituted in Newport.

• The LaCrosse and Milwaukee Railroad tracks reach Kilbourn City and cross the first railroad bridge over the river.

• Methodists offer church services in area.

• Young Morton Holly falls from a cliff in Kilbourn City and becomes the first death reported there.

• P.G. Stroud and Luther Noyes open a law office in Kilbourn City.

• Financial depression bankrupts all Wisconsin railroads; the LaCrosse and Milwaukee defaults on its bonds.

• The Atwood family comes to "Bonnie Oaks" in Briggsville. The Gray family also arrives from Corinth, New York.

• The first post office opens in Kilbourn City.

1858

• The Hydraulic Company hires Joseph Bailey to complete the Wisconsin River dam.

• Land is leased for the Twin Valley School.

• The Stafford School is built in New Haven.

• A sugar mill and carding mill are added in Briggsville.

• Baptist and Episcopal church services are held.

1859

• The first Dells dam is completed; the first lumber raft to pass over the dam, piloted by Kilbourn's Pat O'Hare, is smashed to pieces and three river drivers die.

• The Wisconsin legislature votes to remove the Dells dam, but river drivers have already dismantled it.

• King Thompson sells the first hops harvest in the area.

• Amelia Dutcher is found dead on Blue Mound.

• The Catholic Church is erected in Kilbourn.

• William Steele builds the Newport Hotel.

1860

• The Briggsville Library Association offers 9 books.

1861

• The Civil War begins. Company E, 12th Wisconsin Infantry Division is formed in Lake Delton.

• The Dell Prairie school district is united with Kilbourn.

• Smith, Grundy & Hindes arrive in Briggsville.

• The Leute Brothers Brewery opens in Kilbourn City.

1862

• Jonathan Bowman leaves Newport for Kilbourn City, where he opens a bank and a law office.

1863

• Company E takes part in the Battle of Vicksburg.

• The first Presbyterian Church is dedicated.

1864

• Joseph Bailey engineers the famous Red River dam and saves the Union fleet. Later that year he is promoted to Brigadier General and receives a citation from Congress.

1865

• The Civil War ends.

• Aided by a tax on whiskey that increases demand for beer, and an insect pest on New York's crop, the hops boom begins in the Dells area.

• Jonathan Bowman charters the Columbia Manufacturing Company to rebuild the Dells dam.

• H.H. Bennett founds his photography studio.

• The Sarrington Mill is built on Dell Creek.

• The Seminary (The Institute) moves from Point Bluff to Kilbourn.

1866

• Floodwaters wash away the Gates bridge over the Wisconsin at the Narrows.

• Kilbourn City's railroad bridge is destroyed by fire.

• Fire destroys eleven stores between Oak and Superior Street.

• A Masonic Temple is built in Delton.

1867

• The price of hops peaks at 70¢ a pound.

• Naturalist John Muir visits the Dells.

• More Norwegian immigrants settle in Briggsville.

• Joseph Bailey is murdered by bushwackers in western Missouri.

• Land is purchased for the Kilbourn high school and the first students occupy the new building.

MURDER!

$500 REWARD!

Schuyler S. Gates, of this village, was murdered this morning, between five and six o'clock, in Sauk county, about a mile from this village. The following is a description of the persons who are supposed to have committed the murder:

HUGH SMITH—5 feet 10 inches high; light brown hair; slight moustache colored black; full face; narrow forehead; light blue eyes; thick set; broad shoulders; large neck; light complexion; wears about an 8 to 9 boot, fine; new black velvet cap; light grey coat; dark pants; white shirt, no collar; shaved smooth except moustache; had an open face silver watch, with coarse silver link chain.

PERRY RICHARDS:—About 5 feet 10 or 11 inches high; well proportioned; light brown hair, and moustache, apparently colored; high forehead; light grey eyes; dark complexion; slightly sunken cheeks; dark brown coat and pants, and black wool hat.

A REWARD WILL BE PAID

for the apprehension of both or either of them.

Kilbourn City, Sept. 13, 1869. J. B. SANDERSON, Marshal.

The above reward will be paid for the apprehension of the murderers.

N. STEWART, Sheriff of Sauk County.

BARABOO, September 15th, 1869.

1868

• The hops boom goes bust as prices fall to 5¢ a pound.

• Fire destroys 8 buildings between Oak and Elm Street, as well as the Kilbourn Institute.

1869

• Schuyler Gates is robbed and murdered, his wife Mary Ann raped; the accused criminal, Pat Wildrick, and his attorney, William D. Spain, are lynched by a mob in Portage.

• The first Kilbourn City ordinances regulate taverns, traveling shows, and the running loose of cattle, sheep, and swine.

• G.H. Crandall is born.

1870

• The Stafford School is destroyed by fire.

• German settlers arrive in Briggsville.

• 40 raftsman drown in the Wisconsin River.

• The Washington Temperance Society and the Odd Fellows Lodge are organized.

1871

• The nesting of 136 million passenger pigeons is perhaps the greatest single nesting on record of any bird on earth. 1.3 million nestling pigeons are killed, salted, packed in barrels and shipped to eastern markets from Kilbourn.

1872

• The Kilbourn City Flouring Mill begins operation.

1873

• The first steam-powered tour boats arrive: Captain Abe Wood brings a side-wheeled scow named the *Modocawanda* downriver from Point Bluff and the first *Dell Queen* arrives by rail from Madison; both carry visitors on "jolly excursion trips through the Dells."

• The Universalist Society begins offering church services in Briggsville.

• J. Huntington builds the forerunner of Timme's Mill in Delton.

1874

• The Kilbourn City Flouring Mill is destroyed by fire.

• The steamers *Champion* and the second *Dell Queen* expand the tour boat fleet.

• Federal government makes final and unsuccessful attempt to remove the Ho-Chunk from Wisconsin.

• The *Modocowanda* and the *Dell Queen* now travel through the Lower Dells.

• Chief Yellow Thunder Dies.

• Kilbourn City drills its first artesian well.

1875

• The first walkway is built through Witches Gulch.

1876

• The *Modocowanda* moves to the Fox River and another *Dell Queen* is built.

• The German Lutheran Church is dedicated in Kilbourn.

• Briggsville organizes the "Odd Fellows" with 5 charter members.

• The Dells dam is burnt by raftsmen.

1877

• Pine Grove holds its first school meeting.

• The Village of Kilbourn City maintains a free ferry.

• Joseph Champeny buys a half interest in the Briggs Mill.

• The *Champion* travels the Lower Dells.

1878

• The *Dell Queen* burns and is rebuilt.

• The *Alexander Mitchell* is built in Kilbourn.

1879

• The *Champion* moves to Mirror Lake.

• The Methodist Episcopal Church is built in Briggsville.

1880

• Henry Sarrington purchases the grist mill which was erected by Fox & Topping in 1841.

1881

• Norwegian settlers, including the Cornelius Peterson family, continue to arrive.

Dr. George Jenkins, (second from left) about to embark on a river excursion, c. 1885. Jenkins was the first druggist/physician to practice in the villages of Newport, Delton and Kilbourn. (Courtesy, H. H. Bennett Studio Foundation)

1882
• Delton has its own newspaper.
• The Grand Army of the Republic (G.A.R) charters the John Gillespie Post #50. They have 45 members by December.
• Joseph Champeny buys out the Briggs Mill.

1883
• Edward Munger rebuilds the Dells dam and flour mill.
• Lars Hanson arrives in Briggsville.
• The first frame school building is erected at Fern Dell.
• The steamer *Eolah* travels the Dells.
• A "Broom Brigade" of 20 high school girls is organized.

1884
• The *Alexander Mitchell* is abandoned and sunk in the Dells.
• The G.A.R. is organized in Briggsville, with its first commander Robert Hume and meetings held in Dyer's hall.

1886
• The Kilbourn library is organized.
• H.H. Bennett perfects his instantaneous shutter and photographs a series entitled "The Raftsmen's Life".
• Standards for high school graduation are established.
• The Briggsville G.A.R. Hall is built by Peter Peterson and Thomas Barlow, with money raised at Pork and Bean dances.

1887
• Six pupils become the first high school graduates at Kilbourn school.
• The steamer *Germania* is in the Dells.

1888
• The *New Dell Queen* is built.
• H.H. Bennett photographs his son Ashley leaping to Stand Rock.

1889
• Floodwaters wash out Edward Munger's dam at the Dells.
• Robert Allen, the Dells' first settler, dies at the Juneau county poor farm.

1890
• The last raft floats down the Wisconsin..
• H.H. Bennett opens Kilbourn's first souvenir shop.
• A "Kilbourn Machine" is proposed that will furnish electric lights for village streets. Six are lights at 1200 candlepower and 30 incandescant lights at 32 candle power.

1891
• The *Eolah* is rebuilt and re-named *Escort*. It only operates for 1 year.
• John E. and T.F. Godding, owners of the Dells Resort Company, purchase property and boats.
• The Kilbourn Fire Department is organized.
• The first Bennett Guide Books for boats are published.
• The Briggsville Creamery opens.

1892
• The Briggsville dam goes out and takes the mill.
• The first caucus in 10 years is held at the G.A.R. Hall for the purpose of nominating candidates for village offices.

1893
• The Timme Brothers buy the mill on Dell Creek.
• William Stanton builds a hotel near the depot in Kilbourn City.

1894
• Twin Valley School is destroyed by a tornado.

1895
• William Wilmot rebuilds the Dells dam and W. Munger restores the mill to grind Roller Gem, Gold Brand and Ruby flour.
• Louis Dupless and Jonathan Bowman die.

1896
• A new railroad bridge is built at the Dells.

1897
• Robert M. LaFollette begins his Progressive movement with a speech at Fern Dell.
• The river washes out Wilmot's Dells dam.
• The steamer *Apollo* is built in Kilbourn.
• Kilbourn City sets the bicycle speed limit at 10 m.p.h. and a bell must be rung when approaching intersections.
• J.E. Jones installs telephone & telegraph lines in the village.

The uniforms read "Wm. Hartig Brewer" with a "K" for Kilbourn in between, c. 1890. (standing, l-r) Jake Heimel, Carl Soeldner, Jim Ryan, Andrew Gavinski, unidentified, Fred Soeldner, unidentified (sitting, l-r) Butch Mitchell, Tom Gorman, Freddie Bachman, Norm Magoon, Lawrence Naber.

1898

• The total property tax bill in Kilbourn totals $3500.00.

1899

• The *Germania* is rebuilt and renamed *Eleanor*. It operates only briefly.

• Vandals destroy the Dell House by fire.

• $9000.00 is borrowed to establish a water system in Kilbourn City.

1900

• The first automobile arrives in Kilbourn.

• Confederate spy Belle Boyd dies at the Hile House Hotel.

1901

• W.J. Bell and Frank Conway receive approval to operate telephone lines at Kilbourn City. Prices, for the next 25 years, are set at $12 per year for residents and $1.50 per month for businesses.

1902

• The new post office is located at 211 Broadway.

1903

• Dr. Taylor resigns as health officer and is replaced by Dr. A.A. Duclos. The salary is set at $25.00 per year.

• St. Cecelia's Catholic Church is dedicated.

1904

• Steam heat is added to the Kilbourn school.

• A committee is appointed which will study the cost of an electric plant in Kilbourn.

• A cattle & horse fair is held on Oak Street.

• The "Beautiful America" Club complains about the condition of village ravines, especially the one west of Broadway.

• The Village Utility, with a coal fired, 125 h.p. boiler, will provide electricity at the rate of $.12 per 1000 watts.

1905

• The Southern Wisconsin Power Company begins work on a hydroelectric dam at the Dells.

• Mr. Phillip Spooner proposes building a hydroelectric dam for which he will pay the village $5000.00.

• The total village tax assessment is $4,533.33.

• A committee is formed to study the feasibility of an electric train from Devils Lake to the Dells.

1906

• The Kilbourn high school is accredited by the University of Wisconsin.

• To control alchohol abuse, the Village Board of Trustees is authorized to post residents on a "Black List", which means that taverns can't sell them liqour.

• Henry Van Alstine is Superintendent of Water & Light, with a salary of $110.00 per month. He furnishes all extra labor and if neglected, repairs systems at his own expense.

1907

• A concrete road is built on the River Road Bridge.

• A hospital opens at 211 1/2 Broadway.

1908

• The Village Board votes to publish its minutes in the Kilbourn Weekly.

Motorists (above) about to cross the Kilbourn bridge, c. 1910. (Courtesy, H.H. Bennett Studio Foundation). The Edwin Heilman road construction crew (below) at the Washburn gravel pit on Hwy A.

President William H. Taft campaigning for re-election at the Kilbourn depot, 1912.

• A new brick surface was approved for Broadway.
• H.H. Bennett dies.

1909
• The Dells hydroelectric dam is completed; water levels on the Upper Dells rise 17 feet.
• A grade school is built at the high school site.
• Official village meetings are held in a building on the east side of Oak Street.
• Driving ordinances are set: Autos for hire, 10 m.p.h.; Autos used at night must have lights, brakes and a bell or horn.
• Bill Groothoff falls from Stand Rock.
• The Rood's Glen Resort, formerly the Wayside Farm, is purchased by Adolph Priester.

1910
• A vote to raise the cost of a liquor license to $500.00 loses 135 to 180.

1911
• Southern Wisconsin Power Company offers to sell power to the village and gaurantees to reduce costs 50%.
• The village name is changed from Kilbourn City to Kilbourn.
• The Board of Review values the Dells power plant at $975,000.
• The Mirror Gazette urges road improvement to encourage farmers convenience and trade. *"Kilbourn is making a mistake in building all its business too much on the scenery we have. Will it pay?"*

1912
• In Briggsville, a hotel and meeting hall are erected where the Pheasant Inn now stands.
• Fred Leissman builds a drinking fountain for horses on Oak Street. Water will be furnished by the village.
• The "Wisconsin Dells Band" performs during the summer for $15.00 per concert. A.W. Luettgerodt is band manager.
• The Womens Club petitions the village board for a curfew; children under age 16 to be off the streets by 8:00 p.m. in the winter and 9:00 p.m. in the summer.
• A new library is erected at a cost of $15,000, $6,000 of which is donated by Andrew Carnegie.
• An editorial protests the use of city ravines for dumps, and urges a park commission to develop them.
• The village is asked to build a concrete stairway at the Eddy Street dock for the convenience of tourists. The cost is $200.

1914
• 15 toilet systems are added at the Kilbourn school. Also added are manual training and domestic science.
• Lydia Ely, prominent Milwaukee artist and Kilbourn beautification projects activist, dies.

1915
• All of the village east of Elm Street is declared residential. No factories, machine shops or garages can be built without the permission of taxpayers within two blocks of the site.
• Newport School District #1 is united with Kilbourn.
• Kilbourn village purchases a Pulmotor for lifesaving.
• The Dingee Company purchases the Kilbourn Pickle Plant and contracts over 70 acres.

1916
• An addition is added at the grade school where 51% percent of the students pay rural tuition. Davis Corners also builds new school.
• Henry Loomis founds the Birchcliff Hotel.
• William Federbusch, Sr. purchases a cottage at the Narrows.

1917
• The United States enters World War I.
• Kilbourn develops a street numbering system.
• The John Gillespie post asks the Kilbourn Village Board to purchase flags for veterans gravesites.

Gerald Baggot's rural mail truck mired down in high water, c. 1920.

Wisconsin Dells began as a post office under the name of Kilbourn City in 1857, changed to Kilbourn in 1895, and finally changed to Wisconsin Dells in 1931.

Lake Delton began as a post office under the name of Lauretta in 1850, changed to Delton in 1851, to Mirror Lake in 1926, and finally changed to Lake Delton in 1931.

Village Presidents and Mayors 1869-Present

Village Presidents: 1869, George Smith; 1872, G.J. Hansen; 1873, I.W. York; 1874, C.A. Noyes; 1886, A. Chamberlain; 1890, L. Kleimenhagen; 1897, Frank Snider; 1899 , F.R. Snider; 1904, J.F. Dixon; 1906, L. Kleimenhagen; 1908, Salmon Brown; 1909, A.D. Finegan; 1911, L. Kleimenhagen; 1918, F.A. Field; 1921, Ben Olson; 1923, A.W. Luettgerodt; 1925, A.W. Luettgerodt.

Mayors: 1929, Frank Marshall; 1932, Tom Howley; 1934, Ben Olson; 1938, Tom Howley; 1949, Henry Field; 1951, Henry Field; 1953, Grover Belton; 1955, Tom Howley; 1957, Arnold Borcher; 1959, Merlin Gray; 1961, Ernest Jantz; 1963, Adolph (Monk) Heineke; 1965, Roy Kelly; 1968, Roy Kelly; 1973, Art Hemming; 1975, Bernard Olson; 1979, Dick Schauf; 1983, Jack Waterman; 1985, Tom Christ, Jr.; 1987, Tom Christ, Jr.; 1989, Dick Schauf; 1991, Dick Schauff; 1993, Craig Casey.

Rural Free Delivery of Mail

Written in 1919

The first post office in Adams County was kept by early settler Jasper Stowell, who lived in a house which stood across the road from Harrison Mylrea, just this side of Briggsville.

He was appointed postmaster in 1849. Once a week, a stage line made a two day trip from Portage to Stevens Point. Lumbermen took this same route north, and many drunked men made the road exciting.

When the war of the rebellion broke out, the first news of it for many setlers was when they came to Kilbourn and found the whole union ablaze with patriotism and soldiers drilling on the streets there.

In 1896, rural free delivery of mail was established as an experiment. The convenience to farmers was so great that the country merchants and small post offices who first opposed the plan soon found opposition futile.

Now nearly every farmer in the state can have the news of the world delivered to their door in a daily paper.

This year there are practically five rural routes out of Kilbourn: The Friendship stage serves the families along the river road and by the way of Easton to Friendship; the Baraboo stage delivers mail along the road to Baraboo; Rural Route #1, with the Gillespies as carries, goes across the river, out to the old Red Tavern in Lyndon township, then south through Dellona to the Stein school house, thence to Meyer's Corners and back to Kilbourn. The entire length of the route is 23 miles and serves 478 persons. It runs east from Kilbourn to H.B. Metcalf's, by the M.B. Smith farm, Tibbit's Mill at Big Spring, D. Coty, R.B. Crothers, Hyatt Bidwell, the Cady farm on Dell Prairie, by Dell Prairie Corners, to Alhorn's and back to Kilbourn. Route #3 is 25 miles long with 486 people to supply and Theo Anderson as substitute. This route runs to Jerome Baggot's in Newport, then passes Stearns school house #1, Lewiston Station, Colburn's, H. Mylkrea, Tolef Olson, Ole Ake, the Norwegian church, Nelson's place and back to Kilbourn.

These carriers have wagons made especially for this service, arranged with shelves, drawers, boxes and more. They sell stamps, take money orders, register letters and are in every sense, traveling post offices.

Still another route starts from Delton, runs by the site of old Newport and across Webster's Prairie. This is also supplied with mail from the Kilbourn Post Office.

The south side of the 300 Block of Broadway (above) with the Kilbourn Garage and Bowman bank, c. 1920. The Garage is advertising Ford Roadsters for $390 and Touring Cars for $440. (Courtesy, H. H. Bennett Studio Foundation).

• Dell Creek floods and takes out Timme's and Sarrington's Mills.
• King Henry is shot by a guard on the bridge.
• The Council pays 1/3 of film production costs for a new Dells advertisement. The remainder is paid by the Chicago, Milwaukee & St. Paul Railroad and News Publishing Company of Milwaukee.
• Mrs. H.H. Bennett puts a new front on the studio.
• In one day, the Witches Gulch stand grosses $25.00 from sales of homemade sand bottles at 25¢ each.

1918
• Captain Glen Parsons begins running the steamer *Apollo* to Louis Bluff for "sunset view" cruises.
• Kilbourn declares that soliciting business on the street is illegal.
• Herb Campbell begins his long career on the river, guiding a boat at age 9.

1919
• Prohibition begins.
• Kilbourn passes a $15,000 bond issue to provide a sanitary sewer system.
• Kilbourn loses its first football game, to New Lisbon, by a score of 186 • 0.

Jake Heimel and his saloon customers prior to Prohibition.

The Honeymoon Inn at the Kriegel Farm Resort on Highway 13, c. 1925

1920

• Women vote in a presidential election for the first time.

• William J. Newman of Chicago undertakes his dream of making Lake Delton an exclusive community "up where the pines begin."

• Arson is suspected when the hotel on Blue Mound burns.

• Village receives a new electric schedule from N.A. Landt of the Southern Wisconsin Power Company. Charges are 1 1/4¢ per kilowatt, with a minimum bill of $300 per month.

1921

• The Crystal Theatre presents Norma Tallmadge in *"The Woman Who Gives,"*; prices are $.20 and $.30.

• Kilbourn streets are seldom free from autos limping into town with the help of horses.

1922

• Washington's Birthday ice storm destroys trees and power lines.

• Railroad Freight Depot is destroyed by fire.

• A petition is submitted to forbid the unlawful racing of automobiles on N. Superior St. and Broadway. The village also purchases an American LaFrance combination chemical and hose car, Type E, mounted on a one ton Ford chassis, for the fire department.

• The *Winnebago* is built.

• The Mission Theatre is built.

1923

• The Tourist Boat Company,owned by Harry Radlund, G. Gray, and Fred Dixon, petitions to use part of Eddy Street for a boat dock and ticket office.

• Consideration is given to a proposal to pave Washington Avenue with concrete. Broadway will be widened at the same time.

1924

• In Briggsville, the Catholic Church burns and is rebuilt.

• With Art Koberstein and Stanley Gavinski as proprieters, K & G Restaurant opens at 208 Broadway Street.

1925

• Glen Parsons and George H. Crandall use the steamer *Winnebago* to carry boat loads of visitors to view Indian dancers at Stand Rock.

• A concrete dam is built at Mirror Lake.

• The Kilbourn Village Census is 1,446. The Village becomes a 4th class city.

• Kilbourn Co-op Creamery asks the village for a building site.

• The Larks Hotel is torn down by George Crandall.

• Kremer and Fuechek take over D. McManman's dry goods store.

• G.H. Crandall plants thousands of pine seedlings.

• The fire department asks for a fire alarm to replace the fire bell which did not give a "proper alarm."

1926

• The City develops plans for a new city hall, fire station, comfort room, city ofices, and other apartments.

• The Indian pow wow put on by the Dells Boat Company draws good crowds every night. Approximately 75 indians make up the cast.

• A record crowd of some 15,000 people are in Kilbourn for the Fourth of July. Hotel and rooming housekeepers turn many away.

• Chris Lee purchases Meadowbrook Farm 1/2 mile north of Kilbourn.

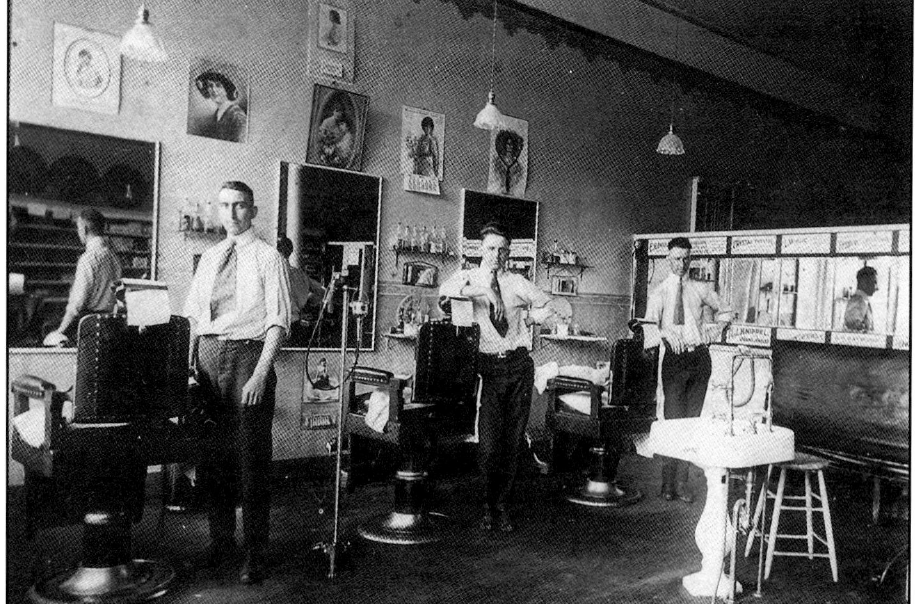

Art Koberstein, Stanley Gavinski and Peter Gavinski at the Gavinski Barber Shop, c. 1925.

The parade for the Firemen's Tournament held in Kilbourn in 1931 was led by a female contingent from Baraboo.

An air show at the Lake Delton airport, 1931. The airplane at right is the same model Ryan machine that Charles Lindbergh flew over the Atlantic in 1927. On its fuselage is painted, "Lake Delton Recreation Company" and "W. J. Newman."

THE DAY THE NAME CHANGED

The official decision to change the name of Kilbourn was made at a city council meeting on Wednesday, April 1, 1931. Presented with a petition signed by three fourths of the voters of the city, the five council members present unanimously passed the rather brief ordinance providing that "the name of said city of Kilbourn City be and the same is changed to Wisconsin Dells." Acting quickly, official publication of the ordinance was made on the front page of the *Events* the next day, Thursday, April 2.

That week's paper was still titled Kilbourn Weekly Events, and several of the local advertisers listed their address as "Kilbourn." By the April 9 issue, however, changes were being made. The title of the paper was Wisconsin Dells Events, and advertisers started listing themselves as being in Wisconsin Dells (Kilbourn).

As far as the U.S. Post Office was concerned, however, the change didn't become effective until June 1, 1931. That date was quite a relief to the local residents who had promoted the change. Some feared it might take two or three years for the post office to recognize the new name.

The post office was already coping with the name change before their official target date, however. The May 28 *Events* noted: "Quite a bit of the mail has been addressed to Wisconsin Dells since the name of the city was changed, and the first few pieces did some wandering before they arrived at their destination, but it did not take postal clerks long to discover there had been a change, and there was no trouble after that."

A recreation guide advertising resorts in "Kilbourn" and published in 1930 was incorrect the following year.

Why was there such an interest in changing the name of the community in that depression year of 1931? Perhaps the reasons can best be understood by quoting from an article in the March 5th *Events*, reporting on a discussion at a Kiwanis Club meeting.

"Those in favor of the change admit that it is a mercenary proposition with them," the newspaper said. "They think that the name Wisconsin Dells would explain better to a person who had never heard of the place what there is here. They claim that it would be an advertising feature. That every time the word Wisconsin Dells were used that it would tell the person who heard it just what there is here and possibly be the means of interesting him to come here and see the Dells.

"This, of course, is not the first time that has been said about changing the name of the city. It is a matter that has been discussed for a number of years past, and many opinions, both for and against, have been expressed on the subject."

The article went on to list 14 advantages of the change as compiled by a local resident who has been immediately connected with the tourist business in Kilbourn.

Among them: *Our name "Wisconsin Dells" would be on all highway and road maps. Tourists would see it and come direct to us. The name Kilbourn does not mean anything to a stranger desiring to come to "Wisconsin Dells" only that he has to go to Kilbourn because "Wisconsin Dells" is at Kilbourn.

*We must capitalize on the $15,000 to $30,000 that is spent each year advertising "Wisconsin Dells" in newspapers, magazines, folders and signs. Why allow ourselves to confuse the tourist when we spend that much money each year?

*We know that last year was not as good as usual. In fact we have to go back several years to find one as poor. This year associations and businesses in the tourist business figure that we will not have as good a year as last. Therefore we need all the publicity we can get for this year.

Not everyone was in favor of the change, however. At that Kiwanis meeting, Mayor Frank Marshall spoke against the change, admitting it was a matter of sentiment on his part. And on the front page of the March 26 Events, nearly a column was filled with a letter signed by "Citizens of Kilbourn" opposing the change. "If we had never been known as a resort, the case for changing our name might be stronger," the letter said, "but we have behind us nearly 60 years of tourist travel, with many thousands of visitors, all of whom know us as Kilbourn. We also have many thousands of dollars already invested in advertising under the present name. Besides all of this past effort, who knows how much printed matter for this year's campaign would have to be scrapped if the name were changed?

Yet, the backing for Wisconsin Dells as the official city name apparently was strong, as indicated by the 75 per cent that signed the petition and the quick action by the City Council to make the name official.

1927

• W.J. Nelson builds the Dell View Hotel.

• The city purchases a Pirsch special fire truck for $6100.

• On Oak Street, a new city hall is built by R.C. Evvin of Minneapolis for $18,870. William Schultz does plumbing and heating work, and K.K. Johnson provides electric service for $388.95.

• Dance Hall Pavilion licenses are granted to the Olson and Riverview Pavillions.

• Property owners in the business district petition for a "White Way" lighting system to be paid for by the abutting property owners. The request is approved.

1929

• G.H. Crandall buys out Glenn Parsons' interest in the Dells Boat Company.

• Developed by W.J. Newman and Ralph Hines, McBoyles Airport opens.

• Talking movies play at the Mission, and later at the Dells Theatre on Sunday and Monday nights. Admission is $.15 and $.25.

• M.H. Stuelke buys the building at the corner of Superior & Broadway from Bertha Wales for his new drug store.

• The Memorial Day Parade is an impressive sight. Three Civil War Veterans ride in the parade, Henry Marston, George Hoisington and Ed Coon. They are the last survivors of the G.A.R.

1930

• The City builds a second water tower on Institute Hill for $10,000.

• Captain Parsons opens his Indian show at Indian Hills on Highway 13.

• Kilbourn grants the railroad the franchise to operate a bus line carrying passengers to Mauston, New Lisbon, Hustler, Clifton, Tomah and Black River Falls.

1931

• Effective April 2, Kilbourn is renamed Wisconsin Dells.

• The high school and grade school structures are combined and a new gymnasium is built.

• The first steamer *Apollo* is scuttled in the Dells.

• The Purple Grackle pavilion is destroyed by fire, sustaining losses of $25,000.

• Olsons build a filling station on the Corner of River Road and Broadway

• New sound equipment is installed in the Mission Theatre

1932

• Wisconsin Dells purchases the Briggsville Utility for $10,000.

Joe Kaiser, Sr., steered the sled and Jack Hall prepared to lower the saw to cut ice on the Wisconsin. Kaiser was the Kilbourn "ice man" for many years.

• The Ringling Hotel is destroyed by fire.

• The Dells Park Trading Post opens.

• Jack Olson, age 12, starts driving a boat with John Jones and Hooky Radandt.

• *Captain Jinks of the Horse Marines*" is performed in the new Dells High School auditorium. The cast of characters includes three ballerinas.

1933

• Liquor is legal again but women cannot hold a tavern license in Wisconsin Dells.

• With members of the Tuesday Club as the cast, amateur movie photographer Miriam Bennett finishes her film, "The Study in Reds."

• The last surviving member of the G.A.R., Henry Marston, dies.

• Mrs. E. Smukal dies, leaving behind 5 sons, one only 2 weeks old.

1934

• An unsuccessful movement begins to create a national park at the Dells.

• Spring drought destroys crops and windstorms create "dust bowl" conditions on area farms.

• Miss Jennie Bowman dies and Wisconsin Dells is a large benefactor. Included is land for a City park as well as a Home for Women.

1935

• The first Hiawatha high speed train roars through the Dells.

The Milwaukee Road's high speed Hiawatha--one of the most powerful steam locomotives ever built--first roared through the Dells in 1935. (Courtesy, H. H. Bennett Studio Foundation).

The Lake Delton Fish House was a popular bar and grill in the late 1930s.

1936
• The State record temperature of 114 degrees is recorded on July 13 in Wisconsin Dells.
• Main Street, Wisconsin Dells, is re-named Bowman Road.
• Land is purchased by City for the Conservation Department to build a fire district sub-station.
• Electric power lines are extended to Big Spring and Lewiston.
• The City requests U.S. grant to build a sewage disposal plant.
• Wisconsin Dells purchases the Beaver Building for $6000.00.

1937
• A freight train wrecks west of the bridge.
• Mrs. Effa Arntz installs an air conditioner in her restaurant.
• The local newspaper urges a municipal swimming pool; the only places to swim are the river, Multnomah swimmimg pool and Silver Beach on Lake Delton.

1938
• The city accepts the Jenkins Park property.
• Wisconsin River water levels rise to an all time high.
• The Upham daughters, Mrs. Carl Henry Davis and Mrs. Caroline Hughes, donate Wawbeek, a 380 acre estate, to the Easter Seal Society to use as a camp.
• George Crandall dies.

1939
• First "Homecoming" celebration is held at Stafford school.
• Kilbourn passes ordinance limiting the number of taverns in the city to 1 tavern per 500 citizens.
• A new sewage disposal plant will be operated by Edward Fitzgerald.
• Hugh Byington sets a course record at Berry's Cold Water Canyon golf course with a six under par 27.

1941
• Pearl Harbor is bombed. The United States enters World War II.
• The Dell View Hotel is sold to Mrs. Kelly.
• Twin Valley annexes Townline and Point Bluff Schools.
• The Harold B. Larkin American Legion Post at Wisconsin Dells accepts sponsorship of the Stand Rock Indian Ceremonial for 1942.
• Fred Stowers and Dana Champlin work six hour shifts counting the 17,572 cars which cross the bridge at Kilbourn on July 4th.
• Planning is underway for Camp Upham Woods on Black Hawk Island, where youth and adults will explore and enjoy nature.

1942
• Badger Ordnance Works is constructed on the Sauk Prairie.
• Dawn Manor is sold.
• Wisconsin Dells passes a zoning ordinance.
• The *New Yorker* magazine reports that the Governor of Wisconsin has made Chief Yellow Thunder an honorary paleface and a colonel.

1943
• County schools begin to consolidate; Moreland joins Stearns.
• "The town is pretty well taken care of by the military police on weekends, for soldier boys from Camp Williams are apt to get a little over-exuberant on nights off."
• The War Production Board complains about the labor shortage and demands that everyone not in essential services either get a war job or join the service.

Waiting in line to eat breakfast at Buckley's Restaurant in 1942. Workers from the Badger Ordnance Works helped bring an end to the Depression at Wisconsin Dells.

Wisconsin Dells High School Football Team, 1945. (front, l-r) Carl Decker, Henry Field, Jack Gray, Ken Meyer, Harold Kaiser, Jerry Baggot, Al Olson, Jerry Fitzgerald, Norm Fedderly. (2nd row, l-r) Jerry Reise, Clinton Fish, Dave Decker, Norb Szymanoski, Bud Gussel, Coach Frank Siewert, Eddy Loofboro, Lyle Cole, Ben Olson, Tom O'Connell, Fred Lowe. (3rd row, l-r) Hans Kneubuhler, Tom Russ, Phil Martiny, Wayne Loofboro, Erv Sobojinski, Dave Baggot, Jerry Hamm, Dan Colby, Ken Martiny. (4th row, l-r) Tommy Tucker, Sidney Dorow, Duke Weber, Jack Wagner, Jim Dixon, Gene Fish, Harvey Christensen, Curt Washburn, Don Donnelly, Frank Russell, Alvin Miner, Howard Rockoff.

Athletics in Kilbourn High School

Written by Ruffina Neumeister for the 1928 Kilbourn High School Yearbook.

The question of athletics involves three points of view held by three different classes of people, as I have recently observed. The first is composed of two groups--(a) disinterested grown-ups who say, "Well, if the school board will pay for the supplies and the young folks wish to take things into their own hands, why, let them; only please don't bother us;" and (b) kindly old ladies and gentlemen who never did such things in their day, but who cast a benevolent eye upon the rising generation of future presidents (and presidents' wives) and who are perfectly willing to concede that times have changed.

The second class consists mainly of fathers with a 60 cent an hour income and six or a half dozen children for whom to pay doctor bills and buy tennis shoes, bats, balls, racquets, chest protectors, and baseball suits. They're not going to buy balls for someone else's kids to cart off and lose, if they can possibly get out of it.

The third and most important class is made up of the student body and this also has two divisions:

(a) The floating mass of spineless jellyfish who drift lifelessly on to destruction without knowing, and possibly without caring, what they are headed for until someone comes along, jerks them into an upright position and tells them to realize what they are doing to themselves.

(b) A consolidated, concentrated, enterprising group, all life and energy, always on the alert for some new way to drive the teachers to distraction. These qualities are a fine thing if carefully handled, but wherever there is misdirected energy there is sure to be an explosion sooner or later and someone is likely to get hurt.

The need for athletics is urgent. Give a child a book and say to him: "Be good and some day you may be president;" ten to one if he is a real boy he will answer you:

"Why, there is only one man in 93,000,000 who is lucky enough for that, and I was born on Friday, the thirteenth of June."

But give him a baseball and bat and tell him that some day he'll be Home Run King for the Chicago Cubs, and ninety-nine times out of a hundred he'll say:

"Sure thing! Give me half a chance and watch this bird develop his wings."

Of course a country like ours cannot exist with brawn and no brains, but how much better is an educated athlete than the president who dies two weeks after his inauguration because of overeating and under-exercising.

The parent is criminally negligent who expects his son to study all day in an ill-ventilated school house and then, at an hour when he ought to be playing hard and breathing good fresh air, lets him kill time in a pool half full of tobacco smoke because there is practically nothing else for him to do. As for the man with the half dozen children and the 60 cent an hour income--well, in any case, the price of six pairs of tennis shoes fades into nothingness when compared to the price of six cases of T.B.

As a student in Kilbourn High School, I ask the citizens of Kilbourn to give this matter a thought before it is too late.

The Lone Tree family line up for a tubercular screening, c. 1955. (l-r) Sam Lone Tree, Mrs.Lone Tree, Kathleen, Rawleigh, Gary, Spencer, Sandra, Janice, Dianne, Jacob, Jonathon, Bernice and Gregory Lone Tree. They are joined by Sauk County public health nurses Dorothy Deitrick and Elizabeth Terry. (Courtesy, H. H. Bennett Studio Foundation).

1944
• Pleasant View School joins Stafford School.
• The American Legion proposes a memorial park complete with swimming pool, athletic field, tennis courts, and parking areas.

1945
• World War II is over.
• Leon Smith of the Dells serves as back-up weaponer for the atomic bomb dropped over Nagasaki in August. Weaponers do the final arming over the target.
• Davis Corners holds its first "homecoming".
• Wisconsin Dells becomes owner of Spring Hill cemetery.
• Owen Gromme wins National Duck Stamp award.
• A. Finnegan retires from a 45 year career with the Milwaukee Road, most of which he spent as an agent at the depot.

1946
• Leon D. Smith is a weaponer on the B • 29, "*Dave's Dream.*" He arms an atomic bomb for a test at Bikini.
• "*When the Moon is a Silver Canoe,*" by Don Saunders is published.
• The Finch Hotel is purchased from Mort Sunderland by Mr. and Mrs. Art Buckley.
• Total cost of the new Hwy 16 project, nearing completion, is estimated at $1 million.

1947
• The first dog jumps Stand Rock.
• James Leary is granted permission to operate the Wisconsin Central Bus Line between Reedsburg and Wisconsin Dells.
• George Isenberg of Baraboo, with his bid of $27,472, is granted the swimming pool construction contract.

1948
• The Union Free High School District is formed.
• Reportedly, 90% of the Wisconsin Dells population serves the tourist trade.
• The Crandall family offers their Dells property to the United States to use for a national park or monument.

1949
• The *Winnebago* is converted to *Clipper Winnebago.*
• The Wisconsin Dells swimming pool is dedicated.

1950
• The Commissioner of Public Land loans $30,000 in order to build a grade school addition in Wisconsin Dells.
• Newport and Dell Prairie rejoin Wisconsin Dells as School District #3.
• The swallows due to arrive on May 2 arrive 10 days late and a chilly summer ensues.
• The Bennett Studio opens its first museum at 213 Broadway.

1951

• Plainville builds a new school.
• Bud Gussel forms Holiday Wholesale.
• Police and fire calls are routed through Ray Booth's Standard Station at a cost of $100.00 per month.
• Director of Public Works and Building Inspector positions are created in Wisconsin Dells.
• Trinity Lutheran Church occupies its new church.
• Parking meters are purchased for the city.

1953
• Tommy Bartlett begins giving water shows in Lake Delton.
• The right-of-way is furnished so a two lane bridge can be built over the Wisconsin River.
• A motion is passed licensing Dr. R.O. Ebert to operate 12 "Ducks" in the city.
• John Dixon goes to the Rose Bowl as a member of the Wisconsin Team.
• Under the leadership of Mayor Grover Belton, the city council passes a resolution providing the right-of-way for a new highway bridge over the river, an extension of Broadway.

1954
• Ralph and Phyllis Crandall Connor, and Howard and Lois Crandall Musson, transfer the Crandall properties on the river to the Wisconsin Alumni Research Foundation.
• The Village of Delton is incorporated with Bill Miller, president.
• Fern Dell builds a new two-room school house.
• The Snider fountain is moved to Library grounds.

1955
• Hans Helland is City Attorney and Chester Harrison is Director of Public Works.
• Storybook Land opens.
• The new Union Free High School is dedicated on Race Street.

1956
• The Sportsman's Club improves Mirror Lake Parks.
• The new highway bridge at the Dells is opened.
• Storybook Land sees first full season of operation.
• Pipe Dyer's Winnebago Indian Village on Stand Rock Road is dedicated.
• The average cost of a 3 day vacation in the Dells, for a family of four, is $127.55.
• 1,210,000 people visit Wisconsin Dells.
• Governor Walter Kohler is in the Dells to officially open the new highway bridge, reveiw the boat fleet, and unveil the plaque at Witches Gulch.

1957
• Newton Landt is president of the City Council.
• The Ramsey addition is added to the city.
• The new post office is located at 713 Superior Street.
• Timme's Mill on Mirror Lake is burned.
• Steak and Stein is built by Bob and Lois Field.
• The new Chamber of Commerce building opens on Broadway and Oak with Les Albertson, Director.
• The new American Legion building is located at 609 Wisconsin Avenue.

1958
• Trinity Lutheran Church opens a parochial school.
• The Chambers of Commerce of Delton and Wisconsin Dells merge.
• Don Sartell holds the first baton-twirling camp at Chula Vista.
• In "Let's Keep Billboards off our New Highways," *Readers Digest*, reports that "... On an 18 mile section of U.S. 12 between Middleton and Sauk City, in the treasured Dells Country, there are 144 signs southbound, 162 signs northbound. On another stretch of only 2.7 miles from Lake Delton to Wisconsin Dells, there are 122 signs southbound and 99 northbound."
• The Dells Theatre is closed.
• Santa Claus Town opens on Highway 12.
• Fort Dells is under construction.
• Riverview opens "Giftland".

1959
• Big Spring builds a new school.
• Chief Samuel Lone Tree, on behalf of the performers at the Ceremonial and the Winnebago Nation, charges "peonage."
• The Chamber of Commerce reports 1,300,000 visitors.
• The national Wally Byam Caravan Club camps for one week at Chula Vista Farms.
• The *Wisconsin State Journal* protests the number of signs in the Dells area. Wisconsin Dells tries to eradicate some.
• Fort Dells opens.

The Reverend William Genzler at the laying of the cornerstone of Bethany Lutheran, 1949. (Courtesy, H. H. Bennett Studio Foundation).

The Wisconsin Dells Area School Board, 1955. (l-r) Superintendent Robert Fenske, Emmett Reynolds, Louis Rockoff, Merton Tofson, Roc O'Connell; (across table, l-r) Tom Crist, Jr., Archie Crothers, Norris Anderson. (Courtesy, H. H. Bennett Studio Foundation).

1960

• School consolidation is complete.

• Lester Clark, Chief of Police, contracts to supply two ambulances at $950 per year.

• Jim Hieneke goes to the Rose Bowl as a member of the University of Wisconsin team.

• The Chamber of Commerce reports 21 main attractions, 478 restaurants, and 210 hotels, motels and rooming houses. The Chamber budget is $90,000.

• Hulburt Creek floods Fort Dells.

• The Northwest Trading Post offers helicopter rides over the Dells and Delton.

• Jack Olson bows out of the race for governor.

• Roger and Bernadine Tallmadge open the Winnebago Indian Museum on Highway 13.

• The Jaycees hold their first raft race.

• The Paul Bunyan restaurant opens.

• Minirama opens at 112 Broadway.

• A fleet reveiw is held at High Rock.

1961

• An estimated 1.2 million tourists visit the Dells.

• Biblical Gardens opens.

• August Derleth is in the Dells to sign copies of "*The Ghost of Blackhawk Island.*"

• With Frank Wiegel as coach, the Dells Land Judging Team wins first place in the North Central Regional Competition and Fifth place in the International contest.

• Water is very high and tour boats must travel through the Old River bed.

• The Jaycees hold their first raft race. Baraboo wins.

1962

• Jack Olson is elected Lieutenant Govenor of Wisconsin, with Warren Knowles as Governor.

• Interstate 90 is routed through Towns of Delton and Lyndon.

• Hanson's Department Store re-opens following a disastrous fire.

• R.D. Potee is panning gold from dirt hauled in from Montana.

1963

• St. Cecelia builds a school for 8 grades.

• Robert & Dorothy Wick's Oaklawn subdivision is annexed into city.

• The City purchases Kellogg lumber property for parking.

• Wisconsin Power & Light obtains the franchise to furnish natural gas in the city.

• Despite strong protest, the City votes to flouridate water.

• The city begins fighting Dutch Elm Disease.

• In New York, H.H. Bennett's work is featured in "The Photographer and the American Landscape", a three month showing at the Museum of Modern Art.

1964

• The Wisconsin Dells Jaycettes are chartered.

• Businesswomen on Broadway spearhead improvements along the street which include planting trees.

• Mike Uphoff gets a skywalk over Hwy 12 for his motel.

• A 46 mile section of I 90-94 from Rocky Arbor State Park to Tomah is opened.

• Charles Van Wie closes his Ghost Town and Wisconsin Dells Trading Post.

• Chief Daybreak, Jim Smoke, retires after 35 years with the Stand Rock Indian Ceremonial.

1965

• H.H. Bennett's photos and equipment are exhibited at the State Historical Society.

• The Sisters of Charity plan a million dollar, multi • unit "Girls Town" for a 60 acre site in the Lower Dells.

1966

• Jack Olson is re-elected Lieutenant Governor of Wisconsin.

• The Wisconsin Dells Fire Department is 75 years old.

• The City Council gives $300 to the Reverend J.W. Davies Memorial fund.

• McBoyles Airport, one of the oldest in the state, closes.

• Mr. & Mrs. Gerald Baggot sell the Dells Pioneer Village Museum to Fort Dells.

• Jack Olson urges the development of a state department of tourism.

• The Totem Tower at Fort Dells is completed.

• Indian Heights, a low rent Indian housing project, is launched on land purchased by the Dells Boat Company and the American Legion on Stand Rock Road.

• Plans for winterizing Camp Upham Woods are underway.

• Leute's Resort, in the family for 110 years, is the oldest business in the Upper Dells.

1967

• Kenneth Weber becomes Director of Public Works.

• The Sauk County area of the city receives sewer and water service.

1968

• A public employee union is established in Wisconsin Dells.

• The alley in Block 41 was closed to expedite the building of the Colonial Apartments by Dells Housing, Inc., Thomas Crist Sr., President.

• Robert Hillman replaces Ken Schanke as Wisconsin Dells Clerk.

• Delton, Town of Delton, Baraboo & Wisconsin Dells establish joint airport.

• Lieutenant Governor Jack Olson is re-elected for a third term.

• Bids totalling $418, 127 for the construction of a new senior citizens home on the corner of Wisconsin Avenue and Oak St. were let Monday.

• Plans are underway for the first annual Wo-Zah-Wa festival.

1969

• City authorizes a 2% room tax.

1970

• N.E. Isaacson & Associates, in anticipation of lake development, purchases 1330 acres near Hulbert Creek.

• Helen Raab dies.

• The high speed train *Hiawatha* makes its last run through the Dells.

• Construction of ski runs and Chalet is underway at Christmas Mountain.

1971

• The Chamber of Commerce receives 75% of room tax revenues, and the City of Wisconsin Dells, the other 25%.

• Snowmobile routes are established through the City.

• The City refuses to take action on the Illinois Avenue bridge issue.

1972

• The *Apollo 2* is built and operates sporadically.

• The Modern Development Company of Madison receives a permit to build the Village Glen Apartment Complex for low to moderate income elderly.

• The City Council agrees to proceed with the dam on Hulburt Creek, despite DNR claims that it is a trout stream.

1973

• St. Cecelia's School closes.

• Vacationland Cable is given permission to operate in Wisconsin Dells for 15 years.

• The police department joins the Teamsters Union.

1974

• City annexes an 80 acre landfill site in Newport.

Nationally-acclaimed artist and Briggsville resident, Owen Gromme.

• Council authorizes 36 ambulance trips per year to Robert Gavinski.

• Hotel Crandall and Multnomah Manor burn, losing everything.

• Captain Soma's boat line offers to pay $10,000 toward abatement of the Illinois Avenue bridge.

1975

• Lake Delton holds its first Balloon rally.

The Bernadine and Roger Tallmadge family at the original Winnebago Public Indian Museum, c. 1960

Lida Dorow, Marge Ennis, Dick Ennis and Francis Bannen at a Rotary dinner, c. 1970.

1976
• A 138 acre property north of the Holiday Inn is annexed into the city.
• Williamson's Dell View Hotel is sold to Lake Delton businessmen.

1977
• The Wisconsin Dells and Lake Delton Sewage Commission applies for a federal grant for a sewage disposal plant.
• Ralph Hines dies.

1978
• A 24,000 square foot parcel of Veterans Memorial Park, to be used for a post office, is sold for $70,000.00.

1979
• Mayor Dick Schauf takes steps to establish a T.I.F. District.
• Many road improvements are made in preparation for construction of the new Holiday Inn.
• The City Council votes to renovate the "stable" at Bowman Park for use as a senior center.

1980
• The Alpha Corporation receives a permit to build a Perkins restaurant and a 120 unit motel in the T.I.F. District.
• City borrows $1,040,000.00 to build a new city hall and subsidize other city projects.

At a 1975 quilt raffle, (l-r) Paula Hofmann, Harriett Gissal, Shirley Olson, and American Field Service student Lisa Reyes draw the name of the winner.

1981
• A step 2 grant is authorized for a sewage disposal plant.
• New post office opens at 310 Minnesota.

1982
• The City approves the issuance of $1.5 million in revenue bonds to finance its share of the sewage disposal project.

1983
• Marshall Knutson is hired to reassess the city for a fee of $25,300.
• A resolution is passed allowing purchase of land for an industrial park.

1983
• "Some people think the new Tidal Wave pool at Family Land is better than the ocean: no salt water, no undertow, and no sand to wash off your feet."
• The Wisconsin Winnebago Business Community opens a new high stakes bingo facility 4 miles south of Lake Delton.

1984
• Sewage disposal operation guidelines are established.

1985
• Complete reconstruction of Minnesota Avenue is authorized.
• Traffic lights are requested on East Broadway, at the intersection of Highways 16, 13, & 23.
• The American Legion pays another $6,000 to the city. They contribute a total of $18,000 for the purchase of a rescue truck.

1986
• The City council sells the Newport Landfill site for $600 per acre or $48,000. Storandt property on East Broadway is purchased for $40,000, to be used for an industrial park. This 55 acre site along with 10 more Storandt acres came into the city.
• The Travelers Motel is ready for razing.
• The Rotary Club pays $3,000 toward the purchase of city playground equipment.
• Mayor Crist appoints Frank Schoeninger acting Chief of Police.
• The Mirror Lake bridge on Ishnala Road is opened.

1987
• Entire community is shocked by disappearance and murder of women in Lyndon and Dell Prairie.
• An Industrial Park Marketing Committee is appointed; called the Wisconsin Dells

Economic Development Committee.
• City sells 2 acres on the intersection of Hwy's 16,13 & 23 for $60,000, where the Dells Clinic is to be built.
• Council approves $53,000 in repairs on the River Road bridge.

1988
• The City approves its 20% share of the Broadway Bridge project.
• Mike Horkan is hired as city engineer and director of public works.
• A recycling ordinance is passed.
• The City borrows $907,000 as its share of the industrial park development project which will include a new well and tower. The U.S. government contributes $520,000.
• For the first time in its 39 year history, the Wisconsin Dells Visitor and Convention Bureau budget tops $1 million dollars.
• The boys basketball team wins the South Central Conference Championship for the fourth straight year.
• Char Walch Davies is the new librarian at the Kilbourn Public Library, which is celebrating its 75th year.
• The Dells Clinic moves into its new Broadway location.
• 400 firefighters and volunteers battle the fire which destroys nearly 2,000 acres north of Wisconsin Dells.

1989
• A new ambulance is purchased for $60,813.
• The Visitors Bureau boasts of 63 Attractions, 70 restaurants, and 141 motels and campgrounds.

1990
• Work is underway on the new $5.8 million grade school.
• Delton township takes over Marshall Hall.
• A River & Bay Committee is formed to manage waterways, shorelines, docks, boat ramps, and parking facilities.
• The City's share of the Broadway Bridge project is $489,000. Sauk and Columbia Counties are asked to share the cost. Sauk declines.
• A 5% room tax is passed. The Visitors Bureau will claim 4 1/2% and the city 1/2%. The Visitors Bureau agrees to contribute $50,000 to the Broadway Bridge project.
• Valley View Apartments opens on Broadway Road.
• The newly remodeled Lake Delton Elementary School holds an open house.
• The Rotary Club finances new baseball and softball fields and a hockey rink.
• Wisconsin Dells Greyhound Park opens as the first greyhound track in Wisconsin.
• A ground-breaking ceremony is held for the new K-8 school in Spring Hill.

1991
• The Dells Country Historical Society begins work on a community history book.
• Lake Delton gets a new municipal building.
• Wisconsin Dells accepts full responsibility for maintenance and operation of the railroad depot.

1992
• Two more lanes have been added to the 1956 Kilbourn Bridge and are dedicated by Mayor Schauf and Governor Tommy Thompson.

1994
• Jason Maniecki goes to the Rose Bowl for the University of Wisconsin Team.
• The old Kilbourn Grade School is demolished.

Long time Wisconsin Dells Santa Claus David Nelson and friends, c. 1980

1995
• Dells Country Historical Society publishes its history book.

Wisconsin Dells appeared in a nationally syndicated comic strip in October, 1991. (Reprinted with special permission of North America Syndicate).

Mary Worth

Index of Families

Families

Eugene Charles and Emma Menges Amann

Eugene C. Amann was born at Lansing, Iowa on August 23, 1879. He married Emma Helen, born October 15, 1876, on May 14, 1902 in Prairie du Chien, her birthplace.

They had five children: Meta, Gretchen, Eugenia, Charles and Paul; surviving are Eugenia, living in San Diego, California; and Paul living in Eau Claire, Wisconsin.

At 16, as a clerk and handyman at the former Bank of Prairie du Chein, he developed an interest in banking. Prior to coming to Wisconsin Dells, he had become a well known and respected banker in the Prairie du Chien area.

Following the serious banking crises of the early 1930s, he accepted a position of executive vice-president of the Farmers and Merchants State Bank, now known as the Bank of Wisconsin Dells. In 1944, the bank consolidated with the former Kilbourn State Bank, and E.C. was elected president and director.

In 1949, he was inducted into the Wisconsin Bankers Association "50 Year Club." He served as president of the Columbia County Bankers Association, as well as on various committees.

He was an active member of the Kiwanis Club, serving as president and committee member. He was also an active supporter of the local Chamber of Commerce. In 1954, after 55 years in banking, he retired at the age of 75.

He and Emma were members of St. Cecelia's Catholic Church. Eugene died on January 21, 1959 and Emma the following April 9.

Theodore Anderson

Theodore Anderson was born on August 16, 1878 to Anders Anderson and Anne Jensen Apland, both of whom were born in Norway.

Anders was a sailor in his youth and later settled on a farm in Newport. He bought his first forty acres in 1854 and later added eighty more. The farm was 7 1/2 miles east of Wisconsin Dells on Ingelbretson Road.

Theodore was born on the farm and spent his entire life there. In the late 1920s he added an additional 33 acres to the property.

Theodore married Marie (Molly) Peterson (1884-1940), the daughter of Ole and Anne Halverson Peterson. They had six sons: Alvin, Lester, Gordon, and triplets Robert, Raymond and Russel. Gordon farmed at the home place from 1946 to 1972 when he retired. The farm was sold after being in the family for 118 years.

Theodore was a life long member of the Newport Lutheran Church. He died on August 21, 1954.

The Armson Family

Olaves (Lavy) Andrias Armson, was born March 9, 1860 in Newport Township and married Mary Ann Schellkopf of Oxford on December 14, 1887.

Olaves was the fifth of seven children born to Ole and Mary Armson. Ole immigrated from Sannidol, Norway, in 1845, and Mary from Skien, Norway, in 1849. They lived in Newport Township until about 1870, and then moved to section 26, Adams County, a 70 acre farm at the west end of Lake Mason.

Engelbert, the eldest, was blinded at age 21 when cleaning a shotgun and was sent to a school for the blind in Janesville. After returning home Engelbert opened a small candy and tobacco store where the New Haven Town Hall stands today. Hendrick August (Henry) married and bought property just west of Big Spring.

The four girls, Lene Marie, Aase Marline, Amale Kirstine, & Marle Karolien were all married and left to make their own homes. Lene Marie was the first white girl born in Newport Township. Harlan Armson (grandson of Lavy), son of Merle & Neita, has the cradle in which Lene Marie was rocked.

Lavy, the oldest able-bodied son, took over the farm. Lavy and Mary had 7 children: Pearl, September 20, 1889; Elmer, December 30, 1890; Merle, March 10, 1893; Ruby, February 10, 1896; Andrew, November 16 1899, (Andrew died in infancy October 4, 1900); Clarence, March 4, 1903; and Alfred, November 16, 1905.

Elmer married Evelyn Learmonth on December 26, 1919, and Merle married Evelyn's sister, Nieta, on July 1, 1920. Elmer bought and farmed property near his home farm, on what now is State Highway 23. Evelyn taught school for many years. They had a still-born daughter, Betty, in 1923 and a son, Duane, in 1925. Merle and Neita stayed at the home farm and raised 6 children. They operated Armson Resort, which offered cabin and boat rentals. Cabin fees were $7.00 per week for a small one and $14.00 per week for a 2-bedroom, with a boat and bedding furnished. In 1945 the cabins were sold and removed.

Lavy and Mary had moved to other property in Big Spring in 1920. After they died their property was left to Alfred; earlier a piece of the property was given to Clarence and his wife, Oline Jacobson, where they built their home and raised two sons, Ralph and Graham. Clarence and Oline had married in 1930 and lived in Big Spring where they operated several businesses; a milk route, a store, and a Ford Tractor Sales and Repair Shop. Oline now lives in Wisconsin Dells.

Alfred, the youngest, never married. After working all over the country, he lived in Beloit and worked for Fairbanks Morse. He died there in 1963.

Lavy and Mary also had 2 daughters, Pearl and Ruby. Pearl married and had 3 children with her first husband, Adolph Kiel Olsen: Leona Mae, Adolph Robert, and Irvin Edward Carl. Pearl's second husband, Fred McQuarters was in the Army and the two of them traveled extensively. Ruby married Fred Hanson, a local farmer, sportsman and fishing guide, and they continued to live in this area.

The original Armson farm near Lake Mason produced another generation when Merle and Nieta started to raise a family. Theo, June 30, 1921; Edward Blake, September 21, 1922; Harlan Merle, March 29, 1924 ; William Henry, November 21, 1926; Mary Lo, January 19, 1928; and Richard Paul, December 10, 1930.

Following nurses training, Theo worked in Chicago and Los Angeles. She married Maurice "Von" Krumrey in 1946. They have 2 sons, Steven Maurice and Ned William. All live in California.

Blake enlisted in the Marine corps in September, 1941. He served with conspicuous bravery and was awarded the Silver Star. He was killed on the island of Saipan, on July 10, 1944.

Harlan Merle married Johanna Delmore in 1948. They have a daughter, Kerry Elizabeth, who is married and has 2 sons. Harlan worked for the SCS for 20 years and upon retirement, opened the Armson Insurance Agency in Waukesha.

William "Bill" Henry married Norma Cowles in 1948. They had 5 sons, Bill; Gary who is married with 2 daughters; Ron and Don (twins); and James "Jim" who is married with 3 children. Bill and Norma divorced in 1980 and Bill married Jean Goodland in 1982.

Mary Lou married Roy Bacon in 1947. They lived in the Janesville and Madison areas where they raised 2 daughters, Derry Lynn and Nita Jo. Derry was killed in an auto accident in 1965. Roy worked with the University of Wisconsin and retired to Branson, Missouri where Mary Lou still lives.

R. Paul Armson married Lada Grunke in 1951 and they bought a farm about 5 miles from the Armson homestead. They had six children: Blake; Rossana, married with 3 children; Margene, married with 2 children; Brenda; Angela; and Brent. Paul had been a Caterpillar Dozer operator for years.

The Armson homestead has passed through many names since Merle and Neita traded it off to Fred Burns for a house in Wisconsin Dells. It is now in the Gussel name. The bay that carries the water from Big Spring to Lake Mason continues to carry the Armson name.

Albert Auerbach

Albert H. (Stub) Auerbach, 78, a lifelong resident of Wisconsin Dells and a former chief of the Kilbourn Fire Department died on Friday, August 2, 1974 in the Baraboo Hospital of a heart attack. Born September 3, 1895 in Wisconsin Dells, he was a retired chief of the Kilbourn Fire Department and a member of the Dells Rifle Club.

He was married on May 6, 1922 to Margaret O'Dell in Wisconsin Rapids.

The Auerbachs owned and operated Shady Lawn Motel on River Road for 35 years. They started Shady Lawn by renting rooms in their home to tourists and eventually built two cabins, added additional cabins and motel units until there were 23 units and a new home.

Auerbach served as fire chief from 1940 to 1946. At his retirement in 1946, he had been a member of the fire department for 22 years. The Memorial Day Parade of 1954 was the 50th parade in which he marched.

He was survived by his wife, Margaret; a daughter, Nona (Rueford) Bork; three grandchildren, Jamie (Paul) Langlie, Ginny and David Bork; and three great grandchildren, Stein, Nina and Kai Langlie.

Gerald P. Baggot

Gerald P. Baggot was born April 14, 1898. He was one of 7 children born to Jerome and Margaret Baggot of Wisconsin Dells. When Gerald started his rural route with the Dells Postal Service, his sister Anna carried mail too. Also Les, his brother, substituted when needed.

The first year, Gerald carried the mail over his 29-mile route with a team of horses. Each trip took him 8 hours. He bought his first car in 1918 but continued to use his horses during the winter. He carried mail for 40 years in Wisconsin Dells and after retiring on December 31, 1957, devoted his time to the Dells Pioneer Village.

He married Marguerite I. McGowan July 23, 1924 in Lyndon Station, Wisconsin and they had 3 children: Joseph P. Baggot (Gail), Dr. Gerald P. Baggot (Mary), and Mary Claire Kutzke (Louis).

Francis Bannen

Francis R. Bannen was born to Richard and Mary Bannen on April 13, 1919 in Fennimore, Wisconsin, and was raised in Boscobel. After graduting from the University of Wisconsin Law School in 1946, he was admitted to the State Bar Association and decided to make the Dells area his home.

Bannen served as attorney for the City of Wisconsin Dells from 1947 to 1953, and for the Village of Lake Delton from 1953 until his death. He was admitted to practice in the U.S. District Court, the U.S. Supreme Court and the U.S. Tax Court. He was also admitted to the Illinois State Bar and was a member of the Illinois Trial Lawyer's Association.

He was a member of many professional and fraternal organizations including the Insurance Trial Council of Wisconsin, Inc., of which he was a past-president; the Association of Trial Lawyers of America; the Sauk and Columbia County Bar Associations; and the St. Thomas More Lawyers Association.

He was a 3rd and 4th Degree member of the Knights of Columbus, and a member of both the Baraboo Elks Club and the Lake Delton Lions Club. He was involved in the WIsconsin Dells Eagles Club and the Rotary Club. He was once named Events Man of the Year. Attorney Bannen was also a member of the Madison Scottish Rites Bodies, the York Rite Bodies (F & AM Baraboo Lodge 34, Baraboo Valley Chapter 49, Baraboo Council 35, and Commandary 28), the Madison Consistery, Zor Vacationland Shrine, and the Eastern Star. He was a past member of the advisory board of the Wisconsin Division of AAA.

Attorney Bannen died on January 2, 1983. He was survived by his wife Patricia as well as a daughter, Catherine Lenahan of Madison; a son Thomas of Wisconsin Dells; and a grandson, Daniel Lenahan.

Carl and Nellie Becker

Carl F. Becker, a Wisconsin River pilot with over 20 years of experience, was born September 30, 1880 in Lomira, Wisconsin. His parents were Julius and Augusta Oldenburg Becker.

Carl was educated there before going to work in a harness shop in Fond du Lac. He soon became an expert harness maker.

On March 30, 1905 he married Nellie Nemitz, daughter of Herman and Amelia Barfjnecht Nemitz. In 1923 Carl and Nellie came to Kilbourn, where Carl earned his pilot's license. Carl worked for both the Olson Boat Company and the Dells Boat Company piloting pleasure launches. He generally spent winters in the leather goods store owned by his brother in Fond du Lac.

Although Carl and Nellie had no children, their home was always open to many young people who came to them with their dreams and problems.

Carl was a member of the Odd Fellows Lodge, and Nellie a member of the Rebekah Lodge.

Carl died on April 23, 1965 in Fond du Lac where he had moved following Nellie's death on January 5, 1945.

The Berry Family

Stiles Peck Berry came to Adams County, Wisconsin in 1847 from Groton, New York. His brothers, Clinton and Buel, settled near Fort Winnebago in Columbia County. They were the sons of Luther Berry who was born at Kent, Connecticut in 1792, son of John Berry. Stiles Peck Berry had five children but only one son, Irwin Storrs, survived to adulthood.

Irwin married Anna Johnson, daughter of Allen and Mary Chalfont Johnson, who came to Portage in 1838.

In 1873, Irwin Berry purchased the Cold Water Canyon Farm, just north of Kilbourn. Around 1884, as the fame of the Dells grew, his family began entertaining summer visitors. By first expanding the family home and later building a number of cottages, the enterprise grew and become Berry's Cold Water Canyon Hotel. Located on River Road and bordering on Cold Water Canyon, it would later be called "one of the most popular summer resort hotels in the Dells".

Irvin and Anna had four children: Stuart Allen, Fay Stiles, Winifred and Clayton DeWitt, of whom only Stuart had children.

Stuart Berry's children were Roland Stuart, Carol Alma, Robert Irwin, Kenneth Ellsworth and Irwin Stiles. Bob and Kenneth moved to Chicago and Milwaukee respectively and have descendants there. Bob became an electrical contractor, inventor and manufacturer, holding many major patents in the electrical equipment field. His son, Robert Donald, was Stuart's only male grandchild.

When Irvin retired, his son Clinton assumed the hotel's management and in 1927 had a nine-hole golf course constructed on the property. The sport of golf was new to the Dells area, and to encourage interest, he hired a Chicago golf pro to provide free lessons to all area residents. As an added convenience for his guests, Clinton purchased the 40-passenger launch *Ramona* which was docked on his property at a river inlet still known as "Berry's Eddy".

Clinton's nephew Roland piloted the *Ramona,* which toured the Upper Dells twice daily and made a nightly trip to Stand Rock where guests could enjoy the Indian Ceremonial.

Roland's granddaughter, Marty Fisher, would later pass the Coast Guard's rigorous licensing exams for this area of the Wisconsin River and become the Dells' first female river pilot. Employed by the Olson Boat Company, her boat crew often included her youngest sister Jimi, an experienced tour guide.

In 1939, Roland picked up the reins of these family enterprises. He discontinued the hotel operation in 1956 following the rerouting of Highway 13, but still ran the Dells Golf Course, with his wife Violet and daughter Marilyn in charge after his death in 1958.

When the Wimmer family of Wisconsin Dells purchased the property in 1960, Marilyn remained manager during the early transition years. A noted amateur golfer, she also designed and built Berry's Par 3 golf Course (later Pinecrest).

The Best Family

Socrates Thomas Best was born in Portage County, Ohio on July 15, 1824. In 1849 he moved with his parents from Ohio to Big Spring, Adams County. He lived with his parents, helping with the farm and teaching school, until he was twenty seven years old, when he married Ellen F. Langson.

Ellen was an Irish Catholic girl, and Socrates was of Irish and Welsh descent and of Protestant faith: a fact which found disfavor in both of their families. Realizing that they would have a hard time living with this disapproval, they decided to move to Texas.

They located there on a ranch where they taught the children of the rancher and his cowhands. There were also many slave children, and although it was against the law to educate the Negro, the rancher asked that his slaves be allowed to attend the school on the ranch.

When the war broke out, the Confederate Army drafted every available man into service. Socrates didn't want to be in the Confederate Army, but the penalty for avoiding the draft was hanging, so he answered the call in May, 1862.

Before he left, he told Ellen that at his first chance, he would desert the Confederate Army and join the Union Army. She was to load what she could into their wagon and take the young children, Augustus, William, and the baby Ellen, and try to get back to Wisconsin where they would all meet if he survived the war.

In December, 1862, the Union Army advanced and captured the hospital where Socrates tended the sick and wounded. Instead of fleeing, he turned himself in to a Union officer. The officer saw a need for him in the hospital, and so Socrates stayed on as a nurse until the end of the war.

Ellen had prepared for the trip as best she could. She gathered up food, clothing and bedding and left with her children. They suffered many hardships and frightening times, often hiding themselves in the forest for fear of being stopped and questioned.

The travel was hard, and baby Ellen couldn't endure the exposure and died. Gus helped his mother bury her in the woods by the trail. Without enough food, they grew weaker and sicker day by day. The horse was also weary and starved to the point that it could barely walk.

One day nearing Fort Smith, Arkansas, some scouts from the Union Army found the sickly family.

When they arrived at the fort hospital, the ward master, Socrates Best, received them and found that it was his own family. Ellen, Gus, and Willie were all in very bad condition, suffering from the measles, starvation, and exposure. Ellen died the same night in his care.

Socrates was left with two boys in the heart of the Civil War. When they recovered, he knew he must send them on to Wisconsin. On paper he wrote down who they were and where they were going, and sewed it to the inside of Gus' coat. He told them to show it to someone if they lost the way.

Socrates found a boat on the Arkansas River and put the boys in a minister's care. He paid passage, lodging and board for the boys to be delivered to Prairie Du Chien, Wisconsin. In 1952, when Willie was 92 years old, he told the story of that trip to relatives:

Gus, eight years old and Willie, three years, traveled on the boat from Fort Smith to Prairie Du Chien. However, instead of traveling first class they were neglected, and the only care or food that they received was from sympathetic passengers. Willie developed diarrhea and became a very soiled, smelly child. Their blankets were stolen and the minister who had promised to look after them did not. When they were put on another boat on the Wisconsin River, they were treated better and reached Portage, Wisconsin without further neglect.

They arrived in Portage and started their search for someone to take them to Big Spring where their grandparents lived. A man named Rob Ramsey from Big Spring was shopping in Portage and heard of the boys, and so took them home to their grandparents. Their grandmother was a little Irish woman and was not too pleased at having two grandsons to care for. Though not very loving, she kept them clean and well fed.

The war ended in 1865, and Socrates returned to Big Spring to find Gus and Willie.He did what he could to make a home for his sons.

Socrates had heard from neighbors of his former student, Sarah Ward Landt, now a widow with two living children, Alana and Warren. Socrates remembered Sarah well. As soon as he could, he called on Sarah, and on January 28, 1866, they were married. It was a good marriage, and the four children were happy to settle into a real home and family.

On March 31, 1867 another child, Judith Geraldine, was born. Socrates continued to teach school and help on the family farm. When Judith was about three, the family moved to Prairie Farm, Dunn County, Wisconsin.

Three more children were added to the family: Samuel, Sylvia and Mildred. Now a family of eight children, they all lived to adulthood near Prairie Farm.

Augustus fell in love with his step-sister, Alana, and they were married and farmed in Prairie Farm. They had seven children: Allie, Eugene, Elsie, Ben, Cleburn, Loren, and Earl. Alana died on August 1, 1895. On February 17, 1897, Augustus married Mrs. Laura Risdon of Necedah and they had three more children: Homer, Laura, and Geneva. They also had an adopted son, Gussie. Augustus died, at age 55, on February 4, 1909.

William married while still in Wisconsin and moved in the early years of his marriage to Coeur d'Alene, Idaho. William and Emma Best had two children: Wilma and William.

Samuel married Ida Harmony, and he also moved his family to Coeur d'Alene where he worked in the lumber business. He was killed in a wagon accident while hauling a load of logs. Ida and Charles had three children: Mary, Nellie, and Charles. In the early 1950's, Ida was living with Mary and Nellie in California, where the daughters were making a successful living supplying retail shops with handmade pottery.

Sylvia married Tom Tibbitts, a miller. Both Sylvia and Tom died quite young leaving their daughter, Margaretta, an orphan at five years old. She was raised by a paternal aunt.

Mildred became an artist of distinction and many of her paintings were hung in prominent places. She married Leon Snyder, and they had one daughter who died of spinal meningitis as a young child. Leon was a photographer with a very good business in Colfax, Wisconsin.

Judith married Delbert Landt, a cousin of her half sister, in 1888. They went on to make their home in the Wisconsin Dells area and had seven children: Newton, Rena, Bryce, Geraldine, Marjory and Janet (twins), and Frances. Delbert had also raised Dan O'Neil, an orphan, from the age of six.

The Blatchley Family

In the spring of 1918, Jess and Mae Lindberg Blatchley came to Kilbourn from Neceedah, driving about fifty miles on mostly dirt roads called the Red Circle Route, which later became part of Highway 13.

They stayed all summer while Jess managed a garage for his brother, William Blatchley. Will had come to Kilbourn in the early 1900's and established a photography studio and a music store. He also had a Stanley Steamer bus which took tourists on sightseeing trips to Devil's Lake.

Jess's family was originally from England, and Mae had migrated with her parents, Per and Karen Forsberg Lindberg, from Sweden in 1898 at the age of 17.

In 1920 Jess and Mae returned to Kilbourn permanently. Jess was a harness maker, and after his death in 1939, Mae worked summers at the Barrett Gift Shop in Wisconsin Dells, and eventually began spending winters in Phoenix. They had three children: Lawrence, Hilda and Glen.

Lawrence moved to Phoenix, Arizona following high school.

In 1926 Hilda married James (Cotton) L. Stephan in Chicago and they lived in Wisconsin Dells. He spent most of his life working as a pilot and in boat maintenance. In December, 1942 "Cotton" enlisted in the U.S. Coast Guard where he served until 1945. He returned home to his work in the Dells until his death in 1963. Hilda also died in Wisconsin Dells.

Hilda and Cotton had four children: James, Joan, Jerry, and Ellen Joyce. James served in the U.S. Air Force from 1944-1947. When he returned he began working for the Wisconsin Conservation Department as a Forest Ranger, and retired from that post in January, 1982. He is now deceased.

Jerry also served in the U.S. Air Force from 1950-1954. He married Patricia Swansby. Joan married a Wilson and worked for the Sheriff in Phoenix, Arizona. Ellen Joyce (McDonald) is an artist, and lives with her husband in Tennessee.

Jess and Mae's son, Glen "Fat" Blatchley, established the Silver Dollar boat line in Wisconsin Dells in 1934. Soon after, he married Josephine "Jo" Arntz, a teacher in Sparta and Kilbourn.

Josephine Arntz Blatchley and her sister, Adeline Arntz Ryan, spent their entire lives in the area. The Arntz family had settled in Lyndon Station after leaving Germany in the 1850's. Jo's father, John, was one of eight children and moved to Kilbourn after he married Effa Bullis.

Adeline married John Ryan, who died suddenly in 1943. Their son, Robert, grew up in the Dells and lived in Hobbs, New Mexico for several years prior to his death in December 1994.

The Bullis family: Effa, Etta, Dick, and Ira, were the children of Edger and Abigail Sly Bullis, who were married in Kilbourn in 1872. Effa and Ira both worked for the Dells Boat Company for several years. Dick was a barber in Kilbourn for several years prior to relocating in Milwaukee with his wife, Mildred.

In 1914, John and Effa Bullis Arntz opened the Arntz Restaurant at 207 Broadway. John died in 1928 and Effa took over. She was a liberated woman long before the life style became popular. Her capable management of the restaurant allowed the business to survive for 60 years.

Jo Blatchley would devote over 35 years of her life to the Girl Scouting Program. She passed away in 1973.

Descendants of Fat and Jo Blatchley include 6 children: Glenda, Peter, Lynne, Dick, Jill and Jacqueline "Jaci"; 11 grandchildren and 2 great grandchildren.

Peter became the patriarch of the Blatchley Family and managed the boat companies after Fat's death in 1975. Peter and his wife, Virginia; his sisters Jill (Bob) Zapuchlak and Jaci Blatchley; Jaci's son Aaron and Jill's children, Tanya (Hans) Backhaus, Peter, Lara, and Nadia, all reside in the Dells area.

Lynne Blatchley died in 1956. Dick has lived in Phoenix, Arizona for over 20 years and Glenda Ladd moved to Illinois in 1960 where her four children, Tom, Dan, Lisa, and Marnie were born and reared. Glenda died January 27, 1995, a resident of Wheaton, Illinois. Peter's children, Tim Blatchley and Belinda (Henry) DeKuiff and their two children, Jeanna and Andrew, also reside in Illinois.

In 1994 the Blatchley family sold the Silver Dollar boat Line.

George Tyler Blood

George Tyler Blood was the third known settler in the town of Lyndon and the homesteader of the oldest known continuously occupied farm in the town of Lyndon and probably all of Juneau County. The property he settled remained in the Blood family for over 100 years. Gordon Johnson, town of Lyndon chairman, is the present owner of the farm.

George was born in Burlington, Vermont, on September 16, 1824. When he was about 16, he and his father drove a team of little brown mares to Chicago. The rest of the family soon followed and all settled in Evanston, Illinois, where George drove the stage coach between Evanston and Chicago.

Later George moved to Thornton, Illinois, where he continued to work as a stage driver. Here he met and married Helen Hurlburt (also spelled Hulbert), a union that was to last over 60 years. Helen Hurlburt was a half sister to Don Carlos Barry, the first white settler in Reedsburg.

Not long after his oldest son Henry was born in 1847, George and other relatives came to Wisconsin, some settling near Lodi. About 1848 they moved to Babb's Prairie (Reedsburg) where Barry made the first claim in 1844 and became a permanent settler in 1845. George's parents are buried near Poynette.

In 1849 Blood moved to the present town of Lyndon just over the Sauk County line and built a cabin at the headwaters of Hulburt Creek (probably named after his wife's family). Here he had a pure water supply, level land and a base for supplies about seven miles away in Newport.

There were still many Indians living nearby. Blood cleared the land and started farming in the center of the east 80 acres where he built his cabin. Within hauling distance of his house, passenger pigeons landed on the trees in such numbers as to break the branches from the trunks. Many settlers took clubs and filled their larders with passenger pigeons they knocked from the trees in the night.

The Bloods had several more children: Hiram, who took over the family farm in 1901; Charles and Ella. Myrtle was born in the 1860's and two other children died in infancy.

Moodie Blood, a 62 year old cabinet maker, was living with the Bloods during the 1860 census. It is possible that this man was George's father, but if so, his grave is unknown in the area.

The 1860 census lists the Blood's nearest neighbors as D.H. Pierce and William Cole on one side, and D.B. Norton and Gerard Burdick on the other. Blood had two horses, three milk cows, three other cattle, ten sheep and four swine. During the year he raised 50 bushels of wheat, 100 bushels of corn and 300 bushels of oats. He also produced 24 lbs. of wool. This was better than average and quite remarkable in light of the fact that he is listed as having only 20 acres of improved land and 20 acres of unimproved land. The land was listed as worth $200 and his machinery, $50.

During the hops boom in the 1860's, Blood prospered with everyone else, building up his land to 160 acres including the previously mentioned west 80 which he had bought from the government in 1854. In 1858, however, he had deeded this land to his mother-in-law, Hannah Hurlburt.

When the hops boom burst in 1868, Blood was forced to sell the west 80 acres to Guildo Hanson for $24 to pay the taxes. Horace Newton and his son Francis later owned the land. The north section of this property not owned by the Isaacson development is now the home of Mr. and Mrs. Frank Dziob and family.

Myrtle Blood Carter often told of quilting bees, molasses pulls, country dances and other long forgotten social activities that the family took part in. Eventually the farm passed to Hiram's son, Willard Blood, whose family kept the farm until 1951.

Three generations of Bloods grew up on this farm and attended the local school three-fourths of a mile away which George helped to organize and serve as clerk. His son Hiram and grandson Willard served on the same board after him. Hiram married a school teacher, Dolly Montgomery, and Willard married Jeanette Clark, who lived in Wisconsin Dells until her death in 1975.

Their descendants number in the hundreds, a great many of which still live in the Wisconsin Dells area. In addition to the Bloods are the descendants of Ella, sister of Hiram, who married Robert Murray in 1880.

George died at his home on July 9, 1915, at age 90. His wife preceded him in death on December 26, 1906, at the home of her son Henry in Minnesota. Both are buried in the Delton Cemetery

George Tyler Blood's life can be best summed up as stated in his obituary:

"During the half century Mr. Blood lived in the vicinity he was esteemed for his moral character, his temperate habits, his frugailty and industry. He was one of the substantial class of citizens who helped build up one of the best communities in the state. His descendants are all occupying prominent and successful places in the communities where they reside, continuing the approved character of their worthy ancestor."

The Bogh Family

Nels Bogh emigrated from Denmark in 1905 to be with a brother, Andrew, and Aunt Matilda (Hans) Anderson. His first contact in Kilbourn was depot telegrapher Henry Tofson. His first job was construction on the Kilbourn dam.

In 1907 Nels returned to Denmark to bring back his bride, Maren Jorgensen. The couple lived in the old Kilbourn Institute. Their first son, Edmund was born there in 1908, and Nels worked as a railroad section hand.

By 1912 they were lonely for home and returned to Denmark for a short time. When they returned they repurchased most of the furniture thay had sold before moving and settled into a house on LaCrosse Street where another son, Laurence, was born in 1914. From 1915 to 1919, they lived in a house on south Superior Street.

Nels was then working at Corning's Feed Mill for $1 per day. He played the accordian for house parties and dances that were popular recreation among the Danish.

In 1919 they moved to a New Haven farm and Marvin was born. From 1925 to 1940 they farmed on the old Paul Anderson homestead in Newport, where Marvin died at age 16 in 1935.

In 1940 Nels and Maren bought their first home, the old Dahl Place, on New Haven Road. This 20 acre parcel is the same, intact parcel deeded by the U.S. government in 1853 to Paul Anderson and precedent to Bertha Dahl. For ten years Nels and Maren enjoyed their "little farm" with 2 horses, 4 cows, 200 chickens and dog, Tuffy.

The Bogh family were faithful members of New Haven and Newport Lutheran churches. Nels died in 1850 and Maren in 1956. Both are buried in the Newport Lutheran Cemetery.

Son Edmund married Marjorie Zietz in 1932. That same year they bought the Theodore Jenson homestead in lower Newport where Edmund lived until his death in 1985. They had one daughter, Gloria (Borkowski), in 1937. Marjorie died in 1952 and Edmund married Pearl Nevar.

Laurence married Helen Anderson, of Swedish-Norwegian parents from rural Elroy. Their first home was the 100 year old Thompson log house in Newport. They had two daughters: Marilyn (Chavera) and Linda (West). Laurence retired in 1980 from a 36 year career with the DNR Forest Fire Control Service.

The Charles Borcher Family

Charles A. Borcher was born in 1883 to parents who had emigrated to Kilbourn from Germany.

Early on, Charles worked for A.C. Dixon in the clothing business. Later he purchased and operated the Stephens farm, plus three commercial buildings owned by A.C. Dixon and Vin Wright. With his partner B.E. Tollaksen, he also operated Borcher and Tollaksen Sanitary Grocery at 224 Broadway for many years prior to and during World War I.

Later he leased the grocery store to George Gray and then to Gordon Winnes. The building at 226 Broadway was leased to Kroger Grocery Company and then to Botsford's Paint and Wallpaper Store. After leaving the grocery business, Charles opened Borchers Variety Store at 216 Broadway. When his health failed, he sold that business to the Schultz Brothers Company.

Charles married Blanche Reuterskoild who was born in 1887 near Edgerton, Wisconsin. Her parents had been born in Sweden.

Both were members of the United Presbyterian Church, where Charles served on the board. He was President of the Kilbourn Co-Op Creamery Association, served on the school board and City Council, and was Chief of the fire department for many years. Charles Borcher died January 11, 1945, and Blanche in January, 1969.

They had three children: Eutella, Charles, and Arnold. Arnold followed in his father's footsteps in 1946 and did business in Wisconsin Dells until his retirement in 1985. His and his wife Catherine had two children: Ben and Jane Heller, who are now involved in operating the business.

Dr. R.D. Boynton

A native of Menasha, Dr. R.D. Boynton graduated from high school in 1906. After attending Lawrence College, he graduated from Marquette University Medical School in 1913.

Prior to locating in Wisconsin Dells, he practiced for a year in Sullivan, was an assistant and acting surgeon at the Wisconsin Veteran's Home at King, and had practiced at Grand Marsh.

He served as local and district chairman, as well as council director, for the Boy Scouts, county secretary of the American Red Cross, secretary of the Chamber of Commerce, member of the council and for many years a commissioner of health.

An active member of the Dells Kiwanis Club, he was a charter member in 1922, served as acting president until 1924, lieutenant governor in 1929, and on the club's board for many years.

He was killed in an automobile accident in 1951 at age 61.

The Brew Family

Gold attracted the attention of many after its discovery in California in 1849, including Daniel Brew, a 22 year old man recently arrived in New York State from the Isle of Man. That winter, Daniel joined others traveling by ship around the Cape of Good Hope to reach California. He was lucky in mining and started back East with two seven pound bags of gold dust. Though he became sick with a fever after passing through Panama, he arrived safely home to the Isle of Man in 1851. In 1853, he married Miss Ann Cormode. The young couple, with Daniel's brother James, came to Newport in 1854 and purchased land on the west side of the river from Frank Blazer.

James Brew had married a girl from New York, Jane Campbell, and when he was killed in a logging accident she and their children returned to New York.

Daniel and Ann raised three children: William, Jennie York and Ella. Three other children died when young. Daniel farmed until his death in 1896; Ann Brew survived until 1909.

Their son, William Arthur Brew, expanded the farm operation. He obtained additional land and in 1915, built a 140' x 50' barn to accommodate 75 milk cows. Milk was delivered to many homes in Kilbourn City by wagon and a team of mules. The barn was dedicated with a huge barn dance; people arriving every 15 minutes by river boat or wagon.

William was in his forties when he married Emma Rothe, a local dressmaker. They had one son, Daniel Conrad.

When very young, Daniel was given a flock of geese to herd but they soon became a nusiance. His father then suggested sheep, and started a seventy year tradition of showing sheep at county and state fairs. Daniel started at the Inter-County fair just north of Kilbourn and was soon shipping his sheep by train all over the Midwest. He once received the National Champion Award on a Dorset ewe at the Ohio State Fair.

Daniel C. married Martha "Mae" Byam in 1931 and they have continued to live on the home farm. Parts of the farm have been sold for Hwy 12, Rocky Arbor State Park, the State 4-H Camp, Dells Industrial Park and Hulburt Creek Trout Refuge. They had three children, Elinor, William and Janet.

William Daniel Brew has managed the farm since 1953. He married Jean Sprecher, who has taught home economics at the Wisconsin Dells High School for many years. They have two sons. Bill has continued raising sheep and cash crops.

The farm was recognized as a Century Farm in 1955 and the family proudly calls it the Brew Century Farm. Four generations have actively farmed the land, located one mile north of Kilbourn City on Stand Rock Road, on the west bank of the Wisconsin River.

Dr. C.F. Broderick

C.F. Broderick practiced medicine in Wisconsin Dells for 25 years. He was born in Fond du Lac and in 1935 became the youngest graduate of Marquette University Medical College.

Dr. Broderick interned and practiced in Milwaukee from 1937 to 1945. He served as a naval Lieutenant in the Pacific during World War II before coming to Wisconsin Dells in 1946. Here he joined Dr. J.H. Houghton at the Dells Clinic.

Dr. Broderick also served as Chief of Staff at both the St. Clare Hospital in Baraboo and Divine Savior Hospital in Portage. He was a charter member of the American Academy of Family Physicians.

In 1970, Dr. Broderick underwent heart surgery and retired from the Dells Clinic the following year. He and his wife Ruth moved to Sun City, Arizona and then later to Peachtree City, an Atlanta suburb, where he died in 1982.

He was survived by his wife, a brother Robert of Brookfield, and eight children: Patrick of Peachtree City; Thomas of Washington

D.C.; Sheila O'Neil and Mary Locke of Topeka, Kansas; Kathleen Stagney of Nashua, New Hampshire; Monica Cook of Columbus, Ohio; Rosemary Broderick of Phoenix, Arizona and Elizabeth Broderick of New York City.

Lawrence Buckley

Lawrence Buckley was born to Leonard and Margaret (Holihan) Buckley on December 28, 1884 in New Haven.

On November 25, 1915 he married Mamie Kane of Kilbourn at St. Mary's Catholic Church in Briggsville. They had three children: Chester of Milwaukee and Las Vegas; Ethel Huber (Stanley) of New Haven; and Lawrence, Jr., deceased. They loved and enjoyed six Buckley grandchildren: Anne, Susan, Denise, Tim, Brian, Kevin and four Hubers: Donald, Kenneth, Gail and Richard.

Lawrence was a life long resident of New Haven and was active in farm organizations for many years. He served on the Adams County Board of Supervisors for 18 years, as New Haven Town Chairman for 11 years and as a Director of the Farmers and Merchants State Bank of Wisconsin Dells for 13 years.

He was honored in 1950 by the University of Wisconsin College of Agriculture for unusual dedication to government and social service. He was also honored at the Adams Coutny Fair as an outstanding community citizen. Lawrence passed away on January 25, 1965.

The Burgess Family

Willard Burgess came to the Dells area in December, 1909. He purchased a 160 acre farm two miles west of town from Menno Leege. In 1910, by wagon from Mercer County, Illinois, he headed for Kilbourn with his wife, 5 children, a cow, a dog, and some chickens.

Though Willard farmed with the help of his son Fletcher, he was a blacksmith by trade. He had a complete shop and repaired machines for his neighbors.

In late years he painted pictures in oils; some were very good. He passed away in 1951 and his wife Margaret in 1956.

With other neighborhood kids, the Burgess children learned to dance on the platform bridge over Hulburt Creek. As they grew older they went to house dances in the area and when the dance was at their home they used the kitchen, the largest room in the house. Everyone helped carry the furniture out, even the cookstove. After they danced all evening they carried it all back in. Someone from the neighborhood usually played a fiddle or accordion.

Fletcher played baseball where the Lower Dells boat docks are today, and to earn the money for his first and only shotgun he trapped muskrats on the creek. He took over the family farm and in 1932 met Edith Hillman from Delton while she taught school at Fern Dell. After a seven year courtship they were married and had two daughters, Carol and Mary. Fletcher continued farming until his death in 1963.

Edith managed the farm after that. She was also treasurer of the Town of Delton for 22 years, and worked summers at the Deer Park. Before her death in 1990 she turned the farm over to her daughters and they are still living there.

Fletcher's oldest brother Schuyler returned to Illinois and married. Ruth married Elmer Collies and moved to Iron Mountain, Michigan; Charlotte married Henry O'Connor of the Dells and Edith married William Henderson and moved to Florida.

The Byers Family

George William and Eva Elvina Evans Byers made their home in New Haven Township, Adams County, where they raised several children.

One son, Arthur Christopher Byers, was born April 7, 1901, and he married Bernice Johnson of New Chester in 1926. They rented Artie's home farm until 1942, when they purchased the Kirchoff farm in New Haven. They were dairy farmers until selling the farm to their son Myron in 1970. They then spent the cold months in Florida and the summers in New Haven. When Artie died June 28, 1991, Bernice moved to Portage. They had three children: Elaine, Myron, and Kenneth.

Elaine married Sheldon Goodhue of Douglas Township, Marquette County. After farming there for several years, in 1989 they moved to Oxford where Sheldon died in January, 1990. They have a son Brian, daughter-in-law Rita (Elliott) and two granddaughters, Dacia and Dawn.

Myron moved to Madison and worked for the Wisconsin Air National Guard. In 1995, he retired and he and his wife Joan (Ellinger) returned to the farm in New Haven. They have two children, Rodney and Rhonda.

Kenny married Lana Kurth, of Easton, and moved to Rockton, Illinois. They have two children, Lisa and Lorinda.

Charles George Byers, second son of George and Eva, was born May 2, 1894. He farmed with his brother William for many years in New Haven.

At age 43 he married a neighbor girl, Eunice Susie Larson, daughter of Lars Peter and Susie (Chapin) Larson, and they had three children: Donald, who died in infancy, Margaret, and Delmar.

When his brother Willie retired to the village of Oxford, Charlie continued to farm with his son, Delmar, until 1970 when he and Eunice retired to Portage. Charlie died March 1, 1971 and is buried in the Briggsville Protestant Cemetery.

Margaret married and has two sons, Charles and Ray. She resides in Baraboo.

Delmar lives in Oxford Township with his wife Mary Lou Lloyd Byers. He works for the Marquette County Highway Department. They have two children: Trent, who married Kim Novak; and Tara. Trent and Kim have one daughter, Brittany Faye Byers.

The third son of George and Eva, Roy Frank, was born January 20, 1896 in New Haven where he attended Jackson School.

He was killed during World War I while serving as a private in the 310th Infantry in France. In September 1919 the American Legion Post at Oxford was named the Roy Byers Post.

The Campbells

Emma and Harriet Campbell were raised in Big Spring, and their brother Bert married Ruby Landt.

Emma married a man named Artnez and had one daughter. Mr. Artnez died soon after the daughter was born. Emma moved to Milwaukee to teach kindergarten.

Harriet married Frank Straw who worked in the Post Office. They had twin daughters and one son. When the boy, Robert, was only two years old, Frank died of meningitis leaving Hat with three children to raise.

She had a large house and her parents came to live with her, and she took in boarders. As time went on, her parents died and she boarded and roomed teachers. She managed well and was a well respected citizen.

So it was that Aunt Em Artnez and Aunt Hat Straw were like relatives to the Landt family and were always at the Landt Thanksgiving table.

Mary T. Conway

Mary T. Conway was born December 8, 1867, near Troy, New York. In 1876 her family moved to Kilbourn. She attended the local school and in the spring of 1884, was granted a teaching certificate. She taught for one year in a Sauk County country school and in 1885, was elected to teach grades three and four in the old second room of the Kilbourn school.

She was successful in her work and every two years was promoted with the class to teach the next two grades. In this manner she taught in each of the grades below high school, having the same class of students from room to room. In 1892 she was elected assistant teacher at the high school.

In the fall of 1908 she began teaching history at the Tomah high school, but returned to the Kilbourn high school in the fall of 1910. She passed a state examination in Madison which qualified her to teach in any high school in the state. On May 13, 1934 the community and Kilbourn alumni gave a banquet in her honor, as a testimonial to her 50 years of teaching.

Thomas D. Crist, Sr.

Thomas D. Crist was born December 17, 1901 in Walton, New York. With his wife Edna and their first child, Thomas, Jr., he came to Wisconsin Dells in 1923. Here he started an ice cream and locker business, the Kilbourn and later the Dells Ice Cream Company. It would flourish until it was sold in 1990 to Cedar Crest Ice Cream of Cedarburg.

The locker plant that Thomas developed to refrigerate meat for businesses and homeowners was one of the first of its kind in Wisconsin. Originally, the total capacity of the Kilbourn Ice Cream Company totalled 60 gallons per day. When it was sold, capacity was at 80 gallons per hour.

Over the years, Thomas became very active on behalf of area senior citizens, organizing the Dells Housing Authority and working to develop the local Colonial Apartments for the elderly. He was also instrumental in developing the Continental Manor Nursing Home as well. In 1969 he was named Man of the Year by the *Wisconsin Dells Events* and was appointed Director of the National Housing Association For Non-Profit Retirement Housing.

As a member of the Columbia County Housing Authority he also helped develop similar complexes in other Wisconsin towns. During vacations to Florida, Thomas offered related expertise on behalf of seniors in that state, and for this, his picture hangs in one City Hall next to those of Spiro Agnew and Rose Kennedy. In 1982 the Wisconsin State Fair Board named him one of the State's Ten Most Honored Senior Citizens.

Thomas spent more than 50 years as president of the Spring Grove Cemetery Association. He was active in the Kiwanis Club, Masonic Lodge and Zor Shrine. He was an elder in the United Presbyterian Church of Wisconsin Dells and served as Clerk of the Session for many years. He served as President of the Dells Housing Authority until ill health forced his retirement. Thomas served on various other Wisconsin Dells City Committees as well.

Edna preceeded Thomas in death, after a marriage of over 65 years. Their family included Thomas, Jr. and two daughters: Barbara Marini and Lu Schwieger. They had eleven grandchildren, eighteen great-grandchildren and three great-great-grandchildren. Thomas Crist, Sr. died at St. Clare Meadows, Baraboo, on May 27, 1994, aged 92.

Archie R. Crothers

Archie R. Crothers was born April 14, 1887, on a farm his grandfather purchased from the government in the late 1840's. There he spent his entire life, and died 100 years later within a few feet of where he was born.

His father, James Morris Crothers, was born in 1847 near Montreal, Canada, the fourth of 10 children born to J.M. Crothers Sr., and Ann (Briggs) Crothers. J.M. Sr. was born and raised near Belfast, Ireland, and was the son of George Carruthers and Margaret Graham. Ann Briggs was the daughter of Robert Briggs, an Irishman who fought in the Battle of Waterloo.

James I and Annie were married in 1840 and promptly emigrated to Canada. In 1856 they purchased the Jordan farm on the south shore of Jordan Lake in Adams County, where they lived for the rest of their lives. James II grew of age there and in 1866 married Julia Ward of Big Spring. Julia, the daughter of Ira C. Ward and Ursula (Edwards) Ward, was born in Lake Mills, Wisconsin in 1847. When she was two, Ira moved his family to this wilderness where bear were a common sight and their closest neighbor was Chief Pretty Man and his family. Ira and his friend, Richard Rose, are believed to be the first two farmers to enter and claim farms in the area now known as southern Adams County.

Ira chose a piece of land on a ridge with white and red oak timber, close to spring water, with rocks in ample supply for building needs. He built a farm and raised his family by trading beef and wheat for lumber at Pineries to the north. Later, he raised hops and, in 1868, erected a hop kiln for processing. The kiln, constructed of hand hewn Wisconsin pine rafted down the river from the lumber camp, still stands today. Direct descendants of these people, as well as their livestock, continue to live on the same farm.

Around 1870, Ira was struck by lightning. After a lengthy recovery he sold his farm to Julia and James Crothers and spent the remaining years of his life operating the Ward Feed Mill in Big Spring.

Archie's parents lived and raised their family on the Ward farm. James II was active in local affairs; serving on the town board, county board, and as Sheriff of Adams County. Julia was active in raising her large family and helping with school and church activities. Julia died in 1921 and James II in 1927. They are buried in the Big Spring Cemetery.

Archie attended the Ward School for eight years and went on to High School in Portage for one year. There he lived with his older brother who was Columbia County Clerk of Court. He then returned home to farm, all of his brothers having pursued other careers. In 1913, he married Laura Clough, born in New Haven in 1889 to Charles and Eva Clough.

Charles Sylvester Clough, known as 'Vet' was the son of Steven Clough and Polly Compton. Steven's father, Moses, was a soldier in the War of 1812. Moses was born and worked in the granite quarries of the East. Following a dynamite blast that blinded him, he and his wife moved to Wisconsin and raised a large family under difficult pioneer conditions. He would live to old age without seeing his new home.

Steven and his brothers were stone masons and carpenters by trade. A surviving example of their work is the Big Spring Church, built in 1875.

Charles Clough died of heart trouble, leaving behind a wife and four young children. Eva Clough was descended from, among others, the Eighme family who were very early settlers near Eighme Pond in Adams County. Re-named 'Amey' Pond by modern map-makers, the pond is about eight miles east of Wisconsin Dells on the south side of Highway 23.

Laura Clough attended the Badger Valley School, graduated from Kilbourn High School and taught until she married Archie in 1913. Archie and Laura farmed in Big Spring for the rest of their lives. Laura died in 1954.

Archie was active in all facets of local politics, serving as Town Clerk for the Town of New Haven and many years on the Ward School Board. He was serving on the Wisconsin Dells High School Board when the new high school was built.

Archie enjoyed keeping abreast of current events and told stories of the good old days to many friends who enjoyed spending time with him during his last years. He died in June, 1987 and is buried in the Big Spring Cemetery. His son Erwin operates the farm today. Erwin and his wife Ruth (Ramsey) have two children: Kenneth and Marie.

The Curry Family

In 1849, at one month old, Joseph Blue Curry, grandson of Irish emigrants, came to Wisconsin in a covered wagon with his parents and siblings James, John, and Elizabeth.

They stopped first at Baraboo where he went to school with the Ringling Brothers, who Joseph called "the wild bunch". Later he moved to Rock Springs where he married Eva Hubbard and their only child, Ross C. Curry, was born. In 1881 the family moved to the town of Lyndon in Juneau County where Joseph died in 1936.

Ross C. Curry married Sarah Burdick in 1918 and their three children were born on the property where he farmed until his death in 1966, aged 92.

Their children were twins, Ross M. Curry and Eva Jane (Melvin) Claussen, born in 1929, and daughter Elizabeth, who married Gordon C. Johnson, the longest serving chairman of the Town of Lyndon.

Ross M. Curry worked more than 45 years in the printing and newspaper business including over 40 years at the *Wisconsin Dells Events*, the longest anyone was so engaged in the Dells area. He wrote numerous historical articles, some of which were also reprinted in book form.

In 1963 he married Sylvia Phillipson, a local school teacher. Their children were Laureen (Bill) Hunter, of Appleton and Ross P. (Kimberly) Curry of Wisconsin Dells. Grandchildren are Tiffany and Crystal Hunter, and Alexander Ross and Ryan Andrew Curry.

Joseph's brother James was born on April 8, 1936 in Jefferson County, Ohio. He made the 1849 trip to Wisconsin with his parents and married Elizabeth McCann. They had one son, James Jr.

James Curry was known as one of the last stage coach drivers. He and Elizabeth operated the stage between Baraboo and Kilbourn's Tanner House from 1860 until the railroads cut into the business and forced him out.

James did a large express and passenger business, sometimes using two teams with Elizabeth driving the other. They frequently travelled through Webster's Prairie (along Highway 12) with a major stop in Delton, and became very well known in the area. They travelled no matter what the weather, and once a passenger froze to death on the trip. James sometimes carried as much as $40,000 with him. Curry gained lasting fame for his part in the capture of Pat Wildrick, the dangerous desperado believed responsible for the death of Schuyler Gates.

James died in 1921 at his farm near Baraboo and is buried there.

The Doughertys

James F. Dougherty was born October 29, 1880 in Kildare, near Lyndon Station. His father came from Tipperary, Ireland in 1861. He married Mary Linehan and settled in Lyndon.

He graduated from the Kilbourn High School in 1899, and from the Wisconsin State University in 1903, then taught school in Omro for two years. In 1905 he returned to law school at the University of Wisconsin and passed the state bar examination in 1906.

On September 1, 1906 he opened a law office in Kilbourn. He married Lillian Rhea of Thorpe, Wisconsin and they had one son, Robert.

In 1910, James was a founder of the Farmers and Merchants State Bank of Kilbourn. He also served on the school board, was city attorney, member of the State Bar Association, charter member and president of the Kiwanis Club, and member of the fire department, Blue Lodge and Royal Arch Masons and Eastern Star.

James died suddenly on February 7, 1942.

Robert was born in Kilbourn to James and Lillian on October 23, 1906. He married Laura Schoeninger on December 27, 1934 and they had three daughters: Mary (Krall), Katherine (Salchert), and Patricia (Birthelmer). He and Laura were able to celebrate their 50th wedding anniversary.

His youth was spent in Kilbourn, driving excursion boats in the Upper Dells, playing trombone with the Harry Peterson dance band and working as an assistant electrician to Chris Lee.

He graduated from Kilbourn High School in 1925, Ripon College in 1928 and University of Wisconsin Law School in 1931. He joined his father's law firm which became Dougherty and Dougherty, located above the post office on the 200 block of Broadway. He practiced for fifty years and was honored as a fifty year member of the State Bar of Wisconsin.

In 1942 he became Vice-president of the Bank of Wisconsin Dells and served in that capacity for thirty five years, becoming an emeritus director.

He served as City Attorney, Harold B. Larkin American Legion Post Commander and County Commander, helped organize the Dells Rifle Club and became secretary and treasurer, Past Master and fifty year member of the Masonic Lodge and Past President of the Kiwanis Club.

During World War II he was a member of the Rationing Board and volunteered for military service as a lieutenant in the Navy. He died on May 19, 1987.

Donovan Deakin

In September 1938, Donovan Sidney Deakin decided to leave his secure job as manager of the Fox Theatre in Milwaukee and move to Wisconsin Dells with his two year old daughter, Penny, and his wife, Arleen. He leased the only movie house in the Dells, located on Broadway.

Success did not come easily in those pre-World War II years when 35¢ for an adult ticket was like five dollars in 1994. Not all movies were like "*Gone with the Wind*" where reserved seats were required, and so to entice patrons to "normal" movies, Don held

"Bank Nights," where money contributed by Dells merchants was raffled off. Merchants received "free" advertising, the winners got the money, and everybody enjoyed the movie.

Many Dells boys earned their first money by ushering, selling candy, and making popcorn. Sometimes the jobs would be passed down from brother to brother. Who could resist 25¢ an hour and all the movies you could sit through?

The movie business prospered in the postwar years and, in August, 1953, Don opened the Winnebago Drive In Theatre on Highway 16, which still operates today. This new concept was very popular during the summer season despite competition from television. The indoor theatre was not as fortunate and lack of business forced its closing in 1958.

Don opened the Coffee Cup Restaurant which he operated, along with the drive-in, until his untimely death in March, 1967.

He loved the Dells and always contributed his talents and energy to the Dells people and organizations. He was the first to organize the Kiwanis Christmas baskets for needy families. He served as Kiwanis President, Alderman, Master of the Columbia Masonic Lodge and became a 33rd Degree Mason at an early age.

The Dixon Family

James Edward Dixon came to Kilbourn in 1857 from Cornwall, Ontario, Canada. He and his four sons established the Dixon Canada Store which prospered until 1866 when it was destroyed by fire. It was reputed to have been "the finest dry goods establishment west of Milwaukee."

In 1862 James' son Adam married Francis Ann Tanner, daughter of the Erie Canal boat captain John Tanner who came to Newport in 1855. When Newport failed to develop, Adam moved to Kilbourn and established the Tanner House, which later became the Finch Hotel.

Adam and Francis had five children: James Frederick, John Tanner, Edwin Church, Jennie Francis and Anna Louise.

Adam owned a number of other properties including Glen Cottage, stores, homes, and property in Newport. He opened the A.C. Dixon & Son store on Broadway with his sons James Frederick and John Tanner. An early trademark of the Dixon store was the life size lion statue which James E. had brought from Canada in 1857. The statue now belongs to fifth and sixth generations of the family.

John Tanner Dixon's son, James Hall Dixon, continued to manage the Dixon and Son store until his death in 1941. James Hall was the father of Elizabeth, James Jr. and John Dixon.

Another of John Tanner Dixon's sons, Fred Gurney Dixon, built and operated Multnomah Resort for many years.

The Drinker Family

Henry Drinker came to Kilbourn City around 1857 from Luzerne County, Pennsylvania. He went into the mill and lumber business with Mr. Hinds at a property located in Happy Hollow on the banks of the river, now the site of the River Inn and the Sunset Cove Condominiums.

In 1870, Henry's sons Albert E. and Robert W. came to Kilbourn and purchased Hinds' interest in the mill. At one point there were nine of Henry's children living near the Dells, but most later drifted away from the area.

Robert Drinker died at Kilbourn in 1903. Another son, Harry, also died in Kilbourn, in 1889. His daughter Minnie, in whose honor the library fountain was donated, married Charles W. Snider. Minnie's son, Harry D. Snider, married Lora Oswald, who died at age 94 in 1989.

In 1930, Francis P. Drinker also came to the area from Luzerne County, Pennsylvania. His great-grandfather was Henry Drinker's brother. Francis P. Drinker died in 1932 at Lake Delton. His daughter, Mrs. Kenneth Stevens, lives on Mirror Lake.

The Drollinger Family

Jacob was born March 1, 1885 in Sherry, Wisconsin. He was the eldest of eleven children born to Clara (Dillinger) and Jacob Drollinger. His father was born in Sheboygan, Wisconsin, and his mother had migrated from Austria when she was sixteen.

At age eighteen, Jake came to Kilbourn where he lived until his death. He first worked as a clerk at the Milwaukee Road Depot, and then learned the profession of harness making and opened his own harness and shoe shop on Oak Street.

On June 21, 1910, Jake was married to Nora Peterson. Nora was born on the Peterson farm, on Peterson Road in Newport, on February 27, 1878. She was the youngest of seven children born to Eliza (Tofson) and Hans Peterson, both of whom had migrated from Norway.

As a young girl, with only two years of high school, Nora taught school in the Newport area. She taught all eight grades and often said, "Some of my eighth graders were much taller than I."

Jake was very active in community and civic life. He held the office of City Treasurer for several years and was an Alderman. He was an agent for the Beaver National Insurance Group and was instrumental in building the Beaver Building. From 1923-26, Jake was treasurer of the local Lutheran congregation. He also served as a volunteer fireman.

Jake and Nora also operated one of the earliest tourist rooming houses, located in what remains the Drollinger family home at 1037 Elm Street. Jake died at the Sacred Heart Sanitarium in Milwaukee, on September 11, 1928 at the age of forty-five. Following his death, Nora operated a successful boarding house for many years. She then accepted a position as hostess at the Jonathan Bowman Home for Women where she stayed for 25 years, retiring at age 80. Nora also spent forty years as an agent for the Beaver (National Mutual Benefit) Insurance Company. Nora's religion was very important to her and she was a charter member of Bethany Lutheran Church where she was buried in 1968.

Nora and Jake had three children: Ronald "Jake", Clarice "Sis", and Wilmon "Bud".

Their son Ronald, also known as Jake, was born in Kilbourn on February 6, 1912. He graduated from the local high school where he was involved in sports, drama and music, and attended Marquette University for one year on a football scholarship.

In 1930, he married Celia Morse and they had four children; Anne, Barbara, Jacob, and Shari.

Beginning at age 14, Ronald spent several years as a river guide and driver. He clerked at A.C. Dixon's Clothing Store, managed the Mobil station at the corner of Broadway and Elm, worked in the office at Badger Ordnance, and managed road construction for the A.T. Rieses Construction Company. At his death he was the owner of the Mobil station and garage at the corner of Broadway and Bowman Road.

Sports were an important part of Ronald's life, both as a participant and as an avid fan. He played football at the high school, collegiate and semi-pro level. He instilled this love of sports in his four children.

He was a volunteer fireman for fifteen years and six months, serving as chief for the years 1949-50. He was elected to the school board for ten years and served as president. He did a great deal of the ground work for the unification of the school district so that the new high school could be built. He was a member of the Masonic Lodge and a charter member of the Bethany Lutheran Church.

Ronald died in March, 1959, at the age of forty-seven.

Louis Dupless

Louis Frank Dupless was born June 10, 1820, in Bordeaux, France. In 1836, at age 17, Dupless found himself aboard a ship sailing to America, where he met the Walklin family of Oxford, England and bound for Wisconsin. Dupless traveled the world as a sailor but he always maintained contact with the Walklin family. After serving in the Mexican War long enough to earn a veteran's land grant, he made his way to Wisconsin and, in 1846, married young Elizabeth E. Walklin. The following year he settled at the Bluff that would bear his name.

After reaching Louis' Bluff in the fall and staking his claim, Dupless wintered there. He left in the spring of 1847 for three months to fetch his bride and belongings.

At the base of the isolated bluff, Louis and Elizabeth Dupless began to trade with the Indians and passing rivermen and to raise a family. Their first son, Charles, was born in 1849, probably the first white child born in Juneau county. The family seems to have maintained good relations with the neighboring Indians. A daughter recalled that:

> *there was a tribe of Indians that were very friendly with father and they came to our house a lot for meals when I was a little girl...I was young but I remember there was an old Indian chief who used to come when the river was frozen over. His canoe was dragging behind him for security, for he could borrow father's rifle to shoot buffalo and deer, and every spring he would bring it back.*

Another family story concerns the time their baby was bitten by a poisonous snake. The neighboring Indians agreed to cure the baby if Louis would let them take it with them. He did, and in a few days the baby was returned sound and well.

As the pace of the lumber traffic quickened in front of Louis Bluff, Dupless turned his nautical skills to the navigation of the Dells. According to local traditions he was the first of the "Dells pilots."

In 1859 a tragedy occurred when the Dupless's eldest son, Charles, slipped from a sand bank and was drowned in the Wisconsin at the age of eleven. Charles was the first to be buried in the small family cemetery by the edge of the river. Four other children had been born by this time - Maria (Thresa) in 1852, Caroline in 1855, Frank in 1857, and Emeline (Emma) in 1859 - and another - Frederick in 1862 - was still to follow from the marriage to Elizabeth.

The passions of the Civil War swept strongly through the Dells from the first outbreak in 1861. Louis Dupless, awaiting another child, had to weigh his family obligations against his stout Republican principles and the ringing appeals for additional volunteers. Finally in 1864, at the age of 44, Dupless enlisted as a substitute soldier with Company G, 6th Regiment, Wisconsin Volunteers, departing for the front in December of that year. He was slightly injured in action at Gravelly Run, Virginia, on March 31, 1865, the basis for a partial disability pension claim, and thereafter performed only light duty in the ranks. In June, he was promoted to the rank of Colonel. Within six weeks the forces of Confederate President Jefferon Davis had surrendered, and Dupless was mustered out on July 14, 1865, barely eight months after enlistment.

Dupless returned to his life as a farmer along the Wisconsin River just as the region was being gripped by the giddy excitement of the hops boom. Like many of his neighbors, Dupless borrowed heavily to expand the production of hops, and when "the bottom dropped out of hops" his property was left significantly encumbered with debt for the first time, a condition that was to worsen in later years.

At about the same time, on August 1, 1869, Dupless suffered another tragedy in the death of his wife Elizabeth, of an epileptic seizure, at the age of 42. She too was buried in the family plot at the base of the Bluff.

Four years later, on April 10, 1873, Dupless married his second wife, Amelia, born Amelia Roessler of Landskron, Austria on March 8, 1846. She was first married to Frank Ressler, and had a daughter Joanna, but that marriage ended in an uncontested divorce a few months before the marriage to Dupless. The circumstances of the divorce on grounds of "willful desertion," with custody of the child awarded to the father, suggest that Amelia had abandoned her first husband for Louis.

The 27-year-old Amelia bravely took up life at the Bluff with 53-year-old Louis and the children from the first marriage. This second union was to result in eight children: Louisa (1872), Helena (1873), Nora (1875), Ida (1876), Daniel (1877), Gertrude (1881), Louis Jr. (1883), and William (1884).

In 1880, Louis Dupless went into partnership with his son-in-law August Blaser, who had married Emma in November of that year. The young Blasers set up household in the former hops house at Louis Bluff. They later bought an adjoining farm near Stand Rock (including "Blaser's Creek" by which early tourists were paddled up to Stand Rock), but Dupless and Blaser continued to jointly farm two islands near the Bluff. Emma Blaser died in 1944 at the age of 85, during all of which time she had lived within a few miles of her birthplace at Louis Bluff.

Neither of the two elder Dupless daughters were to enjoy long lives. "Tress," the eldest, married Peter Weber and moved to Elgin, Minnesota, where she died of measles at the age of 35. Her sister Caroline ("Cal") died still younger at age 32, after a life as unhappy as it was brief. Caroline was married on November 24, 1875, to Hamilton W. Tyler of Plainville, and bore him a son, Arthur. Tyler was the son of a prominent judge and hotel owner, Samuel W. Tyler, but young Hamilton was remembered as a philandering cad who ran through three marriages. After a short, unhappy marriage to Caroline, Tyler abandoned bride and baby and moved to Oregon. Caroline was thereafter regarded by her family members as a tragic figure, frail and weak of heart.

In his later years, Louis Dupless played an active role in the local G.A.R. chapter and in the affairs of the Republican party of Juneau County. Dupless was also an ardent Republican. The year before his death he was elected County Coroner of Juneau County on the Republican ticket.

Louis Dupless died on October 5, 1895, at the age of 75 after a brief illness, survived by his second wife and 11 of his 14 children. The scene at his riverside funeral was described movingly in the *Kilbourn Mirror-Gazette* of October 12, 1895. Louis was the last to be buried in the graveyard at the Bluff.

Wilson D. Eddy

In the 1880's, new homes and buildings were being constructed in Adams County and surrounding areas by an energetic young man named Wilson D. Eddy. He was born in Fort Anne, New York, May 25, 1851, one of seven children. His parents were Thomas Eddy, born in Ireland and Castaria (Mason) Eddy from Granville, New York. They were married on December 31, 1846.

When Wilson was a boy the Eddy family moved to the township of Easton, Adams County.

Wilson learned carpentry from his father and followed the trade until failing eye sight required him to give up active work. Some of his construction work took him to Illinois, Iowa, Missouri and Texas.

Wilson married Lorana Brown, daughter of Amos and Jane Brown in Kilbourn, Wisconsin on June 27, 1881. Seven children were born to them: Effie, who died in infancy; Ethel, Pearl, Iva, Bertha, Eva and one son, Fay. They celebrated their Golden Anniversary on June 31, 1931.

The Davis Corners United Methodist Church in Jackson township, Adams County was built by Mr. Eddy in 1881 at the cost of approximately $800. In 1889, Wilson Eddy also constructed the McGowan home in Friendship, now owned by the Adams County Historical Society and being restored by Wilson's great grandson, Ernie Klicko.

Wilson passed away on February 20, 1936 and is buried in Easton Cemetery, Adams County, along with his wife who died on February 21, 1945.

Dick Ennis

Dick Ennis, grandson of German and Irish immigrants from the Wonewoc area, first came to Wisconsin Dells in 1938 as a summer employee at the Badger Restaurant. Before passing on in 1977, he left his heritage here.

In 1941,he met his bride-to-be, and the same year was called to the service of his country in World War II.

He participated in the invasions of North Africa, Sicily, and Normandy, the Battle of the Bulge and the drive through Europe with the "Big Red One" (the First Infantry Division). By V-E Day he was in Czechoslovakia and served in Europe until October, 1945.

At home two months later, he married a member of a fourth generation Dells family, Marjorie Blood.

The couple farmed for 29 years on a farm they purchased in 1948 from Christine Dunham. The farm is now known as the Trapper's Turn Golf Course.

Dick was the father of six sons and five daughters. Included were four state-qualifying wrestlers and one state qualifying track star. Three of his sons, Steve, Scott and Tony, are still Dells residents. His other offspring are Tim, Corning, Iowa; Rita Heitman, Minneapolis; Peggy Olson, Lodi; Dean, Toronto, Canada; Rich, Mondovi; Carla Karau, Oshkosh; Janet, Madison; and Michelle of Portland, Oregon.

Dick died in 1977.

The Federbusch Family

William G. Federbusch was born on January 18, 1882 in Hanover, Germany. In 1907 a Chicago advertising firm discovered his artistic talent, and procureed a military deferment for him. Six months later William decided to stay in America and he never returned to Germany.

He wrote his fiancee, Else P. Stodelmann, born on October 14, 1888, and she came to the U.S. They married, had two children, and lived most of their lives in Chicago. W.G. became a successful artist creating color illustrations for national publications. He held many of his numerous accounts for more than forty years.

Beginning in 1915 the Federbuschs spent their summers in the Dells. In 1915 and 1916 they summered at "Butternut Ledge", a farm resort owned by "Captain" Walter Pickard just north of the Cold Water Canyon Golf Course.

In 1916, unknown to Else, William bought "Black Hawk's Roost" from Jenny and Emma Bowman. When Else learned of the purchase, she objected and William asked the Bowmans to take it back; which they graciously did. But in 1917 William returned and asked to repurchase, and though the Bowmans doubled the price this time, he did.

William G. died on December 28, 1958, and in 1968 Else moved to the Colonial Apartments in Wisconsin Dells where she stayed until her death on July 31, 1981.

There are four William Federbuschs: W. G., W. H., W. J. and W. S., the last, a great grandson. Thus, Black Hawk's Roost is still owned by William Federbusch, and remains a gathering place for relatives and friends from coast to coast.

The cottage was built in 1898 at the site of the toll house Schuyler Gates built for the first bridge across the river. Externally nothing has been changed, but the inside was upgraded with modern amenities such as electricity, phone, a well and plumbing. The cedar plugs on which it sat in 1916 have been replaced by a stone foundation. A cedar shingle roof was installed to bring it back to its original appearance.

The Field Family

Floyd Augustus Field was born to Henry and Olive Thurston Field on August 3, 1858 in Dell Prairie, Wisconsin. He had one brother George, who later owned several tracts of land along the road which would bear the family name.

F.A. Field was educated in Kilbourn City where he would spend his adult life. He started his career at age 21 as a grain and produce dealer, a business he pursued for eight years. In 1886 he purchased three pleasure steamboats, the *Eolah*, the *Alexander Mitchell*, and the *Dell Queen*. He had begun the first consolidated boat company in the Dells. The original name, the Dell Queen Boat Company, was changed in 1890 to the Dells Boat Company.

In 1892 Field sold the company to the Goddings brothers and pursued other business. He opened a lumber yard in Kilbourn, a cheese factory and a grist mill. He maintained an interest in real estate throughout his life and owned several pieces in Kilbourn City. He served as president of Kilbourn City and was elected Village President in 1918.

On July 9, 1892, Floyd married Ella Mary Kane in Milwaukee. They had two sons: Henry Augustus and Floyd F.

Henry went into business with his father for a time before building his own successful career in real estate. He was elected Mayor in 1949.

Floyd F. became a dentist in Wisconsin Dells. In 1920 he married Leona McGowan of Lyndon Station and they had five children: Floyd, Robert, Mary, Dorothy and Rita.

Melvin Harvey Flath

Melvin Harvey Flath was born in Lake Mills, Wisconsin on September 1, 1914. He was the oldest of five children raised in a German speaking household, and did not learn to speak English until he attended public school.

Melvin enjoyed tinkering with machines or attending circuses much more then going to school. By age 10 he had constructed a small Ferris wheel in his yard for neighborhood children to ride, and by age 12, had developed a chassis able to support large truck loads. Young and naive, Melvin sold the invention, still used by large carrier trucks today, for a meager $100.

By age 20 Melvin had started his own cartage business in Milwaukee. He was married to Ida Sonia Bines and they had four daughters.

When World War II broke out, Melvin was issued a certificate of necessity because his company was hauling scrap iron that the government badly needed. Towards the end of the war, he travelled to a truck surplus sale in California to look for new equipment and was shocked to find that he had travelled 2,000 miles praying to find a good bargain only to find amphibious ducks instead.

Not wanting to leave empty handed, he purchased his first "Duck," and with his brother, spent two weeks driving it home. Neighbors thought him foolish for wasting money when he had three daughters and a pregnant wife. But determined to make it worthwhile, he installed a floor, Milwaukee bus seats, and took some of his friends on a test drive into Lake Michigan. Having never owned a boat before, Melvin was unaware that all boats have plugs, and his first amphibious splish-splash almost became his last.

Melvin began taking his family to Pewaukee Lake on the weekends, and curious onlookers were soon willing to pay 50¢ to ride the Duck from land to water. One passer-by noted that Melvin should take the Duck to the Dells, where everyday is Sunday. Three days later, Melvin did just that.

He opened the Wisconsin Dells Amphibious Lines, and developed trails and a return water route. His tour lasted 1 1/2 hours and he charged $2 per person. He and Ida purchased a home on Lake Delton and for the business, property on Highway 12. Melvin then purchased 65 Ducks at $250 each.

The following year, the Flaths also opened a bar and restaurant called the Old Mill. To fill the grassy open spaces on the highway 12 property, Melvin built a large wooden ship which housed exotic birds and animals to be viewed by Duck customers. In the off-season he started dredging his property and developing lakes. He created one for each of his daughters and named them accordingly.

Next, Melvin developed the area's first airstrip by dedicating a back parcel which he leveled so that small planes could land. Once his lakes were completed, he had fresh, cool spring fed ponds which he loaded with rainbow and speckled trout and opened a trout fishing business.

After six years in the Duck business, Melvin sold it to Dr. Ebert from Beaver Dam, who rented Melvin's Hwy 12 property for several years before moving the Duck Line.

That winter, Melvin drove his family to Pasadena, California where he rented a large home. While the older girls attended school and Ida stayed home with the youngest, Melvin went out exploring. Within weeks he pulled up to his home in a used Greyhound bus. Again, everyone wanted to know why, why, why? Melvin just let everyone get mad at him and later that evening, drove the bus away.

Two months later, he drove it back, complete with kitchen, bathroom, shower, two bedrooms, closets and storage space. Traveling in their "house bus" meant that the family avoided endlessly stopping on the return trip to Wisconsin, as Melvin had intended. Though he didn't know it, he had developed the first motor home in 1953. Whenever the House Bus stopped, mobs of people scrambled to view the unusual traveling machine.

Several winters later, Melvin rented his Hwy 12 parcel to land developers from Milwaukee, who opened Storybook Gardens.

Later Melvin also developed the Dells' first miniature golf course and amusement park, as well as developing another boat tour with his double-decker paddle wheel boat, *Queen of the Dells*. He opened Wisconsin's first dog track behind the present Shipwreck Lagoon Miniature Golf Course. He also started a smaller lake tour on his private Lake Sally.

This gifted inventor passed away in November, 1973.

The Frodin Family

Axel Sanfrid Frodin was born on March 22, 1876, in Billingsfaten Skovle, Sweden. He came to his brother's home in Chicago in 1891. On August 6, 1898, he married Ada Bloom, who had migrated from Scoley, Sweden in 1874, and three sons were born to them: Elmer, LeRoy and Eugene.

In 1908 he built a cottage on property given to him by the Jennings family, who owned the hotel on top of Blue Mound. In 1932, at age 56, Axel died there of a heart attack. Axel was a Master Mason of the Rainbow Masonic Lodge.

At his death, the Dells Masonic Lodge accompanied his body to the train which took him to rest in Chicago. In appreciation, his sons presented the Lodge with a Bible which is still used at meetings.

Elmer Frodin, the eldest son, was born in Chicago on September 17, 1899.

When young, Elmer began working for the Chicago Rawhide Manufacturing Company. In 1922, he married Wilhelmina Reese, daughter of Andrew Reese, a Swedish Methodist Minister. Three daughters were born to them: Jeanne, June and Joy.

Elmer's new family continued spending summers at the cottage in Dell Prairie. In the early 1930s, Wilhelmina's brother and brothers-in-law purchased one of the cottages as a summer home. For years, the women of the families would establish themselves in Kilbourn as soon as the Chicago schools closed for the summer. After Labor Day they returned to the city for the children to begin the next school year. The men would travel to Kilbourn on the weekends via train on the Milwaukee Road or would sometimes drive the 6-7 hour trip.

In time the Frodin cottage became too small for the new Frodin families so in the mid-1940s, Elmer purchased the farmhouse located directly east of Elephant's Back. Elmer's family began living in this house late in the 1940s. Each of Elmer's daughters married men from Wisconsin Dells. Jeanne is married to Harry Priester, June to Adolph Priester and Joy to Bruce Wendorf. They still spend summers in the old farmhouse, known as Wildwood.

Elmer died in January, 1968 and Wilhelmina in August, 1993.

LeRoy, the second of Axel Frodin's sons, was born August 24, 1903. During summers in Kilbourn he made many friends and piloted a launch on the river. As an adult he worked for Standard Oil Company in Whiting, Indiana.

He married Sue Schwartz and had two sons, Robert and James. After LeRoy's retirement he and Susan spent more time at the

Frodin cottage. LeRoy's eldest son, Bob, retired to the Dells and died there in 1994. Roy died in 1972 and Sue in 1971.

Eugene David Frodin, Axel Frodin's youngest son, was born on August 5, 1906. He took his first trip to the Dells when he was a baby and never missed a summer after.

Eugene's fond Dells memories included speakeasies during Prohibition, open air dances at the Olson Family Pavilion and the Purple Grackle, and the first amusement type ride at the Dells, a tilt-o-whirl located near the Grackle. He enjoyed ice cream sodas at Bauer's and O'Neil's Drug Store, or joining in a fire department water fight. He was on the maiden voyage of the *Winnebago* when the paddle wheel got stuck in a sandbar.

Eugene married Kathryn Ladika on February 26, 1944, and they had two children, Linda and Kenneth.

Linda, a village trustee in Glendale Heights, Illinois, is married to William Jackson and has four children: Steve, Tracy, Bill, and Don, and one grandchild, Jennifer.

Kenneth, who drowned in the Wisconsin River on September 10, 1978, spent his senior year at Wisconsin Dells High School. He helped take the Wisconsin Dells Chiefs to the state basketball finals in 1969, and was named All Conference Center for the South Central Conference. He married Ruth Kimball, had two children, David and Leslie, and made Wisconsin Dells his home.

After 41 years at the Chicago Post Office, Eugene retired and in 1974 he and his wife, Kathryn built a home on the side of Blue Mound and finally became residents rather than tourists. Eugene was a Mason and both were members of the Methodist Church. Eugene loved the scenery and wildlife that Wisconsin Dells offered.

On August 18, 1983, Euguene died, taking with him 77 years of Wisconsin Dells memories. All of Axel and Ada Frodin's descendants continue to spend time in Wisconsin Dells each year.

Leroy Gates

"Leroy Gates, Dells and River Pilot - 1849-58."

With these words, carved and painted on the face of a cliff in the Narrows, this early Kilbourn settler made his mark in the Dells. His father was Schuyler S. Gates who, with his family, had come to the area from Vermont. Schuyler operated the toll bridge at the Narrows, and gave his name to Gates ravine on the east side of the river at the Devil's Elbow.

From this convenient location, Leroy picked up piloting jobs in the narrowest and most dangerous part of the Dells. Piloting the Narrows was a great challenge to any raft pilot. An early newspaper reported, "Leroy Gates at the Dells Bridge for coolness, intrepidity and success stands at the head" (of the Dells raft pilots).

The next spring Leroy advertised that his fee for "piloting the Dells" was $2.00 "or 10 dollars if he warrants the trip."

Leroy was a person around whom legends collected. He once undertook to pilot a raft through the Narrows while wearing full formal attire, but this time, the river was too much for him, the raft broke up, and Leroy had to dash for the nearest shore with his coat tails flying.

Before the village of Kilbourn was a year old, Leroy advertised that he had a pleasure boat to rent to sight-seers who wished, as he wrote, to "*penetrate and descry the numerous and occult caves of the Dells.*" Here, he asserted, "*depressed spirits can be aleviated, gloom and melancholy soon be dispelled and the mind become greatly invigorated.*"

In 1860, Leroy appeared suddenly as a portrait photographer. He advertised:

"*Leroy Gates Picture Gallery. Ferrotypes, Papyrotypes, etc. On plate suitable to send in a letter 20¢, and in good sized and fine cases 40¢ and upward...All above 3 years of age taken in cloudy weather with almost as good success as in good weather. Small children and infants taken best on clear days...in 2 seconds.*"

A little later he advertised that his picture gallery was "*open for the reception of all who may be desirous of procuring their life-like shadows to hand down to posterity.*"

In 1865 Gates sold his "picture gallery" to Henry Bennett. The boom in hops was exciting many people in what had become the greatest primary hops market in the United States, and Gates had transfered his interests to the hops field as he tells in this March 1866 letter from Milwaukee:

"Henry Bennett, Kilbourn.
Dear Fellow:

I have a few things I wish you to do - some may be some may not be pleasant and easy.

In the first place I wish you without fail to raise me $100 by the 12 of April and don't disappoint me under no consideration. You see I owe for the hop poles nearly $200...And I have hop roots to buy yet...Now don't fail to raise this $100 and as much more as you can. I shall be back in a few days and then I shall try to settle with those I owe, that is, with your help. If some come to you to inquire if I have run away, tell them I will be back in a few days and settle with them.

Print me one dozen more of my pictures as before and take more pains in toning...

Truly,
Leroy Gates."

Gates was not only growing hops but helping to recruit pickers for the harvest. One September so many girls and women arrived by train from other towns that the newspaper editor wrote of "regiments in calico." However, in a few years the hops louse began to infest the vines and the hops boom evaporated, leaving many people in debt for land, hops roots and poles: a severe economic blow to the community as well as Gates.

"Dells Pilot Captured" was the headline in the October 1868 issue of the Kilbourn paper that reported Leroy's serious courtship of, and possibly marriage to, an unamed lady from Baraboo.

Leroy's father was murdered in the fall of 1869, and though it is impossible to judge of the effect this had on Leroy, the rhyme carved on the grave stone at the Kilbourn Cemetery seems to be in Leroy's style:

"Schuyler S. Gates, born Wallingford Vermont,
January 22, 1805.
Murdered September 19, 1869
A careless and innocent life;
a life of trouble and strife."

Leroy stayed in the Wisconsin Dells area until at least 1878.

The Gavinski Family

Stanley Leo Gavinski was born in Lemont, Illinois on September 27, 1895, one of eleven children born to Mary Ann Hropkowski and Ignasus John Gavinski. Ignasus was a tailor from Pryzce, Poland, smuggled to America in a crate aboard a ship. Stanley's 10 siblings were: Elizabeth, Francis, Tophil (known as Philip), Martin, Sophia, William, Peter, Nellie, Gertrude and Tressa.

The family moved to Adams, Wisconsin when Stanley was a young child.

After his father died in 1914, Stanley went to barber school in Chicago. He moved to Randolph, Wisconsin and then to Wisconsin Dells, in March 1915.

On December 31, 1920, Arthur Koberstein and Stanley L. Gavinski purchased the property at 208 Broadway from Mrs. Annie E. Loomis, where they operated a barber shop, bath facilities, pool hall and bowling alley.

Stanley married Stella Cecelia Hayes on November 25, 1924. Stella was born October 24, 1895, the fourth child of James and Mary O'Connell Hayes. From age three to sixteen Stella lived with her Aunt Kate on the O'Connell farm in Dell Prairie, now occupied by Stanley Gaffney. After attending Adams County's Ward School through grade seven, she spent a year at her mother's home in Dellona where she graduated as salutatorian of her eighth grade class. She then returned to live with Aunt Kate at 1023 Bowman Road in Kilbourn, the same house in which she lived until her death April 11, 1981. The house had been built on land that Stella's great grandfather, Timothy Shanahan, had purchased from Jonathon and Lizzie Bowman on October 10, 1881. Stella attended Kilbourn High School for two years, and over the years spent time working at Dixon's Store, Stuelke's Drug Store and the Marchowsky Dry Goods Store.

In 1925 Koberstein and Gavinski converted their business at 208 Broadway to the K & G Restaurant. In the off season Stanley was a barber and a car salesman. He retired from the restaurant business in 1956. He and Stella also managed the Shady Lane Motel for Phil Van Dyke.

Stanley and Stella had two sons: Stanley Robert, born April 4, 1927 and Donald James, born April 21, 1932. Stanley died on December 20, 1989 at the age of 94.

Stanley's brother, Peter E. Gavinski, was born February 12, 1900 in Friendship, Wisconsin, the eighth child born to Ignasus and Mary Ann.

Peter met Frances Margaret Seger in Kilbourn and they were married at St. Cecilia's Church there on February 12, 1922.

Frances was the daughter of Frank and Mary (Shields) Seger. Her father, Frank, had been born in Germany and was now a painter in Kilbourn. Frances had one brother, Raymond, and a sister, Celia.

Peter started his career as a barber in Kilbourn, where he practiced for more than 47 years. Originally he worked with his brother Stanley and Art Koberstein, at 208 Broadway, presently the Patio Restaurant. Later he opened Pete's barber shop on Broadway, presently the What Not Shop. Martin Gavinski, his brother joined him and later his son, Kenneth (Knute).

He pioneered the first air conditioner in Kilbourn by taking a radiator from a truck, running water through it and putting a fan behind it to cool the air.

Peter belonged to the Wisconsin Dells Business Men's Association and was a charter member of the Knights of Columbus #4392.

Peter and Frances had four children: Lois, Eugene, Patrick and Kenneth. Peter died at the age of 86 on December 20, 1986.

Eugene Gregory Gavinski was the oldest son. He was born in Kilbourn on October 10, 1927. He graduated from Wisconsin Dells High School and served in the armed forces in 1946.

Eugene (Gene) was a sprinkler fitter at Badger Ordinance in Sauk County. He later went to plumbing school in Madison, and graduated with honors as a master plumber. He worked as a plumber for Roser Plumbing and Heating at 729 Oak Street.

Later, when the plumbing shop moved, Eugene worked in Lake Delton and Baraboo. Eventually he worked as head plumber for Tommy Bartlett's in the Dells.

He married Alice Kessler of Baraboo in June, 1956. They lived in Wisconsin Dells and had four daughters: Nana, Gale, Amy and Cheryl.

Eugene died in August, 1992.

The Gissal Family

In January 1947, Dr. Frederick Wilmer Gissal joined Dr. Clifford Broderick and Dr. Houghton in Wisconsin Dells in their offices above Stuelke's Drug Store. They later moved to the second floor of the Co-op building on Oak Street and finally built a clinic on Vine Street. In 40 years of family practice in the Dells, Dr. Gissal delivered over 3,000 babies. He even managed to deliver 3 babies in one day; one each in Baraboo, Portage, and Adams.

Dr. Gissal also loved sports and volunteered as team doctor for the Dells High School football team. He faithfully traveled with the team from town to town for over 30 years.

Although he was on call 24 hours a day, Dr. Gissal and his wife Harriet raised a family of six. Harriet and eldest son Jeff moved from Milwaukee to a cottage next to Frank Trebileak's on the Wisconsin River in June 1947. In the fall, they moved to a new home at 1020 Bowman Road, where they lived for eight years.

Harriet and Fred were quite busy raising children. Cindy was born in 1948, Mary in 1950, and Bill in 1952. They outgrew their house on Bowman Road and moved to the old Greenwood house at 822 Capital Street.

They lived on Capital Street for 25 years. Judy was born in 1956 and Wendy in 1959. Jeff worked for iceman Joe Kaiser and delivered blocks of ice from his ice house in the alley.

American Field Service became a big part of the Gissal family life. Mary was selected to go to Paris in 1967, Bill to Spain in 1969, and Judy to South Africa in 1973. The family also hosted Jurgen Pfeiffen as an AFS student from Germany in the 1971-1972 school year. Mary and Bill were valedictorians at Wisconsin Dells High School in 1968 and 1970 respectively. All the kids spent their summers working in the Dells: wrapping grats bags, clerking at the souvenir stores, waitressing, guiding on the river and selling boat, Duck and Indian tickets.

In 1980, the family sold their house in the Dells and moved to a permanent residence on Jordan Lake.

George W. Gray

George W. Gray was born in Coloma, Wisconsin on April 1, 1890, the only child of Walter and Emma Gray. He grew up in the area and after graduating from Endeavor Academy, attended Carroll College for one year. While at Carroll, he played in the first football game he ever had a chance to even see. One college classmate was Alfred Lunt, who went on to gain dramatic fame on Broadway with his wife, Lynn Fontanne.

George married Mary Bernice Osborn on September 19, 1912 and farmed with the Osborn family in Brooks. Later, he purchased his own farm near Stanley. After having two boys, Willard and Merlin, Bernice passed away on November 18, 1918 during the flu epidemic. After this loss, George sold the farm and moved to Kilbourn in 1919 and became involved with the Kilbourn Co-Op.

On December 25, 1919, George married Margaret Rodger. He bought a Grocery and Meat Market from Borcher-Tollaksen. On November 26,1925, after giving birth to two daughters, Jane and Margaret, Mrs. Gray died.

On June 2, 1927 George married Ottilie Hoedel of Kilbourn. They had one son, John A. (Jack). George sold the grocery business in 1930 to Gordon Winnes and went on the road as a sales representative for E.R. Godfrey & Son (IGA).

In 1933, back problems dictated that he stop travelling, and he bought the Lake Delton Ice Company from Archie Cartright. In 1942, George left the ice business to work at Badger Ordnance.

Following World War II he became an agent for the American Family Insurance Company, whom he represented until full retirement. He also retired from a group he held in high esteem, the Kilbourn Volunteer Fire Department.

George died in his eightieth year, February 3, 1970.

Of his children: Willard made his home in Pueblo, Colorado; Merlin in Wisconsin Dells; Jane in Marshfield; Margaret in Fond du Lac; Jack in Middleton.

Dan Greenwood

Dan Greenwood spent 50 years as an automobile dealer at 305 Broadway.

His first sales job was in St. Paul, Minnesota where he worked for three years at a Ford agency. After time out for Navy service during World War I, he returned to the Dells in 1920 and took on the Cleveland-Chandler automobile franchise. Later he transferred to Overland and Willys Knight, two popular cars in the early 1920s, then to Dodge and Pontiac for a year or two. In 1925 he obtained the Buick franchise and added the Chevrolet line in 1930.

Dan was born in Quincy, Adams County, on June 13, 1897 to Albert H. and Clara Greenwood. He graduated from Wisconsin Dells High School in 1917 and then worked a short time for a railroad contractor in Montana. He married Irene Purcell of Wisconsin Dells on August 26, 1918.

He was a member of St. Cecelia's Catholic Church, the American Legion, the Kilbourn Volunteer Fire Department, and a charter member of the Kiwanis Club. He served on the school board for a number of years.

He was survived by four children; Dan B. of Rockford, Illinois; Jack of Wisconsin Dells; Mrs. Robert Harks of California; and Sheila of Wisconsin Dells.

Ole Gregerson

Ole Gregerson was born to Ole Sr. and Ingeborg Jensen Gregerson on May 6, 1872 in Newport. He lived on their farm on County Trunk O, owned by the family since 1866, for all but the last two years of his life. He attended Laffin School.

Before a well was dug, each day the two oldest Gregerson sons drove livestock from the farm to the river to drink, a distance of about 1/2 mile across the railroad tracks. Ole's brother Greger was killed at age 13 on the railroad crossing, when the horse he was riding bolted and he was struck by the train. When Ole was 18 he worked at logging camps near Corona and Eagle River.

He married Emma Gaalaas on December 6, 1911 in Milwaukee. She was born May 17, 1886 in Norway and emigrated to America when she was 16 years old. Ole and Emma had six children: Olaf, Evelyn, Carole, Gordon, Edith and Edward.

Ole was skilled in blacksmithing as well as the care of sick and injured animals. He repaired all his machinery and mended harnesses with this leather sewing machine.

He served for several years as Newport Town Chairman and on the Stearns School Board. He was a member of Newport Lutheran Church and a charter member of Farmers Union Local 315.

Ole died on October 18, 1962 at 90 years old. Emma died April 26, 1969.

Owen Gromme

Owen Gromme was born in Fond du Lac, Wisconsin in 1886. He became a taxidermist at the Field Museum in Chicago at age 21. After serving in the army during World War I he became a curator at the Milwaukee Public Museum for the next 45 years.

On a museum trip to Africa in 1927, he survived a bout with the deadly Black Water Fever. In 1945 he won the National Duck Stamp award with his painting of Shoveler Ducks. His popular book *Birds of Wisconsin* was published in 1963. A second book, *The World of Owen Gromme*, was published in 1983.

He retired from the museum in 1965 and was commissioned by the M & I Bank of Milwaukee to create 43 magnificent wildlife paintings for the bank's headquarters.

He and his wife Anne then moved to Briggsville. In 1970 he completed the first of many limited edition prints. In 1976, the Leigh Yawkey Woodson Museum named him its first "Master Wildlife Artist." He was named Ducks Unlimited artist of the year in 1978 and the Milwaukee Public Museum named an exhibition hall in his honor.

Owen Gromme died in 1991 at the age of 95.

The Gussel Family

Bernard "Beno" Gussel Sr., his wife Julia and their children moved from Stevens Point to Wisconsin Dells in 1941.

Beno was employed as a millwright foreman at Badger Ordinance Works until the end of World War II. In 1946, he formed Center State Industries, a furniture manufacturing and dry kiln operation. He and his partner, Wayne Boyington, sold the operation in 1951. He was later employed at Storybook Gardens, where through his artistry and fine woodworking abilities, he created many of the attractions there. Beno died of a heart attack in 1967, and Julia died in January, 1990.

They had five children: Beatrice; Bernard Jr. "Bud"; Roseanne; Robert; Thomas.

Beatrice married Clark Winn and had four children: Bill Parchem, Patricia (Mrs. John Johnson), Debbie (Mrs. Curt Konietzki), and Matthew. Her grandchildren are Miranda and Erin Parchem, Melissa and Matthew Johnson and Sarah and Heather Konietzki.

Bernard Jr. "Bud" and his wife Joyce have four children: David, Joseph, Gary and Julie (Keller). Their seven grandchildren are Jordan Keller and Courtney, Tricia, Lauren, Kevin, Caitlyn and Claire Gussel. Bud is founder and general manager of Holiday Wholesale and Vacationland Vendors in Wisconsin Dells.

Roseanne married Harvey Christenson and they had four children: Linda (Schultz), Kenneth, Susan and Richie, and two grandchildren, Kelsie and Hunter. Roseanne passed away in 1991.

Robert and his wife Barbara own and operate Sherwood Forest Campground. They have two children, Lori and Bradley.

Thomas and his wife Lisa have one daughter Andrea. Tom owns and operates Ad Lit Distributing Company in Wisconsin Dells and Florida.

Theodore J. Hagen

Theodore J. Hagen was born in Athens, Wisconsin, the sixth of ten children, to Martha and William Hagen, December 22, 1912. They lived in a log house and Ted's father was a farmer and horse trader.

When Ted was twelve years old, the family moved to Jefferson and later to West Allis. He and his father held jobs in a brick yard and a lumber company. Ted joined him after school and in the summer while attending Saint Aloysius Grade School. After graduation Ted worked full time.

Later he worked at North End Foundry as a coremaker. He met and married Jeanette Brown, a school chum, September 5, 1936. They had four sons: William, James, Dennis and Kenneth.

After taking a farm job for a year in Farmington, Ted and his family decided get a farm of their own. He and Jeanette took a two week vacation and headed toward the Dells, looking at farms on the way. By the time they reached Wisconsin Dells, they knew they couldn't afford a farm.

They visited Ted's brother Lee and his wife Ruth, who suggested they buy the Dell House Park Tavern down the road. The next day they all went down to the tavern, and with owners, John and Martha Schmalze, spent the day visiting, singing and playing music. They loved the Dells scenery and were soon at the Dells bank talking to Mr. Amman and John Kelley.

The Hagens moved to Wisconsin Dells on November 21, 1946. Ted and Marcel (Nibs) Naber tore down the old Drinker House for the lumber to use in remodeling the tavern. The name was changed from Dell House Park to Pow Wow Inn and eventually Hagen's Bar.

The Hagens found cherished friends in the many Indians who became their first customers. The ceremonial singers and actors would come in after the show to relax and sing.

Fish frys were started in 1949. There was no indoor plumbing, and Ted and the boys pumped lots of water to store in large containers. In the beginning there were no french fryers, and fish was fried in frying pans. Potato salad, cole slaw, fish, and bread were served on paper plates for 50¢ per plate.

Ted also worked for Michaels Prepakt Ament Company, Disston Saw Company, and did carpenter work. Ted often played the guitar for his patrons. He passed away on January 28, 1991.

Monk Heineke

Monk Heineke was born in Chicago, Illinois on January 2, 1911, the son of Gustave and Katherine Heineke.

He moved to Kilbourn in 1922, and graduated from Wisconsin Dells High School in 1929. He attended the University of Wisconsin for one year, but due to the depression did not return.

He married the former Helen Thomas on September 12, 1934, and they had two sons, John and Jim.

In 1940 he left for Nevada to work in the gold mines with his two brothers. He returned in 1941 and worked at Badger Ordnance until he was drafted in 1943. He was discharged from the Navy in 1945, and worked for Bill Schultz until opening Monk's Bar in 1947.

He was the only mayor in the city of Wisconsin Dells to be elected as a write-in candidate. He supported the youth of the community in efforts to build the swimming pool and middle school.

Monk died September 4, 1975.

Oliver P. Helland

Oliver P. Helland was born December 25, 1889 on the family farm in Newport. He was the son of Hans O. Helland, of Sogn, Norway and Alice Anderson Helland. He married Irene Stanton in Kilbourn on June 26, 1916.

In 1920, Oliver and Irene bought the old Park Hotel from Eliza Bresnahan. As the hotel was not suitable for year round living, they also bought the Dot Bell home and river frontage.

Oliver's first career was in banking, and he spent 12 years at the Kilbourn State Bank. In 1921, he and his wife, along with Walter and William Stanton, founded the Riverview Boat Line. A few years later they created a partnership with the Crandall family in the Lower Dells. Riverview also operated a free campground and gas station. He owned and operated the Hotel Helland and was an owner in Stanton & Helland properties, which operated several enterprises in Wisconsin Dells.

Mr. Helland was very active in the community, serving as an alderman and as a long time member of the Columbia County Board of Supervisors. He was instrumental in changing the city's name to Wisconsin Dells and in the formation of the present Chamber of Commerce. He was also a member of the Kiwanis Club.

Oliver Helland passed away on November 6, 1957. He was survived by his sons, Hans O. and Peter Helland, and daughters Virginia (Mrs. Richard T. Lucke), and Ragnhild (Mrs. Paul Myklebust), all of Wisconsin Dells. Another son, Oliver, Jr. (Laddie) was killed in World War II.

Jack Heller

John Henry Heller, better known as "Jack," was born in Louisville, Kentucky in 1930. He became interested in 4-H Club work at the age of 10, and worked with 4-H in one capacity or another (as a 4-H Club member and as a professional) until his death in 1988, at the age of 58.

He was educated at the Universities of Kentucky, Maryland and Indiana. His first employment was as a 4-H Youth Agent with the University of Kentucky. He remained on the Kentucky staff until moving his family to Wisconsin Dells in 1970.

He served as Director of the Camp Upham Woods 4-H Environmental Education Center from 1970-1985, when he retired. His appointment with the University of Wisconsin also included working two days a week in the Madison office, implementing statewide 4-H programs in the areas of Natural Science, Recreation, and Environmental Education. He was in charge of Wisconsin's 4-H camping program which included Camp Susan in Langlade County, and Camp Tappiwingo in Manitowoc, Wisconsin. In 1980, he was promoted to Full Professor, and upon retirement, was named "Professor Emeritus" at the University of Wisconsin.

The Kiwanis Club was one of his primary interests, and he served as President of the Wisconsin Dells Kiwanis Club, and Lt. Governor of the Wisconsin-Upper Michigan District. He was also dedicated to the Dells Country Historical Society and the Lutheran Church.

Following retirement he spent winters in Florida, and helped organize Kiwanis and 4-H Clubs on Marco Island. Unable to "really" retire, he began working during the camping season with the University of Florida State 4-H Camping Program.

Jack married the former Betty Jane Hamilton of Mayfield, Kentucky. Their three children are John Gregory and Bryant Scott of Wisconsin Dells and Allison Ann Belisle of Beaverton, Oregon. There are three grandchildren: Kyle and Brittney Heller, and Jordan Scott Belisle.

Walter Helm

Born of German immigrant parents on a farm near Oshkosh, Walter Helm was the seventh son, born on the seventh day of the seventh month in 1887. He had one sister.

Though many believed that all the Government lands in Wisconsin had been claimed, in 1915 land titles were corrected and a 160-acre parcel of unclaimed land turned up west of the Marquette County line, in Jackson Township, Adams County.

Walter was working in the woods of north central Wisconsin, for a man who had a friend in the land office at Wausau.

"One day he came to me and said, 'How would you like to homestead some land?' I said, 'No sir, I tried that on the Blackfoot Reservation in Montana and again in South Dakota during my roving days, and the numbers I drew were too high to wait for.' But when he gave me a description of the land, and it was right here in Wisconsin, I came down to look at it, by train from Merrill to Adams."

It was March 17, 1915, and there was snow on the ground, but the 160 acres had three spring fed lakes, all forest, and Helm saw clover peaking through the snow on a neighboring field. He went back and filed for the homestead. One of the government requirements was that he had to swear he had seen the land.

Helm left his job up north and went back to Oshkosh to gather up his belongings. His mother gave him a stove, couch, bedding, chairs. At a going-out-of-business sale at a lumber yard, he saved $1,000 on lumber, enough to build a shanty. All this he loaded on a box car he'd rented, and came to Oxford by railroad.

Helm's claim surprised the local farmers. His land backed the Adams County Poor Farm and they were using part of it for pasture. A neighbor on the west had fenced into it, too.

He roomed at the Oxford Hotel where they let him store his furniture in the barn. "The hotel was run by a couple who didn't stay long. Bedbugs got into my things!"

Walter walked 10 miles to his claim every day, and back at night because there was no other place to sleep, and it was a while before he could afford horses.

His new neighbors brought their teams to help stump and brush the acreage the government said he had to clear, and to help build his shanty.

"Right after the basement was dug, we had a bad forest fire, but we backfired and with water from the lake saved all but one bundle of shingles." When the shanty was ready to live in, Helm hired 3 farmers for $3.00 each to bring his things out from Oxford.

Government regulations required he live in the shanty six months out of a year for three years. "I had to prove to Uncle Sam I could make a living, then in five years he'd give me the land. I wasn't married, and didn't know if I'd stay around, so I bought the land at the end of three years for $1.25 an acre."

Helm's first crop of corn froze on the 31st of July, but he'd had the foresight to plant rutabagas, too. "Everybody liked the baggies and I made more money from them than the corn that year."

After the two-room shanty, Helm built a granary, and what he calls the 'old barn' where he had room for a team of horses, two cows, and a corncrib. Later he added 200 more acres to the farm, clearing most of it, and built a new barn for twenty-eight cows from lumber it took three men all winter to cut. Rocks used in the foundation of the house and walls were hauled off Helm's fields.

Always a church-goer, Helm walked to Davis Corners to attend services. He met the girl he wanted to marry at a party there. "It took me four years to convince her I'd make a good husband. We were married in 1921. She came to this claim in the woods and afterward told her friends she never had a lonely day in her life."

He added to the shanty so there were kitchen and dining room, living room and three bedrooms.

The Helms had three sons (including twins) and two daughters. They celebrated forty-eight wedding anniversaries.

The family always had a cellar full of potatoes. They raised good alfalfa and corn, but the boys didn't want to farm when they grew up. Walter says that is understandable. They have good jobs.

The last homestead in Central Wisconsin was sold nearly twenty years ago, and the land stands idle now (part has been subdivided and developed).

Walter Helm was past president of Master Farmers of Wisconsin. He was clerk of Jackson Township for twelve years, and Sunday School Superintendant for thirty. He died in 1985.

Fred Hillman

In 1891, at age 17, Fred Hillman came to America from Germany. He got a job on a farm in the Town of Dellona. In 1897 he returned to Germany and brought his brother William back with him. William got a job working for Judge R. Marshall on his farm in the Town of Delton.

Fred married Lillian Foss in 1900. They had six children, two of whom died young. In 1911, they bought a 160 acre farm from Judge Marshall south of Delton, and the family moved from their rented farm in Dellona. They enlarged the house and in 1922 built a new barn. Fred served on the town board for two years.

Lillian was killed in a car--train accident in Reedsburg in 1951. Fred lived to an active 93 years old and passed away in 1967.

His oldest son Edwin farmed with him and later took over the farm. Elsie married William O. Nelson and moved to a farm in Newport. Harold married Lucille Monic and lived in Rock Springs, later moving to Baraboo. They had five children. Edith taught school for 13 years before she married Fletcher Burgess and had 2 daughters. Edwin continued farming until in 1984, at 82 years old, he sold the farm.

Ralph Hines

Named after the 25th president of the United States, Ralph McKinley Hines was born to Frederick and Francis J. Whitaker Hines on April 11, 1896 in Minerva, Ohio. He had one sister, Hazel Mae. He spent his childhood on the family farm, next to the McKinley farm, in Minerva. At age 15 he graduated from the Cleveland Automobile School, and then from a Cleveland technical school of engineering in 1914. He joined the 316th Army Engineers during World War I and after his discharge in 1918, spent five years at the Willing Brothers Construction Company in Bellview, Ohio. In 1923, while attending the Chicago Engineering Works School, Hines was hired by the W.J. Newman.

In 1925, Hines joined Newman's "Lake Delton project."

Newman's dream was to 'create a lake where cows once grazed, up where the pines begin." Ralph Hines made that dream a reality - developing the 2,000 acres around the six mile shoreline. Little known as its true developer, Ralph Hines' made Lake Delton his life from the time he operated the power steam shovel to build the lake in 1926, until his death of a heart attack in 1977 at age 81.

On June 15, 1936 Ralph married Alice Sanden and their daughter Judy was born in March, 1944. Judy married John Skille and they had two daughters, Tara Lynn and Tania Raue.

In the Dells, Ralph was a member of the Harold B. Larkin American Legion Post, the Masonic Lodge, the Kiwanis Club, the Lions Club, the Shriners, and the Consolidated Boat Company. In 1949, he was cited by the State VFW for his contributions to the area. With other local business men, he raised funds to bring industry to the Wisconsin Dells area, and they were instrumental in getting the Ben H. Anderson Manufacturing Company into the area. Big Joe Manufacturing now occupies the Anderson site.

The Hoisington Family

Oliver Hoisington came to the Town of Excelsior, Sauk County, in the spring of 1853 with the Butterfield Settlement. His wife's name is unknown as is information on some of his children.

One of his sons, Warner Hoisington, was born in Utah and is buried in the Revolutionary Cemetery on South Avenue in Dellona. Also buried there is George Hoisington, who may have been Warner's brother. He may have had another brother, Elias, as well.

Warner married Letitia Maria Fuller. Their children were: Merella E., born February 3, 1839; James Elias, a Civil War veteran, born April 28, 1841 at Orangeville, N.Y. and married on June 23, 1867 to Martha E. Rice who was born at Panama, N.Y. on July 23, 1848; and George Henry, born June 15, 1849 in N.Y.

George was also a Civil War veteran who served with Company E, 46th Infantry at the Battle of Gettysburg. He married Frances Helen Rice at Narrows Prairie and they lived most of their lives at 501 Vine Street in Kilbourn, now an apartment building. George had also farmed for a time in the Dellona area. He attended the 75th Reunion of the Battle of Gettysburg, Pennsylvania, in 1938. Frances died on December 31, 1933 and George in September, 1942. They are both buried in Spring Grove Cemetery.

The children of George and Frances were: Cora May, born September 23, 1868 and married on December 21, 1886 to George Montanye at Kilbourn. Cora is buried in Excelsior, and her husband, at the Spring Grove Cemetery; Mary Eunice, born June 2, 1875 and married February 17, 1897 to Willie Newton Stearns at Wisconsin Dells. Mary died October 24, 1920 and is buried in Wisconsin Dells; Elida Letitia, born December 26, 1884 and married in Newport on September 7, 1916 to Edwin Albert Weaver, a Methodist Episcopal Minister born at Smallwood Town, Blain Settlement, Jasper County, Illinois.

Elida Hoisington Weaver attended the Butterfield School on Hwy 23 and Coon Bluff Road and later received her teaching certificate from the Oshkosh Normal School. She taught in various places including Dellona, Wisconsin Dells, and Bismarck, North Dakota. Reverend Weaver preached in these and other places as well. Elida and Edwin Weaver adopted two daughters: Joyce Helen Weaver, born June 30, 1921 and died April 21, 1987 and Frances Lois Weaver, born December 20, 1924, still living at Tripoli, Wisconsin.

Hoyt Orville Hoisington was born on July 17, 1890. He married Mary Alice Johnson on November 7, 1922 at Kilbourn. He and his automobile were found in the river near the bridge at Newport, on February 11, 1932. Friends and family have long questioned the accident, citing the suspicious fact that since 1930, Hoyt had worked for Al Capone, who alegedly kept a bootlegging farm on old Highway 33.

George H. Houghton

This Civil War photographer, born in 1824, learned photography while living in Vermont. He came to Kilbourn with his brother-in-law, George Bennett and his nephew Henry Bennett. His son Fred says, "he had a shop there and made sash, doors and blinds five days a week. Saturdays he had a gallery there and made pictures for those that wanted them so the money he received from both trades gave him a living and that was all." His ad in the *Wisconsin Mirror* advertises his "Daguerrean Salon" in late 1858.

In 1859, Houghton returned to Brattleboro, Vermont and opened his "Photographic Hall" there. During the Civil War, Houghton followed Vermont troops in Virginia and pictured the men and their camps from the autumn of 1861 to the summer of 1862. When he returned home, he sold the photos in his studio.

In October, 1864, he presented a compilation of his war photographs to the Vermont Historical Society. *Military Images Magazine* of November-December, 1992 says "George Harper Houghton left an impressive photographic legacy which includes nearly 100 images of the Civil War. His photos are well balanced and often convey his love of nature and his appreciation for the landscape. His *"Fifth Vermont Being Reviewed, Camp Griffin, Virginia,"* arguably Houghton's most famous photo, is an excellent image conveying the magnitude of a regiment in line. The view was used on the cover of the companion book to Ken Burns' epic television documentary on the War."

After many travels and personal tragedies, Houghton headed back to Kilbourn where he died July 7, 1870 at age 46.

John H. Houghton, M.D.

John H. Houghton was born in Milwaukee, Wisconsin in 1907. He received his medical degree from Marquette University in 1932. On a trip to investigate a medical position in another state, Houghton stopped twice in Wisconsin Dells. He liked what he found so much that he set up a practice here.

In 1936 he left his practice to attend the University of Pennsylvania Graduate School of Medicine, did a years residency at St. Joseph's Hospital in Milwaukee and was married to Elsie Tyrell. The young couple then returned to the Dells.

Dr. Houghton was the senior member of the staff which founded the local clinic. His original office was one room on the second floor above Kleimenhagen & Magoon, now Stuelke's Drug Store. Shortly after World War II he was joined by Dr. C.F. Broderick, then by F.W. Gissal, and the clinic moved to the second floor of the Kilbourn Co-Op Building. During the 1950s a new clinic was built on Race Street.

Dr. Houghton was on the staffs of St. Mary's Ringling Hospital, in Baraboo and Divine Savior Hospital of Portage. He was active in the County Medical Society and in the State Medical Society where he served as president in 1955-56.

In the community, he served on the school board and as a member of the Rotary Club, the Kiwanis, and St. Cecelia's Catholic Church. He was an avid golfer. He was one of the last of the old style country doctors who made house calls.

In 1966 Dr. Houghton was appointed to a seven year term on the State Board of Health, but would not be able to complete the term as cancer claimed his life in March, 1968.

He and Elsie had two children, John Jr. and Judy (Whittaker), four grandchildren and several great-grandchildren, some of whom still live in the Dells.

Dr. George Jenkins

George Jenkins, pioneer Dells area physician for over fifty years, was born in Duanesburg, New York on September 19, 1824. Following graduation from Columbia University in 1848, he left by steamship for the newly opened West, arriving in Milwaukee in 1850. He hired a team and headed North to the newly founded village of Delton.

After a few months in Delton, Jenkins journeyed into Columbia County where he met Joseph Bailey, who, with Jonathan Bowman, had revealed plans to build a new community on the banks of the Wisconsin River named Newport. Jenkins proposed to Bailey that he locate his practice there. Bailey said he'd probably find slim pickings and advised the pioneer doctor to take a walk through the area and see what he thought of prospects.

Jenkins strolled out through Big Spring, Dell Prairie, across the bridge at the Narrows, back south through Delton and on to Newport. Satisfied with what he had found, he told Bailey he would stay in Newport.

In 1856 he married Mary Markham of Newport and they had a daughter, Kate.

His nine years as a physician in Newport was described in the following tribute written by J. E. Jones of Kilbourn: "The record of his life will be an active part of the history of this notable and exciting period in the pioneer history of Wisconsin. Farmers had settled at long and remote intervals around him, and he was called to visit the sick miles away. With the true spirit of the loyal hearts of that day he never failed to answer a call, no matter how far, what the weather, or how uncertain the remuneration."

From Newport, Jenkins moved to Kilbourn, and in 1863, opened the Jenkins Drug Store, which he operated for 30 years. In 1880, he served as president of the State Medical Society. He was also involved in the National Railway Surgeons Association, the American Medical Association, the American Academy of Political and Social Sciences, and as a 32nd Degree Mason. Dr. Jenkins was called too late to the bedside of the infamous Belle Boyd, the Confederate spy who died at Kilbourn in 1900.

Dr. Jenkins died in Kilbourn on November 3, 1913, at the age of 89. In his obituary, J. E. Jones wrote "No other person has been so intimate a part of the lives of Kilbourn from the cradle to the grave." On the day of his funeral, in final tribute, businesses throughout Kilbourn closed and flags were placed at half mast.

Jens Christian Jensen

Jens Christian Jensen was born May 4, 1866 in Copenhagen, Denmark, the eldest child of Nels and Amelia (Sorensen) Jensen. The family migrated to Chicago around 1878. There were four other children: Charles, Alfred, Soaren, Conrad, and Theresa.

Jens married Christina Gertsen on May 25, 1889 in Chicago. They lived in the Deerfield, Illinois area where he farmed and did butchering work.

Jens and Christina had 8 children: Anna (John Borud); Amelia (Fred Storandt); Mamie (Harold Starr); Gilbert (Alma Leege); Harvey (Mary Storandt & Milda Dettmann); Raymond (Ella Tonn & Mary Timlin); Edna (Roy Nielsen); and Alice (Roy Cornwell).

Along with his parents, Jens and Christina moved to Wisconsin in 1900. They lived in Dell Prairie, where their last two children were born, until 1909 when they then purchased the farm on the corner of Hwy O and Hwy 23 in Newport. Their daughter Mamie Starr and her family lived there for many years. The location, known to many as 'Starr's Corner', is now owned by Wilbur Maves.

Jens was a well-known stock buyer and farmer for 38 years. He also owned a milk delivery route called 'Sunrise Dairy', and spent 25 years on the school board.

Jens died in 1939, one year after Christina. Most of their descendants still live in the Dells area.

Kenneth K. Johnson

In 1925 a new name appeared in Kilbourn's business directory–Johnson's Electric Store. The owner was a young man named Kenneth K. Johnson from Tomah, Wisconsin who became known in the community as K.K.

Kenneth Johnson was born in Tomah in 1900 to Dr. and Mrs. H. B. Johnson. He attended and graduated from Tomah High School and, in 1924, from the Milwaukee School of Engineering.

K.K. married Margaret Birkenmeyer, his next door neighbor, in 1926 and brought her to Kilbourn as a new bride. One daughter, Joan, now Mrs. Duane Wilcox, completed their family in 1928.

The Johnson Store was sold to Harris Botsford and Ralph O'Neil in 1932. Mr. Johnson opened a quick service laundry in 1933 and operated that business until he was commissioned into the United States Army in 1943. Following the war, K. K. became the Columbia County Service Officer and held that post until his retirement in 1965.

Boy Scout Troop #66 flourished under K. K.'s guidance and the program was nationally recognized for the large number of young men obtaining the rank of Eagle Scout.

Many years of residence in Wisconsin Dells provided the opportunity for Mr. Johnson to serve on the Presbyterian church board, the Board of Education, the City Water and Light Commission, the city council, the American Legion, and as a fifty year member of the Kiwanis Club. He also served on the Dells Housing building committee that focused on the completion of the Dells Colonial Apartments, and held offices relating to his position as County Service Officer and Civilian Defense Coordinator. K. K. was a member of the Columbia County Board of Supervisors until poor health, in the last few years of his life, forced him from active service.

Mr. Johnson passed away in May, 1975, and Margaret in 1988.

Ingel and Ernestina Jones

Ingel "John" Jones was a Wisconsin River pilot for forty years.

The youngest son of Elias and Pauline Lunden Jones, Ingel was born December 5, 1887 in Blanchardville, Wisconsin. In 1895 the family moved to Kilbourn by way of a three day wagon trip. They wintered at Hile House and in 1896 purchased a farm in Springville, Adams County. Several years after Elias died in 1902, Pauline sold the farm and purchased property in Newport.

When John was 19 he went west with Albert Paulson and joined a threshing crew. Winters were spent on ranches in Montana and North Dakota. He enlisted in the army during World War I and served the country with honor.

He married Ernestine (Tena) Nemitz on September 7, 1921. Ernestine was born April 6, 1888 in West Rosendale, the daughter of Herman and Amelia Barfknect Nemitz. John and Ernestine had one daughter, Helen, born December 25, 1924.

Tena was born April 6, 1888 in West Rosendale, Wisconsin and in 1905 moved with her family to a farm in Jackson, Adams County. She was a charter member of the American Legion Auxilliary and active in church and community affairs.

Along with piloting, John also served as chief boat mechanic and engineer on the *Winnebago*. During winters he worked for Kilbourn Machine and in his spare time repaired everything from cash registers to steam engines. He enjoyed trout fishing, deer hunting and ice skating, and he was never too busy to help a neighbor or make a kite for a child.

He was a charter member of the American Legion, the Drum and Bugle Corps, and the Rifle Club.

Tena died on December 3, 1941. John sold the home they had built and several years later married Agnes Spak. They continued to live in the Dells. Agnes returned to Milwaukee following John's death on June 24, 1967.

J.E. Jones

James Elliot Jones, editor of the Kilbourn *Weekly Events* newspaper for over 30 years, was a versatile and talented writer, well known for his brillant editorials, magazine articles and essays.

According to an article written in 1925, "Probably no more picturesque character has ever appeared in Wisconsin newspaper history." Also in 1925 Charles Elliott, editor of the *Adams Times* wrote, "J.E. Jones was a man of high character and of strong personality. Clear thinking, deep sincerity and an ability to express, without equivocation, the things that were in his mind and heart were evident in all his writing. The article went on, "he stood consistently for the things he deemed right."

Jones' columns never contained scandal or any account of misdeeds of members of the community. Of this philosophy Jones wrote "We are a little community, almost like a family. If one of us steals a horse, we all know it. Why should the misdeed be perpetuated in print? Public opinion in Kilbourn is strong enough to be corrective, so the *Events* leaves out the horse stealing."

Jones was born in 1847 in Tazewell County, Virginia, in an area now called Marion, Virginia. From Virginia the Jones family moved to Dalton, Georgia. He lived with them until he enlisted, somewhat reluctantly, in the Confederate Army at the age of about 15. Shortly after enlistment in 1863 he was captured by Union forces and held in Rock Island Prison. While at Rock Island, Union officials told Jones, who had been a bugler in the Confederate Army, and other young Confederate soldiers that if they would agree to go out West and fight the Indians for the Union army they could get out of prison and not have to go back into the Confederate Army. Jones agreed and at about age 16 he was sent out West. Jones traveled to Kansas, Nebraska, Wyoming, Arizona and New Mexico. In the southwest he learned to speak fluent Spanish and read old Spanish records and studied old Indian legends.

At one point, while he was serving under General Custer and a fierce Indian battle was imminent, Custer turned to the youthful Jones and said "Trooper Jones, does your mother know you are here?" Jones answered that she did not. In fact, at that time much of the Jones family believed that he was dead. Feeling that they would be humiliated to know that he had left the Confederate Army, he'd never written to tell them.

His mother never stopped hoping and continued to inquire about him for many years. Only one person, an old school chum, knew that Jones was alive. He and Jones had met once when the Union Army had sent Jones to Dalton. Jones made the friend swear that he would never tell anyone about seeing him, still believing that it was better his family thought him dead than a member of the U.S. Army.

Not until 45 years later, when the old friend was dying, did he tell the Jones family. Knowing her son was still alive, Jones mother tracked him down through his articles and in 1910, the family was at last reunited.

Jones was to have been with Custer at his "last stand", but according to daughter Vera, "Custer sent young Jones back for something and saved him from the fatal battle. Jones had many fascinating experiences out west, including contact with Kit Carson and Buffalo Bill."

After leaving the Army in 1879, Jones traveled to St. Louis then on to Chicago, where he became a reporter for the *Chicago Daily News*. In 1884, Frank O. Wisner, who owned the *Mirror Gazette* in Kilbourn, became ill and contacted the *Chicago Daily News* for temporary help. Jones was sent. He loved the area and stayed for over forty years. In 1888 Jones bought Wisner's interest in the *Mirror Gazette* and continued publishing until 1902 when he sold out to E.J. Wheeler.

In 1903 Jones began publishing the *Illustrated Events*, a monthly magazine which included historical sketches, short stories, essays and editorials as well as photographs to go with each story, many by famous Dells photographer H.H. Bennett.

In 1906 Jones bought the *Dells Reporter* and in 1911, with B. E. Tollaksen, bought the *Mirror Gazette*. He changed the name of the paper to the *Kilbourn Weekly Events* and continued to publish and edit until his retirement in 1923 when he sold to C.F. Fredricks.

Jones married Anna Bauer around 1886, and they had one daughter, Vera. As a child, Vera's father told her charming and wonderful tales about the Old South, but not until the 1910 reunion, at age 20, would Vera have her first visit there.

It was Jones' promotional efforts that helped establish the Kilbourn Library and he served on the library board for many years. His picture still hangs in the library foyer.

Jones also frequently wrote articles for the *Milwaukee Journal* and other Milwaukee and Chicago papers. It was because of his journalist talent that someone once dubbed him the "Horace Greeley of Wisconsin Dells."

"Even though he lived all but about 16 years of his life in the North, he was at all times a Southern Gentlemen. He wore a suit every day, even in the summertime," his daughter recalled.

Jones had a stroke while in Milwaukee in 1923 and never completely recovered. He died June 10, 1925 leaving behind a rich legacy of writings, for and about Kilbourn and the surrounding area.

The Kaiser Family

Jakob Kaiser was born in Gneibel in the Swabian Alps region of Baden-Wurttemburg, West Germany (the Black Forest) on September 9, 1843. He was the oldest child of six born to Johannes Gaiser (later changed to Kaiser) and Anna Maria Vonbeck. The Kaiser family came to Philadelphia when Jakob was nine years old, where they resided until the Civil War.

At age 13, Jakob joined the Confederate Army in Missouri. Though not legally old enough to serve, he could and did tend the horses. Following the war, Jakob rejoined his family and they moved to Fox Lake, Wisconsin, where his father was promised land at $1.25 an acre. There he married Louise Knoll in 1867. Louise was born in New York on March 14, 1848, to parents who had emigrated from the Plateau Lorraine Province of France.

Jakob and Louise resided on a farm north of the river in Fox Lake. Twelve of their thirteen children were born there, and three who died as infants: Josephine, Jacob, and one name unknown, are buried there.

The Kaisers, with nine of their children, moved to Kilbourn by wagon in 1887. They briefly lived on a small farm in Dell Prairie, where another infant son, Lime, was buried. The family then moved to a farm four miles west of Kilbourn in Lyndon.

Jakob and Louise lived a quiet and comfortable life: Jakob was described as frugal, industrious and respected, and Louise, kind, loving, and of quiet disposition. It is said she was a very modern woman who enjoyed bringing her French etiquette into her home.

During the 1918-1919 flu epidemic, they lost two more children, William Frederick Kaiser, age 47, and Mrs. Emma Peterson, age 37. Jakob died on March 13, 1920, and Louise on April 14, 1925. They are buried in Spring Grove Cemetery.

Seven children were left to Kilbourn: Mrs. Lisabeth Sly, Mrs. Mary Tuttle, Mrs. Louisa Radandt, Mrs. Sara Belter, Mrs. Kate Conway, and Joseph Jacob and Charley Kaiser.

Joseph Jacob Kaiser was born to Jakob and Louise on February 8, 1883. He was a self-taught fiddler who played at many local barn dances. You could often find him and brother Charley, who played guitar and keyboard, on their front porch playing music and singing songs.

As a young man, Joe worked the farm with his father and walked to town to work for the ice company. One of Joe's many ice deliveries was to the Berry Hotel, where he met his wife Wilma Winnes, who worked there. They were married in 1925 in Illinois, then bought a home at 817 Capital Street in Kilbourn.

Shortly after his marriage, Joe purchased the ice company from Cy Barrett. The ice house and business was located along the Wisconsin River on Illinois Ave. near the old Avery Resort. The ice house stood three stories high and was insulated with sawdust. Many horses were used in this business and were housed on the Kaiser farm.

Though it was hard and dangerous work to cut the ice on the river and put it up in the ice house, Joe did well, providing ice for many families and businesses at Kilbourn and Lake Delton.

He and his employees went out on the frozen river and using a gas powered cutter, cut the ice into 6'x3' slabs. After making a channel in the water, the slabs of ice were "jacked" through the channel to the "rack" near the ice house. The slabs were then pulleyed up the rack by horses and into the ice house for storage. Times changed and the winter of 1940-41 was the last year they put up ice. The river didn't freeze as hard and with refrigeration you could make "artificial ice".

Joe built a new ice house along the alley behind his home and bought ice from Oscar Meyer of Madison and Rothe of New Lisbon. He operated from this site until his retirement in 1962. The property along the river was sold in 1946 to the Dells Boat Company, and the ice business was later sold to Morse Enterprises.

Joe was also active in the community and in local government, serving as a city alderman for many years. With two sons active in sports during the 1940's, the Kaisers never missed a local sporting event, and continued to support local sports long after their sons graduated. They were members of the Presbyterian church, where Wilma was very active in many church groups. She made many quilts and fancy work pieces for the church.

Joe and Wilma had four children: Julia (Ron) Lange, Joseph (Deloris) Kaiser, Harold (Shirley) Kaiser, and Jean (George) Hinton.

Joseph Jacob Kaiser died in 1964 and his wife Wilma died in 1984. They are buried in the Spring Grove Cemetery.

William's daughter, Irene Kaiser Evans, also lived out her life in the Dells area.

The Kane Family

Timothy Kane Sr. was born in Ireland and came to Big Springs in 1861 after living in Indiana and Madison for a short time. He became a U.S. citizen in 1870.

Timothy and his wife Julia O'Connor, also from Ireland, had four children: Timothy Jr., Michael, Ellen and Margaret.

Ellen married Floyd A. Field in 1886. They owned three pleasure steamers, the *Eolah*, the *Alexander Mitchell*, and the *Dell Queen*, which they sold to the Dells Resort Company in 1892.

Margaret married Adam Hile and the couple owned and operated the Hile House Hotel. Michael was a bachelor and died at age 75 in 1931.

Timothy Jr. married Celia Hile, Adam's sister, in 1890. He became one of Adams County's most successful farmers. He and Celia had two children: Arthur and Mamie. Timothy and Celia later moved to Kilbourn. At age 59 he died at his daughter's home following a farming accident.

Mamie had married Lawrence Buckley and they had three children: Chester, Lawrence Jr. and Ethel (Huber).

Arthur worked for many years at the local creamery and the Railway Express Office. He married Catherine Conway of Lyndon Station and they had one son, Robert, who married Mary Naber. Robert and Mary had four children: Kay, Kim, Michael, and another who died shortly after birth. Arthur passed away in 1980.

The Kleimenhagen Family

Leonard Kleimenhagen was born on December 20, 1851 in Herrenbreitunge, Germany. He had a twin sister Amyntha, sisters Marie and Wilhelmina, and a brother August. Leonard, Amyntha and Wilhelmina came to America.

After serving over three years in the German cavalry, Leonard set out alone for America, landing in New York November 1, 1874. He spoke no English but secured employment as a butcher in Brooklyn.

In April of 1875 he headed for Minnesota. He stopped off, however, to visit relatives in Portage, and upon their suggestion came to Kilbourn where he found employment at his trade.

On December 15, 1878 he married Augusta Otillie Sorgel of Portage. He also sent for his twin sister Amyntha, who arrived in 1880. In 1882 she was married in Chicago to Ernest Storandt, and they later moved to this area.

In 1877 he opened a retail meat market on Broadway in Kilbourn which he ran for eight years. In the meantime, he began buying and selling livestock, and eventually it took up the greater part of his time.

He remained a stock dealer for 32 years, 25 years of which John Sullivan was a partner. Leonard was one of the largest livestock men in the state and enjoyed the confidence and respect of the biggest men in the meat packing industry in Milwaukee and Chicago. In 1912 he retired from business.

Leonard served for many years as a member of the Columbia county Board, as trustee of the village of Kilbourn and for 12 years as President of the village board.

Leonard and his wife Augusta (Sargel) had four children: Walter, advertising manager at the Harley-Davidson Motor Company of Milwaukee; Karl, treasurer and superintendent of the Carus Chemical Company in La Salle, Illinois; Joan, a home economics teacher; and Arthur in business in Kilbourn.

Arthur was born in Kilbourn on February 7, 1890. He married Anita Michaelis of Milwaukee on January 16, 1932 and they had two sons: Arno K. and Richard A.

Arthur served as Kilbourn's postmaster for about 10 yeras before going into the clothing business. He was in partnership with Norman Magoon from 1928 to 1955, when his son Arno bought out Magoon's share. The business operated until December, 1964.

Arthur A. Kleimenhagen died in March, 1958.

Hans Kneubuhler

Hans Kneubuhler, Sr. was born in Chicago on April 15, 1900. He was the second of three children of John and Bertha Kneubuhler, Swiss immigrants who later settled and raised their family on a farm north of Brooks.

Hans married Isla Stafford in 1928, and they had two children, Jean and Hans, Jr. In 1929 he bought a car repair service to which he soon added a Dodge and Plymouth agency.

Hans retired in 1953 and made the building into a souvenir store. He ran the store, in partnership with Arnie Borcher, until his death in 1965.

Hans was active on the Business Mens Committee, and was a long-time member of the Wisconsin Dells Fire Department.

The Landt Family

Sarah Mahalia Ward was born in Chicago on February 12, 1837, When Sarah was about ten, her family decided to migrate to Wisconsin, traveling with other families in covered wagons. When they reached Newport, the Wards decided to take the ferry across the river and go further northeast.

When Sarah was about twelve, she was picking blackberries near the road when she secretly spied a young man, Socrates Best. Socrates was twenty-five years old, a young farmer and school teacher who lived with his parents on a farm nearby. They had recently moved into the area from Ohio.

When school opened in October, Sarah went bright and early to the school house and started the fire in the stove. The fire was going so well that by the time the teacher arrived, he had to open the windows and door, and Sarah was rather embarrassed.

Sarah stayed in school until age sixteen when she had completed all the available material. She lived with her parents until she was about twenty, when she married Jeremiah Landt, a young farmer in the area.

Jerry and Sarah Landt moved a short distance to Durham where they established themselves on a farm. They had three children: Warren, Alana and Cleburn who must have died as an infant. When the Civil War started in 1861 Jerry Landt enlisted.

Jerry Landt soon found himself in a fierce battle in Tennessee. He was so severely injured in the leg that he was given a discharge, and found himself with no way home. He had no money and a very bad leg, but started the very long and weary journey to Wisconsin. He slept in haystacks and barns and ate what he could find with an occasional meal from some farmer. After many weeks, he arrived home, starved and very ill with his infected leg.

Sarah tried to nurse him back to health, but in a few weeks he passed away. Sarah married her former teacher, Socrates Best, a widower with two children, on January 28, 1866. In addition to the four children that were brought into the marriage, Sarah and Socrates had four more children together: Judith, Samuel, Sylvia, and Mildred.

Her son Warren Landt married his cousin Aura Landt (a sister of Delbert Landt). Their only son, Hugh, died at age twenty of quick consumption.

Aura had also died, when Hugh was a boy, and Warren married a woman named Anna. They had a son, Cleburn, in 1898. When Cleburn was fifteen, he and his cousin Willie Best were handling a .22 rifle. The rifle accidently fired and hit Cleburn in the abdomen, but he soon recovered from the injury.

Cleburn graduated from high school in 1916 and joined the armed forces. During the great epidemic of 1918, he was struck with the flu and died.

Warren and Anna went on to make their home in Coeur d'Alene, Idaho, where many relatives from Wisconsin would travel to visit them.

Alana Landt married her step-brother Augustus Best. Hers and the other Best children's stories are included in the Best family history.

Delbert and Judith Best Landt

Judith Best married a cousin of her half sister, Delbert Allison Landt, on December 24, 1888.

Following some early years in Cadotte, Wisconsin where Bert cared for horses at a lumber company, they moved to Kilbourn, Bert opened a feed store and then a livery stable.

While operating the stable, he learned of an abandoned farm just east of town. The farm, on Hwy 1227, had 160 acres and some ramshackle buildings when Bert purchased it and started to restore it.

First the house was torn down, and in 1898, a two story, nine room house was built. Many people stopped to see the most modern home in the area, with a beautiful fireplace in the large dining room, a bathroom with running water upstairs and a furnace in the basement. A windmill and a large holding tank built into the hill behind the house provided running water with hot water provided by running water through the coils of the fire box on the kitchen range.

Beautiful maple floors covered the ground floor. Judith spent many hours scrubbing the wood to remove stains caused by carpenters spitting tobacco into wood shavings while they constructed the house.

A barn and grainary were soon built and the farm stocked with cows, horses and pigs.

Bert and Judith raised seven children: Newton, Rena, Bryce, Geraldine, Marjory and Janet (twins), and Frances. There was also another member of Judith and Bert's family, Dan O'Neil, who at six years old, along with his older siblings, was left an orphan by the diptheria epidemic.

Neighbors sold the O'Neil farm and property at an auction. Two sisters went to aunts from Milwaukee, and the older boys to neighboring families who could use them to help with work. Dan, a little, frail boy, seemed unwanted. Bert Landt saw him, and though he knew his mother wouldn't like having another mouth to feed, he took Dan home with him. He was a father to Dan from that day forward, and when he and Judith married, Dan was a part of their family. Dan became a pharmacist and was married to Edna York.

In 1921, Delbert Landt suffered a stroke which completely immobilized him, and died five years later.

Following Bert's death, Judith moved into Wisconsin Dells, leaving her son Bryce and his wife Marie to operate the farm. Marjory, Janet and Frances, all working girls in Wisconsin Dells, moved to 1111 Bowman Road with their mother.

After bearing the heavy responsibility of being a farm wife and mother for many years, Judith enjoyed having time for church, Ladies Aid, and afternoon calls to and from friends. She raised a big garden to supplement her table.

Judith Geraldine Best Landt, at the age of ninety-two, died in November, 1959.

Newton Allison Landt was born near Eau Claire February 1, 1890.

Newt was educated in Kilbourn. His original ambition was to be a farmer and he took an agriculture course at the University of Wisconsin. But in his late teens he wanted to try construction and did so at the new dam being built at Kilbourn City. Working among gangs of rough, questionable characters gleaned mainly from Milwaukee Road boxcars, young Landt soon impressed his bosses with his willingness and competence.

When Kilbourn dam was finished in 1909, the Southern Wisconsin Power Company put Landt on other work in the vicinity. Newt tried a short stint out west on railroad construction work but he soon returned home. Back at the power company, he started as a timekeeper at the Kilbourn generating station. Three years later he was made manager of a substation at nearby Portage. In 1919 Landt returned to the hydro dam he helped build and was named superintendent of the Kilbourn plant at age 29.

During 36 years as Kilbourn superintendent he pioneered numerous changes in equipment design and operational procedures. For example, Landt patented a procedure to keep turbine vanes from pitting, but so that others might gain from his research, assigned the patent to Allis-Chalmers, a leading manufacturer of generating equipment.

Company policy forced Newt Landt to retire from Wisconsin Power and Light, February 1, 1955. After a period of restlessness, Landt turned to Dale Prepakt, an old business acquaintance, with the idea of putting his accumulated knowledge and wide acquaintanceship to productive use. It was Intrusion-Prepakt that benefitted in April 1956 when Newt Landt became the newest, one of the oldest and probably the most enthusiastic member of the organization.

Newt Landt married Fay M. Brown on January 14, 1914. They had three children, Nona, Eugena, and Allison, as well as 6 grandchildren and 2 great-grandchildren.

Bryce Sheldon Landt was born to Delbert and Judith on October 11, 1894 in Kilbourn. He attended grade school and high school in Kilbourn, graduating in 1913. He went on to the University of Wisconsin School of Agriculture. While there he played in the band, was a member of the crew and a member of the bobsled team. After two years of college he returned to operate the family farm.

In September of 1924 he married Marie Kingsley who operated a millinery shop in Kilbourn. They had two children: Phyllis Kearney and Shirley Knuth.

For 21 years he served at various times as president, secretary and general manager of the local creamery. He also served as secretary and president of the Wisconsin Co-operative Creamery Association, District #2.

By 1936 Bryce felt that dairy farmers needed a self help organization and after presenting his ideas to the State Board of Agriculture, the Wisconsin Dairy Industries Association was formed. In 1938 that organization grew into the Tri-State Dairy Association which included Iowa, Minnesota and Wisconsin. In 1940 the organization became national and was named the American Dairy Association. He served as president and treasurer at the state level and in 1948 became President of the National A.D.A.

With World War II came the need for dry milk production; Bryce was contacted by the federal government and a production plant was built at Union Center. He served as its manager until 1949, when he died following an auto accident.

Bryce was a member of the Wisconsin Council of Agriculture, the State Fair Association Committee, the Masonic Fraternity, the Eastern Star, the Presbyterian Church, and a 4-H leader.

Shortly before his death, the University of Wisconsin recognized his distinguished service and leadership in the dairy industry.

Menno Leege

Menno Leege was born in Germany May 24, 1867. He came to America with his parents in 1877 at age 10, and settled on a farm near Lake Delton. He had two brothers, John and William, and three sisters, Anna, Lenna, and Wilhelmina. John moved to Los Angeles, California; Anna and Lena to North Dakota; and Wilhelmina stayed in Germany. Menno and William remained in the Kilbourn area.

On April 4, 1894 Menno married Dena Borcher of Kilbourn and they made their home in Dellona. In 1910 they moved to Heda, South Dakota, but returned to Wisconsin after two years. They purchased a farm in Newport and lived there until 1929 when Menno retired to Kilbourn.

The five sons of Menno and Dena were Christian, Walter, Arthur, Ernest, and Rudolph. There were also six daughters - Bertha (Storandt), Arlene (Jensen), Mildred (Froslie), Clara (Lunde), Mary (Anderson), and Adeline (Henke).

The Leege family was active in St. Paul's German Lutheran Church. In 1918 Menno became one of the charter members of the two small Lutheran congregations, St. Paul's and Bethlehem.

Thaddeus and Kunigunda Naber Leute

Thaddeus Leute was born in 1832 and married Kunigunda Naber, born in 1847. They had four sons: Theodore, George, Francis, Eugene and two daughters, Mary and Helene.

Theodore was born in 1869 and his wife, Mary, born in 1881. He owned and operated Leute's Brewery on the north edge of the ravine, Fremont Park, in Kilbourn. In the1910s, '20s, and '30s, their property at 4124 River Road became a farm resort with "outdoor plumbing". That property is now Leute's Resort and is operated by the fifth generation of Leutes: grandson William, and his wife Janice.

Theodore died in 1937, and Mary in 1959.

The Henry C. Luettgerodt Family

Henry Charles Luettgerodt was born on October 11, 1913. He married Lorraine Richter on May 5, 1934.

Henry and Lorraine owned and operated a grocery store in Wisconsin Dells for 33 years. In 1965, they retired to Fort Myers, Florida until they died; Henry on February 28, 1985, and Lorraine on September 18, 1988.

They had 5 children: Shirley, born December 5, 1934; Carole, born March 24, 1936 (deceased 1940 of pneumonia); Helene, born June 21, 1937; Donald, born February 19, 1939; Judy, born March 5, 1940.

Shirley married Bert Milligan on November 8, 1953. They lived in Bayfield, Wisconsin and had 4 children: Sheri, Michael, Patrick and Vicki. They later retired to Florida.

Helene married Eugene Morse on February 23, 1958. They lived in Wisconsin Dells and had 3 children: Tammy, Kelly and Eugene Jr. They live in Wisconsin Dells and own the River Road Motel.

Donald married Barbara Radtke on January 1, 1961. They had 4 children: Doreen, Debora, Denise and David. Don and Barb both worked at Henry's Grocery Store where they later took over the business and operated for 17 years. They continue to live in Wisconsin Dells where Don is a state meat inspector.

Judy married Harley (Ed) Rogers. They had 4 children: Joleen, Kenneth (who died in 1975) and twin daughters Dawn & Diane. They continue to live in Reedsburg, Wisconsin.

Harry Ward Loomis

Harry Ward Loomis was born March 8, 1882 in Lone Rock, Wisconsin, the only son of three children born to Lloyd and Mary Ward Loomis. As a young boy he moved with his family to Kilbourn where his father became a guide on the old *Apollo*, piloted his own tourist boat *#348* and was a caretaker of Waubeek for some years. Harry attended the Kilbourn High School and graduated in 1899.

On March 5, 1907 he married Miss Clara Smelcer in Lone Rock and they had three children: Damon, Marian, and Helen.

In 1916 they purchased a tract of land just north of the Dells next to the Old Orchard Farm Resort. There they built a farm house that was gradually transformed into the resort now known as Birchcliff Lodge. Harry loved nature, farming,and fishing. He had artistic ability and a lively sense of humor.

At various times he was a member of the school board and of the chamber of commerce, justice of the peace and census taker in the town of Dell Prairie, Adams County.

Harry died February 21, 1960 and his wife Clara, May 16, 1974. His son Damon and Damon's wife, Bernice, operated the resort from 1948-1973. They had three daughters: Roxanne, Laurie and Derryn.

Harold A. and Cheridah McClyman

Harold (Harry) was born July 7, 1896 in New Chester, Adams County, to David T. and Myrtle McClyman. He had one brother, Clifford and twin sisters Neva and Nina.

In 1912 they moved to Newport where he graduated from Kilbourn High School in 1916. The following September he went to Stevens Point Normal school for one year. From July 1917 until March 1918 he drove a mail route out of Kilbourn. He then moved back to New Chester and farmed until 1921. In 1921, his father bought out the hardware firm of Martin Brothers in Kilbourn and Harold and his brothers moved to Kilbourn and went into business with him.

In 1936 he married Cheridah Krause, the home economics teacher. Cheridah was born May 31, 1905 to John & Della Krause in Green Lake. She attended school there and graduated from high school as valedictorian in 1922. She attended Stout Institute in Menomonie for two years. She taught one year in Cuba City, Wisconsin and then moved to Kilbourn and began teaching home economics to grades 8-12. She also coached plays and taught gym. She retired from teaching when she and Harold married. They had one daughter, Janet McClyman Krahn, and two grandchildren, Susan Monahan Figi and Robert H. Monahan.

Harold and his brothers later bought out their father and branched out into many different phases of business. They sold Studebaker cars, International Farm Equipment, appliances, televisions, propane gas, and other miscellaneous items. On January 31, 1965 Harold sold his half of the business to his nephew and retired.

Harold & Cheridah were active in the church and stayed in the community until they passed away, Cheridah in November, 1989 and Harold in May, 1991.

The Morse Family

Lyman and Rachel Hazard Morse came to Columbia County, Wisconsin in 1846. They had eight children: Chester, who died in the Civil War, Uri, Henry, Horace, Eli, Polly, Roxana, and Jane.

Uri Morse was born on September 3, 1823 in the town of Guilford, Chenango County, New York. In 1846 he came with his parents to Hampden Township, Columbia County.

In 1849, after climbing a tree and choosing the location of his farm by the character of the trees he saw from his high perch, he filed a squatters claim on land in the Big Spring area.

Uri took grain to Chicago by ox team, often walking the whole distance. Later he went into dairy farming, and also cultivated ginseng. He always had a profitable farm.

Uri was a leader in the community and was quite successful in whatever endeavor he attempted. He was often town chairman and was for many years a county poor commissioner. He loaned money to friends and neighbors, gave advice and was active in church and community affairs. He died on October 25, 1909.

Uri married Miranda A. Morey of Fountain Prairie, Columbia County, Wisconsin on May 13, 1850.

Marinda, one of Big Spring's earliest settlers, was born on February 21, 1831 in Lake Locke, Cayuga County, New York. She was the daughter of Harry M. and Bathia (Hoyt) Morey who came to Fountain Prairie in 1848. She died of a stroke on October 16, 1906.

Uri and Marinda had five children: Lyman Nathan; Andrew H., who married Ida Brooks; Estella B., who married Herbert A. Atcherson of Tomahawk, (Estella died on January 15, 1927, age 69); Justina R., who married B.W. Perry of Fort Barrankas, Florida, and Chauncey W., who married Nellie Hodge. Chauncey was very well known in the Big Spring area as an expert hunter and fisherman.

Lyman N. Morse was born on September 23, 1851, 10 miles northeast of Kilbourn near Big Spring. He was very active within the Methodist church, on several occasions assisting his pastor by filling the pulpit. He was Sunday school superintendent for more than 35 years, and teacher for more than 50 years.

He graduated from the Kilbourn high school and then taught school in Pittsville, Wisconsin. He started farming in 1875. He returned to Big Spring in the early 1880's where he took over the family farm and like Uri, farmed successfully for many years. He died on May 8, 1929 as a well respected member of the church and community.

Lyman married Georgianna Malinda Wells, the daughter of Simeon S. Wells and Mary A. Smith of Big Spring in 1876.

Lyman and Georgia had four children: Lyman Leslie, Arthur Dewitt, Horace Chester and Clara May.

Lyman Leslie, also known as Leslie L. (born April 29, 1880, died February 16, 1948), married Myrtle (Mazie) Wilbur on March 12, 1902. Leslie first lived in Mercer and then Racine. He had two sons, Loren and Lester, and three daughters, Elenor, Mildred and Vivian.

Arthur Dewit (born March 24, 1883), married Stella May Josephine Lunde on November 30, 1904. He died of a heart attack in Woodruff, Wisconsin. Their children were Lena (Jean) Krueger, Lucille Radue, Ada Westphal Wilcox.

Horace Chester (born October 16, 1888, died February 27, 1958), married Clara Procknow on September 20, 1911. He worked as a guard at Central State Hospital in Waupun until he retired. He died in Waupun and was buried in Spring Grove Cemetery in Wisconsin Dells.

Clara May was born June 26, 1886 near Big Spring. She grew up as a neighbor to the J.B. Stowers family, on farms near Big Spring Pond. She married Clarence W. Stowers on July 7, 1904.

Clarence William Stowers was born in New Haven on March 3, 1877, the son of Jeremiah B. and Ellen Stowers. He farmed in the Big Spring area until about 1929, when poor health made farming an impossibility. He moved to Wisconsin Dells and worked as a Police Chief and operated a gas station at the corner of Broadway and Vine Street. Clarence died on January 2, 1944.

Clarence and Clara parented five children: Roland Morse, Irma (Erwin J. Johnson), Mabel (Benjamin T. Wolfram), Herbert and Arnold Clarence (killed in Burma Flying the "Hump" in 1944).

Roland Morse Stowers was born April 12, 1908 in Big Spring, where he was raised. He later moved to Kilbourn. After he married he lived in Milwaukee for a short time, but when the war broke out he returned to work at Badger Ordnance. He also worked at the plant during the Korean and Vietnam Wars.

After World War II he got a job with the City of Wisconsin Dells, but decided he would rather farm. In 1946 he bought a dairy farm six miles east of the Dells on Hwy 23. When his two sons left the farm for their own endeavors, it was sold and he moved back to Wisconsin Dells where he died on September 8, 1984.

Roland Stowers married Gertrude Ruth Mulligan on November 18, 1937. Gertrude Ruth was born in Burnsted, North Dakota in December 1913, and came to Kilbourn with her parents when she was seven or eight. She graduated from Wisconsin Dells High School in 1932 and attended nurses' training at St. Mary's in Milwaukee, Wisconsin for one year. She died August 12, 1978.

Roland and Gertrude had four children: Carol Ruth, Roger, Patrick William, and Steven Thomas.

Carol Ruth (November 1939) died two days after birth when doctors failed to recognize her RH Negative blood condition.

Roger was born January 27, 1942 and married Gaylene Elizabeth Roeker, born March 14, 1943, daughter of Norman and Vanita Roeker, Wisconsin Dells, in 1962. They had two children: Timothy Roger and Tammy Marie.

Patrick William, born May 9,1944, married Glenda Pearson from Rawls, Texas. They were divorced in 1978. He then married Martha Jane Roney Jacobson. Pat and Glenda had adopted two children, Steven and Amy, both of whom live with Glenda in Odessa, Texas. Martha had children by her first marriage, but none with Pat.

Steven Thomas, born September 8, 1946, accidentally hung himself in a wire fence on June 22, 1948. Dr. Houghton drove out to the farm (six miles) in record time and gave Steven a shot in the heart, but could not save him.

The Mulligan Family

The Mulligan and Hurley families left Roscommon, Ireland around 1846 in order to escape the potato famine. They signed up on a ship and their work would pay for their passage to America. For unknown reasons, possibly lack of food, they were put off the boat on a remote island and left to die. Another ship found them and brought them to the U.S., where the two families settled in New York and later in Canada.

Around 1860, the families came to Dellona Township because 10 acre parcels of land were being given to any who would agree to clear the timber.

Patrick Mulligan, born in 1810, and his wife, Eliza, whom he married in Canada, brought three sons to Dellona: Thomas, John and William. Later, Eliza and James were born. James Mulligan, Patrick's cousin, followed a few years later with his eleven children.

James Mulligan (1850-1890), son of Patrick, married Mary Ann Hurley and they had five children: William, Thomas, Arthur, Ellen (Nellie), and Jim.

William was born on January 8, 1879. He was bank president in Kilbourn and later Columbus. He retired as the postmaster of the Portage, Wisconsin office. He first married Clara Stein and then Catherine O'Keefe. He died on June 16, 1969.

Jim, born in 1880, worked for the Dells Boat Company for many years. He died on December 4, 1937.

Ellen (Nellie), born in 1882, married Spencer Fish and they raised a very large family on a farm in the Reedsburg-LaValle area.

Arthur, born in 1890, held various jobs and lived on a farm near Reedsburg. For reasons unknown, the Mulligan family never had anything to do with him. He died October 3, 1956.

James and Mary Ann were victims of a flu epidemic around 1890, leaving the five children orphans. Still a close family friend, John Hurley, already raising several of his nephews and nieces, took them in. After raising 10 children, John Hurley married at age 49 and had seven boys of his own.

Thomas Mulligan was born on May 22, 1885. He married Marion Murray around 1902 and they left for North Dakota where they homesteaded near Burnsted, close to Bismarck. They stayed there about 20 years and had three daughters: Gertrude Ruth (December 24, 1913 - August 13, 1978), Agnes Mildred (June 22, 1908 - December 14, 1973) and Dorothy (February 6, 1917 - November 29, 1973).

After returning to Kilbourn they bought the Pine Grove Farm and operated a small campground and gas station. In 1924, they had another child, Thomas, Jr.

Thomas had made more than enough money ranching wheat and cattle in North Dakota to buy the Pine Grove Farm, and on the advice of his brother, Bill, decided to invest the remainder of the money at the Kilbourn State Bank where Bill was president. Three days after Thomas put the money in Bill's hands the bank closed its doors. The Depression had hit. Supposedly Bill had known the bank was in financial trouble, and Tom, who lost his savings as well as Pine Grove, never spoke to his brother again. None of Tom's kin attended Bill's funeral, and hard feelings lasted many years.

Thomas, the only son born to Thomas and Marion Mulligan was born on February 19, 1924. A medic during World War II, he was killed in action during the Battle of the Bulge on December 12, 1944 near St. Arvold, France. More than once he was honored for his bravery. At one point, he and two other medics were transporting wounded soldiers from the front lines to the hospital when their jeep struck a land mine and burning gasoline was spread on two enlisted men. Thomas risked his life attempting to save theirs by beating out the flames. For this Thomas received the Soldiers' Medal Award for Heroism. He also received the Soldiers Medal of Honor and a Purple Heart posthumously.

Agnes Mildred Mulligan married Frank Cone (1908-1985) and had two children, Harlan, May 24, 1938 and Karen May 30, 1942.

Gertrude Ruth married Roland Morse Stowers and they had four children; Gertrude, Roger, Patrick William, and Steven Thomas.

Dorothy Mulligan married Edward Knapp and they moved to California where they had two children.

Thomas Mulligan, Sr. died on July 10, 1957.

Many Mulligan ancestors are buried in the Dellona Township, Catholic, and Spring Grove cemeteries.

Lorenz Naber

Lorenz Naber was born in Hohenkemmath, Germany in 1828. He arrived in the area and purchased land from Byron Kilbourn in 1855. The family home was built where the KOA Campgrounds are now located on Stand Rock Road.

He and his wife, Elizabeth Hoffman, raised twelve children. In 1915, after both parents had died, the property was sold to William Brew.

Of the twelve children, only one lived to adulthood. Lawrence was a cement contractor and made his home in Wisconsin Dells. He worked on the local dam as well as others including Prairie du Sac, Wisconsin Rapids and Sault St. Marie.

He married Clara Iverson and they had one son, Marcel, who also spent his entire life in Wisconsin Dells except while serving during World War II.

Marcel was a butcher, an electrician, and spent many years as superintendant at the Dells Boat Comapny. He married Doris Vanderbilt and they had two children: Robert Naber of Plymouth, Wisconsin and Mary Kane of Wisconsin Dells.

Lorenz passed away in 1906, and Elizabeth in 1912. They are buried in Calvary Cemetery next to five of their children.

Robert Nauruhn

Robert Nauruhn was born on October 20, 1895, in East Prussia, Germany. He was trained as a tool and die maker.

He came to the United States in 1928 and settled in Chicago, where he worked as a machinery troubleshooter for the Campbell's Soup Company. He met and married Maria Wedeleit in Chicago, and they had no children.

In 1941, the couple bought property on Highway 12 in Lake Delton. The property included some cottages and was later known as Pine Grove Cottages and Motel. Robert did some defense work, first in Milwaukee and later in a machine shop he put in his barn. After the war, he expanded the resort to one of the largest motels in the state.

In 1959, they sold the property and moved to the Fort Myers, Florida area, where Robert hoped to develop moderately priced homes. Tragically, he died in an accident in February 1962, and is buried in the Lake Delton Cemetery.

Maria resides in a nursing home in Kissimmee, Florida.

Palmer H. Nelson

Palmer H. Nelson was born in a log cabin on November 17, 1889 in Lac-Du-Parle County Minnesota. When Palmer was five, his parents, Peter and Gina (Thompson) Nelson moved the family to the Norwegian settlement of Newport. Palmer had two brothers, Clarence and Tennie, and four sisters, Jennie (Thompson), Clara, Tena (Christopherson) and Nettie (Smith).

In his late teens Palmer took a homestead claim in Montana. After some years he returned to Wisconsin and graduated from the Capital City Commercial College, Madison.

On September 24, 1919, Palmer married a young school teacher, Grace Ogle, of Westfield, and they moved to a farm north of Palmer's home. Here Palmer became a successful and progressive farmer, specializing in registered dairy cows. He started with eight cows in 1917, and in 1923 bought two registered cows from the Meadow Brook Farm. Palmer followed with the purchase of a quality bull to produce high butterfat milk.

In 1925 he began testing for butterfat with a hand tester that he had invented. By now his neighbors were certain that he was an oddball. He continued using the test until standardized tests came into popular use in the early 1940's.

Disappointment struck the Nelsons in 1938-39 when the whole herd was completely wiped out by Bangs disease, but eventually Palmer rebuilt and the herd flourished.

Grace and Palmer had three children: Gordon, born December 23, 1921; Grace Lorraine, born June 23, 1924, and Donald Palmer, born September 23, 1930. Gordon was a Lieutenant in the Air Force overseas during World War II. While stationed in England, Gordon volunteered to go with a fleet of 100 planes destined for Germany. 98 planes returned home to England, but Gordon's plane and another were shot down and lost in the North Sea.

Lorraine, a graduate of Stout University, majoring in Home Economics, married Conrad Mayer. Donald remained on the Newport farm where he farmed with his parents.

Palmer was town clerk and was on the school board for many years. He and his family were members of Bethany Lutheran Church. He was a charter member of the Kilbourn and the Wisconsin Farmers Union. Palmer was especially active in the Democrat Party, and never afraid to take a stand on an issue he believed in.

Grace died on February 10, 1977. On January 25, 1979, Palmer passed away at the age of 89, and was buried in the Spring Grove Cemetery.

Ervin and Helen Nemitz

Helen B. Leberg, born and raised at Necedah, came to the area as a young school teacher. She taught at Oak Grove Joint District #7 Lyndon, Delton, and Dellona where she boarded with Zada Hall. She also taught at the Big Spring School, staying with the Hanson family, and the Fairview School on County K.

On June 24, 1931 she married Ervin Nemitz, a young farmer

from Davis Corners. His family, the Albert Nemitzs, had come from near Fond du Lac when he was four.

The couple lived in a log cabin that Ervin built at Jordan Lake. After Helen quit teaching, Ervin built more cabins to rent during the summer, and later they rented boats. Their business became the Nemitz Resort. When Ervin quit farming they expanded the resort into a campground for seasonal trailers.

In 1987, shortly after celebrating their 55th wedding anniversary, they retired and sold the resort. They moved just north of Briggsville to a home beside their daughter and son-in-law, Melvin and Marie Johnson.

Helen died in 1987 at age 79 and Ervin in 1994 at age 90.

Luther B. Noyes

Luther B. Noyes was born in Cortland County, New York, on December 18, 1830. He arrived in Kilbourn City in 1856 and with his partner, Perry Stroud, opened the first law office in the village. Following the Civil War, during which he served as 1st Lieutenant in the 36th Regiment, he moved to Sparta, Wisconsin and was elected a Monroe County Judge. Later he published a newspaper in Sheboygan, then moved to the frontier northwoods of Marinette where he published the area's first newspaper in 1871. In his first editorial for *The Marinette Peshtigo Eagle*, Noyes wrote, "The Eagle has made it's first appearance, the bird is not yet full fledged, but the pin feathers are of good stock and give promise of a victorious future." Today the Eagle is still going strong.

While in Kilbourn, Noyes was recognized as a bitter opponent of Byron Kilbourn. Noyes felt, like many others, that Kilbourn had double-crossed the residents of Newport by moving the promised railroad to Kilbourn. The following letter, found in the Stroud collection, reveals Noyes' hatred of old Byron Kilbourn.

Kilbourn City, Wisconsin *September 23, 1869*
H.W. Emery, ESQ.

Dear Sir,

I wish you would ascertain the state of friend Williams' mind toward our deputy sheriff H. Peabody. He is efficient in performance of his official duties and it is only because he will not succumb to, and be a tool for the most merciless and unscrupulous bloodhounds and scoundrels that ever disgraced God's green earth. I speak of the mutilated and stinking remains of that old hydraulic nest. One of Byron Kilbourn's exploded humbugs. They will approach you with the smoothest tongue, while the rotteness of hell is festering in their hearts, and the knife is unsheathed to stab as soon as darkness will veil the tragedy. Friend Emery you may think this is strong language, but two years experience with the great railroad corruptor has developed the conclusion. It is getting dark and I must close. I cannot see the lines.

Anon
Truly yours,
L. B. Noyes

Phillip (Roc) O'Connell

Phillip (Roc) O'Connell was born in Newport on August 3, 1896. He was one of four children born to Thomas and Margaret (Donahue) O'Connell, including two brothers, Thomas Elmer, and Timothy Raymond, and one sister, Anastacia. Timothy Raymond was killed in France during World War I.

In 1900, Roc moved with his parents to a farm in Dell Prairie, where he lived until he retired. He took over the farm from his father in 1928, and later taught in area schools for several years.

Roc was active in many community organizations, serving for many years as treasurer of the Town of Dell Prairie. He worked on many government programs and was an active promoter of the Adams-Marquette Rural Electric Cooperative (REA). He helped bring electricity to many rural areas. In 1938 he served on the original ACEC board of directors and stayed for several years.

Roc also served on the Wisconsin Dells School Board and was a member of the building committee of the Wisconsin Dells High School and St. Cecilia's School.

Roc and his wife Margaret had three children: Joan, Thomas, and Sarah. They retired in 1963 and moved to Wisconsin Dells. He died July 1, 1967.

The Oehler Family

The Oehler family, though it has disappeared entirely, was once prominent in the Dells area.

The father, Peter, came to Kilbourn in 1871, where he worked for Hansen-Snider Lumber Company for three years. Next he was in the saloon business for about ten years and then established his grocery store about 1884. He married Rose Bayerlein in 1877 and they had four sons and two daughters: Matilda, John, William and Herman of Wisconsin Dells; Mrs. R.W. Miller of Madison; and Albert of Mauston.

Bill, John, and Herman joined Peter in the grocery business, at 308 Broadway, which later became Oehler Brothers. Hermie is remembered as the gentle, smiling man blinded by the explosion of dynamite caps when he was young. His special area was the west side of the store where he weighed out the candy and gave out 5¢ bags of malted milk balls when you paid your weekly bill.

Customers called the "Blue Front Grocery" at number 63 and deliveries were made in their blue van. During the Depression, families were allowed to charge their groceries during the winter and gradually paid this debt when summer visitors brought income.

Albert returned to Kilbourn and established a jewelry store a few doors away from the grocery. About 1956, Oehler Brothers, one of the Dells oldest businesses, was sold to Bob Seger.

Ben Olson 1869-1952

The son of Norwegian immigrants, Ben Olson was born in Newport on July 4, 1869. He married Nellie Ryan in 1888 and they had one son, Grover. After farming for several years, Ben opened the Olson Boat Company, and later the Olson Hotel.

He was an innovator in bringing modern power on the boats so that more people could see the now famous Wisconsin Dells.

Mr. Olson was active in city affairs and served as mayor. He passed away in 1952 at the age of 84. Almost 100 years after Mr. Olson began rowing tourists on the river, his great grandson continues the family-operated Olson Boat Company.

Grover Cleveland Olson was born November 4, 1892, in Guelph, North Dakota to Ben and Nellie. He was educated in Kilbourn and at Carroll College at Waukesha.

Grover married Jane Zimmerman of Reedsburg in 1917. They had three children: Mary Jane Van Hout, of Appleton; Jack Olson (Eleanor Lang), Wisconsin Dells; and Ben Olson (Shirley Hill), Wisconsin Dells.

Grover served in both World Wars. In World War I he saw service in the U.S. Navy aboard the battleship Pennsylvania. In World War II he served in the U.S. Coast Guard, in charge of the vessel inspection base at St. Louis, Missouri. He became a founding member of the Harold B. Larkin American Legion Post #187.

In 1920, he joined his father in the Olson Boat Company as co-owner and operator. In 1921, together with his parents, he purchased the Joseph Bailey property at Broadway and River Road. The property became the location of the Mission Theater, the Olson Dance Pavilion, a gift store, restaurant, arcade, and ticket offices for the Olson Boat Company.

In 1946, Grover designed and commissioned construction of the first all-steel, double-deck, motorized sightseeing boat to operate on the Wisconsin River, the *Chief*, which began operating on the Upper Dells in 1947.

Grover retired in 1954, selling all real property plus the Olson Boat Company to his sons, Jack and Ben. He and his wife, Jane, lived in a home which they built next to the Blackhawk Hotel. They divided their time between that home and their winter home in Fort Lauderdale, Florida.

Grover died in Wisconsin Dells of a heart attack, in 1974, at the age of 82.

Otis Wilcox Palmer

Otis W. Palmer was the oldest son of James and Jessie Wilcox Palmer. He was born on August 29, 1899 and as a child he lived on a farm in the Town of Lemonweir, near Mauston, except for a year when his father took a job as manager on a wheat ranch near Edmonton, Alberta, Canada. Otis loved the year in Edmonton where he rode a pony to school.

While attending the University of Wisconsin at Madison he met Rena Landt of Kilbourn. They were married at her parents home in Newport on September 13, 1924. They lived on a farm near Mauston until moving to Kilbourn in the fall of 1927 to manage a farm at Wawbeek for the Upham family. They lived there until the Uphams gave the property to the Wisconsin Association for the Disabled. In March of 1940 they purchased the Thompson farm in Newport where they lived until Otis died as the result of a dynamite explosion on November 9, 1950.

Their oldest child, Loris Jean Palmer was born at Mauston on August 28, 1925. Their oldest son, Lloyd Landt Palmer, was born at Kilbourn on September 18, 1927, and their youngest son, Leland Bryce Palmer was born at Wawbeek on September 13, 1932.

While working at Wawbeek, Otis raised purebred Guernsey cattle and developed an excellent herd. He also raised purebred pigs, Barred Rock chickens, and produced excellent corn, rye, and other crops on a sandy farm. He developed a crop rotation system for the farm and vetch for hay. He also raised good alfalfa, and took an interest in the large orchard at Wawbeek, producing many varieties of apples and plums.

Otis always kept abreast of new developments in agriculture, and liked to attend Ag experiment showings. He was one of the first in the area to try contour farming.

At Wawbeek he kept the woods on the farm and on Blackhawk Island cleared of dead wood. Roland Weber often helped and likes to tell of the time they decided to walk around Blackhawk Island on the ice. When his wife Rena heard about this adventure she was very upset because of her great respect and fear of the river, and especially the danger that the ice might have broken while they were in the Narrows.

Otis was an active member of the American Legion in the Dells, having served in the "student army" while at the university. He never missed a Memorial Day Parade, and taught his children to revere the flag and be a participant in community functions.

He was a member of the Dells Masonic Lodge and was often called upon to give lectures for initiations and other occasions. He became a 32nd Degree Mason. He and his family were members of the Wisconsin Dells Presbyterian Church, and involved in 4-H. Following his death on November 9, 1950, portions of his memorial went to the completion of the Newport Town Hall and 4-H Memorial building.

The Pickel Family

John Pickel (1819-1900) and his wife Anna Myers (1818-1885) were both born in Buren, Germany. They came to America in 1847 and settled in Port Washington, Wisconsin.

Andrew, born in 1848, was the first of their eight children. About 1869, Andrew journeyed to the Kilbourn-Delton area to look for land. He purchased a 120 acre farm near what is now County Hwy H. The area was known as Pickel Road. The whole Pickel family moved from Port Washington with ox drawn wagons.

Andrew Pickel married Katherine Funk. In the late 1870's, Katherine, with her brother John, had migrated to America from Wurtenburg, Germany to work in the Woolen Mills at Reedsburg. John married Andrew's sister.

Katherine and Andrew's first child was George Michael Pickel (1883-1971). He had four brothers and sisters.

In 1913, George married Augusta (Gussie) Christiana Storandt, daughter of Carl and Christiana Heimel Storandt of Kilbourn City. George and Gussie were active in the Lutheran Church and in other community affairs, especially in organizing the Farmers Union, Kilbourn Equity Co-op, Kilbourn Co-op Creamery and the Wisconsin Progressive Party. George was a long time member of the board of the Town of Delton.

After selling the family farm in 1948 they moved to Wisconsin Dells and George worked for that city for a time before his retirement. George and Augusta had one son, Hilbert.

Hilbert and his wife Prudence presently live in Chariton, Iowa.

William Playman

William Lyle Playman was born in Stevens Point on March 15, 1900, and raised there, where his father was a building contractor.

As a young boy, William worked on many building projects with his father. He served in World War I, stationed in France with Battery C, the 120th Field Artillery. After the war he attended Stevens Point Normal and graduated in 1923.

William met his wife Katherine Pliet in Stevens Point where she worked at the Five and Dime. He always said, "I met my million dollar baby in the five and ten cent store." They were married on August 13, 1923, and moved to Kilbourn where William had his first teaching job.

He taught high school math and physics from 1923-25. During this time he was also the high school basketball and football coach. He left the Dells in 1925, moving to Eau Claire, then LaCrosse, as a Standard Oil representative. He moved his family back to the Dells in 1939 when he became the Standard Oil bulk agent there. He sold that business to Howard Heitman in 1958.

William was a business and civic leader in the Dells for many years. He and Katherine owned and operated a motel in the Dells until shortly before his death. William was a past commander of the Harold B. Larkin American Legion Post and a past president of the Wisconsin Dells School Board. He also served on the Columbia County Board of Supervisors.

He and Katherine were members of St. Cecilia's Catholic Church, where she played the organ for many years. She donated her organ to the church when she died.

William and Katherine had three children. James Richard was born in 1925 and died in 1990. Deloris Jane was born in 1928 and is married to Joseph F. Kaiser. Robert Eugene was born in 1930 and is married to Betty John Tilton. Both Deloris and Robert still reside in Wisconsin Dells.

William died in 1979 and Katherine in 1988. They are buried in Calvary Cemetery in Wisconsin Dells.

The Priester Family

Adolph and Sophia (Meier) Priester moved from Eldridge, Iowa in 1909 to a farm three miles north of Kilbourn at Rood's Glen. They farmed at first and then started a resort, gradually adding buildings, using the name Rood's Glen.

During the 1920's and 1930's, before modern refrigeration, feeding guests required 5:30 AM trips to Kilbourn for fresh meat and supplies. Grocery stores and meat markets were open to serve the needs of the resorts. Other produce came from a large garden, and chickens for Sunday dinner were raised on the property.

The resort closed during World War II when gas and food shortages reduced travel and service. For several years, rooms at Rood's Glen were rented by Chula Vista resort and long-time guests continued to return there. Adolph Priester, Sr. died in 1952, and Sophia in 1968.

Adolph and Sophia had one son, Arnol in 1899. He helped at the resort and operated the launch *Hawkeye*, and later the launch *Milwaukee*.

In 1922 Arnol married Crystal Ruth Lee. They had eight children: Harry, Adolph, William, Jerry, Thomas, Vivian, Peggy and Robert.

In addition to the resort, Arnol's career included operating the launch, *Ramona*, at Berry's Golf Course; working at the Pines Hotel; cutting ice at the Kriegel farm and filling ice houses for summer refrigeration. During World War II he worked at the Badger Ordnance ammunition plant in Baraboo. Later, as a river pilot for the Dells Boat Company, he forged a river tradition that he would hand down to all six of his sons. They all earned their way through college working for various boat companies. In total, Arnol and his sons piloted 51 boats over 68 years.

Arnol Priester's six sons all earned their way through college working for various boat companies. His sons worked on Dells river boats during the following years: Harry 1941-1947; Adolph 1942-1959; Bill 1941-1951; Jerry 1948-1965; Tom 1954-1958; Bob 1974-1979.

Jack Purcell

J. J. Purcell was a well known and much loved resident of Wisconsin Dells.

Mr. Purcell was born in Hartford, Wisconsin on May 3l, 1856, and the family moved to the area when he was only nine months old. His grandmother was the daughter of Englishman Sir John Tilly. His father, Joe, was looking for Punkintown.

Jack married Nora Tangney and they had two sons and three daughters. From the 1890s through the 1920s, Jack was the Kilbourn depot agent. Nora passed away in December 1919. Three of their children also preceded Jack in death.

In 1921, he married Kate Slowey. They lived together on Washington Avenue until, in 1945, Kate's health began to fail and the couple moved to the Masonic Home in Dousman, Wisconsin. Mrs. Purcell passed away shortly before Jack did, and his tender and unwearied devotion to her during her long illness exemplified his fine spirit and endeared him to his relatives and friends.

Jack himself was in rapidly failing health when he died on September 10th, 1951 at age 92. Jack was a mine of information on the early days of this community; an honest, upright and independent American citizen. At his death he left one son, William C. of Alhambra, California, and one daughter, Irene (Mrs. Dan Greenwood) of Wisconsin Dells.

Helen H. Raab

The historic Dawn Manor on Lake Delton was the home of Helen Raab between 1942 and 1970.

Born in Lincoln, Nebraska in 1889, she moved to Milwaukee at age 17. While working at the Layton Art Gallery she met, and later married, artist and lecturer George Raab. They had a son, Kirby.

Helen Raab began acquiring property along the lower Dells of the Wisconsin River in 1929. Each year she stayed in the Dells area and was attracted to Dawn Manor. The large stone house, built in 1855 for Mr. Vanderpoel, had been converted to tourist rooms and was in disrepair. Helen purchased the property in 1942 and carefully restored the mansion to its original grandeur. She filled the house with her priceless collection of paintings, rare porcelains, fabrics and antiques acquired on numerous world tours.

Helen Raab had a wide range of friends who were frequent visitors at Dawn Manor. Among them was Mrs. Frank Lloyd Wright who left Mrs. Raab her collection of rare and original Japanese prints. She enjoyed the outdoors and often hunted, fished and trapped (she once trapped beaver for her own coat). She loved animals and pets at Dawn Manor included goats, a donkey, dogs, cats and geese.

In 1956, the Wisconsin Alumni Research Foundation acquired three miles along the Wisconsin River from Helen Raab. Mrs. Raab died at the age of 81 from complications following surgery.

The Radlunds

John and Katherine Radlund came to the United States from Sweden and Denmark in the 1880's. In 1900, they purchased the Pine Glen Resort on the Lower Dells, with 100 acres of land and 1.5 miles of river frontage, for $7,000.

Six children came with them and lived there for varying numbers of years. Carl became a carpenter in Beaver Dam. Emma married and moved to Elmhurst, Illinois. John became superintendent of the Wisconsin Power and Light Company dam at Prairie Du Sac. Emil built Ravenswood Resort. Olga and Harry were associated with Pine Glen until its sale to the Wisconsin Alumni Research Foundation in 1964.

Emil had worked for the Wisconsin Power and Light Company until purchasing eight acres of river frontage north of Pine Glen from Jenny Bowman. He named it Ravenswood, for the section of Chicago from which the family came. He and his wife, Julie Eckhart of Rock Island, Illinois, whom he met as a guest at Pine Glen, built Ravenswood into a resort.

Their son, Donald, served in the 94th Infantry Division in World War II and then joined his parents in operating the resort. In 1966, Ravenswood was sold to the Alumni Research Foundation as part of their program to preserve the river frontage of the Lower Dells from overdevelopment.

With the death of Harry's daughter, Dorothy Kazanecki, in 1983, the 80 year saga of the Radlund family in the Dells ended.

The Ramsey Family

James Ramsey was born in 1804 and in the 1840's picked out a home in the Indian Territory of Wisconsin. He and his family moved to the new farm from Northeast Ohio on July 28, 1850. James was elected the first Town Chairman of New Haven in 1856. One of his sons served and died in the Civil War. James died in 1880 and is buried on his farm.

His wife, Sally Best, was born in 1804 into a family of seven children. Her mother, Eleanor (McClarity) Best was born in 1771, married a Revolutionary War Soldier name Thomas Best (1768-1807) who drowned in Ohio. Eleanor moved to Wisconsin with Sally's family at age 79, and lived there until she died at age 89. Sally died in 1881, and is buried in the Ramsey graveyard along with her husband, her mother, some children, some neighbors, some hired men, and Jake, the big lead ox in her son's draft team.

James and Sally's son, Robert M., born in Ohio in 1829, became a very influential and well known citizen of the area. Rob eventually owned over 400 acres of land and a large herd of cattle, including over 20 draft oxen. He once produced over a ton of butter in one year's time. The oxen pulled a 24 inch breaking plow which cleared much of the land in southeastern Adams County, and in the winter, Rob took them to work in the pineries to the north. Rob also had a large wheel scraper which he used for road building, dam construction, and other related tasks.

"Old Rob" died in 1895, and is buried with his wife Rebecca in the Big Spring Cemetery. Rebecca was also born in Ohio, in 1834. They raised a large family. She spent most of her life in Wisconsin living in a log home with a dirt floor and removable rifle ports in the walls. In 1890 they built a new brick home . She died in 1910.

Wallace James Ramsey was born to Robert M. and Rebecca in 1854. Wallace had four daughters from his first marriage, and had two sons with his second wife, Etta. Following Wallace's early death in 1902, Etta remarried and had another daughter.

Robert L. Ramsey was born to Wallace and Etta on July 23, 1888 in New Haven. He lived and died on the farm his great grandfather had carved from the wilderness many years earlier, and except for the farms unusual prosperity, Robby's early childhood was typical. The prosperity soon dwindled, however.

His grandfather, Robert M. suffered a stroke in 1895 and the empire began to crumble. Robby's father was also stricken with cancer and died when Robby was fourteen. The winter of 1901-1902 was especially hard. His mother, father, and younger brother had moved to Kilbourn, where his uncle Clint ran a livery stable, and where doctors could better help the dying father. Most of the livestock and much of the land had been sold to pay doctor bills and no hired men were left. Robby and his aged grandmother, Rebecca, were left to tend the remaining stock. Robby said that at Christmas his grandma gave him the best gift he ever received in his life – a quart of lamp oil so he needn't milk the cows in the dark each day.

Soon his grandmother also became ill and moved to Kilbourn. The remainder of the cattle and standing crops were sold and his mother and brother moved to a better house in Big Spring.

Robby took the train from Kilbourn to Washington State where his great uncle owned a ranch. He might have remained there but when Rebecca died, in 1910, he was named executor for the combined estates of Robert M., Wallace J., and Rebecca Ramsey. When he returned from Washington he found what remained of the Ramsey farm abandoned and falling down.

With the few dollars he had saved, he bought a few cows and a horse to team with an Indian pony his father had bought from Chief Pretty Man many years before, and began farming in earnest. In September of 1911, he married a girl who waited on customers at Hanson & Hindes Store in Big Spring, Alice Amelia Evans.

Alice was born in 1891, the sixth of eleven children born to George and Sarah (Schellkopf) Evans. George Evans (1860-1949) was the son of Jacob Evans (1835-1910) and Thurrissa Jackson Evans (1841-1902) of Jackson, Adams County. Sarah was the daughter of John Schellkopf (1824-1907) and Mary Byers (1824-1898) also of Jackson Township.

When Alice was twelve years old, she went to work and live at the Adams County Poor Farm south of Jordan Lake. Working away from home was common for children of large families. Later she secured a better job from Parson Hindes.

Robby and Alice moved into an old hired man's cabin on the Ramsey Farm. They bought out several other heirs to the Robert M. Ramsey estate, and re-assembled about two thirds of the original farm. Later they moved into the old farm house to raise their children: Arthur; Nina McClyman; Archie (who died soon after D-Day in 1944); Eva; Helen Treadwell; Wayne (died in infancy); and Ruth Crothers.

Robby continued to farm until he died in May, 1980, and Alice died in 1987. All of the Ramsey property has since been sold, except for the old graveyard on the hill which has remained in the family for 145 years.

Fred A. Sauger

Fred A. Sauger was born August 14, 1889 at Egg Harbor. He graduated from the University of Wisconsin in 1926, where he had played on the varsity football team for three years.

Following graduation, he taught biology and physical education and coached the football squad for six years at Reedsburg. He also was a member of the staff at Culver Military Academy in Indiana for six years. He married Norma Schweke at Reedsburg on June 12, 1928. He went into business at Lake Delton in 1938 and worked only on a part-time basis after 1948 because of ill health. He served as a Sauk County deputy sheriff for many years.

Mr. Sauger was a member of the Lake Delton Masonic Lodge, of the Reedsburg St. John's Commandery, and the Madison Consistory and Shrine.

The Schoeninger Family

Adolphe, Frank and Lena Shoeninger came from Stuttgart, Germany to the United States with their parents, William and Lena, when Adolphe was seven years old.

Adolphe lived in Chicago until he moved to Kilbourn and resided at Pine Glen Farm. Following his marriage to Hattie Miller on February 28, 1901, he returned to Crystal Lake, Illinois until 1912. Then with daughters Marie, Madeline and Laura, he and Hattie returned to Kilbourn.

The couple owned property on the west side of Cedar Street, from Minnesota Avenue to, and including, land bordering Taylor's Glen. They built log cabins near the Glen in 1925, which they rented for one dollar per person/per night.

At Taylors Glen, the Schoeninger daughters gave guided tours, pointing out rock formations, wild flowers, ferns and natural spring waters. Tours ended with a trek through a dark tunnel beneath the railroad tracks which led to the Lower Dells.

Adolphe was a bookkeeper for the I.W. York Company–Squire Dingee Pickle Company, located along the railroad tracks near the swimming pool. He was active in civic affairs, serving on the city council for ten years.

Adolphe died on September 9, 1946.

His brother Frank J., arrived to live at the old house at Pine Glen farm in 1899, with his wife Rose and son William J. Another daughter, Louise, was born there on September 21, 1900. Finding the soil on the farm too sandy, Frank returned to Chicago in 1901, but continued spending summers in the Dells.

He and his family lived in several different homes on Washington Avenue, near brother Adolphe, and during 1917 and 1918, rented Dawn Manor for the summer. In 1922, Frank bought the Peter Bauer farm, and spent the the next few summers at the old grainary while building a home above the river.

During the early 1920's, Frank and his children, William and Louise, used their large open car to take local youth to the lower Dells for swimming lessons. Frank J. Schoeninger died on August 1, 1943 at his home on the river, and Rose died at Louise's home in Arizona in 1962.

William married Marie Schmit and their son, Frank M., was born in Chicago on December 8, 1937. Frank spent his early summers in the Dells and in 1964 moved to the area permanently. He joined the Police Department that same year and in 1987, was appointed Chief of Police by Mayor Tom Crist.

William also relocated permanently in 1979, after serving the state legislature and holding various real estate management positions in Chicago. He retired as an Illinois state senator and Democratic ward committeeman.

William J. Schultz

W.J. Schultz was born on March 4, 1875 in Reedsburg, Wisconsin. As a young man he worked on a farm and later purchased a custom threshing machine and did threshing for farmers in the area. In 1900 he moved to Kilbourn City and was employed as a plumber for the Snider Hardware Company. The plumbing shop was located on the second floor of the old McClyman Building on Broadway.

Mr. Schultz married Myrna Borcher in the early 1900s and they had four children: Avis, Norman, Helen, and Margaret. Avis and Margaret are deceased.

In 1910 W.J. started his own plumbing business and purchased a building at 759 Oak Street. His first service vehicle was a two wheel cart which he pulled from job to job. His son Norman joined his father in 1932.

W. J. died in 1950 and Norman operated the shop until his retirement in 1976. The business was sold to Don Vander Sande.

W. J. was a member of Bethany Lutheran Church and both he and Norman were members of the Kilbourn Volunteer Fire Department. W. J. served as fire chief during his last years.

Joseph W. Shourds

Joseph W. Shourds was born on April 18, 1826. His birthplace is unknown but as a young man he walked to California as a '49er. His trip was less perilous than some because, with foot care so vital on the long walk, he had the forethought to take a large bundle of socks.

It is also unknown just how successful his gold-seeking efforts were, but his great-grandson, Percy Seamans of Lake Delton, has two tiny gold nuggets that Joseph brought back as proof of his adventures.

In 1852, Joseph married Elmina Bloomer and settled in Newport where they had two children, Lenora and Milo. Lenora's school was located where the Helen Raab estate now stands.

Joseph invested in land in Newport, planning to subdivide it into lots. When the railroad went to Kilbourn instead, his plans were shattered and he had to move elsewhere. He was a skilled artisan and inventor but his later life was relatively uneventful He died January 18, 1897.

The Shumway Family

Oliver Arden "Ollie" Shumway, one of six children, was of French descent. His father, Fred Albert, was a carpenter from Waushara County. His mother was Maggie Wilson, also a native of Waushara County and of English lineage.

Oliver was born in Ashland, Wisconsin on December 28, 1904. He moved from Stevens Point in 1922 to become a member of the Kilbourn High School athletic teams. He operated a boat on the river for a time and later, like his father, was a carpenter.

On September 5, 1923, Oliver married Margaret "Peg" Tolleth, who was born September 23, 1906, to Henry and Lena (Hanson) Tolleth, who later came to this city from Wild Rose.

Oliver died on October 17, 1972 at the age of 67 years. His wife, Margaret joined him on October 19, 1987 at the age of 81. They are both buried in Spring Grove Cemetery.

Ollie and Peg had three children: Norma Phyllis, born at Kilbourn, May 9, 1925 in a house on River Road; Mary Louise; John Edward.

After Norma graduated from Wisconsin Dells High School in 1943, she attended the University of Wisconsin in Madison where she met her husband, Edward Joseph Marz of New Britian, Connecticut, at the time a smiling young man in uniform. They were married in Boca Raton, Florida on January 15, 1945.

Upon discharge from the Army and completion of his Masters Degree in Education from Columbia University in New York City, Edward and Norma moved to Carroll, Iowa with their young family and there Edward was employed as an insurance salesman and substitute teacher. Norma and Edward returned to Wisconsin Dells with their family in 1974 and Edward became a salesman of specialty items and Norma a souvenir store clerk and bookkeeper. He died on July 13,1982 at the age of 62 and is buried in Spring Grove Cemetery. Since her husband's death, Norma has operated the Sherman House Bed & Breakfast. Their children are John Edward of Greenwood, Wisconsin, married to Suellyn Kay Schmitz (with children Susan Jane of Wisconsin Dells and Sara Jane, a student in Madison); Peggy Ann of Wisconsin Dells (her son is Christopher James Pitts, a student in Madison); Peter William, of Roselle, Illinois, married to Barbara Ann Bonnan (with children Timothy Peter and Anthony Jacob "A.J."); Jane Elizabeth of Middleton, married to Steven Alan Sheline (their children: Zachary

Steven and Chad Alan); and Daniel Joseph of Wisconsin Dells.

The second child of Oliver and Margaret Shumway is Mary Louise Shumway, born in Portage on August 21, 1926. She was an editorial assistant for academic journals at the University of Chicago; instructor of English and Anthropology at George Williams College; a social worker for Los Angeles County, California; a dean of women, coordinator of undergraduate studies and instructor at the San Francisco Art Institute; a newspaper reporter; an editorial assistant; a waitress; a book clerk; accident insurance underwriter; a statistician on a horse farm; a clerk in an Indian trading post. She received her bachelor's degree from the University of Chicago in 1957 and her master's degree from San Francisco State College. Her Ph. D was obtained at the University of Wisconsin, Stevens Point and she was a professor of English. Prior to retirement she was given the Excellence in Teaching Award. Mary is the author of the following books of poetry: *Son of the Archer, Headlands, Time and Other Birds, Practicing Vivaldi*, and *Legends and Other Voices*. She later moved to Plover, Wisconsin.

John Edward was born in Wisconsin Dells on November 30,1935. He graduated from Wisconsin Dells High School and attended the University of Wisconsin--Stevens Point. While serving as a Marine, in 1957 he married G. Corrine "Corky" Hudson in San Diego while she was a U.S. Navy nurse. They moved to Wisconsin Dells where they had five children: Andrew John of Los Angeles, California, married to Brenna Joy Ellis; Julie Ellen of Dodgeville, Wisconsin, married to David Lee Hill (with children Rachel ann, Paul David, Lydia Margaret and Jordon John); Paul Alan, deceased; James Clifford of Madison, married to Cynthia Marie Teml; and David Michael, also of Los Angeles.

Corinne has worked since 1963 at the Dells Clinic, John worked as a police officer, restaurant owner and accountant prior to his death on November 18, 1989. He is buried in Spring Grove Cemetery.

Of the three football teams from Wisconsin Dells High School that had undefeated seasons, each had a Shumway playing.

Gerhard G. Smukal

Gerhard was born July 15, 1922 in Wisconsin Dells, one of twin sons, to Rev. and Mrs. E. Smukal. He graduated from the local school in 1940. He was an all round athlete, winning letters in football, basketball, track and boxing. He spent 39 months in the service, in the anti-aircraft division in the United States and the infantry in the European Theater, four months of his time overseas being in the hospital due to wounds. He received his discharge in January, 1946.

On September 4, 1946, he was married to Miss Wilma Christensen of Copenhagen, Denmark whom he had met overseas and brought to the United States.

In partnership with Dennis Stroede, he started the Superior Ice Company, and had built up a fine business before his very untimely death. Gerhard drowned after rescuing a swimming companion from the same fate.

At his death in 1947, he was survived by his father, four brothers, Robert, his twin Luther, Henry and Ewald and his grandfather Rev. R. Smukal of Detroit. He was preceded in death by his mother in 1933, and by a brother, Vernon.

The Snider Family

The Snider and Drinker families came from Pennsylvania to Columbia County. They settled in Newport and later moved to Kilbourn. Early history shows that John R. Henry Snider and his son, Charles Wilson, were raftsmen on the Wisconsin River.

Henry, known as "Cap" Snider later piloted the steamer *Apollo* "up river", transporting early tourists through the Dells, "Cap", in fact, died on the lower deck of his boat. He had taken a load of passengers to the Larks Hotel to a dance, and while waiting, quietly died as he was seated, smoking his pipe on the deck.

Charles' mother was Joseph Bailey's sister. When Charles was young, he went to work for Hansen's Hardware in Kilbourn. He worked so well that after a year he was rewarded with a bonus of a new suit. He stayed with the firm and later he and Mr. Hansen established the Hansen-Snider Lumber Company.

Charles married Minnie Drinker, whose family built the Drinker saw mill, and they had one son, Harry. Charles opened a hardware store on Broadway, and later a lumber and hardware yard on the corner of Washington and Superior Street. Charles was president of the board of the Presbyterian Church, president of the school board and the library board, and spent four years as mayor.

While Charles was Mayor, Kilbourn saw its first street lighting and a lamplighter was employed. He was instrumental, and also contributed financially, in the purchase of the public library property.

When young, Harry worked summers on a steamboat, and daily made the jump at Stand Rock. His Uncle Henry was the pilot of the *Dell Queen* and the *Apollo*. On the *Apollo's* maiden voyage, a young girl named Lora became drenched with spray and Harry helped her dry off. He later married her.

After Harry graduated from Beloit College, Colorado School of Mines, and worked as an engineer in the west, he returned to settle in Kilbourn. He and Lora, daughter of William F. and Josie (Edson) Oswald, were married in 1905. Lora's parents were very active in local church and Red Cross activities. Josie made countless hospital garments for the Red Cross during World War I.

Harry joined his father at the Hansen-Snider Lumber Company. For many years, he was a volunteer fireman, president of the library and cemetery boards, President of Wisconsin Retail Lumber Dealers Insurance Board, and active in other civic groups. Lora worked with the Bennett family on Christmas Seals, and was engaged in Presbyterian Church activities.

Harry and Lora had two children, Charles and Beverly (Mrs. William Van Orden French of Pompano Beach, Florida).

Lora and Harry were nearing their 64th wedding anniversary when Harry passed away at the age of 90.

The statue which now graces the lawn of the Wisconsin Dells Public Library was dedicated to Minnie Drinker Snider, and also to Charles' brother, Frederick Bailey Snider.

The Soma Family

Peder Laurits Soma was born March 10, 1878 near Sannes, about 12 miles south of Stavanger, Norway. He was one of eight sons and one daughter born to Ingebert and Kirsten Ingebertson. When he was 20 years old, he ventured to America and arrived at his sister and brothers-in-law near Austin, Minnesota.

Bertha Steinsland from Bjerkreim, Norway, sixty-five miles south east of Sannes, arrived in America in early March, 1899. She married Peder at Austin, Minnesota, on March 29, 1899. They rented a farm and worked it with horses. They had eleven children: Milla, Ingebert, Oscar, Paul, Almer, Laida, Arlie, Laurie, Beatrice, Sherman (Stanley) and Nenfred.

They farmed in Minnesota until 1920 when they purchased a farm one mile north of Kilbourn on old Hwy 13, which had river frontage with the famous rock formation called High Rock. Peder also purchased a piece of land on the corner of Hwy 13 and Town Line Road. Along with his sons, he operated a saw mill powered by a steam engine. They also did custom threshing, silo filling and corn shredding as far north as White Creek, east to Briggsville and south as far as Lewiston.

In 1926, he sold this parcel of land to Roland Dyer. Peder also purchased a number of city lots on east Broadway which he sold to Norman Coapman and Alfred Preissel in the 1930's. In 1929, Pedar sold his farm to the Crandalls. He then purchased a farm one and a half miles east of Kilbourn on Hwy 23 in Newport.

In 1939 while doing custom shredding, he lost his right hand. He was still very active and kept on with his custom work until September 17, 1943 when he was killed by his tractor.

Peder was a proud and honest man. He planted five thousand pine tree seedlings around the Hwy 23 farm with his one hand. These trees are now 30-40 feet tall.

Peder and Bertha have 24 grandchildren and 78 great grandchildren, many of whom remain in the Dells area. They were members of the Trinity Lutheran Church in the Dells. When Peder became a U.S. citizen, he took the much shorter name of Soma, from the township or farm where he was born in Norway.

Bertha was stricken with multiple sclerois and parkinsons disease in 1922 and passed away November 1, 1944.

The oldest son, Ingebert (Cap) Soma was born March 29, 1901 in LeRoy, Minnesota. Ingebert and Marie (Gibson) Soma purchased property on Crandall Bay and in 1942 founded Soma Boat Lines on River Road. The boat line was a landmark in Wisconsin Dells until 1958.

Ingebert and Marie's children were Sharon, Ruth, Margaret and Harold. Margaret's (Hartwig) children are Lynn, Mike and Joan. Harold remained here and carried on the river boat tradition, retiring in 1992 after 40 years as a river pilot. He and his wife (Judy Blood) raised four more river pilots.

These grandchildren of Ingebert (Cap) Soma are Dave, Dan and Chris Soma and Monica Meyers. Even though Dave and Monica have pursued other careers and Dan has a reputation as an entertainer, he and Chris can be found on any summer day following in their grandfather's footsteps along the Wisconsin River. Cap Soma died in Wisconsin Dells in 1986.

Of the other Peder and Bertha Soma children, Oscar farmed near Rochester, Minnesota. Paul and Arlie farmed near Briggsville. Almer worked for the City of Wisconsin Dells and also did custom butchering for the Fred Zinke Food Market. Laurie, Sherman and Nenfred served in World War II. Laurie served in New Guinea and Australia. Sherman (Stanley) was in the Norwegian Battalion Special Unit, and trained for the invasion of Norway. This unit fought across Europe including the Battle of the Bulge. When the Nazis surrendered, they were on the Danube. On June 6, 1945 they were sent in triumph to Oslo, and hailed as conquering heroes. Stanley then worked for the City of Wisconsin Dells for 25 years prior to his retirment.

Nenfred was stationed in Alabama, Wyoming and Colorado. After service he worked and retired from Oscar Mayer of Madison and now lives in Sun Prairie.

Milla, the oldest, is now 93 years old and resides at the Winnebago Nursing Home. She was married to Peder Tovdal, a World War I veteran. They farmed near Blue Earth, Minnesota.

Laida married Martin Platt who operated a garage and wrecking business along with his sons.

Beatrice, the youngest girl, spent most of her time caring for her invalid mother. She later married Alfred H. Nickel and they had five children: Bonnie, Melvin, Darlene, Gene and Jerry. Following her mother's death, Beatrice spent 18 years as a waitress at Uphoff's Rotunda in Lake Delton.

Oscar, Paul, Laurie and Laida are deceased.

Alonzo Stearns

"The first settler [in the township of Newport] was Alonzo Stearns who came here in March, 1849, and located on Section 17. Mr. Stearns erected a small log cabin, and commenced to clear the land for a farm," wrote the author of the 1880 history of Columbia County. He purchased this farm when the land came into market in the fall of 1852.

The first sermon preached in town was at the house of A.B. Stearns, July 5, 1852, for the death of L.W. Stearns.

Alonzo married Antoinette Calkins in June, 1852. They had eleven children and later built a large house on their 200 acre farm. Though busy on the farm, he held many Newport town offices.

After living in Newport for nearly 50 years, the Stearns' moved west to Heckla, South Dakota to be near their children.

Alonzo died in 1911 and his wife in 1915. Both are buried in the Spring Grove Cemetery.

The large farm house built by Alonzo burned about 1907. His son Willis' house still stands at fire #14025. The former Stearns School was converted to a residence and stands across the road.

Eugene Steele

Eugene Steele was born in White Creek to Thomas and Elizabeth Steele on July 16, 1917.

Thomas was born and raised in White Creek and later moved to Illinois to look for work. There he married Elizabeth Cook and they returned to White Creek to farm and raise a family. They also had three other children: Lorene, Julia, and Albert.

Eugene attended school in Wisconsin Dells. He loved farming and owned several farms in the area throughout his life. He also worked outside the farm at Storybook Gardens, Fort Dells and Badger Ordnance.

He married Medie Richardson of Adams, who had three children: David, Sharon and Shirley. Eugene and Medie had four more children together: Marilyn, Gary, Cindy and Albert.

Eugene was a World War II veteran and a member of the American Legion and St. Cecelia's Church. He died of cancer on October 26, 1970 and is buried at Calvary Cemetery in the Dells.

The Stomner Family

Orville Herbert Stomner was born in Newport on April 7, 1892, to Charles Ole and Mattie Peterson Stomner. Charles had come to America at age eleven from Kongsvinger, Norway. The family settled at Fairfield, across the river from Newport.

In June, 1916, Orville and Cora Serena Bartness from Albert Lea, Minnesota were married. After farming for a few years in Newport, they moved to Kilbourn in 1920.

Buying out Mr. Wirtz's part of the business in the meat market at 308 Broadway, Orville entered into a partnership with Mr. Meinicke. The partnership ended in February, 1925. The Modern Meat Market specialized in homemade sausage and home dressed meats. Upon retiring from business he was hired to buy cattle for Oscar Mayer Company of Madison, Wisconsin. For years area residents enjoyed Clara's cooking, developed while cooking meals for eight brothers and her parents, who worked out in the fields. She cooked every Monday night for the Kiwanis Club, at each of 20 annual Firemen's Banquets, and spent summers cooking pies and other delights for the Finch and Blackhawk Hotels in the Dells, and for Uphoffs in Lake Delton.

Orville was a member of the Kilbourn Volunteer Fire Department for many years. He died on Christmas Day, 1980.

Orville and Cora were the parents of six children: Charles, Claire (Fulmer), Phyllis (Angsten), Ruth (Lee), Dorothy and Beverly (Shander).

Charles Theron Stomner was born in Newport on July 14, 1917 to Orville and Cora Stomner.

In June, 1940, he married Dorothy Krueger of Reedsburg, and they had two children: James Todd and Sally Kay (McGowan).

Charles was a lifelong resident of the Wisconsin Dells area. For some years he was in the grocery and meat market business at 308 Broadway. He then managed the kitchen at Uphoff's which later became Kahler's and, and for many years he worked in building.

Being involved in the Kilbourn Volunteer Fire Department was of great importance to "Butch" Stomner. He was generous in giving of his time and talent. Serving as chief for six years was a highlight of his life.

Charles passed away on May 1, 1990.

Vivian O. (Peterson) Steiner

Vivian O. Steiner was born to Joseph and Carrie Peterson in Kasota, Minnesota, on February 24, 1986. She had two older siblings, Harry and Effie, and later a sister Grace.

On April 4, 1901, the family came by train to Kilbourn in order to help care for Vivian's paternal grandmother. After a night at the Kilbourn Inn, they hired a livery buggy to take them to the 200 acre farm through a driving rain. Vivian and Effie had a delightful summer with plenty of room to play in the yard and adjoining wooded area. There was a hops kiln in which the hops crop was hung to dry. Grandma died that November, and was laid out in a wooden casket in one of the two living rooms.

Though Vivian's father had chronic asthma, he loved to talk with good friends Hans and Tillie Anderson and Ollie Christopherson, who frequently came to help with planting and harvesting. In 1904, Joseph became deathly ill with a strangulated hernia. Two surgeons, brought to the farm from Portage, draped the kitchen with sheets and operated on the kitchen table. While the chloroform caused him to sleep for five hours afterward, he did recover.

The family stayed on the farm for four years before building a new three bedroom house in town.

Joseph Peterson was a temperance man. He showed lantern slides by gas lamps that depicted the terrible outcomes of drink and was often hired to take his traveling show, along with songs and stories, to surrounding towns.

The entire family were musicians and travelled from town to town to play fairs. Their orchestra was well known in the area for fifteen years and hired other musicians to a total of twelve pieces at times. Clayton Rodwell and Huet Johnson were often part of the band. They played all the proms and traveled, with all their instruments, by train and Model T Fords.

A violinist, Louis Steiner, moved to the area with his family in about 1917. He played in the Peterson Harp Orchestra for about six or seven years. In the winter, he often returned to Chicago to play at the Palmer House with Al Henke. On October 26, 1926, Vivian Peterson and Louis Steiner eloped to Gary, Indiana to be married.

Louis and Vivian worked at Parsons Trading Post for many years. When Captain Parsons opened his small Indian ceremonial, Louis helped with lighting and landscaping and Vivian accompanied the Indian singers on the harp. In 1942, Phyllis Connor asked Vivian to return to the show at Stand Rock, and she did, until 1954. She and Louie also played on the steamboat to and from the show.

Vivian and Louie had one daughter, Rita, who married in 1954. After Louie died in 1956, Vivian worked in sales, moved to La Crosse for a while, and returned to the area in 1963 when Rita's family moved to Lake Delton.

She had an artistic flair in decorating and built three homes in her lifetime. The little red cottage on the corner of Elm and Oak in Wisconsin Dells is one of them. Her final home was a log cottage in Lake Delton that she purchased from Joe Kaminski. After redecorating this home, she enjoyed her retirement years there watching the progress of her three grandchildren nearby. She died at Rita's home in 1981.

The Storandt Family

During the 1800's, Ernest, Wilhelm, and Karl Storandt migrated to America. Their brother Heinrich and sisters Sara and Marie remained in Germany. These were the six children of Bernard Christian Storandt and his wife Gund Elizabeth Rommel of Germany.

The three brothers, and their families, lived out their lives in the Kilbourn area.

Wilhelm married Anna Seabert and they had four children: Frederick (Amelia Jensen); Marie (Harvey Jensen); Bertha (Carl Herwig); and Amelia.

Karl had married Christiana Heimel in Germany before coming to America and their sons, Richard and Ernest, were also born there. They had two more children in America: Augusta (Pickel) and William.

Ernest Storandt was born in Herrenbreitungen, Germany in 1852. In Chicago, Illinois, on March 14, 1882, he married Amynta Kleimenhagen of Kilbourn City. She had come from Germany to join her twin brother Leonard Kleimenhagen. The Storandts and Kleimenhagens came from the same area of Germany and had known one another before coming to America.

In 1883 Ernest and Amynta had a son, Wilhelm August, and in 1885 a daughter, Lydia Augusta. In 1885 the family moved to Wisconsin and established themselves on a farm in New Haven, seven miles from Kilbourn City. One wall in the kitchen of their farm house was what remained of an old stagecoach stop that had been on the property.

In 1909 Ernest, Amynta and Lydia moved from the farm to their newly built home at 731 Elm Street in Kilbourn, presently owned by Ronald Newell. The Ernest Storandts were charter members of the Trinity Evangelical Lutheran in Kilbourn.

Son Wilhelm (William) had remained on the farm. He married

Bertha Wilhelmina Leege on September 10, 1917 at the home of her parents, Menno and Dena Borcher Leege, in Newport. Wilhelm and Bertha had nine children: Geraldine, Walter, Mabel, Homer, Irene, Betty, twin sons Earl and Erwin, and Ima Mae.

Their children attended the same one room school known as Badger Valley, School District #8, New Haven Township, which their father William and his sister Lydia had attended before them. During High School, Geraldine Storandt lived with her grandmother and helped to care for her.

Lydia was married on April 8, 1912 to Harry Horton Sabin from Iowa. Harry was in the construction business and helped build the Kilbourn Dam and power plant. They eventually moved to Marley, Illinois where they operated a Clover Farm Store for 33 years. Their children were Eleanor, who married Francis Nelson of Marley, and Homer, who married Lillian Cooper of New York.

The Stowers Family

J. B. Stowers was one of at least five children. He was reportedly born in Dedham, Massachusetts in 1846, but no records have been found. Two brothers, J. B. and Joe, came west about 1870. Joe settled in the Chicago area and J. B. continued to Wisconsin. He arrived in Big Spring in 1872 and lived with the Ed Sargeant family.

While J. B. was hauling grain to the mill near Pardeeville, he stopped to water his horses at the French farm, where Ellen Isadora French was born and raised. J. B. and Ellen were married when Ellen, born in 1855, was only 17 years old.

Ellen Isadora was a direct descendant of John Milton French. The John Milton French family history is very well documented, going back to at least 1791 in Mainstone, Vermont. John French married Tirzah Day.

John Milton French moved his family to Wisconsin in 1840 and first settled in Dodge County. A few years later they moved near Fort Winnebago. John built the first sawmill on a branch of the Fox River, later called French's Creek. Tirzah died in 1863, the mother of 18 children, most of whom died in infancy.

J. B. Stowers lived on rented property and share cropped most of his life. In his later years he operated a livery stable, on the corner of Wisconsn Avenue and River Road, in co-operation with Mr. French. The eight children of J. B. Stowers and Ellen French were Austin, Clarence, Fred, Bernard, Charles, Mildred, Nellie, and Archie.

J. B. died in 1919 and Ellen Isadora died in 1947.

The Stuelke Family

Mondus H. Stuelke was born on December 11, 1880 at Milford, Wisconsin, attended high school in Marshfield and then graduated from Marquette University. On April 4, 1905 he married Pauline Ahrens of Kilbourn and they had one son, Gordon.

He worked as a pharmacist in Milwaukee for some time and then opened a drug store in Kilbourn on October 8, 1908. For some time the drug store was operated in what is now the east part of "Nig's Bar" (formerly the Farmers and Merchants State Bank). It moved across the street to the corner of Broadway and Superior street in 1923. Mondus died in 1946, and Pauline in 1948.

Their son, Gordon A. was born in Kilbourn on December 15, 1909. He attended Kilbourn High School and graduated from the University of Wisconsin in Madison. He joined his father as pharmacist in the drug store in 1932, and continued to operate the drug store until his retirement in December, 1974.

Gordon and his wife Blanche had one son, Stephen, who was born on October 3, 1939. He graduated from Wisconsin Dells High School and attended the University of Wisconsin in Madison and Rochester Institute of Technology in Rochester, New York receiving an Associate of Applied Science degree in Commercial and Industrial Photography. Stephen briefly operated a photo studio above his grandfather's original drug store. He worked for three years as assistant manager of the Wisconsin Dells Regional Chamber of Commerce before joining the Academic Staff of the University of Wisconsin Extension in Madison in 1966. Stephen continues to reside in Wisconsin Dells.

His mother, Blanche, died in 1983 and Gordon in 1987.

Adolphe and Selma Sunderland

Adolphe "Dade" Sunderland was born in Paris, France on July 31, 1883, to A.F. (Frank) and Hermance Defour Sunderland. He came to the U.S. with his mother in 1886, to join his father in Lake City, Minnesota. Later that year the family moved to Kilbourn where they purchased the Finch Hotel. Adolphe and his younger brother Mortimer were raised at the hotel, which became a popular place known for its comfort, service and excellent food.

On October 26, 1920, Adolphe married Selma Nemitz, daughter of Herman and Amelia Barfknecht Nemitz. Selma was born in West Rosendale, Wisconsin on December 9, 1891. Her family moved to a farm in Jackson township, Adams County, in 1905.

Adolphe and Selma made their home at the hotel, where they helped Hermance with its management until eventually Adolphe and Mortimer took over the establishment. Selma was active in business and community affairs, as was Adolphe, a long time member of the Kilbourn Volunteer Fire Department.

The couple enjoyed fishing and in the fall, duck and goose hunting. They maintained a cabin on the river to which they could escape from the pressures of business.

Adolphe died on May 6, 1936 and Selma on April 18, 1937.

Margaret C. Sweeney

In the fall of 1958, Margaret C. Sweeney came to Wisconsin Dells to help her daughter recuperate from surgery. Margaret had been a widow for five years and decided to stay through the winter to welcome a new grandson in January of 1959.

When spring came, Mr. William Gaffney needed special care and Margaret assisted the family.

As summer neared, another friend, Mrs. Frances Daugherty, who was in charge of the Bowman Home, asked her to cook for the guests there. When Frances retired, Margaret Sweeney became the hostess. While Margaret was at the Bowman Home, from 1959 through 1976, she introduced many guests to the special attractions of the Dells area.

Margaret was the fourteenth child born to Patrick and Margaret Lonergan Havey, on February 17, 1897. She attended the Mauston High School, the Sauk County Normal School in Reedsburg, and Milwaukee Teachers College. She taught school for three years before she married John T. Sweeney on June 26, 1918. They had three sons and one daughter. Margaret died in 1977.

The Tangneys

Two Tangney families settled in the Dells area in the late 1850s. They were Irish immigrants and connected with several other Irish families: the Prindables, Sullivans, Connors, Connells, Bresnahans and Costellos.

Because the immigrant Tangney men were named either Thomas or Patrick, they were given nicknames. Patrick J. was called "Curly Pat" because of his curly hair. His cousin was called "By J Pat" but no one seems to remember why. Another cousin Thomas was called "By God Tom" because he ended each sentence with the sentence, "by God."

The Tangneys were also differentiated by where they lived. Curly Pat and By God Tom were the "West Tangneys" and By J Pat was the "East Tangney."

Patrick J. Tangney (c. 1824-1900) and his family came to the Dells area in 1855 by way of Indiana. Curly Pat had been part of an Irish labor gang laying track for the Terre Haute railroad. He brought his wife, Catherine Connor (1823-1905), and their two year old daughter, Mary Ann. Their next four children, Patrick Michael, Honora, Catherine and Julia Martha, were born in Dell Prairie. Jeremiah J. was born in New Haven.

In 1858, Patrick J. bought 40 acres in Dell Prairie. In 1863, he bought 80 acres on the north edge of Lake Mason in New Haven. In 1872, he moved again and bought 80 acres on the south side of Gillette Avenue where he lived until he died in 1900.

Patrick and his family worshipped in St. Cecilia's Catholic Church and many members of his family are buried in Calvary Cemetery. His daughter, Mary Ann (1854-1933), married James George Hoey and after homesteading in South Dakota for 21 years, the Hoeys moved back to Wisconsin and settled in Polk County.

Son Patrick Michael (1856-1930), married Catherine Costello and Norma Jane Day. He tried homesteading with the Hoeys in South Dakota, but returned to New Haven township in 1891 and bought a farm on Gillette Avenue.

Nora (1858-1919), married John Joseph Purcell, a depot agent and telegrapher in Kilbourn. Kate (1860-1945), married three times (Higbee, Miller and Moffett) and lived in Minneapolis, Minnesota.

Both Julia (1862-1948) who married Patrick Bresnahan, and Jerry (c. 1865-1937) who married Julia Cusak, lived in the Dells area.

The Thomas Tangney family also settled near Kilbourn. Thomas (1801-1882) was Curly Pat's uncle. By J Pat, By God Tom and Mary (Tangney) Crowley were his cousins. Both Thomas Tangney Sr. and Jr. immigrated in 1860 but By J Pat was living in Wisconsin sometime before 1858.

By J Pat (1832-1892) was married to Julia Bresnahan and Mary Agnes Sullivan, and was father to seventeen children. By J Pat and Julia had three sons, Thomas (1858) who settled in Idaho and Washington, Michael (1861) who probably died young and Patrick (1861) who went to Australia.

With Mary, By J Pat had fourteen children: John William (1866-1931); Daniel P. (1868-1918); James J. (1870-1934), who married Martha Lyste; Jeremiah V. (1871-1954); David Walter (1873-1957); Catherine Agnes (1874-1952); Michael A. (1876-1894); Mary Aurelia (1878-1952); Ellen (1880-); Honora Cecelia (1881-1965) who married Charles Hiram Barlow; Henry (c. 1883-died young); Margaret Ida (1884-1972); Julia F. (1885-1963); and William Arthur (1887-1966). Of these seventeen children only James is known to have married and had children. Most of By J Pat's children did not marry and are buried in the Tangney family plot in St. Mary's Catholic cemetery in Briggsville.

Mary Tangney (1834-1911) married Patrick Daniel Crowley and lived in Portage. Their children were Ann, Ellen, Catherine, Julia and Dennis.

By God Tom (1838-1911) was married to the Prindable sisters, Margaret and Nora. Tom and Margaret were the parents of: John Michael (1864-1946) who married Mary Kinney; Ella (1865-); Mary Agnes (1867-1950) who married Alfred H. Smith; Catherine (1870-1899); James E. (1872-1947) who married Clara Hagen and lived in Oregon; and Patrick William (1875-1933) who married Mary Ida Moran.

When Margaret died following childbirth, Tom married her sister, Nora, and they four children: Jerry (1884-) who disappeared; Margaret Mary (1886-1953) who married Frank Nelson; Julia (1887-1909); and Ethel Mae (1893-) who married a man named McIntrye and lived in Oregon and Iowa.

Descendants of Curly Pat and By God Tom still live in the Dells area.

S.A. Thayer

Stephen Augustus Thayer, better known as "Gus", was born in Warsaw, New York in 1853. He came to Dell Prairie in 1866.

In 1876, he married Delia Hutchinson of White Creek. They continued to farm and had six children, only two of whom survived their parents: Carrie Rich and Clate Thayer of North Dakota.

In 1914, the Thayers bought land in Kilbourn and built a Sears Roebuck home on Main Street, now the site of the Coca Cola plant. The house was later moved to 817 Race Street.

Mr. Thayer loved music and was a violinist of considerable ability. He and his family had an orchestra and officiated at many town and country dances. He was humorous and enjoyed "jam sessions" with old cronies including Otto Bohn on clarinet and A.K. Olson on the organ.

Mr. Thayer died in 1929 and Mrs. Thayer in 1937. The only living relatives in this area are granddaughter Doris Naber and Mary Naber Kane, a great granddaugther.

The Thompson Family

Christjahn C. Thompson was in the wagon making business in Baldwin, Wisconsin before he moved to Kilbourn in October of 1919. He and his wife, Martha Caroline Falck, brought their five children: Stewart, George, Carl, Belva and Emma, with them.

Stewart Herman Thompson was the second son, born October 7, 1902. He graduated from Kilbourn High School and attended Lawrence College in Appleton.

In 1923, he married Iness Waterman, daughter of Villie Belle (Hayes) and Andrew Seth Waterman. They had two sons, Stewart Andrew (Kicker) and Thomas Waterman Thompson.

Shortly after his marriage, he was employed in Beaver Dam as a carbon movie machine operator at the Odeon and Davidson Theaters. Later he helped with construction of the Multnomah Lodge in Kilbourn and worked as manager and lifeguard of the Multnomah Swimming Pool.

In 1929, he and Iness opened the Thompson Restaurant on Broadway, which was famous for its 5¢ hamburgers. They continued operating restaurants in the Dells area for over 50 years. His sons, "Kicker" and Tom and their wives, Kaye and Marilyn, later took over operation of the businesses.

Stewart was on the Wisconsin Dells School Board for many years and served as president for some of this time. He was a very active member of the Holy Cross Episcopal Church and was on the building and financial committees that constructed the new church.

Stewart was a proud member of the Kilbourn Fire Department and upon retiring was succeeded by his son, "Kicker". His grandson, Peter is presently a member of the fire department. Stewart died on May, 1983. He and Iness had been married 59 years.

George Phillip Thompson, the youngest child, was born on October 20, 1910 to Christjahn and Martha and was nine years old when he came to the Dells. George did yard work and cared for the beautiful gardens of the Schoeninger family while in high school and after graduation from Kilbourn High in 1929, continued working for them until the mid 1930s. George's nickname was Rabbit, and in his younger years he had a band called Rabbit and His Little Bunnies. George played the trumpet in the band which played dances for $4.00 a night.

On September 26, 1936, he and Stella Louise Ellison were married at the Trinity Lutheran Church parsonage. They purchased a home at 1036 Oak Street from Ernest Newell and after spending one year in Mount Horeb, returned to the Kilbourn residence and George went to work for Wisconsin Power & Light.

In 1938, he purchased a flower business from Robert Kimball and moved the business to his home on Oak Street.

Five children were born to George and Louise; Lee, of Sandwich, Illinois, Linda of Grand Rapids, Minnesota, Sandra of Wisconsin Dells, Christine of Mauston, and Tobias of Stevens Point.

George was an active member of the Kilbourn Fire Department as well as a charter member of Bethany Lutheran Church. He passed away on November 13, 1979.

Of the other children of Christjahn and Martha: Carl made his home in Las Vegas, Nevada; Belva in Waukesha; and Emma in Tampa, Florida. All are deceased.

The Tofson Family

In 1877, Henry M. Tofson was born in Newport to Martin and Anna Tofson. He began his career in business as a ticket agent, day operator and Western Union manager with the Milwaukee Road in 1900. During the evenings, he began to dabble in insurance on the side. He was later employed as a cashier at the Farmer's and Merchant's State Bank, but continued to sell insurance.

After a few years Henry was elected to serve as bank director, but in 1927 decided to devote himself full-time to his Tofson Insurance Agency. His interest in the local bank remained active, however, and he was elected its president in 1934 and later served a 20 year period as chairman of the board.

He was active in other areas of the community as well, including the Kilbourn Volunteer Fire Department, the Kiwanis Club and Trinity Lutheran Church.

Henry married Nina Montgomery in 1906 and they had five children: Doris (Waterman), Donald, Merton, Geraldine (Smith), and Wanda (Counsell).

Like his father before him, Merton W. Tofson was born, raised, and remained in Wisconsin Dells for his entire life.

He was born, the third of five children, to Henry and Nina Montgomery Tofson on July 21, 1916. He worked summers on the river as a tour guide and later earned a business degree from the University of Wisconsin-Madison. Throughout his education he distinguished himself as a scholar and an athlete.

In 1940 he married Ruth Davis and they had four children: Toby, Tim, Tom and Tami.

After serving four years in World War II, Mert returned home and joined his father at the H.M. Tofson and Son Insurance Company, which Henry had established in 1911, adjacent to the Tofson family home on Elm Street. Mert remained in the business, later named Tofson Insurance, Inc., for 25 years.

In 1970 the business purchased and renovated the former St. Paul's Episcopal Church building. The building, which once served as the first school in Wisconsin Dells, continues to proudly display the original school bell at its entrance.

The same year, Mert's oldest son Toby entered the business, making it a third generation enterprise.

Sadly, Mert did not live to see his other sons, Tim and Tom, enter the business, as he was stricken with cancer and died at age 54.

Mert loved the Wisconsin Dells area and was very active within it. He was a member of the Kilbourn Fire Department, the Rotary Club, Bethany Lutheran Church, Columbia County Welfare Commission, and the Bank of Wisconsin Dells. He also served as President of the Wisconsin Dells School Board, and during his tenure, was honored to dig the first shovelful of dirt for the new Wisconsin Dells High School.

Many Tofson descendants remain in the Dells area today.

The Tollaksen Family

Hazel Seuberth was born in Chicago, on May 28, 1892, to Emil Edward Seuberth, a merchant, and Emelie "Rock" Seuberth. She had nine brothers and sisters: Edward, Lillie, Roy, Victory, Mabel, Lyda, Emily, Jane and Myrtle. In the early 1900's Emil moved his family to Wauwatosa where in 1904, Lillie and Lyda were accidently drowned while playing.

In 1910 the family moved to Wisconsin Dells where Emil started a small manufacturing plant. In 1916 he built a new building on Broadway and opened a Ford automobile dealership there. He built another building next to the garage which served as "The Ray Murray Tire Shop".

On May 31, 1911 Hazel married Bert Emil "B.E." Tollaksen who, along with J.E. Jones, operated "the Dells Events and Printing Office." "B.E.", a dedicated Kilbourn Fire Department veteran, had the wedding postponed so that he could march in the Memorial Day parade, an event Hazel would carry on about for the next 60 years.

B.E.'s mother, Carrie was born on January 29, 1847 in Lourdale, Norway. At age six she came with her parents, Mr. and Mrs. Ole Halverson, to Stoughton, Wisconsin. In 1855 they settled on a farm in Newport. After Carrie finished school she moved to Chicago where she met and married Emil Tollaksen. They moved to Riverside California where B.E., two brothers, and one sister were born. Some time went by, one son and then Emil, died, and Carrie and the children returned to Wisconsin Dells. Carrie passed away on February 17, 1932 at "The Whitehouse" where her son B.E. and Hazel had cared for her. She was survived by one son, B.E., one brother, Hans Halverson of Newport, and one sister, Mrs. William Paulson of Fort Benton, Montana.

In the fall of 1914, B.E. left the paper and with Charles Borcher, got into the grocery business. In 1922 he contracted tuberculosis went to the sanatorium at Wales for the winter. The illness kept him inactive for almost two years.

During this time Hazel made renovations to their home, named it "The Whitehouse," and began to take in tourists during the summer. An annex was added, more porch rooms built and it became a "thriving" hotel and motor court.

Hazel also became involved in wholesale beadwork and supplies for area Native Americans. The business thrived as customers came from miles away to buy beads, bones, feathers, looms, wires, threads and needles.

Following his illness, B.E. opened "The Whitehouse Cottages" on Vine Street. In the late 1950's he sold the business to Mel Kuikmann who renamed it the "Dutch Mill".

B.E.'s anticipated retirement was short lived, as he soon went to work for his sons at the Deer Park Store where he remained active until his death in 1965.

Hazel was always a bundle of activity, she was very active in the Presbyterian Church, and for many years was active in the arts. One group was "The David Garrick Players" and was made up of adult and youngsters from the community.

When B.E. died in 1965, Hazel got out of the hotel business but continued to take in young seasonal summer help as boarders. Her home was always the center of family activity, and relatives from near and far would come to visit and stay.

Hazel loved her big sprawling house at 912 Capital Street and remained there until her death on May 15, 1974. Her daughter-in-law, Mary, stayed with her and cared for her until the end.

Hazel and B.E. had four sons: Gordon K. "Tux", born in 1914; Russell Bert in 1916; Woodrow C. "Jim" in 1918; and Herbert Arthur "Sam" in 1921.

Gordon later made his home in Racine, Wisconsin, and Sam in Chicago.

Woodrow C. (Jim), was born in the Dells on November 11, 1918. He attended Dells schools and was a graduate of the University of Wisconsin. He married Mary Eagan on September 8, 1945. They had five children: Gregory, James, and Michael, Susan and Marcia.

Jim was associated with many Dells area businesses and civic organizations. He owned the Moccasin Shop, a souvenir store on Broadway, was associated with his brother Russell in the Wisconsin Deer Park attraction, was a partner with George Willard at the Super Dime 'N Dollar store, was connected with Charles Van Wie and Arnold Borcher in a number of enterprises, and also had other business interests in the area.

He was a member and congregation president of United Presbyterian Church, a veteran of World War II, a member of Harold B. Larkin's American Legion Post, a charter member and president of the Wisconsin Dells Rotary Club, a longtime member of Kilbourn Volunteer Fire Department, served for many years as Boy Scout Clubmaster, Vice President of Dells Housing Inc., sponsor of the proposed new senior citizen's home in the Dells, and was active in many other civic groups and projects.

Russel was born to B.E. and Hazel on August 3, 1916. While in high school he was active in band and football. During the summers he guided and later piloted on the Wisconsin River for Blatchley's Silver Dollar Boat Line. He graduated from high school in 1934, and spent a few years traveling the U.S. and doing odd jobs.

In 1937 he took a job selling lace for the Russell Rohner Company of Chicago. On July 30, 1938 he was married to Virginia Ruth (Ginny) Norling of Wisconsin Dells.

Ginny's family lived on Elm Street in the Dells where her father was a banker. They also had a summer home and resort known as "Camp Cummings," later known as the "Cove," on Lake Mason near Briggsville. Before her marriage Ginny worked at O'Neil's Drug Store.

Russ and Ginny lived in Chicago and had three children: Peter in 1942, John in 1944 and Stephen in 1948.

The March 30, 1945, *Wisconsin State Journal* reported that there were 3 Tollaksen's, Woodrow, Herbert and Russell, serving in World War II.

Upon his discharge, Russell and family moved from Georgia back to Edison Park, outside Chicago, and Russell started his own sales firm.

In 1950 Russell and Woodrow began building the "Wisconsin Deer Park." The doors opened in 1952, and the partnership continued until "Jim's" death in 1968. In the mid-1950's the four brothers opened Beaver Springs Trout Farm. Both businesses continue to be operated by members of his family.

Russell was active in the community, including the American Legion Post, and in the Chamber of Commerce where he spent nine years as president. Shortly after he stepped down as president of the Chamber he was appointed to the Columbia County Board of Supervisors, on which he served until his death in 1979.

Russell was an active hunter and fisherman, and he and a group of other "local sportsmen" banded together to form "Tamarack Hunting Club." They acquired some swamp property east of town and built a club house.

Russ and Ginny had nine grandchildren, all living in the Dells, and he often waited for their school bus with some activity planned. He would attempt to get some work out of them but soon they would all pile into his "Blazer" to go to "Tom's", "Fitzgeralds" or the "Diary Queen". Ginny would come by in her red convertible, she had three, all red, and take them one place or another.

At one point she enrolled everybody's pet in obedience school including her own poodle. Once a month she would drive around and pick up one child and one dog from each family, and they would all head to Portage for school. Thus one grandmother, two or three grandkids and three or four dogs who did not get along, all piled into one red car.

Ginny taught piano lessons for many years and once decided that her grandkids needed a little culture so enrolled them for free. At first they were opposed to this but soon connived a way where they could all go on the same day, of course she could only work with one at a time so the rest were free to play together and ransack her house, where there were always plenty of cakes and cookies that she had baked.

Russ passed away in January of 1979, and Ginny in April of 1985. One son, Stephen, preceded them in death. They were survived by two sons, Peter "Ann", and John "Shirley", and nine grandchildren.

The Tolleth Family

James Tolleth, of Scotch descent, emigrated to the United States and became a pioneer of Wisconsin. His wife, Martha Jones, was a native of New York State and of Welsh lineage. Their son, Henry, was born in Fredonia, Wisconsin on September 25, 1865.

Henry became a carpenter, and in the off-building season, was a potato buyer. He was employed by the A.M. Penny Company for thirty years. For a period of time he acted as Supervisor, Trustee and Justice of the Peace for the village of Wild Rose. He belonged to the Independent Order of Odd Fellows. He grew up in the Baptist faith, and when he found no church after arriving in Kilbourn in 1911, he became a very active member of the local Methodist Church. Henry supported the Republican Party.

On February 11, 1885, he married Miss Lena Hansen in Waupaca, where she had been born on October 21, 1867. Her parents were Ole and Margaret (Knutsen) Hansen, who had come to the U.S. from Denmark. Lena was also active in the church as well as the Daughters of Rebekah and the American Legion's Women's Auxiliary. Henry Tolleth died on April 11, 1953 and Lena on November 13, 1962. They are both buried in Spring Grove Cemetery.

Henry and Lena had eight children: Gertrude, Agnes, Hale Robert, Florence, Fred, Dewey E., Claire Hudson, and Margaret.

Gertrude (Gert) was born in Ogdenburg, Wisconsin on February 10, 1886, and attended school there. In 1911 she came to the Dells with her family. She was hired by the Commonwealth Telephone Company in 1916 and won rapid promotions. For eight years she was chief operator. After dial service was introduced here, she was employed as a sales clerk. Gertrude was identified with the Telephone Pioneers of Wisconsin, the Dells Chapter of the Eastern Star and also with the Daughters of Rebekah. She was a charter member and historian of the American Legion Auxiliary of Harold B. Larkin Post #187. Like her father she was a Republican and a member of the Baptist Church. Gertrude died on July 7, 1973, and is buried in Spring Grove Cemetery.

Agnes was born at Waupaca on October 22, 1888. On February 10, 1910 she married Claude Edmonds, Chief of Police at Oshkosh. Their daughter, Evanda Irene, married Leonard Sly of Wisconsin Dells, and the couple owned and operated the Sand Bar on Eddy Street for a number of years. Evanda and Leonard had two children: Jack M., who now resides in New York and has two children, Terry and Toni; and Corinne Elizabeth (Mrs. Arno Carl Meyer) of Wisconsin Dells. Agnes Tolleth Edmonds passed away following a brief illness on May 31, 1918, at only 30 years old.

Hale Robert Tolleth was born in Elderon, Wisconsin on January 26, 1890. He was educated in Ogdensburg and at the state university, and became a truck driver for the Texaco Oil Company. In Kenosha, on May 24, 1917, he enlisted for service in World War I and was assigned to Company B, attached to the 107th Supply Train off the coast of Ireland on February 5, 1918. Later he went to Germany and was stationed on the Rhine until April 1919. He was discharged, a Corporal, on May 29, 1919.

On October 15, 1939, at age 48, Hale married Vernice Julson Fabian, and they had three daughters: Janice; Alice "Mickey"; and Marlea. Hale died in Wisconsin Dells on April 22, 1964.

Florence "Flossie" Tolleth was born at Ogdenburg on June 4, 1892. She married Walter Risinger and they made their home in Milwaukee before returning to the Dells. Walter went overseas with the 20th Division during World War I, and after returning, worked for the railroad until his retirement. They were devout Baptists. Although they had no children, Flossie and Walter were dearly loved by many nieces and nephews. Walter suffered a stroke, so, in 1970 they moved to the Wisconsin Veterans Home at King where Flossie died on April 17, 1976, following her husband's death two years prior. She is buried with him in the Wisconsin Veteran's Memorial Cemetery at King.

Henry and Lena Tolleth's fourth child, Fred, born at Ogdenburg, March 7, 1894, completed his high school education at Wild Rose. He enlisted in World War I at Portage on May 19, 1916 and went overseas in March, 1918. He returned to the United States in May, 1919, and received an honorable discharge at Camp Grant. He married Mable Etta of Loyal, Wisconsin, and was a postal clerk at Wisconsin Dells until his retirement. Fred was an avid golfer, a member and past commander of the Harold B. Larkin American Legion Post, and a member of the Wisconsin Dells Masonic Lodge. Fred died at age 90 and Mabel at 93.

Dewey E. Tolleth was born May 8, 1898, at Ogdenburg, where he obtained his early education, and was graduated from high school at Kilbourn. Entering the army April 7, 1917, he became a member of the 120th Field Artillery Band of the 32nd Division, and went to France in January, 1918. In April, 1919, he sailed for America and was discharged in May. He worked as a Postal Clerk in Chicago but resided in Libertyville, Illinois. He married Madolyn Zook. Their only child, Ida Marilyn, married William Decker and had one son. Ida died on January 11, 1992. Dewey died at the age of 76 on February 12, 1975.

Claire Hudson Tolleth was born August 9, 1902 in Wild Rose. He graduated from Kilbourn High and was later employed as a signwriter. He married Theresa Domagalski and they had 3 children: Hale Robert, born April 25, 1930, a plastic surgeon in California (who now owns the Fred Tolleth homestead here in Wisconsin Dells); Alan Charles, born August 20, 1931, a steel fabricator and bridge builder of Oregon; and Clifford Fred, born January 8, 1933, an aircraft design engineer and vibration/stress expert.

Claire later married Violet Cramer Meyer, and their children are Vincent William; Helen Elizabeth, a broker/realtor in California; and Margaret Mary Wright, a psychologist in California. Claire died on January 21, 1964.

The youngest child, Margaret Martha "Peg", was born January 23, 1906, in Wild Rose. She graduated from Kilbourn High and on September 5, 1923, married Oliver Arden Shumway in Milwaukee. She played the piano and organ for various local organizations as well as her church and the old Dells Theater. She and Henry had three children: Norma Phyllis, Mary Louise and John Edward. She was a life member of the Wisconsin Dells Order of the Eastern Star. Margaret died on October 19, 1987.

Aris Vanderbilt

Aris Vanderbilt was born in New York around 1844, the son of Philip Vanderbilt and Sarah Bullock. His mother passed away shortly after his birth. It was her wish that he be raised by a member of the Bullock family of Big Spring. Her sister, Mrs. Martha Bakeman of Big Spring, went to Poughkeepsie, New York and brought Aris back with her.

He grew to manhood and married Armenia Hagerman. Three sons were born to them: Evert in 1869, William in 1872, and Andrew in 1874.

Evert married Ruth Ettie Mowers of Douglas Center, Marquette County and fathered eight children. William married Eva Whipple of Davis Corners and they had two children.

Andrew married Cora Kelly of White Creek and had two sons. Andrew was Adams County Superintendent of Schools for several years, then moved to California.

Through a misunderstanding of his birthright, he wasn't fortunate enough to claim any of the family fortune. According to old records, his uncle George was the founder of the Biltmore Castle in Asheville, North Carolina.

His wife, Armenia, or Grandma Minnie, as she was commonly called, died in 1918 and is buried in Spring Grove Cemetery, as are two of his sons. Aris died in 1924 of cancer and is buried at Big Spring in the Bullock lot.

They left many descendants who still reside in the Dells area.

The Van Dyke Family

In 1850, Samuel Van Dyke came from Pennsylvania to Wisconsin and settled on a large farm on Nashotah Lake in Waukesha County. The Van Dyke's were members of the Episcopal Church, and were one of the first families with Bishop Kemper's Missionary to the Indians, presently the Nashotah Theological Seminary.

Samuel's son Norman E. Van Dyke, came to Kilbourn City after receiving his law degree at the University of Wisconsin. With him was his wife, Tommie Shi Van Dyke, a lovely girl from Texas. They immediately became a part of the community and its growth. Mrs. Van Dyke was a founder of the Tuesday Club and served on the Library Board for many years. Their son Phil was born in Wisconsin Dells on December 3, 1896, and always made it his home.

Norman had one daughter, Madge Van Dyke Carpenter, who made her home in Milwaukee.

The Van Ells - Ressler Family

Clara Ressler Van Ells was born near Lyndon Station, the oldest of six children born to William Ressler and his wife Agnes (Blaser). Agnes Blaser's parents were John and Mary (Cragor) Blaser, and they had come from near Portage and settled near Stand Rock.

William had been christened after his father as Joseph Willebald but in order to distinguish between them he was always called Willy or Will. The elder Joseph Willebald was married to Rose Hebl.

The Resslers first settled 4 miles north of Lyndon Station and it is there that generations were raised, including Clara's. Clara's siblings were: Ernest, Irene, Herman, Richard, and Marvin. Herman died in 1900 at age eight, and Ernest drowned in 1908, aged 21.

Young Clara went to Chicago, to work as a dressmaker. There she met Emil Van Ells, a Milwaukee native of Dutch descent. He was a window washer at that time. They were married in Lyndon Station in 1905. Emil and Clara continued to live in Chicago where Emil was a switchman on the Santa Fe Railroad. They had two daughters: Isabel, born in 1908 and Eleanor, born in 1910.

When Isabel was six, Emil lost his right arm in a railroad accident. He was unconcious for two weeks and came out of the coma calling for Isabel. Because of Emil's disability the family moved to Kilbourn, and Emil purchased the Ford garage which he continued to operate for 23 years. He was also the propietor of the Sinclair Service Station.

Emil and Clara's third child, William, was born in Kilbourn in 1921. All three Van Ells children attended and graduated from high school there. William Van Ells lived in several different cities before settling in Birmingham, Alabama where he is a mining engineer. He and his wife Lois, a teacher, have one son, Joe, who lives in Texas.

Eleanor married Chuck Anchor in 1936 and they had no children.

During the 1920s Isabel served as a "tour guide" for the patrons of her mother's rooming house, where room and board was offered for $5.00 a week.

Isabel married Frank Schultz in 1939. They reared five children: Monica, Dick, Robert, John and Marie. After 29 years of marriage, Frank died from complications from an accident five years earlier when he was employed by the city of Wisconsin Dells.

Isabel was a dance teacher for many years. She also worked for several Dells businesses for many years, including the restaurant operated by Eleanor and Chuck. She worked at Uphoff's, now Copa Cabana, and at the Ponderosa Steak House.

She married Ed Golembiewski in 1972, and they are active in senior citizen groups, like to travel, and she is the instructor of the senior exercise class at the municipal building.

The Van Wie Family

The Van Wie family has lived in the Dells area for almost 150 years and seven generations. Members of the family have served in the Revolution, Civil War, World War I and II and Vietnam.

After leaving their homestead in Holland, brothers Teunis Gerritse Van Wie and Henrich Gerritse Van Wie came to North America among the first settlers of Albany, New York.

The Van Wie family continued to live in Albany until Henry Van Wie and his son, Lorenzo, claimed 168 acres of land in 1847. This property was located north of Wisconsin Dells on Highway 13 in Adams County, and the Van Wies were also among the first settlers in this area.

Andrew Van Wie, Henry's brother, was born in 1816, at Jakway's Corners, Cayuga County, New York. He was the youngest of four boys and two girls. He had lost both his parents by age 16, and lived with his uncle Frederick until 1835, at age 19, when he married Anna Elizabeth Cushman.

Andrew lived in Albany, New York for another ten years. In 1845, he and Anna and five sons moved to Michigan. In 1852, Andrew received a letter from his older brother Henry, in the Dells, asking the family to move to Wisconsin. Henry would sell him eighty acres of his 168 acre farm. So Andrew, Anna and Edward, William, Daniel, John, David Carl, Develo, Cecilia, Mary Elizabeth, and Helen, moved to Wisconsin. In 1855, their tenth child, Sarah, was born.

In 1858, Anna died at age 42. Andrew was left with a young family to raise. A year later he met Almeda E. Phelps, a widow with a 7 year old son, Franklin Phelps, and the two were married. After only three years, on May 30, 1862, Almeda also died at the age of 42 years. Andrew remained a widower and dedicated his life to raising his children.

In 1861, Andrew's sons William, Daniel, John A., and David Carl went to train as infantry men to fight in the Civil War. Edward, the oldest, remained home to help his father with the farm. Youngest son Develo, only 14, also remained at home for a time, but in a few years he also went to fight in the Civil War and lost his life.

David Carl, born in 1843, fought with Company G 16 Regiment of the Wisconsin Infantry Volunteers and Company K 6th Regiment Wisconsin Infantry, serving his country through two terms. After returning he resumed his career as a logger on the Wisconsin River.

In 1875, David Carl became one of the first pilots on the Wisconsin River, piloting the steam boat *Champion.* During this time he became known as Captain Dave, and was also regarded as a friend and interpreter to the area's Indians. Four years later Captain Dave built his own boat, the *Alexander Mitchell*, and piloted it on the river for five years.

Captain Dave, age 41, married Jennie A. Fish, age 26, on September 15, 1884. They had one child, David Carl Jr, in July 1887.

On September 1, 1891, Captain Dave and Jennie settled on a farm which included parts of a ravine later known as Cold Water Canyon. Around 1900, they built a two story inn where they served meals to visitors arriving by boat. It was soon a major boat landing and resort. In 1909, Southern Wisconsin Power built the Kilbourn dam which raised the water level 17 feet and flooded the inn, but the family rebuilt, and the inn stands today. Cold Water Canyon remains in the Van Wie family, and though a souvenir stand is all that still exists, it remains one of the most beautiful river landings on the boat tours.

David's father, Andrew, lived with David and Jenny until David's death on August 14, 1903. Andrew then stayed with his son John A. in Minneapolis until he died on March 26, 1905, at nearly 90 years of age. He was buried with his son William in their family plot in Mauston, Wisconsin.

Jennie A. Van Wie died at her home in Cold Water Canyon on June 8, 1920 at the age of 61.

David Carl Jr. (known as Carl) was now 33 years old. As an only child, he had spent his boyhood at Cold Water Canyon where he kept many pets and befriended area Indians. On January 5, 1910, he married Alma Balsmedier in Kenosha, Wisconsin, and they soon moved to Kilbourn. In 1922 they bought a home on the site of the present Gables Motel swimming pool. They continued to run the Canyon and later passed the business down to their children.

Carl served the area as chairman of the Chamber of Commerce, as member of Kilbourn's Fire Department and Water and Light Commission, and in other important capacities.

Carl and Alma had four children: David Charles born December 5, 1910; Robert Harry, 1916; Ralph Jack, 1922; Helen Jenette, 1926; all of whom are now deceased.

Robert H. married Mary Dauterman. They adopted a daughter Constance and had a son Kurt.

Helen married Delman Keubke and had no children.

David Charles was born December 5, 1910, above the old Farmers and Merchants State Bank. He was very active in high school,participating in football, orchestra, operetta, class plays, glee club, pep club and on the yearbook staff. He studied Business Administration at Madison Business College, graduating in 1931. From 1932-39 he lived in Chicago and played semi-pro football.

In 1942, he opened a bakery shop in the former Quality Market building on Broadway, a venture cut short by World War II. He served as procurement section head of the administration division at Badger Ordnance Works prior to enlisting in the Navy's construction battalion in 1944. He served on active duty in the South Pacific for two years.

Following the war, David Charles and his wife, Clarine (Shettl) moved to Milwaukee, where he worked for the Veterans Administration.

In 1948, the Van Wies moved back to Wisconsin Dells and began a long business career in the summer tourist trade. He purchased the corner building and opened the Totem Pole Souvenir Shop. Later he purchased the Northwest Trading Post property, which consisted of several cabins and a gas station.

The Van Wies also owned the Wonder Spot, Ghost Town, Devil's Lake Boat Company, the Enchanted Forest, the Chuck Wagon Restaurant and Molly's (formerly Call of the Wild). He also managed Dells Park Indian Village, and worked with the Stand Rock Indian Ceremonial. He was instrumental in starting the Wisconsin Dells Regional Chamber of Commerce, and served on the board of directors and in other executive positions for many years.

He was always very active in community affairs including the Boy Scout Council and the Masonic Lodge. He was general chairman of the first Wo-Zha-Wa Fall Festival, and a judge at the first Jaycee Raft Race. He was president of the Wisconsin Dells Kiwanis Club, and also a member of the American Legion, the Shriners, and the Wisconsin Dells Art Association. He was secretary-treasurer of the local American Field Service organization, and helped create the Kilbourn Historical Society. He was an active member of the United Presbyterian Church.

At the time of his death, his daughter Nancy had married James Hopkins and lived in Madison and his son, Gregory Charles, lived in Wisconsin Dells. He had four grandchildren. Clarine Van Wie died in 1965.

Carl and Alma's son, Ralph Jack, known as Jack, was born December 13, 1922 in Wisconsin Dells. He attended grade and high school in Wisconsin Dells, graduating in 1940 and then attended Ripon College. On June 5, 1943 he married Dorothy Bisely. While he was at Ripon, World War II broke out and he left school to join the service. He was turned down because of an ear problem and went to work as a foreman at the Badger Ordnance Works near Baraboo.

Following the war, Jack returned to the Dells and went into the insulation business. He later added roofing and siding and in 1947 started Dells Lumber Company. In 1962 he purchased the Westfield Lumber Company. Jack was also a land developer and three of his major projects were Castle Rock Gardens, the Oak Lawn Subdivision and River Bay, Inc.

His love of children led Jack to organize the first Dells Little League and Babe Ruth baseball teams. His 1959 team was second in the state tournament. Highly active in the community, Jack was involved in the Holy Name Society, the Kiwanis Club, the Knights of Columbus, the Wisconsin Retail Lumbermen's Association and was a charter member of the Dells Eagles. He was a sports lover and an avid golfer.

On August 19, 1978, Jack underwent a second open heart surgery and died at the age of 55. Evidence of his love for children was in the will he left, which stated that a party was to be held for 27 children he had befriended on his daily walk to the office over the past 8 years, and that each should be given a gift.

The Media Center at the Wisconsin Dells High School athletic complex was erected as a memorial to Jack, in honor of his love for children and athletics. His tombstone reads a favorite saying of his, "Children are the key and the closest thing to God."

Ralph Jack and Dorothy had six children: Robert, John C., William, David, Mary and Elizabeth. They also considered a former AFS student, Alexander DeCarli, another son.

Robert married Evelyn Tessmer and had three children: Robert, Melissa and Thomas Jack. John C. married Joanne M. Amend and had four children: Suzanne, Jeffrey, John B and Joseph.

William married Paula Meister and had four children: Anne, William, Elizabeth and Andrew. David R. married Bonnie Nachreiner and adopted her daughter Heather and had three children: Matthew, Heidi and Amanda.

Elizabeth married Clifford Wolfram and had two children: Brenda and Christopher. Mary remained single.

The Walker Family

Mack Walker, born in 1842, came to Necedah from Montreal, Canada, around 1850. He worked as a blacksmith there before moving to a farm north of Big Spring.

He married a Lutheran girl, Happy Lange, changed his religion, and later became the head of the Masonic Lodge in Kilbourn. They had three sons, Clifton, Edward and William.

Mack later bought a farm on the river at Plainville, selling it to his two oldest boys a few years later. Clifton bought out his brother Edward, who purchased a farm west of Big Springs. William married a local girl and moved to Milwaukee.

Clifton married Emma Jesse Billings and they had two children, Jesse who died in infancy, and Ray Clifton. As part of their farming operation they made and sold ice cream to many of the hotels in Kilbourn. Clifton also helped start the Farmers Telephone Company of Kilbourn.

Ray Clifton graduated from Kilbourn High School in 1903, and later from the Agriculture Short course at the University in Madison After working for a few years, he took over the home farm. He married Harriet McBrayer of Lime Ridge and they had one son, Harold.

While on the farm they developed a fine herd of pure bred Holstein cattle. Ray also helped start both the Kilbourn Co-op exchange and the Co-op Creamery.

His son, Harold Walker took over the home farm in 1938. He married Marie Jacobson and they had five daughters: Marjorie (Francis) Fitzgerald, Dorothy (Charles) McFalrin, Nancy (Daniel) Sayre, Jean (Ray) Ford and Janet (David K.) Jones.

The Waterman Family

In 1895, the following news item appeared in Kilbourn's *Mirror Gazette*:

"The Rose House has again changed hands, having been purchased by the Andrew Waterman family, and their popularity will tend to change the character of that once popular former hotel."

The Watermans have been in business here since 1895, except for a 10 year period following the death of Drute Waterman.

The name Andrew Waterman has been around a long time, as his son was also Andrew, known as "Drute", and Drute's son was Andrew III, followed by another Andrew (the IV) known to all as "Turk."

Andrew Shepard Waterman, like many of the settlers coming to this area in the 1800's was from New York state. He was born in Baldwinsville, N.Y. in 1827.

In the 1850's he purchased a farm northeast of Kilbourn in Twin Valley. His wife, Almira Goff, was a Yankee from Vermont.

After serving in the Civil War, Andrew became the first of many Watermans to open a business in Kilbourn. Farmers from as far as 15 miles away brought their cattle and grain to Kilbourn to be shipped by rail to Chicago, and the Hotel Waterman, as the Rose House was renamed, was a popular farmer hotel for many years. The Watermans also cared for the tired work horses.

Andrew's son Drute and his wife Vinnie operated the hotel with a crew of hired girls. These girls were paid $3 per week, plus room and board. For 35¢, the farmers were able to eat a hearty meal of meat, potatoes, vegetables, pie and coffee.

The Waterman Hotel and barn were on the site of the present Telephone Company and Laundromat. The original barn burned about 1910, and a concrete one was built in its place. Drute and Vinnie Waterman had six children, all born at the hotel.

Besides Iness (Mrs. Stewart Thompson) and Andrew Victor, who have been in local business for almost 50 years, the children were: Charlotte and Vera, deceased; Harriet (Mrs. Clarence Wessel); and Mary (Mrs. Claude O'Neil).

Other descendants of Andrew Shepherd Waterman in business in the Dells area today include Stewart (Kicker) Thompson, Tom Thompson, Andrew IV (Turk) Waterman and Jack Waterman.

The Weber Family

In the early 1900's, the Martin Weber family moved from LaCrosse, Wisconsin to Kilbourn. Martin worked for the Milwaukee Railroad, and was also talented as a tin smith. He and his wife, Amelia (Thiel), built a large Victorian-styled home on Vine Street, and eventually built another home next-door for rental purposes.

Martin and Amelia had five children: Samuel, Martin, Jr., Edward, Albert, Roy, Clara and Ida. Ida died at the age of 21 from pneumonia.

Clara earned a college degree in business, married, was widowed in her middle years, and continued in the insurance business in California. Clara lived next door to the then Governor's Mansion, and socialized with many dignitaries of her time.

Sam, the eldest son, went to California where he worked for R.K.O. Studios. He later returned to Kilbourn and built the first motion picture theatre on Broadway, which served the Dells community until it closed in the 1950's. Sam also built another large building across the street from the theatre, where along with other family, he operated a restaurant during World War I. It was not uncommon for the restaurant staff to handle 400 customers on a busy day. Sam owned many other properties in Kilbourn and Portage, including the Beaver Building and the Little Norway Bar. Many dances and parties were held over the years in the Beaver Building, which also included a stage for plays.

Martin, Jr. traveled with the Ringling Brothers Circus and worked in management. Later he returned to Kilbourn and became a police officer. Martin bought a farm and built homes and rental property. He remained in the Dells area until his death.

Edward became a traveling salesman in California and in Oregon, where he later established a men's clothier. Albert had a newspaper and magazine business in California. Both brothers lived out their lives on the West Coast.

Roy, the youngest brother, remained in Kilbourn and married Sadie Streiff in 1908. Sadie's ancestor, Fridolin Streiff, was one of the founders of New Glarus, Wisconsin. Sadie's father, John Streiff and family, had come to Kilbourn from Monroe, Wisconsin. The Streiff family lived on a farm and operated a butcher shop in Kilbourn. Later, the family moved back to Monroe, where John went into the cheese business. Sadie held a diploma in nursing from the Milwaukee School of Nursing.

Roy worked for the Milwaukee Railroad as a fireman on the old locomotives. He also helped build the Kilbourn dam. Roy had been a mailman, a restaurant owner, and the owner of a wallpaper and paint store in the Dells. During World War II, he worked as an engineer at the Badger Ordnance Works. He also served in many Wisconsin Dells civic organizations.

The Weber family was in the tourist business for many years, and owned much property at the northeast corner of Hwy 13 and Broadway. Beginning in the 1930's, the Route 13 and Broadway site emcompassed campgrounds, cottages, riding stables, and later, the addition of motel units. The years passed, and Roy and Sadie were no longer able to handle the operation of the business by themselves. Roy's eldest son, Chester, and his wife Marion eventually assumed full control over the business until their retirement.

Roy also owned the Oak Lawn subdivision, which is adjacent to the Hwy 13 and Broadway site. The subdivision, today, includes a park named in honor of Roy Weber. The Weber family remembers the area when Indians would camp in their wigwams during the summer months, beating drums, singing and dancing into the night. The subdivision was also the site for many a gypsy caravan.

The home that Roy built in 1929, not far from the Weber's original homesite, still stands at 1022 Race Street.

Roy and Sadie had nine children, six sons and three daughters. Five of the boys served in the military. Today, Harold lives in Dubuque, Iowa and Bernice (Mola) lives in Munster, Indiana. The remaining children Chester (Reedsburg), Madge (Friendship), Roland, John, James, Kenneth and Dorothy Wick are all living in the Dells area.

Sadie Weber died on May 29, 1954, and Roy on August 6, 1967.

The Wenkman Family

In 1859, Mr. and Mrs. Maximillian Wenkman arrived in New York from Germany. That same year they moved to Wisconsin Dells where Max was a carpenter until his death.

The couple had four sons: Mike, John, Max and George.

George married Nellie Peterson of Wisconsin Dells and had two sons, Henry and Arthur. George owned and operated a retail shoe store at 737 Superior Street. He retired in 1928 and sold the building to Harry Landry, who operated it as a furniture store. Arthur, died at age 12 of head injuries sustained during a fall while ice skating. Nellie died at age 34 and George died in 1955.

The other son, Henry, married Ida Bandfield of Mauston and they had five children: Lorraine, William, Dorothy, John and James. Henry purchased a building at 741 Superior Street and organized a radio sales and service store. When he found that he actually had to service what he sold, he converted it to a restaurant which he and Ina ran together. In 1934, Henry purchased the Helm restaurant at 321 Broadway and operated it as a tavern until 1939 when he added bowling alleys. Ina ran the Superior Street restaurant until it was sold in 1944.

When sons Jim and Bill returned home from World War II they joined Henry in business. They purchased the adjacent building (Harry Landry's Furniture), added more bowling alleys and a restaurant. In 1949 Henry sold his interests to his sons, and in 1955 Bill sold his share to Jim. Jim Wenkman operated the business until 1977 when he sold it to Bud Gussel.

Ina Bandfield Wenkman died of cancer in 1961. Henry married Ruth in 1970. He died in 1988.

Of Henry and Ina's five children: Lorraine married Tom Sheridan in 1938 and they had two children; Bill married Frances Hillebrandt and had four children. They were divorced and Bill married Georgia Schattner in 1969; Dorothy married Floyd Field and had two children; John returned from service, graduated from the Marquette Dental School and practiced dentistry in Milwaukee until retirement to Murphy, North Carolina. He died in August 1995; Jim married Margaret Sweeney of Lyndon Station in 1946 and they had six children. Margaret, his first wife and Beverly, his second wife, both died of cancer and he is now married to Delia Griffin of Oxford, Wisconsin.

Bert Wharry

Bert Raymond Wharry was born to George and Ella (Spade) Wharry on October 31, 1880 in Lyndon, Juneau County. He had a brother Leonard and sisters Clara and Minnie.

Bert married Mayme Maxfield, who died during the birth of their daughter, Louella. Louella lived most of her life in Milwaukee, where she raised four children.

Bert married Lucreta (Lucy) Selchow in Kilbourn in 1923, where they lived until the time of their deaths.

Burt spent some time in the livery business, and then in the 1920s, started a taxi business which he operated until his death in 1959. The taxi met all the trains arriving in Kilbourn. In the 1940s, it cost 25¢ to hail a taxi in the Dells.

Members of his family all helped with the business; Lucy answered telephones, and their children, Gertie Ann and Bert, Jr., became drivers as soon as they were old enough.

Bert Jr. was born on October 13, 1925. He had one son, Patrick, who married Marilyn and has two children, Timothy and Julie. They live in Crest Hill, Illinois where Pat is with the Army Corp. Bert Jr. died on May 13, 1975.

Gertie Ann was born on January 3, 1929 and married Gordon Gregerson in February, 1953. They lived on a farm in Newport and had five children: Paul, Lief, Thor, Olaf, and Kristen.

Ella Spaide Wharry died in December, 1980.

The Winnes Family

George Winnes was born in Waldorf, Germany in 1830. He came to Ohio in 1849, and then in 1856, when the village was still very young, settled in Kilbourn.

He married Margaretha Schmidt, from Wurttenburg, Germany, in 1861. Her family had migrated to New York in 1849, moved to Milwaukee in 1854 and by 1859, settled in Kilbourn.

In 1868, George and Margaretha purchased from Elizabeth Titus, sole heir to Alfredd Mott, a 160 acre tract one mile west of Kilbourn on County H and began farming. Alfred Mott had homesteaded the property in 1850 and immediately leased an acre for the Fern Dell School. In compliance with the Winnes will, the Wisconsin Dells School District administration building occupies the site today.

George spent 17 years working for the Railroad Company on the water tank. The Winnes' were active members of the Presbyterian church, as George spent many years as a deacon in the German Presbyterian church.

George died on June 29, 1901 and Margaretha in 1914. They are buried in Spring Grove Cemetery.

George and Margaretha had six children: George Jr.; Anna (1864-1940); Elizabeth; Frederick; Frank (1870-1934); Edward; and Emma (1877-1954).

In 1902, Frank married Julia Steffen (1873-1938), an Elroy native, and in 1903 they made the Winnes farm their home. Emma married Fred Schmidt and they also raised their family in this farming community.

When the children were grown, Frank and Julia sold the farm and moved into town, residing at 1117 Bowman Road. Over the years he worked for Harry Corning at the local feed mill, was a section foreman for the railroad at Lewiston Station, and was a gardener for the Upham family. Julia was an excellent candy maker and sold many of her delicious creations to families in Kilbourn. She was also an active member of the Woman's Relief Corps.

Frank and Julia had five children: twins George and Gordon, Anna, Wilameana, and Frank Jr., who died in infancy. All of the surviving children graduated from Kilbourn High School. Gordon became the proprieter of the local IGA. grocery for many years, and George operated an IGA in Reedsburg. Wilameana (Wilma) married Joseph Kaiser Sr., who owned and operated the ice company for many years. Anna married P.A. Carey who operated the Meadowbrook Lodge.

Of George and Margaretha's other children: Anna and Emma were very involved in the community and various business enterprises. Anna never married and operated a millinery shop next to the H.H. Bennett Studio, made hats and taught many local girls to sew and knit. Later, she operated a beauty shop from her residence at 306 Washington Avenue, which also served as a boarding house. Emma acted as housekeeper and assisted Anna in operation of the beauty shop.

Anna and Emma are also buried in the Spring Grove Cemetery.

The Worthy-Larkin Families

Peter Worthy was born June 20, 1825 in the county of Yorkshire, England. In 1847 he married Mary Ward, a native of Leppington, Yorkshire, where she was born March 22, 1818. They had three sons before leaving for the United States in 1850. On the summer voyage, eight month old Alfred died at sea.

The Worthy family settled in Dodge County, Wisconsin. Peter purchased and later sold land throughout Wisconsin and Minnesota. Six more children were born to them in Dodge County. In 1869, Peter bought the Four Mile House Inn at Rolling Prairie. The family lived at the Inn which was also a community center.

In the 1980's the Four Mile House was moved to Old World Wisconsin, an outdoor museum run by the State Historical Society. The last residence of Peter and Mary was at Davis Corners in Adams County where they also owned farm land. Both Peter and Mary died in 1906 and were buried at Davis Corners.

The Worthy's daughter, Margaret, (1859-1918) married J. Weedin Larkin (1860-1912) in March, 1885 at Oxford.

J. and his brother, Charles (1859-1918) were the sons of David W. Larkin (1817-1900) and Margaret Ottman (1821-1903). David W. and Margaret Larkin were both born in New York but later farmed in Jackson township, Adams County.

J. and his new bride Margaret then left for Dakota territory where they homesteaded and farmed for 20 years. Their five children were born at New Rockford, North Dakota: Claude Worthy (1887-1962) David Ward (1889-1913). When Margaret's parents were ill and needed assistance, J and his family returned to Adams County where they farmed in Davis Corners for several years.

In 1912 when J. Larkin was very ill with tuberculosis, his family took him to Rocky Ford, Colorado where he died after a few months. He was brought back to Kilbourn for funeral services and buried at Davis Corners.

Oswald (Ossie) drowned in the Wisconsin River at the age of 17 on July 8, 1913. He was woking on the new Kilbourn dam when he slid off the concrete apron.

Maggie (Mrs. J.) Larkin died in Kilbourn on June 15, 1918. Claude, who was the only son who went to college, worked at the Kilbourn bank. He married Cora Mac Murtrie and they moved to Montana and later farmed at Catawba, Wisconsin. They had six children: Charles Russell (Wanda), Faye (Raymond) Mabie, Harold Edgar (Virginia), Howard Mac (Leta), John Stanley (Thelma) and Darrell Jay (Doris).

David Ward attempted to file a claim in North Dakota in 1910 or 1911 but was called back to Wisconsin by the poor health of his father. Later, he was employed by Wisconsin Power and Light at the Kilbourn plant for 37 years. He married Helen Waite (1900-1965), they had three children: Robert Ward (July 4, 1929-1974), Harold Wallace (July 4,1933) and Shirley Helen (August 15, 1931).

After David Ward passed away, Helen Waite Larkin went to Madison Area Technical College and then worked as bookkeeper at Schultz Plumbing and Heating in Wisconsin Dells.

Robert joined the Navy and while stationed at Norfolk, Virginia, married Lillian LeLeche. They had four children: Timothy (Cynthia), Ronald, David (Sandy) and Deborah Mason (Billy Joe). Bobby's family all live in Portsmouth, Virginia.

Harold married Evelyn Hewitt and they have four children: Michael (Patty), Teresa Richards (Gary), Robert and Jeffrey. Harold served in the Navy for four years after high school. He then worked at Wisconsin Power and Light for 38 years. Evelyn is employed by the Wisconsin Dells High School.

Shirley married Clarence (Junie) Nelson, Jr. and they had five children: Heidi Leeck (Mark), Genevieve Houston (Kevin), David, Tennie and Tena Thompson (Rathe). Junie sill works the same farm, four miles east of the Dells, that has been in his family for 140 years, and Shirley is employed as a LPN.

Bettie and Al Abrams live in Columbus, Wisconsin where Al was the city clerk for many years and Bettie worked at the local library. The Abrams have two children: Jacquelyn Jeanee Newman (Jim) and Jill Christine Miels (Jerry).

Don De Lap served in both the Army and Navy for many years and he and his wife lived in Rantoul, Illinois. They have two children: Don, Jr. (Robyn) and Darice.

Albert Yellow Thunder

Albert Yellow Thunder Sr. was the grandson of Wa Kun Cha Koo Kah, or Yellow Thunder, who was among the area Ho-Chunk Indians who travelled to Washington in 1837.

Albert was born at Green Lake, Wisconsin on July 7, 1877. He attended public school at Berlin, Wisconsin, and then entered Haskell Institute at Lawrence, Kansas. After his graduation he served in the Spanish American War. In 1899 he married Ella White at Tomah.

Albert was the heir to the last recognized Chief among the Ho-Chunk Indians, and has been known as Chief Yellow Thunder. He also enjoyed the title of Colonel, an honor conferred on him by the late Julius Heil while he was Governor of Wisconsin.

He played an active role in the Stand Rock Ceremonial for many years, and spent winters lecturing at schools or clubs where his knowledge of Ho-Chunk history and customs was always of great interest. It was his life's ambition to be a missionary and he worked for three years among the Seminole Indians in Florida. Due to his close association with both the white and Ho-Chunk peoples in this community, he did much to bring them together.

He had four children: Albert, Jr., Chadwick, Miles, and Maria. Albert, the eldest, succeeded to the title of Chief.

Anna Ziegenhagen

Anna Ziegenhagen was born in 1874 on the family farm just west of Wisconsin Dells. An ambitious young girl, she sought work in Kilbourn City at age 14.

For more than 50 years she was the night operator at the local telephone switchboard. People depended on the telephone girl to provide help of any kind, at any time, to all those in need. Residents knew that no matter what the hour, Anna would find it for them. Alert to every emergency, she always knew just where to locate local doctors, police and firemen.

She worked six nights a week and sometimes more if others were sick. After plodding through the rain and snow to work, she had to keep the fire going in the upstairs office as well as plug in the switchboard connections.

When she left the telephone office in the early morning hours, Anna's activity did not stop. She devoted her life to helping others; stepping in when tragedy struck, providing assistance to others, baking, cooking, comforting and taking over a household when necessary. As a dependable mid-wife she delivered many babies. Her tireless energy was always available to those in need.

In 1960, at the age of 86, this tiny dynamo moved to the nursing home in Portage where she remained a constant inspiration to residents, visitors and employees. She died a few months short of her one hundredth birthday after a lifetime of devotion to those less fortunate than she.

Fred Zinke

Fred Zinke, the youngest of Frank and Bertha Zinke's thirteen children, was born in Newport on March 17, 1899. Fred's youth was spent on a farm in Newport. As a young man, he worked as a "gandy-dancer" on a maintenance gang for the railroad. In 1924, he courted and married Emma Nelson. During this time he was employed at a tire factory in Cudahy, Wisconsin.

Just prior to the onset of the Great Depression, Emma's father became ill and Emma was needed at home in Wisconsin Dells to help care for him. It was about this same time that the tire factory closed. Fred returned to Wisconsin Dells and found employment in a meat market where he learned the butchering and meat cutting trade.

By 1937, Fred no longer wanted to place his family's security in someone else's hands. He and partner, Ingebret Soma, started the Modern Meat Market at 310 Broadway Street. When Soma left after two years, Fred went into business with Todd Bartness, a butcher, for another three years at the Broadway location.

He started out for himself by opening City Market at 725 Oak Street. Fred's reputation as a first-class butcher, his homemade ring bologna--and the help of his two sons--Gordon and Ken, made his store such a success that by 1946 he was looking for a larger location and bought out Louie Miklic's store at 721 Oak Street.

This was a general business type store and after several years Fred eliminated shoes and clothing to make room for more groceries. He was one of the first to start a supermarket: he bought Indian baskets so that customers could pick out their own groceries rather than having a clerk do it for them.

In January of 1952 Fred's oldest son Gordon joined him in a partnership and by August of 1964 they built the present Zinke's Shop-Rite supermarket at 216 Washington Street.

In December of 1967 Ken retired from the Air Force and returned home to buy his father's share of the business. This allowed Fred the freedom to retire and spend more time doing what he most loved to do, hunt and fish.

Fred was a member of the Wisconsin Dells Gun Club and was known as one of the area's top sportsmen. He spent many summers in Canada fishing, and hunted elk in Montana and North Dakota. During one of his trips out west, he shot and killed an elk from five hundred yards.

In their youth, Fred and his brother Rob spent many hours fishing. Rob later discovered that attaching a small piece of metal to the mouth of a bait made the bait swim and wiggle as if it were alive. The new bait, called Zinke bait, was the first of its kind and became so popular with the area's fishing crowd that even with Fred's help, the hundreds of orders they were receiving could not be filled. Fred proposed a partnership to market the invention, but Rob declined, and the bait was never mass produced. A few Zinke baits can still be found and are considered collector's items.

Fred died in 1979, preceeded in death by Emma who died in 1969. He was survived by his four children, ten grandchildren, twelve great grandchildren and one great, great grandchild.

His legacy lives on through his son Ken and grandson Dan who bought Gordon Zinke's share of the store in 1988. Together they engineered a complete remodeling as well as a 10,000 square foot expansion which more than doubled the size of the store.

Index

D

E

F

G

H

I

J

K

L

M

N

O

P

R

S

Bibliography

Books

Adams County Plat Book, 1947.
Goc, Michael J., *Stewards of the Wisconsin;* Friendship, Wisconsin: The New Past Press, Inc., 1993.
Goc, Michael J., *Juneau County: The First 100 Years*; Friendship, Wisconsin: The New Past Press, Inc., 1988.
Goc, Michael J., *Many A Fine Harvest, Sauk County 1840-1990*; Friendship, Wisconsin: The New Past Press, Inc., 1990.
History of Columbia County, 1880.

Articles

Curry, Ross. *Ross's Reminiscences*, 1993.
Dixon, E.C. *The Raftsmen, Wisconsin's Vanished Race*, 1948.
Dixon, E.C. *Logging, the Drive, Running the River*, 1948.
Dixon, E.C. *More on Rafting Days From Personal Experience*, 1948.
Dixon, E.C. *More About Old Rafting Days*, 1948.
Dells Booklet Brings Memory of Early Days, 1939.
Durbin, Rick. *The Kilbourn Dam*; unpublished manuscript.
Durbin, Rick. *Two Wisconsin River Stories*, Wisconsin Magazine of History, v. 77, n. 3, spring 1994.
Greenwood, Donna. *Kilbourn Klippings*, 1985.
Houghton, Fred. *Biography Verifies Tales*, 1986.
Illustrated Events 1903–1905.
Lovesy, Carla with Marie Beyer and Katharine Green, *The Early Days of Briggsville*, 1950.
Lumber Rafting, Gus of Gisholt, Gisholt Machine Company: Madison, Wisconsin, April, 1953.
Merrill Historical Society, *Assembly of Cribs*.
Musson, Lois, *Water over the Dam*; unpublished manuscript.
Weinhold, Frank. *Louis Bluff*.
Weinhold, Frank. *The Wisconsin River Hydraulic Company*; unpublished manuscript.
Weinhold, Frank. *The Rise of Tourism and the Kilbourn Dam*.
Wisconsin Dells Events

Taped Interviews

Blatchley, Peter
Baggot, Ed
Helland, Hans
Johnson, Tim
Olson, Jack
Priester, Adolph
Reese, Oliver
Sly, Phil
Tagney, Ed
Whaley, Sheila

Documents

Adams County School Histories, 1950s.
The Arrowhead, school annual, 1916.
The Arrow, school annual, 1928-1929.
City Council proceedings, notes by Tom Crist.
Consolidated Boat Company minutes.
Fern Dell School *Souvenir Booklet*.
Pine Grove School *Souvenir Booklet*.
School District #3, 6 and 9 School Registers.
The Senior, Kilbourn High School Annual, 1907.

No history of Wisconsin Dells would be complete if it did not include H. H. Bennett's stop-action photo of his son Ashley leaping to Stand Rock in 1888. (Courtesy, H. H. Bennett Studio Foundation).